1913

1913

In Search of the World before the Great War

CHARLES EMMERSON

PublicAffairs
New York

First published in Great Britain in 2013 by The Bodley Head
Published in the United States in 2013 by PublicAffairs™,
a Member of the Perseus Books Group

Typeset by Palimpsest Book Production Limited, Falkirk, Stirlingshire

Library of Congress Control Number: 2013935895
ISBN 978-1-61039-256-3 (HC)
ISBN 978-1-61039-257-0 (EB)

First Edition

10 9 8 7 6 5 4 3 2 1

To my father

Contents

Introduction

In 1913, Francis Wrigley Hirst, the editor of *The Economist* magazine, published an essay entitled 'Foreign Travel'.[1] In it, he described the globalisation of his day, a process which seemed to pick up speed with each passing decade.

'Already', Hirst wrote, 'railways and steamers have made the journey from London to Chicago quicker and pleasanter by far than was the journey from London to Edinburgh two centuries ago':

> English comforts and American luxuries, French dinners and German waiters, are everywhere at the service of wealth. Wherever there is plenty of sport, good air for invalids, or good markets for merchandise, good hotels will be found. The watchful eye of capital, which knows no national prejudices in its unceasing search for high interest and adequate security, is always looking for opportunities, and the taste for travel grows with the facilities. Switzerland was the first playground of Europe. The world is now covered with playgrounds, to which active idlers and weary money-makers flock in obedience to the varying fashions of smart society, of sport, or of medical prescription. The African desert, Kashmir, California, Japan, the Canary Islands, Bermuda, the isles of Greece, Uganda, British Columbia, are not too remote for the modern globe-trotter. The commercial traveller is ubiquitous; and 'our own correspondent' pursues wars and rumours of wars as keenly as the hunter tracks his quarry.

Travel – not just that of wealthy tourists in search of new experiences but that of migrants in search of brighter tomorrows – had become much cheaper over the course of Hirst's lifetime (he was thirty-nine years old in 1913). 'No wonder, then', he wrote, 'if the number of those who travel for pleasure or profit steadily increases'.

A trip around the world, once fraught with danger, could now be sold to the curious traveller as a cruise, to be completed in the lap of luxury. The Hamburg-American Line offered regular round-the-world journeys on the SS *Cleveland*, from New York to Europe and then via the Suez Canal to India, Burma, the Philippines, Hong Kong, Japan, Hawaii and San Francisco, all for as little as $650. 'So momentous an undertaking [as travelling around the world] has always been pervaded by an atmosphere of romance and a spirit of adventure', declared the prospectus for the trip.[2] In the modern age, however, the traveller was provided with a degree of comfort unimaginable to his or her ancestors. On the SS *Cleveland*, electric elevators connected the decks, and telephones allowed one to make calls from cabin to cabin. The ship was equipped with a darkroom for amateur photographers, a library stocking books in English, French and German, and a gymnasium with electrically operated machines, including several in the form of a saddle. In 1913 the last leg of the journey – from San Francisco back to New York – was still by transcontinental railway. The opening of the Panama Canal in 1914 would allow future travellers to complete their trip by sea.

This book is a circumnavigation of a different sort. Starting in the capital cities of Europe – London, Paris, Berlin, Rome, Vienna, St Petersburg – it journeys to the cities of North America – Washington, New York, Detroit, Los Angeles, Mexico City and then to the four corners of the wider world – Winnipeg, Melbourne, Buenos Aires, Algiers, Bombay, Durban, Tehran and Jerusalem. Finally, it travels into the hearts of the chief cities of the great non-European empires of 1913 – Constantinople, Peking, Shanghai and Tokyo.

The intention is not to capture everything that happened in a single twelve-month period in every corner of the globe, still less to deliberately seek out the causes of the Great War which broke out the following summer. The origins of the First World War are the subject of an enormous and ever-expanding body of historical scholarship. Debate over the attribution of responsibility for the war has raged since its outset. Various historians at various times have pointed the finger of blame towards the militarism of Prussian society, German ambitions for world domination, the internal political crisis of the

German state, Austro-Hungarian adventurism, the internal crises of
the Austro-Hungarian state, Russian imperialism, the internal crises
of the Russian state, the European alliance system, fears of European
cultural degeneration, the remorseless logic of train timetables or a
combination of a number or all of the above.[3] Acts of commission
and omission by particular individual diplomats inevitably influenced
decisions made in the chancelleries of Europe. Relative assessments
of power and intention – and of how these were likely to evolve in
the near future – all changed the calculus of war in the minds of
different politicians, monarchs and generals. Historians do not now
generally believe that war was inevitable from the moment that the
Austro-Hungarian Archduke Franz Ferdinand was shot in Sarajevo
in June 1914. Exactly when war became inevitable – much earlier or
much later, if ever – is an open question.[4] Most historians accept that
Britain's participation in the war was not pre-destined in 1914, indeed
some historians argue that it was a grave error.[5] Even once it started,
the course of the war – like any set of historical events – depended
on a range of contingent factors, as well as more unalterable factors
such as economic strength, administrative efficiency, population and
so on.[6] 'Virtual history', where one or other of the contingent factors
is changed, can help us think afresh about causality, chance and path
dependence in history.[7]

Seeking to understand why the world went to war in 1914, and
how that war then lasted for four years, is a vitally important
historical and political endeavour. Only through attempting to understand the past – however imperfectly – can we possibly hope to
learn from it. And yet, as one leading historian has written, the
single-minded quest for the causes of the war may, perversely, carry
the risk of distorting the past as well as uncovering it:

> . . . causes trawled from the length and breadth of Europe's pre-war
> decades are piled like weights on the scale until it tilts from prob-
> ability to inevitability. Contingency, choice and agency are squeezed
> out of the field of vision.[8]

Knowing what ultimately happened – a war which would turn the
world upside down – can narrow our view of what the world was
like before it happened. Because the war started in Europe, there is
a natural tendency to focus on the magnificent cauldron of European

hopes and ambitions in the pre-war era at the expense of the world as a whole.[9] Listening for the voices of those who predicted war in 1913 can lead us away from the many others who did not expect it – and indeed who were surprised when it eventually came.[10] In 1910, the writer and propagandist for peace Norman Angell famously declared that the idea of a profitable war was, in the interdependent world of the early twentieth century, a 'great illusion' (though he did not go quite so far as to say it was impossible).[11] Even amongst those who did believe war was possible or even probable, the prospect was often greeted with a certain equanimity, for it was thought that any war would be a short shock to the system rather than a four-year bloodbath. Perhaps inevitably, asking a single question of the past – why did war happen? – risks making everything else a piece of evidence to be used or discarded according to its utility in providing an answer to that question. The world of 1913 risks becoming viewed as nothing more than an antechamber to the Great War, rather than being looked at on its own terms – 'as it really was', as the great German historian Leopold von Ranke famously put it.[12]

Of course, it is not possible to escape hindsight. We cannot but look at the world of 1913 through the prism of what happened after it – indeed part of the interest of that year is our knowledge of what happened next. But we can at least attempt to look at the world in 1913 as it might have looked through contemporary eyes, in its full colour and complexity, with a sense of the future's openness. We can do this, in part, by looking at what individuals were writing about at the time and what newspapers were reporting. We can do this by reading the confidential reports put together by diplomats on the spot in Tokyo or Buenos Aires to inform their superiors as to the situation in a particular country at a particular time. We can do this too by looking at those parts of the world which tend to receive less attention from Western historians – the non-Western world – because they were less obviously and directly involved in the lead-up to what started as a European war.

The objectives set for this book are thus in one sense more modest and in another more ambitious than many books written about this time. Modest, because it does not seek to explain the Great War – this book should be taken as a complement to histories of the war's origins, not as a replacement for them. Modest also because it takes a single year as its focus, rather than describing the entirety of the long nineteenth century, as some other historians have done so brilliantly.[13] Its sweep is geographic, more than chronological. But therein lies its peculiar ambitiousness: to paint a truly global picture of the world in 1913, often from the perspective of contemporary travellers and writers – many of them Western – but also from the perspective of protagonists both high and low, famous and unknown, Western and non-Western. This book attempts to bring back to life *their* world. It is a book self-consciously engaging with the idea of 1913, and the years before it, as a period of unprecedented globalisation, rich in encounters, interconnections and ideas.[14] 1913 was a year of possibility not predestination.

Writing about the world in 1913 often involves digging further back. Sometimes it involves the arresting realisation that our perspectives on the passage of time are skewed by familiarity or by proximity – we tend to mentally compress time when it falls within our own lives, and extend it when it falls in the lives of past generations. And yet for those alive in 1913, the 1880s and 1890s were no more distant than the 1980s and 1990s are to us: the fall of Communism in eastern Europe, Tiananmen Square, the advent of the personal computer, the presidency of Bill Clinton. The Boxer Rebellion of 1901 – when foreign troops marched into the Forbidden City in Peking (Beijing) to put down a rising which targeted Western interests – is as close in time to 1913 as the events of September 11, 2001 are to us today. In 1913, only a hundred years ago, tens of thousands of veterans who had fought in the American Civil War met in Gettysburg, Pennsylvania, on the site of one of that war's most important battles. The shadows of the nineteenth century loomed large into the early twentieth century.

Similarly, the world of 1913, though separated from us by two world wars and the rise and fall of Communism, is not entirely foreign to our own times. It is not just that many of us have known grandparents or great-grandparents who were alive a hundred years ago. (My own grandparents were all alive in 1913; my grandfather was a young boy who took a steam train to school in rural Australia.) It is also that the world of a hundred years ago was in many respects decidedly *modern*.

In 1913, *our* world was alive and kicking. Globalisation, which is often casually assumed to be a phenomenon of the second half of the twentieth century, was well underway in 1913 – indeed in some respects one might argue that global integration was more advanced then than it is today. The ideas of global society or a world ordered by international law were commonplace in the year before the Great War even if its institutions were less well-developed. As the liberal British historian G. P. Gooch put it in 1912: 'civilisation has become international'.[15] The Peace Palace in The Hague, the building housing the forerunner to the International Court of Justice, opened its doors in 1913. There are striking and unsettling parallels between the geopolitics of the world today – shifting from a period of American unipolarity to a period of potentially much more competitive multi-polarity – and that of a hundred years ago – with Britain in relative decline, Asia re-awakening, and rising powers trying to carve out a place for themselves in a global system established by others. Furthermore, much of what we take to be quintessentially modern in terms of culture or technology – the modern art of Cubism and Expressionism, the aeroplane, the telephone, the automobile, even aerial bombing – was already around in 1913.

This book offers a selection and an interpretation – in that sense, it is a portrait. But it is also a journey into the world of a century ago – which, it turns out, is not so long ago at all.

The Exposition Universelle et Internationale of 1913, Ghent. The exhibition served as a celebration of human progress and a statement of the primacy of European civilisation. Within eighteen months the city would be occupied by the German army.

PART I

CENTRE OF THE UNIVERSE

A European could survey the world in 1913 as the Greek gods might have surveyed it from the snowy heights of Mount Olympus: themselves above, the teeming earth below.

To be a European, from this perspective, was to inhabit the highest stage of human development. Past civilisations might have built great cities, invented algebra or discovered gunpowder, but none could compare to the material and technological culture to which Europe had given rise, made manifest in the continent's unprecedented wealth and power. Empire was this culture's supreme product, both an expression of its irresistible superiority and an organisational principle for the world's improvement. The flags of even some of Europe's smaller nations – Denmark, Portugal, Belgium or the Netherlands – flew over corners of the wider world, whether a handful of islands in the Caribbean, a south-east Asian archipelago, or a million square miles in central Africa. Among Europe's Great Powers only Austria-Hungary remained without a colonial empire. To be a European – to be a European man, in particular – was to see oneself at the centre of the universe, from which all distance was measured and against which all clocks were set.

In a world made smaller by the distance-destroying innovations of technology, and made more integrated by flows of goods, money and people, it was inevitable that Europe, the engine room of these developments, would be most densely interconnected, criss-crossed by railway lines and telegraph wires. In a world where the remorseless logic of scale pointed to ever-larger industrial enterprises, and where economies seemed to be ever more interlocked with one another, Europe represented the summit of interdependence: each country relying on its neighbours for resources, or markets, or access to the rest of the world. And just as Europeans saw it as the natural

order of things that they should venture forth to colonise and control
the world, so it was inevitable that Europe would be where, in turn,
the world came to display itself.

In 1913, it was perhaps in industrialised, peaceful, bilingual, constitutionally neutral Belgium where the force fields of European integration most overlapped. In that year the medieval Flemish city of
Ghent hosted the Exposition Universelle et Internationale – more
commonly referred to as a world fair – as had Brussels a few years
before. Each country taking part commissioned its own pavilion,
celebrating every aspect of its ascent towards the common uplands
of industrial civilisation, from education to fine arts, electricity to
sport. With the peaceful sound of fountains in the background one
could promenade along the Avenue des Nations from the pavilion
of neighbouring Holland to distant Persia. One could visit the
elegant pavilion of Paris, host of the iconic world fair of 1900, or
the neo-classical Palais du Canada, or that of Germany, more modern.

Because this was the age of empire, and because this was Belgium,
one might also stop inside the Palais du Congo and leaf through a
book commemorating the heroic endeavours of Belgian colonisation.
'Does she [Belgium] not owe it to herself, to her honour', its author
asked, 'to continue the work of civilisation begun by the valiant
colonisers, sleeping in the African bush, far from the Mother-
Country?'[1] No mention was made of the thousands of Congolese
sacrificed in the greedy quest for the African rubber on which so
many Belgian fortunes rested; nor of the dishonouring episode of
1908, when international revulsion at Congo's mismanagement under
the personal ownership of the previous King of the Belgians had
led to its formal annexation to the Belgian state.[2] But no matter
– a world fair celebrated the progress of the nations of the world.
It did not investigate its underpinnings.

Within eighteen months Ghent would be a city occupied by a
foreign army, languishing behind German barbed wire. But in 1913
Albert, King of the Belgians, could still welcome an invasion of
commercial displays, of German furniture and of British arts and
crafts. 'The Ghent exhibition', read a brochure encouraging participation, 'should be an eloquent affirmation of the incessant progress
for which the genius of humankind is responsible, in every field of
its peoples' activities'.[3] The gold and white exhibition buildings were
set in extensive, well-ordered gardens. At night the whole place was

lit up with electric lights, bright symbol of a new age. An arriving visitor could be forgiven for thinking herself at the centre of a European universe, at the crossroads of progress and destiny.

Suitably enough it was a Belgian, Social Democrat Henri la Fontaine, who was awarded the Nobel Peace Prize in 1913 for his work at the International Peace Bureau (he was also the founder of the Union of International Associations, headquartered in Brussels). And it was only a hundred miles from Ghent to the Dutch city of The Hague, where in August the Peace Palace opened its doors – a home for the Permanent Court of Arbitration, dedicated to the resolution of states' differences by force of argument rather than by trial of arms. Underwritten by the generosity of American steel magnate Andrew Carnegie, the building incorporated materials from all over the world: bricks from the Netherlands, sandstone from France, granite from Sweden and Norway, and the wood for its floors from Austria. Inside, British stained glass overlooked American bronze statues, rosewood and satinwood panelling from Brazil, silk cartoons and vases from China and Japan, and carpets from Turkey. Switzerland provided the clock tower that adorned the top of the building. Germany provided the Peace Palace's wrought-iron gates.[4]

To those of a certain class in particular, 'Europe' was not just a geographic description of a continent, or the dream of wide-eyed internationalists, it was a lived reality. For men such as Harry Kessler, an Anglo-German aristocrat who dabbled in writing – he was the author of the libretto to Richard Strauss' wildly successful comic opera *Der Rosenkavalier* – Europe was an open book, to be picked up at any page, all equally intelligible to his European sensibilities. His diaries from 1913 find him dining with England's part-German Queen Mary (whose conversational skills he denigrated), supping with the Irish playwright George Bernard Shaw (who advocated a Franco-German-British alliance), lunching with the Russian ballet impresario Nijinsky and visiting the French novelist Octave Mirbeau (who confided to Kessler that 'we won't have war because within thirty days it would turn into a stampede ... and our [French] politicians know it').[5]

Kessler was no doubt remarkable in the breadth of his social and political contacts – but he was not exceptional in treating Europe as a single entity, separated by national rivalries to be sure, yet entangled by common bonds of culture and class, trade and travel.

Aristocrats had always been able to travel across Europe; now it was the turn of the middle classes. Young Russian composer Sergey Prokofiev accompanied his mother on a trip to Berlin, Paris, London and Switzerland that summer. When Cambridge economist John Maynard Keynes finished a draft of a major book earlier in the year, he hopped on a train from London to Milan (and then a boat to Cairo) to celebrate; December found him at Roquebrune on the French Riviera.[6] British Prime Minister Herbert Asquith travelled to Venice that May, revisiting the Adriatic shoreline along which he had cruised the previous summer on the Admiralty yacht the *Enchantress* with his wife, daughter and Winston Churchill in tow. Now, clutching his *Baedeker* to his breast in Venice, he became just like any other exacting European tourist of the age, interrogating his fellow gondola passengers as to 'who had painted what saint, in which church'.[7]

For Europe's leisured classes – and increasingly for the professional middle classes, or at least those who had money and the time to spend it – the continent might be experienced as a succession of train journeys from spa town to seaside resort, periodically interrupted, if at all, by the polite enquiries of differently plumed customs officials. These Europeans inhabited a continent of palace hotels, from the newly opened Carlton in St Moritz (which its owner claimed had been built as a retreat for the Russian Tsar) to the gold and marble gaudiness of the Negresco in Nice. Those seeking a health retreat might travel to the Radium Kurhaus of St Joachimsthal (Jáchymov), where Marie Curie had acquired pitchblende for her studies of radioactivity. Those seeking sun and inspiration might repair to the Grand Hôtel des Bains on the Venetian Lido, the setting for a popular German novel of the previous year.[8] In Monte Carlo, say, it would not be surprising to find an English gentleman conversing with an Austrian surgeon in French while he observed the losing streak of a Russian general at cards.

Patriotism, real though it was, did not negate the active cosmopolitanism of this European society. Love of one's own homeland did not preclude identification with one's social peers from foreign climes, nor appreciation of the finer qualities of their countries. So it was that when Archduke Franz Ferdinand was assassinated in Sarajevo in the summer of the following year – the event which unleashed the final approach of European war – politicians, generals and writers all found themselves on holidays on the wrong side of borders they were accustomed to cross without a second thought. Russian General Alexei Brusilov was in Germany.[9] Serbian army commander General Radomir Putnik was in Austria-Hungary. Winston Churchill was at an Anglo-German naval event at Kiel, in northern Germany. British author Joseph Conrad was in Zakopane, in his native Poland.

Writing about these years later, after they had passed into much-mourned history, author Stefan Zweig recalled a French-speaking Belgian poet crying when he heard of the crash of a German Zeppelin airship, because this was a tragedy for *European* progress. Zweig remembered himself, an Austrian, cheering the exploits of French aeroplane pilots:

> . . . because of our pride in the successive triumphs of our technics, our science, a European community spirit, a European national consciousness was coming into being. How useless, we said to ourselves, are frontiers when any plane can fly over them with ease, how provincial and artificial are customs-duties, guards and border patrols, how incongruous in the spirit of the times which visibly seeks unity and world brotherhood![10]

Just as Europe's leisured classes might have their sense of commonality forged by common social experience, so Europe's progressive women shared the cause of seeking the vote, so Esperanto speakers shared the hope of a new language. And so Europe's working classes had their sense of solidarity enshrined in the doctrines of socialism and in the practice of workers' internationalism. European aristocrats had their rounds of regattas, casinos and social engagements with distant foreign cousins; Europe's middle classes had their *Baedeker*s and museums; Europe's working classes had their socialist Second International, with its permanent bureau in Brussels. This was the Europe of Jean Jaurès, the French socialist leader, Victor Adler, the Austrian socialist, and August Bebel, founder of the powerful German Social Democratic Party – then the largest single party in the German Reichstag. Even Britain's leftist leaders, Keir Hardie and Ramsay MacDonald, attended congresses in Stuttgart and in Basel. Most members of the European working class could not dream of foreign travel – but their representatives could, availing

themselves of the same forms of transport which brought coal from
the mines, and steel from the foundry.

And although socialism was riven with its own doctrinal disputes
– the extent of reform that could be achieved within a bourgeois
society, the potential for revolution in an agrarian society, the relationship of socialism to colonialism – international solidarity of the
working classes cut across all of them. In November 1912, five hundred
and fifty-three delegates from twenty-three countries gathered in
Switzerland to rededicate themselves to the causes of unity and
peace.[11] The greatest threat to the Ghent world fair in 1913, it turned
out, was not the threat of war – it was the threat of a Belgian general
strike. Faced with workers' solidarity, was not war in any case a
practical impossibility? Would not the very concept of the nation
eventually become a quaint remembrance, evoking no more loyalty
than one's region or one's city had a generation or two previously?
Would not the nation, like the state, wither away?

The continent's cultural and intellectual elites were not immune
to myths of national character, to outright nationalism or even, more
worryingly, to the glorification of war. French composer Maurice
Ravel pronounced that there was an 'abyss' between the music of
the Austrian composer Arnold Schoenberg and 'my way of feeling,
that of France'.[12] Italian Futurism, which managed to be both fiercely
nationalistic and hypercritical of Italy at the same time, proclaimed
that the 'world's only hygiene' was war.[13] Darwin's science and
Nietzsche's philosophy, similarly bastardised, appeared to announce
the inevitability of human conflict (though Nietzsche also penned
the rather less famous observation that, in the meantime, 'Europe
wants to become one').[14] French 'culture' was frequently compared
to German 'Kultur' (the Germans thought their sort more manly
and more intellectual and that of the French more effeminate and
conversational). Nor were artists or composers indifferent to their
own cultural hinterlands, above, beyond and below the level of the
nation. Folk culture, both of supranational groupings such as the
Slavs or sub-national regions such as Brittany or Catalonia, enjoyed
increasing popularity at the turn of the century, albeit alongside a
wider interest in more 'primitive' (and not necessarily European)
forms, in which fresh inspiration was thought to reside.

Yet in some respects the continent's intellectual and artistic scene,
like that of its working or its leisured classes, was evolving towards

a set of common European movements, defined more by their relationship to what had gone before than to their relationship to any
particular national school.[15] European architects built in remarkably
similar styles, took up frequent commissions abroad, and dealt with
the same problems of the modern city in Berlin as in London or
Vienna. Europe's leading artists and authors frequently exhibited,
and even lived, outside their home country: French painter Robert
Delaunay enjoyed a one-man show in the Berlin Der Sturm gallery
in 1913, while Irish author James Joyce lived in Italian-speaking
Austro-Hungarian Trieste, Russian painter Wassily Kandinsky in
Munich, Russian author Maxim Gorky on the Italian island of
Capri, and Italians Modigliani and de Chirico in Paris, alongside
the Spanish Picasso and the Russian-Jewish Chagall. In the realm
of the unconscious, Freud's *Interpretation of Dreams* was first
published in an English edition in 1913.

European tastes in art and music were not only defined by national
publics, but by an active class of international collectors, and by
pan-European magazines of cultural criticism which would be as
available in Viennese coffee houses as in Parisian cafés. In dance,
all of Europe was preoccupied with the popular craze for the tango
in 1913 – to the extent that some church and political leaders
attempted to ban it. At a rather more elevated level, European tours
of musicians and dancers – Diaghilev's Ballets Russes being the
outstanding example – helped create a protean European contemporary culture.

In music in particular, while there were certainly definable national
composers over the last few decades of the nineteenth century and
the first of the twentieth – Wagner in Germany, Bruckner in Austria-
Hungary, Elgar in England, not to mention Grieg in Norway,
Tchaikovsky in Russia, Smetana in Czech-speaking Austria-Hungary
– nationality was hardly an insuperable obstacle to transferability.
Music from fellow European countries could be heard in most cities.
It could be studied anywhere: Vera Brittain remembered how, before
the war, her brother fully intended to study musical composition in
Leipzig or Dresden.[16] The nationality of artists or composers neither
guaranteed popularity in their own country, nor excluded it in others.
Even in Paris, capital of the country that coined the word 'chau-
vinism', the most played composer in the city's concert halls in 1913
was Beethoven – featured in no fewer than 716 concerts. (The most

popular French composer, Saint-Saëns, featured in just 279 concerts, behind Wagner – whose centenary was celebrated in 1913 – as well as Schumann and Chopin, the famously French-speaking Pole.)

In *Jean Christophe*, a ten-volume novel published between 1904 and 1912, Romain Rolland, the French biographer of Beethoven, aspired to write a truly European novel charting the career of a German composer Johann Christopher Krafft, and his French comrade Olivier Jeannin, the two united by a common European musical canon.[17] This was a vision of a transcendent culture, and one that found readers both in France and in Germany. It was not universally shared, of course: the Belgian ambassador in Paris noted applause for French anti-German sentiment in the city's theatres, and the success of an anti-German play, *L'Alsace* (and even Rolland himself drew the line somewhere, believing that Alsace and Lorraine should certainly be French not German).[18] But in amongst such disputes, and in amongst the petty everyday nationalism that percolated popular life, the idea of a wider European culture was not yet extinguished – in many respects it was being rejuvenated.

In the summer of 1913, when Europe's intellectual aristocracy gathered for a cultural festival in Hellerau – itself a German garden city inspired by a British model – they formed a truly European artistic avant-garde. This was not quite the European unity of the Middle Ages, defined by the cultural autocracy of the Catholic Church and Latin script – though that still counted, of course, for millions who worshipped in the same language each Sunday. It was a fractious, dynamic artistic scene. It was nonetheless more European than it was national, aspiring to be more universal than particular.

At the apex of society were the grandest Europeans of them all, the continent's monarchs, forming a dynastic web of kinship thick with common European blood. There were three monarchs in particular whose own reputed qualities and defects defined the countries of which they were the head: the United Kingdom's George V, dependable and dull; Wilhelm II of Germany, erratic and proud; Nicholas II of Russia, loyal and conservative to some, easily led and weak to others. Together, these three – all cousins to one another; all descended from Queen Victoria; George and Nicholas so alike in looks that they could be mistaken for one another – personified the European family of nations.

In mid May 1913 the three cousins gathered in Berlin for a royal wedding between Princess Victoria Luise, popularly referred to as

Symbols of the permanence of European order. Cousins Tsar Nicholas II and King George V at the wedding of the daughter of Kaiser Wilhelm II – also their cousin – in Berlin, 1913. 'Guests who rule a third of the world', ran a newspaper headline.

the *Prinzesschen* ('the little princess'), the only daughter of the German Kaiser, and Prince Ernst August of Cumberland. A 'galaxy of princes' were in attendance.[19] Billed as a final reconciliation between the royal house of Hohenzollern, of which Kaiser Wilhelm was the head, and that of Hanover, of which Prince Ernst August was the scion, the wedding settled a private dynastic quarrel. But it also played a public role. It provided a focal point for a social season 'without precedent for prosperity and gaiety'.[20] The story of the royal couple overcoming dynastic differences under the star of true love seemed a royal magnification of the universal themes of popular cheap novellas. Souvenirs of the bridal pair were depicted with 'the unbridled sentimentality dear to all true Berliners'.[21] Victoria Luise, rather better at managing the modern press than her father, who liked only to be photographed in a pose of stupendous magnificence, happily 'smiled, posed and changed position, so as to give each photographer his chance'.

The wedding occupied the social pages of Europe's newspapers for a week. Inevitably the presence of the British King and Russian Tsar gave the occasion a wider meaning to those who read about it, or to those who watched newsreels rushed back from Berlin to picture houses in London, Paris or St Petersburg. The presence of the three rulers confirmed, perhaps, the value of monarchy as a conciliatory, if waning, force in European politics. While no one expected much diplomatic business to pass between the monarchs themselves – indeed much effort might be spent by the monarchs' respective diplomats ensuring that they did not freelance their way beyond their intellectual (or constitutional) limits – the meeting would, at the very least, reinforce trust. 'When great potentates who are near relatives can meet in public and give full rein to their natural affection', opined the *Daily Graphic*, 'it is always legitimate to assume that the political horizon is clear'.[22] Berlin shops sold portraits of the British King and Queen, and Union Jacks to wave at them. King George took the opportunity to speak to the British community in Berlin, telling them that 'by fostering and maintaining kindly relations and good understanding with the people of this, your adopted home, you are helping to ensure the peace of the world'.[23] (Later that summer the King would send his son Edward, Prince of Wales, to Germany, where he took a motor trip up the Rhine, dropped in on his cousins, and visited the Kaiser in Berlin.)[24]

Given the frayed nerves of the past couple of years – with war in the Balkans and Franco-German stand-offs over North Africa – King George's words were a valuable reminder of common interests, and an antidote to the outbursts of the hotheads. In 1913, retired German general Friedrich von Bernhardi was still basking in the popularity of his book *Germany and the Next War*, which advised Germany that her best hopes of greatness lay in waging war within the next few years.[25] The preface to a patriotic book issued by the Crown Prince Wilhelm only a few weeks earlier had denigrated contemporary society as 'only too willing to boast of its international cosmopolitanism' and declared 'visionary dreams of the possibility of an everlasting peace' as un-German.[26] Just as lightning represented the inevitable release of electrical tension between differently charged clouds and land, so war would be a natural release for the dynamic energy of a young power unreasonably constrained, he suggested.

These were intoxicating ideas for some. They certainly had their backers amongst pan-Germans who imagined a titanic settling of scores between Germany and Britain or, more ethnically inflected, between Teuton and Slav. But they were not particularly new. Europe was accustomed to linguistic flourishes of German militarism, and conventional wisdom had generally learned to discount them. After all, Britain had its jingoes too, Russia its pan-Slavists and France, perhaps most shrill of all, its ultra-nationalists. More to the point, Crown Prince Wilhelm was not the Kaiser, he was the Kaiser's rebellious son. And Bernhardi was a retired general, not an active one. The Emperor himself used the occasion of the royal wedding to return to his favoured roles as a man of the world and peacemaker, magnanimously releasing two British subjects, Captain Trench and Bertrand Stewart, both imprisoned in the fortress at Glatz (Kłodzko) for having conducted espionage of Germany's naval defences while posing as tourists. Was not the presence of the British King and Russian Tsar at the home of the German Emperor sure evidence that no harm could befall the world so long as Europe's dynasties remained so intertwined? Were not the cheering crowds on Berlin's streets a testament to the underlying bonds of goodwill between the nations?

Choreography reinforced the sense of royal concord over and above any political disagreements. When King George arrived at Berlin's Lehrter station he rode together with the Kaiser to the imperial *Schloss*, the British King wearing the uniform of the Prussian Dragoon Guards and a sash denoting him as a member of the Prussian Order of the Black Eagle while the German Emperor wore a British uniform, set off by the broad blue ribbon of the British Order of the Garter and topped with a brass helmet. As the carriages entered the grounds of the *Schloss* a 101-gun salute was fired. The next day the Tsar arrived with somewhat less fanfare but with rather more security, 200 burly Russian detectives manhandling the crowd. Tsar Nicholas, it was noted, travelled without his German wife and his reception from the public was somewhat colder. But the German court made up for it by covering the roof of the opera house with Russian and German flags.[27] 'Guests who Rule a Third of the World' ran a headline of a British newspaper story of the events.[28] It was only a very slight overstatement.

From Olympus then, level-headed, well-informed, internationally minded Europeans – not cynics, but not dupes either – could still view the world in 1913 with a certain equanimity, their civilisation unmatched, their superiority unchallenged, their peace disturbed only by a few rabble-rousers, martinets and revolutionaries at home, their future guaranteed by the march of progress. Things might come to some kind of scrap at some point, of course. But not today, nor perhaps tomorrow. When over, equilibrium would be re-established and calm restored. Olympus would remain inviolate, the dangers to it not negligible, but not unmanageable either.

As it was, the sun still rose each morning over Europe from behind the Urals and still set each evening into the wide Atlantic. The stars above remained fixed in the firmament. The universe continued on its steady, silent course.

LONDON
World City

The capital of a small group of islands off the north-western coast of the European landmass, London had become, by 1913, the most populous city the world had ever seen, the metropolis of the largest empire the world had ever seen, the fulcrum of global order, and the core of global finance. Ghent might be the world's shop window for a few months that year but London was, in the words of one contemporary, a 'permanent world's fair'.[1] Lord Curzon, the classically minded former Viceroy of India, described the city as 'becoming what Rome was in the first three centuries after the coming of Christ, what Byzantium was rather later'.[2] Within a Europe that was the centre of the universe, London could reasonably lay claim to be the centre of the world.

At more than seven million, the city's population was half again that of New York or Paris, and nearly double that of Berlin. London was still, as the American novelist Henry James had described it some years before, 'the biggest aggregation of human life – the most complete compendium of the world'.[3] As a consequence of London's overwhelming scale even the smaller national communities in its midst might have passed for whole cities elsewhere, including in their home countries. 'In London', noted one guide, there are 'more Irish than in Dublin, more Scots than in Aberdeen, more Jews than in Palestine and more Catholics than in Rome'.[4]

But the city's position in the world depended on more than the number of its inhabitants. For British subjects in far-off Australia, Canada, South Africa and New Zealand, London represented imperial Anglo-Saxon order – to some it represented 'home'. In the corridors of Whitehall and the chambers of Westminster, with Liberal Prime Minister Herbert Asquith presiding, political decisions were taken that affected the futures of millions in Asia and Africa and, closer to home, in Ireland. In the to and fro of Europe's ambassadors to the British Foreign Office, overseen by the archetypically English Sir Edward Grey, could be discerned London's central diplomatic role in maintaining the world's peace, attempting to enforce a great power solution to troubles in the Balkans. Behind the newly ornamented façade of Buckingham Palace resided a King-Emperor whose impressed profile was as familiar to the palms of a merchant in Singapore as to a shop-owner on Oxford Street. In the city's docks, the world's largest, goods would arrive each day to match the fortunes and tastes of every Londoner – cinnamon from Ceylon, furs from Canada, rum from Jamaica, tea from India – and goods would be sent around the globe to pay for them. In the City of London, lapped by tides of rumour and by the silent currents of the world's money, reports from far-off business interests in South Africa or Argentina could inflate or puncture the global market for a particular good, or for a particular security, making fortunes or destroying them in a matter of hours. The lesser cities of the world – from Moscow to Rio de Janeiro – relied on London to raise their finance, as did the countries of which they were part. 'A bill on London', stated *The Economist* with satisfaction, 'is a form of international currency'.[5]

Through all this ran the River Thames, from the neat boathouses of Henley which opened on to it, through the centre of London which turned its back against the polluted river's stench, to the estuary which led to the sea. Down this stream, reflected Joseph Conrad, chronicler of Britain's empire, had floated 'the dreams of men, the seeds of commonwealths, the germs of empire'.[6] Up this river had returned imperial conquerors, the wealth of nations and the peoples of the world.

Foremost amongst these were King George's imperial subjects. Most exotic, but hardly unfamiliar in the city's East End, were lascar seamen from Yemen, Somaliland and the Indian sub-continent, constituting one in every seven seamen on British merchant ships. Settled now in London, lascars formed some of the city's first Muslim communities.[7] More familiar in the city's central districts were the studious young men of empire – from Ghana, Nigeria and India – who arrived in London to study law, as had Mohandas Karamchand Gandhi some twenty-five years before. Some would perhaps settle to practise law in London; others would return home, while still others might take their skills to other corners of the empire where English legal practice and principle prevailed. Most familiar of all – so much so as to be barely noticeable – were Londoners' British-origin kin from the self-governing colonies, perhaps only a generation or two distant from a farm in Kent or a village in the Scottish lowlands. Amongst these returnees from empire was the leader of His Majesty's Loyal Opposition, Andrew Bonar Law of the Conservative Party, who was born in New Brunswick, Canada. And then there were the Irish, split between the southern majority that had been seeking a parliament in Dublin and Home Rule for their island for the past fifty years, and the Protestants of Ulster, who saw Home Rule as a Catholic plot, and committed their lives to preventing it.

To the average Londoner of 1913, empire was a habit of mind. The sight of a visiting colonial premier or an Indian maharajah was a commonplace. Memories of King George's coronation two years previously, and the mass visitation of imperial personalities which this occasioned, were still fresh. The city's bus routes advertised themselves by imperial analogy. 'Just as the flag links the empire's commerce', ran one, 'so does the General link up the world's greatest city'.[8] The *Evening Standard* ran an advertisement for holidays in Sudan: 'Presents a perfect winter climate, invariably dry, sunny and bracing; offering express steamers and sleepcar trains-de-luxe'.[9] The country, it was reported, offered excellent big game shooting.

Scattered across the city were the agencies of the different colonies and dominions of empire: Canada, West Australia, Tasmania, New Zealand and South Africa on Victoria Street, Quebec on Kingsway, New South Wales on Cannon Street, Nova Scotia on Pall Mall, Queensland on the Strand, and Victoria on Melbourne Place. For Earl Grey, former Governor General of Canada, this was not enough. A single 'Dominion House' should be built, he argued, 'a great landmark, it should dominate the entire district in which it is situated, and should imprint upon it its character so as to advertise the grandeur and significance of the great Dominions far and wide'.[10] In July 1913 King George laid the foundation stone for what would become Australia House, which merged the various Australian agencies into a single building. The city's Australian population met the event with a national shout of 'coo-ee', 'a long-drawn, plaintive cry', the *Daily Express* reported, 'which swelled and died again and again, coming to Londoners' ears with almost startling novelty'.[11]

Everyone found their place in London. Whatever imagined slights existed between Germany and Britain in the realm of high politics, a student from the Baltic city of Königsberg or the Silesian city of Breslau could feel at home in London, joining a German gym near St Pancras station or visiting the offices of the German cultural society near Oxford Street, taking any medical complaints to the German hospital in Dalston, while avoiding the German Officers' Club which met every Wednesday morning at the Gambrinus restaurant on Regent Street or the Association of German Governesses in England, with its offices on Bryanston Square.[12] Some 100,000 Germans lived in Britain.[13] Though young German men embarking for Britain from a German port were required to show they were not fleeing military service, no passport was needed for them to enter Britain, whether by boat from Bremen or Hamburg (for Berliners and north Germans) or from Dutch Vlissingen or Belgian Ostend (more convenient for southern Germans). An Anglo-German exhibition opened at Crystal Palace in June 1913 (following an Anglo-French one in 1908). 'Cousins should not be allowed to drift apart', said one of its English promoters.[14] The sentiment echoed that of *Our German Cousins*, a book published some years before by that supposedly rabidly anti-German rag, Lord Northcliffe's *Daily Mail*.[15]

The summer months – May, June and July – were the best times to visit the city, *Baedeker* advised its German readers. This was the 'season', when Britain's grander classes made London the centre of their social calendar – as opposed to the rest of the year, when the over-titled British aristocracy retreated into draughty country houses and to Scottish moors. And by 1913 London society was, more than ever, international. On the evening of 5 June – the day after suffragette Emily Davison had thrown herself under the King's horse at the Epsom Derby in the cause of votes for women – Europe's hybrid aristocracy gathered at the Royal Albert Hall for a charity event themed as a ball at the seventeenth-century French court of Versailles. Prince Felix Yusupov of Russia had been meant to play Louis XIV himself, but at the last minute passed off his role (and costume) to the German Grand Duke of Mecklenburg-Strelitz, preferring to attend as a French sailor. The

Russian ballerina Anna Pavlova danced. 'The *bal masqué* was in its hey-day in Paris of the Second Empire when the City of Light was the social centre of the world', noted the *Daily Mail*, 'is not London's rise to social pre-eminence amongst her sister capitals shown by the ever increasing vogue of these splendid costume fêtes, each one more magnificent than the last?'[16]

Wealthy German visitors who did not wish to impose on friends and family might stay in one of the city's grand hotels (with 'all the modern comforts', *Baedeker* advised) and be serenaded by small orchestras at set mealtimes. 'Somewhat less demanding' travellers – the hard up – could seek out lodgings in the temperance hotels of Bloomsbury, or at a guesthouse run by German immigrants. While French food predominated in restaurants, and most hotels would put on a mixed grill of some sort, vegetarians could choose between Food Reform on Furnival Street or the glorious Shearn's Fruit Luncheon Saloon on Tottenham Court Road. Those seeking a taste of home could retire to the Löwenbräu and Zum Lahmen Pferd restaurants, or the Café Vienna.

For twenty-two-year-old Sergey Prokofiev, on his first trip outside the Russian Empire, critically hamstrung by the fact that his only English words were 'jockey club' and 'water closet', London none-theless seemed to open a world of possibility.[17] Walking along Regent Street and Piccadilly:

> My eye kept being caught by the abundance of shipping-line offices, whose plate-glass windows were dignified by huge and artistically represented models of ocean-going liners, some of them with sections cut away so as to show the internal construction and layout. There were also brilliantly coloured images of India and America, with piles of the appropriate guidebooks and brochures. Such appetizing displays, beckoning from afar, are not to be found in St. Petersburg, or even Paris, and they make London seem somehow more closely connected to the world, so that a trip to India or South America, which seems to a Russian a virtually impossible fantasy, here appears a relatively normal, even simple, undertaking.

It was to prove more complicated to get to nearby Windsor, but repetition of 'Vindzor' eventually obtained him the required ticket. In London just for a few days, Prokofiev nonetheless managed to

spot King George V and visiting French President Poincaré in Hyde
Park, enjoy an evening at a London music hall (at which he laughed
uproariously without understanding a single word), form an opinion
that 'one is more likely to encounter a beautiful face in London
than in Paris' and make an earnest resolution: 'to learn English; it
will be essential for my future travels'.

From an entirely different corner of the globe, Mr N.
Ramunajaswami, a young lawyer glimpsing Britain for the first time
after a four-week voyage from India, set down his excitement in his
diary:

> It was past three o'clock when I sighted the chalky shore of that
> great and free country which distinguished itself by winning laurels
> in the memorable and historic battles of liberty and good conscience.
> The sight of the English shore, longed after with devout expectation,
> sent a thrill of joy through me, and though the surrounding atmos-
> phere was chill I was kept up by the warmth of my pleasure which
> the sight of Dover produced in me.[18]

In London itself, Ramunajaswami explored the city first from the
upper deck of a London bus, travelling from his lodgings in
Bayswater to Marble Arch and Oxford Street, and then to the City.
Over the following several weeks, Ramunajaswami attended a lecture
by Mrs Ellen Terry on Shakespeare's women and went several times
to the theatre. He visited Westminster Abbey, St Paul's, the horse
races at Epsom, both Cambridge (where there were said to be one
hundred Indian students) and Oxford, Lord's Cricket Ground, the
House of Lords, the London Zoo (where he admired the polar
bears), Madame Tussaud's (where 1913 saw the introduction of wax
models of the various warring Balkan monarchs), the British
Museum, and the Tate, National and National Portrait galleries. At
the Royal United Services Museum on Whitehall he saw a model
of the battlefield of Waterloo, the order of execution of King Charles
I, and a pendant of diamonds said to have been given to Admiral
Lord Nelson by the Sultan of Turkey after Nelson's victory over the
French at the Battle of the Nile in 1798.

The political preoccupations of Britain and its empire were never
far away. Ramunajaswami heard a suffragette haranguing passers-by
at Speakers' Corner in Hyde Park – an event which he referred to

in Hindi as *tamash*, 'a spectacle' – and went to a larger meeting presided over by Mrs Pankhurst herself. He was present at the unveiling of a plaque at the headquarters of the Independent Labour Party in Bermondsey, whose members were now in Parliament. He went to a meeting of the British offshoot of the Indian National Congress, held under the auspices of one of its British founders, Sir William Wedderburn, and with future Labour Prime Minister Ramsay MacDonald in attendance. He visited the offices of the Universal Races Congress, devoted to the improvement of relations between the constituent nations of the British Empire. Everywhere, he came across representatives of a broader British Indian community, firmly entrenched in the capital city of empire.

Ramunajaswami was impressed at the city's hugeness, of course, but also at its orderliness, and at the politeness of its policemen. He admired the British combination of conservatism and liberalism, the distaste for grand ideas yet the willingness to constantly adapt themselves to novelty – which he compared favourably with India. He marvelled at the British obsession with hats. One day he ventured into the working-class, poverty-stricken East End of London, remarking that 'if the eastern portion alone were London, then London would not have been far better than even some of the inferior portions of Madras'. But overall he accepted London as a symbol of the Empire's greatness and of that Empire's rights of tutelage over India.

Ramunajaswami made two purchases – a bicycle and a gramophone player – to take back to India. Steaming back from Dover to Calais, the journey of a lifetime behind him, Ramunajaswami proclaimed the impression London had left on him:

> O mighty London! How I love thee! . . . I can never forget thy parks and thy gardens, thy heaths and thy meadows, thy towers and thy monuments, thy tunnels and thy bridges, thy tubes and thy undergrounds, thy busses and thy cars, thy theatres and thy galleries, thy shops and thy hotels, thy halls and thy churches, thy mansions and thy palaces, and, above all, thy police and thy people.

Ramunajaswami had come to Britain an imperial Indian. He left with the attitudes of an Indian imperialist, convinced of the virtues of empire while seeking improvement in India's position within it.

London – world city, national capital, imperial metropolis – had performed its role: to awe all those who came near it with its scale and variety, forcing upon them the impression of London as the inevitable concentration of global power, the acme and justification of empire.

Yet there was something unsatisfactory about this London. When Ramunajaswami came to take his leave of London, his expression of love for the city came in the form of a catalogue. Was London really no more than the sum of its many and varied parts – an agglomeration of people and buildings, squares and gardens? The city was imperial – imperious, even – but it had no culminating point, a place where all its different aspects came together. It lacked structure – it lacked a theme. To Theodore Dreiser, an American writer on a tour through Europe: 'It seemed to me at first blush as if the city might be so vast that no part was important'.[19]

Perhaps history was to blame. Unlike Berlin, which had exploded from Prussian backwater to imperial capital in forty years and which was jam-packed with the heroic avenues of a nervous parvenu, or Paris, which had been extensively remodelled by an emperor worried about civil unrest, London had grown slowly over many years, spreading out along the Thames, gradually turning sleepy villages into outlying city boroughs, extending roads along the uneven lines of Domesday hedgerows set down eight centuries before. The city had been added to, yet nothing had been taken away. To the east in particular, in and around the City of London, crooked streets, narrow houses, the absence of public spaces and a jumble of archi-tectural styles defied the modern edicts of scale and unity. Although London had come to contain one-fifth of the population of England and Wales, it had done so with no master plan. The city was the product of a conservatism deep in British culture, an innate suspicion of grand ideas.

For Lord Curzon, former Viceroy of India, London's haphazard development bore comparison with the growth of Britain's empire, acquired 'in a fit of absence of mind' as John Seeley's famous formulation had put it.[20] In a public speech at the Mansion House, the residence of the city's Lord Mayor, Curzon argued that while 'we all of us recognize that this London of ours is the greatest, the most populous, the most amazing city in the world', yet there had never been anywhere in the history of the world a 'great city that grew up with less forethought, or that rested less definitely on a plan'.[21]

Both London and its empire, Curzon opined:

> . . . have sprung up almost unawares, their great position being due partly to advantages of geographical situation, partly the blessings of Providence, partly to accident, partly, we like to think, to the genius of our own people; and both Empire and capital have now reached a point at which we have to take stock of our position, and see what we are to do for the future, because in both cases, one of two conditions must result; either the Empire and the capital will break down from their plethoric condition, and from the operation of the numerous centrifugal tendencies that are at work; or, on the other hand, by counsel, by consideration, by forethought, it may be possible both for Empire and for capital city to create a new unity, to obtain a more commanding influence, to ensure a future not less wonderful than their past.

More parochially, Curzon argued that London did not play the same role for England – which for Curzon was interchangeable with Britain – as Paris did for France. Each small town in France measured its provinciality against the capital, aspiring to be a Paris in miniature. For French citizens, time spent in Paris was to be sighed over, savoured, celebrated. London, on the other hand, represented obligation, pomp, power and industry. It commanded pride and loyalty, but not longing or affection. Paris was an idea, refashioned in each retelling; London was a fact, made gross by practical experience. While Frenchmen might dream of becoming Parisians, Englishmen rarely dreamed of becoming Londoners. Rather it was images of the English countryside, of the leafy lanes around the county town, which stirred an Englishman's deeper emotions. 'The first thing an Englishman does in the outlying portions of Empire', Curzon told his Mansion House audience, 'is to make a racecourse'. The second was to make a golf course; the third was to 'sever all connexion with London by putting away his silk hat and frock coat, and appearing on all occasions in a straw hat'.

The city itself was fragmented, with numerous different town centres and high streets, each with their own character and history. 'London' incorporated the established residential areas of Belgravia, Mayfair and Kensington and the newer areas of Shepherd's Bush and Queen's Park; it could mean the mansions of Hampstead or the intermixed factories and slums of the East End. Pushing out, the city's boundaries were becoming ever more frayed. Local rail lines brought dormitory villages in rural Essex and Hertfordshire into London's orbit, while the electrified Metropolitan line extended the city's reach westwards into Middlesex and Buckinghamshire. To the east, the villages of Walthamstow and Leyton gradually merged with the expanding city, as Streatham and Balham already had to the south. To the north, the new semi-urban 'garden city' of Letchworth aimed to provide a happy medium between town and country, taking the pressure off London's expansion and providing a model for future new towns not just in Britain but for the world. In 1913 Ewart Culpin, one of the founders of Letchworth, travelled around the world lecturing on how such new towns would be the handmaidens of social reform.[22]

Even within the central quarters of the sprawling metropolis there was a multiplicity of cities: a London of business, a London of government, a London of entertainment, a London of museums, a London of monuments and, finally, as Curzon said, 'the London of the submerged millions, that mysterious, unknown, inscrutable London that always baffles and bewilders'. London might be the centre of the world, the chief city of empire, the capital of the United Kingdom, but where was its own heart?

For some, the heart of London lay somewhere in the West End. Australian landscape artist Arthur Streeton, one of those who had judged the choice of architect for Australia House, picked Trafalgar Square. His painting *The Centre of Empire*, finished in 1902, shows the square enveloped in mist yet shimmering with light, pigeons circling Nelson's Column, that celebration of Britain's greatest naval hero. In the background lie the chimneys of London's political and royal quarter with the dome of Horse Guards, headquarters of Britain's armed forces, clearly visible. The painting invited the viewer

One vision of the centre of London, the political heart of a worldwide empire.
Trafalgar Square, as painted by the Australian artist Arthur Streeton in 1902,
with the government offices of Whitehall off to one side.

to peer down Whitehall, the seat of imperial government, home of
its various government ministries. Here, Streeton suggested, at the
nexus of political authority, military power and royal prerogative lay
the centre of empire – and therefore the centre of London.

But it was another nexus – that of trade and money – which was
more commonly viewed as the city's true centre. In *The Heart of
Empire*, painted in 1904, Danish-born artist Niels Moeller Lund
placed Bank junction at London's geographic and moral core. At
street level, Bank junction was a congested intersection, thronged
with vehicles, faced on three sides by the Bank of England, the
Royal Exchange and the Mansion House, where Curzon gave his
1913 address. But Lund chose a more elevated perspective on the
place, taken from above the hubbub of the street. St Paul's Cathedral
hovers above the scene, suggesting the sanction of an Anglican God
for the pursuit of imperial Mammon below. It was not the stately
squares and wide streets of London's West End that Lund placed

at *The Heart of Empire*, as Streeton had. Rather, following the views of the City merchants who had commissioned the painting, it was the streets and alleys of the City of London.

From London's seven million strong population, only 20,000 actually lived in the square mile of the City. But nearly twenty times that number worked there each day, uniformly bowler-hatted figures arriving at their places of work each morning, to be penned in behind a ledger in a bank or behind a desk in an insurance company. 'From the hour of 6 a.m. until nearly noon', wrote Ellis Powell in *The Mechanism of the City*, 'a constant stream of humanity, numbering thousands and tens of thousands in its aggregate of individuals, pours into the small area, the "one square mile" which we call the City of London'.[23] (*The Economist* calculated that passenger journeys on public transport were now approaching two billion annually.[24]) At 4 p.m., the tide reversed, and the City's workers were gradually expelled:

> The phenomenon may be seen on every day from year's end to year's end. At certain points where the mass of humanity is more than usually congested . . . the spectacle is really startling, alike in the magnitude of the aggregate, and in the hurried, serious, preoccupied aspect of the human units who compose it. No thoughtful observer, whether of this or of another world, could possibly look upon it without asking himself the question, 'Who are all these people, and what is the purpose of their daily anxious oscillation between their suburban sleeping places and this teeming arena of diurnal activity?'[25]

For the City clerk, poised between working-class poverty and middle-class respectability, the City's square mile contained within it the totality of professional aspirations, hopes of advancement and fears of slipping into London's poorer underworld. 'All men are equal', thinks Leonard Bast, the tragic clerk of E. M. Forster's novel *Howard's End*, 'all men, that is to say, who possess umbrellas'.[26] When City men referred to 'the House', they meant the Stock Exchange, not the Houses of Parliament, still less their own homes.

In January 1913, the City was broadly optimistic about the future. 'If Sir Edward Grey [Britain's Foreign Secretary] could guarantee us a year of peace in Europe and a friendly understanding with Germany', *The Economist* editorialised, 'a year of even greater prosperity than the

An alternative vision of London as the world's financial hub. The City of London depicted in *The Heart of Empire* (1904) by Danish-born artist Niels Moeller Lund.

last might be confidently predicted'.[27] The prospects for peace appeared brightening at the beginning of the year, with Europe's great powers working more closely than ever to secure it. The men of the City, though thoroughly imperialist, were nonetheless amongst the most avid consumers of Norman Angell's thesis that economic and financial integration made war unprofitable. The previous year Angell had delivered a well-received address to the Institute of Bankers, flattering them with the observation that simply by continuing to operate internationally, binding the world ever tighter with rings of gold, they were contributing to the cause of peace.[28]

The City's role as meeting place of the world's money seemed unchallenged. Indeed it seemed mandated by economic law. 'Free-trade and a free gold market', thundered the free-market *Economist*, 'are two of the key different advantages which we enjoy over all our competitors, and the chief means by which London maintains itself as the banker and financier of the universe'.[29] The stability provided by gold as the anchor of the world's economic system was axiomatic. All currencies were fixed against each other through the medium of gold. When there were trade imbalances, these would be settled by flows of bullion from one country to another. The consequent interest rate differentials between these countries would, over the long term, bring them back into alignment. 'This is the known established theory of international trade', President of the Board of Trade Winston Churchill told his Manchester constituents in 1908, 'and everyone knows, ever single businessman knows, it works delicately, automatically, universally, and instantaneously'.[30] 'It will be the same', he concluded, 'when the year 2000 has dawned upon the world'.

Nonetheless, for the more thoughtful observers there was the seed of a worry in the City's pre-eminence – a concern for the possibility of divergence between the internationalist interests of finance and the more parochial interests of the country at large, or of the empire of which it was a part. As the City loomed larger and larger in the national economy, as it became more and more global (rather than more and more imperial) the scope for divergence would inevitably increase. In time it might become acute.

Britain did not, of course, depend wholly on London's money men for its prosperity. The country was still, in 1913, a large exporter both of manufactured goods and of raw materials. One million men worked in the country's coal mines. Although each British miner produced less than half the tonnage of his American counterpart, Britain remained the world's second-largest producer overall, digging far more out of the ground than could be consumed in the country's furnaces and fire-grates. Three-quarters of German coal imports, four-fifths of those of Sweden, and two of every five tons of coal imported by France and Spain came from Britain.[31] The United Kingdom was still responsible for fourteen per cent of the world's manufacturing production, a dramatic fall from one-third as recently as the 1860s, and half the share of the United States, yet only just behind Germany, and more than double either France or Russia.[32] 'Almost all branches of British industry have been booming since the recovery from the coal strike', *The Economist* reported in January 1913, 'shipbuilding and shipping, in which Great Britain leads the world, have never been so prosperous'.[33]

Yet in all these sectors Britain's relative position had been diminished over time, growing more slowly than those of other countries while retaining the habits and ideologies of a previous era of industrial preponderance. The only area where Britain remained splendidly dominant – indeed more dominant than ever before – was in managing the finances of globalisation, and in exporting the nation's capital. Nearly half of all the world's foreign direct investment came from Britain – as much as the United States at its peak in 1960.[34] Some returned each year in profits and dividends, most stayed invested abroad. Other returns came in from Britain's £4 billion in portfolio investments in foreign securities, from Russian railway bonds to shares in rubber companies in Malaya.[35] But the growing importance of the City to Britain's economic arrangements was not uniformly welcomed. Was the country not simply living off its wealth, the product of its former labour? Did the City strengthen both nation and empire by placing itself at the crossroads of global finance, lowering the cost of money in London into the bargain? Or was the City, so important and yet so vulnerable to a changing international scene, a source of potential weakness? By creating opportunities for British investors to send their money abroad, was not the City denying investment to industry at home?

Around the turn of the century, some British industrialists and some British politicians had become convinced that free trade – the twin sister of open capital markets – no longer served them as well as once it had. In Joseph Chamberlain, the former Secretary of State for the Colonies, they found an able advocate of the position that greater protection for home industries and empire trade was required. Britain's exports to empire – one-third of the total – were greater than ever. But should this trade now be consolidated within some kind of common imperial trading area, with a high wall around it to keep other countries out?[36] The call for protection ran counter to long-held principles of free trade, principles that were inculcated into Britain's economic intelligentsia from a tender age. It also risked cutting across the interests of the City, which lay in the maintenance of open and free flows of money and goods. One option was to deny that the divergence existed at all, taking refuge in the argument that what was good for finance was good for industry. 'If there is prosperity in the country there will be prosperity in the City of London' and vice versa, argued one City grandee in 1906, a familiar refrain a hundred years later.[37] Many others feared the City's influence was now outsized, undermining any clear-sighted imperial economic strategy and weaving the money and tastes of the financial *nouveaux riches* into the fabric of the nation. Was Britain simply becoming, in the words of David Lloyd George, a self-seeking people of 'footballers, stock exchangers, public-house and music-hall frequenters'?[38]

In 1913 a scandal appeared to answer this question in the affirmative. At the centre of the scandal was the Marconi company, founded by the Italian electrical engineer who had first transmitted a wireless signal across the Atlantic. Three years previously, the British government had opened discussions with the Marconi company with the intention of commissioning a chain of wireless stations across the world, to allow wireless communication between the empire's most distant reaches. This was to be the nervous system of empire – allowing the whole to function effectively in peace, and in war. Though these negotiations were in theory secret, the price of Marconi's stock had risen ten-fold over the course of 1911 and 1912 on the expectation of a deal. It was alleged that government ministers were amongst those who had purchased shares. It was implied that they had abused their positions to gain – and then exploit – market insight.

Two ministers, in particular, were in the frame: Attorney General Rufus Isaacs, whose brother worked for Marconi, and the Chancellor of the Exchequer David Lloyd George, the very man who had worried about Britain's decline towards becoming a nation of stock exchangers. Both had indeed bought shares in the company, it emerged, though both denied that they had traded on privileged information. A parliamentary enquiry was called. Winston Churchill leapt to the defence of his fellow Liberal ministers, attacking the enquiry for giving credence to 'unsupported tittle-tattle' and for allowing accusations to stand against men's honour (including his own). The whole affair, he argued, reeked of party politics, usefully undermining the credibility of any parliamentary report before it had even been issued. When the enquiry did report back it was indeed split on party lines – with the Liberals whitewashing their colleagues, and the Conservatives blacklisting them. Britain's politics descended further into the partisan abyss.

Isaacs and Lloyd George survived. Already Britain's first Jewish Cabinet minister, Isaacs would later become Viceroy of India and Foreign Secretary. Lloyd George would become the country's wartime Prime Minister. Churchill, the stout defender of his Liberal colleagues, would subsequently defect to the Conservatives, and become Prime Minister in a later conflict. But the Marconi scandal left a bitter taste at the heart of London and the heart of empire, implying the corruptibility of both.

The fortunes flowing daily through the City did not make London uniformly rich. And while the City employed a good number of Londoners as clerks, lawyers and stockbrokers, many more laboured in the rest of the city's sweatshops, docks and factories. These were low-paid workers, with limited certainty of a daily wage, often risking life and limb in the course of their work, sometimes at the mercy of employers who saw their labour force as a stock of human brawn to be drawn upon at will rather than as a set of individual employees. Living conditions had improved since Victorian times. Further improvements were forecast, with the 1910 Town Planning Act aiming at 'the home healthy, the house beautiful, the town pleasant, the city dignified and the suburb salubrious'.[39] Yet inner city conditions remained unenviable. Many buildings were blackened by smoke, flecked white by rain. When Ramunajaswami had taken the bus to East Ham he had remarked it worse than the Indian city of Madras. He could have taken a bus in any other direction – except perhaps to the west – and found similar pockets of deprivation.

Maud Pember Reeves, a member of the left-wing Fabian Society's Women's Group, focused her attentions on a nest of streets between Lambeth, Wandsworth and Lansdowne roads in south London, penning *Round About a Pound a Week* as an investigation of the social conditions of its inhabitants.[40] She described the relative illiteracy of many of Lambeth's women, the mortality of their children, the costs of burial insurance alongside food and rent, the 'filling, stodgy' diet which was all that they could afford to eat, the problems of the underemployed (though few were entirely without work), the inevitable rows resulting from houses where everyone was in the way of everyone else all the time, and yet the sense of local community which prevailed.

Whereas London's well-off might pay a tiny portion of their income for a sumptuous residence in South Kensington, Reeves calculated, the city's poor would pay a third of their income for a few dark, damp rooms, which they would nevertheless call home, in neighbourhoods where they knew everyone and were known to all. The divergence between the lives and attitudes of the middle classes and the poor was stark. In summer, when a well-meaning Fabian investigator commented on the lovely warm weather, a Lambeth resident grumbled: "Lovely fer you, miss, but it brings out the bugs somethink 'orrible".'[41]

Reeves drew a picture of urban poverty that translates depressingly well over a hundred years. She mocked restrictions on family size as the solution to the problem, calling for greater state intervention instead. She voiced a righteous anger at a group of people living in the world's greatest city, yet seeing less of its prosperity than they should. From these neighbourhoods men, women and families emigrated to all corners of the British Empire, though always with a glance back at 'their' neighbourhood, in 'their' city.

Another chronicler of London, Thomas Holmes, painted on a broader canvas than a patch of Lambeth, taking as his subject 'the odds and ends of humanity' consigned to the city's extensive underworld: the near-blind sixty-year-old man making artificial flowers by the light of an evil-smelling lamp, and the young widow making cardboard boxes while her children sleep. Holmes estimated at least 50,000 women were in a similar position: 'working, working day and night, when they have work to do, practically starving when work is scarce'.[42] Thames Embankment, not far from the Houses of Parliament, had nightly soup kitchens. In this world, he wrote, 'the funeral of one child is only a pageant for others'.

Some of Holmes' solutions were harsh: the permanent confinement of the 'indisputably feeble-minded' or the committing of tramps to detention camps. Unplanned emigration, Britain's traditional safety valve, was no long-term answer, Holmes argued. Rather 'it increases the evil, for it secures to our country an ever-increasing number of those who are absolutely unfitted to fulfil the duties of citizenship'. It was the ambitious and the self-starters who tended to leave, not the dregs. Still, compulsory emigration for those convicted of a third criminal offence might help.

Most measures proposed by Holmes, however, involved the state as a guardian of welfare, not as a stony-hearted provider of punishment and detention. This was the active state supported by Britain's many progressive social movements and by the forty MPs of the Independent Labour Party. This was the dream propounded by socialist intellectuals who, at the beginning of 1913, would anxiously pore over the first edition of the *New Statesman*, a high-minded magazine devoted to the cause of social reform. Germany, though its political system might be roundly condemned, was seen as a model to emulate when it came to welfare policies. Increasingly, reform was not a slogan for the left, it was an expectation.

In the summer of 1913 London was in the grip of ragtime. One older gentleman complained of being massaged in ragtime at his Turkish bath. Another said that he was sure his typists now clattered away to the same rhythm. But the city could still put on more stately airs, turning itself to the formality of a great occasion. Coming hot on the heels of King George's trip to Berlin, London prepared itself for a state visit from the leader of Britain's oldest enemy, now become its closest friend: President Raymond Poincaré of France.

It was a remarkable turn of events for two countries more prac-tised in denigrating each other's achievements than in celebrating them, more used to killing than embracing each other. English kings had contested the crown of France for centuries. In the seventeenth century the two countries' armies had clashed on European battlefields, and their ships on the high seas. In the eighteenth century, as dynastic conflict evolved into an imperial rivalry, Britain and France fought the first global war, crossing swords and exchanging bullets in the Americas, in Asia and in Africa. The French had sought revenge in supporting America's war for independence. At the time of the French Revolution, Paris had become the source of the dangerous heresies of *Liberté, Egalité, Fraternité*. In the Napoleonic Wars the countries had been at each other's throat for a generation, deepening mutual animosities. For the British, the French language was proverbially considered equiv-alent to swearing.

The passage of time and a short war fought jointly against the Russians in Crimea in the 1850s tempered the feelings of the time of Napoleon. But if France's existential threat to Britain receded, and the enemies became mere rivals, there were still plenty of opportunities for the two to collide. Though forever dislodged from North America and from India, France made up for serial defeat at the hands of the British by creating an empire in the Far East and in Africa. Even here, the two powers clashed. In the Fashoda Incident of 1898, a small French force marched halfway across central Africa to assert claims to the area around Fashoda, in southern Sudan. But British pressure brought about a French diplomatic capitulation, and an agreement on spheres of influence in Africa was reached. As recently as the turn of the century French intelligence agents were in Ireland considering how to help the nationalists, and what the ground might be like for the introduction of French military forces.[43] After France's last Emperor, Napoleon III, was overthrown some forty years before, he had sought refuge in the English countryside. His widow still lived there.

Yet now, in June 1913, the President of the French Republic was received with genuine warmth. First, in Portsmouth, where his yacht arrived, by the booming guns of the Royal Navy and a rendition of the 'Marseillaise'. Then that afternoon in London, where King George awaited President Poincaré in a Victoria station that was bedecked with tricoloured banners, and shields bearing the letters *R. F., République française. 'Nous sommes camarades'* – 'We are friends' – ran a banner hanging high above the road from the station to Buckingham Palace. After jointly inspecting a detachment of Irish Guards, King George and President Poincaré toured around central London in an open-topped landau carriage, escorted by the Household Cavalry. 'The crowd broke into loud cheers', wrote a newspaperman from the *Daily Graphic*. The ovations at Hyde Park, where Sergey Prokofiev caught sight of King and President, were reported as being particularly rousing.[44] That evening, at a state banquet, the English King addressed the republican President in French.

The trip was mostly ceremonial, mood music for the work of others behind the scene. Poincaré travelled to Windsor to lay wreaths on the tombs of King Edward VII and Queen Victoria. He visited London's French colony, conferring the Légion d'honneur on the London correspondent of *Le Figaro*. He paid homage to the City, visited a horse show and inspected a display of motor cars at Marble Arch. But the visit was not, for all that, simply a round of meetings, without a wider message. Indeed that message was made explicit by President Poincaré, and it was addressed to the British people:

Not only in Europe but throughout the world the restless billows on the ocean draw together and unite the shores of the two great colonial Powers in a constant exchange of ideas and interests. Does not the very nature of things will it that the two peoples of Great Britain and France should ever be associated for the progress of civilisation and the maintenance of peace in the world. Never, perhaps, have the necessity and benefits of that solidarity in good made themselves more strongly felt than in the course of recent events.[45]

The recent events that Poincaré referred to concerned the status of the European Great Powers in north Africa. In 1905 and 1911 Germany had forcefully protested creeping French colonisation of Morocco which, it argued, ran counter to France's diplomatic undertakings not to upset the regional status quo. In 1905 Kaiser Wilhelm II had landed in Tangiers on a white horse to make the point; in the summer of 1911 the German gunboat *Panther* was sent to Agadir on the flimsy pretext of protecting German citizens, sparking a war scare in Europe. Berlin hoped that Britain would maintain a position of studied neutrality, giving free rein to German intimidation. In the event, Britain supported France, demonstrating that the Entente Cordiale established between the two countries a few years earlier was here to stay. It was to cement this sense of Franco-British solidarity, and of common challenges presented by rising powers around the world, that Poincaré travelled to London.

Not everyone was willing to have Britain tied so closely to France. What if France took British support as an invitation to challenge Germany in Europe? 'If they think they [the French] can stand upon their bonds like Shylock for so many tons of English flesh', said an English guest at a private dinner at the German embassy that February, 'we shall be appreciably nearer to a general war'.[46] 'They can wait a long time if they're waiting for that', added Lady Randolph Churchill, American-born mother of Winston. (In fact, British and French army officers had already discussed the eventuality of British military support in the event of a European war – though this remained a plan for a possible contingency, not a blank cheque.)

The Economist agreed with Poincaré that it was in the nature of things for France and Britain to be friends – indeed it was 'the expression of tendencies which are slowly but surely making war between the civilised communities of the world an impossibility'.[47] But, the magazine continued, 'a man who is a chum of Jones may also be a friend to Robinson, and, indeed, if Jones and Robinson should happen to have a difference of opinion they will be fortunate in being able to confide in a mutual friend'. After all, Britain's commercial ties with Germany were progressively removing that country from the list of potential foes, *The Economist* contended, on the basis that it would be 'the highest folly to fall out with one's best customer'. Better to remain a little bit aloof, therefore, in order to be more useful to the cause of peace.

The new-found friendship between Britain and France should not be seen as placing those two countries (and Russia) in mutual antagonism with Germany and Austria-Hungary. Rather, intoned the sweet voice of liberal reason, shaped by a century of ever-increasing global integration, 'our common interest with France is the maintenance of European peace – and that is an aim which we share equally with Germany'.

Just as the City of London both provided and received money from all around the world, regulating global finance as a result, so Britain could be a friend to all, with London as the world's great aggregator, above the fray, in a world at fractious peace.

PARIS

The Eternal, The Universal

Already in 1913, plans were on the table for a tunnel linking Britain to France under the Channel, tying the two countries together with bands of steel. Until such a tunnel was built, however, a traveller from London to Paris, even a President, ran the risk of a choppy sea crossing from Newhaven to Dieppe, London to Boulogne, or Dover to Calais. Taking this last route it would take only six or seven hours to travel from London, capital of the world, to Paris, a city which aspired to be something both grander and more nebulous: capital of the twentieth century, just as it had been capital of the nineteenth.

Sweeping through northern France, trains from London would cross the Somme river at Amiens, deep in the heartland of Picardy. Here, if not too pressed for time, a tourist might pause to be inspired by the city's thirteenth-century cathedral, amongst the finest examples of Gothic style in Europe, famed for its stained glass, a symbol of Europe's ancient common Christian heritage. The American writer Theodore Dreiser stopped here on his way to Paris. Paying a guide two francs, he went up into the roof of the cathedral and, peering down at the play of candlelight on the statues of the saints, found a 'splendid confirmation of the majesty of man, the power of his ideals, the richness and extent of his imagination'.[1]

In the early summer of 1913 a visitor might catch some of the excitement of the French Grand Prix to be held around the city in July, heavy with expectations of victory by Frenchman Georges Boillot driving a French-made Peugeot EX3. If the hour was late, one could do worse than spend a quiet night in Amiens at the Hôtel de France et de l'Angleterre, a reminder of the distant age of Joan of Arc – burned at the stake in Rouen in 1431, a statue of whom stood in Amiens cathedral – when England and France had been hereditary enemies. The story of Joan, a Catholic saviour of a French king against foreign invasion, still had resonance in France in 1913. Both royalist Catholics and French republicans could rally around her as a symbol of national defiance. The previous year Poincaré and other republican nationalists, men who wished no return to an age of Catholic kings, had proposed a national holiday be established in her honour. But the object of French nationalist defiance had changed since the age of Joan. After all, it was not the troops of perfidious Albion who had occupied Amiens within living memory in 1870, it was, briefly, the Germans.

For many French, Poincaré included, such facts were not easy to forget in 1913. Poincaré's own corner of Lorraine, in eastern France, had been trampled over by Prussian troops forty-odd years before. Initially, his family had fled from the Germans, spending several weeks moving from hotel to hotel in northern France and southern Belgium, through the very same fields and orchards now cut across by the train from Calais to the French capital. Later, they returned to Bar-le-Duc to find their home occupied. 'Disgusting soldiers are in the house', wrote the young teenage Poincaré afterwards, 'one paints a skull and crossbones on our sideboard, the other spits, like a Cossack, in our stew'.[2] Then, in 1871, France's humiliation had been doubly sealed by the proclamation of the new German Empire from the old French royal palace of Versailles, and by the incorporation of the French provinces of Alsace and Lorraine into the new German Reich.

The loss of land and people rankled. Poincaré was himself a senator for that part of Lorraine which remained in France. On the Place de la Concorde in Paris a statue representing the city of Strasbourg, now in the German Reich, was regularly draped in black. In French newspapers the 'Lost Provinces' were depicted as a young orphan girl, exemplar of virginal French womanhood, in the evil clutches of male militarist German thugs.[3] (In Germany, of course, the provinces were presented as the daughters of *Mutter Germania*.[4]) The loss of Alsace and Lorraine was seared into the consciousness of French nationalists as a daily affront to national honour. More extreme rabble-rousing nationalists called for *'la revanche'*, revenge. But for most, and indeed for Poincaré, that was a step too far: revenge would be sweet, and the provinces should of course return to France, but a war to achieve that aim alone was neither likely nor desirable. French writer Remy de Gourmont was reported to have said that the provinces were not worth the little finger of his right hand, which he needed for writing, nor the little finger of his left hand, which was needed to flick cigar ash.[5] More importantly, though often missed in the French nationalist press, it was unclear whether the people of Alsace and Lorraine actually wanted to be part of a French *revanche*: in early 1913 a leading French Alsatian, Henri Kessler, wrote to a French newspaper saying his people would rather seek autonomous status within Germany than be the cause of broader Franco-German tensions.[6] (A few months later, after the actions of the German army in the Zabern [Saverne] affair, he might have felt differently.[7])

Maurice Barrès, the French nationalist writer who Poincaré himself proposed as a member of the prestigious Académie française in 1905, summed up the gloomy right-wing cult of the French fatherland with the words '*la terre et les morts*', the earth and the dead.[8] In northern France, slipping past Amiens towards Paris, these words might come back to Poincaré as a recollection of past losses – and perhaps as a prefiguring of the future. A few months earlier Germany had expanded her army, leading the French government to introduce a law to extend military service from two to three years, a highly controversial move. French socialists, and perhaps the majority of the French population, opposed the measures, thinking them unnecessary for the purposes of French territorial defence and unduly influenced by the more aggressive interests of the Russians, who wanted a French army that would carry any future war to the Germans, and who paid parts of the French nationalist press to make their argument. Socialist leader Jean Jaurès brought 150,000 French protesters out to the Pré-Saint-Gervais in May – adding to a petition signed by five times that number – haranguing the government for not pursuing a more active policy of peace. The same month, nearly two hundred French politicians – including deputies and senators – attended a peace conference in Berne, joined by several dozen German colleagues. But for a man such as Poincaré, all this was by the by: it was only by remaining alert and ready that France would prevent history from repeating itself. His was a policy of peace – but it was a policy of peace through strength. Poincaré would ultimately be successful, pushing the three-year law through parliament later that summer.

French socialist leader Jean Jaurès in characteristic pose, arguing against the extension of military service from two to three years.

In many ways, a patriotic Frenchman could contemplate France's position in 1913 with a degree of satisfaction. For a start, the country was perhaps more united than at any time in its recent history. It was more united than in 1870, when France had buckled under the pressure of the Prussian advance, and ended up fighting a civil war on the streets of Paris between the forces of law and order and those of the Paris Commune. And it was more united than at the turn of the century. Then, the heat of the Dreyfus affair had divided families against themselves and turned old friends into sworn enemies. France had torn itself apart over the question of whether Captain Alfred Dreyfus – convicted of spying for Germany by a court martial in 1895 – had been wrongly imprisoned in an army cover-up or whether he was evidence of Jewish treachery at the heart of the Republic.

For some, Dreyfus' guilt was preordained by his religious background. For others the question was more a national one. If the army said Dreyfus was guilty, then guilty he must be: to dispute this was to impeach the army's honour. For the Dreyfusards, however, the whole case was an appalling miscarriage of justice, anti-Semitic prejudice parading itself as patriotism. This was a fight, therefore, for the principles of justice, it was a fight for the soul of the Republic. It was a fight the Dreyfusards won, with Dreyfus ultimately rehabilitated eleven years after his original court martial. But by 1913 Dreyfus had retired from the army, and the affair which had carried his name was old news. Anti-Semitism was still virulent, but it was submerged in the wider cause of French nationalism.

Many of the older wounds to the French body politic, those dating from the French Revolution, had been cauterised, if not healed. In spite of the separation of church and state in 1905, the Republic was now broadly accepted by Catholics as the expression of the nation. When Joan of Arc was beatified in 1909, both republicans and Catholics rallied around her as a symbol of one eternal France. In Rome, Pope Pius X pointedly kissed the French tricolour at the beatification ceremony.[9] In Paris, Paul Déroulède, a leading French nationalist, could pay homage to Joan of Arc, in phrases unthinkable a few decades previously, 'as the Christian patriot I have always been and the Catholic Republican I shall always be'.[10] A Catholic republican, indeed! In the 1870s a royalist restoration of some sort, whether of the Orleanist or the Legitimist branch, had been a real possibility. By 1913 some were still romantically attached to royalism, but they were on the fringes of political power. Instead, France had forged a new common ground around a love of the French *patrie*, of which the Republic was now the accepted political form. It was precisely this kind of national *ralliement* which Poincaré himself represented. The form of French government was increasingly accepted on all sides. Politics now revolved around more mundane issues such as electoral reform and tax.

By any measure France was still a great country and a first-rank power. The French navy was amongst the world's largest; its army was the equal of any, though parity with Germany was becoming harder to maintain. France had amassed the world's second largest empire, from Indochina to Guyana, reaching into every continent on earth, even Antarctica. This empire was still expanding – not least in north Africa. While France had no continent or sub-continent to itself, as did Britain in India and Australia, it had Algeria, relatively sparsely populated yet close to the fatherland. The empire was a source of pride for many, and of wealth for some. It was also an increasingly important source of troops. At the Bastille Day march past at Longchamp in July 1913, Poincaré presented the flag to twenty-five colonial regiments, from Algeria, Morocco, Senegal, Indochina, Madagascar, Chad and Gabon.[11] French investments around the world were second only to those of Britain. In Russia, in particular, French investment was dominant. And while London was the undisputed clearing house for the international gold standard, France had been instrumental in forming a Latin Monetary Union with Paris in a leading role, making the currencies of several European countries interchangeable.

If French industry was far smaller than that of either Germany or of Britain, it was nonetheless technologically advanced, pioneering both moving pictures (the Lumière brothers, Pathé) and the European automobile industry (Michelin, Renault, Peugeot). The Germans might have their lumbering Zeppelins, portrayed in French magazines as both ugly and dangerous, but the French were masters of the aeroplane, more graceful, more manoeuvrable, and faster. A Frenchman had already been the first to cross the Channel in 1909, and first to fly to Rome in 1911, sailing above the Vatican and an awestruck Pope. The year 1913 saw a Frenchman be the first to fly across the Mediterranean, a Frenchman be the first to land a plane in the Holy Land, French pilots flying higher than any man had ever flown, and a Frenchman perform the first loop-the-loop (which was then reperformed for adoring crowds at the Ghent world fair). Like French pilots, French engineers – educated in the École Polytéchnique or the École Centrale – had a daring and a flair of which their German counterparts could only dream. Only a Frenchman such as Gustave Eiffel, a graduate of the École Centrale, could have built the tower which bore his name in Paris. (In keeping with the time, by 1913 Eiffel was working on aerodynamics.)

Besides these material considerations of its power and influence France was, more to the point, still a great civilisation. It was the French language, not English, that was the *lingua franca* of society and diplomacy, if not commerce. French cooking was deemed the standard of elegance, and French chefs the most capable exponents of the art. French fashion set the trends for the world. France's universities, though perhaps less famous than Oxford and Cambridge, and without quite the same status at home as German universities, nonetheless housed great philosophers, Henri Bergson being the most famous, the advocate of intuition and the prophet of *'l'élan vital'* – the vital force of life. France produced great mathematicians, including Raymond Poincaré's cousin Henri. Over the preceding twelve years French scientists, authors and humanitarians had been awarded no fewer than fifteen Nobel prizes, close to the German total of seventeen, and far ahead of the British total of six, let alone the American three.

Above all, France still had Paris. While London dominated the terrestrial plane, did not Paris reign supreme on a more ethereal plane? It was, at the very least, more beautiful. Even a loyal subject of the British Empire such as Mr Ramunajaswami, stopping briefly in Paris on his way back to Berhampore, was forced to admit its beauty, though he worried this might appear disloyal to London. 'I may be pardoned', Ramunajaswami wrote, 'for hazarding my opinion that, in the best portions of Paris, were traceable more artistic beauty and greater symmetrical arrangements [than in the British capital]' though 'in respects other than those of artistic beauty, my predilec-tions are unhesitatingly in favour of London'.[12]

But there was something more. For the two and a half million Parisians who lived there – with a further one and a half million in the city's suburbs – and for thousands of visitors who arrived every day to catch something of the city's spirit, Paris was still the *cité-lumière*, the metropolis of light: a beacon to humanity. It was still in Paris that eternal verities of the human condition might reveal themselves, and universal principles of life be laid down. Paris, as a city of myths as much as one of bricks and stone, was a product of the collective imagination of its inhabitants, its visitors, and those who dreamed of visiting. As long as those myths were believed, Paris would retain its allure. And as long as Paris maintained its allure, France would be great.

For a visitor to the French capital, looking out from the observation deck at the top of the Eiffel Tower, the tallest man-made structure on earth, Paris unfolded itself voluptuously.

To the west and far below lay the Bois de Boulogne, the city's pleasure gardens, the former hunting grounds of emperors and kings, now crowded on any given afternoon with men in straw boaters promenading with their mistresses. To the north-west were the Place de l'Étoile and the magnificent Arc de Triomphe, reminder of the past victories of Napoleonic France. Down the Champs-Elysées, a more majestic avenue than any in London – and one marched down by German troops in 1871 – was the Place de la Concorde, home of the Hôtel Crillon and the Automobile Club de France, where Parisian high society celebrated the cult of speed and danger. Directly in front, beyond the gilded Opéra, at the summit of the hill of Montmartre, stood the Catholic basilica of Sacré-Cœur, largely built with donations from the public, erected as a bright reminder of France's Catholic heritage and as a symbol of penance for past godlessness – now surrounded by irreligious cafés, cabarets and dancing halls for every budget and every taste.

Below, at one's feet, lay the seventh *arrondissement*, home of the French parliament, military school, foreign ministry, and of the ministers and officials who worked there – the seat of French empire. To the east, the older districts of Paris on either side of the Seine, and the cathedral of Nôtre Dame on the Île de la Cité, in the middle of the river's flow. On the 'left bank' (though on the right viewed from the Eiffel Tower) the Latin quarter of the Sorbonne, crowned with the Panthéon, to which were committed the ashes of heroes of nation and Republic. On the 'right bank' (though on the left from this vantage point) stretched out the elongated elegance of the Louvre, the grandest gallery in the world, from which the Mona Lisa had been stolen in 1911 and to which it had not yet been returned. Further on, almost out of view, the district of the Marais, the former working-class heart of Paris and now home to the city's Jewish immigrants. Behind these, in an arc around the city's northern and eastern fringes, the *quartiers populaires* of Paris, the Paris of the street, Belleville and Ménilmontant, where the Commune had made its last bloody stand forty years before.

'Modern Paris', noted *Baedeker* in 1910, 'has been criticised for the uniformity of its general appearance'.[13] It was indeed true that large parts of the city had been rebuilt in the 1860s under the watchful eye of Baron Haussmann, widening the city's boulevards so as to make the construction of barricades more difficult and facilitate the movement of troops. This required that apartment blocks be built in a similar style and of a similar height, creating a city of greater aesthetic unity, and one which the rising bourgeoisie could claim as their own, rather than a city of poor artisans, shiftless vagrants and wealthy aristocrats.

Yet Haussmann's work had enhanced the city's grandeur, not

destroyed its charm. Some quarters of Paris struck *Baedeker* as almost Italian, others medieval. Surveying the city from the Eiffel Tower one caught a suggestion of its variety:

> The Seine, with its flotilla of merchant ships and barges, conveys, especially after dark, the impression of a sea-port. The boulevards at night with their electric lights and brilliant illuminations, suggest a city of pleasure, always *en fête*. And the charming environs, with the woods of Boulogne, Vincennes, Meudon and Montmorency, add a final touch to the variety that is one of the charms of the seductive capital, which no one quits without regret.

The Eiffel Tower had now stood for twenty-five years, the priapic symbol of French modernity, instantly recognisable to the city's visitors, and to many more around the world. In the first years of the twentieth century it had been slated for demolition. But it had been ingeniously repurposed as a radio mast, exciting a renewed burst of artistic appreciation for the tower as a symbol of modernity, painted by French artist Robert Delaunay and by Russian artist Marc Chagall, eulogised by Blaise Cendrars, the Swiss-born poet, and by the Italian-born writer Guillaume Apollinaire (briefly arrested on suspicion of having stolen the *Mona Lisa*). In a gesture which surely appealed to every Parisian's sense of their place in the world it now became, from July 1913, a planetary clock tower, the 'watch of the universe'.[14] Once in the late morning and then again at midnight a powerful radio signal would be sent around the world. The world would be reminded that Paris still existed, and it was against this signal that the world's clocks should be set. Robert Delaunay completed one of his canvases with the words: '*La tour à l'univers s'addresse*' – 'The tower addresses itself to the universe'.

Thus was the myth of Paris as a force of universalisation maintained. The truth was somewhat more complex, itself a parable of how much France had become a single country over the last few decades, its regions and identities welded together by the force of the republican French state. It was not so long ago that there had been no commonly agreed time zones for the world, nor even a single time zone within France itself. In the past this had not mattered. In a world where 'all human existence played out in the shadow of one's native bell-tower' place determined the hour. But

Robert Delaunay, *The Eiffel Tower* (1910). The tower, symbol of France's '*élan vital*', beloved of artists of the time, had been slated for demolition at the beginning of the twentieth century. By 1913 the tower had been repurposed as a radio mast, broadcasting Paris time around the world.

what was accepted in that world seemed anachronistic in the world of the telegraph and the railway, set to standard rather than local times. 'According to local time', noted Louis Houllevigue in the *Revue de Paris* in 1913, 'the train seemed to take fifty-four minutes less to travel from Paris to Brest, than from Brest to Paris; a news item sent from Nice at midday arrived in Paris at eleven-forty'.[15] (To make this more confusing for the foreigner, clocks in French train stations ran five minutes behind in order to provide a cushion for hard-pressed passengers.)

To overcome these discrepancies, in 1891 France set her national time – and that of French Algeria – on Paris. Now, clocks in Calais and in Biarritz would show the same hour. But internationally, standardisation had already moved ahead from setting national times to aligning and setting regular intervals between them. This required establishing a starting point, a time zone against which to set others. Greenwich Mean Time, based on the Greenwich observatory outside London, had become the standard, a few minutes behind Paris. The establishment of a universal benchmark was a matter of practicality in an interconnected world, for much the same reason that local time was necessarily superseded by national time. But it was also a matter of safety: sending time signals by radio to ships at sea allowed them better to determine their exact location. In 1911 France bowed to the inevitable and renominated France's national time as being nine minutes and twenty-one seconds slower than Paris Mean Time, equivalent to that of Argentan, a village in Normandy on exactly the same line of longitude as Greenwich. Having failed to make the world adopt a system based on its geographical position, Paris now manoeuvred itself to be the world's time-setter nonetheless. In 1912 Paris hosted an international conference on the subject, preparing the Eiffel Tower for its new role, and Paris as the host of the new Bureau International de l'Heure.[16]

For much of the nineteenth century the claim of Paris to universality related to its politics: forever at the leading edge of history. In 1789 that had been the guillotine and the storming of the Bastille. In 1830, after a period when France had seen its first republic, then its first empire, and then the restoration of the monarch, Paris

deposed a Legitimist Bourbon king for a second time, replacing
him with a more liberal Orleanist monarch, and setting itself up
as a bastion of individual freedoms and political liberalism. It was
around this time that German writer Karl Ludwig Börne moved
to Paris and declared it the capital of the nineteenth century.[17] In
1848 another French revolution occurred, sparking off a wave of
European popular uprisings, and encouraging a young Karl Marx
to move back to Paris from Brussels, to what appeared to be the
revolutionary heart of Europe once more. In 1871, Paris became a
focus for political violence once again, establishing the radical Paris
Commune against both the Germans and the new conservative
French government which emerged from the disaster of the Franco-
Prussian War. The re-establishment of national order in Paris cost
10,000 lives on the barricades. Another 10,000 were summarily
executed; further thousands were exiled to New Caledonia in the
Pacific.

But alongside the image of Paris as a city of political radicalism,
occasionally violent, was the idea of Paris as a capital of pleasure
– forbidden pleasures included. Over the course of the long nineteenth century it was ultimately this idea which came to predominate:
Paris as a worldly city of good taste and luxury but also a romantic
city of artists and poets, poverty and its tragedies.

The idea of Parisian Bohemianism – passionate, flamboyant,
unconventional – was already established in literary culture by the
1850s, though it had to wait another forty years to be immortalised
in music by the Italian composer Giacomo Puccini.[18] By the 1860s,
in the midst of the Haussmann boom, the city acquired a reputation
for moral licence and for excess, described as the new Babylon, or
as 'the entertainer of Europe'.[19] This was the city of Manet's *Olympia*,
depicting a naked courtesan staring confidently out of the canvas
at any one of her surrogate clients amongst the male crowds of the
Paris Salon.[20] It was the city described in Zola's *Nana*, which tracks
the career of a teenage star of the operetta stage who seduces men
only to ultimately destroy both them and herself. In 1867 the city
created a new aspect to its universalism, hosting the Exposition
Universelle, and making itself the world's shop window, with exhibits
from as far away as Japan and Burma.

The Commune briefly revived the city's reputation for political
radicalism. But unlike the revolutions of 1789, 1830 or 1848 – which

had become foundation myths for the following regime – the Commune was something rather to forget than to commemorate. There was no glory attached to it for most republicans – socialists excepted – only the reminder of disaster. Instead Paris regained her former insouciance, coupled with an expansion in outlets for the consumption of alcohol, sex and amusement. Populism transferred from politics to entertainment. Between 1870 and the mid 1880s the number of Parisian cafés rose from 22,000 to 42,000.[21] Paris became the city of Seurat, who painted girls delicately lifting their skirts in dance halls for the inspection of orchestra and audience in *Le Chahut* or the Parisian bourgeoisie taking their ease on the island of La Grande Jatte, a top-hatted dandy promenading with his mistress. It was also the city of Toulouse-Lautrec and Degas, sculptor of tender ballerinas, painter of circuses, brothels and dance halls.

The *fin de siècle* saw Paris resplendent, at the height of its reputation – origin of all the latest fads, and capital of the arts. Only in Paris could one visit the Louvre in the afternoon, listen to an operetta in the evening and then, if feeling adventurous, listen to gypsy music until dawn at the Rat Mort in the still largely unmodernised Montmartre, or take in the plebeian scene at the Moulin de la Galette. Around the Grands Boulevards, Paris became the playground for Europe's wealthy and dissolute, choosing each sunset between the Folies Bergère on rue Richer, the Moulin Rouge or the Étoile Palace, where each night a different cast of spectators was unburdened of their worries and of their money by the same cast of singers and dancers. In Paris one could eat well, the city having practically invented the modern restaurant, lunching at the Ritz and dining at Durand's or at Paillard's. And Paris remained, of course, the city of sex, whether purchased directly from one of the city's many brothels or more indirectly and delicately acquired through the taking on of a mistress.

If London was where the world came to invest its money, Paris sold itself as the place where the world came to spend it. In London people did business; in Paris they came to international conferences: 426 were held in the French capital between 1900 and 1913, compared to 168 in Brussels, 141 in London and 96 in Berlin (New York, off the beaten track of such things, held just 14, fewer than the Norwegian capital Oslo).[22] In the 1890s the German Kaiser disparagingly called Paris 'the whorehouse of the world' – but he knew that his own capital, however much it might have grown, could not yet compare with it for charisma or international pull.[23] In 1900 Paris hosted the Exposition Universelle for the fourth time, each time more successful than the last. Some fifty million visitors saw the Exposition of 1900 – more than the entire population of France or Britain. Paris thus laid claim to the twentieth century.

Americans, in particular, had long been in love with Paris, the antidote to American puritanism and the narrowness of its commercial spirit.[24] Increasing numbers of Americans took advantage of fast ships to Le Havre to consummate that love – and, in a novel twist, to find themselves in the process. In Henry James' novel *The Ambassadors*, published in 1903, the fifty-five-year-old Lewis Lambert Strether is sent to Paris to rescue his fiancée's son Chad from the city's moral dangers – Chad has taken up with an elegant (and older) Parisian companion – and instead finds himself quite taken in by the city, leading him to re-examine his own life in its light.[25] In the same year *The Ambassadors* was published, a well-off young American, Gertrude Stein, moved to Paris with her brother Leo, where she established an intellectual salon at their apartment at 27 rue de Fleurus, its walls dripping with contemporary art of the Paris scene.

Thus visitors to Paris serviced the city's mythology, and became part of it themselves. 'Paris', observed an American visitor from the Midwest in 1913, 'is the magnet that attracts all the tribes of the earth; it is the dumping ground for the gold of the world'. The city left her breathless – something no one would ever say of London, except perhaps in reference to its smog:

> Once you have lived in it [Paris], drunk in its beauties, absorbed its mysterious atmosphere, and become fascinated with its inscrutable personality and its *sans-gêne* joy of life, you are part of it forever. It is a city full of noble beauty and of fascination. You cannot define this fascination, but you feel it – it takes possession of you. You breathe it in, in long delicious drafts. You live tremendously and nerve-rackingly; you expect it, it is Paris.[26]

So much for the city of revolution. Paris was now the quintessential city of seduction, sensation and spectacle, to be consumed without moderation, to be experienced rather than to be comprehended: the city of pleasure and occasionally the city of risk. This was a mythology to which Parisians themselves could subscribe, flattering, as it did, both their sophistication and their worldliness.

By 1913 Paris had become the first global tourist brand: its allure to the world undiminished. Paris was a commodity, reproduced on postcards and posters, bottled and sold as perfume. A thousand Cafés de Paris opened their doors around the world, aspiring to recreate, even for one instant, the atmosphere of the street of the genuine French capital, with its *boulevardiers*, elegantly-dressed *flâneurs*, and its colourful criminal gangs of *apaches*. Visitors to the real thing could not leave it without having some tacky keepsake thrust upon them. An *'Article de Paris'*, as such souvenirs were known – *'souvenir'* meaning memory in French – could be anything from artificial flowers to a leather bag.

In truth, such articles were more likely to have been mass produced in the city's east end than hand-crafted in a studio within earshot of Nôtre Dame. But this did not matter. Like relics from the Holy Land a thousand years previously, the object's significance lay partly in its provenance, but equally in the meaning with which the owner imbued it, and the worship to which it was subjected, displayed proudly on a mantelpiece or above a doorway. Souvenirs were, of course, ephemera – but ephemera touched by eternity. Sergey Prokofiev sent back twenty-nine identical postcards of the Eiffel Tower to friends in St Petersburg to prove that he had indeed made it to the city of light. He also ordered a black suit with black-and-white checked trousers, experimented with whisky and soda, and stayed in his first double bed. 'Altogether Paris, as a city, is astonishingly beautiful, alive, gay and seductive', he wrote in his diary, 'I felt on top of the world there, surrounded on all sides by novelty and interest'.[27]

But was not Paris a little tawdry in 1913 compared to the magnificent city of 1900? Trainloads of tourists arrived each morning from Calais with a day's hectic sight-seeing before them. Was the city's romance not diminished by industrial-scale tourism, and by the cheap pedlars and swindlers who sought to profit from it? On stepping outside his hotel on the rue Helder, Prokofiev found himself immediately assailed by a Frenchman who sold him a map and a dozen postcards and who 'offered me from under the counter a packet of indecent pictures'.[28] Dreiser chased away a similar approach by asking the vendor if he had a mother, or a sister, and what they would think of such things.[29] *Baedeker* presented card sharps as being a particular hazard on suburban trains and warned its female readers not to frequent cafés north of the Grands Boulevards, where they risked being misunderstood and possibly harassed. Tourists of both sexes were advised not to travel to less-frequented parts of the city after nightfall, and to be vigilant at all times against 'the huge army of pickpockets and other rogues who are quick to recognize the stranger and skilful in taking advantage of his ignorance'.[30] Prokofiev's mother, perhaps a little less impressionable than her young son, was rather less bowled over by the city: '"Well, here it is, Paris", said Mama as we came out through the gates of the Gare du Nord and she looked around her. "Nothing special though."'[31]

Some Parisians worried: was not Paris losing some of its charm and originality? *Parisia* magazine fulminated in January 1913 against the commercialisation of the Champs-Elysées. 'An illuminated sign over there, a pylon to be erected over here; further on, an advertising hoarding freshly mounted; emboldened building-owners agree to hire themselves out for business with ever more aggressive and provocative displays and advertisements', wrote a journalist, criticising the trend to place advertisements across the front of buildings, breaking up the visual rhythm of the avenue and prostituting it to baser purposes. 'See those enormous golden letters hanging from the balcony, look at the flamboyant sign which "makes eyes" at you in the same way a pickpocket "does" your pockets', the tirade continued, 'see if you can stand the glare of a tawdry electric advertisement which would burn the pupils of a blind man'.[32]

Worse, perhaps, was the demolition of parts of Montmartre, the former crucible of the Parisian art scene and of the city's romantic appeal. On the very day that Raymond Poincaré was being feted in London, the London papers reported on the area's gradual transformation. 'Old Montmartre', one noted, 'is being pulled stone from stone, and soon will be nothing but a memory':

> The wide-trousered, floating-tied, long-haired Bohemians of all the Quat'z'Arts, who had found their last refuge in this forgotten village are in despair, and know not where to hide now to be at peace. Paris

is invading the sacred Butte, and all that gave it character and charm is vanishing before it.[33]

The artists were now elsewhere. Matisse lived on the city's south-western outskirts, in a bourgeois villa in Issy-les-Moulineaux. Pablo Picasso, the Spanish artist but long-time Paris resident, had his studio on rue Schoelcher, opposite the Montparnasse cemetery in southern Paris. Montmartre was now a tourist trap, a pale imitation of former glories.

Paris remained Europe's capital of culture in 1913, though it wore the crown a little more uneasily than in 1900. Vienna and Munich, even London and Berlin, had made inroads into the French capital's former unquestioned supremacy. Yet 'France still sets the tone', wrote Jacques-Emile Blanche, critic and artist, 'from everywhere they come to Paris to see what we produce and to gain our sanction for their cosmopolitan baggage'.[34] Paris remained a centre of artistic innovation, giving rise to the Cubism of Picasso and Braque. It remained the place where artists exhibited, and where they sold their work. Paris was still the place to launch a career or to launch a movement. When Italian Filippo Marinetti launched the Futurist manifesto in 1909, proclaiming the birth of a self-consciously incendiary artistic movement dedicated to speed, novelty and violence, he did so on the front page of the Parisian newspaper *Le Figaro*, in French, only two weeks after it had appeared, with much less fanfare, in an Italian newspaper:

8. We are on the extreme promontory of the centuries! . . . What good is it to look behind us at the moment when we must smash in the mysterious doors of the Impossible? Time and Space died yesterday. We live already in the absolute, because we have already created the eternal omnipresent speed.
9. We want to glorify war – the world's only hygiene – militarism, patriotism, the destructive actions of anarchists, beautiful Ideas which kill, scorn for women.
10. We want to demolish the museums, libraries, combat moralism, feminism and the all opportunist and utilitarian cowardice.[35]

The very notion of the avant-garde, the permanently shifting vanguard of modern art, emerged in Paris.

But while Paris remained the arbiter of cultural modernity, and a platform for artistic endeavours, its role now was as much a *vitrine* for European culture – a shop window – as an advertisement for that of France. Unlike Impressionism, which had been dominated by the tastes of Paris and by French artists, the newer movements within the visual arts were not identifiably French at all. Expressionism's chief exponents were based in Germany. Futurism may have been launched in a Parisian newspaper but its leaders were Italian and, in a somewhat different form, Russian. The theatres of Paris, meanwhile, had held Viennese, Italian and even Belgian seasons in recent years.[36] The artistic event of 1913, one which famously caused a riot amongst the audience for its daring, was almost entirely foreign: the staging of *The Rite of Spring*, with Russian ballet dancers dancing to music composed by a Russian composer, Igor Stravinsky, in a theatre criticised for its Germanic lines as 'the Zeppelin of the Avenue Montaigne'.[37]

'The French are barely tolerated on their home turf these days', wrote Jacques-Émile Blanche. It was only by force of habit that Paris was still asked to pronounce its supreme verdict on the world's art at all. And so rather than Paris conquering the world, it was the world which was conquering, colonising and internationalising it. Paris, Blanche concluded, was fast becoming the 'central station of Europe', its originality and impetus now imported.[38]

In 1913, despite all the accolades and superlatives heaped upon France by her sons and daughters, there was a lingering sense of apprehension behind French pride and posturing.

There was perhaps more menace to the future now than ten years ago, in the bright sunshine of the Exposition Universelle. In 1913 the film *Fantômas* occupied the capital's cinema screens; the elaborate crimes of its eponymous anti-hero were committed against the everyday backdrop of the modern world. The poster for the film showed Fantômas top-hatted and masked, a spectre dominating a blood-red sky, leering over Paris, the Eiffel Tower barely reaching above his knees. Fantômas suggested the almost occult power of modernity, a dark and mysterious side to quotidian experience, a world from which spectres of evil had not been exiled, but rather

The spectre of fictional master criminal Fantômas occupied French cinema screens in 1913, symbol of the occult power of modernity.

one to which they had returned in new and more dangerous forms.

Perhaps these apprehensions of modernity, balanced though they were by the positive cult of speed, aeroplanes and automobiles, were tied up with a broader set of questions about France's relationship to the changing world around it. Was France past its prime? Was French greatness a reality – or was it a sense memory, like the texture of a madeleine dissolving on the palate, as in Marcel Proust's elegiac novel *À la recherche du temps perdu* (*In Search of Lost Time*), the first instalment of which was published in 1913? Above all, was France slipping quietly behind its rivals – Germany, in particular?

To even ask such questions was considered by some to be too fatalistic, if not defeatist. Poincaré himself had on occasion declared discussions of French decadence to be unpatriotic. For every ten books proclaiming the causes of decadence – German-Jewish conspiracy being a staple of far-right writers such as Léon Daudet, and the internationalist socialism of Jean Jaurès offering another target – there were a couple proclaiming the glorious renewal of France around the ideas of patriotic union and sacrifice for the nation. French nationalism was shrill because it was born of weakness, intended as an exhortation to renewal, as if greatness depended only on self-belief, and not on material facts.

For some, France's population statistics showed all that one needed to know about the country's historical decline, and provided all that one needed to worry about for France's future. 'One single agonising problem should occupy all the thoughts of France', wrote Jacques Bertillon starkly in a surprise best-selling treatise on the issue: '"How to prevent France from disappearing? How to maintain the French race on earth?"'[39] How was it, Bertillon asked, that France, with some of the best agricultural land in Europe, supported less than half the number of citizens per square mile than did Britain? How was it that France's population had increased by only two million over the previous thirty years, while Britain's had grown by ten million and that of Germany by eighteen million? Even Italy was now almost as populous as France.

The reasons for France's relative depopulation were various: low levels of childbirth amongst France's leading classes, laws of succession that tended to discourage large families (as this would lead to ever-greater fragmentation of estates), and French couples' sexual habits, in particular the 'crime of Onan' (coitus interruptus or masturbation). Bertillon cited additionally the popularity of Parisian music halls – dens of 'light music [and] inept and immoral refrains' – plays which implied that smaller families were better, the availability of contraceptive prophylactics, and campaigns against childbirth which he associated with socialists and anarchists. He applauded the actions of a police chief across the border in Belgium, who had closed down an educational display of contraceptive methods on the basis that this fell under the category of an immoral publication. In order to try and reverse the depopulation trend, Bertillon formed the Alliance nationale pour l'accroissement de la population with Charles Richet, a physiologist who won the Nobel Prize for Medicine in 1913, tirelessly lobbying the French parliament to act (though without great success).

The fact of France's relative depopulation entailed a string of dangers, as Bertillon saw it. Already, a higher proportion of the country's male population was required to serve in the military in order to achieve parity of numbers between the French and German armies. Indeed, this was one of the reasons Poincaré campaigned in 1913 for an extension of military service from two to three years in the wake of a German expansion.

In the future, this problem would become more acute. France would be required to rely more and more on its less physically robust conscripts, and those from its colonies. These were facts not lost on German military planners, or their acolytes. 'A people who do not want to be soldiers and whose women refuse to have children, is a people benumbed in their vitality', wrote one German a decade previously, 'fated to be dominated by a younger and fresher race'.[40] Weakened militarily, Bertillon asked, would France ultimately become like Poland, carved up by Europe's other powers?

But this was not all. High levels of British emigration had historically strengthened the ties between the British motherland and its far-flung overseas possessions, particularly the settlement colonies of Canada, Australia, South Africa and New Zealand. Emigration from France to its empire, however, had traditionally been low, partly the consequence of slow population growth overall. This, Bertillon thought, tended to enfeeble the impulse of colonial expansion, and weaken the bonds of empire. Even in Algeria, the jewel of the French Empire, much of the non-Arab population was not of French origin. Within Europe, meanwhile, the decline in the number of French speakers compared to those who spoke German (now more than double), would mean that the language of Voltaire would lose its universality, and with it France would lose her cultural influence.

To read Bertillon's analysis was to read about a France sleepwalking to her political, economic and cultural doom. How much would French achievements be worth without the men ready to fight for them? If the scales came to be weighed between France and Germany, as men such as Poincaré believed possible – perhaps likely – what would tip the balance France's way? Faith, perhaps? National unity? The patriotism of the young?

In 1913 two Catholic intellectuals, Henri Massis and Alfred de Tarde, published *Les jeunes gens d'aujourd'hui* (*The Young of Today*), writing under the pseudonym 'Agathon'. They vigorously rejected the idea that demography was destiny. Instead, they described a generation of 1890, their generation, those born twenty years after French defeat in the Franco-Prussian war. This generation, they claimed, was different from that of their parents, accused of pessimism and dilettantism. The younger generation, in contrast, was inspired by the ideal of action and sacrifice, by the culture of sport and by the adventure of travel, a rediscovery of Catholic faith in place of the libertinage of the precedent generation, that which had flourished around the turn of the century. Their intellectual heroes were Maurice Barrès and Henri Bergson – the philosopher of *'l'élan vital'*. Their exponents were Paul Claudel and Charles Péguy, the Catholic Dreyfusard and nationalist. Disciples of Jaurès, once numerous in the 'cosmopolitan' Sorbonne, were now outnumbered by nationalists.

This generation, Massis and de Tarde explained, would rather undertake a colonial campaign than sit comfortably at home. They provided the examples of Klipfell, a recent graduate of the École normale supérieure, who joined the army so as to serve in Morocco, and that of Ernest Pischari, the grandson of Ernest Renan, the great theorist of French nationalism, who wished to serve in the African bush. 'For such young men', Massis and de Tarde wrote, 'exalted by their patriotic faith and by the cult of war-like virtues, all they need is the opportunity in order to become heroes'.[41] This, they argued, would be the generation to save France.

BERLIN
Powerhouse

'Paris has had its day', wrote Theodore Dreiser, approaching the end of his European tour, 'and will no doubt have others'. 'London is happy with an endless conservative day', he continued.[1] But Berlin's brightest days lay before it. 'The blood is there, and the hope, and the moody, lustful Wagnerian temperament', wrote Dreiser, suitably enough in the year of Wagner's centenary.

Visitors to Berlin, over a million of them in 1913, found a city full of nervous, unchannelled energy; a city that wrapped itself in the mantle of the German Reich but which was, inside, still the provincial capital of Prussia; a city which was reckoned the most modern in Europe, an industrial powerhouse and a capital of science; a city on parade. Their reactions were mixed. Some saw a metropolis more suggestive of the future than any other, more urban and more modern, the very expression of the global economic force which the German Empire had become. But other visitors found a parvenu, blaring its new-found prosperity but with no finer sensibilities, an ugly and uncouth city. Many found both.

Russians, who made up over a third of tourists to the city, might breathe a little more freely here than they could at home, and perhaps see in Berlin an intimation of what a rapidly industrialising, semi-democratic state could achieve.[2] Austrians, the second most frequent visitors, looked nervously at Berlin as a rival capital of the German-speaking world. Americans, the third most numerous group, tended to find the city modern at least, reminding them of home. But they would not stay long. 'They'll only stay three days here', noted the owner of the Hotel Adlon melancholically, 'then they will scatter to the spa towns . . . it's Paris which will get the bulk of their money'.[3]

Theodore Dreiser's first glimpses of the city were from a

horse-drawn carriage, jogging from the glass and iron splendour of the Friedrichstrasse railway station down the tree-lined Unter den Linden, Berlin's ostentatious answer to the Champs-Elysées, with the Brandenburg Gate ahead:

> Everything, literally *everything*, was American new – and newer – German new! And the cabbies were the largest, fattest, most broad-backed, most thick-through and *Deutschiest* looking creatures I have ever beheld.

Charles Huard, a French artist, sketched the same view on a sheaf of paper, later incorporating it into a caustic book on Berlin which played to the popular French stereotypes of the Germans: haughty, disdainful, unattractive. Unter den Linden, he had been assured by an acquaintance from Berlin, was finer than the Corso in Rome, more aristocratic than the boulevards of Paris or Piccadilly in London. Instead, he found 'a wide avenue, certainly, but planted with common trees, unwelcome chestnuts and shrivelled linden trees; unsightly carriages drawn by emaciated horses . . . My disillusion was complete'.[4] On the terrace in front of the Kranzler patisserie Huard noted 'a fat man trying greedily to lick his spoon' and, on the pavement, 'a succession of heavy, thick, robust people, with arrogant and forbidding faces'.

Arriving from the east, Sergey Prokofiev marvelled at the number of railway stations in the city, unsure of which one he should alight at: 'Berlin something-or-other, that must be ours, no, must be further on, then Berlin-something-else, no, this still isn't it; finally, Berlin Friedrichstrasse, and we had to scramble out quickly as the train waited there only for two minutes before continuing to yet another Berlin-something'.[5] Prokofiev and his mother lunched on lobster and champagne at the Kempsinsky hotel to recover. The city, he found, was 'Germanically impressive', with broad, straight avenues through the Tiergarten, the central city park and former hunting grounds of the Hohenzollern kings. No beautiful women though, he noted, or at least none as attractive as Umnenkaya, the Russian girl from St Petersburg who occupied his thoughts.

Berlin für Kenner, a guidebook from 1912, advised the new arrival to the city, fresh off the train from Paris or St Petersburg or Vienna, to head straight into the crowds.[6] Starting conveniently from

Friedrichstrasse – the station where Dreiser, as well as Prokofiev and Prokofiev's mother had disembarked – the guidebook suggested walking first south down Leipziger Strasse towards what was one of the city's premier sights: the Wertheim department store, one of the city's largest alongside A. Jandorf & Co., Tietz, and, newest of all, the Kaufhaus des Westens (KaDeWe) in the city's west. 'Naturally one goes inside', the guidebook explained, 'and then is immediately cast helplessly into the delirium of Berlin life'. Wertheim was indeed a city within a city, offering shopping, but also a library, art gallery, roof garden, photography studio, ticket agency and several restaurants. Such stores were a crucible of the Berliner identity, some observers noted, because these were places where aristocrats and the middle classes mixed, where the city's population was united in a new culture of conspicuous consumption.[7] More prudish Germans, scandalised that a department store should feature alongside Berlin's museums and art galleries amongst the city's highlights, saw department stores rather as proof of Berlin's worsening dissipation, an assault on traditional middle-class virtues of thrift and self-development through education, and perhaps a softening of that famously upright Prussian spine.

Continuing down Leipziger Strasse from Wertheim one arrived at Potsdamer Platz, Berlin's Trafalgar Square and Place de l'Étoile rolled into one. Here, above all, one could sense the vibrancy of the city: 'the picture of unbelievable movement of people, lights and cars that presents itself to the eyes – THAT is Berlin!' This was the square that suggested itself to Ernst Ludwig Kirchner and to Ludwig Meidner, painters of the city, as an expression of the modern metropolis. 'A street', Meidner wrote the following year in his instructions on how the modern city should be painted, 'is composed not of tonal values, but is a bombardment of whizzing rows of windows, of rushing beams of light between vehicles of many kinds, of a thousand leaping spheres, tatters of people, advertisements, and droning, formless masses of colour'.[8]

This, then, was Berlin: colourful, large, impressive in a showy kind of way, above all, modern. Berlin was a city of vending machines and newspaper kiosks, telephones and trams. In 1895 the city had eight times as many telephones per head of population as London; by 1911, even after the prodigious growth of telephony all across the world, it still had twice as many as the capital of the British Empire.[9] Berlin's electric tram network was equal in length to the distance between Berlin, in the north-east of the German Empire, to Frankfurt-am-Main, in the south-west. Its most recent subway station – Alexanderplatz – had opened in 1913. At the very end of that year, the world's most famous physicist, Albert Einstein, prepared to take up his new post at the Kaiser-Wilhelm-Gesellschaft zur Förderung der Wissenschaften (the Kaiser Wilhelm Society for the Advancement of Science). After all, Berlin was a city of science – and it was not unfriendly to the Jews. The World Zionist Organisation had its headquarters here.

Less visible to the casual visitor to Berlin was what Walter Rathenau, the German Jewish son of the founder of the Allgemeine Elektricitäts-Gesellschaft (AEG), called the 'Fabrikstadt', the factory-city of Berlin, lining the city's eastern canals and the ring railway, forming a huge arc around the centre from north-west to south-east, from the Siemens plant at Charlottenburg past AEG's various factories. For it was here in Berlin that the German electrical engineering industry – makers of world-famous turbines and gener-ators, telegraphs and telephones – had made its home, close to some of Europe's finest technical universities, and to many of the indus-try's major clients: the German military, the railways and the post office.[10] While Paris might retain the crown of the *cité lumière*, Berlin gloried in the title of '*Elektropolis*', city of electricity.

American Walt Kuhn, visiting Berlin to acquire European art works to show at an exhibition at the Armory in New York certainly found the city an energising jolt, if not perhaps the pleasantest of places. 'Town and people not "Gemütlich"', he wrote home to his wife.[11] He compared the traffic to New York: 'the police make a bluff of it, but you've got to jump or get bumped'.

The origins of Berlin as a garrison town, and Prussia as a militarised society, still persisted in a certain air of officiousness in the city, attempting to tame Berlin's restlessness and contain it within the straitjacket of Prussian order. The Belgian ambassador remembered that, whereas one could lie down on the grass in the Bois de Boulogne or in a London park, one was met in the Tiergarten with the sign '*Verboten*' – 'forbidden' – stuck in the perfectly tended lawn.[12] Dreiser described the everyday presence of high officialdom:

The German policeman with his shining brass helmet and brass belt; the Berlin sentry in his long military gray overcoat, his musket over his shoulder, his high cap shading his eyes, his black-and-white striped sentry box behind him, stationed apparently at every really important corner and before every official palace; the German military and imperial automobiles speeding their independent ways, all traffic cleared before them, the small flag of officialdom or imperialism fluttering defiantly from the foot-rails as they flash at express speed past you.[13]

The spiky-helmeted officer was such an instantly recognisable symbol of Prussia that it was chosen as the cover of an English guidebook to Berlin, understood in a single glance across a crowded London bookshop.[14]

In Berlin, the suggestions of Prussia's military origins and traditions were never far away, in the monuments to past military victories, in the endless parades, in the military brass bands in the city's parks, or in the presence of soldiers in fantastic uniforms, the Kaiser chief amongst them, on Berlin's grand central avenues and in its smart cafés. In 1906 traditional Prussian deference to the outward signs of military office had turned to farce when a humble cobbler Wilhelm Voigt, dressed in the second-hand uniform of an army officer, picked up some real German soldiers in the street, ordered them to follow him to Köpenick town hall, where he proceeded to claim 4,000 marks from the borough's mayor – with nothing more than his self-assurance and his soldiers as his warrant – and then made off with the money, changing later into civilian clothes. So confident was he of the effect of his military uniform that he had commandeered a train on the way. Voigt was picked up, and eventually pardoned by the Kaiser in 1908. After all, Wilhelm felt, had not Voigt's escapade shown that the spirit of hierarchy and authority was alive and well in Berlin? By 1913 the 'Captain of Köpenick' was part of Berlin lore.

There were more subtle signs of society's latent militarisation, too. The city's apartment buildings, occupying large blocks of land, were referred to as *Mietskasernen*, literally 'rented barracks', a reference to the size of the apartments they contained as well as to their anonymous, uniform and quasi-military character. In Grunewald, the forested areas to the city's west, one might easily come across groups of young men on a *Wandervogel* of an early morning, part of a scouting society under the patronage of Germany's militaristic Crown Prince Wilhelm, the same man who published his paean of praise to the manly virtues of war in 1913. Even in the public gymnastics practised by the beach at Wannsee there was a fondness for the display of military precision and bodily preparation. No surprise then that the president of the German Imperial Board for the Olympic Games, charged with improving the country's Olympic performance for the 1916 Berlin games – to be held in the new stadium inaugurated with great fanfare in June 1913 – was a military man, General Victor von Podbielski.[15]

The organisational virtues of the Prussian state were in evidence in Berlin's streets, kept spotless by an army of cleaning trucks (though this made it dangerous for cyclists). The city had made great strides since the 1870s in the matter of public sanitation. By 1913 one English guidebook could comment: 'Berlin drinking water is excellent, so clear and so refreshing it is a wonder the working-classes do not prefer it to beer, but unfortunately they do not'.[16] Whereas Hamburg had experienced a cholera outbreak as recently as 1892, Berlin's city authorities kept the city safe through the regular application of disinfectant.[17]

Whatever the role of officialdom in making Berlin function efficiently as a city, and whatever its military undertones, there was ample room for private distraction and frivolity too. Society could not be managed entirely from above, as some conservatives would have liked. There was the Luna Park at Halensee and the flirtatious atmosphere of the five o'clock tea dances in any one of the city's leading hotels. Like the rest of Europe, Berlin was in the midst of a craze for the tango in 1913, though the Kaiser forbade military officers in uniform from dancing it. There was perhaps even a hint of counter-culture in the city's vegetarian restaurants (which numbered 152 in 1902) and nudist societies – not to mention in its nightlife.[18]

For it was at night the city's gloves came off, exchanging its daylight officiousness for its night-time licentiousness. 'The nightlife of Berlin', remarked *Berlin für Kenner* in the exaggerated tones of a promoter, 'cannot be compared to that of any other city, not even Paris, and it marks out Berlin as a *Weltstadt*'.[19] In the centre of town, around Friedrichstrasse and from Unter den Linden until Mohrenstrasse, the guide promised visitors plenty of *Nachtlokalen*, the late closing bars frequented by smartly-dressed Berliners. 'Why don't you follow them in?' it suggested, 'one doesn't need to drink champagne in the Moulin Rouge or the Palais de Danse, one can be quite happy with Mosel or Bordeaux'. (Dreiser's experience was different: he found he could buy only champagne at the Palais de Danse at the cost of twenty marks a pop, about a third the cost of a good new suit.[20]) These places, not far from the city's new hotels, the grand Adlon (located at number one, Unter den Linden) or the only slightly less grand Esplanade, were relatively tame. Here, noted the guide helpfully, 'one can take one's wife without fear'. Later, one could continue the evening at the Lindencasino or at Toni Grünefeld's bar, open till four in the morning at least.

An alternative expedition, or *'Bummeltour'* as the guide called it, would take the (male) visitor to the northern part of Berlin, more industrial, more grimy, more risqué. For this, it 'would be better to leave the wife at the hotel'. Here the night could stretch until after dawn. At six in the morning one could continue drinking toasts to Berlin the glorious, Berlin the superlative, Berlin the drunk, at Café Stern or at the bars of the Elsässer Strasse, just opening, the Erlanger Krug, Café Goethe or Walhalla. Now would be the final hour for the city's prostitutes, estimated at 20,000 plus perhaps an additional 2,000 male prostitutes.[21] (Though homosexuality was illegal in Germany, Berlin was the homosexual capital of Europe – and therefore the world.) In some of these early morning bars it might be wise to hide one's identity papers in case the police decided to conduct a *razzia*, a raid. But then, *'Auch das ist Berliner leben!'* – 'THAT too is Berlin life!' – proclaimed the guide triumphantly, as if a trip to Berlin were not complete without a run in with the forces of law and order. So much for unquestioning deference to authority.

And it was perhaps coming back to one's hotel in the morning that the foreign visitor might catch sight of that other Berlin, the Berlin of the urban proletariat, the workers in Rathenau's *Fabrikstadt*. Whereas fewer than four out of ten Parisian workers were employed in industry in 1913, six out of ten Berliners were.[22] 'At best we find out how it [the proletariat] starts the day when we get home tired, at five or six', wrote sociologist Werner Sombart in 1906, 'after a night spent dancing or in an extended game of poker, or when we go to the railway station to catch an early train':

Then we are amazed to suddenly catch a glimpse of a totally alien world. We didn't know that they were there, these hundreds, these thousands, 'going to work' at a brisk walk, in twos and threes, mostly without speaking, working tools or coffee jar in hand, in long columns. They . . . hurry now into the arms of the giant Moloch, the factory whose shrill whistle at 6 o'clock, when we once more turn comfortably round in our beds, announces that its inmates' individual life is now over for eleven or twelve hours.[23]

This was Berlin's social underbelly – the 'reverse side of the gleaming medal' as *Berlin für Kenner* put it. This was the Berlin of the trade unions, which counted 224,000 members in 1905.[24] This was the Berlin of the 150,000 workers who protested for a change in Prussia's electoral laws in 1910, or the 200,000 who came out to Treptower Park in 1911 to condemn the Reich's foreign policy in Morocco. This was the city of Marxist sociological analysis and social democracy. It was the Berlin which conservative Berlin might like to forget, but which was nonetheless brought back to them by a strike, or by an outbreak of disease. Rosa Luxemburg, a Jewish Polish Social Democrat and later one of the founders of the German Communist Party, described the cases of three poor, relatively anonymous Berliners Joseph Geihe, Karl Melchior and Lucian Szczyptierowski, whose contraction of a mystery illness suddenly transformed them from dark shadows on the streets of the city to subjects of lively middle class interest and concern. 'In their entire lives [these three] never excited such interest', Luxemburg noted scathingly, but 'now – what an honour! . . . The contents of their stomachs, to which the world was once frankly indifferent, is now painstakingly examined and spoken about in all the newspapers'.[25]

Everyone agreed that while Berlin might not yet be as important as London, and was far too industrial and brash to ever be as charming as Paris, it was nonetheless the coming city, as unmissable as Shanghai today.

At the opening of the nineteenth century Berlin had been little more than a dusty garrison town in the middle of the Prussian plain, its population barely 200,000, royal seat of the kings of Prussia, the artificial capital of a north German state with pretensions above its station. 'The capital of Prussia resembles Prussia itself', wrote Madame de Staël in 1814, 'the buildings and the institutions are of the same age as men, and nothing more, because they are the creation of one man' – Frederick the Great, though he had preferred speaking French and spending his time in nearby Potsdam at the Sanssouci palace, rather than in Berlin itself.[26]

In 1871 however, the Prussian capital was catapulted into a new role as the capital of the German Empire, freshly proclaimed in Versailles. Since then it had grown prodigiously, becoming one of Europe's main industrial cities and gradually acquiring the trappings of a *Weltstadt*, or world-city, just as Germany aspired to become a *Weltmacht*, or world power. As much as possible, it was felt, Berlin should reflect the dynamism and international reach of Germany itself, a country which now produced more steel than Britain, France and Russia combined, which exported more than any country on earth other than the United Kingdom, and which produced the bulk of the world's chemicals (shipped to their consumers on British

Peter Behrens' modernist turbine hall (1909), built for AEG. Berlin was not just the capital of the German Empire, but an industrial powerhouse in its own right, both '*Fabrikstadt*' (factory city) and aspirational '*Weltstadt*' (world city).

ships), not to mention leading the globe in electrical engineering.[27] As Germany's bankers and businessmen looked around the world they saw markets to be conquered and consumers to be satisfied. In 1913 they set up a research institute in Kiel to study the issue.

By 1913 Berlin's population was nearly four million, and rising. It was only a matter of time before it passed five million, then six, gaining on London all the while. The Berlin of the mid nineteenth century – 'Alt Berlin', as the old-timers called it – bore only limited resemblance to the urban behemoth which had grown up in its place, from the city's poorer central districts, to the industrial north and east, and out into newer districts of the west and the villas of the bourgeoisie in Grunewald, where Rathenau had a highly ornate house on the Königsallee that was quite unlike the industrial buildings which daily made his fortune.

Kaiser Wilhelm II had invested heavily in memorials and monuments to emphasise Prussia's historical claims to greatness, and to give the place some gravitas. (Dreiser termed the resulting sculptures 'a crime against humanity'.[28]) The city already had, of course, the Siegessäule – a bombastic victory column topped with a golden statue. The Kaiser added to this by building a memorial church to his grandfather, also Kaiser Wilhelm, at the top of the Kurfürstendamm. He built a cathedral, which he hoped one day would be to Protestants what St Peter's was to Catholics. Himself an amateur archaeologist, who regularly turned up 'finds' on his holiday island of Corfu in the Ionian Sea, Wilhelm took a personal interest in Germany's acquisition of the archaeological treasures of the ancient world, enticing the famous archaeologist Heinrich Schliemann to leave his hoard of treasures to the city of Berlin. He had presided personally over the inauguration of a new space to house the Pergamon Altar in 1902, before construction began on the Pergamon Museum in 1912.[29] He inaugurated the Victory Avenue, a sculpture park of famous figures from the Prussian past, stretching back to the twelfth-century Albrecht der Bär, though some statues looked suspiciously like sycophants from the contemporary court.

At the beginning of the twentieth century the city's boroughs followed their Kaiser's cue, building town halls which outdid each other in the height of their towers and the grandeur of their façades, a mishmash of historical references which characterised the city as a whole. The *Rathaus* of Köpenick attempted something approaching north German Gothic, that of Rixdorf (Neukölln) fused the styles of northern Germany with a tower which imitated the thirteenth-century Palazzo Pubblico of Siena.

But even as the decades passed, as it built town halls suggestive of Gothic heritage, and monuments to past heroes, Berlin never shook off its newness, the Johnny-come-lately of Europe's capital cities. As art critic Karl Scheffler, one of Berlin's main biographers, was famously to describe it, the city was condemned *'immerfort zu werden und niemals zu sein'* ('always to be becoming, never to being').[30] Yes, the city was a parvenu, admitted Berliner Walter Rathenau in 1899. Indeed 'Berlin is the parvenu of cities, and the city of parvenus'.[31] But this was nothing to be ashamed of. 'In German', he countered, 'parvenu means self-made man'.

In a sense the very rate of the city's growth precluded Berlin from being anything other than a parvenu, where buildings were built at a rate of knots just to keep pace with the increase in the city's population. (As it was, some 60,000 Berliners lived in cellars in 1911.[32]) Many visitors identified the city as more American than European. 'Chicago would seem venerable beside it', wrote Mark Twain in the 1890s, 'the main mass of the city looks as if it had been built last week, the rest of it has a just perceptibly graver tone, and looks as if it might be six or even eight months old'.[33] And the American label was one that stuck. Karl Scheffler went further, suggesting in 1910 that Berlin was not only American, but it was *Americanising* – an influence on the rest of Germany about which he was ambivalent at best.[34]

As it was, wrote Scheffler – a native of Hamburg – most Germans themselves simply did not feel at home in Berlin. It was not 'their' city in the same way that Bavarians might feel about Munich, or Rhinelanders about Cologne, both of which had been centres of local political activity when Berlin was still a glorified village, and which were important cities in their own right. While one in five Englishmen lived in London, and one in eight Frenchmen lived in Paris, only one in every twenty Germans lived in Berlin – most of them originating from the eastern half of Germany, Prussia, rather than from the west. Thus, Berlin was not so much a natural capital for the nation as a whole as a super-imposed colonial capital, out in the sticks of East Elbia, inhabited by a 'species of pioneer, hard and dry'.

Worst of all, Scheffler lambasted the artificiality of the city's cultural life: 'no one knows Goethe so badly, and last season's poets so well'. Lacking its own artistic traditions, and insufficiently creative to generate its own style, Berlin simply cannibalised those of others, but voraciously, without any discretion. 'In no other place in Germany', Scheffler wrote, 'are second hand national and international tastes more cultivated'. And so it was with the city's architecture. Scheffler was sympathetic to the elegant simplicity of modernism – just as he was sympathetic to the medieval grace of Gothic. He suggested that Peter Behrens' turbine hall recently built for AEG would find its way into future *Baedeker* guides.[35] But most of Berlin's new buildings were much less fine, he thought. They showed questionable taste, a confusion of styles and ideas, borrowed not made. As a result, Berlin's architects cast a clumsy shadow over the rest of the country – a *'Weltstadt* shadow'.

But then this shadow had a very particular form – it bore the outline of the Kaiser himself. 'He has the same nervous restless need to do things as modern Berliners', Scheffler wrote, 'the same enterprising spirit, the same optimism and materialism, the same instincts, the same desire for show, and in taste the same uncertainty'. More to the point, 'he has developed a lust for construction just at the time when architecture is its most degenerate'. Just as the Kaiser felt inclined to intervene in the acquisitions policy of the national gallery, so he felt equipped to wield his blue imperial pencil when confronted with plans for buildings in Berlin which he did not like, and to push projects of which he approved. 'There are probably few successful artists, architects, engineers or shipbuilders who have not at some time been indebted to the Emperor for his many professional suggestions', an English observer of the court wrote diplomatically.[36] Berlin was thus built with the defects of its ruler.

Kaiser Wilhelm II liked to think himself a man of the world. He liked to travel. He was keen to be up on the latest technological developments, and to provide his insights on them. Though he attempted to exude self-assurance, he was prone to fits of depression and self-doubt, the perfect German of his time. In terms of court life he could be both an infuriating stickler for tradition and a welcome breath of fresh air, on friendly terms with men such as Albert Ballin, a Jewish shipping magnate, who would not have had a look-in a generation before. But then that was something else the Kaiser liked: to make the rules.

The year 1913 was to be the Kaiser's year. It was a quarter-century since he had become German Emperor, succeeding his father Friedrich III at the age of twenty-nine. But it was also a century since Prussian forces had been victorious over the armies of Napoleon at Leipzig. For Wilhelm, a man who sought to be the bride at every wedding and the corpse at every funeral, the coincidence presented a unique opportunity. The anniversaries were welded into a single year-long celebration: of himself, of Germany, and the Hohenzollern dynasty of which he was the head. All this reflected the Kaiser's startlingly conservative conception of how the country's politics should work: the Kaiser led, the German nation followed.

That this was not, in fact, the case was self-evident: both constitutional law and German history intervened. For a start, to whom exactly did the German nation refer? The population of the Reich was predominantly but not exclusively German in its ethnic and linguistic composition, with a Polish majority in some eastern provinces. Even within the German population there were divisions. Catholics had historically been made to feel that they were not quite part of the German nation, at least not as the Prussians saw it. Suspicions remained on both sides. Nor did the Reich contain all German speakers: a large number still lived quite happily under Habsburg rule in the Austro-Hungarian Empire.

Constitutionally, although the Kaiser stood alone as Emperor in Germany – Franz-Joseph being the Austrian, not German, Emperor – he was not the only royal German sovereign: Bavaria maintained its King, and other former kingdoms retained their local potentates, or their successors. These states retained a large degree of political autonomy from Berlin and thus from the Kaiser; as Scheffler had noted, their people did not necessarily look to the city on the Spree for political or any other kind of inspiration. Germany's constitutional and cultural federalism was to some degree offset by the fact that one state, Prussia, far outweighed the others in population and economic clout. And in Prussia, where state elections were conducted on a grossly unfair three-class voting system heavily weighted towards the wealthy, conservative majorities were essentially assured.

At the imperial level the Kaiser was head of both army and navy, giving him a certain military prestige and allowing him to spend time in the ordered military surroundings he loved. He was responsible for the appointment of the Imperial Chancellor, who also served as the Prime Minister of Prussia, giving him a double mandate and enhanced influence over the German political system as a whole. Still, the Kaiser's Chancellor was far from all-powerful in imperial matters. He was constrained in his activity by the imperial German parliament, the Reichstag. And whereas the Prussian parliament was elected according to a franchise which assured a conservative majority, the much wider franchise for Reichstag elections – every man above the age of twenty-five – made for a less docile group of parliamentarians, with far greater democratic legitimacy to boot. Required to vote on imperial laws, the imperial Reichstag could in theory block the imperial budget, providing parliament with a blunt but potentially powerful tool for influencing government. Although Wilhelm had insisted that the inscription above the new Reichstag entrance read *Der deutschen Einheit* (To German Unity) – instead of the more liberal *Dem deutschen Volke* (To the German People) originally proposed – the Kaiser's ministers could not command German political unity in the same way one might command an army; they could not cajole or bully the electorate to vote only for placemen or conservatives, and once a Reichstag was elected they would have to live with the consequences.[37] In the 1912 elections over one-third of the German people voted for the Social Democrats, returning 110 to parliament. In Berlin – imperial capital but also capital of German socialism – the Social Democrats won three-quarters of the vote.

At the end of 1913 the principle that the Kaiser alone could choose the Chancellor, a fundamental part of his power, was indeed challenged over the Zabern (Saverne) affair. The initial spark for the challenge was rather trivial: a military officer in the garrison town of Zabern had angered the citizenry by calling them *Wackes* – a term of abuse – and appearing to incite his soldiers to kill locals if they got into a brawl with them. The issue could have been dealt with by the officer in question, Lieutenant Günter von Forstner, being disciplined in some way and local feelings calmed. In fact, the ensuing public outrage was met by a mixture of military high-handedness, appalling management of local sentiment and a fastening of bayonets.

The high-handed behaviour of the German army in the town of Zabern (Saverne) in the lost French provinces of Alsace-Lorraine in 1913 led to calls in the Reichstag for the resignation of the Chancellor.

The army was made to look absurd, and when the locals laughed about it, they were summarily arrested. Who ruled in Alsace-Lorraine – indeed in Germany – parliamentarians in Berlin asked: the army or the civil authorities? The Reichstag sought Chancellor Bethmann-Hollweg's resignation. And although they did not get it – he refused to resign himself, and only the Social Democrats and a small Polish party were willing to push it to a vote on the budget – the gauntlet had been thrown down. The tendency towards greater parliamentary independence, indeed opposition, was clear. The willingness of the Reichstag to question the role of the army – and for this to have wide public backing – was also clear. Was Germany evolving towards a more parliamentary system, like Britain?

The cracks in the idea of a subject people, operating only on the instructions of a well-loved emperor, were thus already gaping by the time 1913 came round. Nationalists felt the Kaiser too timorous, and set up extra-parliamentary organisations such as the Pan-German League or the German Army League, beyond his control yet stirring up public opinion on matters of foreign policy. Even conservatives, congenitally sympathetic to the idea of monarchy, found the Kaiser himself a little clumsy – prone to confident statements of boundless banality, misjudged interviews, and tin-eared speeches. Even in this Hohenzollern year, wrote an editorialist of the *Berliner Tageblatt*: 'we cannot write without restraint: the Kaiser and *his* people; or the German people and *their* Kaiser'.[38]

Wilhelm's reign had long been noted for its love of festivities of all sorts. A left-leaning paper noted 'the amount of official celebrations that the German Empire has had to endure has been seemingly endless. They follow each other as uninterruptedly as do film reels in a cinema'.[39] But in 1913, combining national, dynastic and personal elements was nonetheless a unique opportunity for the Kaiser – who had always considered himself to have the popular touch – to attempt once more to elevate his personal prestige, and to identify himself yet more firmly as the nation's unifying force. Could he perhaps rekindle some of the excitement of his accession in 1888, when he brought a flash of youth and style to what had become a rather dour royal house, sparking a craze for moustaches to be worn with their ends defiantly turned upwards, as the Kaiser dynamically wore his own? Might not the complexities, weaknesses and archaism of the German political system be forgotten in a benign dynastic-nationalist glow? And if Germany did not yet have its place in the sun, could at least Kaiser Wilhelm have his?

As in every year, national celebrations greeted the Kaiser's birthday on 27 January. In Berlin, the event was marked by a *Lustspiel* at the Opera House, under the Kaiser's personal direction. (Wilhelm rated himself as a music critic, as well as a connoisseur of painting and sculpture in general, frequently intervening when the mood took him, or expatiating on the public role of art itself.) Three days later the royal palace issued the following press release:

My birthday has in this year introduced a series of commemorations which once again bring alive before us the events of the national uprising of Prussia one hundred years ago. May this remembrance of the past always help to remind us in the present what we owe the Fatherland and incite us to apply the same loyalty, devotion, and

unity in those tasks Providence presents to our generation just like
our forefathers one hundred years ago.[40]

Through the year, the Kaiser's celebrations took him all across
Germany: to Kelheim in Bavaria, where the rallying of Bavaria to
the standard of Germany was celebrated (albeit historically remas-
tered, and viewed through the prism of the Bavarian royal family
rather than any broader national awakening). In October he travelled
to Leipzig, where he unveiled the Battle of the Nations monument
(and missed out on the industrial fair being held in the city at the
same time, much to the disappointment of its local industrial not-
ables). In Berlin, the Kaiser had not only the royal wedding in May
to contend with, but the opening of the Grunewald Olympic Stadium
in June (at which the Kaiser's entourage attempted to engineer a
rather more popular festival than that created by the standard military parades). Later that same month the Kaiser oversaw the Festzug
der Innungen, a positively anti-modern parade of Berlin's various
medieval guilds paying homage to the monarch, criticised as a
'medieval masquerade' in the socialist press.[41] Some no doubt liked
the show, although the military turnout made it hard to get close to
any of the action. Many found such celebrations pompous, and rather
divorced from the modern Germany in which they lived. Far from
arresting the Kaiser's diminishing appeal, therefore, the celebrations
of 1913 perhaps accelerated it.

The Belgian ambassador recalled the thaler coins – worth three
marks – issued for the celebration. On one face of the commemorative coin the king was depicted on horseback with soldiers brandishing
their swords and guns, *'Mit Gott für König und Vaterland'* – 'With
God for King and Fatherland' – printed below the scene, and above
it, *'Der König rief und Alle, Alle kamen'* – 'The King called and everyone
came'.[42] On the reverse of the coin, an eagle towered victoriously over
a serpent, and a device underneath read *'Gott mit Uns!'* – 'God with
us!' The words referred to 1813 when, according to the mythology
proclaimed a century later, the Prussian king had called on his people
to defend Prussia, and they had responded to a man (the historical
record was rather different, but this was to quibble). The seeds of
German unity lay in royal initiative as much as in the political mach-
inations of Bismarck, such coins suggested.

A hundred years later the notion of a warrior king, a unifier of the nation, and a magnifier of its prestige, certainly appealed to Kaiser Wilhelm's martial side. It was Wilhelm who had declared that he and the army were made for each other. He appreciated its pomp, and its hierarchy – with himself, of course, at the summit. He gloried in the prospect of a new Imperial Navy with which to impress his English cousins (despite the obvious fears this raised in London). He spoke encouragingly of Germany's *Weltpolitik* – the natural corollary of Germany's commercial reach, as he saw it – keenly supportive of the schemes of his foreign office to extend German influence in the Middle East through the construction of the Berlin–Baghdad railway and his country's alliance with the Ottoman Empire. He never missed an opportunity to show off his military knowledge and inclinations: the British Prince of Wales recalled visiting Wilhelm in his office in 1913 and finding that he sat at his desk not in a chair, but in a military saddle, claiming that this was more conducive to 'clear, concise thinking', before whisking the young Prince off to the opera in a fast car, wearing a deep green uniform with a gilt hunting dagger and a plumed hat.[43] More importantly, the Kaiser supported a further expansion of the German army in 1913, the expansion which sparked off the French extension of military service from two to three years. Occasionally he expressed dark expectations of a coming clash between Teuton and Slav.

But alongside the image of Kaiser Wilhelm as the warrior – albeit a chocolate-box warrior – there was the image of Wilhelm as a peacemaker. Both competed in the public mind, both nationally and internationally. And why not? After all, by 1913 the Kaiser had overseen not just twenty-five years of German economic expansion, but twenty-five years of continuous peace. Despite the odd flare-up, things had never come to war, and Germany had always stepped back from the brink (much to the chagrin of nationalists and militarists who thus saw the Kaiser as weak and ineffectual, incapable of being a true Prussian leader). The language of international pacifism was German. In 1913 the Kaiser intervened forcefully with Vienna to dissuade Austria-Hungary from getting more deeply involved in the Balkan mêlée, though some in Vienna wanted to use the opportunity of an ongoing Balkan war to discipline Serbia and prevent it from becoming either a magnet for its own Slav population, or too strong a power on its southern flank. The Kaiser saw himself as the master of European diplomacy, attempting to make and break alliances right and left, although his diplomats might privately differ from such a warm assessment.

In 1911 the president of the University of California at Berkeley, Germanist Benjamin Ide Wheeler, had nominated Kaiser Wilhelm II for the Nobel Peace Prize. In 1913, a spate of articles in Germany and abroad labelled him the *Friedenskaiser*, 'Emperor of peace'. In June that year, the *New York Times* published a long article by Alfred Fried, founder of the German peace movement, who wrote:

> His glory as a man of peace, great enough now, will become greater, and his wish to figure in history as a hero of peace will be fulfilled. And historians of the future, in a position to appreciate fully this great and restless epoch through which we are passing ... such historians will speak of Wilhelm II as the compelling force in that process of change and will bestow upon him the title of 'The Great Conciliator'.[44]

ROME

The Pope's Aeroplane

Most European thoughts tended to Berlin when they considered Europe's rising powers in 1913. Italy was rather the country of the *passeggiata* and the *dolce far niente*, a playground for the wealthy and artistically minded, who allied themselves with the impecunious Italian aristocracy, renting a distressed palazzo for less than a small house in Grunewald, or spending a pleasant month in Venice amongst Europe's finer sort. Italy was thought picturesque and poor, equal charm residing in both qualities, the southern European antithesis to northern European wealth and dynamism.

In the patronising northern European formulation, Italy was an aesthetic experience, a living museum. For such travellers Florence was the essential destination to be visited, at least as much as Rome. Florence, after all, was the city of Dante Alighieri and the Medici chapel, and the city of the Renaissance. Italy was a showcase of natural and human beauty, a land where opera – the most famous popular composers of the time were Italian – was simply a natural expression of life. 'I do believe that Italy really purifies and ennobles all who visit her', says Philip Herriton in E. M. Forster's novel *Where Angels Fear to Tread*, 'she is the school as well as the playground of the world'.[1] Such sweeping statements were typical of north Europeans intoxicated by Italy – just as Goethe had been more than a hundred years before. It was against these views of Italy that Italian Futurists such as Filippo Marinetti so consciously rebelled. 'It is in Italy that we are issuing this manifesto of ruinous and incendiary violence', wrote Marinetti in 1909, 'because we want to deliver Italy from its gangrene of professors, archaeologists, tourist guides and antiquaries'.[2]

What pretty foreign accounts of Italy's art and architecture tended to overlook was the country's contemporary power. While Italy was certainly the least of the continental great powers beside Germany, France, Austria-Hungary and the Russian Empire, the Kingdom of Italy nonetheless sought her place amongst them. True, Italy had only been unified under the royal House of Savoy in 1861, and the nation was not yet fully forged. Some Neapolitans and Sicilians might feel stronger attachment to their region and to their church than they did to the Kingdom of Italy, perceived largely as an extension of the northern Kingdom of Piedmont, just as the Milanese looked down on their southern compatriots as being as anciently primitive as the populations of north Africa over whom they aspired to rule. 'North and south are two nations', wrote a socialist commentator, 'and one, the most wretched, is fleeing across the seas', emigrating permanently or seasonally to America or to Argentina.[3] True also, that essentially all of Italy's industry – such as the Fabbrica Italiana Automobili di Torino, or Pirelli – was in the north. Much of the rest of the country was still an agricultural land of peasants, many of them illiterate. 'In a place like this', writes one of Forster's characters, 'it seems impossible that the middle ages have passed away'.[4]

Yet Italy was also becoming a modern, imperial European nation-state. Recently introduced electoral laws extended the vote to over eight million Italians in the election of 1913, more than double the previous electorate (as in France, female suffrage was not granted until much later). Taking aim at those of his fellow northern Europeans who persisted in seeing in Italy a polity of little importance, underdeveloped and chaotic, the English writer Richard Bagot wrote:

> I often have occasion to wonder whether my compatriots, who visit the country for a few weeks or months, realise, even to the most superficial degree, the true significance of what they see all around them, and whether they have the remotest conception of what has been accomplished in Italy in the course of the last fifty years. I imagine, from the remarks and criticisms I so frequently hear made by them, that they neither realise the one nor possess the other . . . They forget that if Rome was not built in a day, neither was England; and they do not reflect that it is entirely unfair, and not a little absurd, to judge a people that has fifty years of national life by the standards rightly appertaining to a people which lives under an organisation

that has needed nearly twenty times as long a period in which to attain to its actual development.[5]

Perhaps, he hinted, they preferred to see in Italy a country forever archaic and forever weak, just as they uttered 'indignant wails over vandalisms daily perpetrated by the modern Romans', or wrote letters to the London *Times*, whenever 'some ancient piece of building is removed in order to meet the ever-increasing exigencies of a great city such as Rome is rapidly becoming'.[6]

In January 1913, 10,000 Italian troops marched through Rome fresh from a colonial campaign, part of an army close in size to that of Britain. Italy had its first dreadnought, the *Dante Alighieri*, part of a navy which might tip the balance of power one way or the other in the Mediterranean. Italy had African colonies: Eritrea, in the Horn of Africa, and now Libya, which had been acquired from the Ottoman Empire in a small and superficially victorious war the previous year – the first conflict in which aeroplanes were used, mostly for reconnaissance but also, in a sortie led by Lieutenant Giulio Gavotti, to drop bombs on Ottoman troops.[7] Filippo Marinetti, brought up in Alexandria and suckled by a Sudanese wet nurse as a baby, celebrated the war's violence as reconnecting Italy with the energies of 'barbarian' Africa, while affirming the country's modern élan.[8] Just as the Franco-Prussian War had helped weld Germany into a single political unit, so the war in Libya was a crucible for the remaking of Italy and Italians, argued Giovanni Pascoli, a well-known Italian poet:

> Whoever wishes to know what [Italy] is now, behold its army and its navy . . . Land, sea and sky, mountains and plains, peninsula and islands are perfectly fused. The fair-skinned solemn Alpine soldier fights beside the slim dark Sicilian, the tall Lombard grenadier rubs shoulders with the short lean Sardinian fusilier . . . Run your eye over the lists of the glorious dead, and wounded – who rejoice in their radiant wounds: you will find yourself remembering and revising the geography of what was, but a short time ago, just a geographical expression . . . Oh, you blessed men who have died for the fatherland! . . . Fifty years ago Italy was made. On the sacred fiftieth anniversary . . . you have proved that Italians too have been made.[9]

Such writers looked scornfully upon *Italietta* – the notion of a quiet little Italy, comfortably bourgeois, but essentially picturesque – the image of the country associated with its Prime Minister, Giovanni Giolitti. Rather, they pictured a glorious future for Italy, a country respected by its European peers, and a suitable inheritor of the still-visible past of the Roman Empire.

Such grandiose ideas of the country's national destiny fed additional colonial aspirations for Italy in Africa, particularly Ethiopia, from which the Italian army had been ingloriously turned back at the Battle of Adowa in 1896. They stoked Italian interest in the Balkans, where some Italians dreamed of a renewed zone of Italian influence along the Adriatic. And just as some nationalist French had revanchist ambitions towards Alsace and Lorraine, so some extreme Italian nationalists demanded their government act to return the once Italian, but now French, city of Nice to the fatherland, and claim Italian-speaking Trieste and Tyrol from Austria-Hungary, a nominal Italian ally. The inconvenient fact that the people of Nice had actually voted to stick with France in a referendum fifty years earlier was forgotten. The reality that neither France nor Austria-Hungary was likely to concede territory without a fight was glossed over. Perhaps it did not matter. After all, a fight was precisely what some Italians wanted. Marinetti referred to Trieste as *'notre belle poudrière'* – 'our beautiful gunpowder keg'.[10]

Thus while Italy was not on the main line of European diplomacy in 1913, she could not be ignored in Balkan diplomacy, nor discounted in wider calculations of European power. Rome was granted the status of a city to which the great powers now accorded a full embassy, a mark of regained status on the diplomatic circuit. She could no longer be left happily to tourists, who would provide no more annoyance than the occasional consular enquiry over the whereabouts of an errant husband or a stolen bag. Italy would have to be taken seriously.

If there was one city which had a greater claim on eternity than Paris it was surely Rome. Here the Roman empire had risen and fallen, now visible mostly in the city's plentiful ruins, lying within

the Passeggiata Archeologica in the centre of the city. After the fall
of Rome, the city had declined, and then found a new role as the
intermittent home of the papacy, capital of the Papal States, and
seat of the Roman Catholic Church. It had become a place of priests
and nuns, churches and monasteries, its population a fraction of
what it had been at the height of empire, industry discouraged, and
its Jews corralled into a ghetto. Now, however, Rome was the capital
of the young Italian kingdom, liberal and anti-clerical, with bureaucrats of the new state taking up residence in the city. From a population of less than 200,000 in 1861, by 1913 Rome numbered half a
million or more: less than either Milan or Naples, a fraction of that
of London, Paris or Berlin, but impressive nonetheless. Unlike Paris,
which had a reputation to maintain, and Berlin, which had a
desperate need to show it had arrived, Rome was a city recovering
its rank.

Although the Kingdom of Italy had been proclaimed in 1861 –
and 'Rome or death' had been Giuseppe Garibaldi's cry for the
Risorgimento, which unified Italy through war – Rome had only

Old and new. The first flight over the Vatican in Rome in 1911.

been incorporated into the kingdom a decade later. It was in 1870, when the French Emperor Napoleon III was forced to remove the garrison which had been protecting the Pope's temporal power in order to defend France itself, that the opportunity arose for the Italian army to occupy Rome. In the following decades projects were conceived, under the title of 'Roma Capitale', for the capital of the Kingdom of Italy to be transformed from a papal enclave into a city that would bear comparison to other European capitals. *Romanità* – the spirit of ancient Rome – was to be reborn, and Italy lifted from the pages of books of archaeology and *Baedeker* guides to the pages of world history of the twentieth century, glorying in both Italy's past and her future.[11]

In June 1911, the fiftieth anniversary of the proclamation of a united Italy reached its climax with the official inauguration of a huge and still unfinished marble and blinding-white limestone monument to Vittorio Emanuele, the king whose troops had occupied the city. Reaching into the Roman heavens, the monument, designed by Italian architect Giuseppe Sacconi, raised an equestrian statue of Vittorio Emanuele above the goddess of Rome. Above them both, the sixteen regions of Italy were represented by sixteen figures apparelled in classical dress. The symbolism of the monument, harking both backwards to ancient Rome and suggesting Italy's glorious future as a nation-state – without making reference to the church – was inescapable. Its location, on the Capitoline Hill from which the Roman Empire had once been ruled, expressed its ambition. It was to dominate Rome; buildings around it were moved in order to provide more impressive vistas to it, and to magnify its visual monumentality.[12] It was called the 'altar of the nation', wilfully adopting a term imbued with religious meaning. Indeed, the monument physically hid a church, and it provided an alternative focal point to the dome of St Peter's Basilica on the other side of the River Tiber. As if to confirm the liberal nature of the new Italy, events around the inauguration included a beauty contest in which 300 girls competed to be crowned 'Queen of Rome'.[13]

As it was, the rather more formally instituted second-crowned head of Italy – Pope Pius X – refused to recognise the full legitimacy of the Italian state, following in the traditions of his predecessors, though perhaps more ritualistically than in the past. Pius X's predecessor but one, Pius IX, had declared himself a prisoner in the

Vatican in the 1870s, unable to step outside its bounds. Though Italian, just as all popes had been for the last 400 years, Pius IX did not celebrate the creation of an Italian state. Rather, he viewed the Kingdom of Italy as an occupying power in what had formerly been papal territory. Since then, the conflict between church and state had been kept alive in Rome by bull-headed anti-clericals on the one hand and by a stubborn papacy – bolstered by a claim of spiritual infallibility – on the other, with fierce partisans on either side. In 1899, the deliberately provocative erection of a statue of the heretic Giordano Bruno on the site in Rome where he had been burned by the Inquisition led to a papally inspired riot on the Campo dei Fiori. Up until 1913, the papacy forbade Italian Catholics from voting in Italian elections, since casting a vote might be seen as conferring legitimacy on an illegitimate regime. Only in that year, under the so-called Gentiloni Pact, was the ban partly lifted by the Pope, and only then in order to prevent the victory of socialist candidates.

How much such edicts were ever taken to heart by Romans, living in the reality of a united Italian kingdom, its life now stretched into decades rather than being an aberration as the Catholic Church proclaimed, was open to question. Nearly all counted themselves Catholic; most who were eligible voted nonetheless. Foreign Catholics might yet discern a semi-divine atmosphere in the Vatican – even lapsed Catholic Americans such as Theodore Dreiser relished an opportunity to get near to the Pope – and there were still so-called 'Black' salons in Roman high society where only those who shared the political leanings of the church were admitted.[14] But most Romans were less ideologically or spiritually inclined than these ultra-conservative zealots. Even if they regularly attended church out of custom and allowed their lives to be pleasantly punctuated by the celebration of this or that saint's day, most Romans were more cynical about the intrigues of the Vatican and more sceptical about its holiness. 'His [the Roman's] seat is too near the stage, and the working of the *mise en scène* is too familiar to him', wrote Bagot.[15]

Some Italians disparaged Rome as being too archaic, too trapped in history, too corrupt, too concerned with parliamentarianism rather than action. 'Fish begin to stink from the head', ran one article in

a nationalist journal, 'Italy, from Rome'.[16] In his 1912 poem 'The
Pope's Aeroplane', an extraordinary Futurist imagining of a plane
flight across Italy which combined the archaic and the ultra-modern,
Marinetti saw Rome as a 'giant molehill', its smell of political petty-
dealing rising to high heaven. Such refrains were not uncommon.
While Italian governments had made Rome the capital of Italy,
Rome's destiny was not complete. For nationalists and for their
acolytes – men such as Benito Mussolini, flirting with combinations
of socialism and nationalism – Rome had been re-established, not
yet restored.

Yet this much was clear to most Italians by 1913, and to some
visitors: Italy could no longer be discounted as the victim of European
history – broken up, fought on and over, occupied. It was now a
great power. Might it not rise further? Not to the level of Britain
or France perhaps, but as an equal to Austria-Hungary, its compet-
itor in the Adriatic, and the only other European country (besides
Switzerland) which contained a significant indigenous Italian
minority. 'The Pope's Aeroplane', a hymn to speed and to danger,

Giacomo Balla, *Abstract Speed (The Car has Passed)*, 1913. Italy, country
of the *dolce far niente*, was also the country of Futurism. Wrote Marinetti: 'we
want to deliver Italy from its gangrene of professors, archaeologists, tourist
guides and antiquaries'.

planes swooping down and then rising up vertiginously, trains winding like serpents on railway tracks below, ended in Marinetti imagining war between Italians and Austrians, but only as the expression of something deeper, a war of liberation from Italy's past:

> I am free and powerful! . . .
> I am an Italian delivered all of a sudden
> From his Christian ballast
> And from his Catholic fetters! . . .
> Onward to Vienna! . . . Onward![17]

VIENNA
Shadows and Light

The Kingdom of Italy ended, and the lands of the Habsburgs began, in the Adige valley, in the foothills of the Alps, south of the city known as Trento in Italian and Trient in German. In the sixteenth century Trento had been made famous as the site of a council of the Roman Catholic Church. Since then it had slipped back into obscurity, occasionally being transferred from the authority of one dynasty to another, but always returning to the Habsburgs, a fixed element in the ever-changing scene of European politics. Now, Trento was one of the last remaining pieces of that family's once vast Italian holdings, a dynastic hangover, an anomaly in the Europe of nation-states, ruled over by the greatest and most historically freighted anomaly of them all: the Austro-Hungarian Empire.

In 1909 Benito Mussolini had briefly lived in Trento, invited by the local socialist party to be their coordinator. In 1913, the city's chief significance was as a railway town lying on one of the main arteries between southern and central Europe. To the north lay the Brenner Pass, nature's gateway through the Alps. On the other side of it was Austria proper, where one spoke German, albeit in an accent and dialect that would make a north German shudder.

From the Brenner Pass it was only a few dozen miles to Innsbruck, and then a few hours further to Vienna – to St Stephen's Cathedral, to the Hofburg palace and its now eighty-three-year-old occupant, Emperor Franz Joseph, to a favourite corner in one's favourite café. Approaching the Austro-Hungarian Empire's capital city, one could anticipate barging through the double doors from a wintry street into the café's pleasant fugginess, the head waiter calling out one's name in smiling greeting, bowing slightly as he did, and surreptitiously ordering his staff to prepare one's favourite coffee for that hour of the day: from a *kapuziner*, if it was early, to a *fiaker* (with rum) if it was late, served the right way in the correct glass or cup, as it always had been. As it always would be.

To unfold one's map of the Austro-Hungarian Empire in 1913 was to be struck, first, by its extent. The Habsburg lands stretched from Switzerland in the west halfway to the Black Sea in the east, and from the Russian and German empires in the north, deep into the Balkans in the south. In 1908, much to the chagrin of Russian nationalists who saw their country as the natural guardian of the Balkans, Austria-Hungary had taken one further step into the Balkan arena by formally annexing Bosnia to the empire, a territory which had been administered from Vienna for thirty years but which had nonetheless hitherto remained formally part of the Ottoman Empire. Belgrade, the capital of Serbia, was already within a stone's throw, or a cannon shot, of the Austro-Hungarian border, a point not lost on Austrian generals in 1913 as they considered whether to intervene in the Balkan wars and, at the risk of war with Russia, shut down a troublemaker on the Habsburg doorstep. (*Baedeker* included Belgrade, and Bucharest, as side-trips in its edition on Austria-Hungary.[1]) The population of these realms was fifty million souls – a little more than France or Britain, a little less than the German Empire. Within the ample girth of the Austro-Hungarian Empire lay mountains and lakes, vineyards and fishing villages, snow and sun. The Habsburg empire yielded iron and coal from Bohemia; in Galicia it produced its own oil, making the Habsburg lands self-sufficient.[2] It contained areas as rich and as industrialised as Germany, and other areas as poor as Russia. It was as varied as the world itself. It traded with itself, it invested in itself: it was perhaps a world to itself.

But therein lay the rub. Because to look at any more detailed maps of the Austro-Hungarian Empire – ethnographic, religious or political – was to be struck by something rather more worrying: the remarkably disparate, if not downright fissiparous, nature of the Habsburg realms. *Baedeker* advised that, while in Bohemia, Styria, Upper and Lower Austria, Salzburg, Carniola, Moravia, Galicia, Austrian Silesia, Bukowina and Hungary one drove on the left; in Carinthia, Tyrol, Istria and Dalmatia, one drove on the right.[3] 'Nowhere in Europe', noted an American book on Austria-Hungary, 'is the past so intermingled with the present'.[4] Imperial climatologists called the empire a 'laboratory of nature'.[5] The socialist leader

Victor Adler, perhaps more appropriately, called the empire a 'laboratory of world history'. (In 1914 the Vienna satirist Karl Kraus would call it a 'proving ground for world destruction'.[6]) It seemed a miracle that such a variety of lands could be held together under any political structure.

A linguistic or ethnographic map of Austria-Hungary, such as those drawn up in the wake of the 1910 census, looked rather like the canvas of a particularly adventurous abstract painter, splattered with a multitude of different colours, few tones dominating over others, the overall impression one of kaleidoscopic variety. Around Trento, Franz Joseph's subjects spoke Italian. In a large swathe of land from the Swiss border to the Danube, and then all along the borderlands with the German Empire, they spoke German. In the heartlands of Bohemia, and in Prague, the Czech tongue was predominant, but not exclusive. Further east, linguistic supremacy passed to the Poles on the northern side of the Carpathian mountains and, below them, to the Slovaks, though with German-speaking exceptions. At the eastern extremity of the Habsburg lands the peasants, by and large, spoke dialects that linguistics experts loosely grouped as Ruthenian (essentially, Ukrainian), while Polish would be the first language of those in the region's largest city: Lviv, Lwów or Lemberg depending on who was speaking to whom. Moving clockwise around the edges of the Habsburg empire, one alighted upon areas where the locals spoke Romanian. Interspersed with Romanian-speakers in the south-east, but forming the clear majority of the population as one moved towards Budapest, were the Hungarians, the second-largest linguistic group under Habsburg rule. Finally, in the Balkans proper, the Habsburg standard flew over Serbs, Croats, Bosnians and Slovenes.

All of these linguistic groups had different attitudes towards the empire as a whole, and different places within it. Some fell under different administrative systems within the empire, some were more or less unified. Some could look to compatriots outside the Habsburg lands: the south Slavs (to Serbia), the Poles (to their fellow Poles under German and Russian rule), the Romanians (to Romania), the Ruthenians (to Ukrainians in Russia, though their lot was not necessarily one to be wished for) and to some extent the Austro-Germans (some of whom followed a pan-German credo, preferring imperial Germany to imperial Austria). Other groups were contained entirely within the empire, including the Czechs and the Hungarians.

Taking a religious map of the Habsburg realm, one faced a similar picture of diversity, though not quite as daunting, and one less of clear lines than of shadings. Most subjects of the Austro-Hungarian Empire were Catholic. But not all. In parts of Hungary, around the city of Debrecen for example, the population was Protestant. Serbs tended to be Orthodox, feeling greater religious kinship with Russians than with Catholic Austrians. In Romanian-speaking areas, meanwhile, the Orthodox Church battled with the Unitarian for confessional supremacy. Bosnia was different again, with a substantial Muslim Bosniak minority in a sea of mostly Orthodox Serbs. There were Jewish communities in every part of the empire, but particularly in the north and east of the Habsburg lands – and in Vienna itself, where Jews played a key role in the city's cultural life, and in its courtrooms, hospitals and consulting rooms.

The political map of the Austrian-Hungarian Empire was by far the simplest, with two halves: one supposedly Austrian in the west (known as Cisleithania in reference to the river Leitha, or simply Austria) and one supposedly Hungarian in the east (known as Transleithania, or simply Hungary). But this apparent simplicity was deceptive – indeed it created its own problems. For the dual structure could not mask the far more complex linguistic and religious make-up of Austria-Hungary on the ground. In Austria, the Austro-Germans were the largest group, yet they represented little more than a third of the population. In Hungary, the Hungarians accounted for under half the population.

That the Habsburg lands had a dual structure at all was the result of a moment of weakness, born of an impulse of dynastic survival – and it showed. It dated back to 1867, when Emperor Franz Joseph was a young man. The previous year his armies had been defeated by those of Prussia, the Habsburgs' upstart rival for influence in Germany, at the battle of Königgrätz near the town of Sadow (in Czech, Sadová). In the shadow of defeat, Franz Joseph had delegated a Saxon, Baron Beust, to negotiate a deal with the Hungarians, the empire's second-largest grouping, so as to ensure that they did not take this opportunity to escape from Habsburg rule altogether as they had threatened to do in previous years.[7]

The result was the *ausgleich*, or compromise. The Hungarians agreed to stay, but demanded a new constitutional formulation, and insisted that the ancient lands of St Stephen (Hungary's warrior patron saint) be ruled from Budapest, irrespective of their current population. Both halves of the Habsburg lands would have their own premiers and parliaments, in Vienna and in Budapest – with the Budapest parliament elected according to a system that entrenched the supremacy of the Magyar (Hungarian) landed gentry. But they would share an army, foreign policy, and common financial burden. There would be three central ministries (foreign, defence, finance) in regular written contact with delegations from the two parliaments. The three central ministers sat alongside the two premiers in a joint council chaired by the imperial foreign minister. All of these governments would be responsible to the sovereign, Franz Joseph, though he was styled Emperor in Austria but King in Hungary. His government was thus, in 1913, 'K. u. k', 'Kaiserlich und Königlich', 'Imperial and Royal'. (The 'und' was added after 1867, to make clear that empire and kingdom were indeed separate, and yet part of the same body, a concept which no doubt made sense to those brought up with the mysteries of the Holy Trinity.) Later, when Austrian novelist Robert Musil wrote a fiction about the empire in which he had grown up, he described the K. u. k as 'Kakania'.[8] Franz Kafka's sense of the absurd no doubt owed something to the political structures by which he was surrounded in Prague.

Even in the 1860s few thought that such arrangements were a perfect compromise – for a start, aspects of the compromise were to be renegotiated every ten years, thus guaranteeing an almighty dust-up between the two entities with alarming regularity. But then the *ausgleich* was the best that could be mustered at the time. From Franz Joseph's own perspective the compromise had initially been a temporary expedient, to be revisited later, perhaps when the armies of the empire were able to regroup, inflict a defeat on the Prussians, and find themselves again at the heart of German politics. This was not to happen. By 1871 Prussia had been victorious again, over France this time, and the German Empire had been proclaimed. There was no going back. But the Austro-Hungarian Empire was stuck with the *ausgleich*. The deal of 1867 had become practised constitutional reality by 1913 – and, imperfect though it was, by then it had lasted longer than most of the Emperor's subjects had been alive.

At the imperial level, some worried about the effect of duality on military preparedness. Franz Joseph's nephew and heir apparent,

Archduke Franz Ferdinand, fretted about the issue of the languages of command in the army, particularly after experiences with the Hungarian portion of the forces, where they insisted on speaking only Hungarian (against regulations) even in front of him.[9] At the turn of the century the Hungarians demanded an independent Hungarian militia (the Honvéds). Franz Joseph rejected the idea. The issue festered, a constant worry.

The structures of empire inevitably created their own dynamics for its different nationalities. The Poles became accustomed to dualism, providing a number of key ministers over the years, enjoying more freedoms than their fellow Poles under German boot and Russian thumb and lording it over the Ruthenians. The Czechs, in contrast, felt let down by the whole dual structure, which promoted the Hungarians above them, and made them a second-class nation: where was there a recognition of the lands of St Wenceslas to match those of St Stephen? This feeling was accentuated by the fact that Bohemia and Moravia, in which the Czechs were in a majority, were fast becoming industrial powerhouses for the empire as a whole, with forty per cent of their population working in industry, producing the bulk of Austro-Hungarian iron, and hosting the giant Škoda armaments works.[10] True, the economic position of the Czechs was improving, and an increasing share of the factories was owned by Czech-speakers, but disagreements over language in the administration of local government – German or bilingual German-Czech? – were a running sore.

Ultimately it was these divisions, on top of other political divisions between and within linguistic groupings, which meant that the Austrian parliament in Vienna had become something of a pantomime parliament by 1913. Ten languages were admitted (German, Czech, Polish, Ruthenian, Serbian, Croat, Slovenian, Italian, Romanian and Russian), yet there were no interpreters, and everything was set down only in German.[11] Desks were rattled, insults exchanged – there was even the occasional punch-up. The introduction of universal male suffrage in Austria (but not Hungary) in 1907 did not make politics more manageable, as Franz Joseph had hoped. The government ruled by decree where necessary. Tourists came to visit parliament in Vienna, and to gawp at the spectacle. One was a young and failing artist from upper Austria, Adolf Hitler, his fists clenched in excitement.[12] Leader of the Russian Bolsheviks Vladimir

Lenin, living now in Austrian Galicia – 'almost Russia', as he termed it – read about such things in the Kraków papers, a diversion from work preparing for the next meeting of the party, in between skating in winter and hiking trips up into the Tatra mountains in spring.[13] The Georgian agitator and bank thief Josef Djugashvili, otherwise known as Stalin, was sent to Vienna (under a Greek cover name) to study what lessons could be gleaned from the experience of the socialists in Austria for the application of Bolshevism to the nationalities question in Russia.[14]

In the kingdom of Hungary, the Hungarians pursued an aggressive policy of Magyarisation of everyone else – Romanians and Slovaks in particular – insisting on the exclusivity of Magyar culture. Other nationalities protested; Franz Joseph failed to register their anger. Despite official autonomy within the Hungarian Kingdom, the Croats were suppressed by a Hungarian-appointed ruler. Some looked towards their fellow south Slavs, the Serbs – within and outside the empire – for support. Others sought a reconstruction of the empire along tripartite lines, with Austrian, Hungarian and South Slav entities. The position of the Serbs in the empire was worst of all: divided between 100,000 in Dalmatia under Austrian administration, half a million in Hungary, a further 650,000 in a supposedly autonomous Croatia-Slavonia and 850,000 in the newly acquired province of Bosnia.[15] All the while, the relationship between Vienna and Budapest remained difficult – at one point plans were prepared for the army to be used to re-establish Habsburg order in Hungary if the situation were to deteriorate.[16]

Thus the Austro-Hungarian Empire in 1913 was a heap of paradoxes and anachronisms, a mix of peoples and religions, a hotchpotch of political regimes and relationships, a jumble of dynastic possessions assembled by a long process of canny marriages, good fortune, and temporary compromises which then became permanent. Though some Viennese, and certainly the heir apparent Franz Ferdinand, might spend long hours poring over maps and trying to work out some ideal solution for the Habsburg lands – perhaps a tripartite federation, perhaps a federation of all the nationalities rather more like the United States of America, perhaps a unitary state – the truth was that a solution did not exist, or at least not without a major political opposition. Given the costs of full-scale constitutional reform, rebalancing here and there was the best that could be hoped for in the immediate term. Perhaps this would change when Franz Ferdinand became Emperor, a man who saw the need to cut the Hungarians down to size, and who intended to brook no opposition in doing so, to the point of considering military force.

And yet, despite its extraordinary complexity and variety, and despite years of crisis and dark warnings about its integrity, the empire, like the giant wheel in Vienna's Prater gardens, still turned. Discussions about the constitutional structure of the empire would go round and round in circles, but one would always end up at the same point in the end. Like the Riesenrad, the empire went on and on, through summer and winter, storm and sun. Perhaps muddling through, as the Austro-Hungarian Empire did, was a kind of system anyhow, if not a very glorious one. (The long-serving Chancellor of Austria at the end of the nineteenth century, Eduard Taaffe, referred to his technique of government as 'preserving all the nationalities of the Monarchy in a state of balanced and well-modulated discontent'.[17]) In any case one could chose to ignore politics too if it got too heated or if it got too dull . 'The first glance of an average Viennese into his morning paper', Stefan Zweig later recalled, 'was not at events in parliament or world affairs, but at the repertoire of the theater'.[18] There were more important things to life.

For many, the most persistent feature of the Austro-Hungarian Empire was, quite simply, its existence. Did not this fact prove the empire's fundamental resilience? Did it not justify its continuance? Perhaps it even proved its necessity. For if the Austro-Hungarian Empire was not to exist: what then? German domination? Russian domination? War? None were attractive options, except to a minority of pan-Germans who would have quite liked to team up with their stronger elder brother. The empire at least provided a frame for steadily increasing prosperity, albeit unevenly (average incomes in the central districts of Austria were three times those in Polish-majority Galicia).[19] Though primarily agrarian – over half the population of Austria and two-thirds of the population of Hungary was still on the land in 1910 – Austria-Hungary was steadily industrialising, albeit running along a slower French track than the high-speed industrialisation of Germany.[20]

And, in unifying diverse forces, did the empire not create something greater than the sum of its parts – a great power which none of its constituent peoples, including the Hungarians, could

conceivably hope to be without? Thomas Masaryk, later to become
the father of independent Czechoslovakia, and one of the leaders
of Czech nationalism in the Viennese parliament, declared in 1893:
'we want Austria to remain a great power, but we also wish that
Austria should be great and powerful inwardly'.[21] He did not seek
independence but, even in 1913, reform: 'our . . . plans are not designed
to weaken the others but to strengthen the whole. We know that
if the whole is no good, we, alas, must share in it'. The problem, he
said, was that the process of reform seemed stuck. Nothing seemed
to really change. An Austrian statesman, he said, was like a man
who had swallowed an umbrella, unable to move, afraid it might
open at any instant.

One might even hear it said that perhaps this immobility was
not so bad after all. It acted as a check on overbearing government.
It made for an Austria-Hungary which was rather like a large
rambling house with many interconnected rooms, a place which had
seen better days, and yet where it was pleasant to lounge around.
In Kakania, remembered Robert Musil, 'there was a tempo too, but
not too much tempo':

> Of course cars rolled on these roads too, but not too many! The
> conquest of the air was being prepared here too, but not too inten-
> sively. A ship would now and then be sent off to South America or
> East Asia, but not too often. There was no ambition for world markets
> or world power. Here at the very center of Europe, where the world's
> old axes crossed, words such as 'colony' and 'overseas' sounded like
> something quite untried and remote. There was some show of luxury,
> but by no means in such overrefined ways as the French. People went
> in for sports, but not as fanatically as the English. Ruinous sums of
> money were spent on the army, but only just enough to secure its
> position as the second weakest among the great powers. The capital,
> too, was somewhat smaller than all the other biggest cities of the
> world, but considerably bigger than a mere big city.[22]

So, the permanent crises of the Austro-Hungarian Empire, for all
its internal shenanigans, were a condition, but not a necessarily
terminal one. As respected British journalist Henry Wickham Steed
put it in a book published in 1913:

Errors, weakness, or prejudice on the part of the Monarch, of statesmen, or of races may, it is true, bring the Monarchy again to the verge of ruin; disaster may seem to portend the fulfilment of prophecies of disintegration; but I have been unable to perceive during ten years of constant observation and experience – years, moreover, filled with struggle and crisis – any sufficient reason why, with moderate foresight on the part of the Dynasty, the Hapsburg monarchy should not retain its rightful place in the European community. Its internal crises are often crises of growth rather than of decay.[23]

In 1913, as in 1813, as in 1713, a Europe without the Habsburgs was barely imaginable, least of all in Vienna, their capital. A Viennese picture postcard of the time showed the ageing Emperor Franz Joseph bent double over a small desk, signing documents, approving promotions, agreeing to the transfer of an officer from one garrison to another. In 1908 Kaiser Wilhelm II himself had led a delegation of German princes to Vienna to pay homage to the Austrian Emperor on the sixtieth anniversary of his accession, a living embodiment of Habsburg history. The old man had already been there for an eternity. Why not another?

In Vienna, so long used to the theatrics of Habsburgian government, life was taken as a stage on which to exercise, in public, the collective myths of Viennese life. Splendours past – or, at least, their evocation – provided a confident sheen to a more troubled present. The city's inhabitants played their allotted roles, and congratulated each other and themselves on their performance. The city's 100,000 annual tourist visitors from outside the empire experienced heavy doses of Viennese nostalgia – and lapped it up obligingly.[24] Vienna's mantra was perhaps best expressed in one of its most popular operettas, Johann Strauss' *Die Fledermaus*, first performed in 1874, when Vienna was trying to take its mind off a stock-market crash, but just as relevant forty years later: '*Glücklich ist, wer vergisst, was doch nicht zu ändern ist*' ('Happy is he who forgets what cannot be changed').[25]

Lev Bronstein, otherwise known as Trotsky, living precariously as a journalist in Vienna during these years, described Vienna as 'a centre of political and intellectual interests, of love of music, of four

Leon Trotsky, a Russian resident in the Austro-Hungarian capital in 1913. Lenin lived as an exile in Galicia. Stalin visited Vienna to learn about Austro-Hungarian nationalities' policy.

European languages, of various European connections'.[26] Although statues of Schiller and Goethe proclaimed the city as culturally German, its imperial status made it supranational, while its population made it multinational – exotic, even. The city's gypsies and *Ostjuden* (eastern Jews) showed that Asia no longer started at the Landstrasse, as Metternich had declared nearly a hundred years previously – the east began in the very shadow of St Stephen's Cathedral.

Though it still had considerable old-world cachet amongst European cities, Vienna was no longer in the same category as London either as a political force or as a modern metropolis. Its population was just two million. For better or worse, it had fallen behind Paris as Europe's pleasure capital. Nor did Vienna have Berlin's energy and drive. In comparison, the Austro-Hungarian capital seemed elegantly shabby around the edges these days, and much quieter. 'Vienna has no nightlife', complained the *Wiener*

Montags Journal, 'the Viennese are asleep by ten. At ten o'clock the front door is locked', and this to avoid the superintendent's fee, a small amount to be paid to each doorman at each apartment block after that time.[27] Another article criticised Viennese dust, complaining that 'in Berlin, where in one day there's more people in the street than in Vienna all year round, it's cleaner'. Another wrote that, whereas department stores in Berlin were listed as tourist sights, in Vienna they were simply 'junk stores'. Underlying all this, of course, was the full knowledge that Berlin was the true powerhouse now, and that in the military alliance agreed between the two empires back in 1879 (just thirteen years after the defeat at Sadowa), Germany was undeniably the senior partner.

Most Viennese nonetheless preferred their own city, with its own charm, its own imperfections, and its character – a reflection of their own. While Berlin dressed itself in military uniform, Vienna put on fancy dress. Whereas Berlin turned its energies to the thrills of power, wishing to impress others with its greatness, Vienna was a touch more modest, capable of laughing at itself even as it touted its imperial birthright. Karl Kraus, the most famous exponent of the typically Viennese art of satire, is alleged to have said: 'in Berlin things are serious but not hopeless; in Vienna they are hopeless but not serious'.[28] Perhaps, noted Stefan Zweig, having given up on political supremacy in Europe or in the world, Vienna had turned to artistic supremacy as the key to its own particular self-expression.[29]

Physically, Berlin was huge and impersonal, alienating the individual by making him feel insignificant in relation to it. Vienna's grandeur was on a more manageable scale, impressive certainly but not overbearing. (If the city alienated some of its visitors – Adolf Hitler, for example – that was because of its society, out of reach to those who could never grasp the all-too-human combination of Viennese frivolity and seriousness, one eye laughing, the other crying.) The magnificent buildings of Vienna's Ringstrasse – replacing the city walls torn down in the 1850s – were rather elegant in an old-fashioned way, with far more aesthetic unity than the crude architectural adventurism which Karl Scheffler had identified in the German capital.

In the old heart of Vienna there was more romance than in all of the German capital, and more room for gothic imagination. An

American book on Vienna at the turn of the century recommended a tour by moonlight:

> Note the romantic beauty of the scene, the exquisite effects and unexpected revelations that meet one at every turn. One half of the town is plunged in a sea of black shadow; the other is bathed in floods of light, limpid and silvery as the dawn, and under the influence of these alternate reflections of agate and opal the bearded faces of the caryatides seem to work with the grimaces and contortions of living creatures . . . Utterly alone in the deserted streets, which wind about like silver ribbons, a sensation of dreamy melancholy gradually steals over the senses, and one lingers to gaze in silence over the city, sleeping beneath its silvery canopy . . .[30]

Above all, Vienna had what Berlin did not: tradition. A popular Viennese song ran:

> There is only one imperial city,
> There is only one Vienna,
> There is only one den of thieves,
> And its name is Berlin![31]

(In the years before 1913, in reference to Vienna's growing Czech population, the last two lines were reworked to read: 'the Viennese are outside, the Bohemians within!'[32])

In the Austro-Hungarian capital, tradition began at the top: at the court, with Franz Joseph himself, the imperial metronome for sixty-eight years. At the beginning of the year British newspapers reported the Emperor's failing health, but this was dismissed as nothing more than a tiresome cold, which he was finding more difficult to get rid of than in previous decades:

> The Emperor, who retires at eight, gets up before five a.m., and Dr Kerzl likes to watch him while he inhales steam. Persons who meet the doctor walking across the Castle yard of Schönbrunn forget what an early riser the Emperor is, and think he has been summoned in haste. The doctor is always with the Emperor at five in the morning, and again at noon, when the Emperor paces up and down the Great Gallery, where a small forest of pines has been placed and where he

enjoys the perfume exhaled by the trees. He very much misses his daily smoke, which Dr Kerzl cannot allow while the cough shows no improvement.[33]

The regularity of court life, his imperial duties performed unceasingly for over six decades, was perhaps comforting to the Emperor himself, who had little else now that his wife was gone (assassinated by an anarchist terrorist in Geneva fifteen years previously), as was his son (who committed suicide in 1889 in a pact with his much younger lover, Baroness Marie Vetsera). The Emperor had a long-standing relationship with Katharina Schratt, an actress from the Burgtheater, as was pretty much expected from any self-respecting Austrian aristocrat. But this was a relationship of diligent letters of affection, rather than one of lusty passion.[34]

Even when interspersed with the occasional romantic scandal, the essentially unchanging nature of the court provided comfort to the Viennese, a calm centre in the maelstrom of Austro-Hungarian politics. The fact that most Viennese were far too low-born to ever be able to attend one of the grander court functions merely reconfirmed the point that, in Vienna, traditions were diligently maintained. John Lothrop Motley, an American ambassador to Vienna in the 1860s, had remarked that 'an Austrian might be Shakespeare, Galileo, Nelson, and Raphael in one person, but he would not be received in good society if he did not possess the sixteen quarterings of nobility which birth alone can give him'.[35] 'Quite right', would have been the response fifty years later of Franz Joseph, a man entirely unwilling to have his habits changed by the passage of time, who thought the telephone a nuisance, who lit the Hofburg palace with kerosene lamps not electricity, who gloried in his old-fashionedness and was, to boot, a stickler for court etiquette – indeed court etiquette of the eighteenth century, inherited more distantly from the Spanish court of the sixteenth century.[36]

In 1913 his rigorous application of tradition led him to slight his nephew and presumptive heir, Franz Ferdinand, for having married a Czech aristocrat beneath his station, Sophie Chotek. This poisoned irretrievably the relationship between the two men (while Kaiser Wilhelm II cannily exploited Franz Ferdinand's feeling by inviting the Archduke and his wife to dine with Kaiser and Kaiserin à quatre, thus emphasising that he was more a man of the times, albeit arch-conservative in his own way). Yet the habits of courtliness in wider society, even if artificial, absurdly formalised and hidebound, could be a pleasure to at least some of Vienna's inhabitants. Stefan Zweig was delighted when, a play of his having been accepted at the Burgtheater, he received a return visit from the director himself, an indication of Zweig's own social elevation to the rank of gentleman.[37]

The court gave its royal impress to galleries, and to theatres and, of course, to the opera house – the Hofoper – which Hitler painted many times from the outside and in which he was transported by the operas of Wagner, performed under the baton of the Austrian Jewish composer and conductor Gustav Mahler (before he was appointed as conductor at the Metropolitan Opera in New York in 1908).[38] In 1913, the Hofoper, now under the direction of Weingartner, met the centenary of Wagner's birth with the traditional round of his operas. Those of Verdi, composer of *Aïda*, were not given any special prominence – not least because Verdi's music was so strongly associated with the Italian *Risorgimento*, as a result of which the Habsburgs were reduced to their twin Italian holdings of Trento and Trieste.[39]

But music in Vienna was far from being a royal prerogative – Franz Joseph himself, unlike Kaiser Wilhelm, was rarely seen at the opera house, his tastes being distinctly simpler. Nor was music the preserve of the aristocracy, who had hunting instead. Music, rather, was a Viennese religion – for the bourgeoisie in particular (many of whom were Jewish), but ultimately for the city as a whole. Music and theatre were serious. In Vienna, noted Zweig, 'every flat note' was remarked upon. 'Control was exercised at premières not by the professional critics alone', he wrote, 'but day after day, by the entire audience, whose attentive ears had been sharpened in constant comparison':

> Whereas in politics, in administration, or in morals, everything went on rather comfortably and one was affably tolerant of all that was slovenly, and overlooked many an infringement, in artistic matters there was no pardon; here the honor of the city was at stake. Every singer, actor, and musician had constantly to give his best or he was lost. It was wonderful to be the darling of Vienna, but it was not easy to remain so; no letdown was forgiven.[40]

The city had an unerring tradition of celebrating some of its greatest composers after it had allowed them to die in poverty – Mozart, Beethoven, Schubert. The notable exception was Johann Strauss, the 'waltz king', to whom in 1913 a museum was opened in his wife's house.[41]

In these years, Vienna counted eight major orchestras (including the Vienna doctors' orchestra). There were 247 male choirs, including those of the grocers' association, the workers of the Ottakring brewery, of individual factories and companies and of particular branches of the civil service. The Wiener Kaufmännischer Gesangverein, the Viennese Salesmen's Choir, sang concerts of Weber, Liszt and Wagner. (Arnold Schoenberg, the modern Austrian composer, directed the Chormusikverein, the choral music association.) Operettas were professionally performed at the Theater an der Wien, at the Volksoper, or at the Johann-Strauss – including eleven new operettas for the single year 1913. Richard Strauss' *Salomé* was not performed in Vienna, failing to pass the Viennese censor. *Die Fledermaus*, in contrast, was promoted to being acceptable at the Hofoper, thus given the benediction of the guardians of Viennese tradition.

However, there were problems with the picture of Vienna as the city of the waltz, the city of tradition rigorously upheld, a city decaying yet joyous. It underplayed Vienna's role as a crucible for cultural experimentation. This was Vienna's signal paradox: that such a bastion of tradition could also be a forcing-house for modernity.

Perhaps the Viennese themselves understood better than anyone else how much the brilliant surface of the city concealed. Sigmund Freud, in his mid fifties by 1913, psychoanalysed his patients (and his society) on a daily basis, publishing *Totem und Tabu* in that year, uncovering neuroses both individual and collective. The city's picture-postcard image could be a foil for Vienna's modernists – be they Karl Kraus, who deconstructed sentimentalism every fortnight in his paper *Die Fackel* (*The Torch*) or Adolf Loos, who responded to the over-decoration, and therefore decadence of Viennese architecture as he saw it, by declaring that '*ornament ist vebrechen*' ('ornament is crime'). Loos famously put his dictum into physical form with the '*Haus ohne Augenbrauen*' ('House without eyebrows') – so-called because the windows had no decorative lintels – on Michaelerplatz in 1910. (It was said that as a result Emperor Franz Joseph never

Sigmund Freud, an assimilated Jewish intellectual in Vienna, dissected the
psychoses of a class, a city and an empire on permanent display. 'Nowhere
in Europe', noted an American guidebook, 'is the past so intermingled with
the present'.

looked out of his favourite window in the imperial palace again;
Hitler got over the problem of the building's existence by simply
putting another in its place in his paintings.[42])

Modernity touched even that which was most sacrosanct to the
Viennese, music, but not without controversy. On 31 March 1913
Arnold Schoenberg conducted a concert of music by himself and
fellow Austrian composers Alban Berg and Anton Webern. Berg's
Altenberg Lieder led to a riot – as did the much more famous performance of Stravinsky's *Rite of Spring* in Paris a couple of months
later – leading to the entry of the police.[43] Arthur Schnitzler challenged the hypocrisies of Viennese society by writing about sex with
scandalous frankness. Egon Schiele displayed such frankness on his
canvases, as did his mentor Gustav Klimt, the leader of the *Sezession*
('Secession') movement. In the midst of all this Ludwig Wittgenstein,
the son of a Jewish steel magnate and patron of the arts, began

to develop his challenge to traditional philosophical thinking.[44]

That such an outpouring of challenges to the established cultural order should happen all at the same time, at the same place, in so many fields, was not pure coincidence. It was, in part, the product of a community, many of whom were Jewish, which viewed German *Bildung* (self-cultivation) as one of the highest of human objectives. It was also a product of the smallness of this community, an extraordinarily interconnected intelligentsia. Arnold Schoenberg, a noted expressionist painter linked to the Blaue Reiter school as well as a musical composer, wrote in the flyleaf of satirist Karl Kraus's copy of his *Theory of Harmony* that 'I have learned more from you, perhaps, than a man should learn'.[45] Sigmund Freud considered Arthur Schnitzler his intellectual double. Stefan Zweig wrote that 'nothing has contributed as much to the intellectual mobility and the international orientation of the Austrian as that he could keep abreast of all world events in the coffee-house and at the same time discuss them in a circle of his friends', Zweig's own favourite being Café Griensteidl, next to Adolf Loos' *'Haus ohne Augenbrauen'* on Michaelerplatz.[46]

But this coincidence of cultural effervescence was also perhaps the product of the particularities of the city in a deeper sense, both as reaction against the city's tradition and a reflection of the deeper undercurrents in Viennese life. Freud wrote about dreams as wish fulfilment, and about jokes as a product of inner psychic tension: a laughing image concealing a darker reality.[47] He could not have written a better description of the city in which he lived.

'In Europe one knows of Vienna, the place where it is forever Sunday', wrote Hermann Bahr in 1906. 'This reputation of a happy city, swaying with dance, of harmless people, a little dissolute, not very active, not very efficient, but of good and kind people, has been retained in the wider world', he continued.[48] This, Bahr suggested, was an illusion. 'Perpetually swearing', he wrote, the true Viennese nonetheless wishes to be 'permanently praised . . . always complaining, always threatening'. Bahr's book was banned by the imperial authorities.[49] It was too critical. More to the point, it was perhaps too accurate.

In politics, it turned out that the easy-going Vienna of myth was in fact a city which experimented with populist politics – theatrical politics, indeed – which frequently shaded into the lowest common denominator of anti-Semitism. Jewish migration to Vienna had increased over the 1880s and 1890s, with Jews fleeing persecution and poverty further east, particularly in the Russian Empire. Vienna at the time offered the protection of law – equal rights had been guaranteed since 1867 – and the possibility of economic advancement (though Jews were still blamed for the stockmarket crash of 1873). New *Ostjuden* settled in Leopoldstadt, adding to Vienna's more long-standing and generally assimilated Jewish population. According to the 1910 census there were 175,000 religiously defined Jews in Vienna, out of an overall population of two million. This was a lower proportion than in Prague or Budapest. Vienna nonetheless developed a particular strain of populist anti-Semitism, led first by Georg von Schönerer and then by Karl Lueger, the city's mayor from 1897 to 1910.

The newly-arriving *Ostjuden* were popularly portrayed as poverty-stricken pedlars of cheap goods, foreign and mysterious. (This view was sometimes shared by their assimilated co-religionists, who saw the newcomers as a benighted community apparently unwilling to change their dress, speech or *shtetl* traditions in order to be inducted into the higher values of German culture.) At the same time, Viennese envy was given full rein against the city's commercially and professionally successful Jews, who constituted forty per cent of medical students at Vienna university, one-quarter of law students, a large proportion of journalists – and, of course, so many of the city's intelligentsia: Freud, Mahler, Kraus, Zweig amongst them.[50] Karl Lueger did not shy away from using 'the Jews' as shorthand for the various forces of modernity ranged against 'the small man'. To this witches' brew was added one final, contradictory, element: the image of Jews as anarchists and revolutionaries. The fact that the leader of Austria's social democrats, Victor Adler, was Jewish was presented as evidence. In the wake of the Russian revolution of 1905, Karl Lueger warned Vienna's Jews that 'we in Vienna are anti-Semites' and that 'should the Jews threaten our homeland' no mercy would be shown them.[51]

In some of the city's more fevered minds these disparate images of Vienna's Jews combined to become a picture of an extraordinarily wide-ranging Jewish conspiracy to take over the world – starting with Vienna. For most Viennese such attitudes, while not necessarily being shared in their extreme form, became an accepted part of the city's background noise, building on an older tradition of Catholic anti-Semitism. Many of the city's assimilated Jews, however, did not feel particularly threatened in 1913, viewing the whole thing as an exercise in populist rhetoric. Lueger, after all, was not so determinedly anti-Semitic all the time. And Vienna's assimilated Jews were not only loyal upholders of German culture, they were protected by law. Whether he was remembering or misremembering the past, Stefan Zweig wrote: 'I personally must confess that neither in school nor at the University, nor in the world of literature, have I ever experienced the slightest suppression or indignity as a Jew'.[52] Intermarriage between Jews and Christians was common.

Yet the anti-Semitic refrains of everyday Viennese life serviced a dangerous set of entrenched assumptions and prejudices – prejudices which would later prove fatal. To some Jews, they already suggested that assimilation was a dead end. Theodor Herzl, an Austrian journalist who had accepted Stefan Zweig's manuscripts for the *Neue Freie Presse* during his editorship of that journal's essay pages, began to see a Jewish homeland as the only way out. Zionism, which became the name of Herzl's movement, was criticised by many of Vienna's Jewish intellectual elite for appearing to give up on assimilation, and its rabbis for being essentially ethnic rather than religious. But the movement gathered pace nonetheless, eventually selecting Palestine as a possible home for Europe's Jewish population and supporting Jewish emigration there. In September 1913, nine years after Herzl's death, the eleventh Zionist congress opened its doors – in Vienna.

In the same month that Vienna hosted the Zionist congress, the city hosted a much larger set of meetings on public health and the prevention of disasters. Dr Rosner of the Vienna ambulance corps delivered a paper on the first dressing of injuries. Mr Greil spoke of the importance of fireproof curtains in theatres, separating the stage from the audience. A Mr Wortmann spoke about something still more important, and more concerning, the indication of a society which was perhaps psychically unwell. In 1912, he told his international audience, there had been 1,387 cases of suicide in Vienna, a number that was 'constantly and rapidly increasing'.[53]

The year 1913 had started no differently to previous years. In January, London's *Standard* newspaper opened its New Year's coverage of the Austro-Hungarian capital, a city it already described as having the highest rate of suicides in the world, under the headline 'Morbid Vienna Youths: Triple Suicide in a Café'.[54] Three boys, aged eighteen, seventeen and sixteen, were reported as having gone to a coffee house together around midnight, where they ordered coffee, added potassium cyanide to it, drank it, and died writhing on the floor a few minutes later. One of the boys wrote a letter to his mother and father explaining that he had had some trouble with work. The others wrote no such notes. Instead, the three had a photograph of themselves taken together, and they sent this picture on to their parents. A girl was supposed to have received a further copy of the photograph but, the *Standard* reported, 'there appears to be no love affair'. The story was off the newspapers the next day. Three dramatic and tragic deaths amongst many others, rapidly forgotten – a statistic.

It was another suicide, later in the year, which was to give Stefan Zweig 'waking dreams' of fear – a personal episode that nonetheless stood as the symbol of the extent to which Austria-Hungary was now morally and politically compromised, a contribution to an uncertain atmosphere beneath a surface insouciance.[55] It concerned the case of Alfred Redl, former chief of military intelligence. In 1912, it had emerged that Russia, Vienna's prospective military opponent should Austria-Hungary ever decide to intervene against Serbia in the Balkans, was fully apprised of the main Austro-Hungarian battle plan. The plan had been stolen. The armed forces, one of the few pillars of the Austro-Hungarian Empire, had a mole.

Redl had by this time moved from his position as head of military intelligence to a role in Prague, as chief of staff to the local force commander. He was therefore unaware of extraordinary measures taken by his successor to uncover the spy within the army's midst. Suspicious letters were opened and read, hundreds daily. One in particular invited the attention of the investigation, a package addressed to Nikon Nizetas, posted from Eydtkuhnen in eastern Prussia, a few miles from the Russian border.[56] The package contained

6,000 Austrian shillings, a not inconsiderable sum to leave in the trust of the Austro-Hungarian postal service. It was, moreover, linked to an address known to be used by Russian intelligence. The package arrived at the main Vienna post office on the Fleischmarkt – and there it remained, awaiting the mysterious Mr Nizetas to pick it up. Police officers were installed in a room in a building close by, connected to the post office by an electric wire. When Mr Nizetas showed up, a post office employee would press a hidden button, and a bell would ring at Postgasse, number 10. Here they waited for six weeks, from seven in the morning till eight in the evening.

On Saturday 24 May 1913, a man in a grey suit and dark hat arrived at the post office just before five in the afternoon, claiming a package for him under the name Nizetas. Accounts differ as to exactly what happened next. One version suggests that the policemen lost track of Nizetas, and only caught up with him through multiple strokes of luck: someone remembered the number of the taxi in which the man in the dark hat had departed, the policemen stumbled across the same cab twenty minutes later, and, although its original passenger was no longer at the Café Kaiserhof to which he had been taken, a boy at the taxi rank remembered a man answering to Nizetas' description had taken a second cab on to the Hotel Klomser. Another version suggests that the policemen followed the cab themselves, a little behind, arriving in time to interrogate the cab driver as to his customer's destination, to which Nizetas had proceeded on foot. But the accounts do agree that the police had an additional piece of good fortune. In the back of the cab Nizetas had left the sheath of a pocket knife he used to open his correspondence. The sheath of the pocket knife was taken to the Hotel Klomser and left on display at the reception, where the receptionist was to say it had been left by a cab driver. Nizetas picked it up. Nizetas was Alfred Redl.

Why had Redl done it? Principally because he was blackmailed over his homosexuality, of which the Russians had been aware for over ten years. But he had been impelled to continue because he had then developed expensive tastes, and a dangerous sense of his own inviolability. He made the mistake of claiming the pocket-knife sheath, which, as an experienced intelligence officer, he should have known to leave alone. A subsequent search of Redl's apartment in Prague would reveal unfinished love letters to Stefan Horinka, a

lieutenant in the army who wished to break off a homosexual relationship, and with whom Redl had argued on the day that he was
picked up. Redl was said to give Horinka some 900 crowns a month.
Such details inevitably leaked out over the next few weeks and
months.

It would at least be possible for Redl and the army to avoid the
embarrassment of a drawn-out court case. That evening, no doubt
already aware that the net was closing around him, Redl dined with
an old friend, observed by the police. On returning to his hotel, he
was confronted with his treason. He requested and was lent an army
pistol. Some time after one in the morning the cobbled streets
around the Hotel Klomser echoed briefly with the sound of a gunshot
as Alfred Redl became the latest of Vienna's suicides for 1913.

Then the calm of night returned. In a few hours' time dawn would
break over the imperial palace, and the Emperor Franz Joseph would
awake again. News of the previous day's events would be summarised
for the emperor, and a plan for the day ahead laid out. The Riesenrad
would begin to turn. The Habsburg empire would carry on.

ST PETERSBURG
Eastern Colossus

At Easter 1913 Tsar Nicholas II gave his wife Alexandra a remarkable present: a golden Fabergé egg. Its exterior was sumptuously decorated with golden double-headed eagles, imperial crowns and eighteen exquisite miniature portraits of the Tsars and Tsarinas of the Romanov dynasty stretching back to Nicholas' distant forebear Tsar Michael, who had become Russia's leader exactly 300 years previously.[1] But the egg's true masterwork was on the inside. There, a globe of blued steel showed the frontiers of Muscovy in 1613, and those of the Russian Empire in 1913. The contrast was suitably impressive. For now the double-headed eagle could be seen from the Baltic to the Pacific, from the Black Sea to Central Asia, from the borders of China to those of Prussia. All in all, these domains constituted the largest contiguous empire on the face of the earth – the largest contiguous empire in world history – one which had continuously expanded, decade-by-decade, over three centuries, the absolute justification of Romanov rule.

Over the course of that year the Romanov tercentenary was celebrated everywhere across this vast territory. Biographies of Tsar Nicholas were published, monuments erected, crosses and icons blessed, and new churches dedicated, including one that could hold 4,000 worshippers near St Petersburg's Nikolaevskaya railway station. Countless performances of Glinka's *A Life for the Tsar* commemorated the heroic sacrifice of Ivan Susanin, who was said to have saved Tsar Michael Romanov's life by tricking the Tsar's foreign enemies into following him deeper and deeper into a midwinter forest, from which neither they nor he would ever escape alive.

That summer, Tsar Nicholas and his family travelled down the Volga from Nizhny Novgorod to Kostroma and Yaroslavl, places intimately connected with the foundation legends of the Romanov dynasty. With a politician's eye, premier Count Kokovtsov detected only 'shallow curiosity' amongst the crowds along the riverside, 'handsomely ornamented descents' of peasants to the shore to see the Tsar, thinned out by biting winds. But in Kostroma, where a Romanov monument was unveiled, the enthusiasm seemed genuine enough: 'the return of warm weather had thawed out the crowd'.² The imperial family experienced manifestations of Russian fidelity to the Tsar that they would never forget: 'artisans and workmen falling down to kiss his shadow as we passed. Cheers were deafening'.³ In Moscow there were more processions, more speeches, more moments of high symbolism to invoke the identity of Russia's national destiny with that of her imperial family, more rituals of power.

Two rival films were made covering key episodes of Russia's recent history, indistinguishable from that of the Romanov family itself. Commemorative mugs, biscuit tins and cigarette cases were produced, and postage stamps bearing the likeness of the Tsar were issued – though traditionalists feared that this risked his imperial visage being besmirched by Russia's postmasters. In Orthodox churches across the empire a manifesto issued by the Tsar was read out, reconfirming his commitment to the development of Russia's national life. In St Petersburg's newly built mosque, the Emir of Bukhara, the Khan of Khiva and Muslim members of the Russian Duma were reminded that 'devotion to the throne and love of the motherland are ordered by God himself and by his Prophet Muhammad'.⁴

In the Russian capital, the city's bankers demonstrated both their generosity and their lack of imagination by presenting the Tsar with a cheque for one million roubles to be cashed at the state bank, delivered on a golden platter.⁵ Government officials in remoter corners of empire sought to remind St Petersburg of their existence by organising the sending of more modest offerings to the Tsar, a token of their respect. In the south-west Siberian town of Tobolsk, once a centre of Russian colonisation but now sidelined by the construction of the trans-Siberian railway, it was decided to send local priest Dmitri Smirnov to Russia's capital city to present the Tsar with a copy of the miracle-working Abalakskaya icon to which Nicholas had prayed as a young man in 1891.⁶

The highlight of the tercentenary celebrations came in St Petersburg on 21 February 1913. The date was historically significant, and freighted with contemporary pertinence. It was on this date in 1613 that Michael Romanov had been acclaimed Tsar by an assembly of Russia's nobles, the Zemsky Sobor. Acclaimed, not elected: the difference was important. According to the tercentenary committee set up to manage the commemorations, Michael Romanov had been raised to the position of Tsar by the Zemsky Sobor, with one voice and with one soul, to deliver Russia from domestic strife and from its foreign enemies. The contemporary implication was clear: in 1913, as in 1613, the Tsar was to be understood as bound directly and irrevocably to the Russian people, in a mystical union with them, acting as their father, their guide and the defender of their faith. Nothing should be allowed to bring this bond into question, or to take away from the wholeheartedness of faith and obedience that it implied. A Duma, for example, an elected parliament – as the Tsar had been forced to concede after the 1905 revolution – should aid the sovereign in his responsibilities, not undermine his autocracy. Nicholas did not like the title 'Emperor', which for him implied simply the grand figurehead of the state. He preferred the ancient Russian title 'Tsar', with its Byzantine connotations of absolutism and spiritual authority, of a leader at one with his people.[7]

Although the signs and symbols of Orthodox Christianity would run through the celebrations from start to finish, the tercentenary committee had rejected the suggestion of the church elders of the Holy Synod that the highlight of the tercentenary be on July 11, the date on which Michael Romanov had been crowned Tsar in church. To raise this date above any other, it was felt, would appear to suggest that the Tsar derived his legitimacy from the Orthodox Church itself. Rather, the Tsar should be considered the defender of the Church, not its subject; anointed by God and the Russian people, not by priests.

At precisely eight that February morning, a thunderous twenty-one-gun salvo was fired into an overcast sky from the Peter and Paul Fortress. At this signal a number of processions, mostly religious but with nationalists and monarchists in support, began to converge on the city's central Kazan Cathedral. Church bells rang, military bands played. St Petersburg's streets, emptied of traffic, shop shutters drawn down, were decorated with portraits of the Tsar, flags, double-headed eagles and garlands of electric lights. 'Lack of taste and poverty reigned', leading Petersburg artist Mikhail Dobuzhinsky complained; but for most the impression was more positive. 'Everything looked more smart, better and more brilliant than the day before', reported a journalist from the local *Petersburgskaia gazeta*.[8] Dmitri Smirnov, overwhelmed by the contrast with the quiet dirt tracks of his Siberian home town of Tobolsk, reported streets of 'unprecedented movement' as he hurried to arrive at the Kazan Cathedral at nine in the morning – hours before the main ceremonies were to begin – ticket clutched firmly in his hand.[9]

Inside the cathedral a crowd of 4,000 assembled slowly, noisily, from all corners of the Russian Empire. Smirnov found himself 'astounded and blinded' by the reflections of candlelight on chandeliers, on swords and on gold braid. Equally overwhelmed, the reporter from *Novoe vremia* described 'the brilliance of the ladies' diamonds, the brilliance of the medals and the stars, the brilliance of the gold and silver of the uniforms'.[10] Having found himself a place near the front of the cathedral, where he could command a view over the proceedings and over the arrival of the Tsar, Smirnov now waited diligently. Others were less pleased with their placement. Michael Rodzianko, the president of the Duma, protested vigorously that Duma deputies had been placed behind members of the appointed state council, seeming to suggest their secondary importance. He demanded this be reversed, a small political battle that he was able to win.

As the congregation settled, a celebratory liturgy began, conducted by the Patriarch of Antioch, supported by priests from Russia and from other Orthodox countries, including Serbia, then in the midst of a Balkan war. The Tsar and his family made their way in open carriages from the Winter Palace down Nevsky Prospekt to the Kazan Cathedral, the most exposed the Tsar had been to a large mass of the public in years, albeit surrounded by a guard of mounted Cossacks keeping the crowds well back. Smirnov described the scene as the Tsar arrived:

Everyone's eyes moved to the south main entrance. Enthusiastic shouts of 'Hoorah!' could be heard from the streets as the doors opened, greeting the beloved monarch and his family . . . Then He entered – He who was wanted by all, awaited by all, adored by all . . . Him, whom you are used to respect with all your soul as the chosen one and the anointed one of God, for whom you feel the greatest reverence and boundless commitment, as the sole support, protection and hope of all Russia, as its Red Sun (to use a popular expression) . . ."

The priest's eyes filled with tears at the sight. 'From time to time', he wrote afterwards, 'I have thought: have our values stumbled and weakened?' The last years, he could recall, had seen industrial unrest, protests on the streets, a political revolution in 1905, military defeat by Japan, the diplomatic embarrassment of Russia over the Austro-Hungarian Empire's annexation of Bosnia in 1908, the assassination of a prime minister in 1911, and ongoing war between Slavs and Turks in the Balkans. But at the sight of the Tsar, at the sight of his subjects assembled under the dome of the Kazan Cathedral, surrounded by the icons of the Holy Church, doubts about Russia's unity and status evaporated, like a morning mist burnt off by the warmth of the sun. 'Where has all the gloom gone?' he asked. 'It is as if it was never there at all'.

Later that afternoon the police estimated that a quarter of a million St Petersburgers, approximately one in ten of the city's inhabitants, attended popular fêtes in public parks, the crowds finely balanced between the steadily plummeting mercury of the thermometers, the effects of alcohol, and the promise of festivities to come. The Peter and Paul Fortress was now lit up, adorned with three massive portraits: of Tsar Michael, the founder of the Romanov dynasty, Peter the Great, the founder of St Petersburg, and their successor, Nicholas II.[12] In the gilded hall of the St Petersburg conservatory, the whole bathed in light from crystal chandeliers, the twenty-two-year-old composer Sergey Prokofiev conducted a small concert in the Tsar's honour (though not in his presence) including, inevitably, excerpts from *A Life for the Tsar* – performed two days later in full at the Mariinsky Theatre in front of the imperial family themselves.[13]

At around seven-thirty in the evening, the sun having already sunk below the horizon, a barrage of fireworks was unleashed into the cold clear sky, lighting it up once more in an effusion of Romanov magnificence. Then darkness fell once more.

The Russian Empire gloried above all in the extent of its territory, secondly in the size of its population, and thirdly in the diversity of the peoples which fell under Romanov rule. All three were prodigious, all three had increased constantly from the crowning of Tsar Michael to the tercentenary celebrations of Tsar Nicholas II.

The empire might yet increase in size. To the north, the Russian Empire's border was the icy seas of the Arctic. Here, exploration left open the possibility of the discovery of more islands. To the east, Russian expansion had been checked by defeat at the hands of Japan in 1905, a loss of prestige that Russian patriots found hard to bear (including the Tsar himself, who had toured Japan as a young man, was nearly assassinated there, and who persisted in calling the Japanese *makaki*, 'monkeys').[14] But even this military defeat was not necessarily a permanent barrier to Russian growth into northern Manchuria or into Mongolia, where a government under Russian protection had recently been set up, suspected of being little more than a Russian puppet. Further west, in the borderlands of Central Asia and the Middle East, where Britain and Russia had long vied for influence, holding agreements had been reached. But competition between the two imperial powers remained in the shadows – neither side imagined that the last move of diplomatic and military chess had been played. Finally, along the uncertain borderlands between the Russian Empire and the Ottoman Empire there reigned mistrust – the Russians were, after all, long-time sponsors of the Slav nations against which the Turks were fighting for their lives in 1913. The Russians had long coveted Constantinople itself (both a seat of Christian Orthodoxy and a gateway to the Mediterranean), and might yet use the defence of Christian Armenians as an excuse to extend itself into central Anatolia.

It was not known with any great precision how many lived within the Russian Empire. But the Central Statistical Bureau estimated the population to have increased by some thirty per cent between the last census in 1897 – riddled with inconsistencies, in which Tsar Nicholas had characteristically listed his occupation as 'landowner' – and 1913.[15] In the tercentenary year, therefore, the published figure amounted to no fewer than 175,137,800 souls – nearly double the population of the United States, and more than the populations of the Austro-Hungarian Empire, German Empire and France combined.[16] (The majority of these were in European Russia, on the near side of the Urals, but that still left perhaps forty-five million subjects of the Tsar in Siberia, Central Asia and in the Far East,

closer to Peking and Tokyo than to Paris or London.) Such a population translated into a standing army larger than any other – well
over a million-strong in 1913 – and reserves of manpower far in
excess of those available to any other country.

Russia's vast population was ethnically and religiously mixed,
Russians themselves constituting less than half the total. Adding
the Poles, Belorussians (White Russians) and Ukrainians (who the
Austro-Hungarians called Ruthenians, and who the Russians dimin-
utively called Little Russians) took the proportion to just under
three-quarters. The remaining share comprised Armenians and
Azeris, Kazakhs, Kirghiz and Kalmyks, Latvians and Lithuanians,
Estonians, Finns and Germans. Some of these groups were assimilated to Russian society, others grudgingly accepted its predominance, others were suppressed. (Russia's Jews formed another still
more problematic group, not considered yet a 'nation', and subject
to laws which restricted their rights even beyond those of other
Tsarist subjects.) In 1913 the Russian Empire published books in
forty-nine different languages.[17]

So massive was Russia, so diverse: but how well understood? Even
those responsible for ruling over a part of the empire recognised
the limits of their information about it. 'We knew as much about
the Tula countryside', admitted a local nobleman responsible for the
area's affairs in the 1890s, 'as we knew about central Africa'.[18] No one
could deny the success of the Romanovs in assembling such vast
domains – but did they or anyone else truly rule Russia? Did the
Romanov regime simply provide cover for a mass of Russian contradictions, a barely managed chaos?

In his novel *Petersburg* Andrei Bely neatly captured both the self-
importance of St Petersburg's *chinovniki* (bureaucrats) and their
impotence to control the sprawling reality of the Russian Empire,
by acidly observing that the imperial capital existed, above all:

> – on maps: as two little circles that sit one inside the other with a
> black point in the centre; and from this mathematical point, which
> has no dimension, it energetically declares that it exists; from there,
> from this point, there rushes in a torrent a swarm of the freshly

printed book; impetuously from this invisible point rushes the government circular.[19]

In truth, many Russians had long considered St Petersburg an artificial city, the capital of the Russian Empire, but not truly the capital
of Russia. Bely was not the first to depict the city as a phantasm,
almost as an apparition.

The city had not emerged naturally at the crossroads of ancient
trade routes. It had been commanded into existence by imperial
diktat, Peter the Great decreeing that the capital should be pulled
from Moscow to a still-empty plot on the Gulf of Finland, where
the smell of Baltic sea air would encourage Russians to look west
and free them from the stench of incense in the churches of Muscovy.
St Petersburg was thus the symbol of the absolute power of an
autocrat or, as he preferred it, an enlightened despot. For much of
its life the city was viewed as Peter's folly, a city of impeccable classical façades built on marshland at the cost of tens of thousands of
Russian lives. But the city was also intended as a political project:
the advance guard of Russia's modernisation, its window on the
world and the world's window on it, a city dedicated to the proposition that Russia was and must be European. 'Petersburg' and
'Moscow' became slogans dragooned into the service of different
visions of Russia's future.

Everything about the Russian capital bespoke the Europeanising
ambitions of its founder, starting with its name: German Peters-*burg*
rather than Russian Petro-*grad*. (The locals themselves referred to
the city simply as '*Piter*', the Dutch version of the Tsar's name,
recalling time spent in Holland in Peter the Great's youth.) While
the city's first building had been a fortress – the Peter and Paul
Fortress from which the opening salvo of the Romanov tercentenary
was fired, now converted from military use to be Russia's most
exclusive prison – St Petersburg had no traditional raised '*kremlin*',
as did more ancient Russian cities such as Moscow, Smolensk or
Nizhny Novgorod. Instead, the city fronted on to the magnificently
broad Neva river, frozen solid in winter, a site of ice-skating and
markets. The city's networks of canals, semi-circles radiating outwards
from the shoreline of the Neva, called to mind the layout of
Amsterdam, where Peter the Great had lived and worked as a young
man, learning the basics of ship construction. The rectilinearity of

St Petersburg's grand central thoroughfare, Nevsky Prospekt, evoked the rationalistic mindset of the European enlightenment rather than Russian spirituality. The city called one of its grandest quaysides the English Quay, and one of its islands was given the name New Holland.

The city's architecture – the Admiralty Building, the Tauride Palace, even the Orthodox Kazan Cathedral – reflected European models. Some of the city's grandest buildings had indeed been designed by European architects. The Tsar's Winter Palace, and many other famous St Petersburg edifices, were the work of Francesco Bartolomeo Rastrelli, born in Florence, Italy. Many of the city's statues, too, were by foreign sculptors. The most famous was that of Peter the Great, commissioned long after his death by the German-born Empress Catherine the Great in the hope that Petersburgers would recognise her as the inheritor of his imperial mantle, and executed by the Frenchman Etienne Maurice Falconnet. Bursting with national pride, Louis Réau, director of the French Institute in St Petersburg, wrote that: 'if the capital of Peter the Great must necessarily earn the admiration of any cultivated European, this must particularly be the case for the French, for they alone have done more for it than all the rest of Europe'.[20]

In 1913, some found St Petersburg's northern elegance a little cold, a little too European, as intricately symmetrical as a snowflake but deprived of Russian warmth. They yearned rather for something more Slavic, redolent of a deeper past. (Nicholas II had himself a seventeenth-century style village built at Tsarskoe Selo, not far from St Petersburg, where he could imagine himself cast back to an earlier age.[21]) Alexander Benois, a leading figure in the city's cultural elite, told them to get out of their 'Slavophile nappies' and look on St Petersburg as something uniquely beautiful because it was both Russian and European, rather than carping that it was neither.[22] He co-edited *Starye gody* (*Bygone Years*), a highly successful magazine dedicated to the art and elegance of old St Petersburg. In the pages of the art journal *Mir iskusstva* (*World of Art*) – founded with Petersburg impresario Sergei Diaghilev – Benois disseminated an architectural vocabulary of classical harmony, emphasising open spaces (without people, some said) and panoramas. (Some suggested clearing the area around the Kazan Cathedral of *lavochki*, petty traders, in order to purify its aspect.) Together with like-minded Petersburgers – the so-called Preservationists – Benois set up a Museum of Old St Petersburg in 1912, and dedicated himself to protecting the city's classical unity from Muscovite or modern encroachments.

In this, he was not entirely successful. Many St Petersburgers loathed the new Church of the Saviour on Spilled Blood for example – a virtual copy of St Basil's Cathedral in Moscow – inaugurated by Nicholas II in 1907 on the site where his grandfather Alexander II had been assassinated thirty-six years previously. Entirely out of keeping with the rest of the city – but entirely in keeping with Nicholas' preferred view of Russia – the church's golden onion domes punctured the flat evenness of the St Petersburg skyline with a reminder that one was still in Russia, not in some idealised European city of the eighteenth century.

More importantly, neither Benois nor anyone else could halt the broader developments of St Petersburg – its expansion, its need for new housing and new office buildings, its gradual transformation from a city of aristocratic palaces to a city of the middle classes, from a city of government to one of commerce, from a city of art to one of industry. For by 1913 St Petersburg was Europe's fourth-largest city, with a population of two million, including 200,000 industrial workers. When Dmitri Smirnov, the Tobolsk priest, disembarked at the Nikolaevskaya railway station that winter, arriving in a place he had not clapped eyes on for thirty-three years, he found himself caught up in a city that had graduated from being an imperial stage set to being a European metropolis. 'I was staggered', he wrote, 'and deafened by the noise, movement and bustle'.[23]

As 1913 progressed, the memory of the Romanov celebrations began to fade. As the gold tercentenary leaf began to peel, the full complexity of the Russian empire was revealed, the true extent of the challenges it faced – and its mixed prospects for the future.

In many ways things were not that bad; indeed they were perhaps better than they had been for several years, and getting better. Granted, most Russians were still poorer than a citizen of France or a subject of the Habsburgs. But their sheer numbers meant that the empire as a whole had a national output double that of the Austro-Hungarian Empire, already greater than of France, and growing faster than either.[24] Russia's larger cities were covered in advertising hoardings for European products. Was this not a down payment on a still-larger consumer market to come? London's *Times* newspaper ran special supplements on Russia throughout 1913, boosting the country's profile to foreign investors. Its message of Russia's future economic prospects was plain enough.

By 1913, the Russian colossus was not just stirring economically, it was exploding. Rural incomes were rising, with 1913 promising to be a bumper year for the country's agriculture. Russia's share of the world's industry had increased consistently for thirty years, but now this growth was accelerating still faster. The empire's exports – timber, metals, grain and oil from the south Caucasus – poured through the country's ports on the Baltic and on the Black Sea. Foreign capital flowed in, constituting four-tenths of the capital behind Russian banks and an equal share of investment in Russian industry, in Russia's trams and trains, mines, metalworks and power stations.[25] Europe was awash with fashionable theories pronouncing the consolidation of world politics around a few world empires – no one doubted that Russia would be one of those empires. As Halford Mackinder put it 'the spaces within the Russian Empire and Mongolia are so vast and their potentialities in population, wheat, cotton, fuel and metals so incalculably great that a vast economic world . . . will there develop'.[26]

All this might be disturbed by war, of course. As traders bought and sold on the St Petersburg stock market, they might hear the sounds of marches outside calling for stronger Russian involvement in the Balkans. In March the Bulgarian General Radko Dimitriev was met in the city with adoring crowds, a service in the Resurrection Cathedral and shouts of 'Shumi Maritsa', the Bulgarians' bellicose national anthem.[27] But as the economy of the Russian Empire grew it was becoming more enmeshed with that of its most significant political antagonist, the German Empire, source of half of Russia's imports and destination for a third of its exports.[28] This, surely, was a positive sign for Europe's political stability as a whole. 'What Russia wants most at present is external peace', wrote Count Kokovtsov in a much-reported memorandum to the Tsar, 'in order that, enjoying its blessings, she may develop her productive powers to the necessary extent'.[29]

And should war come there was less and less reason for Russia

to fear it, her army recovered from 1905's blow of defeat, rearmed
and reformed. Although the governments of the various European
powers disagreed on the strength of the Russians in 1913 – not
untypically the most caustic were the Russians themselves – all
considered the country to be growing daily more powerful.[30]
(Whether that made it a factor of stability in Europe, calming any
German thoughts of conflict, or a factor of instability, enticing Russia
deeper into adventures in the Balkans or near East, remained to be
seen.) 'The future belongs to Russia', confided the German Chancellor
to his private secretary the following year.[31]

Above all, it was far from obvious that Russia was heading inevitably to revolution. Industrial strikes in St Petersburg and elsewhere
were an evident cause for concern, and in 1913 the number of industrial stoppages was multiplying. But Russia had no monopoly on
labour unrest, nor were the demands of workers particularly political
– they were the same as those of workers in Glasgow, Düsseldorf
or Milan: improved wages and conditions, less intrusion from the
bosses, a safer working environment. There were signs that the
revolutionists were in fact losing their grip on the proletariat, if they
had ever had them fully in their grasp. St Petersburg metalworkers
criticised the Bolshevik paper *Pravda* as the 'imaginary leaders of
the working masses', accusing them of twisting 'the meaning of
certain decisions and resolutions of the workers out of internal
considerations that in no way correspond to the interests and attitudes of the workers'.[32] In the meantime, increased factory inspections
were improving labour conditions. Health insurance was being introduced which promised to lessen the precariousness of industrial life.
The growth of Russian civil society offered an avenue for social
cooperation between workers and the middle classes. Newspapers
provided a common culture of aspiration. An assessment made by
English historian Bernard Pares of Russia a few years earlier still
held true in 1913:

> Despite the ominous pronouncements of a number of untrained
> correspondents, who have by their exaggeration almost killed public
> interest in this great country, the crops go on growing and life goes
> on developing. What we have to watch is the gradual formation of
> a middle term between despotism and revolution . . . With or without
> convulsions . . . the great main factors are slowly but surely changing,

and Russia will eventually issue on the path of renewed life, with loyalty to the past and with confidence in the future. So far from being weakened, she will be better able to take her natural part in the common affairs of Europe.[33]

In the Romanov's tercentenary year, wrote a journalist for the London *Times*, 'no hope seems too confident or too bright'.[34]

And yet – and yet. The challenges to Russian development, both economic and political, remained daunting. The darker forces within Russia remained strong, the structure of Russia's government remained creaky. While the extent of Russian territory was impressive, not all the gold leaf in the world could hide the fact that much of that land was empty wasteland, frozen in winter and a swamp in summer, without roads, railways or people. Despite improvements in rural incomes the country was saddled with a massive rural population that was uneducated and poor. The diversity of the empire's population was impressive in itself – but it increased the challenges of governability. More often than not, cack-handed coercion of individual nationalities had achieved the opposite of its objective, and had consolidated opposition to Romanov rule. Russian nationalists, meanwhile, lived in permanent suspicion that the empire served the interests of its subject peoples better than those of the Russians themselves.

In no other country did life seem so precarious or violence so quotidian, barbarism so near the surface. Accidents of all sorts – fires, industrial accidents, mineshaft collapses, breaking ice on rivers, road accidents, train accidents, tram accidents – casually carried Russians off to early deaths by the dozen every day. In the countryside, although serfdom had been abolished fifty years, feudal attitudes remained alive and well. Justice, such as it was, was rough and immediate: the mother of an eight-year-old child who threw a stick between the legs of a General's horse was reported to have been struck with a whip, a ten-year-old flogged for having thrown stones into the yard of a neighbouring house.[35] In the cities, the Russian papers were full of tales of *khouliganstvo*, or hooliganism, taken as the sign of a society where established principles of order were breaking down.[36]

Russian Futurists embraced the spirit of hooliganism in their art and poetry, expressing a desire to shock the public out of their

St Petersburg in the tercentenary year of the Romanov dynasty, a shop window of Russian modernity with a vast undeveloped hinterland behind it.

bourgeois values. In 1912 they published a manifesto for their move-ment entitled *A Slap in the Face of Public Taste*. In December 1913 they put on a Futurist opera in St Petersburg's Luna Park theatre in which the sun itself, symbol of enlightenment, was taken captive and then killed. 'They want to transform the world into chaos, to smash the established values into pieces', said Matiushin and Kazimir Malevich, two of the opera's creators, in an interview.[37] 'Who is more crazy?' asked the *Petersburgskaia gazeta*, the Futurists or the public who paid nine roubles for a seat in order 'to see ugly decorations and some freaks dressed in large shirts, and to listen to a senseless selection of words clearly meant for whistling and abuse'.[38]

Memories of blood on the streets were fresh. During the tercen-tenary celebrations in February 1913, Tsar Nicholas had walked into the Kazan Cathedral over the same ground where a throng of students had been cut down by Cossack soldiers in 1901 while they celebrated the assassination of a government minister. It was only eight years since the revolution of 1905 and the moment when imperial troops had fired indiscriminately into a crowd of 60,000 workers – a crowd led by a priest bearing a cross and carrying a loyal petition to the Tsar – in front of the Winter Palace. In the previous year striking miners in the Lena goldfields of Siberia had been fired on, with several hundred killed or wounded. In the first years of the twentieth century, pogroms of Russian Jews, carried out by the marauding Black Hundreds while government officials looked on – or even with their connivance – had made rural Russia a byword for anti-Semitic butchery.

Despite legal reforms passed in the wake of the 1905 revolution, the state retained extraordinary and often arbitrary power over individuals and over society. A public meeting could be broken up by a policeman who heard a word – 'constitution', for example – to which he took exception. Internal migration was controlled, a system which was applied with particular ferocity to Russia's Jews, who were excluded from living outside an area known as the Pale of Settlement, with limited exceptions, such as for Jewish women prepared to be labelled as prostitutes. Even for foreign nationals, the Russian state evoked real fear. As Luigi Villari, an Italian traveller to Russia, described it, 'you arrive with your head full of passports, gendarmes, the secret police, nihilist novels and Siberia'. Nervously, 'you cannot help looking again and again at your papers . . . visions of Russian prisons rise up before your eyes, searching examinations into your past history by an all-knowing chief of police'.[39]

In many respects the Russian state was a scrawnier creature than the double-headed eagle suggested, its grip weak even if its talons were sharp. It was not the case that there was a policeman on every street corner in Russia – in fact there were fewer per capita than in Germany or Britain. In the end, Villari's fears of Russian border guards turned out to be unfounded – the checks at the border were a fiasco. 'I might have had a whole boxful of revolutionary literature for all the customs officers knew', he wrote.[40] But this was a consequence of despotic capriciousness rather than thought-out policy, a trait that applied throughout Russian officialdom. The very structures of Russian administration – multiple layers, multiple jurisdictions, different organisations with the same ostensible purpose – seemed calculated to impede effectiveness. Such a state might serve to keep the people sufficiently on edge to ensure sullen submission, but if this was order, it was skin-deep. When it came to more complex tasks of modern government – raising money or prosecuting wars – it was blunderingly incompetent. The story of Russia's military defeat in 1905 was riddled with shocking examples of disorganisation.

The closer one got to the centre of things, to St Petersburg, to the Duma and to the Tsar himself, the more disheartened one became about the mechanisms by which Russia's challenges might be addressed. The Duma was housed in Potemkin's Tauride Palace – and it provided a democratic Potemkin façade to the realities of the Russian political system. Although the existence of the Duma was a welcome advance, and it certainly made popular sentiment ever harder to ignore, the road to true constitutional parliamentary government in Russia was a crooked path strewn with obstacles, not an open highway of political development. As the tercentenary celebrations had made quite clear, the Tsar saw the Duma as subordinate, consultative and, quite possibly, temporary. The Duma itself did not speak with one voice, but was divided between liberals and conservatives, socialists and nationalists, modernisers and those who sought to turn the clock back to simpler times.

The Tsar's own theory of government, as one former Russian premier described it in 1912, was positively infantile: 'I do what I wish, and what I wish is good; if people do not see it, it is because they are plain mortals, while I am God's anointed'.[41] Perhaps this was Russia's way. 'Let Europe boast of its constitutions', wrote Vladimir Mescherskii, a favourite of Nicholas II, 'Russia alone in Europe requires her own path toward development and the future . . . complete authority and complete freedom for the supreme power, since it alone remains pure and untouched by the poison of corruption'.[42] Still, if Tsarist autocracy was to be enlightened absolutism rather than plain old despotism, then the Tsar himself had to be enlightened. But Nicholas was no Peter the Great. His intellectual limitations were well known. Even to those who believed in the system that he represented, the Tsar was a disappointment. His impressionability was legendary; the most powerful man in Russia was said to be the man who had most recently spoken to the Tsar. It was difficult to know what Nicholas really thought, or to predict how he would act. 'In general one can say about our Tsar in that he is an enigma', confided one politician to his diary, 'today he is a rightist, what he will be tomorrow is shrouded in mystery'.[43]

To the uncertainty of his own mind was allied a willingness to disrupt the work of others. 'A veritable passion for secret notes and methods', inexpertly put into effect, invariably landed the Tsar in 'a mud puddle or in a pool of blood', wrote a former minister.[44] Most recently, the reforming premier Pyotr Stolypin had been undermined by the Tsar behind his back. (Stolypin finally bullied the Tsar into accepting proposals for local government reform in western Russia by threatening to resign.) In 1911, Stolypin was assassinated in the Kiev opera. The Tsar was said to have asked for forgiveness for his meddling. Too late.

And behind the Tsar lay – what? A nine-year-old boy afflicted with haemophilia who invited shocked gasps when seen in public, a brother who had been cut out of the succession for having married a previously married commoner against the Tsar's will, a German-born wife who refused to show herself in public and when she did seemed on the verge of a nervous collapse, and the *starets* Rasputin, a so-called holy man who many believed to be an out-and-out fraud with far too much influence, poisoning the life of the imperial court.

Towards the end of the year, the world was reminded of a continuing canker on the Russian body politic, that of anti-Semitism, as its attention turned to a courthouse in Kiev in Ukraine. There, a Jewish clerk, Menahem Mendel Beilis, was on trial on trumped-up charges of ritually murdering a local lad in order to use his blood in a religious service. Under a full-length portrait of Tsar Nicholas II, wrote journalist Vladimir Nabokov, a travesty of justice was underway, 'poisoned with hatred, suspicion and lies'.[45] Witnesses were blackmailed and the police lied through their teeth. The only 'evidence' was provided by the whispered statement of a local professor of psychiatry, Ivan Sikorskii, who was disowned by his profession for his testimony, of which Nabokov wrote:

> No matter how many years will pass, when the future historians of our trial, of our public life, open the pages of the shorthand reports . . . they will read the delirium, the assurances taken from anti-Semite literature of the lowest rank presented under the flag of scientific authority by a professor of psychiatry [and] he will ask in amazement, how could this happen?

Like the Dreyfus case in France, Beilis became a worldwide cause célèbre, provoking letters to the newspapers and public information campaigns both for and against. Many wondered whether it was not Beilis in the dock, but Russia itself.[46] Ultimately, even a specially selected Ukrainian peasant jury could not stomach the injustice and acquitted Beilis. But the Russian Empire was tarnished. So was the Tsar, believed to be supportive of Russian anti-Semitism as a rallying point for the regime against liberalism, and against the future.

The imperial court still loomed large in St Petersburg in the Romanovs' tercentenary year. Russia's politics largely revolved around the relationship between the Tsar, his government and the Duma. But the imperial family preferred to live in the relative privacy of Tsarskoe Selo, fifteen miles distant. The Tsar was nowhere near as visible in St Petersburg as Franz Joseph was in Vienna, or Kaiser Wilhelm in Berlin, speeding from the opera house to the palace in a motor car several times a day, in a different uniform each time. The Tsarina was virtually invisible in St Petersburg's aristocratic social life, a black mark against her name. Walking around the city streets one could perhaps forget the Tsar and the buzzing of the Duma and take in St Petersburg itself: a modern city now, a crucible of modernity, perhaps a harbinger of Russia's future alongside the other modern great powers of Europe.

Though dominated by the various nationalities of empire, and above all by the Russians, the city had an international feel. An English colony flourished. French was widely spoken in polite company, while a French-language newspaper offered a blend of news of home, French coverage of Russian politics and, inevitably, reminders of France's unquestionable grandeur. (The French Institute provided courses on Voltaire; the *Journal de Saint Pétersbourg* ran a series of articles on Napoleon, arch-enemy of Nicholas' forebear Alexander I.) A 50,000-strong German community boasted no fewer than seven churches, five choirs, a theatre and two daily newspapers.[47]

The city still bore the hallmarks of its aristocratic upbringing and its aristocratic wealth in 1913, in the city's liveried servants and grand palaces. 'No capital in the world has more porters than St Petersburg', noted Wladimir de Belinsky in the *Journal de Saint Pétersbourg*, 'they comprise a people, no, a nation, no, a state!'[48] But alongside the old palaces of the nobility were the new palaces of the middle classes. Opposite the Kazan Cathedral stood the Russian branch of the Singer sewing machine company, built in the *style moderne* of Paris or Budapest rather than the traditional style of Petersburg. A little further down the Nevsky Prospekt was the Elisseeff delicatessen, advertising its wares in French, German and Russian. On the street itself, advertising hoardings enticed customers with everything from English tea to French perfumes.[49]

Years later, the novelist Vladimir Nabokov – son of the journalist at the Beilis trial – was still able to reel off the British commercial products of his Petersburg childhood:

Pears Soap, tar-black when dry, topaz-like when held to the light with wet fingers, took care of one's morning bath. Pleasant was the decreasing weight of the English collapsible tub when it was made to protrude a rubber underlip and disgorge its frothy contents into the slop pail. 'We could not improve the cream, so we improved the tube', said the English toothpaste. At breakfast, Golden Syrup imported from London would entwist with its glowing coils the revolving spoon from which enough of it had slithered onto a piece of Russian bread and butter. All sorts of snug, mellow things came in a steady procession from the English shop on Nevski Avenue: fruitcakes, smelling salts, playing cards, picture puzzles, striped blazers, talcum-white tennis balls.[50]

Twenty-eight of the fifty-five buildings on Nevsky Prospekt between the Admiralty Building and the Fontanka canal contained banks, reflecting a newly prosperous bourgeois society which both saved money and speculated with it.[51] (In 1913 Prokofiev invested 4,000 roubles in the Nikopol Mariupolsky metallurgical company, and later in cement – both were industries expected to do well in times of economic expansion and urban construction.[52])

Ten minutes' brisk walk from Nevsky Prospekt, the Astoria Hotel, St Petersburg's grandest and newest, was thoroughly modern in style and would not have been out of place in Berlin, Stockholm or Copenhagen. Equally striking was the building opposite it, the new embassy of the German Empire, Russia's largest trading partner, designed by Peter Behrens, the same man who had designed the AEG turbine factory in Berlin a few years previously. Though its façade sported classical columns in a nod in the direction of the St Petersburg style, these were thoroughly without any prettifying Petersburgian adornment.

British journalist George Dobson found a city that was 'hurrying up', as he put it, picking up its pace as it strode towards modernity.[53] 'Less than ten years ago', he wrote:

> ... it could still be said with a certain amount of truth that St. Petersburg consisted of only two main avenues, towards which everybody seemed to gravitate – the Nevsky Prospekt and the Great Morskaia Street – the Oxford and Regent Streets of the Russian capital. To-day many other important thoroughfares, such as the Sadovaya and Gorokohovaya Streets, and the Litainy, Soovorofsky and Voznesensky Prospects are equally busy and crowded arteries of traffic. The crowds also have mended their pace, which was formerly a crawling one in comparison with the bustling throng of other European capitals.

Dobson noted the spread of cinemas – 130 in St Petersburg by 1913 – where one might watch a film of the tercentenary celebrations or, more probably, catch a silent account of unrequited love played by Russia's most popular film actress, Vera Kholodnaya.[54] He noted the spread of electric lighting, particularly brilliant in winter. Although many buildings on the outskirts of the city were still built of wood, elsewhere they were steadily becoming colonised by bricks and stone. He remarked on the introduction of motorised transport in the city, mourning the loss of wintry silence conferred by sledges running silently over snow-covered roads. He noted the introduction of electric trams, replacing their horse-drawn equivalents from 1907 onwards, fifty or sixty at a time.

Those who looked up into the skies of St Petersburg in 1913 might see something still more remarkable, further evidence of the way in which Russia was bounding ahead into the future, unshackling itself from the past: Russia's latest aircraft, the four-engined *Grand*, compared to which other planes were nothing better than 'air kayaks'.[55] Interviewed by a St Petersburg paper, the aircraft's designer Igor Sikorsky – son of the Kiev professor who provided anti-Semitic 'evidence' against Mendel Beilis – declared that 'having started later than others ... we [Russia] gain more experience day by day in flying and in construction: we are not behind our teachers, soon we will overtake them'. Edward Acheson, an American inventor speaking in front of the Imperial Technical Society in St Petersburg in early 1913 declared simply 'Russia – country of the future!'[56]

Yes, the city still had its tenements, *naemnye kazarmy*, after the German *Mietskasernen*. The city had its homeless, their survival through a hard winter dubious. Most workers' apartments had no running water at all, and excrement was still removed by cart at night. Large red-letter placards on the city's trams warned residents not to drink raw water, but to boil it first. St Petersburg's death rate was higher than Constantinople. In 1908–1909, some 30,000 fell ill with cholera; in 1913 the Tsar's own daughter contracted the disease.[57]

But these were perhaps the inevitable growing pains of a city undergoing galloping change, in a country experiencing a transformation from archaism to modernity. Such problems were experienced a few decades later than other European cities, certainly, but they were not fundamentally different from them. Would they not also be overcome, as they had been elsewhere in Europe? A matter of time perhaps. A matter of time.

The Exposition Universelle in Ghent in 1913 was not as successful as some earlier international exhibitions. Some reasons were easy to find: Ghent, charming though its lace shops were, was not Paris. The organisers were unfortunate: in May that year a fire destroyed the pavilion of French Indochina, in September another fire started in a German restaurant and spread. But perhaps there was a deeper reason too. By 1913, international affairs and exhibitions had become routine, run of the mill. Rather than exceptional events, they were expected, the anticipation lessening with each repetition. Internationalism was, as John Maynard Keynes later put it, 'normal, certain, and permanent, except in the direction of further improvement'. [58]

To many a European, he continued, 'the projects of militarism and imperialism, of racial and cultural rivalries, of monopolies, restrictions, and exclusion, which were to play the serpent to this paradise, were little more than the amusements of his daily newspaper'. Such projects were never off the front pages in London, Paris, Berlin, Vienna, Rome or St Petersburg, of course. The war in the Balkans received ample coverage. So, too, the related movements of pan-Germanism and pan-Slavism, not to mention French nationalism, Italian colonialism, Prussian militarism, British imperialism and

Russian anti-Semitism. But they had competitors for space: royal weddings, parliamentary debates, political scandals, social scandals, industrial strikes, celebrations and anniversaries, the prices of bank shares, Russian railway stocks, South African gold and Canadian wheat. For some, war was a word which denoted the facts of modern life, a scramble for position. For others, it was a word from the past, and something which should be forever kept there. For many, war was just a word. If it ever actually happened it was generally in other parts of the world, between people who were either impossibly heroic or inconceivably dastardly, and were almost certainly poorer and less well educated.

In the meantime, the world came to Europe, the world went from Europe, and Europe remained its midpoint, steady on the seas of change.

The inauguration of President Woodrow Wilson, March 1913. 'It would be an irony of fate', Wilson had commented to a friend a few months earlier, 'if my administration had to deal chiefly with foreign problems'. Reform of America's financial system stood at the top of his list of domestic reforms.

PART II

THE OLD NEW WORLD

In 1913, travelling from the Old World to the New World meant taking a boat. From Southampton, Cherbourg or Hamburg one could take fast steamships, cutting their way through the North Atlantic. More lumbering vessels made their way to America from Naples or Genoa, Trieste or Fiume. On the upper decks, sea air refreshed those travelling for business or leisure. On the lower decks, whose inhabitants were more likely to be migrants, the intermingled smells of tar and sweat predominated.

There was perhaps a slight frisson of fear for some travellers on the fourth or fifth day at sea when a ship might come close to the spot where, the previous year, the *Titanic* had struck an iceberg and sunk, taking with it a host of the transatlantic elite – John Jacob Astor, Benjamin Guggenheim, the British journalist William Thomas Stead, the military aide to the American President – and many, many others whose names did not register in the public mind. But most voyages passed without incident. The safety of Atlantic shipping was constantly being improved. When the SS *Volturno* caught fire in October 1913, wireless signals brought nearly a dozen other ships to her rescue.

Americans travelled to Europe to conduct business, to see the sights of the Old World and perhaps to marry into an aristocratic European family. Europeans travelled to America to seek a better life, attracted by the political freedom of the United States and by the boundless economic opportunities it appeared to offer for the common man. There was no shortage of European enquiries into the causes and consequences of America's fantastic economic growth over the past fifty years – the multiplication of each American's industrial output by a factor of six, while that of each Briton rather less than doubled. W. T. Stead, late of the *Titanic*, had written of *The Americanization of the World* as early as 1901. In 1913, the Italian historian Guglielmo Ferrero published an essay on 'The Riddle of America'.[1] The French Nobel Prizewinner, aristocrat and politician Baron Paul-Henri d'Estournelles de Constant, following in the footsteps of his compatriot de Tocqueville some eighty years previously, added his contribution to the pile in the form of *Les État-Unis d'Amérique*. The idea of America pressed itself ever more firmly into the European imagination, just as the products of America were ever more frequently to be found in European homes.

Had the European traveller chanced upon *Philip Dru, Administrator*, a novel published anonymously the previous year about an America of the near future, they might have felt their curiosity particularly aroused – or perhaps, on further inspection, they might have wished to get off the boat. Here was an American book with a strange and unlikely vision of the United States, imagining that country in 1920, and on the eve of a second civil war. They would not have realised that the New York address, 'Mandell House', given to the book's hero, Philip Dru, provided the clue to its author: Texan businessman and Democratic Party fixer 'Colonel' Edward Mandell House (the military title was honorary). And only if they followed American politics extremely closely would the name have meant anything to them – it was that of the closest political adviser to the newly elected President of the United States, Woodrow Wilson.

As *Philip Dru, Administrator* begins, its eponymous hero regales his high-minded girlfriend, Gloria Strawn, with observations on the recent American past. 'Wealth had grown so strong', he tells her, 'that the few were about to strangle the many, and among the great masses of people there was sullen and rebellious discontent'.[2] The gap between winners and losers from America's industrial growth has widened. For 'the laborer in the cities, the producer on the farm' the outlook is 'gloomy and hopeless'. From the dismal state of American economics, Dru explains, flows the dismal state of American politics. In an America bereft of true leadership from its natural governing class – of which House would consider himself and Dru honorable members – political initiative has passed to the manipulators and the conmen. A bloody denouement is anticipated:

> Nowhere in the world is wealth more defiant, and monopoly more insistent than in this mighty republic . . . and it is here that the next

great battle for human emancipation will be fought and won. And from the blood and travail of an enlightened people, there will be born a spirit of love and brotherhood which will transform the world; and the Star of Bethlehem, seen but darkly for two thousand years, will shine again with steady and effulgent glow.

In the novel, Dru leaves the army and takes up residence in New York, observing the harsh and unjust realities of modern city life at close quarters.

Meanwhile, the plot of *Philip Dru, Administrator* turns to the national scene. It describes an unfolding political conspiracy master-minded by the deviously intelligent Senator Selwyn, manipulating American democracy by focusing efforts and money on just a thousand swing voters in each district in twelve key states and then finding out everything necessary to persuade, cajole and bribe them to vote the 'right' way. This is the way to win elections, Selwyn realises, not by running a wasteful national campaign of ideas, but appealing to the baser instincts and vanity of the few voters who really matter. Selwyn selects an obscure Midwestern state governor, James R. Rockland, to be his candidate for the presidency. In turn, Rockland uses classic techniques of political manipulation – holding out the possibility of visits to Washington and the power of high office – to attract additional support from the politically influential men in key states, using Selwyn's database of information about them to know just how much, and what, to offer.

Rockland wins the presidency, but the conspiracy which delivers his victory is ultimately undone in true Nixonian fashion: by a voice-activated recording device that Selwyn uses to capture conversations in his personal rooms, revealing the extent to which he has debauched American democracy. As the conspiracy is made public Philip Dru bounds back on to the scene, at the head of a military insurgency against Selwyn and Rockland, a kind of political crusade for a new politics. The states of the West rise in his favour. So, too, the South, recalling bitterly the impoverishment brought on them by the last Civil War and by the misnamed period of 'Reconstruction' which followed it.

Dru wins a striking victory at Elma, in upstate New York. Subsequently acclaimed 'Administrator of the Republic', he embarks on a dramatic programme of radical reform: introduction of a federal income tax, nationalisation of key industries, limitation of the working week, more stringent controls on concentrations of industry and the introduction of profit-sharing with employees in return for the abolition of strikes. Not content to rest there, he ensures women are granted the vote, and the Constitution is rewritten.

Abroad, Dru negotiates a geopolitical deal between the United States, Europe and Japan to keep the global peace. Canada joins the United States, while American troops intervene in Mexico to 'bring order out of chaos'. Dru assures the defeated Mexicans that he does not intend annexation or indemnity, yet:

> . . . in the future, our flag is to be your flag, and you are to be directly under the protection of the United States . . . There will be an equitable plan worked out by which the land now owned by the few will be owned by the many. In another generation, this beautiful land will be teeming with an educated, prosperous and content people.

After seven years of dictatorship, America is renewed. But, following the example of George Washington, Dru refuses to remain permanently at his country's head. He and Gloria sail into the sunset. Well-wishers watch 'in silent sadness' as their ship fades into the Pacific: 'Where were they bound? Would they return? These were the questions asked by all, but to which none could give an answer.'

Edward Mandell House was no great novelist, and *Philip Dru* is no great novel. But, as a book of the time, written by a man with a close understanding of the political system and of the pressures within it, it is revealing. On the eve of President Wilson's inauguration in Washington in March 1913, House was offered his choice of position in the Wilson administration. But, like the fictional Selwyn, he preferred the role of *consigliere* behind the scenes.

The themes of *Philip Dru* are those of America during the progressive era: a country grappling with a half-century of dramatic economic and social change, a country not at ease with itself, a nation incomplete.[3] The fear that big business – the huge companies dominating the country's railways, steel mills and Wall Street – would crush the enterprise and spirit of America was a commonplace of the late nineteenth and early twentieth centuries. While Europeans looked at the New World as a rising global force, Americans looked back to the Old World for their culture and, for good or ill, for their immigrants. Fifty years after the end of the Civil War, the South remained a sullen partner in the country's construction. Though the American economy was now the richest in the world, having surpassed the United Kingdom on measures of industrial production as early as the 1880s, politically that economic power was only dimly mastered. The mechanisms for its management were weak: until 1913 America did not even have a central bank. The United States was only halfway along a course from being a country of small villages and towns, each with their own political hinterland, to being a nation of great cities, connected over vast distances, and expressing the dynamism of a single nation.

Some of the means for America's completion as a nation were obvious to any observer in 1913. In January of that year the Parcel Post introduced a nationwide parcel service, allowing a business in Boise, Idaho, to ship direct to a customer in Savannah, Georgia. In October, President Wilson's finger on a button in Washington launched the explosion of several tons of dynamite breaching the last obstruction in the Panama Canal, and connecting the east and west coasts of the north American continent. Throughout the year, under the motto 'One Policy – One System – Universal Service', Bell telephones advertised the nation-building role of their system:

> The telephone, by making communication quick and direct, has been a great cementing force. IT has broken down the barriers of distance . . . The Bell System, with its 7,500,000 telephones connecting the east and the west, the north and the south, makes one great neighbourhood of the whole country. IT brings us together 27,000,000 times a day, and thus develops our common interests, facilitates our common dealings, and promotes the patriotism of our people.[4]

The first transcontinental phone call did not take place until 1915, but the march of progress – and the spread of railways – brought America closer together, just as it brought the globe closer together.[5]

This raised a supplementary question. As America completed the work of becoming a nation, what was to be its role in the world? In *Philip Dru*, Colonel House imagined the United States as a global peacemaker, intervening in Mexico and – through a combination of military strength and attraction – placing the entire North American continent under its wings. But in 1913 the United States was no military superpower, nor did it have the trappings of global diplomatic supremacy. Walter Hines Page, appointed ambassador to London that year, found his embassy in a converted flat entered through a dark and dingy hallway between two cheap stores. Such surroundings hardly proclaimed the twentieth century as American.

Yet perceptive observers understood that as the United States became more powerful economically – and as its population grew, partly through immigration from Europe – it would necessarily be drawn into the affairs of the wider world. As Page wrote to President Wilson: 'we are in the international game – not in its Old World intrigues and burdens and sorrows and melancholy, but in the inevitable way to leadership and to cheerful mastery in the future; and everybody knows that we are in it but us'.[6] The United States could no longer be aloof from the world, secure in its singular uprightness, a distant 'city upon a hill'. Rather, in the future, America would have to live in the world, examining its moral purpose in the light of the realities of global politics: how to exert power both in the name of principle and in the service of the nation, and what to do when others failed to adopt its chosen determination of their best interests. Would America as a rising power, emerging into its rightful place in the global order, become more and more like the European powers on the other side of the Atlantic? America had been the New World for a long time; would it now become more like the Old?

The United States, like any other powerful country in an age of imperialism, was subject to the temptations of empire. In the Pacific and in the Caribbean an American empire had begun to take shape at Spain's expense at the end of the nineteenth century, from the Philippines to Puerto Rico. This first flush of imperialism took place under the auspices of two Republican presidents: William McKinley and Theodore Roosevelt. But this was an American, not a party-political, enterprise. In 1901, the Princeton academic Woodrow Wilson stated America's imperial duty in plain terms. It lay not in giving the peoples of the Philippines 'the full-fangled institutions of American self-government'. These things, he argued, 'are not blessings, but a curse, to undeveloped peoples, still in the childhood of their political growth'. Rather, his country's responsibility was to give the Philippines a 'government and rule which shall moralize them by being itself moral, elevate and steady them by being itself pure and steadfast, inducting them into the rudiments of justice and freedom'.[7]

And if this was a familiar sentiment to a European mind, that is because it was drawn from a wider imperial culture. For many years Wilson carried the poem 'If' by Rudyard Kipling, the great poet of the British Empire, neatly tucked inside his jacket pocket.[8] Although Americans preferred not to use the word 'empire' to describe their overseas possessions, the arguments used to justify continued over-lordship did not differ substantially from those made by right-thinking imperialists in France or Britain. Others saw it differently, worrying that America might gain an empire but lose itself. Mark Twain, America's most famous essayist and one-time 'red-hot imperialist' suggested that the flag of the United States should be adapted for the Philippines, with its white stripes redrawn in black and the stars replaced with skull and crossbones.[9]

As House published *Philip Dru* in 1912, four men contested the presidency of this half-formed, half-united United States. William Taft, the sitting President, ran as a Republican. Theodore Roosevelt, his predecessor as President, deserted the Republicans and ran as a Progressive candidate, earning the nickname 'Bull Moose' for his characteristically robust response to an assassination attempt while on the campaign trail. Eugene Debs, from Indiana, ran as the socialist candidate. Woodrow Wilson, one-term Democratic Governor of New Jersey, ran as a Democrat. Edward House had already committed to Wilson, helping to swing Texan support behind his candidacy within the Democratic Party. Now he was to see if his man could make it all the way to the White House.

No one doubted that there were only two likely winners, Wilson and Roosevelt, with Wilson clearly favoured by the Republican split. Both offered an image of American renewal. Roosevelt, under the banner of the 'New Nationalism', proposed to harness the dynamism of the modern world in the service of the nation. The energies unleashed by the scale and efficiency of modern business would be expertly redirected by a newly powerful state. Wilson, instead, proposed the 'New Freedom', a wide-ranging political manifesto proclaiming support of the common man and the taming of the industrial giants – the so-called 'Trusts' – which had emerged over the previous half-century. Freedom of competition would be restored to the marketplace, Wilson promised, and hope would be restored to small-town America.

Both candidates agreed on the extent of economic concentration over the last few decades, both in terms of wealth and in terms of the power of the few to influence the country's economy as a whole. 'The life of America', Woodrow Wilson suggested, 'is not the life that it was twenty years ago':

> We have changed our economic conditions, absolutely, from top to bottom; and, with our economic society, the organization of our life. The old political formulas do not fit the present problems; they read now like documents taken out of a forgotten age.[10]

The question now, then, was how to adapt to these changed conditions: by a radical centralised overhaul, or by unlocking the traditional forces of competition and initiative which some said the new economy had stymied.

The differences in Roosevelt's and Wilson's prescriptions for the future were ultimately as much temperamental as analytical. Roosevelt, with a superabundance of confidence, put faith in his personal ability to remould America from above. Wilson, more temperamentally conservative, inspired by classic English political philosophy, saw Roosevelt as a dangerous showman, destined to become a strongman were he elected. His own vision of society was more organic, one of constant renewal from below, from the striving classes from which he himself sprang. 'The flower does not bear the root', he opined on the campaign trail, 'but the root the flower'.

Roosevelt was a serious challenger, Wilson noted, a 'real vivid person, whom they [the voters] have seen and shouted themselves hoarse over and voted for millions strong'. Wilson himself was, in the public mind, 'a vague conjectural personality, more made up of opinions and academic prepossessions than of human traits and red corpuscles'.[11] Roosevelt would no doubt have agreed, viewing Wilson as an old-fashioned, pusillanimous conservative, rooted in the past.

Yet Wilson made his strength felt. He issued a highly partisan campaign film: *The Old Way and the New*. In speeches across the country, he railed against the closeness of business and government – symbolised by the various import tariffs used to protect special interest industries in the United States – declaring this to be 'un-American'. He attacked the rise of 'great, impersonal' corporations as threatening to stamp out competition and turning individuals into subservient employees. The enterprising middle classes, he warned, were being 'squeezed out by the processes which we have been taught to call the processes of prosperity'. The spirit of freedom of American communities, in which lay America's true vitality, was under threat. 'If America discourages the locality', he warned, 'she will kill the nation'. 'The amount of money in Wall Street', he pronounced, 'is no indication of the energy of the American people'.

In all this, Wilson, the son of a Presbyterian minister and himself deeply guided by his Christian faith, purported to see a challenge to the very moral fibre of American society. The impersonal nature of the corporation threatened to turn people away from notions of personal responsibility. This more corporation-driven America might make people forget the America of values forged in small communities:

> . . . when America lay in every hamlet, when America was to be seen in every fair valley, when America displayed her great forces on broad prairies, ran her fine fires of enterprise up over the mountain sides and down into the bowels of the earth, and eager men were every- where captains of industry, not employees; not looking to a distant city to find out what they might do, but looking about among their neighbors, finding credit according to their character not according to their connections, finding credit in proportion to what was known to be in them and behind them, not in proportion to the securities they held . . .[12]

So Wilson turned a set of economic questions into a set of moral questions. He turned himself from the leader by default, favoured by the electoral arithmetic of a split Republican Party, into the insurgent candidate, at the head of a moral movement for change. He aligned himself with progress, but proposed organic change, advising that 'you cannot take a sheet of paper and determine what your life shall be tomorrow' but rather 'you must knit the new into the old'. He responded to the anxieties of an America undergoing deep social change, and provided level-headed reassurance. He reflected America's mood at the close of 1912, the year of *Philip Dru*, winning forty of the forty-eight states in that year's election. By early 1913, Woodrow Wilson was President.

WASHINGTON, DC
Republic, Nation, Empire

Wilson took the oath of office on 4 March 1913. Four years earlier, Taft's inauguration had been forced inside by a snowstorm. This year, Wilson was able to take the oath outside on the east portico of the US Capitol building, in full view of a crowd of a quarter of a million.

The presidential inauguration was, by now, established as a national occasion, providing a rhythm to the country's public life and drawing tourists to the nation's capital. The touring department of the Automobile Club of America provided advice on how to drive from New York to Washington along the pike roads and dirt tracks that connected America's financial capital to her political capital, taking in Philadelphia but avoiding Baltimore at all costs.[1] The *New York Times* reported, a few days earlier, that the spirit of commercial enterprise was alive and well in Washington. Rooms in the big city hotels could be had for $20, but would have to be taken for a full five days. Those on Pennsylvania Avenue were more expensive, at $50 a night. Offices and private residences along the procession route could be rented out at similarly steep rates. On inauguration day itself, the crowd swarmed with young Princeton undergraduates wearing the orange and black colours of Wilson's old university. Ex-President Taft, 'the worst-licked, the least-sore and best-liked of any defeated Presidential candidate we ever saw', was all smiles as he passed on the office of the presidency to Wilson.[2] Though Taft had run third in the election he had, at least, prevented the renegade Roosevelt from returning to the White House by channelling off enough votes for the official Republican candidate.

The city was built to impress. Visitors were to be inspired by the republican virtues of Washington's classical architecture and civic statuary, by the national coming together represented by the inauguration of a new President – only the second Democrat since the Civil War – and by the imperial magnificence of the city's layout, with grand vistas in every direction. Arriving by train at Union Station, out-of-towners could feel the granite gaze of Louis Saint-Gaudens' *The Progress of Railroading*, six stone figures atop the station's main entrance which proclaimed both America's modernity – in the statues of Prometheus representing fire and Thales representing electricity – yet reiterated the ancient values of justice, and reminded an urbanising America of the values of toil in the fields. Next to a proud statue of Ceres, the Roman god of agriculture, were inscribed words of which Thomas Jefferson himself would have approved: 'The Farm. Best Home of the Family. Main Source of National Wealth. Foundation of Civilized Society. The Natural Providence.'

The British Ambassador, James Bryce, noted that while New York was 'almost as much foreign as American', Washington had a higher calling:

> . . . to be the embodiment of the majesty and stateliness of the whole nation; to be . . . a capital of capitals . . . representing all that is finest in American conception, all that is largest and most luminous in American thought, embodying the nation's ideal of what the capital of such a nation should be.[3]

The inauguration was an opportunity for Washington, not only the chief political city of the United States but the private domain of the federal government, to show off.

Wilson, standing in front of a Capitol decked with American flags, fronted by the Great Seal of the United States in coloured electric lights and topped by spectators peering down from the roof, offered to 'interpret the occasion' for the crowds. 'There has been a change of government', he intoned. But this was merely the outward sign of a national demand for renewed moral purpose. Government had been debauched for 'private and selfish purposes' by lobbyists. The country had become rich, but 'the evil has come with the good, and much fine gold has been corroded':

> We have been proud of our industrial achievements, but we have not hitherto stopped thoughtfully enough to count the human cost, the

cost of lives snuffed out, of energies overtaxed and broke, the fearful physical and spiritual cost to the men and women and children upon whom the dead weight and burden of it all has fallen pitilessly the years through.

The task ahead, therefore, was one of restoration: 'to cleanse, to reconsider, to restore, to correct the evil without impairing the good, to purify and humanize every process of our common life without weakening or sentimentalizing it'. Wilson enumerated his priorities: tariffs on imported goods were to be removed; a national banking system was to be created that would ease access to credit and remove overweening power from the holders of capital; an industrial system which restricted competition and wasted the nation's natural resources was to be reformed; the health of the nation's workers was to be protected by law.

The burden of expectation lay on Wilson's shoulders. As one breathless editorial put it, his inauguration was more than the passing of the presidential baton from one man to another, it meant that 'the old days have died and that a new era has come'.[4] A German journalist, writing a few months previously, forecast that Wilson would be not only 'the head of the government, but a leader in American political thought'. In St Petersburg, a Russian paper expressed the expectation that 'if the sinister party forces will not paralyze the will and initiative of the future president he, maybe, will inaugurate a new era in the United States, an era of real political honesty'.[5] Having touted the 'New Freedom', Wilson would now have to provide it. There was no word in Wilson's inauguration speech of international affairs. 'It would be an irony of fate', Wilson had commented to Princeton biologist Edward Grant Conklin a few days after his election, 'if my administration had to deal chiefly with foreign problems, for all my preparation has been in domestic matters'.[6]

The speech reflected Wilson's understanding of government, and his role in providing it. It was sincere and ambitious. *The Economist* contrasted Wilson's cogency to earlier inaugural addresses, which had probably been 'the work of secretaries, assistant secretaries, and short-hand writers'.[7] The new President's speech was economical in length. It did not match the rhetorical flights of Lincoln or Jefferson. 'Evidently', commented one editorialist, 'the new President understands that the Presidency is not a medal to be worn, a prize to display, but a troublesome undertaking to be approached warily. We suspect he is right'.[8] As Washington soon found, Wilson took seriously his role as head of America's executive branch and as an impartial defender of the public interest. The following month, Congress was recalled to Washington, earlier than either tradition or the constitution dictated. Supporters seeking preferment – a federally appointed position or an ambassadorship somewhere or other – found the doors of the White House barred to them, earning the unreadable, apparently impassive Wilson the moniker 'the sphinx'. He appeared before a joint session of Congress and, later in the year, delivered a State of the Union address in person, which few of his predecessors had bothered to do.

On the evening of 4 March there was no traditional inaugural ball, deemed too frivolous. Instead the President dropped in on a dinner at the Shoreham Hotel, retreating into the presence of those amongst whom he felt most comfortable, the Princeton class of 1879. Later he wrote to one of his former classmates: 'You may be sure that I only followed the dictates of my heart on Tuesday night and that my visit to the '79 dinner was the best part of the day for me'.[9] Colonel House, author of *Philip Dru* and now Wilson's closest political confidant, stayed away from the public ceremonies, though he attended a lunch with the newly minted President and his Cabinet, many of whom House had been instrumental in selecting. He preferred to sit out the inauguration itself in the Metropolitan Club, a few blocks from the White House.

As night fell, the American nation had a new champion, the federal government had a new leader and Washington a new master.

Even in 1913, Washington had a reputation to live down. Its introspection was famous. As Henry James put it, 'Washington talks about herself, and about nothing else'.[10] At his first meeting with the 'gentlemen' of the press Wilson urged them not to tell the country what Washington was thinking but rather to 'tell Washington what the country is thinking':

> . . . and then we will get things with a move on, we will get them
> so refreshed, so shot through with airs from every wholesome part

of the country, that they cannot go stale, they cannot go rotten, and men will stand up and take notice, and know that they have got to vote according to the purposes of the country, and the needs of the country, and in the interpreted general interests of the country, and in no other way.[11]

At a press conference in May, Wilson raised another familiar and related gripe. 'This town is swarming with lobbyists', he complained, 'so you can't throw bricks in any direction without hitting one – much inclined as you are to throw bricks'.[12]

The intensity of lobbying was partly a matter of the import tariff, which Wilson proposed to radically reduce. In the early summer of 1913, as the Underwood Tariff Bill made its way from the House of Representatives to the Senate, lobbyists made the case for the continued necessity of some sort of tariff protection for *their* particular industry. A centrepiece of Wilson's 'New Freedom' agenda – the wholesale reduction of import tariffs, to be paid for by the introduction of a federal income tax – was threatened with a slow and painful death, only avoided by the President's personal intervention.

But the presence of so many lobbyists in the city at all was also a reflection of Washington's growing importance in the political and economic life of America. In the eighteenth century the city had been chosen as the nation's capital, rather than Philadelphia or New York, so as to place the federal government beyond the narrow political life of the various states. So it was natural that as the national element in politics grew, so Washington grew in importance. 'Whether designedly or unconsciously, the American people have become Federalists', editorialised Alfred Maurice Low, 'and Washington symbolizes Federalism'.[13]

There had been a time, Low remembered, when 'Washington was shunned by everyone who was not compelled by stern necessity to go there'. In those days, the city was 'a mud-hole, a slattern among cities, unkempt, sprawling, elbows out of sleeves, unashamed of its patches, and in ignorance glorying in its dirt and general untidiness'. This, he argued, had now changed. Honeymooners were now as likely to go to Washington as to go to Niagara Falls.

Only a few decades previously the 'big places' politically and socially had been the state capitals, characterised by little formality and much hospitality, where everyone would know their elected representative personally. Washington, in contrast, was a distant 'stony-hearted step-mother'. There, your average State Assemblyman Bill Jones, everyone's best friend, would become the more austere Congressman William Jones 'known only to a handful of the voters, and . . . nothing but a name to the rest'.[14]

Now Washington was becoming the big place politically, bringing more formality to politics and making the city both more familiar to most Americans, and more refined. People who, in the past, had gone to Washington on business, now made it their business to live there. The population of the District of Columbia, of which Washington was the major part, more than quadrupled from the Civil War years to 1913: from 75,000 to over 330,000.

> The big, sprawling girl, all legs and arms with awkward feet and hair uncombed, is now a finished woman of the world, proud of her beauty and conscious of her power. Washington, the mud-hole, is now only a memory – memory that no one cares to revive. The mud and slush have gone with the old customs and the old ideas. Broad and well-paved streets; stately tree-lined avenues; public buildings that have not sacrificed use to beauty but, in remembering use, have not forgotten art; hotels and restaurants of the first class, theaters and shops and many fine residences – make Washington one of the most attractive capitals in the world.[15]

The confirmation of Washington's place amongst the great cities of the world – smaller than most European capitals, but elevated to their rank by its political status and urban beauty – was surely to be found in the judgement of Frenchman Baron Paul-Henri d'Estournelles de Constant. Travelling through America, he recalled with pleasure that Washington's layout had been set out by his compatriot, Pierre-Charles l'Enfant. He noted the central location of a statue of the Marquis de Lafayette – the French General who fought in the American War of Independence with George Washington, after whom he named his only son. He celebrated 'the creation of a large city, yet giving its streets the charm of a park or a garden . . . the dream which has made Washington one of the most beautiful cities in the world'. Above all, he rhapsodised on the elegance of Washington's women, reflecting the beauty and newfound worldliness of the city itself:

I can see them coming, sure of themselves, certain of their attractions, and satisfied by this certainty . . . Ah, American women of the world! Elected queens, aristocrats of a democracy, how much money will your husbands, fathers and your country have to earn to continue to dress you! Let us be reassured that a fair bit of this money will be spent in Paris . . .[16]

Constant celebrated the European inspiration behind Washington's progressive refinement. But he also saw it as a challenge to Washington's enduring Americanness. When the city was established as capital, Constant wrote, no one could have predicted that the United States would expand so quickly to the point where Washington found itself not in the geographic heartland of the American people, but on its eastern fringe, several thousand miles from its coastline on the Pacific.

Which way, then, will she [Washington] face? Towards the past, towards the Old World which lies across the ocean, or towards the New World of which she is only nominally the centre? Which of the two worlds will influence the other more? Will the New be infected with the ills of the Old or, on the contrary, will they be resisted?[17]

What such observers overlooked – or perhaps consciously ignored – was that, behind the classical façades and porticos, behind the celebrations of republican values of justice, and behind the question of whether European-inspired Washington would Europeanise America or whether imperial Washington would Americanise the world, Washington remained, in its heart, a city of the American South. One in three of the city's inhabitants was black, and they tended to be the poorest, the least educated and the least healthy of the population. In October 1913 journalist John Palmer Gavit wrote to Oswald Garrison Villard, a white newspaper owner and one of the founders of the National Association for the Advancement of Colored People:

Washington is essentially a Southern city; the great majority of white people here hold the Southern view of the negro, and as for the Northerners here, it takes but a little while for them to become infinitely more anti-negro than any Southerner.[18]

While a number of the black population of Washington were clerks in the federal government, with some hope of advancement as a result, a significant minority of the city's black population were desperately poor. Around one in five, at least 16,000, lived in the unsanitary back alleys of the city, often within sight of the gleaming white dome of the Capitol. These were the 'neglected neighbors' written about by social reformers Charles Frederick Weller and Eugenia Winston Weller.[19] The inhabitants of the alleys, suggested the Wellers, 'have no connection whatever with those of the streets and avenues', the larger tree-lined thoroughfares down which Washington's wealthier, mostly white denizens – and foreign visitors – could cast their imperial gaze.

The hidden dwellings are reached by distinct, winding roadways. Resourceful people live for years in attractive residences on the avenues without knowing or affecting in the slightest degree the life of the alley hovels just behind them. Such is the ground plan for some striking social contrasts in the National Capital.[20]

Church Alley. Within sight of the Capitol, the promise of the republic remained unkept. Behind its grand exterior, Washington, DC remained a city of the South.

The names of the alleys gave a sense of them: 'Slop Bucket Row', 'Moonshine' or, sarcastically, 'Constitution Alley'. Closer inspection revealed the social conditions to which the alleys gave rise – appalling health, petty crime, illiteracy, unstable families, dependence on alcohol:

> On a soiled and broken lounge, in a little room which was crowded with children and adults, Annie Sammons lay one afternoon, rolling her head about weakly and gasping for breath. Her little baby was feeding fretfully at the consumptive's wasted breast while Hattie, a child of seven, was playing about the room with seven other young-sters. Altogether there were fifteen people, including six adults, living permanently in the little four-room house, while improper lodgers also were accommodated from time to time. Although Maria Sammons, the mother of the household, is a large fine-looking woman who does not show bad character in her appearance, every one of her five grown daughters has had illegitimate offspring. Mrs Sammons herself has borne sixteen children, of whom five are happily dead. One son is in the insane asylum. The daughter Annie is dying of tuberculosis.[21]

All rapidly growing American cities – and European cities – had slums. In most cities populations grouped themselves according to their origins. In Paris, Bretons concentrated themselves around the Gare de Montparnasse, where the trains arrived from Brittany. In Vienna, Jews tended to settle in Leopoldstadt, near to the Nordbahnhof station, and in proximity to a number of synagogues. Nowhere, however, was the physical distinction between slum and non-slum so clear, nor the racial connotations of the slum so obvious, as in Washington. For some, this meant that the alley problem was not really one of poverty, but something else and, as such, it should be accepted – or ignored:

> 'Why they're all negroes', some will say, and conclude either that it does not matter in what condition members of that race may live, or that the evils and problems of alley life are merely the result of the intrinsic characteristics of the colored race . . . 'Those high death rates, the large record of arrests, the low standards of life in the hovels and alleys, are simply due to the negro'.[22]

Others took a different view. By 1913, the population of the alleys was falling. The Wellers' book had brought renewed attention to a social crisis that had been festering for decades. In 1912, the Monday Evening Club, an organisation of social reformers, had published an inventory of Washington's inhabited alleyways, so as to make the average citizen aware of the conditions that prevailed in parts of a city held up by the world as the exemplar of America. Ellen Axson Wilson, the President's Southern-born wife, made the cause of cleaning up Washington's slums her principal social endeavour. On her deathbed, in August 1914, she was gratified to learn that the Alley Dwelling Act – a law to renovate the alleys and improve housing – was making an accelerated passage through Congress, the body constitutionally responsible for the nation's capital city.

The election of Ellen Axson Wilson's husband to the White House was greeted by many as a return of the South from political no man's land. For the first time since 1865, when a bullet lodged in Abraham Lincoln's head had elevated Andrew Johnson to the presidency, Washington's new ruler was one of its own. In February 1913, the month before Wilson's inauguration, *Harper's Weekly* ran an article entitled 'The South in the Saddle'. But the attitudes of Woodrow Wilson on the South – and, inextricably linked to this, on race – were far from obvious. The President was indubitably from the South, but could he be called a Southerner?

Born in Staunton, Virginia, in the Shenandoah Valley, Wilson grew up in Augusta, Georgia, in the midst of cotton-growing country. Half the population of the surrounding countryside were slaves and one-third in Augusta itself. Four years old when the Civil War began in 1861, Wilson remembered whispers of the election of Abraham Lincoln and what that meant for the peace of America. His family was split by the war. Two uncles rose to be senior officers in the army of the Union. His father, though born in the northern state of Ohio, became one of the founders of the Presbyterian Church of the Confederate States. His mother was born in England. In an address that Woodrow Wilson gave to the University of South Carolina in 1909 he declared that 'a boy never gets over his boyhood' and that in his case this meant 'the only place in the country, the only place in the world, where nothing has to be explained to me is the South'.[23]

All this helped electorally in 1912. In Rome, Georgia – birthplace of Wilson's wife, Ellen – the editor of the *Tribune-Herald* declared the Democratic candidate 'of southern blood, of southern bone and of southern grit'. In an election where Wilson carried forty states overall, it was only in the South that he won more than half the votes cast. In Alabama he took four times as many votes as those cast for his nearest rival. The electors of Mississippi awarded him nine out of every ten of their ballots. Wilson won outside the South as well, but nowhere by such convincing margins.

Yet Wilson was not quite a true son of the South – at least not in the full meaning and prejudices of his electors. He saw his career play out on the national, not the provincial stage. He was keen to expunge Southernness from both his and his wife's accents. He studied in the north, at Princeton, though he returned to law school at the University of Virginia. Whilst there, in 1880, he celebrated the 'failure of the Confederacy', arguing that 'the damnable cruelty and folly of reconstruction was to be preferred to helpless independence' for the South.[24] The concord of the nation featured more highly in his political philosophy than the sectional interests of one region. His interpretation of the Civil War was not that the South had fought to defend the right to hold slaves, but that it had fought for the constitutional right to secede, which he thought reasonable but misplaced. As he put it in his chapter in *The Cambridge Modern History*:

> The South fought for a principle, as the North did: it was this that was to give the war dignity, and supply the tragedy with a double motive. But the principle for which the South fought meant standstill in the midst of change; it was conservative, not creative; it was against drift and destiny . . . Overwhelming material superiority, it turned out, was with the North; but she had also another and greater advantage: she was to fight for the Union and for the abiding peace, concord and strength of a great nation.[25]

On 4 July 1913, fifty thousand veterans from that war gathered on the low fields of rural Pennsylvania, at Gettysburg, site of one of its most crucial battles, fought half a century previously. The overall estimated cost of the event, financed in large part by the state of Pennsylvania, but also by the federal government and the other states, was a million dollars.[26] The oldest veteran present, Major Weiss from upstate New York, answered to the age of 112 years; the youngest was 61. The message of the gathering was clear. 'These old soldiers', wrote a reporter, 'who know what real war means (no body of men in the world today has learnt the lesson more thoroughly) are determined, as a final service to their country, to show the world that between North and South no bitterness survives'.[27] 'Blue' and 'Gray', 'Yankee' and 'Johnny Reb' embraced each other on the field where, fifty years previously, they had tried to kill each other in a hail of gunfire.

Wilson attended the commemorations. As he admitted to Ellen, he did so more out of a sense of obligation as President than because he felt personally invested in it: 'Find so long as I am President, I can be nothing else'.[28] But he was doubly compelled to attend: by the office he held and his Southern birth. Failure to show up at Gettysburg could be misread as disapproval of the war's outcome.

Fifty thousand veterans met at Gettysburg in 1913 to commemorate the fiftieth anniversary of the great Civil War battle. 'But has it yet squared itself with its own great standards set up at its birth?' asked President Wilson of the United States.

At the commemorations, Wilson made a speech. He celebrated 'the vigor, the maturity, the might of the great Nation we love with undivided hearts'. He invoked the need to press the energies of war into the service of domestic peace and the national cause of economic development. Now, he said, 'the quartermaster's stores are in the mines and forests and fields, in the shops and factories'.[29]

What he did not do – not once – was mention the words 'slave' or 'slavery'. He used the word 'race' on a single occasion. He alluded to the incomplete fulfilment of America's promise by asking whether the nation had 'yet squared itself with its own great standards set up at its birth'. But these standards were general, not specific, applying to all Americans rather than to any particular section of the population. He reiterated the 'naïve appeal to the moral judgement of mankind to take notice that a government had now at last been established which was to serve men, not masters'.

To be sure, these words of Wilson were noble in themselves. They echoed those of Abraham Lincoln's own Gettysburg Address – shortly to be inscribed in stone in a grand memorial in Washington, the design and location of which was formally approved that year. Lincoln himself had not explicitly spoken of slavery in his more famous speech – he had alluded to it through his reaffirmation of 'the proposition that all men are created equal'. But then Lincoln was speaking in 1863 in the midst of a Civil War, the deeper origins of which were understood by any listener. From Wilson's speech alone, it would have been impossible to have divined why men fought at Gettysburg – only that they did, and that the matter was now settled.

But it was not. In Washington it was about to get worse. Wilson had long found the issue of race an embarrassment. Like many liberal-minded men and women he saw it as secondary to the growth of the nation, to be worked out over the course of time, as what was seen as the lower level of civilisation of the black population was slowly and steadily improved. Some African-American leaders advocated a similarly gradualist approach, including Booker T. Washington, the former slave, now head of the Tuskegee Institute.[30] The belief that 'white' civilisation was more advanced than that of other peoples was hardly an exclusively American trait – indeed it was a commonplace shared around the world, far beyond the countries and peoples to which it accorded such imperial privileges.

Ellen Axson Wilson's commitment to cleaning up Washington's alleys showed a certain sense of responsibility towards less fortunate sections of the city's population – though perhaps more in the tradition of charitable almsgiving than in the nature of a fiery protest against injustice. Wilson, like his wife, expressed basic sympathy with the plight of the black population. But he was never prepared to stick his neck out even one inch in a cause he felt best taken care of by the passage of time. Booker T. Washington was invited to Wilson's installation as president of Princeton in 1902, but he could not be housed with the faculty, as were the other guests, nor could he attend the official dinners. When Wilson received an enquiry as to the possibility of an African-American studying at the university, he responded that: 'while there is nothing in the law of the University to prevent a negro's entering, the whole temper and tradition of the place are such that no negro has ever applied for admission, and . . . [it] seems unlikely that the question will ever assume a practical form'.[31] It was not until 1947 that Princeton had its first black graduate.

Despite this, black political leaders had supported Wilson for the presidency in 1912, breaking with the tradition of support for the Republicans, the party of Lincoln, the party which had campaigned to end slavery in the Southern states, even to the point of Civil War. During the campaign Wilson told an influential bishop of the African Methodist Church that they [African-Americans] could count on him for 'fair dealing', saying that 'my earnest wish [is] to see justice done them in every matter, and not merely grudging justice, but justice executed with liberality and cordial good feeling'.[32] He said he would speak out against lynching – America's parallel to the pogroms of Russia – though he qualified this by saying that he did not have the constitutional power to actually intervene to stop it. It was widely thought that Wilson's Presbyterianism would make him a stalwart defender of black interests in the White House. 'We sincerely believe', wrote an editorialist at *Crisis*, the magazine of the National Association for the Advancement of Colored People founded by W. E. B. Dubois:

that even in the face of promises disconcertingly vague, and in the face of the solid caste-ridden South, it is better to elect Woodrow Wilson President of the United States and prove once for all if the Democratic party dares to be Democratic when it comes to black men.[33]

They were soon disappointed. In August of that year, the president of the United Colored Democracy of New York, Robert N. Wood, wrote a letter to Wilson. 'In order to voice the feeling and thought of the ten million persons of Negro blood who justly aspire to the maintenance of their privileges as citizens in this great democracy', he began, 'I am reluctantly compelled to express to you a respectful, but none the less earnest, protest at the course your administration is pursuing with regard to the status of the colored people of this country'.[34] He accepted that Wilson had been busy with affairs of state. Yet he endeavoured to make the president aware of a campaign to reduce African-Americans to a state of 'serfdom', led by reactionary elements in the Democratic Party, now the majority party in both houses of Congress and amply represented around Wilson's own Cabinet table. It had been hard to persuade black voters to abandon their 'superstitious reverence for the Republican Party'. It was galling that, despite this, a country 'so rich in opportunity to the most degraded refuse of Europe' was now turning its back on opportunity for black American citizens.

The issue here was not the countless evils perpetrated in the name of racial peace in Southern states under so-called Jim Crow laws, beyond the reach of the constitutionally limited federal government. The issue here was one of segregation within the federal government, in Washington, under Wilson's nose and amply within his power to rectify. Departments of government under the authority of Southern Democrat cabinet members had begun to segregate their offices, reversing a half-century of integration. 'We resent it', wrote Wood, 'not at all because we are particularly anxious to eat in the same room or use the same soap and towels that white people use'. But rather because:

. . . we see in the separation of the races in the matter of soup and soap the beginning of a movement to deprive the colored man entirely of soup and soap, to eliminate him wholly from the Civil Service of the United States.[35]

Wilson's Chief of Staff, Joseph Patrick Tumulty, attached a note to the letter recommending that the President read it in its entirety. Perhaps he did. But whether or not he found the time to read the letter, he did not muster the energy to respond to it.

A few days later, a widely published letter from three leaders of the National Association for the Advancement of Colored People stated the case unambiguously. 'Never before has the Federal Government discriminated against its civilian employees on the ground of color', it pointed out. Now, however:

> It has set the colored people apart as if mere contact with them were contamination . . . To them is held out only the prospect of mere subordinate routine service without the stimulus of advancement to high office by merit, a right deemed inviolable for all white natives as for the children of the foreign born, of Italians, French and Russians, Jews and Christians who are now entering the Government service.[36]

Wilson evaded meeting black leaders on this subject. He reversed his commitment to set up a race commission to enquire into related issues. When directly challenged on race issues Wilson lost his cool, vigorously reproaching his accusers for their impertinence.

The National Association for the Advancement of Colored People persisted, setting up their own investigation, producing a report in September which was then forwarded to the White House.[37] The examples of slights both petty and gross were numerous. In one, in the Treasury, a bookkeeper called Tyson was demoted, and moved. He told the investigation that 'he had cried like a baby when he was moved not so much because of the reduction in work, but because he felt that taking him out of the room where he had sat for ten or more years with white people, including women, was a reflection on him personally'. But, at base, the motives of segregation were not personal, they were systematic, and both racist and economic:

> Competition in work has been eliminated so far as the colored employees are concerned. It is only a question of time before the few colored people who are now so expert as to prevent their being segregated, will leave the government service, and their positions, of course, will be filled by white people . . .[38]

To those who argued that the separation of the races allowed for a smoother working of government and a better appreciation of the relative skills of different groups the report retorted that one 'might as well test the comparative ability of women and men by insisting that the former devote themselves exclusively to the three K's [housework] and forbid their entry into any other fields of effort'.

Wilson's high-mindedness, his passion for the 'New Freedom' and his willingness to take on vested interests – so evident in his championing of tariff reduction – did not apply within the corridors and office buildings of Washington. He prevaricated, he ignored, and he pointed to the prejudices of his Democratic colleagues in the Senate. Here, in its capital city, an older America reasserted itself.

NEW YORK

Metropolis

If, in 1913, Washington stood for the incomplete fulfilment of America's past, New York stood as the ambiguous symbol of America's future. To some, New York was America's beacon to huddled masses of the world, making good on the promise inscribed at the base of the Statue of Liberty. To others, New York's immigrant population was a harbinger of America's coming degeneracy, transplanting European vices into American soil.

For New Yorkers, the city could be viewed as the dynamo of American business. In 1913, it surpassed London to become the world's busiest port; it was already America's pre-eminent financial centre. New York's wealth, therefore, could be interpreted as evidence of the city's vitality and national utility – and as an assurance of future national prosperity. But for others, New York had come to represent everything that was wrong with the nation's economic development, a city living off wealth created elsewhere, a machine for concentrating money and power into the hands of a cabal of Wall Street money men. As far as the rest of the world was concerned New York, for all intents and purposes, *was* America; as the British journalist W. T. Stead remarked, 'the rest of the country is but the pedestal on which New York stands'.[1]

New York shared many of the ills of any other large and growing city of its times: social deprivation cheek by jowl with enormous wealth, crowded conditions for the city's working population, inadequate housing. In all of these, New York excelled. Being the city's mayor, one government official wrote, was 'the largest administrative task entrusted to any municipal official in the world'.[2] But New York's corruption was in a class of its own.

Its government had become 'a byword, a hissing and reproach', with public contracts doled out and electors bought on the instructions of the city's shadow government, the local Democratic Party machine, Tammany Hall.[3] In 1913, the city temporarily shook off Tammany in a wave of reformist anger. After the previous mayor had died suddenly on a transatlantic steamer, probably from the lingering effects of an attempt on his life back in 1910, a young and inexperienced anti-Tammany candidate was elected. But many doubted whether New York's turn towards reform – both political and social – would last. 'On the Reformers' side there is human nature as it ought to be', wrote a cynical but astute observer, 'on the side of Tammany there is human nature as it is'.[4] In the final analysis, he remarked, Tammany was really the city's way of rebelling against the inclination of Puritanical legislators at the level of New York state, sitting up in Albany, to dictate to their city brethren what they could and could not do:

> The Tammany method, after all, is the most convenient and the easiest. To the proprietor of the saloon and the gambling den and the disorderly house Tammany simply says, 'Pay me so much a month and I will protect you'. In the result, everyone is satisfied. The law remains on the statute book, a glowing testimonial to the 'morality' of New York; it is not put into action, so nobody feels its inconvenience; and Tammany grows rich on the proceeds of non enforcement.

In 1913, the state itself was embroiled in political scandal. Governor William Sulzer, a former Congressman, was successfully impeached for violations of electoral law in October 1913. (His true crime may have been to refuse to take instructions on appointments from Tammany.) But in the topsy-turvy world of New York politics he was elected to the New York State Assembly the following month.

The widely publicised political corruption of New York was perceived as being strongly linked to the city's moral corruption. The sins of New York's poor were traditional and well established: prostitution, gambling and petty crime. A 1913 report sponsored by John D. Rockefeller Jr estimated that there were 15,000 prostitutes in New York City, many of them managed by immigrant networks. Others put the number twice as high. Lyman Beecher Stowe, grandson of the famous abolitionist Harriet Beecher Stowe, asserted that the police themselves were compromised by corruption 'almost entirely from their contact with gambling, liquor-selling and prostitution'.⁵ The city thus created the conditions for its continuing immorality.

The failings of the well-off were more subtle, but no less real from the perspective of the small-town or upstate observer, and perhaps more worrying for the country's long-term health: a tendency to have things done for you rather than doing them yourself, a tendency to love of money, a tendency to selfishness. A Manhattan doctor, John H. Girdner, diagnosed 'Newyorkitis' as a communicable condition affecting a large portion of his fellow New Yorkers. In extreme cases, he wrote, 'the gray matter of the brain is never used to think with, except when the patient is engaged in getting money, or gratifying some physical appetite'.⁶ As America became more citified, observers worried, was it to become more dandified, more greedy and more individualistic – more like New York?

The sins of the rich were the most sophisticated, and perhaps most strongly linked to the image of New York as a city of unearned privilege: the new depravities of excessive wealth. The *New York Times'* unfavourable review of Upton Sinclair's novel *The Metropolis* mocked the book's portrayal of the city's upper classes as an absurd 'debauch of interior decorations, orchids, bathtubs, and other wicked features of Babylonian luxury' – but accepted that Sinclair would readily find an audience willing to believe them.⁷

All of these images – New York as the apex of American capitalism, New York as the new Babylon – sprang from a period of prodigious demographic, physical and economic growth. A few decades previously the city had been made up of five or six-storey buildings concentrated on lower Manhattan, bounded by the Hudson on one side and the East River on the other. Farm animals were only legally banned from the streets of Manhattan in 1867.⁸ The city then sprawled over the waters that surrounded Manhattan Island, reaching into its neighbours' backyards with a series of mile-long bridges and, in 1910, a tunnel under the Hudson. In 1898, Brooklyn, Queens and Staten Island were annexed to the behemoth across the water. Only Jersey City preserved its independence.

New York was not just the nexus of American trade and finance, however. It was a large industrial city in its own right. Midtown Manhattan remained a centre of garment making, with its immigrant workforce squeezed into tenement blocks along the city's edge while wealthier residents migrated up Fifth Avenue towards the open spaces of Central Park. Heavier industries – refineries, shipyards and railway repair yards – were kept at a safer distance, in Brooklyn, the Bronx and on Staten Island. Not content with setting the pace of the country's economic life, New York dictated the nation's taste in culture – both high and low. The city boasted 900 cinemas, several aspirationally named 'opera' houses (including a brand new one in the Bronx) and over one hundred theatres, always ready for a 'new producer willing to gamble on a lucky hit'.[9] Or take the hit for an expensive flop. 'What New York doesn't happen to care for', one observer noted, 'remains in the city for a quiet little burial near Forty-second street'. The city vibrated with the nervous energy of a true metropolis. It impressed itself violently upon the consciousness of all those who visited – and many who did not.

In 1913, the best-travelled man of the age, French writer Pierre Loti, described his arrival in the city in terms of sensory overload. Like travellers before and since, he marvelled at the combination of naivety and clumsy intrusiveness that greeted him on the arrivals form at US Customs and Immigration: 'Are you an anarchist? Are you a polygamist? Are you an idiot? Have you ever shown signs of mental alienation?'[10] Once past the meaty guardians of the republic's sanctity he found himself caught up in a symphony of movement, noise, colour, and commercialism.

'This mish-mash of all the races', as Loti put it, 'Japanese, Chinese with European haircuts, Greeks, Levantines, Scandinavians with pale hair'. Like his compatriot Constant in Washington, Loti commented on the elegance and beauty of the women – 'as long as they are not too crudely displayed under electric lights, which give them the pallor of corpses'. He saw 'opulent shops, with long shelves behind the glass, as long as our boulevards'. He wondered at the sovereignty of electricity across the city, 'one thousand times more aggressive than at home'. But it was electricity that made New York possible – air conditioning keeping larger and larger buildings cool in the summer, electric lighting illuminating corners darkened by the massiveness of the buildings surrounding them. New York, Loti said, 'seems to vibrate and crackle under the influence of these countless currents, radiating strength and light – one is oneself electrified, and left quivering by it'. Under the elevated railway at West Broadway was nothing but noise: 'monstrously-sized train carriages, packed with people, running vertiginously above one's head, without pause, sparks flying'. 'Returning from here', Loti sighed, 'Paris is going to seem like a nice old-fashioned little place'.[11]

Above all, Loti was fascinated by the large electrically lit advertisements all over the city, complementing the electric bulletin board on Times Square that had been put up the previous year:

Everywhere these multi-coloured lights, which sparkle and change, forming and re-forming letters, rushing cascades down the fronts of buildings, or crossing the tracks like taut banners. But it's up into the air that you have to look – in spite of the din of subway trains which instinctively makes you cast your eyes to the ground. It's in the air that one sees the most extravagant constructions of light, above the rooftops. There, there are the advertising hoardings, offering a dancing vision of new products to consume . . . An umbrella salesman has put up a lady gesticulating with her open umbrella. A haberdasher shows off a huge cat, all lit up in fiery yellow, unpicking a red ball of string and getting caught up in its threads . . . Quickly, quickly, the apparitions are drawn in lights, change, disappear and return, quickly, so quickly that one can hardly follow them with one's eyes. And then sometimes, on top of an unlit skyscraper, the peak of which is invisible amongst the fog and the smoke, a huge display lights up, as if suspended from the heavens, and hammers a name in electric red letters into your soul, only to dissolve as rapidly as it appeared. All this, to the mind of an Oriental [European] is bewildering and even a little diabolical. But it's so amusing, and so ingenious that I enjoy and almost admire it.[12]

Viewing New York from the twenty-fifth floor of the *New York Times* Building, Loti declared the city the 'capital of modernism', announcing himself both fascinated and frightened by what he saw. 'Seen from here', he wrote in his diary, 'the city looks infinitely large: as far as the eye can reach, electricity traces zig zags, palpitates, winks, dazzles, and finally, towards the horizon, merges in a diffused glow as of the aurora borealis'.[13]

Loti missed a still more spectacular illumination a few months later. On 24 April 1913, at half-past seven in the evening precisely, President

Wilson hit a button in the White House. Two hundred miles north-east the Woolworth Building, the tallest building in the world, was bathed in electric light flashing into the cold night air.[14]

In 1910, when the construction of the Woolworth Building had first been proposed, its cost had been estimated at $5 million and its height at 625 feet.[15] Both had escalated by the time the building opened in 1913. When Cass Gilbert, the building's architect, asked Frank Winfield Woolworth, its commissioner, how tall the tower should ultimately be, Woolworth was said to have responded: 'Fifty feet higher than the Metropolitan tower', the then-tallest building in New York, finished a couple of years previously.[16] And so it was, with Gilbert's design edging up to 750 feet, and then to 792 feet.

Woolworth, the founder of a chain of cheap stores across the United States, intended the building to be a permanent advertisement for his shops (he himself appeared as a grotesque with a nickel in the foyer).[17] The advertising alone justified his investment. But he also intended the building to be a profitable venture in itself, with the highest office rental rates in the world. It boasted an enviable location, within easy reach of Wall Street and the Brooklyn Bridge. Looking up Broadway at St Paul's Chapel, with the Woolworth Building dead ahead and City Hall off to the right, it was said that in this one place you could see the most splendid examples of three centuries of New York architecture. But it was Cass Gilbert who best expressed why the skyscraper really took off in New York City. A skyscraper, Gilbert explained, was a 'machine that makes the land pay'.

Not everyone approved. In 1913 the Heights of Building Commission was set up to investigate. It was noted that on the shortest day of the year, 21 December, both the Woolworth Building and the Singer Building cast shadows of well over 1,000 feet at midday. While the Woolworth building promised 'permanent light and air' to the 'lawyers, financial institutions and high-class businesses' it intended to attract, it denied these conditions to nearby offices. There were considerations of public safety to be borne in mind. Two years previously a fire in the Triangle Shirtwaist garment factory, on the top floors of a ten-storey building in Greenwich Village, had claimed well over one hundred lives. Since then, the city's workshops had been plastered with no smoking signs, in

The tallest inhabited building in the world, the Woolworth Building, opened in New York in 1913, symbol of a city on the make.

English, Italian and Yiddish. But many considered it a matter of time before something went wrong in a tall building, with little that the fire service, on the ground, could do to help. A month before the inauguration of the Woolworth Building, George McAneny, the Manhattan Borough President, told the members of the New York City Club that the 'day of the skyscraper is passing'. He predicted a time, in the not-too-distant future, 'when there were no more skyscrapers built in this city, and when that type of architecture would be regarded as a curiosity'.[18]

Over time, of course, the skyscraper would be viewed as the quintessentially American building, marking a radical divide between the urban landscape of the Old and New Worlds. No buildings in Europe could compare to the audacity of New York's tallest skyscrapers – even if the Eiffel Tower, pride of European modernists, overtopped them all in sheer vertiginous height. Nonetheless, American skyscrapers rendered themselves less brutal by appealing to the aesthetics of older civilisations. The ceiling of the lobby of the Woolworth Building evoked Byzantine mosaics, while its marble floor was hewn from a quarry on the Greek island of Skyros. The tower was made out in the Gothic Flamboyant style with a tourelle on each corner. The building accordingly became known as the 'cathedral of commerce', though Gilbert himself preferred to think of an analogy with the great town halls of northern Europe, while Woolworth had advised his architect to take the neo-Gothic Victoria Tower of the Houses of Parliament in London as his model. The next tallest building in New York, the Metropolitan Life Tower, owed its form to the campanile of San Marco in Venice. (The president of Metropolitan Life, John R. Hegeman, was said to have admired the campanile – which had collapsed in 1902, but been rebuilt in 1908.[19])

What went for the skyscrapers went for everything else. The recently built Penn Station was modelled on the Roman Baths of Caracalla. The New York Public Library was designed by men who studied at the École des Beaux-Arts in Paris, and who contributed to the flowering of its elegant, recognisably Parisian, style with pillars, pediments and pilasters on public buildings, office buildings and theatres all across America. The Central Post Office building, which opened its doors in 1913, was one of the best examples in New York. The new Grand Central Station, completed the same year, combined American efficiency and scale with European grace.

In many respects, the New World defined itself against the Old. Yet when educated New Yorkers came to think about culture – and particularly high culture – their minds journeyed fondly back across the Atlantic to Europe, the birthplace of modern civilisation.

John Pierpont Morgan might be considered the titan of American high finance at the turn of the twentieth century, but when the Swiss and German-educated Morgan came to art he looked to Renaissance Italy. When Puccini played back an image of Gold Rush America to an appreciative New York audience in the 1910 première of *La Fanciulla del West*, the opera was, of course, sung in Italian. William Frick, the steel magnate on whose Fifth Avenue home construction began in 1913, as a rule did not collect art by American artists. (The house itself was built in the Beaux-Arts style, using the same Paris-educated architects as for the New York Public Library.) Only in later years did Frick purchase works by his compatriots: a portrait of George Washington by Gilbert Stuart, chosen more for the subject than for the artist, purchased in 1918, and, from 1914, a substantial body of work by James McNeill Whistler, who spent much of his career in Europe painting European subjects. Europe was where art was produced. America's role was to acquire.

But only if an artwork was bought in Europe by an American, shipped back to the United States and given to a public gallery such as the New York's Metropolitan Museum (which was provided with the foundation of its collection this way) would it be seen by Americans other than the minority who could afford regular travel abroad for leisure. New York was rich, and a number of its leading citizens highly cultured. Educated Americans took seriously the role of the arts in rounding off the country's rough edges – John H. Girdner prescribed it as the only cure for 'Newyorkitis'. But the elite got their cultural education the old-fashioned way: they went to Europe, a few months spent in the museums of Italy to familiarise themselves with great art, and a few more in Parisian cafés turning their earnest American appreciation into urbane European sophistication. Returning American artists and a few brave Europeans aside, New York was barely touched by Europe's main currents in contemporary art.

In February 1913, that changed. The International Exhibition of Modern Art gathered over a thousand modern art works – many of them European – at the Armory on Lexington Avenue. The previous autumn, travelling to Cologne, Munich, Berlin and Paris in order to identify suitable European art works and secure them for the exhibition, the young American organiser Walt Kuhn had worked hard to persuade European galleries of the spectacular nature of the planned New York show. '*Gang und gar ausgeschlossen!*' – roughly translated 'never in a million years' – exclaimed Berlin art dealer Cassirer when Kuhn enquired about the possibility of taking a couple of Cézannes and Van Goghs over to New York.[20] But Kuhn hoovered up anything he could find. Meanwhile, an American resident in Europe, Walter Pach, used his personal connections to cajole artists and Parisian galleries to part with their work.[21] A significant proportion of the artworks which eventually made it across the Atlantic reflected Pach's biases and relationships. New York, the city Loti had extravagantly declared the 'capital of modernism', was now to be exposed to the contemporary art of Europe for the first time, on a truly American scale.

Pach estimated that, over the course of a month, some 100,000 New Yorkers came to see the International Exhibition before it moved on to Chicago and, in slimmed-down form, Boston. Held under the auspices of the Association of American Painters and Sculptors, much of the exhibition was given over to American artists. But most spectators came to gawp at works by modern European artists never before displayed in America in such numbers, or at all: Picasso, Duchamp, Brancusi, Van Gogh, Cézanne, Braque, Matisse, Degas, Renoir, Gauguin. Of these, it was the more shocking exponents of modernism – the Cubists in particular – who grabbed the attention of the public, and who raised the ire of the critics, breaking away from plainly figurative art in a leap towards deformation and abstraction. That the Armory Show would cause a scandal was, of course, expected by the organisers. Indeed, that constituted a critical element of success. This was not to be just an exhibition, it was to be a cultural event, a revolution even.

Former President Theodore Roosevelt thanked the organisers for putting on such an important and necessary exhibition. But this did not mean that he accepted the artistic proclivities of those he termed 'European extremists'.[22] Granted, he wrote, 'there can be no life without change, and to be afraid of what is different or unfamiliar is to be afraid of life'. Nonetheless, it did not follow that all change was life – sometimes change meant death, 'retrogression instead of development'. The Armory Show, he contended, was just such an instance. But perhaps such philosophical reflections were to take some of its art too seriously, he wrote:

> It is likely that many of them [the pictures] represent in the painters the astute appreciation of the power to make folly lucrative which the late P. T. Barnum [a circus-owner] showed with his faked mermaid. There are thousands of people who will pay small sums to look at a faked mermaid; and now and then one of this kind with enough money will buy a Cubist picture, or a picture of a misshapen nude woman, repellent from every standpoint.

Most professional art critics agreed. Kenyon Cox, writing in *Harper's Weekly*, proclaimed his belief that 'there are still commandments in art as in morals, and still laws in art as in physics'.[23] He had no doubt that the art of the Armory Show would not last – but it could yet do serious harm, corrupting public taste and leading some young artists to abandon the hard graft of study in the belief that success could be won through scandal instead. He advised the public: 'If your stomach revolts against this rubbish it is because it is not fit for human food.' But he saved his most stinging criticisms for the artists themselves. Of Van Gogh, Cox wrote: 'All I can be sure of is an experiment in impressionistic technique by a painter too unskilled to give quality to an evenly laid coat of pigment.' In the works of Rodin, 'how far mental disease mingles with inordinate self-esteem . . . it is difficult to say'. Finally, in the paintings of Matisse, 'it is not madness that stares at you . . . but leering effrontery'.

Others showed less drama, and more wit, in their denunciations. *Puck* magazine pictured hens laying Cubist eggs.[24] A group of artists mocked the pretensions of the Armory Show by promising to 'out-cube the Cubists' with an exhibition held by the 'Academy of Misapplied Art' in the auditorium of the New York Association of the Blind. Invitations promised 'an exclusive exhibit of works of the most distinguished American artists from the Cubistic, Post-Impressionist, Futuristic, Neurotic, Psychopathic and Paretic schools'. Robert Sewell, one of the artists involved, said that he intended to 'put the Futurists into the middle of the past tense'. Some reviewers called the Armory Show 'freak art'. 'Wouldn't it be awful if someone got locked in here overnight', a reporter heard an exhibition-goer say.[25] But whatever the papers said, it was a commercial success – and that, in New York, counted for a lot. When the exhibition moved to Chicago in March the *New York Sun* ironised: 'Cubists migrate; Thousands Mourn'.

American art would not be the same after the Armory Show. Joseph Stella, an Italian-born American who had spent the previous few years in Europe, painted his first Futurist painting – *Battle of Lights, Coney Island* – in the show's wake. New York had begun the journey from a city which bought and revered European art, to a city which would ultimately surpass it.

For Americans who could trace their families back more than a couple of generations to the fields of northern Ireland or southern Scotland – President Wilson himself claimed Scots-Irish heritage – New York presented a paradox. While foreigners thought of New York as the symbol of America, many Americans viewed the city, with some suspicion, as the country's most foreign. The figures backed them up. In 1910, the thirteenth national census revealed that fully four-fifths of New York's population, more than any other major city, were of 'foreign stock' – either born outside the United States or natives born to foreign parents. Was New York still an American city, or was it increasingly a European city stranded on the wrong side of the Atlantic?

In truth, the attitudes of the city's latest European arrivals towards their European past were mixed. Many had come to America from Europe to escape hardship, marginalisation and persecution. For some – the Irish or Italians, for example – the national homeland could, in time, acquire a warm glow. Its finer points were recalled and celebrated; inconvenient facts were forgotten. Occasionally, distance simplified politics, sharpening distinctions between right and wrong, between us and them. For many others – particularly those who had no land to call their own, driven across the Atlantic by targeted persecution rather than by generalised poverty – Europe was a much more problematic inheritance. For these immigrants, particularly Jews from Russia, America was not only a land of economic opportunity, but a refuge from the rest of the world. They were often viewed as the most 'foreign'. Yet as all these groups met and forged their new identities as hyphenated Americans – Jewish-American, Italian-American, Polish-American – they began to forge a new identity for America itself.

Around two million New Yorkers had been born outside the United States. Of these, a quarter of a million each were born in Germany and Ireland, with a further 100,000 from Great Britain. They joined communities that were well established in New York, and which had sister communities in cities, towns and villages across America. They were the backbone of the migrants of the previous century. Every President the United States had ever had was of North European heritage – mostly English, Scottish and Protestant Irish. What was relatively new to America, and most acute in New York, was the prominence of immigration from Europe's southern and eastern fringes. Over 300,000 New Yorkers had been born in Italy. Nearly 800,000 were from central and eastern Europe: from Russia, the Austro-Hungarian Empire, and Romania. In 1870 these countries had accounted for one in a hundred of New York's foreign-born population; now they constituted one in four. Many were Jewish, doubly distant from the Protestant ascendancy. In 1913, over 100,000 Jews arrived in America. Most settled in New York, contributing to the ethnic kaleidoscope of the city's Lower East Side.[26]

John H. Girdner had described New York as a 'huge mill, into the hopper of which is annually thrown raw material in the form of brain, brawn, money, and character drawn from the outside world'. Out of these elements was produced 'the metropolis'. Israel Zangwill, a British Jewish playwright and essayist, chose a different metaphor: the melting pot.

His 1908 play of the same name, performed for the first time in New York in 1909, was set in one of the city's outlying boroughs. In the Jewish Quixano household a picture of Wagner – a great German composer, but a renowned anti-Semite – hangs on the wall, and a book by Nietzsche stands in the bookcase, symbolising the family's German-language culture. Mrs Quixano speaks only German. Her nephew David, brought to America when his parents are murdered in an anti-Semitic pogrom in the Russian town of Kishineff, is more readily assimilated – in love with the idea of America as a new start, a place purged of the ancient feuds and vendettas which plagued Europe:

> Oh, I love going to Ellis Island to watch the ships coming from Europe, and to think that all those weary, sea-tossed wanderers are feeling what I felt when America first stretched out her greater mother-hand to me![27]

In New York, David falls in love with a Russian Orthodox immigrant, Vera (meaning 'truth' in Russian). Later, he discovers that she is familiar with Kishineff. Still later, he discovers that the Russian military officer in charge of the district during the pogrom – whose face is etched into David's nightmares – is Vera's estranged father, Baron Revendal. With the help of an unscrupulous American Christian, Quincy Davenport, Revendal travels to New York in an attempt to win back his daughter, and to dissuade her from marrying a Jew. 'Don't you lynch and roast your niggers?' Revendal enquires of Davenport by way of explaining his attitude towards the Jewish problem in Russia. But even the arrival of David's tormentor cannot keep him apart from Vera.

The final scene of the play takes part on 4 July, Independence Day. David and Vera declare their intention to marry – and David declares his love for America:

> Yes, East and West, and North and South, the palm and the pine, the pole and the equator, the crescent and the cross – how the great Alchemist melts and fuses them with his purging flame! Here shall they all unite to build the Republic of Man and the Kingdom of God. Ah, Vera, what is the glory of Rome and Jerusalem where all nations and races come to worship and look back, compared with the glory of America, where all races and nations come to labour and look forward! [28]

At the 1908 opening of the play in Washington Theodore Roosevelt exclaimed, 'That's a great play, Mr Zangwill'. Not everyone agreed. In the Jewish press, some accused it of condoning effective 'race suicide' by intermarriage.[29] The *New York Herald* ran a front-page debate between Zangwill and American industrialist Daniel Guggenheim under the banner 'Should Jews marry Christians?' New York's different communities were not quite so willing to be tossed into a single crucible as David Quixano might have hoped.

Nor was the rest of America quite as welcoming. 'God is making the American' in New York, Quixano exclaims in *The Melting Pot*.[30] But many existing Americans felt God had already done His work. In 1911, a congressional commission chaired by Senator William P. Dillingham of Vermont produced a forty-one-volume report into the changing patterns of migration into the United States. The report suggested a number of possible measures to restrict immigration, as a means to ensuring its appropriate 'quantity and quality'. One suggested approach was to limit immigration to some fraction of existing ethnic communities, thus acting as a brake on newer flows of migration. Another was to institute a test for reading and writing. The overall message was clear: unrestricted migration could not continue.

Others felt that it had already gone too far. One of America's most famous medical doctors, Henry Smith Williams, reported that while only one in a hundred Scandinavian or English migrants were illiterate, forty out of every hundred Russian immigrants, half of Italian and two-thirds of Portuguese immigrants could not read.[31] Nearly half of the inmates of New York State's hospitals for the criminally insane were foreign born. Charles B. Davenport, director of the Eugenics Record Office in Cold Springs Harbor, NY, was quoted as arguing that:

> A new plague that rendered 4 per cent of our population, chiefly at the most productive age, not merely incompetent, but a burden costing $100,000,000 a year to support would instantly attract universal attention. But we have become so used to crime, disease and degeneracy that we take them as necessary evils.

Williams went further. The consequences of this latest wave of immigration – 'the incubus of this alien horde' – threatened the survival of the country's values, even its democracy, he argued. The ghettoisation of migrant communities sustained the politics of 'bossism' of the kind which had become so prominent in New York City. 'Cosmopolitanism' was compared unfavourably to 'Americanism'. Williams warned of the decline in the nation's average intelligence, and thus its economic prospects. It would be no bad thing, he said, for the population of America to fall by a quarter if this were to result in a corresponding increase in average quality.

Edward Alsworth Ross, a prominent sociologist and former chair of the American Economic Association, painted a still more dramatic picture of America's future under conditions of unrestricted migration, symbolised by the cosmopolitanism of New York. The immigration of southern Europeans, he argued, was only the start of a slippery slope:

> Already America has ceased to allure, as of yore, the British, the Germans, and the Scandinavians; but it strongly attracts the Italians, Greeks, and Slavs. By 1930, perhaps, the opportunities left will have ceased to interest them; but no doubt the Khivans, the Bokhariots, the Persians and the Afghans will regard this as the Promised Land. By 1950, even they will scorn the chances here; but then, perhaps, the coolies from overpopulated India will be glad to take an American wage. By the last quarter of this century there will remain, possibly, no people in the world that will care for the chances left in America. Then, when immigration has ceased of itself, when the dogma of the sacred right of immigration has wrought its perfect work, and when the blood of the old pioneering breed has faded out of the motley, polyglot, polychrome, caste-riven population that will crowd this continent to a Chinese density, let there be reared a commemorative monument bearing these words: 'TO THE AMERICAN PIONEERING BREED, THE VICTIM OF TOO MUCH HUMANITARIANISM AND TOO LITTLE COMMON SENSE'.[32]

In this reading of multicultural, multi-ethnic, multi-religious New York, the city was not America's noble vanguard, it was rather a warning of things to come.

On 31 March 1913, word reached the city that one of the grandest men of old New York was no more. John Pierpont Morgan, titan of Wall Street, scion of New York's once-dominant Anglo-Saxon ascendancy, leading figure in the Episcopalian Church, the most powerful economic figure in the New World, had passed away in Rome, capital of the Old World.[33]

The following days saw a flood of testaments to J. P. Morgan's greatness. The New York Stock Exchange declared he had done more for America's economic development of the last half-century than any other man – an exaggeration, but an idea widely shared on Wall Street. With more than a hint of self-interested sycophancy the photographer Edward S. Curtis, whose documentation of Native American culture had been supported by Morgan (and by Theodore Roosevelt), declared him 'the greatest citizen of the time'.[34] Morgan received grand treatment in journals as diverse as *The Churchman*, *Banker's Magazine* and the *Nautical Gazette*. In the *American Review of Reviews* he was termed 'the Napoleon of finance'. Sir William Boyd Carpenter, former chaplain to Queen Victoria, steaming to America aboard the RMS *Adriatic*, was so moved as to write a poem in Morgan's honour: 'Dip flags, the Commodore has come to port!' Morgan's son Jack received telegrams from friends, admirers and business colleagues around the world: from Havana, Melbourne, London and Hamburg. The *Independent* magazine quoted a London-based correspondent as declaring that, to the average Englishman, Morgan was 'the personification of America's wealth, energy and financial organization'.[35]

At his death, Morgan was a wealthy American at a time when America was famed for the wealth of its richest citizens, a fact which Woodrow Wilson's income tax, levied at only seven per cent for incomes above $500,000, barely dented. The precise extent of Morgan's wealth was anyone's guess. It took a full three years after his death for a comprehensive account of his estate to be made. When it was finished it showed him poorer than many expected (and much poorer than oil baron John D. Rockefeller) but in good company alongside Henry Clay Frick, Andrew Carnegie, or the heirs of Jay Gould and Cornelius Vanderbilt.

But it was Morgan's generosity, as well as his wealth, which formed the subject of his obituaries in 1913. The Metropolitan Museum applauded the man's 'inherent greatness of character' – a greatness backed up with the dollars needed to add countless artworks to New York City's finest public collection. On a different scale, Theodore Roosevelt recalled an occasion on which Morgan had privately given a substantial sum to the widow of a prominent senator, to whom he had no connection, on hearing that she had been left without money on his death. Philanthropy squared red-blooded capitalism with Christianity. To men such as Morgan, grown rich in the moralising world of the late nineteenth century, there was only one thing more American than making money – and that was to give it away to causes or museums of which one approved. One could thus be a gentleman, a good Christian, an American, a capitalist, a man of European culture, a benefactor of the arts, a tycoon, and a servant of the public good rolled into one. This was the paternalistic, imperial model of the leadership of the rich. Characteristically, Morgan was reported to have more respect for bishops than for presidents.

Morgan's public spiritedness manifested itself chiefly through his informal role as the nation's banker, and through his cultural invest-ments. In 1907, in the absence of an American central bank, Morgan had averted a full-scale financial meltdown by gathering Wall Street's money men in his high-ceilinged study and, under the gaze of the European Renaissance, browbeating them into providing the American market with additional liquidity. Morgan's appetite as a collector of art was gargantuan. His estate included $2,800,000 of tapestries, rugs, furniture, snuff boxes and decorative pieces. One London house alone was packed with candelabras and commodes, goblets, clocks, faiences, Japanese lacquered boxes, vases, and a collec-tion of 138 watches.[36] But, over his life, much else was given away. Morgan sat on the boards of numerous museums. His extraordinary library, his inner sanctum, was turned over to the public in 1924. 'As he has led America out of financial provincialism', noted the Union Club of New York, 'so he has done his utmost to educate his fellow Americans in good pictures and good books', providing his compat-riots with the opportunity to be 'refined by their beauties'.[37]

In late 1912 Morgan had faced a congressional grilling on a supposed 'Money Trust'. The Money Trust, it was alleged, was a system of cross-holdings that allowed a small number of Wall Street bankers to squeeze their investors, control access to credit, and therefore determine the fate of individual businesses over the entire United States. The theme of more democratic access to credit, and Wall Street's predatory influence over the national economy, had been taken up enthusiastically by Woodrow Wilson in his presidential campaign, with crusading lawyer Louis Dembitz Brandeis at his side. (In 1913, Brandeis wrote a series of articles subsequently published in a book as *Other People's Money – and How the Bankers Use It.*) In 1912, under cross-examination, Morgan had acquitted himself well, batting away questions that hinted at conspiracy, and declaring himself an unambiguous advocate of the American free market.[38] He received a slew of supportive letters, including one from the Bishop of Albany. Another congratulated him for 'having floored that shyster', in reference to his cross-examiner on the congressional committee.[39]

But Morgan had been tired by the experience. Now, he travelled to cities with more ancient connotations. First to Cairo, city of the pharaohs. Then to Rome, where he stayed in rooms at the Grand Hotel said to be those occupied by crowned heads of Europe when passing through, with a view towards the dome of St Peter's. He had intended to travel on to Aix-en-Provence. When he did ultimately leave Rome it was in a coffin, on a ship bound for New York owned by a company in which Morgan had a financial interest.

'He is worthy to lie at the central city of the world [Rome]', one American journalist wrote after his death, 'and to have the world quiet, thinking and talking of him'.[40] Rome had seen the passing of none so powerful as 'the man of the New World, accidentally dead in the heart of history'. Asked about Morgan by an American reporter, Italian socialist Leonida Bissolati noted his admiration for his financial genius, while adding that 'had he directed his splendid talents to the realization of Socialist ideals the world would mourn his loss far more sincerely than is now the case'.[41] Historian Guglielmo Ferrero noted the 'sociological anomaly' of Morgan's wealth, and declared that 'America has a big problem to grapple with in this respect'.[42] They, and others, were chided by the director of the American Academy in Rome, Jesse Benedict Carter: 'No one but ignorant persons ever thought of Mr Morgan as a "rich man". Those who had come in any way near to him . . . thought of him as a great man, whose greatness had brought wealth with it'.[43] In contrast to the 'new era' some proclaimed for America, Carter asserted the virtue of a man 'steeped in the old tradition', the tradition of individuality.

On one thing everyone agreed: the death of J. P. Morgan was a larger event than the death of a man. 'It's not just a grand financier – the grandest – who has passed', wrote *Le Figaro* in Paris, 'it is a whole regime which has disappeared: the system of financial feudalism'.[44] Over the course of the rest of the year 1913, New York, the self-appointed metropolis of American business, the epicentre of freewheeling financial capitalism, had its wings clipped by Washington.

In place of the private arrangements of private bankers running the finances of the world's largest industrial economy – the system symbolised by Morgan – the hybrid Federal Reserve System was established, a kind of decentralised central bank. Under this system, power was shunted away from Wall Street by setting up regional Federal Reserves – including one in New York – able to report back on credit conditions on the ground. Public officials were to be appointed to the Federal Reserve board in order to allow the views of Wall Street to be tempered by those of Main Street, and those of Washington. Interest rates, which had tended to fluctuate seasonally in the past, with a major impact on farmers, would now be smoothed over the course of the year. Financial panics would be more easily controlled. Although not necessarily foreseen at the time, the creation of such a system would have still-larger consequences for the long term. The introduction of greater stability into America's domestic finances would eventually, particularly in the period after 1945, provide the springboard for the increasingly important role of the United States dollar in the global economy, from which it was almost absent in 1913 where the British pound sterling predominated.[45] Thus the Federal Reserve Act of 1913 would ultimately form the basis of New York's emergence not as the nation's financial capital, but the world's.

Two weeks after Morgan's death, his body arrived back in New York, his coffin wrapped in the American flag and topped with Jacquemot roses. More flowers arrived later, as the body lay in state in the Morgan Library: a cluster of palm leaves bound with silk streamers from the German Emperor, a wreath of lilies of the valley from the Italian government, palm leaves from a tree at Mount Vernon reputed to have been planted by George Washington. The funeral was held a few days later in St George's Episcopal church. As a mark of respect normally reserved only for presidents, the New

York Stock Exchange stayed closed. Later, John Pierpont Morgan's coffin was put on a special train for Hartford, Connecticut, and there his body was committed to the firm New England ground of his birth.

For America, the death of J. P. Morgan represented the end of a particular era of capitalism – born of nineteenth-century precepts of unfettered free markets – which had given rise to the trusts and the tycoons, the tremendous enrichment of the elite, and the cultural affectations of New York's aristocracy of wealth. Now, in its place, there began to emerge an era where the state would play a more directive role in the national economy and where mass production and mass consumption would become America's hallmarks, rather than the prosperity of its elites. In 1913 America jolted decisively, from the age of Morgan to the age of Ford.

DETROIT
A Model Future

As Cass Gilbert celebrated the opening of the Woolworth Building in New York, his attention turned to his latest commission in one of America's fastest-rising cities: a grand public library in Detroit, Michigan. The plot chosen was on Woodward Avenue, a wide road running from the city's centre up towards its northern fringes. Gilbert envisaged a classical building of white marble, a symbol of learning and culture for Detroit's burgeoning aspirational classes. A mile or two further up Woodward Avenue stood another building, of brick and glass this time but every bit as grand in its way, and equally symbolic of Detroit's rise: the Highland Park factory of the Ford Motor Company, home of the Model T.

By 1913 Detroit already claimed half a million residents, and the number was rising. 'Probably no place in the United States has grown so rapidly since the last census', proclaimed a tourist guide produced a few years later.[1] 'Detroit is Growing Northward' screamed an advertisement in the *Free Press* for the North Woodward area, estimating that the city's population would top one million by 1920, even as notices for chicken farms jostled with those for suburban property.[2]

Like New York, the city's population was cosmopolitan, including a large number of recent immigrants in search of work in the city's factories. 'Half a dozen cities' lay within Detroit's limits.[3] A 'large colony' of African-Americans from the South had begun to grow up in a nest of downtown streets – Clinton, Macomb, Monroe and Beaubien – though Detroit was still the whitest large city in America. Around West Jefferson Avenue 'almost all the names on the stores are Hungarian, Romanian and Armenian'. East Canfield was a Polish stronghold. 'Little Roumania' had established itself around Highland Park itself, but several thousand more Romanians lived by the wharves of southern Detroit, in an area once dominated by French Canadians. Elsewhere, there were streets of Greeks or Russians, and city blocks of Serbians or Belgians. 'Although foreigners are adapting themselves to American life generally', the guidebook noted, 'different nationalities follow different trades':

> Greeks are florists, waiters, and have monopolized the bootblacking business. Sicilians are fruit dealers. Other Italians are laborers. Syrians are laborers. Belgians are farmers, laborers and many of them are good mechanics. The foreigners are among the best workmen and very valuable in the industrial world.[4]

At Highland Park, the city's largest factory, more than half the workers had been born outside the United States, 'men of every race and creed' wrote one visiting journalist approvingly. The plant was to be Ford's own version of Zangwill's 'melting pot', churning out not just Model Ts but a truly American workforce: hard-working, conscientious, well-paid, consumers as well as producers. Within a few years, graduations from the company's English school saw foreign-born employees enter a giant cauldron marked 'Ford English School Melting Pot' in foreign costume, from which they emerged a few minutes later dressed in American clothes waving American flags.[5]

Established in 1913, the Ford English School, along with Ford's other social innovations, was partly a matter of enlightened self-interest. Company managers observed that a common language, alongside high wages, comfortable working conditions and the enforcement of standards of personal discipline led to greater efficiency and higher rates of workforce retention. The Highland Park building itself was designed to be the very opposite of the traditional, dark industrial complex. The size of the place, the largest building under one roof in Michigan, was impressive but not new – German architect Walter Gropius compared the scale and ambition of American industrial buildings with the pyramids of Egypt.[6] But under the direction of another German architect, Albert Kahn, fully three-quarters of the wall space of the huge Highland Park building was glass, increasing natural light for the workers and earning the factory the nickname the 'Crystal Palace'.[7] Both the building design and the company's programmes to educate the workforce were part of a broader Fordist vision of society: as something to be constantly improved upon in the light both of modern science and the values of the traditional American homestead, such as that on which Henry Ford had grown up. Following these twin principles, Ford believed, Highland Park could be a successful model factory, and Detroit a successful model city.

Alongside work for Detroit's workers, of course, there was leisure for its citizens. In the summer of 1913 the city's inhabitants could take in *Nero Burns Rome* at the Detroit Opera House. The Polish-language Fredro theatre opened that year on the corner of Chene and Kirby. For visitors there was the prospect of midnight excursions on the water separating the United States from Canada, or dancing on Wednesday and Saturday evenings in the pavilion on Sugar Island.[8]

Confidence in Detroit's future was written in its skyline. The city claimed its own skyscraper, the Dime Building, with four more planned for the year ahead. On the edges of downtown stood the proud Michigan Central Station, both 'mammoth and beautiful', designed by the same architects as Penn Station in New York.[9] With eleven tracks for passenger trains, and one for freight, Michigan Central opened its doors at the end of 1913, a reminder that while the future might belong to the automobile the present belonged to the railway train. From here, travellers could take trains to nearby towns, or to the next state, or as far as Florida. The fact that the station was brought into service eight days early – the result of a fire in the old depot – was taken as a sign of efficient organisation rather than a portent of the station's future obsolescence. 'There was no fuss or feathers about the matter', reported the local newspaper, 'the fire broke out at 2.10; at 3.30 the Wolverine Express from Chicago steamed importantly up to the new 16 storey terminal and at 3.50 steamed out again . . . and by supper time outgoing trains were leaving as if they had been accustomed to it for years'. The clock on the old depot had stopped still at 2.40 a.m. – but Detroit had already moved on.

It was not inevitable that Detroit would become the unquestioned centre of the American car industry, nor that this industry would do more to shape America than any other. Ford had many national rivals in the first decade of the twentieth century: Cole Motor Company and National Motor Company in Indianapolis, the Willys-Overland Company in Toledo, Ohio, Borland-Grannis in Chicago, the White Company in Cleveland and the Pierce Arrow in Buffalo, New York, to name a few. While some made gasoline cars, like Ford, others thought the future lay with electric vehicles. Where roads existed at all they were generally poorly maintained, hampering the use of automobiles beyond a specified radius of homes and making interstate travel an expedition into the unknown. The first motoring hotels were only just emerging; the route of the interstate Lincoln Highway was only drawn up in 1913. In late September Detroit hosted the American Road Congress, a nod to the city's increasingly dominant role in the automobile industry and to the beginnings of a mass automobile culture in the Midwestern states, with twice as many cars per thousand inhabitants as the South, and nearly as many as New England.[10] But, even now, Detroit's position was not necessarily unassailable.

Ford was not the city's only automobile manufacturer, nor were cars the city's only industry. Detroit had long been associated with the fur trade. It also turned out cigars, elevator cabs, picture frames and furniture. In September the city organised a Made in Detroit exhibition across the city, running late into the evening, which included a number of mechanical displays and forty-five different types of car. The organiser, Mr Zenner, told a reporter that the exhibit 'will give Detroiters a better idea of the greatness of their own city and will impress visitors with Detroit as a city of large and varied enterprises'.[11] Whereas New York had earned itself a reputa-tion – unfairly, perhaps – as a dandified city of personal convenience, where 'you can be shaved, manicured, have your shoes shined, smoke a cigar, and read the paper all at the same time', Detroit presented itself to the world as an industrial workshop, able to turn its hand to anything.[12] Alongside the lessons learned from the failures of his predecessors, it was these smaller industries – proving grounds for innovation, incubators of practical engineering skills, suppliers of all the parts needed to build a car – that enabled Ford's success. In this crucial sense, it was not Henry Ford who made Detroit, it was Detroit that made Henry Ford.

Yet Ford had the ability to capitalise on the advantages which

Detroit provided him and, above all, the vision to create and sustain a wholly new market for his products. Unlike most of his competitors, Henry Ford designed a car not for the elite but for the masses, for the average citizen of smalltown America rather than the wealthy city-dweller for whom the automobile signified status above all. While most automobile manufacturers built cars that were strong, heavy and powerful – great for cruising down city streets, but prone to sink into the mud of unpaved country lanes – Ford built a car that was light and flexible, cheaper to make and run, and less likely to break down. The Model T was a car for everyman.

There was commercial logic to the proposition of a cheap car that would not break down. But there was also a moralising side to it, and ultimately a vision of American economic development driven by the automobile. In 1906, Woodrow Wilson had declared that 'nothing has spread socialistic feeling in this country more than the automobile; to the country man they are a picture of arrogance and wealth with all its independence and carelessness', responsible for the accidents on the front page of each newspaper, every day.[13] Ford sought to reverse that picture, making the car a symbol of individual empowerment and social responsibility rather than one of wealthy high-handedness. Ford owners were advised of the consequences of speed on the 'smashing power' of collisions, and instructed that 'the men who buy this automobile [the Model T] prize safety more than speed. They are not joy riders'.[14]

The pages of the *Ford Times* – distributed to Ford dealers, owners and prospective customers, allowing the magazine to claim the widest circulation of any industrial publication – were filled with conservative homespun wisdom. 'It may have taken a million years to make a man out of a monkey; but it doesn't take a million drinks to make a monkey out of a man', warned the magazine.[15] 'The one thing we need most to fear is fear', it advised.[16] Fun was made of the vanity of a Michigan woman who bought a $5000 automobile for the same reason that she 'had diamonds set in the fillings of her teeth'.[17] Smoking was banned from Ford showrooms, and salesmen were told to dress down, rather than appear know-it-all or flashy. In one edition, a story ran about how a Model T Ford hooked up to a generator had allowed the telephones in a rural Kentucky community to keep going after a power failure, showing the automobile embedded in a community as much as the horse and cart in previous years.[18] In another, space was given to the story of a group of girls who had sold 1,900 copies

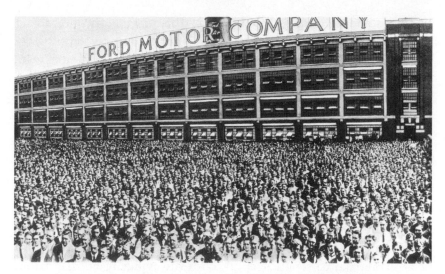

The employees of the Highland Park plant, which churned out Model T Fords on the world's first production line. The most expensive photograph ever taken, according to the Fordist maxim that time equals money.

of a calendar in order to raise money to get their local church pastor a Model T.[19]

In the January 1913 issue of *Ford Times* a prospective customer – in this case, a male farmer – was painted a picture of freedom and development brought by ownership of an automobile and, under the title 'Better Roads – Bigger Farm Values', enlisted in a campaign to improve the nation's byways:

> The roads are so easy to travel, you go to town more frequently than you used to, and once in a while you bring back something to make her work easier. Then there are the papers and magazines that come to you regularly each month . . . Telephone companies are more anxious to extend their lines to communities where the roads are good, for they know there is more business than in backwoods localities. So you have the telephone . . . Soon you will be able to buy your goods at city stores and have them delivered right to your front door . . . This would be an impossible task if your roads were unimproved.

'A new Declaration of Independence is made by every man who resolves to own a Ford', declared the magazine a few months later.

In all this, Henry Ford widened the appetite for modernity, resolving its urban anxieties into an older creed of self-advancement. [20]

As the practical vehicle for the aspirations of the common man, the Model T was to be built – and sold – at scale. Rather than building one car at a time, in line with the principles of artisanal craftsmanship, Fords would be produced with industrial efficiency, and sold by professional salesmen all over the country, 'Ford people' or 'Fordites' as the *Ford Times* liked to refer to them. Endless innovation in the manufacturing process led, by 1913, to the world's first fully-fledged production line. Six years after the first prototype Model T had been built at the Piquette plant in Detroit, a single nine-hour shift at the much larger Highland Park plant assembled one thousand cars. The company estimated that it now produced one-third of all American cars.[21] In keeping with the typically Fordist axiom that time equals money, a posed photograph of the entire 12,000-strong workforce of the Highland Park factory was reported as being the most expensive photograph ever taken, 'costing many thousands of dollars for employees' time and loss of production'.[22]

Thus Henry Ford envisaged, evangelised, and came to personify an American economy of mass production and, crucially, mass consumption. A country brought up to believe itself a nation of tinkerers and inventors was made to see, in Henry Ford, one of their own. So while Ford himself ultimately became far richer than J. P. Morgan ever was, he was the acceptable, populist democratic face of American industrialisation where Morgan was its haughty, distant aristocratic face. Henry Ford may not have made Detroit, but his success supercharged its ascent – and changed America.

Henry Ford's vision of mass production and mass consumption did not arise from nowhere. It grew out of an American obsession with innovation and constantly improving productivity, and out of an infectious belief in material progress.

In 1913, efficiency was an all-American cult. The tenets of the gospel of industrial efficiency were cited in Congress and in the country's courts as revealed truths.[23] Its prophets were hailed as bringers of a new American revolution. In 1911, Frederick Winslow Taylor published *The Principles of Scientific Management*, asserting that vast amounts of time and money could be saved by analysing and improving how holes were dug, or buildings built. Through scientific analysis – essentially photography and stop-watches needed for time and motion studies – the manufacturing process could be disaggregated into a series of similar, standardisable steps. These snapshot views of individual steps in the industrial process, studied, improved and then accelerated through time, would produce stupendous increases in productivity. (In the *Made in Detroit* exhibit of September, Taylorian 'motion exhibits' – otherwise known as films – showed Detroiters how individual products were manufactured.)

Many of Taylor's actual results were statistically spurious. Yet they appealed to managers now in a position to claim the authority of science over their workers. Basic Taylorian principles were applied to workplaces across America, chiming with wider notions of continuous improvement through learning, work and ingenuity. America in 1913 was awash with would-be inventors, who filled four pages of *Scientific American: The Weekly Journal of Practical Information* with announcements of patents for tyre inflaters, moveable cuffs and automatic plant seeders. With Taylor, as with Ford, scientific method, rather than God, would now light the way to industrial nirvana.

And beyond. Another guru, Harrington Emerson, offered a home course of study in personal efficiency in just twenty-four lessons, available by writing to a New York address. In 1913, the Sears Roebuck catalogue advertised a range of labour-saving devices, from the cedar-wood High Speed Wizard Washer at $6.95 – 'probably your neighbor has one' – to the Eckhard Electric Suction Cleaner, available in both alternating and direct current designs to account for variations across the United States. 'Make 1913 the electric year', suggested an advertisement in the *Los Angeles Times*, accompanied by a picture of a single woman cooking on an electric hob, under an electric lamp.[24]

Efficiency at home and at the factory was all very well, but with basic needs now so readily fulfilled, how would the economy be kept busy? The answer, the gurus argued, was much greater consumption, creating the demand that mass production could then supply. 'Take your pencil – follow these figures', advised N. A. Hawkins, the sales manager of the Ford Motor Company, walking his audience through the mathematics of mass consumption. There were a hundred million Americans, he reasoned, and twenty-five million families. Of these, five million could afford a new car, while existing automobile owners would buy new ones down the line. Conclusion: 'Ford sales can never stop – they must increase!'[25] A few years later, Ford passed the one million mark. 'A million of anything is a great many', Henry Ford told an adoring audience.[26]

But Ford's ambitions did not stop with a million, and did not stop with America. According to the *Ford Times*, 'The Universal Car' was the most popular automobile in Vladivostok, and elsewhere in Russia it was used by 'two Grand Dukes and nineteen Princes' as well as being inspected by the war department. The Model T turned up in China with a machine gun mounted on the back to protect a government official. Japan had already been 'conquered' with Ford's service culture acting as the company's forward artillery. The *National Geographic* described the delivery of a Ford, via the Gobi desert, to the 'Living God' (the Dalai Lama) of Mongolia. It was used on coffee plantations in Brazil and sheep farms in New Zealand. A cartoon showed a startled Martian looking through a telescope at earth – to see it swarming with Model T Fords.

Ford learned his creed of mass consumption by looking around him – and studying its prophets. In 1907, Simon Nelson Patten had written of the 'pleasure or surplus economy' as a 'new basis for civilization'.[27] An age of relative plenty changed the meaning and purpose of economic life. 'Cleanliness ceases to be the more or less onerous requirement', Patten wrote, 'and becomes a widening aesthetic joy in the scrubbed floors of the worker's own house, the shining windows, the ebony stove, and in his well-washed children about a white-clothed table'. 'Tawdry, unmeaning and useless objects' became objects of affection in the home, and 'the mark of superiority and success' to oneself and to others. Leisure and meeting new aspirations – indeed creating and defining new aspirations – had become a growth business.

The Sears catalogue of 1913 was eloquent testimony for the emergence of a society of mass consumption, with new and varied tastes. At the more serious end of the scale, Sears offered gasoline engines, a range of ploughs, and almost everything else the American farmer could want or need to produce food in American quantities for American plates. For those who had recently left the countryside, Sears offered reminders of it in cheap reproductions depicting scenes from rural life: 'Homeward Bound', 'Fishing' or 'The Old Homestead'.

The patriotic could adorn their walls with carbon tints of Washington or Lincoln. Pyrography equipment for burning designs on to wood or leather would keep Americans busy on dark nights.

Although in 1913 Sears abandoned the sale of patent medicines, for which it could vouch neither for their contents nor efficacy, it offered hundreds of other products intended to smarten or beautify. The Nu-Life Truss, for example, a men's corset designed to force deep breathing, 'creating perfect circulation and preventing decay'. Or an obesity belt 'to give shape to the pendulous or relaxed abdomen'. There was special elastic for cyclists' ankles, an ear cap to restrain children's protruding ears, thirty types of soap, various cold creams, Carmichael's Peroxide freckle ointment, Gervaise Graham's Hair Color to dye hair, Princess Hair Tonic to grow it and De-Miracle Non-Irritant Depilatory to remove it. Sears carried a range of twenty face powders, many with Japanese names evoking the pale skins of Japanese women. The results could be contemplated in mirrors with German silver handles, or Parisian ivory, or anything in between.

More frivolously, Sears offered two dozen types of doll (including Eskimo dolls), three different decks of cards for magic tricks, an eight-key toy clarinet, toy aeroplanes, German-made teddy bears, metal warships of different sizes, Ouija boards (known as Egyptian luck boards) and, in the year when the National Association for the Advancement of Colored People was protesting at racism in Washington, a 'negro makeup outfit' described as follows: 'Consists of woven-black cotton hood and realistic large eyes, thick red lips and large teeth . . . A great item for masquerades or Halloween'.

But this was not all. There were pruning knives, hunting knives, imported German knives and the full range of Wilbert pocket knives, including the Cowboy knife and the Teamsters' knife. Before the cigarette had become the nation's preferred means of consuming tobacco Sears offered sixty types of smoking pipe, including carved Meerschaum pipes in the popular Hungarian shape. For one's leisure and for the home, one could buy boats, curtains, fishing bait, reels and rods, hammocks, tents, dog muzzles, baseball horns, college pennants, tennis rackets, roller skates, pedometers, and traps for otters, deer and vermin with such names as Kill-Um and The Sure Death Trap. Bullets, axes, gun stocks, air rifles, pistols and revolvers were all on offer, alongside cuckoo clocks, rosary beads, crucifixes, fountain pens, pins of all types for every lapel, pocket watches (including the interstate chronometer for $17.45), telegraph transmitters, adjustable electric shock providers (for 80 cents), Westinghouse fans, telephone switchboards, binoculars, telescopes, automobile goggles, postcard projectors, a full range of cameras (including those for just a few dollars), metronomes, gramophone players, guitars, rugs, dresses, suits, hats – and a United States flag with forty-eight stars.

Some in America worried about the health of a society based on consumption – just as they did in Berlin, Paris or Vienna. In *Philip Dru*, Colonel House wrote of 'unhappiness for all and disaster for many', which would follow a society of competitive consumerism. Woodrow Wilson had been elected while criticising American society's growing materialism. Italian historian Guglielmo Ferrero saw mass consumption and mass production as America's challenge to civilisation: the victory of quantity over quality.[28] But ultimately any fears about consumerism were outweighed by the market imperatives of American business. The logic of Henry Ford was the logic of the twentieth-century economy.

As a rash of consumer choice spread across America, it spread across an increasingly Americanised world. As early as 1901 W. T. Stead quoted an English account of the new world being built by American business in Europe:

> The average man rises in the morning from his New England sheets, he shaves with 'Williams' soap and a Yankee safety razor, pulls on his Boston boots over his socks from North Carolina, fastens his Connecticut braces, slips his Waltham or Waterbury watch in his pocket and sits down to breakfast. There he congratulates his wife on the way her Illinois straight-front corset sets off her Massachusetts blouse, and he tackles his breakfast, where he eats bread made from prairie flour . . . tinned oysters from Baltimore, and a little Kansas city bacon.[29]

In the 1901 version of this account of global Americanisation, the Londoner proceeds to go to work by tramway, and by American electric railway. Perhaps, twelve years later, he would venture out by car, and probably a Model T.

Woodrow Wilson, who had criticised the automobile in 1906, was won over to it by 1913, enjoying his regular pleasure drives around Washington as President. He too came to espouse the creed of ever-expanding American business as the handmaiden of American power. What sweet music to the ears of Henry Ford when, in his hometown of Detroit, President Wilson addressed 3,000 managers at the first World Salesmanship Congress in 1916: 'Go out and sell goods that will make the world more comfortable and more happy, and convert them to the principles of America'.[30]

LOS ANGELES

Boom!

Henry Ford's success with the Model T Ford depended on one other crucial factor: a steady supply of gasoline. Internationally, there were concerns about how long petroleum supplies could match skyrocketing demand. In London, while armchair strategists fretted about the decision to begin the Royal Navy's move from coal to oil-fired ships, rising petrol prices led cab drivers to strike. *The Economist* reported that 'the associated automobile clubs of the world have decided to offer a prize of £20,000 to anyone who will produce a suitable substitute for petrol'.[1] The British government began an era of oil diplomacy, ultimately leading it to deepen its stake in the Middle East, particularly in Persia.

In the United States, and especially in California, the position was somewhat different. Around 1913, America produced two-thirds of the world's petroleum; of that, California was responsible for four barrels out of every ten. The United States Geological Survey reported that:

> the United States being omitted, California produced more oil than any other nation; and if Russia and the United States are omitted California far surpassed the production of all the rest of the world, including Mexico, India, Rumania, Galicia, Japan and South America.[2]

This was a remarkable development for such a young industry, born in far-off Pennsylvania in the 1850s, when the US state of California was barely a decade old. The first commercial well sunk in Los Angeles dated only from 1893 when Edward L. Doheny, a Wisconsin-born oil man who had prospected in Kansas, South Dakota, Arizona and New Mexico, had struck oil at 150 feet on the corner of Patton and State streets, so close to the centre of town that the hard-up

Oil derricks outside Los Angeles. The first man to strike oil in the area,
Edward Doheny, rode out to the patch twenty years previously in a streetcar. By
1913 California alone produced more crude oil than any country in the world
(bar the United States).

Doheny rode a streetcar out there the first time he visited the patch.

But by 1913 Doheny was one of America's richest men, and Los
Angeles was established as the capital of the oil industry of southern
California, the nation's largest. Doheny's oil interests now stretched
across the border into Mexico, and his fortune was prodigious. From
rooms in a cheap hotel twenty years previously, he now lived in a
palace, decorated with 10,000 orchids. In 1913, his wife Estelle,
inspired by a long trip to Europe, commissioned a marble and glass
ballroom that became known as the Pompeian Room, designed by
Louis Comfort Tiffany.[3] Doheny bought more estates, gave money
to the Catholic Church, and supported Irish causes with his munif-
icence. Estelle Doheny's soirees were compared to those of the White
House. The area around Los Angeles, meanwhile, was now dotted
with hundreds of oil rigs, some dipping their feet into the Pacific
Ocean. Floating on oil, California boasted more cars per head
of population than anywhere else, more even than Detroit itself.
But then California boasted more of everything: more telephones,
more tramlines, more sunlight, more opportunities, more bright
tomorrows.

Like gold and cheap farmland before it, and the movies after, oil
became the symbol of California's promise of easy riches. 'It is true
that there are some persons in California who are making oil a
gambling device', wrote the self-styled historian of the state's oil

industry Lionel V. Redpath in 1900. 'There is something about the oil business', he continued, 'which prompts men to dream dreams at the expense of the most common of common sense'.[4] But where could one dream dreams if not California? Men such as Doheny had become rich, why not others? In the old new world of America, as one writer put it, Los Angeles was the 'old new land of promise'.[5]

For visitors, the area around Los Angeles was a picture of natural wealth converted into individual prosperity. 'I have been fortunate enough to live in France', wrote Paul-Henri d'Estournelles de Constant, 'I know England, the shaded vales of Oxford or Cambridge, have greeted the stirring of spring in our Algerian oases, I thought myself blasé':

> Yet I note that the Americans have covered the most beautiful valleys of California with lawns, flowers and fruit and have created . . . veritable outposts of paradise on earth . . . Each villa in Pasadena sits on its own carpet of green; each cottage, different from its neighbour, nestles under leafy bowers and the flowering of roses and climbing geraniums . . . In these gardens, created by Americans, reigns the inspiring idea of America.[6]

Californian wines, Constant noted, were 'not less good than ours, but more full bodied'. He suggested setting up a school of French cooking as a complement to Californian culture. He recounted the story of a land surveyor who had been astute enough to accept payment for a job in land. Now that oil had been struck he had a thousand dollars a day to his name.

With stories such as this, the idea of California as a land of opportunity was constantly embellished and enriched, its reputation reaching across the country and enticing migrants from cold Detroit, crowded New York – or even from across the Pacific. In most respects, Los Angeles was not particularly cosmopolitan. Although three-quarters of American-born Angelenos were from outside California, only a fifth of the city's overall population was born outside the United States – a far smaller share than in New York or Detroit. Of these, most came from England and Germany rather than from Italy or Russia, let alone Asia. The Mexican era of California's history, meanwhile, survived as much in architecture and place names as in people.

While enticing domestic migrants, Californians nonetheless had long feared foreign immigration, particularly from Asia, and had periodically sought to limit it. While the Chinese preferred San Francisco, Japanese migrants preferred the area around Los Angeles. The numbers involved were small – 8,000 Japanese in the whole of LA county by 1910 – but fear and prejudice were amplified by local politics, and a push-button issue was constructed out of little more than worked-up imaginings of the 'Yellow Peril'. 'My neighbor is a Jap', one farmer told a journalist:

He has an eighty acre place next to mine and he is a smart fellow. He has a white woman living in his house and upon that white woman's knee is a baby. Now what is that baby? It isn't white. It isn't Japanese. I'll tell you what it is. It is the beginning of a problem – the biggest race problem the world has ever known.[7]

In 1913 the California legislature in Sacramento prepared to pass legislation which would disbar Japanese farmers from owning land in the state. Washington advised California against it, on the basis that it would offend Asian sensibilities and might, as Japanese diplomats insisted, run counter to the United States' treaty commitments. The *Los Angeles Times* appealed to the legislators' common sense, leaving 'the Japanese in our midst to cultivate their vegetable gardens, and clean clothes, and make and sell kimonos without molestation'.[8] Secretary of State William Jennings Bryan was dispatched on a five-day trek to Sacramento to try and negotiate a form of words which would allow all sides to claim a measure of victory. But the law Bryan lobbied against was passed in spite of him. Wilson tried to play the whole thing down in public. In private, the President and his Cabinet received the US Navy's startling assessment of the possibility of war with Japan and its outcome. 'It is conceivable', read Secretary of the Navy Josephus Daniels, 'that Japan may conclude – *may have already concluded* – that, if she should go to war with the United States, she could, by enduring a period of privation and distress lasting about two years, acquire possession of both the Philippine Islands and the Hawaiian Islands'.[9]

Paradise was untroubled by the prospect. As Los Angeles boomed, land values soared and the city stretched along the coast, building out rather than up, the very opposite of New York. Confidence filled the air. The Los Angeles and Pacific Electric railways 'extended into the open country, ahead of, and not behind the population', explained the company's owners, justifying their investments.[10] An advertisement in the *Los Angeles Times* promised returns of 200 or 300 per cent to those investing in The Palisades, a coastal development by Santa Monica, soon to be connected to the Pacific Electric and enjoying 'four beautiful macadam boulevards' to the city.[11] While the much more established San Francisco repaired itself after the 1906 earthquake and prepared for the 1915 Panama Pacific International Exposition, the population centre of California moved south. It was commonly anticipated that Los Angeles, whose population had increased from 1,500 in the 1840s to nearly 500,000 by 1913 would pass the million mark in 1920. Some felt this would happen even sooner. One journalist predicted that the population in 1920 would stand very precisely at 1,193,086.[12] A *Times* editorialist imagined Los Angeles in 1938 as 'the Wonder City of Los Angeles', 'the Mecca of art, culture and learning', 'the Athens of the modern world'. Another, more humorously, pictured an eighteen-storey Los Angeles department store, staffed by the deposed monarchs of the globe.[13]

But though California was floating on oil, Los Angeles was running short of a still more important commodity: water. The city's response, typically grandiose, was the Owens River aqueduct to bring water 225 miles, the same distance as between Washington and New York, from the verdant countryside to the thirsty city. 'The impossible', rhapsodised the *Times*, 'was again met and driven by the invincible city of Los Angeles':

> . . . a great river has been turned from its course – a course it followed since the hand of God raised the mountains and laid the oceans in their place on the morn of creation – and brought down to serve the people of Los Angeles who are here today, and the millions more who are to come tomorrow, tomorrow, and tomorrow.[14]

On 5 November, the Catalina Island band played 'I Love You, California', the Stars and Stripes were unfurled, and Owens River water gushed towards the thirsty city.[15] Thirty thousand looked on. Later, a celebratory dinner was held at the Hotel Alexandria, Los Angeles' finest.

To the south, another opening, that of the Panama Canal, was

Water for the thirsty city of Los Angeles, the city of 'tomorrow, tomorrow and tomorrow'.

expected to bring new trade routes to Los Angeles, and new travellers from Europe. In preparation, the city's deep-water port was expanded. By early May 1913, five shipping companies had announced around-the-world routes that would stop in Los Angeles, prompting a local shipping agent to proclaim: 'If no others come, these five concerns assure this harbor of the rosiest of futures, a place on the premier trade lane, that around the world'. 'The tri-color of France, the Union Jack of old England, the sun-rayed flag of the Mikado's kingdom will flaunt jauntily from the taffrail of ships entering this harbor', continued the *Los Angeles Times*. The Chamber of Commerce, in addition to publishing *Los Angeles Today*, a book extolling the natural wealth, climate and prosperity of the city, proposed a Spanish pamphlet to advertise California's products to the Latin American market. 'It is to be the opening wedge', a journalist wrote, 'by which it is hoped to not only foster closer relations with our neighbors to the south, but also trade relations, that will put money in our purses'.[16]

For those who had come to the city with grand dreams only to find that sunshine and hope did not put bread on the table, all this reeked of industrial-scale boosterism. In October 1913 the *Los Angeles Record* asked Angelenos their thoughts on the city's problems. The readers' responses were instructive. 'Of course it is to the advantage of "big business" to advertise the country and circulate ads stating that the population in 1913 is so and so, and in 1915 will be so and so', one wrote in, 'but it is very noticeable that they do not place under those same ads statistics showing the large percentage of that population who are eagerly seeking work to keep bodies and souls together'. 'Long hours and small wages', diagnosed another reader:

> . . . too much grafting; the mistake of not getting municipal owner-ship, the main object – to make a smooth road for the RICH and a rocky one for the POOR, too much of the 'Los Angeles spirit' – ('how much money has he got and how can I get it away from him?') . . . IF you question the EMPLOYERS regarding the continual changing in their staff they will tell you that Los Angeles has a 'floating population', apparently failing to realize that the population would be permanent if living wages were paid.[17]

After a few weeks of such letters the *Record* summed up its findings across the front page on 5 November 1913: 'What's the Matter with Los Angeles? It is G-R-double E-D, GREED!' Perhaps the journalists of the *Record* were amongst those who had invested in the Los Angeles Investment Company, a debt-financed real estate company that worked hand in hand with the Chamber of Commerce to build mile after mile of cheap bungalow housing in order to entice new low-paid workers to Los Angeles. In a cycle all too familiar for California, the boom produced the bubble, and the bubble, eventually, burst. Over the course of a few weeks at the end of 1913 the Los Angeles Investment Company share price collapsed from $4.50 to just 23¢.[18]

Rags to riches, riches to rags, whether from land purchases or from oil or from orange groves, Los Angeles was already a city which conjured up popular dreams of novelty, success and prosperity in the minds of visitors, out-of-towners and prospective migrants. It

had not yet claimed full ownership over the medium which so
effectively packaged these dreams: the movies. Los Angeles was
not yet Hollywood. In 1913, it was only just embarking along the
road to becoming the metropolis of mass entertainment, just as
Detroit, a little further ahead, was becoming the metropolis of the
automobile.

Over the previous fifteen years film had exploded across the
United States. By 1910 there were 10,000 cheap cinemas in the
country. Twenty-six million Americans – one-fifth of the country's
population – went to one of these, known as a nickelodeon, each
week.[19] (As Henry Ford might have observed, a nickel might not
be much, but twenty-six million nickels is a great many.) The country,
and particularly its working class and immigrant communities, was
in the midst of a moving picture craze. 'You wonder', wrote author
Olivia Howard Dunbar, 'how it can be possible, in an alleged busy
world, to secure this magnificent total of leisure – to assemble daily,
and for long, blank periods, so many people who have nothing to
do and who are obviously not worrying about it'.[20] Three-quarters
of movie-goers were men.

Most nickelodeons showed short silent films, one after another,
irrespective of continuity or subject, with the expectation that spectators would arrive and leave at different times. Many films were
news items. For those used to the stage there was something two-
dimensional about this form of entertainment, bereft of narrative
structure, and without the support of the spoken word:

> . . . companies of shadow-soldiers are assembled and drilled; parades
> of a dozen kinds trail their blurred length across the curtain; foreign
> cities flash out glimpses of their characteristic scenes; ships are
> launched, cornerstones are laid, medals are presented, and laboratory
> experiments demonstrating some feature of popular science are pains-
> takingly performed.

Storylines, if there were any, tended to be intellectually undemanding.
'An altercation, a practical joke' in one film; 'a chase of anything by
anybody' in another. As each individual film was short – as little as
one or two reels – there was no time for character development.
Roles had to be easily grasped by the audience, and plots straightforward:

. . . disputes between an impossible mistress and an unnatural servant in which the maid tumultuously triumphs; or farcical interruptions of the love-making of an ill-suited couple; or rowdy street scenes in which people tumble over each other and somebody gets beaten for an offense he didn't commit, while the culprit leers from a neighboring corner.

'Reasonably good eyesight', Dunbar concluded, was the only requisite for the movie-goer.

In 1913, the centre of the national entertainment industry was still New York, driven by the business model of smash-hit theatre productions which could then be replicated nationally. But unlike theatre, film could be made in places far distant from key markets. And, as a place to make movies, California had distinct advantages. Consistent weather and sunlight increased the number of hours and days available to film – though the same applied to Cuba, Texas or Florida, and as much to San Francisco, a more established and only slightly smaller city, as to Los Angeles. Diverse landscapes – desert, forests, mountains – meant different kinds of film could be shot relatively nearby. An army of cheap labour, for as little as $1 a day, provided all the extras one could wish for.[21] Finally, and perhaps crucially, Los Angeles was distant from the litigious Motion Picture Patents Company – the trust which controlled patents associated with movie-making – and it was only a hundred miles to Mexico, which provided a convenient bolt-hole if representatives of the trust got too close. Distance from the establishment meant more innovation, and as the patents of the trust eroded and the public's tastes evolved towards longer films with stronger storylines, the California independents started to steal a march on their eastern rivals.

Still, at this time the movies were a peripheral economic activity, not a core business for Los Angeles. When the *Los Angeles Times* imagined in 1913 how the city would look and feel in 1938 – by which time film and Hollywood would be synonymous – the movies did not crop up once. Though the Chamber of Commerce was supportive of filming taking place in Los Angeles, a booklet produced touting the city's economic prospects in 1913 did not mention it. In September the *Times* produced a seven-part guide to 'Writing a Movie Play', but there was nothing to suggest that the city was crawling with budding screenwriters. Only at the very end of 1913 did filming begin on Hollywood's first feature-length movie – *The Squaw Man* – just as Charlie Chaplin was signing his first contract with Keystone Pictures in Los Angeles.

For an industry that prided itself on its modernity, and for a state that prided itself on its future, it was perhaps ironic that the first films shot entirely in Hollywood – *In Old California* and *Ramona*, both from 1910 – were romanticisations of California's recent past, set in the years shortly after America's victory over the Mexicans in the war of 1848 and the incorporation of California into the United States in 1850. (Historical dramatisations became something of a speciality for D. W. Griffith, who later directed *The Birth of a Nation*.) *Ramona*, starring Mary Pickford in the title role, was only seventeen minutes long. But its story, lightly adapted, was familiar. The book *Ramona*, written by easterner Helen Hunt Jackson and published in 1884, had intoxicated a generation of readers with its description of the beauties of the land and its dramatisation of Mexican life in the young state of California.

Part love story, part tragedy, the novel opens at sheep-shearing time on a *rancho* somewhere in southern California, with Spanish Señora Moreno 'amiable and indolent, like her race' struggling to maintain her ranch in the face of the encroachments and requirements of American rule:

> It was a picturesque life, with more of sentiment and gaiety in it, more also that was truly dramatic, more romance, than will ever be seen again on those sunny shores. The aroma of it all lingers there still; industries and inventions have not yet slain it; it will last out its century – in fact, it can never be quite lost, so long as there is standing one such house as the Señora Moreno's.[22]

Brought to the *rancho* by the Señora's sister is Ramona: beautiful, kind, good. She falls in love with Alessandro, a Mexican Indian farm worker. At the same time Ramona is admired by Moreno's handsome son, Felipe. When he puts on his father's ceremonial clothes, Felipe appears the spitting image of his father, General Moreno. 'Wear them', Señora Moreno tells her son, 'and let the American hounds see what a Mexican officer and gentleman looked like before they had set their base usurping feet on our necks!' The

Señora tries and fails to stop Ramona's love for Alessandro, both when she appeals to Ramona's faith and her supposed Spanish heritage – placing her far above the status of an Indian – and when she reveals Ramona's true parentage, born of a Scotsman and a Californian Indian. Finally imprisoned by her mistress, Ramona manages to escape with Alessandro, fleeing to an Indian village. But life is hard. They lose their first child; Alessandro loses his mind. Ultimately, he is shot dead by an American who falsely thinks him a horse thief. In the film version, Felipe turns up as Ramona is mourning her husband's death and the film ends. In the novel, Felipe and Ramona return to the rancho, Señora Moreno now passed away. But they are forced to leave. They travel to Mexico City and finally they marry in its cathedral.

However sympathetically Ramona and Alessandro were portrayed, and however unsympathetic the Americans were in the book, and however much *Ramona* was enjoyed as entertainment, there was no desire on the part of white Angelenos to return to the life of the *ranchos*. This was the past from which, in the Anglo-Saxon vision of the city, Los Angeles had escaped: from the nineteenth-century Catholic obscurantism of the pueblo to the pleasures and riches of a twentieth-century metropolis. Yet the very recentness of this past – within the living memory of the state's Spanish-speaking elders – underscored Los Angeles' progress, and emphasised its headlong trajectory into the future.

Meanwhile, it provided both romance and tourist revenues. Southern California had, after all, its fair share of Spanish names, from its own abbreviation of Nuestra Señora la Reina de los Angeles, the original Spanish settlement founded in 1781, to Santa Monica, or the state's *presidios*. California's Catholic missions, once active with monks and priests attempting to spread the word, in Spanish, amongst the indigenous population, had now fallen silent except for the snap of tourists' photographic shutters. The picturesque Spanish-Mexican culture was partially revived, but as a quaint memory rather than a political project. In the 1890s the Fiesta de las Flores became an annual, week-long celebration – though later Americanised in preparation for a visit by US President McKinley in 1901.[23] *Ramona* had already fostered an active tourist trade: visitors seeking out where Ramona was married and where she lived, happily mixing real places with Jackson's fictional creations.[24] El Camino Real, the coastal road running from one Mexican-era mission to another, was sold as a tourist destination.

Where the monks had left, the mission ruins of the California of just sixty years ago were treated by many as a civilisation as ancient as the Aztecs or the Incas: a Mexican past left behind by history, surpassed by modernity. Yet that past was not quite effaced from the architectural record or erased from Californian culture. Nor, as Californians looked anxiously south into Mexico itself, was it entirely irrelevant to the present.

MEXICO CITY
Monroe's Bequest

The tourist trail of the El Camino Real went as far as San Diego. But for the adventurous it was possible to drive further south – deeper into California's past, and further into Mexico's tumultuous present. This was the oldest part of the Old New World. It was where the contradictions of American power and principle reached their climax in 1913.

Where exactly America ended and where Mexico began was hard to say. In principle, the boundary between the two countries was defined by a line on a map: gently east from California, then skirting the southern limits of Arizona and New Mexico, fully-fledged states for less than a year, and then following the twists and turns of the Rio Grande down to the Gulf of Mexico. But lines on maps do not always correspond to the realities on the ground. How different, really, was San Antonio, Texas, from Monterrey, Mexico?

The line on the map was, in any case, perhaps temporary. In his novel *Philip Dru*, Woodrow Wilson's Texan adviser Colonel House had fantasised about a future where Mexico was incorporated into the United States. This did not seem so far-fetched. To many Americans, it would be the natural continuation of manifest destiny which had gathered Texas and California into the American fold, and which had made America responsible for the fates of the former Spanish colonies of Cuba and the Philippines. But even if the line would not be redrawn, would it not fade away over time as Mexico and America were welded together in the common fires of economic development? If Mexico was California's past, was California not Mexico's future? Even in 1913, as Mexico was falling apart in the fires of civil conflict, Wilson's personal representative, holed up in Veracruz because the capital was too dangerous, contemplated that American civilisation was percolating south over the border, unstoppably:

> . . . we must not overlook the contact of the Mexican peon with our civilization along the National boundary, in our schools, and along the lines of the National railways for upwards a quarter century. Many have tasted the sweets of personal independence and security and of a higher plane of living . . . They are breathing the atmosphere of the twentieth century in rarefied form. A middle class is in the making. They have become democrats by contact with democracy and force of circumstance . . . and in the degree that the Mexican of the North becomes a democrat his hatred grows against the social and economic conditions of the South and against the old 16th century regime . . .[1]

In the first years of the twentieth century, American companies were already the largest investors in Mexico, well ahead of the Mexicans themselves (and ahead of the British, French or Germans). American mines had American foremen, American engineers, American accountants and American doctors. Edward L. Doheny, the man who had first struck oil in Los Angeles, was also the first to produce oil in Mexico, at El Ebano, near Tampico on the Gulf of Mexico. His Mexican Petroleum Company, controlling 600,000 acres of Mexican land, was incorporated in Los Angeles.[2] Although Mexico's foreign-built railway system had now come under Mexican control its official language was still English, and its principal railway lines still ran north. A strike of workers at the American-owned Cananea Copper Company in 1906 was put down with the help of Arizona rangers from across the border in Bisbee, though the local Mexican governor softened the blow to national pride by insisting the Americans be temporarily sworn in as soldiers of the Mexican border state of Sonora.

At the same time, Mexican political leaders often found refuge on the north side of the Rio Grande when things were not going well for them on the south side. From the revolution of 1911 onwards, Mexican oppositionists frequently launched their campaigns against whatever government was in charge in Mexico City from American soil. In February 1911 the teetotal spiritualist landowner Francisco Madero entered Mexico with 130 men, crossing at the border post at El Paso on his way to overthrow Porfirio Díaz, Mexico's President since 1876. In March 1913, Francisco 'Pancho' Villa, the peanut-brittle-eating revolutionary, crossed the same border to wage war against Madero's successor, General Victoriano Huerta. 'Poor Mexico', Díaz was said to have once remarked, 'so far from God, and so close to the United States'.[3]

Mexico's capital city bore its ancestry proudly. The Zócalo, the city's huge central plaza and stage for the most dramatic episodes of the nation's history, lay on the same site as the main square of the Aztec city of Tenochtitlan. The first stone of the city's ornate Catholic cathedral – in which Felipe and Ramona are married in Helen Hunt Jackson's novel – was laid by Spanish missionaries fifty years before the *Mayflower* made landfall in North America at Plymouth, Massachusetts. In the national museum one could compare the gilded state coach of Mexico's last Emperor, the Vienna-born Maximilian, with the 'severely simple, well-worn, eminently republican vehicle of Benito Juárez', the restorer of the republic in 1867.[4] In the Academy of San Carlos one could contemplate, besides the Rubens and the Titians, Felix Parra's painting of Bartolomé de las Casas, the sixteenth-century bishop credited with protecting the Indians against the depredations of the Spanish conquerors. On a hill to the west of the city itself lay Chapultepec castle, started the year before the American Declaration of Independence – and overrun by American troops in 1847. Now the castle served as a military school and the residence of the President of Mexico: Porfirio Díaz before the revolution, and Francisco Madero after it. On Sundays, the good and great of Mexico City would take their carriages up to the park around Chapultepec – to be seen and, at dusk, to admire the view back towards their city on the plain below.

The best time to see the Zócalo, assured Charles Macomb Flandrau, the Minnesota-born essayist, was between five and six in the morning:

Beyond a few laborers straggling to work, and the men who are making the toilet of the Alameda with large, green bushes attached to the end of sticks, the city appeared to be blandly slumbering, and just as the face of someone we know will, while asleep, surprise us by a rare and unsuspected expression, the great, unfinished, unsympathetic capital smiled, wisely and a trifle wearily, in its dreams. It is at this hour, before the mongrel population has begun to swarm, that one should walk through the Alameda, in the first freshness of wet roses and lilies, the gardenias and pansies and heliotrope in the flower market, and, undisturbed among the trees in front of the majestic cathedral, listen to the echoed sob of history.

But the city was changing, too. A new theatre was under construction in the Alameda park, with elaborate glass stage curtains designed by Louis Comfort Tiffany of New York – the same man commissioned to design Estelle Doheny's ballroom in Los Angeles. In the very centre of town, a nest of streets built in the old Spanish and Mexican styles was slowly being transformed with more modern buildings. The effect, Flandrau remarked, was that of a 'small city in a large town'. The architecture was suggestive of Europe, but 'the multitude of American signs, of American products, and American residents, by which one is on all sides confronted, makes it impossible to decide where'.

Before the revolution of 1911 a traveller from the north might almost have felt at home, or at least not very far abroad in Mexico City, reading the English-language, American-owned *Mexican*

Mexico City, emerging market capital, early twentieth century.

Herald while sipping morning coffee in a downtown café. He or she would be likely to quickly recognise compatriots, whether visitors or residents:

> Though it may have been two or three weeks since you landed in Vera Cruz, probably the tall American with the long nose or some equally remembered fellow-passenger will be sitting within reach of a nod; and there will also be some of last nights 'arrivals' who will tell you, if you ask, that they were just four days coming from Buffalo or three from St. Louis, with Pullman and dinner car service all the way.[5]

Cosseted in the centre of Mexico City it was easy to misjudge the potential for revolution in the first years of the twentieth century. Sporadic strikes and local unrest did not challenge the central assumptions of President Porfirio Díaz, his technocratic supporters – collectively, the *científicos* – or his international backers. For them, the last thirty-odd years, known as the *porfiriato*, had been ones of the steady march of progress: rationalisation, industrialisation, education. International investment, the construction of the railways and now oilfields were all symbols of Mexico's advance towards modernity. The process was incomplete, but the course had been set. And as Porfirio Díaz celebrated his eightieth birthday at Chapultepec castle in September 1910 the regime hardly seemed to be on its last legs. At the celebrations of the centenary of Mexico's independence from Spain, falling in the same month as Díaz's birthday, some 100,000 Mexicans came to the Zócalo, which was lit up in green, white and red lights.[6] '*1810: Libertad*', read a neon sign at the base of one of the cathedral towers; '*1910: Progreso*', read the other.

Conscious of the projection of Mexico's international image, the Díaz regime invited foreign journalists to cover the celebrations, ordered the indigenous locals of Mexico City to swap sandals for shoes so as not to show up the proximity of poverty to wealth around the Zócalo and showered official international delegations with generosity. This paid off. The leader of the American delegation, Special Ambassador Curtis Guild, Jr, former Governor of Massachusetts, called Díaz 'the greatest living American'.[7]

As it turned out, this was not the crowning glory of the regime but its swansong. Some were already sceptical. John Kenneth Turner, an American investigative journalist who had first come across Mexican revolutionaries in a Los Angeles jail, wrote a searing indictment of the *porfiriato* for an American audience in 1910. He disabused his American readers of characterisations of Mexico as 'Our Sister Republic', a place they mistakenly believed to be 'much like our own, inhabited by people a little different in temperament, a little poorer, and a little less advanced, but still enjoying the protection of republican laws'.[8] He challenged the vision of the country as seen 'through a car window' or through speculation in Mexican mining stocks. He described a country poor, corrupt and unfree. In the Yucatan he uncovered debt slavery and, worse, Americans complicit in it. 'After freeing his black slaves', Turner wrote, 'Uncle Sam has gone to slave-driving in a foreign country'. Above all, he found assumptions of the unassailability of Díaz's rule to be baseless:

> I found that the people do not idolize their president, that the tide of opposition, dammed and held back as it has been by army and secret police, is rising to a height where it must shortly overflow that dam. Mexicans of all classes and affiliations agree that their country is on the verge of a revolution in favor of democracy; if not a revolution in the time of Díaz, for Díaz is old and is expected soon to pass, then a revolution after Díaz.

What no one predicted fully was that, less than a year after the crowds had gathered in the Zócalo to celebrate a hundred years of Mexican independence, Díaz would be in exile in Paris, Francisco Madero would be president, and Mexico would be launched into the first phase of a drawn-out revolution.

There was not, in reality, one Mexican revolution.[9] Once fully unleashed by Díaz's overthrow there were rather waves of unrest, sometimes mobilised by one or another political figure or military commander – Francisco Madero, Francisco 'Pancho' Villa, Emiliano Zapata, Pascual Orozco, Victoriano Huerta, Venustiano Carranza – sometimes coming under their control, and sometimes engulfing them. Political instability flowed, in part, from economic volatility: fluctuations in international investment, in prices or in the amount of rain falling on different parts of the country. But it also rested on the pent-up anger of the Díaz years. Anger at the *hacienda* system of farming, which reduced some Mexicans to the level of slaves while providing enormous wealth for absentee *hacendado* landlords living in Mexico City or Paris, without a care for Mexico's broader modernisation, often to the frustration of Díaz's *científicos*. Anger at the arbitrary justice meted out by representatives of the state – often the stooges of local power-brokers – symbolised by the *ley de fuga* allowing government authorities to kill those attempting to escape the law, with the authorities themselves as sole witnesses and judges of any such attempt. Once unleashed, revolt became its own end.

In such a large and fragmented nation as the United Mexican States, the official name of the country, there were bound to be regional variations, key to the ebb and flow of the revolution. As in Helen Hunt Jackson's description of Mexican California in *Ramona*, in Mexico proper there were distinctions between Mexicans of Spanish descent and those of Indian descent, with racial prejudices overlaying economic rivalries. The *porfiriato* had tried – and failed – to crush a long-standing rebellion of the Yaqui Indians of the Pacific coast by forcibly transporting them to the Yucatan peninsula on the other side of the country. And, as anywhere else, political instability provided an opportunity for local scores to be settled, for personal grievances to be aired, for heroes to be acclaimed and discarded, giving full rein to the fickle fortunes of war. Charles Macomb Flandrau summed up all of Mexico with the response he was given to a simple question about the likelihood of rain: '*No hay reglas fijas, señor*' – 'there are no fixed rules'.[10]

If anything united the vast majority of Mexicans it was distrust of the Americans – the 'Gringo', the *yanqui*. Less than two months after the celebrations of Mexico's independence in the Zócalo, the lynching of a young Mexican in Texas led to an attack on American interests in Mexico City, including the *Mexican Herald*.[11] After the revolution, the spectre of American invasion would consistently be raised as a rallying cry for political support for whoever was in control in Mexico City.

In May 1911, Francisco Madero had forced out Díaz, the *porfiriato* ending with protests on the street, the massacre of 200 protesters on the Zócalo and, in the wake of that disaster, a crumbling of the Díaz leadership. The old man was bundled on a slow train to Veracruz and a boat to France. But Madero – 'a little man, of unimpressive presence and manner, highly nervous, overwhelmed by his troubles' – had been elevated to the presidency on the shoulders of an uprising which he did not control.[12] He won as a result of Díaz's errors – belief in his own propaganda – as much as his own qualities. After Díaz had been dispatched to Paris – where Edward Doheny took tea with him the following year – Madero won an election virtually unopposed in October. At which point the new President, rather than launching himself into land reform, published a *Spiritualist Manual* based on the Sanskrit epic the *Mahabharata*, an epic of ancient India, under an assumed name.[13] Madero had neither the steel to suppress dissent, nor the vision to push through reform. Fatally, as it turned out, he did not know who to trust.

Madero's presidency itself unravelled within little more than a year. He could not put down an uprising by Emiliano Zapata in Morelos province, in the centre of Mexico. His inaction on reform led erstwhile supporter Pascual Orozco to start a fresh revolt in Chihuahua, in the north. The political capital of victory was rapidly squandered. Even as the country became more militarised and the army more powerful, central government authority could not be re-established. Madero, it turned out, was not Mexico's saviour from itself.

At the end of 1912 Porfirio Díaz's nephew, Félix Díaz, rebelled. In itself, the rebellion was easily contained and rapidly defeated. Díaz was imprisoned, along with Bernardo Reyes, a former minister and general. But the intervention of the *porfiriato* supreme court saved the younger Díaz's life, and right-wing elements conspired to free both him and Reyes from custody. On 9 February 1913 the plan was put into action. Porfirio Díaz's former army chief, General Manuel Mondragón, marched to the barracks where Reyes and Díaz were held. When the commanding general refused to hand over the two men to Mondragón, he was shot dead. Reyes was taken to the Zócalo, where he confidently expected to be proclaimed the new President. But troops still loyal to Madero had been warned. Reyes and 400 others were killed in the Zócalo in a hail of gunfire. So began the *decena trágica* – the tragic ten days.

Government forces and those of Díaz now settled into a stalemate in the centre of Mexico City. Downtown became a battlefield, littered with corpses. 'Capitalists have sunk much money into the country's undoubted resources', wrote a journalist from the British magazine *The Economist*, 'and it is perhaps unlikely that a state of anarchy will continue long . . . But at the present moment it is hard to see where the restoring hand of authority will come from'.[14] In fact, the restoring hand of authority was nearer than suspected. On the day the coup began, rushing into the city to restore his authority, Madero ran into General Victoriano Huerta, minutes after an assassination attempt. Knowing Madero's military commander was wounded, Huerta offered his own services to the President. Madero, fatefully, accepted. According to a later account submitted to Woodrow Wilson, the Mexican President then made a speech to the crowd with Huerta at his side.

Huerta, under the pretence of faithfully serving Madero, played the next few days with consummate Machiavellian skill, assisted by the American Ambassador, Henry Lane Wilson. The battle between government forces commanded by Huerta and rebel forces commanded by Díaz seemed strangely choreographed. This was because it was. With Wilson's encouragement, the two bided their time. Huerta sent units loyal to Madero into battle to be shot; Díaz's troops made no serious attempt to dislodge him. Meanwhile, Ambassador Wilson encouraged Mexico City's elite in the belief that the United States would imminently restore order through military invasion. To forestall such a shameful eventuality, Mexican senators called for the President's resignation. Huerta, having previously sworn his loyalty to Madero, now sent his men to the National Palace to arrest him.

The orgy of betrayals continued. Huerta invited the President's brother, Gustavo Madero, to dine with him at Gambrinus, a downtown restaurant. When Madero turned up he was arrested and taken to jail, where he was blinded and shot dead. Huerta then surprised Díaz by announcing that he wanted to be President himself, rather than turning over the presidency to Porfirio's nephew. Faced with Ambassador Wilson's support for the move, Díaz had no choice, later accepting a diplomatic appointment from Huerta. Meanwhile, the minister of foreign affairs, Pedro Lascuráin, persuaded Madero – unaware of what had happened to his brother – to resign the presidency. The office then skipped to Lascuráin, who held it for less than an hour before turning it over to Huerta, thus maintaining the fiction of constitutional due process. *'VIVA DÍAZ! VIVA*

HUERTA!' topped the *Mexican Herald* the next day: 'After a year
of anarchy, a military dictator looks good to Mexico'.[15]

Finally, though safe passage abroad had been supposedly guaranteed by Huerta to Madero and his Vice-President Pino Suarez, the
two were murdered on 21 February 1913. The false story was circulated
that they had been killed in a shoot-up when an attempt had been
made to rescue them. The *ley de fuga* lived on. According to a later
confidential dispatch to US President Wilson, the place where
Madero and Suarez were shot became a shrine: 'passers by piled
stones in a little mound over the two blood-soaked spots of ground
and stuck lighted candles on top'.[16]

Towards the end of 1913 President Woodrow Wilson went to
Congress to give an account of his first year, and to outline his
observations on the state of the union. It was a mostly upbeat affair,
and mostly concerned with domestic affairs. 'There is but one cloud
upon our horizon', Wilson said. 'That has shown itself to the south
of us', he continued, 'and hangs over Mexico'.

For Wilson, the problem of Mexico had started on the day of his
inauguration, when he received a telegram from Huerta: 'In the name
of the people and government of Mexico, and in my own, I have the
honour to offer to your Excellency my most cordial congratulations
on your elevation to the first position in your great Republic'. It was
not easy to know how to respond. President Wilson was not ready
to recognise Huerta's coup through a formal diplomatic exchange.
A neutral response was prepared, to be sent a few days later, addressed
non-committally to General V. Huerta, Mexico City, Mexico: 'I
thank you for your cordial congratulations'.[17]

The dilemmas of how to deal with an unstable military-led regime
on the doorstep of a democracy which pronounced itself a beacon
of liberty to the world – and which increasingly wore the mantle
of a great power – were inescapable. Was it better to extend diplomatic recognition to an unattractive regime and thereby hope to
achieve a measure of political stability – or to refuse to recognise
the regime on principle, thus emboldening its opponents and running
the risk of losing both American investors' money and the lives of
American residents in the widening civil war which might follow?

Victoriano Huerta (seated left), brutal military strongman. 'After a year of anarchy, a military dictator looks good to Mexico', wrote the editors of the American-owned *Mexican Herald*. But the anarchy did not end with Huerta's coup.

Was it preferable to intervene militarily to protect American interests and bring stability and freedom to the Mexican people – or rather to maintain the purity of neutrality and avoid a potential quagmire, but run the risk of appearing weak, and leave the outcome in Mexico to be determined by forces beyond one's control?

In April 1913 Colonel House confided that he thought military intervention would require 50,000 men, but that there might be guerrilla warfare after the initial pacification. (A subsequent War Department contingency plan suggested that the United States could have 3,000 men in Veracruz within a week, and 40,000 within a month – the minimum required for an expedition against Mexico City.) In May, Wilson's own Assistant Secretary of State urged the US President to recognise Huerta's government, arguing that non-recognition was itself a form of intervention, that it ran counter to normal diplomatic practice, and that the United States lay open to charges of hypocrisy as long as it dithered on recognition and yet failed to prevent American arms sales to the government in Mexico City.[18] Wilson would not be the last President to grapple with the quandary of how to square American interests with American principles, or how to manage inconsistency in how those principles were applied.

Nor would he be the last to realise the very real limitations to American power, even in the country's backyard. The Mexican problem was not an academic problem which could be dealt with philosophically by Wilson alone, at his leisure. Whatever the Monroe Doctrine might have said about the western hemisphere being off limits to European powers, the reality in Mexico was that other players were inevitably involved from the outset. And they would act according to their calculations of national interest, affecting the calculations and interests of everyone else, including the United States.

Britain, for one, was ready to go ahead and recognise Huerta, leading some in the US Cabinet to conclude that the Mexican situation was in reality 'a contest between English and American Oil Companies to see which would control [the country's resource wealth]', with British-owned Mexican Eagle jockeying for concessions with Doheny's Mexican Petroleum Company and Rockefeller's Standard Oil.[19] German grand strategists took an interest in what was happening in Mexico.[20] Arms sales from outside parties could help tip the balance of forces within Mexico. Direct foreign military intervention could not be excluded. Japan, locked in dispute with the United States over the Californian land ownership law, was happy to take the opportunity presented in Mexico to show that it could affect American interests on Washington's doorstep if it wanted. In July 1913 the new Japanese Ambassador to the Huerta regime, Minechiro Adachi, arrived in Mexico City to ecstatic cries of 'Viva Japan'. A few months later Felix Díaz was sent on a diplomatic mission to Tokyo as the envoy of Victoriano Huerta.

Wilson's dilemmas in Mexico were further compounded by the lack of sound information as to the situation on the ground. 'Did you ever know a situation that had more question marks around it?' complained Wilson to the press in May 1913:

> Whenever I look at it, I see nothing but exclamation points. It is just a kaleidoscopic, changing scene. Nobody in the world has any certain information about the situation that I have yet found.[21]

Not trusting the dispatches provided by Henry Lane Wilson, President Wilson resorted to sending William Bayard Hale, a journalist who had played a key role in Wilson's presidential campaign, to see how things stood and to report back, informally.

Hale's reports in June and July made for depressing summer reading. They repeated circumstantial evidence that Madero had been murdered with Ambassador Wilson's foreknowledge and that the ambassador had far overstepped his instructions in bringing Huerta to power. Huerta himself was described as 'an ape-like old man . . . said to subsist on alcohol'. Whatever his military credentials or political intentions, he was not restoring stability. Emiliano Zapata was still active in the south. Unrest in the north had now come under the banner of the Constitutionalists led by Venustiano Carranza, a former supporter of Francisco Madero. Mexico, Hale reported, was reaching rock bottom:

> There is no security for any sort of property or life. Lands are going out of cultivation; mines are closed down; only the most necessary labor and trade is carried on. Bandits and Government troops vie in cruelty to each other and towards the population. The Mexican is a savage and finds sport and pleasure in horrible excesses of cruelty. Except in its chief cities, life in Mexico counts for nothing today; non-combatants are shot to death merely by way of amusement . . . The abuse of women is extremely common.[22]

Despite – or because – of all this, American engagement was more necessary than ever before:

> We are, in spite of ourselves, the guardians of order and justice and decency on this Continent; we are, providentially, naturally and unescapably, charged with the maintenance of humanity's interest here. Civilization and humanity look to us, and have a right to look to us, for protection on this Continent . . . It is more necessary to maintain civilization than to pay fantastic deference to the formal prerogatives of a Government that has lost the ability to maintain civilization.

So much for America's responsibilities in Mexico: how was she to act on them? Hale himself did not recommend military intervention. 'Perhaps', wrote Ellen Axson Wilson to her husband, 'it would save us trouble in the long term to give them [all] arms and let them exterminate each other if they so prefer'.[23]

Wilson opted for a more diplomatic course. He recalled and fired Henry Lane Wilson. In his stead he sent John Lind, the former Governor of Minnesota, as his personal representative, on a peace mission. But Lind's mission was dismissed in Mexico. Federico Gamboa, Huerta's foreign minister, responded archly to Lind that an American peace mission was odd given that the two countries were not at war. He claimed that most of Mexico was under government control, and that if the United States wished to show true friendship to Mexico it could simply 'watch that no material and monetary assistance is given to rebels who find refuge, conspire and provide themselves with arms and food on the other side of the border'.[24] He rejected the notion of an armistice, pointing out that 'bandits, Mr Confidential Agent, are not admitted to armistice'. Finally he expressed surprise at the American call for elections, as elections were already planned for October, and refused the American suggestion that Huerta pre-emptively rule himself out of the presidential race, arguing that 'this point can only be decided by Mexican public opinion when it may be expressed at the polls'. At the end of August Wilson reported back to Congress on the initial rejection of Lind's mission – now calling on all Americans to leave the country and announcing a ban on the sale of weapons to Mexico. September found John Lind and his wife in the sultry heat of Veracruz, on Mexico's Caribbean coast. 'I confess that I have almost given up hope', Lind wrote in a letter to Secretary of State Bryan.[25]

For the rest of 1913, with his diplomatic options now close to exhausted, and not ready to order military intervention, President Wilson was reduced to 'watchful waiting' as Mexico pulled itself apart. Huerta was becoming weaker, but perhaps not fatally. Venustiano Carranza was holed up in the state of Sonora, in Mexico's far north-west. Zapata's guerrilla operations in southern Mexico continued, with sporadic risings against federal targets. Francisco 'Pancho' Villa waged a media campaign in the American press from his stronghold in Chihuahua state, presenting himself as the only true alternative to Huerta, and cultivating the radical image of an insurgent revolutionary.[26] In November Villa took the northern city of Ciudad Juárez by capturing a federal train, filling it with his soldiers, and riding it straight into the city, taking the garrison entirely by surprise.

As calendars flipped over from 1913 to 1914, American eyes looking south to Mexico saw a cautionary tale. Somewhere south of the Rio Grande the promise of the New World seemed to have been blunted by the demons of the Old.

———————

Within little more than a year of the novel's publication, much of the political programme Colonel House had fictionalised in *Philip Dru* had come to pass. Washington had seen more activity in the last twelve months than in the previous twelve years, bringing the rest of America with it. On the economic front, tariffs had been reduced and an income tax introduced. A Federal Reserve system was under construction. A casual traveller through the United States in that year might not have fully grasped the importance of what had happened. For others, however, the significance of the moment was beyond doubt. Walter Hines Page, on a golfing holiday in Dornoch, Scotland, wrote to President Wilson that 'the passing of commercial supremacy to the United States will be dated in the economic histories from the Tariff Act of 1913 . . . It is so good to be alive at such a time that I have driven my golf ball clean over the greens and lost the game from excitement'.[27]

Perhaps the tone of the country had changed too. America's richest citizens were maybe less high-handed; maybe the country's poorest had a touch more confidence in their future, notwithstanding an economic slowdown which gathered pace towards the end of the year. The nation was perhaps more bound together in a common purpose of renewal. America was a little closer to operating as a single whole, rather than as an aggregation of cities and their regional hinterlands.

However, much more remained the same. *Philip Dru* envisaged women being granted the vote – but despite Wilson's pledges of private support this moved no closer to being realised, except at the state level. Nationally, the situation of the country's African-American population remained unchanged – in Washington itself, it had worsened. Colonel House's fantasy of Mexico being drawn closer to the United States had been spurned by events.

Above all, the United States remained, for most Americans, a continent unto itself, inviolate. A continent on whose shores arrived people from around the globe, to be sure, and a continent from whose shores flowed goods and people to the earth's farthest corners, but nonetheless a protected country – perhaps even a country with a singular destiny – floating above the world's troubles. Although accounts of fresh atrocities in Mexico were splashed across their evening newspapers, these events did not touch the average American directly. News of battles in the Balkans, or of war scares in Europe, merely emphasised the advantages of having the depths of the Atlantic ocean between America and Europe.

The assurance of America's invulnerability was rarely disturbed – and then only momentarily. In May 1913 a senior British delegation visited the United States by way of planning for the celebration of a hundred years of Anglo-American peace, which was to fall on 17 February 1915. The delegates dined with former President Roosevelt. In Washington they were granted an audience with President Wilson. At their final meeting at the Plaza Hotel in New York, Anglo-American delegates adopted the proposal that the centenary – a hundred years to the day since the end of the misnamed War of 1812 – should be marked by a five-minute silence across the English-speaking world and by the simultaneous inauguration of two monuments, one in America and one in Britain, by King George V and President Woodrow Wilson.

Professor Hugo Münsterberg, well-known in America as one of the fathers of industrial psychology, head of Harvard University's institute on the matter, interrupted proceedings. Were the delegates aware, Münsterberg asked: 'a general idea prevails in other countries that Great Britain and America are getting together to join in a war against Germany'? Charles Peabody, a member of the New York committee, quietened him down. Neither country was contemplating war, he said. Indeed, he continued, all nations could be part of a universal bond of brotherhood which would abolish it. Everybody clapped.[28]

The celebration of Empire Day in Winnipeg, Canada, May 1913. Similar celebrations were held on the same day in Australia, India, New Zealand, South Africa and all across the British world.

PART III

THE WORLD BEYOND

There were few blank spaces left on a map of the world in 1913. Bar a few dotted lines in the far northern and southern hemispheres, the landmasses of the world would be confidently filled in, their outlines firmly marked in thick black ink. The South Pole had been reached little more than a year previously, and the North Pole only a few years before that. The world was now, for the first time in history, cartographically complete, its different parts coloured according to the kingdom, republic or empire under whose sway they fell, particular colours – red and blue, above all – standing out to denote the extent of European empires. The age of exploration was coming to an end. The world map showed unruly nature being increasingly ordered by man, and by the empires of men.

Connected by man, too. On most maps, notched lines showed railway lines spreading across continents from city to city and dotted lines the routes of passenger ships across the seas from port to port. On more specialised maps one might find routes of telegraph lines, criss-crossing the earth and the depths of the sea, connecting Vancouver to Brisbane via Fiji, or Europe to Latin America via the islands of the mid-Atlantic and Brazil. Rudyard Kipling wrote a hymn of praise to the world's deep-sea cables, bringing a single world to life through communication:

> They have wakened the timeless Things; they have killed their
>   father Time
> Joining hands in the gloom, a league from the last of the sun.
> Hush! Men talk to-day o'er the waste of the ultimate slime,
> And a new Word runs between: whispering, 'Let us be one!'[1]

Kipling was suggesting that time and distance had been slain. This was an overstatement – they had been tamed, not abolished. After all, communications were accelerated, not instantaneous: information flowed around the world at the speed of the telegraphist's tap certainly, but only between telegraph stations themselves, and only when the line was free. Cargoes travelled around the world more securely, more cheaply, and with greater certainty of their arrival in a given place at a given time, but only at the speed that infrastructure and technology allowed. Human travel was quicker and easier than in the past, but unevenly so. It could still be a laborious and time-consuming process, particularly in inland areas where roads might be poor to non-existent, and railways still just a glint in the promoter's eye. Large sections of the planet remained remote, even if none of it was now truly inaccessible.

Yet this was a world increasingly interconnected and in motion. There were now few parts of the globe that were entirely untouched by foreign travellers or tourists, by goods produced in a different corner of the planet, by the ready money of a foreign investor, or by the political edicts of some distant metropole. Different parts of the world could no longer evolve along parallel lines of development, meeting only occasionally. Now, when crop returns in Canada were reported on a Tuesday as more promising than had been expected, this would affect prices in London the following morning and demand for Russian wheat by the week's end. News of battles won and lost, of famines, massacres, floods and revolutions, would spread more swiftly and more widely, sparking sell-offs, celebrations or demands for retribution. Nationalist Irish, Indians and Indochinese could now more readily communicate and share their grievances, viewing themselves as similar groups, engaged in a common struggle for greater autonomy against control exerted from London or Paris. Arabs, Africans and Asians could all more easily articulate and sustain a common identity in 1913 than at any time in the past. In 1905, Japanese victory in a naval encounter with Russia ricocheted around the world, and was celebrated in Cairo and Calcutta. In 1913, a march of Indians resident in South Africa against unequal laws in the province of Natal provoked comment in London and protest in Bombay. Was this a sign of something new, an emergent globalism or even, as some saw it, the emergence of a global moral conscience?[2]

The disparate corners of the globe were being pulled steadily towards each other. In many cases, this was a matter of money. The flowering of such far-off places as Winnipeg, Melbourne and Buenos Aires shared common roots: the demand for food and raw materials in wealthy and industrialising Europe, the abundance of these resources in Canada, Australia and Argentina – and the ability to match up the two. The hopes, dreams and ambitions of European and American investors and prospectors, and their search for raw materials and for markets, shaped what happened in Persia and in central Asia, in China and in Argentina, in South Africa and in India. 'Capitalism has triumphed all over the world', wrote an exiled Russian Marxist living in Austrian Galicia, Vladimir Lenin.[3]

But the wider world was still a messy place, shaped by more than capital, and by more than the demands and tastes of Europe and America. Most countries and regions followed weaker and more elliptical trajectories around the European continent, drawn in different directions by their own histories, their own perceptions of the universe around them and how they aspired to relate to it. They had their own hinterlands and their own horizons. What Europeans perceived as the planet's edgelands were to others their backyard.

The bold colours of a few empires on a map hid variations between and within them. After all, empire, a political form so dominant all over the world, meant different things in different places to different people. In Jerusalem, a multi-confessional Jewish and Arab city within an Ottoman Empire run above all by Turks, empire could be seen as a guarantee of security, as an imposition from above or simply as a fact of political existence. In Persia, empire meant being crushed between the Russian quest for territorial expansion and the British quest for the security of India, a chessboard for others' imperial ambitions and anxieties. In Algeria, formally a part of centralised Republican France yet not quite administered as such, empire meant (to the French) the aggrandisement of the metropole, the spread of French civilisation and influence, the bringing of light to the dark corners of north Africa. In India, empire meant something different again, an enterprise in which Indians themselves were active participants, a sort of British tutoring for Indian political development – as some saw it – within a wider British Empire where, despite some very general overarching principles, expedient recalibrations of local relationships were the empire's modus operandi, and where a virtue had been made of what was essentially haphazard.[4]

Empire Day, ostensibly a day of imperial commemoration common to all corners of the British Empire, was a case in point. It meant subtly different things wherever it was celebrated. In Melbourne and Winnipeg, to genuflect before the empire was, for the mostly British-origin residents of those two cities, to reconfirm the covenant of Britannic people around the world and to recommit to the principles of mutual defence. In Durban, Empire Day reminded the white British population of the city of their status as a politically dominant minority in a country populated by far more black Africans than whites, and where even amongst the white population power was shared with Dutch-speaking Afrikaners, many of whom felt no allegiance to an empire which had defeated them in war, interned their families and deprived them of their independence a few years earlier. In Bombay, for the Indian elite of the city at least, to celebrate Empire Day was to remind oneself of British promises of greater self-government and of the practical advantages of British rule – notably security, railways and the rule of law.

And everywhere over the globe, differing perceptions of race and civilisation shaped people's attitudes towards each other and towards their own place in the world. That some civilisations and races were superior to others was axiomatic to the existence and practice of European empire. As Jules Harmand, a French colonial official, put it in 1910:

> One must accept the principle and point of departure that there is a hierarchy of races and civilisations, and that we belong to the superior race and civilisation . . . Our dignity rests on that quality, the foundation of our right to direct the rest of humanity. Material power is simply a tool.[5]

But an account of the world in which some civilisations had progressed further than others was hardly the unique preserve of the colonial administrator seeking to burnish the mantle of his own political authority with the gold leaf of superiority. In 1913, one could find Indian nationalists, too, sadly commenting on the decline of Indian civilisation – while at the same time heaping praise on European civilisation, and the individual qualities of Europeans in which it had resulted. In French Algeria, one could find a group of assimilated Young Algerians – the Jeunes Algériens – arguing that it was precisely their Europeanness, as compared to the Arabness of the old-fashioned *vieux turbans* ('old turbans'), which qualified them for leadership in Algeria, and on which basis they demanded the redistribution of political power. In China and Japan, many saw Westernisation as related to modernisation – and possibly even to political independence, for was not the acquisition of Western technology the best means of achieving the capability to protect themselves against the West's political encroachments?

The habit of looking at the world through the prism of race, meanwhile, was not limited to European colonisers either – even if they were sometimes the most ardent defenders of the 'whiteness' of their settler societies against perceived threats from outside and from within. While Mohandas Karamchand Gandhi was in 1913 militating for the repeal of laws which persecuted the Indian community in South Africa, he was quite silent on the treatment of the '*kafirs*' – South Africa's majority black population. If anything, Gandhi wanted to ensure that Indians and blacks were not confused in the mind of the governing whites, but rather distinctly separated. The idea of the importance of race – and the validity of thinking of individuals in terms of assumed racial characteristics – was widely shared.

So, within a global context of increasing integration and interconnectedness, articulated around the centrality of Europe, the world beyond was something more: a space of encounters of money and goods, but also people, ideas, hopes and fears.

WINNIPEG–MELBOURNE

Britain Abroad

In May 1913 the imperially minded citizens of Winnipeg, Canada prepared themselves for the 'Pageant of Empire', a lavish commemoration of the British Empire to be held in the newly built Industrial Bureau building. Proceeds from the pageant, staged over several days, were to go to the local branch of the Imperial Order of the Daughters of Empire, a Canadian women's organisation set up a decade or so previously to foster the identification of Canadian nationhood with the broader conception of the British worldwide empire, stretching from Canada to Australia, from India to South Africa. The pageant was made up of a series of *tableaux vivants* representing different parts of the empire. 'Five hundred ladies, gentlemen, boys and girls and even tiny tots of tenderest years' were dragooned into the show, according to the *Manitoba Free Press*.[1] The impression it left was one of 'solemn loyalty and thrilling appreciation of the meaning of the British Empire and its flag'.

The first tableau involved Britannia herself, resplendent with a trident in one hand, the symbol of Britain's dominion over the seas. Behind her marched representatives of the imperial armed forces, entering to the strains of 'Rule, Britannia'. England, Scotland, Wales and Ireland arrived next, accompanied by national songs, dances and instantly recognisable historical figures – an exercise in education as much as entertainment. The English danced around a maypole, joined by the figures of King Alfred, the medieval father of the English nation, and Queen Victoria, the contemporary mother of empire. Scotland appeared reeling on to the stage, the national bard Robbie Burns accompanied by Flora MacDonald, heroine of the Highlands. The Welsh Dramatic Society sang 'God Save the King' – the national anthem of both Britain and Canada – in Welsh.

Ireland was represented by harpists, lace-makers and the shipbuilders of Ulster, singing 'The Dear Little Shamrock'.

Canada's entrance was still grander, with hundreds of Maple Leaf girls and all the symbols of the Dominion, as vast as an empire in itself: Inuit, fur traders, wheat farmers, miners, cowboys, the North West Mounted Police, Canadians in canoes, Canadians in snowshoes and Canadians singing 'O Canada' at the top of their voices, national patriotism happily allied with imperial affiliation. Next came the separate imperial territories of Newfoundland and Labrador, followed by the West Indies and South Africa. 'A Zulu dance, though apparently exaggerated', noted a newspaperman, 'was doubtless true enough to life in "Darkest Africa"'.[2] Then Australia – the 'sister of Canada' – and New Zealand, including women wearing badges declaring boldly 'We Vote!' (in contrast to the women of the Dominion of Canada). New Zealand Maori warriors were accompanied by figures representing Fiji and Polynesia, chased off stage by Egypt. Then the jewel in the crown of the British Empire: the princes and princesses of India. The global reach of the Britannic people was further represented in the British Empire's 'world girdling fleet of naval and merchant vessels' and the network of coaling stations which fuelled it: Gibraltar, Malta, Hong Kong, Aden, Suez, Bermuda, Ascension Island, St Helena, Mauritius and Singapore. In a final *tableau*, recorded by newspaper photographers for the next day's paper, the entire cast assembled on stage, grouped around Britannia in the centre, an affirmation of British greatness – and of Canada's part in it.

A few days later, on 23 May, as the Manitoba spring began to turn to summer, it was the turn of Winnipeg's schools to sing out their loyalty to the mother country and to the Crown in celebration of Empire Day. A private initiative which had gained public support across the British Empire, Empire Day was now celebrated more in the empire's farthest corners than it was in London. This year, 10,000 children in Winnipeg's schools were given Union Jacks, the national British flag. 'Nothing apparently could have made them prouder and happier', noted the *Free Press*.[3] In Norquay school the local Anglican clergyman reminded schoolchildren that 'we belong to a great empire', great in numbers and in extent but above all great in its level of civilisation. 'No Empire in the world has laws so good as ours', he declared, 'one king, one flag, one fleet, one empire – a mighty confederation of nations linked together in the most wonderful way'.[4]

On the other side of the world, in the southern hemisphere city of Melbourne, Australia's temporary federal capital – a few weeks distant from Winnipeg by rail and ship, via Vancouver and Fiji, but linked to it securely by telegraph cable and familial ties of Britannic unity – the Australian subjects of the crown celebrated Empire Day in much the same way. As in Canada, children were at the centre of events. 'It is the duty of all teachers employed in State schools', read a circular from the education department of the State of Victoria, 'to foster in the minds of their pupils the sentiments of love of country, respect for its laws, and loyalty to its Sovereign . . . opportunity should be taken from time to time to impress upon children that they are citizens, not merely of Australia, but also of a great empire'.[5] Flags were to be hoisted high into the autumn sky above the state's school playgrounds, and three cheers given for the King, the empire, and the newly formed Commonwealth of Australia, now entering its teenage years. The saluting of the flag, suggested a local newspaper, would be the most pleasing part of the day's proceedings for the children (although the fact that school closed in the afternoon was perhaps nearer the mark). In the evening, there were electric illuminations in the Melbourne suburbs of Camberwell and Surrey Hills, following a local tradition set over the last few years.

The Melbourne *Argus* reminded its readers of the true meaning of Empire Day as an affirmation of an essential Britishness which could be found in every corner of the world, on every continent. The empire, in this conception, was not only about reason but about emotion; not only about strength in numbers but about opportunities afforded to the individual:

> The Australian in Britain, as in Canada or in South Africa, is at home. He is a citizen with all the rights of citizenship and that without losing in the least his Australian citizenship, which he can resume when he pleases. This world-wide British citizenship which makes him at once of the old world and of the new – a man with civic rights on every continent and on multitudinous islands, the representative everywhere of a vast pervasive world-power whose flag flies near by every land as the sign of ubiquitous influence – is in itself a precious gift to the Australian tourist and trader alike . . .[6]

Above all, noted the *Argus*, national and imperial identities should be seen as mutually enhancing rather than antagonistic: 'to be a good imperialist one must first be a good Australian or a good Canadian'. Put another way, to strive for British ideals of self-government (and for freedom from the direct control of London) was not to question the imperial ideal, but to honour it more perfectly in a free partnership of Britannic nations, each evolving their own policies and interests, but bound by custom and culture to British ideals. In its widest sense this communion of Britannic nations allowed Britain to exist, not only in the countryside of England or the mountains of Wales or the hills of Scotland, but in the bush of rural Victoria and the wheat fields stretching from horizon to horizon in the open farmland of Manitoba. Melbourne and Winnipeg could be seen as being as British as Manchester or Glasgow; the names of their streets and buildings recalled local heroes of the construction of their cities, Britons abroad building a new Britain over the seas.

That was the theory. The reality was more complicated. Canadians and Australians were not *just* expatriated Britons, though their parents or grandparents might have been. They had developed a relationship to the land, a sense of national destiny wrapped up in imperial destiny, a sense of having cut loose from Britain as well as recreating it. Australians congratulated themselves on having created a paradise for the working man, more liberal and more equal than in Britain. Canadians had built a continental nation, with almost unlimited promise for the future. What, then, was owed to the mother country? Affection? Loyalty? Money? Men? As Australia and Canada emerged from the status of colony, and took on a life of their own, how was their relationship with Britain to alter?

There was another change afoot. While the majority of the populations of Canada and Australia could still point to heritage from the British Isles – importing into their new homes, amongst other things, the squabbles of Catholic and Protestant, the Church hierarchy of Catholic Irishmen and the Orange Order bands of Ulstermen, the pride of the Scots and the songs of the Welsh – some new Australians, and many new Canadians, had origins in Germany,

Poland, Ukraine, Russia or Italy. In 1913, immigration into Canada reached 400,870 – more than in any year before or since, and from increasingly diverse origins. If things were simply left to run, would Canada and Australia cease to look and feel British, and become American melting pots in miniature? Empire Day, then, was not just an affirmation of imperial identity, it was intended to be a creator of it.

'First of all', wrote English-born Canadian Stephen Leacock in 1907, asserting his vision of Canada as an engine of empire rather than as a dependency of it, 'we must realize, and the people of England must realize, the inevitable greatness of Canada'.[7] This, suggested Leacock, was 'not a vainglorious boast . . . no rhodomontade':

> It is a simple fact. Here stand we, six million people, heirs to the greatest legacy in the history of mankind, owners of half a continent, trustees, under God Almighty, for the fertile solitudes of the west . . . Aye, such a little people, but growing, growing, growing, with a march that shall make us ten millions tomorrow, twenty millions in our children's time, and a hundred millions ere yet the century runs out. What say you to Fort Garry [essentially, Winnipeg], a stockaded fort in your father's day, with its hundred thousand of today, and its half a million souls of tomorrow?

The nineteenth century had been that of the United States, the twentieth century would be that of Canada, went the line first expressed by Sir Wilfrid Laurier, Canada's Prime Minister up until 1911, now leader of the Liberal opposition. Although Australia was less populous than Canada, with less immediate prospect of rapid advancement and fewer European immigrants – partly a matter of distance, partly a consequence of the effective advertisements of Canada's boom and partly, one visitor wrote, 'because stories reach Europe at intervals of drought and commercial disaster [in Australia]' – it too could look to its future as a growing part of the empire, steadily opening up its vast land to farming and development.[8] Australia's first Prime Minister, Edmund Barton, coined a phrase almost as grand as Laurier's for Canada, and considerably more realistic: 'for the first time in history we have a nation for a continent, and a continent for a nation'.

But who would defend these new nations? Would they in turn defend Britain? The questions of imperial defence, partially but unsatisfactorily answered during the South African Boer War by the contribution of Canadian and Australian troops to the British war effort, reached an ever-increasing pitch of intensity in the years leading up to 1913. The interests of Australia or Canada, it was accepted, would not necessarily match those of Britain on every issue – on issues of trade, or political relationships, it was natural that there would be differences. Nor could Britain herself always provide an assurance of unlimited security, with her extensive commitments elsewhere in the world, and facing the prospective competition of Germany, or Russia, or even Japan at some distant point in the future. Increasingly therefore, Canadians and Australians might see themselves both as members of a triumphant Britannic race, custodians of the Britannic future – and yet perhaps as vulnerable, too.

For Australians, it was not just the relatively slack rate of British immigration that was a worry but, ultimately, how the sparsely populated continent of Australia – with fewer than five million inhabitants in 1913 – could remain inviolate in a crowded neighbourhood. 'Japan is packed to the bursting point', noted British traveller John Foster Fraser, '[it] must have somewhere to send her surplus population . . . [it] is looking around the eastern world and marking the spots where her statesmen want that population to go'.[9] Since 1902 Britain had had a military alliance with Japan – an admission both of Japan's increasing status in the world and of British overstretch – but that might not last. And what if Britain was dragged into conflict elsewhere? 'Australian statesmen with imagination may possibly glance into the future, and contemplate the possibility of the British Navy being worsted in the Western Seas', Foster Fraser continued, 'it is fit that such statesmen should contemplate what would be the action of Japan under such circumstances'.

In Melbourne, the newspapers were full of Asian scares. 'The day of the horde is past', noted the *Argus*, 'but there may be a subtler menace to-day from beyond the pale, and the wardens of the marches where West impinges upon East may be instinctively bracing themselves'.[10] Visiting London in July 1913 the Premier of Victoria, William Watt, told his British audiences of Australia's desire to build up a 'Southern Pacific nation' but warned that should Australia weaken, 'the yellow man will come'. He went on: 'The present generation may see little of this anticipated development, but it must come sooner or later, and then the theatre of the great struggle may be transferred from the northern to the southern hemisphere'.[11] A few days later, in Melbourne, Major C. A. Mitchell of the Intelligence Corps delivered a public lecture on the subject of Australian defence, raising the prospect of invasion.[12] The aims of a Melbourne Overseas Club, inaugurated in the presence of leading political figures from across Australia, were described as 'unity, comradeship, and readiness for defence'.[13] Suitably enough, prospective members were asked to sign up at the clubrooms in Empire Arcade on Flinders Street. As it was, the state of Victoria boasted 325 rifle clubs in 1913, and 15,000 boys between the ages of twelve and fourteen were members of the Junior Cadets, while permanent militia and volunteer forces, shown off proudly to a visiting British parliamentary delegation that September, numbered nearly 17,000.[14]

On the more expensive question of a navy, the Commonwealth of Australia had bitten the bullet a few years previously under Labor Prime Minister Andrew Fisher and invested in a flagship for its own navy, the HMAS *Australia*, in order to replace departing British vessels. In 1913 the battleship and her escorts steamed from British shipyards towards their new station, stopping in South Africa to impress the locals there with the loyalty and sacrifice of the Australian taxpayer, before powering across the Indian Ocean. 'From out of the morning mist, the long grey line came in', wrote a reporter for the *Sydney Morning Herald* in October, describing the arrival of the Australian fleet near the spot where Captain Cook had landed in 1770:

> The thing was done. The talking time was past . . . There, in front of their eyes, on this bright morning, was the splendid realisation of the dream of years – a dream that was born of our Nationhood. Not the full realisation of it, in truth, but the beginning of it, the nucleus of the Fleet that is to be. And all knew, as they looked, that there could be no turning back. The full meaning of it, with all its responsibilities, shot home, as these terrible engines of war, withal so stately and majestic, rode in triumph through the Heads.[15]

Like the country as a whole, the navy was to be in one sense separate from its British mother, and yet attached to it 'with the same traditions to live up to, the same worlds to keep'. Being Australian, it would also be imperially British: 'a thing apart, and yet a part of a glorious and indivisible whole'.[16]

As in Australia, most English-speaking Canadians accepted the case for Canada taking up a greater burden of imperial defence. There was broad agreement with the proposition made by the Canadian Conservative MP George Foster in 1909 that Canada was now, whether she liked it or not, 'launched upon the world's waters . . . open to every storm . . . exposed to every danger'.[17] 'She cannot escape the common burden', Foster warned, 'she cannot neglect the common duty, she cannot ignore the common responsibility'. As in Australia, the case was made in reference in part to the stronger powers which surrounded Canada, and in part to the complications of geography. 'East and west, across two mighty oceans, she is face to face with two immense masses of human activity', Foster opined, 'on one side, in the Orient, 350,000,000 people waking up into a new life . . . on the other side, the activities of the old and well-known nations of Europe'.[18] To the south lay the United States, seen by some as the perennial threat to Canada's Britannic identity, and by others as a natural British ally, being both predominantly white and of largely Anglo-Saxon stock. In the other direction, 'the wide cool reaches of the north, silent and mysterious'. As with Australia, a vast sea lay between Canada and the geopolitical centres of Europe, though in Canada's case it was a matter of a few days' sailing rather than several weeks. In any event, Foster reminded the Canadian parliament, 'we must not think that because we are not within sound of the artillery, or in sight of the vessels that are engaged therein, that it is not our battle'.[19]

But whatever Foster's eloquence or the cogency of his imperial reasoning, there were vocal groups opposed to the principle of the matter – the idea that Canada was bound to fight the wars of the mother country – and heated differences over the practical form that any Canadian contribution should take. By early 1913, as Winnipeg's citizens crowded into the Industrial Bureau building to see the Pageant of Empire, the issue of naval defence had become the most divisive issue in Canadian politics, fraught with allegations of disloyalty, and entangled with questions of constitutional legitimacy.

Some Canadians saw greater military expenditures as an excuse for greater taxation which, in turn, would act as a brake on the economic development and prosperity that was Canada's true birthright and its best protection. Others argued that additional spending on defence would be more likely to encourage war than avert it. 'What need is there for a navy now more than there has been for the last fifty or a hundred years?' asked James Scallion, the Irish-born president of the Grain Growers' Association in Winnipeg, in a letter to the local newspaper. 'Are the people of Canada going to encourage European militarism and the estrangement of nations by spending millions in the construction of warships?'[20] At its annual meeting at Brandon, just outside the Manitoban capital, the association voted overwhelmingly against any naval policy at all. 'They [the grain growers] seem to weigh all public issues on their grain scales', commented one observer caustically.[21] In French-speaking Quebec, Henri Bourassa led the charge against British imperialism. Having broken with Laurier for having caved in to London in sending Canadian troops to fight in the Boer War, he now warned darkly of a warlike imperial clique dragging Canada into more bloody adventures in the future, with conscription just over the horizon.

But even amongst avowed patriot-imperialists, those who accepted the need for a Canadian naval contribution to imperial defence, there were stark divisions on how to achieve it. The middle course charted by Laurier between English-speaking jingoists and French-speaking refuseniks – essentially offering a small Canadian-run naval service – satisfied no one. It still left Canada on the hook for British wars, argued Bourassa; it left Canada with a 'tin-pot navy' made up of second-hand British ships which would otherwise have ended upon the scrapheap, argued the Conservatives. Having won the election of 1911 on an imperial platform – against free trade with the United States, and in favour of a stronger contribution to imperial defence – Conservative leader Robert Borden found himself in 1913 in the middle of an ill-tempered debate over which was more patriotic: an immediate financial contribution to the British Treasury of $35,000,000 to allow for the construction of dreadnoughts (the Conservative proposal), or a Canadian naval service (even if that took longer, was less capable, more restricted to Canadian waters, and came less directly under a broad imperial command, except in wartime).

The Conservatives argued that their policy was necessary, and that it was welcomed in London – although in truth British politicians were divided on the issue too, both whether more ships should be built, and whether a direct financial contribution was the appropriate way for a dominion to proceed. The Canadian Liberals argued that the Conservative policy amounted to a new subjugation to Whitehall; Laurier himself stood up in parliament to argue that 'if we pass this bill we will certainly interrupt, and perhaps put an end to, the spirit of self-confidence and self-reliance which has made Canada what it is today'.[22] Attacked on all sides, and with the government accused of parliamentary bullying tactics in trying to get its way, the Borden plan ultimately died, unloved and unmourned. Canada – seen by many as the elder brother of Australia for having confederated thirty-four years before her – was left in an embarrassing mess. By the end of 1913, while Australia had proudly formed a Royal Australian Navy dedicated to South Pacific security – and to keeping Australia white – Canada had a limited naval service with no naval policy for the future, even as most of Canada's politicians proclaimed their Britannic identity, their unswerving loyalty to the crown and their commitment to imperial security.

But then this was perhaps the new reality of Britain abroad in 1913 – more complex and more challenging than in years past, celebrated on Empire Day in the same way in Winnipeg as in Melbourne, in Toronto as in Auckland, in Cape Town as in Sydney, but subject to national variations within imperial unity, and a layered sense of identity, self-interest and obligation.

If Manitoba's real-estate boosters, immigration agents and local politicians (often the same men) were to be believed, Winnipeg was a sure-fire city of the future. Fuelled by the powerful combination of rising commodity prices, immigration, foreign investment and hard graft, Canada had boomed in the decade up to 1913. 'The poor relation', noted one British economist, explaining the flow of capital from London across the Atlantic, 'has come into her fortune'.[23] Within Canada, nowhere had boomed as much as on the prairies, where the four ingredients of the dominion's economic success came together most intoxicatingly. The new visitor was to be left in no doubt: Winnipeg was a city which was going places.

Winnipeg, capital of the prairies, a city destined for worldwide greatness.
Or so its promoters claimed in 1913.

'Winnipeg', noted an illustrated souvenir booklet of the time with
only a little exaggeration, 'can boast of the most rapid growth of
any city in the world'.[24] 'Just thirty years ago', it reminded its readers,
the area where they now stood had been 'bare prairie with a few
rough buildings occupied by the Hudson Bay Company and a score
or so of aggressive pioneer settlers'. How things had changed.
Winnipeg was no longer a settlement but a city; not the end of the
line but a crossroads; not a hard-scrabble outpost but an entrepôt
for the world economy, collecting and then sending out an ever-
increasing stream of grain. 'Winnipeg the Wonderful' it was dubbed,
giddily:

> Immense buildings of brick, stone and marble . . . replace the few
> shanties and their Indian and half-breed inhabitants; whilst the many
> lines of Railway and Electric Street Cars take the place of the groaning
> and squeaking Red River Carts . . . Churches, Colleges and first-class
> Educational facilities abound. The Dominion and Municipal Public

Buildings are a credit to any city. Many miles of Asphalted Streets and Granolithic Sidewalks bear witness to the 'go ahead' character of Winnipeg's citizens . . . The whole of the Transcontinental Railway Traffic goes through the city. Main Street both in its length and width is one of the finest streets in the world.[25]

Admittedly, all these glories were still doled out to a relatively small number of actual live Winnipeggers, numbering only 150,000-odd in 1913. (In typical booster fashion, the *Canada Newspaper Directory* of that year estimated Winnipeg's population at much more: 205,000.)[26] But there was plenty of room for expansion, the city limits extending to 14,861 acres, roughly the size of Manhattan Island.[27] In 1913, the tram-line extended to the outskirts of the suburb of St Vital, which then consisted of little more than a grocery store, a few scattered homes, and a long line of telegraph poles stretching into the distance. 'Welcome', read a makeshift triumphal arch representing entry to St Vital, with 'Prosperity' and 'Progress' painted in large letters on to smaller arches to the left and right, alongside two shields bearing the word 'Enterprise'.[28] Build it, and they will come, was the philosophy of Winnipeg's city fathers.

Thus far, it had worked. After all, there were three times as many Winnipeggers in 1913 as in 1900, a far cry from the 241 recorded in the Canadian census of 1871 – or from the 1,600 canny inhabitants who, two years later, had got their scrawny frontier town ennobled as a city so as to allow them to borrow more money for its expansion. The 'Million for Manitoba' league, founded in 1911, urged ever-greater migration in order to populate and farm the plains of central Canada. According to the *Canadian Annual Review* of 1912, Winnipeg was already the largest grain centre in North America, having edged out Minneapolis a few years previously.[29] In 1913, the doors of the opulent Fort Garry Hotel, even grander than the city's Royal Alexandra Hotel, opened for the first time. Postcards advertised Fort Garry's $2,000,000 cost. The assessed value of Winnipeg's land reached $259.4 million that year, $100 million more than in 1912, and twenty-five times the total in 1900.[30] Winnipeg's banks cleared over $1 billion. And there was more to come. 'As the Canadian West and North unfold their almost limitless wealth in lands and forests and mines', asserted a publication of the Industrial Bureau, 'so the importance of Winnipeg must grow and the fundamental resources of

Winnipeg expand'.[31] 'Thank God for Now!' wrote one optimistic Winnipegger in an article in May 1913, 'these present times are the greatest and the best the world has ever seen'.[32]

The hub of Winnipeg was, as it is today, where Portage Avenue meets Main Street. Around that nexus, and along those two streets, lay most of Winnipeg's main buildings, each proclaiming in their own way the city's confidence and verve. To the north, on Main Street, lay the Union Bank Building, a skyscraper which would not have looked out of place in downtown New York, a dozen storeys high. To the west, on Portage, was situated Eaton's department store, occupying a whole city block, said to employ over a thousand staff and the jewel in the crown of a retail and distribution empire. Close by, on Lombard Street, was the Winnipeg Grain and Produce Exchange. Here, on the floor of one of the largest commodity exchanges in the world, the price of grain was determined by reference to the wholesale price achieved in Liverpool, England, from whence the information was cabled under the Atlantic three times a day. An electric wheat clock registered the Winnipeg price from minute to minute.[33] A little further out, in 1913 the first stones were laid for the new Manitoba Legislative Building, intended to be one of the most impressive and most stately edifices in Canada, if not the world.

The names under a collection of snapshots, marked 'Representative Business and Professional Men of Manitoba', in the 900-page *Twentieth Century Impressions of Canada* left no doubt as to British supremacy in the city.[34] Beside one 'Kelly' lay two more. Around a 'Davidson' lay 'Black', 'Robinson', 'Prior', 'Kelly' (again), 'Thomson', 'Hall', 'Hudson' and 'Wheatley'. Yet there was more to Winnipeg than just its Britishness – its Masonic clubs, fox-hunting and marching bands – important though it was. As in Canada as a whole, and western Canada in particular, the face of the city was changing. Thirteen countries had consular representatives there, including Austria-Hungary, Italy and Sweden.[35] The city had five synagogues for its bustling Jewish community, with one part of the city called 'Jerusalem' as a result. It had German, Swedish and Icelandic Christian congregations. Winnipeg's population in 1913 was sufficiently diverse to sustain an astonishing variety of newspapers: four German (one with a circulation of 21,000), two Hungarian weeklies, five papers for the super-literate Icelanders, three for the Swedes, as well as the Polish *Gazeta Katholicka* and papers for the Norwegian, Jewish and Ukrainian communities.[36] One of Winnipeg's richest men, who died in the United States in 1913 – and so did not feature in the snapshots of the *Twentieth Century Impressions* – was William Leistikow, born in the German city of Stettin (now the Polish city of Szczecin).

Most immigrants were less fortunate than Leistikow. Visitors venturing to the area around the Canadian Pacific Railway yards, known as the North End, were faced with tightly-packed wooden houses, without sanitation and with little protection against the harsh Canadian winter. Here, voices spoke in languages strange and foreign to most Winnipeggers: Polish, Yiddish, Russian, Ukrainian. While infant mortality ran at 112 for every thousand live births in Winnipeg's Ward 1, the district that was the home of the prosperous elite, in Ward 5, around the CPR yards, it ran at 282 per thousand.[37] In a series of broadly positive articles on immigration in the *Manitoba Free Press* in May 1913 James Shaver Woodsworth, a Methodist who worked in the North End, warned of the corruption that new immigrants brought to local politics when they became new citizens, and of the end of the 'quiet Canadian Sunday of our childhood', to be replaced with more raucous European beer-drinking.[38] However, like most in the city, he also welcomed the spirit and colour of the new migrants, their musical culture and their vivacious engagement with life. 'At a joyous Polish wedding festival at which I was a guest', Woodsworth recalled, 'I saw some of the strange old [Polish] folk-dances, survivals of by-gone days, and heard the bursts of patriotic music that at home [in Europe] alien authorities had for years tried in vain to crush out'.[39] 'As the strong faces glowed with an almost reverent enthusiasm', he continued, 'I caught a glimpse of qualities and gifts that will yet bring honor to this Canada of ours.' There was work to be done to build Winnipeg, and these were the men and women to do it.

Would the boom last forever? There were signs in 1913 that it was running out of steam. 'Facts are proverbially stubborn things', editorialised the *Free Press*, 'they have to be faced sooner or later . . . there is, for example, the fact that the production of wheat in western Canada is advancing at a vastly greater rate than the capacity of available markets to absorb it'.[40] This could be used as an argument in favour of reciprocal free trade with the United States, with its large and growing market for grain against which Liverpool and even Europe as a whole could not compete. There were other signs that the good times were coming to an end. In 1913, the wages for labour in the farms around Manitoba, having risen hugely over the last few years, began to fall. More and more immigrants to Canada, stopped only briefly in Winnipeg in 1913, before making their way further west to Saskatoon, or Calgary, or Edmonton. These were the new frontier towns – perhaps the new Winnipegs. Ultimately, would Canada's grain continue to flow west to east (with Winnipeg on the railway line in the middle) or would it increasingly flow west to Vancouver (to be shipped across the Pacific) – or directly south to the United States, circumventing the Manitoban capital entirely? Were Winnipeg's glory days beginning, or was its moment already past?

Melbourne was in some ways a cautionary tale for Winnipeg. It too had been the boomtown of the British Empire. It too had been the future, in its day. Back in the 1870s and 1880s, as Melbourne's central grid layout took shape and as its suburbs began to spread, the city had been awarded the popular moniker 'Marvellous Melbourne'.[41] Grown rich on gold and sheep, Melbourne seemed destined to become the premier Britannic metropolis of the southern hemisphere, and one of great cities of the world. In 1880 the upstart city hosted an International Exhibition, opened with a thousand-strong choir under the dome of the newly completed Royal Exhibition Building. From 139,916 inhabitants in 1861, the population of the city had soared to very nearly half a million by the time of the 1891 census.[42]

Then disaster struck. Boom turned to bust. A banking collapse in 1893 frightened off the British investors on whom construction depended. Business slumped. For a decade, Melbourne's population flatlined. Sydney – viewed by upright Victorians as the centre of uncouth, convict-settled New South Wales – began to catch up. When the various Australian colonies came to federate in the Commonwealth of Australia in 1901, Melbourne was still a mite ahead and was duly pronounced capital – but only temporarily, until a new federal city was established, a rural site in New South Wales being selected for construction in 1908, and given the name Canberra in 1913. Two decades after the bust of the 1890s, a British visitor to Melbourne in 1913 found it still a constant topic of conversation. 'Every one talked to us about it, and told us tales of well-to-do ladies who in a day became penniless, and were thankful to get situations as domestic servants', wrote Alex Hill, former Master of Downing College, Cambridge, 'of rich men who were reduced to begging for a clerk's stool in a shop; of crowds of employees of every kind, who, owing to the sudden bankruptcy of so many firms, did not know where to turn for work.'[43]

As Melbourne's story demonstrated, circumstances could change quickly at the outer edges of the world, bound as they were to the global economy, yet distant from its heart. A loss of confidence could be catastrophic. But Melbourne had ultimately proved resilient. Perhaps it was too big a city to fail economically, exerting its own force field on its hinterland of farms and mines and vineyards, and already sufficiently rich to fund its (more steady) future growth out of savings at home rather than relying on money pouring in from abroad. Federation had made it the nation's political capital. So while the days of headlong, unrestrained expansion were over by 1913, the city had recovered its poise, its population rising at a more leisurely, but nonetheless quite rapid, pace to 651,000, making it the same size as Montreal – the largest city in Canada – more populous than Madrid, Rome or Amsterdam, nearly twice as large as Washington, DC, and four times the size of Winnipeg.[44]

Melbourne was back. On Swanston Street, the Library of Victoria showed off its new dome, the largest reinforced concrete dome in the world, reminding Melburnians of their city's capacity to be world-beating (albeit only for a few months, until the opening of Max Berg's Jahrhunderthalle in Breslau, Germany [now Wrocław, Poland]).[45] A promotional film of the city was made by fixing a camera to the front of one of the new electric trams that rode down St Kilda Road and through the wide streets of the city. Resurrecting the title 'Marvellous Melbourne', the film cut from Flinders Street railway station to the famous Exhibition Building to the tall build-ings of the business district to Henley-on-the-Yarra, Australia's answer to the English rowing regatta.[46] The city had regained some of its old verve, and some of its appetite for risk. 'Its financiers are perennially engaged in preparing fresh "booms"', wrote Alex Hill, marvelling at the rebound of the 'elastic country':

> Such gamblers are the Australians! On board ship they were always
> gambling. As soon as they landed they began to go in for little 'flut-
> ters' . . . Every town has its racecourse. The Melbourne Jockey Club
> claims that theirs is the finest in the world. They have spent £750,000
> on it and its surroundings.[47]

In the Melbourne Cup horse race of November 1913, the most keenly
attended in Australia, Posinatus came in first, edging Belove and
Ulva's Isle out of the running. Tens of thousands of pounds were
won and lost by Melburnians, rich and poor. No matter – the future
was bright. Debts would be repaid and new fortunes made.

Above all, Melbourne was a good place to live. 'The beautiful
harbour is all very well', pointed out the *Argus*, but it was cheaper to
live in Melbourne than in Sydney, with cheaper housing and cheaper
food.[48] There were a few complaints about increasing pollution from
the city's industry, but Melbourne had more parks than other cities
too, and was far less densely populated than its New South Wales
rival. Relatively well housed, well fed and well paid, Melburnians were
also well entertained in 1913. In addition to sporting events – cricket
matches, football games – which regularly attracted crowds in their
thousands, Melburnians could choose between numerous touring
theatrical shows, cheap thrills at the newly opened Luna Park by the
beach, or, for those with a week of free evenings, the first full performance of Wagner's *Ring Cycle* in Australia (sung in English) at the
cost of four guineas. In no other part of the world was the party of
the working man so well represented politically, or his interests so
well protected. A total of 134 wage boards in Victoria were involved
in the setting of workers' minimum wages by the end of 1913, covering
every occupation from bedstead-makers to brewers, nail makers to
nightwatchmen, pastry cooks to plumbers.[49]

Employers and their allies warned of the unions' 'skilful manoeu-
vring and irresponsible lung-power' and even of their 'tyranny'.[50]
They railed against the 'dissemination of syndicalist ideas' and of
the dangerous tendency towards disruptive strike action, such as the
stand-off which had developed at the Broken Hill mines earlier in
the year.[51] Workers, meanwhile, fought hard to defend their accrued
rights against a range of perceived threats. The Labor Party's support
for equal pay for women, some alleged, was simply a ploy to have
women removed from the workplace, reducing the competition for

men. The desire to keep Australia 'white' was not only about a sense of cultural separateness, it was also about preventing Australian workers from being undercut by imported Asian labour (Indians, Chinese or Japanese). This could be taken to absurd lengths. The *Argus* reported furious union complaints made in Western Australia about the engagement of a Sri Lankan doctor on an Australia-bound ship when the English doctor on board fell ill.[52]

Yet wages in Australia could not be expected to rise forever: long-term growth depended on some level of immigration; specific labour shortages would have to be met. The answer, as the government saw it, was to encourage British migration – which by 1913 flowed far more to Canada and the United States than to Australia – tripling its spending on assisted migration schemes from the British Isles. Farm labourers and domestic servants could expect particularly high reductions in their fares, mirroring the two greatest labour shortages in Victoria. In the end, however, these schemes brought relatively few new migrants, and certainly not enough to change the established demographics of the state. Unlike in Manitoba, where there were few born-and-bred Manitobans, the vast majority of Victoria's population had been born locally – not just within Australia, but within the state. As for those born outside Australia, the overwhelming majority were British or Irish, outnumbering the next most populous group of immigrants – the Germans – by twenty-five to one. Melbourne, it seemed, would remain British for a while yet.

Or Anglo-Celtic, as some preferred it. One of the newest migrants to Melbourne in 1913 was the city's new Catholic Archbishop, Daniel Mannix. He was, he said, an Irishman, leaving little doubt as to his views on Home Rule for Ireland, the domestic political issue which convulsed the British Parliament for much of the year. 'For years the Irish people were walking, as it were, through the desert', he told the cathedral congregation at his welcome speech in March 1913.[53] Now, they were on the brink of reaching the promised land. These were hot political issues in Melbourne. Earlier in the year, towards the end of January, over a thousand Catholic Australians had sailed down to the Mornington Peninsula in the annual outing of the United Irish League, who were supportive of Home Rule. The very next day, the Loyal Orange Order held a picnic at Aspendale Racecourse. 'Orangemen', they were told, 'were the watchdogs of liberty', stirring every sinew to save Ulster from the dangers of Home Rule.[54]

Mannix did not intend to be a quiet Archbishop, a pacifier. He intended to be an activist on behalf of what he saw as his own down-trodden and misrepresented people, Victoria's Irish. He launched into attacks against the casual anti-Irish attitudes of the establishment newspapers of Melbourne, where the Irish, who were generally poorer than those of English or Scottish origin, were presented as habitual whiskey drinkers, uneducated and unreliable. That the iron-mask-wearing bushranger Ned Kelly – a cold-blooded murderer to the establishment, but a fighter for economic justice to others – had been an Irish-Australian was not lost on Victorians. A quarter of a century after his death in a shoot-out in 1880, the population of Melbourne was treated to a feature-length movie of his story and that of his gang, the first feature made in Australia, or anywhere else in the world. There had, of course, been Irish judges, Irish politicians and Irish premiers as well as Irish criminals. Mannix sought to remind Victorians of these contributions, and challenge anti-Irish prejudices.

He also intended to be a stout defender of his religion, to which his nationality was so closely related. As in other parts of the British world – including Manitoba, where the Catholic population was predominantly French-speaking, adding another layer of mistrust – the debate between Catholics and Protestants covered the question of mixed marriages (recently made more difficult by the Catholic Church) and, perennially, the dispute over the proper relationship between the Church and state education.[55] To that end, Mannix aimed to turn the city's Catholic population – between a fifth and a quarter of the total – into a powerful bloc of voters he could ultimately mobilise for confessional causes. To some, this looked like gang politics. Secular-minded Australians saw an unwelcome attempt to stir up religious feeling. Mannix's suggestion that Catholics in Victoria had not just been slighted in living memory, but actively persecuted by the police and the courts, brought a stark warning from the *Argus*: 'there is danger in persons in high places making misstatements – danger to themselves'.[56]

What went almost completely unmentioned in Melbourne were the people who had come before the British: Australia's aboriginal people. Occasionally they were thought of as an ornamental addition to

Australian culture, as a curiosity. More often, they were ignored. Aboriginal people were counted quite separately from the rest of the population in the Australian census statistics. The *Victorian Year Book 1913–1914* noted that their number in Victoria had fallen from between 5,000 and 15,000 at the creation of the colony in 1851, to just 643 in 1913. 'The race is gradually but surely dying out', noted the *Year Book*. This, the reader was invited to conclude, was both natural and good – ignoring the role whites played in creating the conditions under which the aboriginal population in Australia had fallen in the first place, through disease and conflict. In accounts of Australian history, aboriginals appeared at the moment of Australia's 'discovery' by Captain Cook, and then more or less disappeared from the historical record. There was only 'one ending' possible to the conflict between 'stone and steel' – between the backwardness of aboriginal societies and the industrial metal-working whites – noted a history book *Australia Unlimited* in 1910, and that conflict had ended long ago.[57] As far as the law was concerned Australia had been *terra nullius* – an empty land – when white men arrived to colonise it. In 1913, in Melbourne, aboriginals were seldom seen, never heard.

In Winnipeg, things were different. The native Assiniboine people were more present than aboriginals were in Victoria – in the name of the city's main river and even in the name of the city itself, as well as in parts of the countryside around. Amongst the pictures of bank buildings, new houses, bustling streets, and harvested fields which made up the bulk of *The Illustrated Souvenir of Winnipeg* there was room for one picture marked 'Indians of the North-West'.[58] The Métis, a mixed-race group who had been the masters of Manitoba in the heyday of the Hudson Bay Company in the eighteenth and nineteenth centuries, were less easily dealt with. Their role in Winnipeg's history was more recent, and more raw.

Canadian veterans parading on Dominion Day in July 1913 included those who had fought against Métis rebellions on two occasions, in 1869–1870 and in 1885. In the first rebellion, the Métis were protesting against the 1869 transfer of Rupert's Land – a large area of central Canada comprising all of what would become Manitoba, and parts of what would later become Saskatchewan and Alberta – from the authority of the venerable Hudson Bay Company to the ownership of the newly created Dominion of Canada. This transfer, the Métis correctly feared, would push them off their land – to which they had historic access but not legal title – bring in more outsiders to run their lives, and challenge both their culture and habits of government. A local French-speaking Métis leader, Louis Riel, established a provisional government in the Red River colony to defend Métis interests. This was deemed illegitimate and ultimately treasonable by Ottawa. Troops were sent to suppress the colony. Riel was forced to flee. In 1870, the province of Manitoba was born, built on the ashes of a failed rebellion.

A number of land treaties were subsequently signed by representatives of the government of Canada with native indigenous groups, under which any rights they had to large tracts of land across Manitoba and other parts of north-western Canada were given up, in return for the confirmation of rights on smaller portions of territory and some assistance with adapting to their changed circumstances. But Louis Riel and the Métis remained a thorn in the side of central government for years. Some suggested an amnesty for Riel. Others hoped he could be bribed or otherwise compelled to disappear, perhaps by moving to the United States (which, for a while, he did). But Riel was not easily shunted aside. Instead, he was elected as a Manitoban representative to the Dominion parliament in Ottawa – but prevented from taking his seat there. Later, in 1885, the increasingly unhinged Riel led another rebellion, this time in the Northwest Territories (in an area which is now part of Saskatchewan). This time he was caught, tried for treason and hanged. Many Canadians, particularly French-speaking Canadians – including some in Manitoba – criticised the way in which the trial was handled, and the harshness of the sentence. Some chose to see him as a romantic hero, even as a political martyr. English-speaking Manitobans, on the other hand, saw Riel as a treasonous brigand, a reminder of just how recently they had assumed control over their province and, because French-speakers seemed to cherish the memory of Riel, a reminder of the questionable loyalties of some of their compatriots.

The majority of the population of Melbourne and Winnipeg in 1913 would no doubt have considered the slow extinction of the aboriginal population of Australia, the effective cantonment of the indigenous population in Canada, and the suppression of the Métis rebellions as the price to be paid for the spread of Britannic culture, civilisation and order. Was this not the lesson of history? Older peoples

were superseded and pushed out by newer and more dynamic populations. Was that not what frontiers were about? Indeed was this not
what progress – British progress – demanded? As they saw it, the
continuing challenges posed by indigenous peoples to the Britannic
fabric of Canada and Australia in 1913 would be overcome by the
march of time. Soon enough, prior peoples would be assimilated,
crushed, or forgotten.

BUENOS AIRES

Southern Star

In the mind of the foreign investor in 1913, there was perhaps one destination with more promise for the future than Canada, Australia or even the United States: Argentina. 'In Capel Court, the home of the London Stock Exchange', wrote Reginald Lloyd a few years previously, 'the names of the Argentine railways are as familiar as those of India, and the stock of its towns vies in publicity with British municipal scrip'.[1] The darling of the world's largest financial market, Argentina borrowed more money from London than Australia, and soaked up nearly as much British investment as Canada.[2] Despite having been forced to renege on her national debts in the 1890s, Argentina was generally seen as a safe bet by 1913. The convertibility of the peso into gold, coupled with the surer financial footing of the country, provided adequate assurance of the country's fundamental economic health to investors. Within the last forty years the population of the country as a whole had swollen from two to seven million. Buenos Aires had grown from the size of Melbourne in 1869 to more than double the Victorian capital by 1913, her exports flooding on to the world market.[3]

The speed and scale of change in the country was vertiginous. In the 1870s Argentina had imported wheat. Now she was one of the world's largest exporters, the massive grain elevators along the shore of the Rio de la Plata the first thing that a visitor arriving in Buenos Aires from abroad would see, long before they caught sight of the city itself. Shipments of frozen beef had increased five times over between the first years of the twentieth century and 1913; these were carried to European markets, principally Britain, by *frigoríficos* – huge refrigerated vessels. The local *Baedeker* – really more of a thinly disguised prospectus – recommended tourists visit the La Negra slaughterhouse in order to marvel at the efficiency of the system of

slaughter and refrigeration, every bit as impressive as the manufacture of Henry Ford's automobiles in Detroit, a wonder of the modern
world.[4] Georges Clemenceau – French journalist, newspaper proprietor and former Prime Minister – was one of the many prominent
foreign visitors drawn to the allure of Buenos Aires' success. He was
shown around the La Negra plant by the half-French son of the
owner, and found the whole process of slaughter and refrigeration
performed with 'a rapidity so disconcerting that the innocent victim
of our [meat-eating] habits finds himself in the sack ready for
freezing, with all his insides neatly packed into tins, before he has
had time to think'.[5]

Alongside the *frigoríficos* – and sometimes carrying cargoes of
meat themselves – passenger vessels plied routes to Southampton,
Liverpool, Naples, Marseilles, Genoa and Hamburg.[6] The Italian
lines were particularly busy, carrying the bulk of Argentina's new
immigrants and many of the 100,000 seasonal workers who came
to help at harvest time and returned to Italy when their work was
done in Argentina. On land, a map of the country showed a network
of railway lines running into tens of thousands of miles, stretching
out from the capital city to reach large inland estates – the *estancias*
– where so much of Argentina's wealth was generated. Nearer to
the capital, 1913 saw a bumper harvest of peaches, pears, apples,
grapes and figs, all of which could now, with the introduction of
the automobile and motor trucks, be brought to Buenos Aires market
stalls within twenty-four hours of being picked.[7] 'One wishes to
conjure up this image in front of the readers' eyes as with the
cinematograph', *Baedeker* noted of the change in Argentina's countryside.[8] It was an apt metaphor: any photograph of Argentinean
economic prosperity would be out of date before it was developed.

Observers concurred that this was a moving picture that, in 1913,
had only just started. The same forces which were at work around
Winnipeg or Melbourne had been evident in the transformation of
the hinterland of Buenos Aires from colonial subsistence backwater
into industrial-scale farming over the last few decades: the availability
of good land, the global demand for agricultural commodities, and
the integration of global transport. And those forces had ample
scope to run for years to come on the *pampas*. There was land aplenty
in the provinces of Cordoba or San Luis, noted the local *Standard*
newspaper, cheap compared to land around Melbourne and 'not

infested with rabbits or drought'.[9] What Argentina needed above all, then, was money and people, investment and immigrants – the first to build Argentina's future, the other to populate it with Argentineans, a hundred million of them one day perhaps. 'It is a truly wonderful prospect that lies before the country', opined Reginald Lloyd, considering Argentina's future development, 'some of its features may be marred by world changes of which we at present have no conception, but if Argentines are only true to themselves no ordinary vicissitudes can arrest the steady march of their destiny'.[10]

Well-heeled Argentineans, already renowned for their fierce patriotism, dared to dream that one day, not so distant, Argentina would be to southern America what the United States was to the north. When Theodore Roosevelt paid homage to the star of the south in November 1913, the man who had extended the Monroe Doctrine into a creed of American imperialism recognised that in Argentina, at least, American guardianship against European depredation, even if only theoretical, had been overtaken by events. 'You need no protection', he flattered an audience of upper-crust Argentineans gathered in the Teatro Colón, a newly built opera house the locals considered the equal of any in Europe, 'you are fit to be the champion of your own Monroe doctrine'.[11] Coming from a former US President, at a time when Mexico was under threat of US

Twins: The Manitoba Legislative building in Winnipeg, begun in 1913.

intervention, with the so-called ABC countries – Argentina, Brazil, Chile – demanding they be consulted on matters concerning the Americas, Roosevelt's recognition of Argentinean greatness could not but be rapturously received. 'Thunders of plaudits made the great theatre re-echo', wrote a reporter from the *Buenos Aires Herald*, 'ladies assembled in hundreds in the boxes showered down bouquets of posies and flowers to show their appreciation'.[12]

Buenos Aires was front and centre in the Argentinean economic miracle. The city dominated the country, home to one-fifth of its population. It had no serious rival, whether as a centre of commerce – the northern port of Rosario handling one-sixth the amount of international trade passing through Buenos Aires – or as a political, cultural or administrative centre. To foreigners, the city represented Argentina as much as Paris represented France, or New York the United States. Its splendour became a matter of national honour.

As recently as 1880 the city had consisted mostly of single-storey buildings, an overgrown Spanish village centred on a main square, the Plaza de Mayo. Since then the government had spent a small fortune gentrifying the place, commissioning new buildings – including the Italian-designed Congress, which Clemenceau

Twins: The Congress of the Argentine Republic, Buenos Aires, finished in 1906.

compared to the US Capitol – widening the city's streets, and transforming Buenos Aires into a European metropolis which combined ornate turn-of-the-century grandeur with the blessings of modern engineering.[13] In a relatively short space of time, Buenos Aires had become:

> A city of great docks and private palaces, imposing public and commercial edifices, well paved, scrupulously clean streets, and almost too many electric trams; a city of handsome railway termini, into which are daily poured the seemingly illimitable riches of Argentina; an admirably lighted city . . . a city of plazas and parks, stately avenues and attractive racecourses . . . a city of fine theatres, very modest churches, elegant shops, and surpassingly graceful women . . . The metropolis of the Argentine nation easily invites comparison with the Babylons of the twentieth century. The stranger, whom she absorbs in tens of thousands yearly, involuntarily salutes her with the epithet of the great, and speedily falls beneath her spell![14]

In December 1913 the city opened its first underground railway line, the first in the southern hemisphere. 'Nothing so much as the convenience of this important modern means of urban transport . . . could serve to make eloquently manifest the colossal development of the city', the local representative of the Anglo-Argentine Tramways Company said at the inauguration ceremony.[15] The Mayor of Buenos Aires, Joaquín Samuel de Anchorena, continued: 'To us has fallen the good fortune to be the first to enjoy the enormous benefits such as exist in London, Paris, Berlin, Vienna, New York, the model cities par excellence in urban development'.[16] The builders of the line were promptly dispatched to give lectures about it in Brussels and Berlin.[17]

Porteños (as inhabitants of the great port-city were known) were growing used to Buenos Aires being mentioned in the same breath as the great cities of Europe or the United States. Already their city covered more land than central Paris and its population was within striking distance of Vienna's. The zoo had as wide a range of animals as any around the world, boasting a polar bear, lions, cheetahs, elephants, rhinoceroses, giraffes, and Latin American jaguars. Buenos Aires was a favoured destination for transatlantic tours of the great opera and ballet companies of Europe. A few months before President Roosevelt spoke at the Teatro Colón in September 1913, the boards of the theatre creaked to the acrobatics of 'Russian dancers who took London by storm', Diaghilev's Ballets Russes (though Diaghilev himself, being prone to sea-sickness, did not follow his company on the Latin American leg of their tour).[18] For a month, Tamara Karsavina and Vaslav Nijinsky, whose performance of Stravinsky's *Rite of Spring* had scandalised the Parisian critics earlier in the year, charmed the audiences of Buenos Aires with a repertoire stretching from popular favourites such as *Swan Lake* to *Scheherazade* and the shocking *L'Après-midi d'un Faune*, via ballet choreographed to the music of Weber, Tcherepnin, Borodin and Schumann. (Between performances, Nijinsky found time to get married.) A few snarls aside – Nijinsky described as 'rather ape-like' in *Scheherazade* – the performances were counted superb, every bit the equal, if not better, than presentations in London or Paris.[19] 'The vast theatre was packed from stalls to gallery', noted the *Buenos Aires Herald* on one of the Ballets Russes' last nights in Buenos Aires, 'and from all parts the applause was spontaneous as it was sustained'.[20] Twelve curtain calls ensued. No longer living in the shadow of the European metropolises but instead participating in the most sensational aspects of their common cultural life, would Buenos Aires one day be their equal?

As in many other parts of the world, though Argentina was not formally part of the British Empire, the tentacles of British influence wrapped themselves around Buenos Aires' commercial life. The language of business was English. In the boardrooms of most Argentine railway companies the vast majority of the board members – and always the chairman – was British (or at least Anglo-Argentine). One-third of Argentina's imports – including the bulk of its machinery – came from Britain.[21] So did three-fifths of its investment (including nearly the totality of foreign investment in the railways). Many of the British community in Buenos Aires worked as clerks in British-owned banks. All this was a reflection of a long-standing economic partnership between the two countries, established as long ago as 1825, when Britain, having given up on direct imperial control of the Argentine, recognised the independence of the new republic of Argentina in return for a free trade agreement.

A newly arrived Briton in Buenos Aires, though a member of a British community which numbered only in the tens of thousands, could find corners of the city where he or she was quite at home. On Calle San Martín, the Phoenix Hotel declared itself 'The English Hotel of Buenos Aires'.[22] The suburb of Belgrano was colonised by wealthy British families. In the docks, the majority of ships bore the British flag, and were manned by British sailors – to which locals ascribed the disproportionate number of arrests of *Ingleses* for public drunkenness.[23] Elsewhere around the city, on dates fixed months in advance, British businessmen, clerks and doctors met discreetly in one of Buenos Aires' seventeen Freemasons' lodges, which bore names such as Albion, King Edward VII, Victoria and Star of the South. Buenos Aires boasted a few dozen British schools, a British hospital – believed by the British, of course, to be the best in the city – and an English Club. The Buenos Aires branch of Harrods department store, combining convenience with British style, was operated, the English-language *Buenos Aires Herald* noted, 'as at home . . . the absence of petty molestations at the hands of shop assistants greatly appreciated'.[24] Empire Day celebrations in 1913 confirmed to a local English reporter that 'sentiment towards the Motherland and the Empire is truly alive in Buenos Aires'.[25]

Remarkably for such a small community, British influence on the sporting life of Buenos Aires was considerable. Quite apart from cricket – which was sufficiently popular in the city to lure the most famous cricket team in the world, that of the Marylebone Cricket Club, on a tour there in 1912 – the Argentine Football Association was in 1913 presided over by a Briton, Hugo Wilson. A series of English football teams had visited in recent years: Southampton in 1904, Nottingham Forest in 1905, Tottenham Hotspur and Everton in 1909. In 1912, Swindon Town beat San Isidro Athletic Club, the Argentine national champions, 4–1. On the water, the British Buenos Aires Rowing Club dominated, having beaten the German R. V. Teutonia in the HM German Emperor's Cup three years in a row. The Hurlingham Club, home of Argentinean polo, opened its doors in 1889 and benefited for a while from its own railway station. It set the tone for a combination of British sport and sociability.

Outside the sports clubs, the banks and the railway companies, however, it was Latin-accented influences which prevailed in Buenos Aires. Upper class *Porteños*, renowned for their sartorial splendour, tended to be Spanish-speaking Argentineans of long standing, a small elite of a few thousand families who lived in the centre of the city, around the Plaza de Mayo, as they always had – and increasingly in the Barrio Norte a few blocks away. These, along with the fabled rural *gaucho*, were the carriers of Argentinean tradition, from the European settlement of the country in the sixteenth century to the wars of independence under Belgrano and San Martín and the celebrations of Argentina's centenary in 1910. They were also the country's major landowners and conservative political elite. Their social preserve was the Jockey Club – founded by a future President of Argentina in 1882 – where the wealthy men of the city would dine at widely spaced tables covered with sparkling white linen table cloths and gleaming silver cutlery, while discussing the country's political and economic future, which by and large they felt was theirs to determine.[26] Argentina, as they saw it, was by right their country; Buenos Aires was their city.

The British population was negligible compared to the communities from other European countries, which comprised by far the larger part of the foreign-born residents of the city, half of the city's overall population and two-thirds of its working-age men.[27] One and a half million Italians, as well as over one million Spaniards, had streamed over the Atlantic to Argentina over the past quarter-century. Though a number returned home within a few years, disappointed with the reality of economic opportunities for workers (as opposed to investors) in Argentina, many stayed, living in the houses by the Buenos Aires waterfront or in the tightly packed tenements (*conventillos*) in the centre, or in more outlying low-rise *barrios*. These areas were a constantly changing patchwork of Piedmontese and Neapolitan, Castilian and Andalucian, where the dialect spoken varied from street to street. On carnival week, when the local and Latin immigrant population took to the streets with gusto, the British drew down the shutters. In 1913 the *Buenos Aires Herald* criticised the carnival festivities for their 'rowdyness' and 'disorder', launching a broadside against the licentiousness of the Venetian-style masked ball held at the Tigre Hotel.[28] The *Standard* was similarly scathing of events elsewhere:

> The Argentine newspapers refer with satisfaction to the 'enthusiasm' which prevailed, but, unfortunately, this degenerated into disorder in some parts of the city, particularly in Calle Independencia at the corner of Catamarca, where two men persisted in throwing water on

passers-by (formerly a general custom during Carnival); the police interfered, the delinquents were supported by a crowd of people, revolvers were used, and two policemen and numerous other persons were wounded, the unfortunate policeman mortally it is feared.[29]

Such things would not happen in a British city, the newspaper implied. Latin passion had got the better of the crowd.

In its grander parts, the feel of the city recalled the influence of France. This was most obvious in the fondness for official buildings in the French Beaux-Arts style, though Clemenceau noted a more recent 'epidemic of Italian architecture', highly decorative, with 'astragals and florets amid terrible complications of interlaced lines'.[30] The statuary of the city – hastily erected over the past quarter-century in order to provide Buenos Aires with a suitably noble-looking set of heroes – was mostly in the French style, soaking up the surplus sculptors of the French Republic, and adorning the city's numerous parks. Buenos Aires' cafés brought to mind those of the Grands Boulevards, its bookshops were stocked with the latest French literature, and its department stores with the latest French fashions. Each morning, as part of her *toilette*, a leisured *Porteña* might apply to her neck a few dabs of French perfume – more heavily taxed than in the past, noted angry newspaper columns – before breakfasting on *medias lunas* (croissants).[31] No wonder Buenos Aires was proverbially known as the 'Paris of Latin America'. Some went further. Playing to the crowd, a visiting American, James Logan, vice-president of the Boston Chamber of Commerce, put things somewhat differently: 'Paris', he told an appreciative after-dinner audience, 'is the Buenos Aires of Europe'.[32]

It was gratifying for *Porteños* to hear the praise of European or American visitors. It was just as gratifying for European visitors from countries such as France to find in Argentina such a dynamic Latin-dominated country. Here lay the Latin world's future, and a reservoir of influence on which the older Latin countries could perhaps draw in the future. Georges Clemenceau noted that 'we French have allowed ourselves to be outstripped in economic affairs' in Argentina as elsewhere. But, he comforted himself, the French still had 'a patrimony of moral authority'.[33] The original emblem of the Argentine Republic had borne a Phrygian cap, the symbol of the French revolution. Giving a lecture, in French, on the subject of democracy, the publisher of Zola's *J'Accuse* found that the *Porteños* understood him perfectly. 'By the grace of winged words', he wrote, 'the mind of France has flown across the ocean, and we may rejoice in the fact and found great hopes for the future on it.'[34]

If France could not outstrip British investment, it could nonetheless endeavour to convince Argentineans of France's cultural authority, a claim to leadership through aesthetics rather than through money. In 1910, the French Ambassador had penned letters back to the foreign ministry in Paris recounting his attempts to influence an Argentinean jury to choose a French entry in a competition for a new centrepiece monument to the Argentinean revolution of 1810, to stand in the middle of the Plaza de Mayo – the heart of the city, the centre of national attention. A French sculpture, it was felt in Paris, would not only confirm the supremacy of French art, but act as a permanent reminder of Argentina's political inheritance, much as the Statue of Liberty in New York was intended to remind Americans of what they owed France in their own War of Independence.[35] The French foreign ministry trembled at the thought of a German victory in the competition.

In the end, after much prevarication, and an extension of the shortlist from five to seven, the Argentinean jury selected an Italian entry designed by Gaetano Moretti. This was acceptable, thought the French; it was a Latin victory, after all. An alternative Franco-Argentinean monument was erected on the Plaza Francia, a Marianne-like figure representing France bearing a torch of liberty, leading two girls and a young boy towards the republican enlightenment which France still claimed to embody.

Moretti's obelisk, meanwhile, was delayed year to year. Three years after the centenary had passed, in 1913, it amounted to no more than some foundations in the middle of the Plaza de Mayo and special reinforcements of the subway tunnel below.[36]

Perhaps an unfinished sculpture more eloquently described the Argentine nation in 1913 than a completed project would have done. What was the Argentine nation, after all? Who was the Argentine nation? Many Argentineans were indubitably proud of their country, both of its past and, more particularly, what they deemed to be its inevitably bright future. Travelling the country, Clemenceau remarked upon the 'rabid Argentinism' he found there, and the 'inherent jingoism' of the country's people.[37] There was the perennial rivalry with Chile to stoke feelings of nationalism, as well as competition with Uruguay and Brazil. British ownership of the Falkland Islands was hotly contested. A particular state-sponsored reading of Argentine history was evident in Buenos Aires' statues, and in the textbooks of the country's schools. 'There is a stereotyped ideal of Argentine History which must be adhered to . . . to depart from this is regarded as an educational crime', editorialised the *Buenos Aires Herald*, 'it would be an actual crime if any Argentine personage . . . were to be represented as other than a whole-hearted patriot and a hero'.[38]

Yet having thought it through, many new residents of the country chose not to become Argentine citizens, preferring to remain legally French, Italian, Spanish or German. Their affiliation to the Argentinean state was muted. Unlike in the United States, where the acquisition of citizenship was considered a mark of success, opening the way to greater opportunities ahead, foreigners felt they had little to gain from Argentinean citizenship. They already had the right to own land, and to travel freely. To many, citizenship simply conferred the dubious right to be conscripted into the Argentinean army. And although some nationalists railed against the failure of immigrants to be naturalised as Argentineans – periodically suggesting enforced naturalisation and Spanish classes to remedy the matter – the arrangements ultimately suited many conservatives. Why needlessly introduce a new element into the country's political system through the grant of citizenship, by which men (but not women) would acquire the right to vote? Foreigners could remain foreigners if they wanted. The political status quo would be retained.

As it was, though elections were held in Argentina, the process of voting in public meant that those in power were in a strong position to ensure that the voters followed their line. 'The Government is republican in name', wrote Lloyd in 1910, 'but the elective principle is largely farcical, and the executive power is as autocratic as that of Central Europe'.[39] Politics continued to be dominated by the elite, with political bosses – *caudillos* – running the show in the provinces. For those in charge, the system seemed just fine. Argentina should be led from above, by the old Argentinean elite. Why change?

But the pressures on the country's political system were increasing. Opposition demands for reform were accompanied by occasional bouts of political unrest, as in 1892 and 1905, sometimes with the support of sections of the army. As conservatives saw it, dangerous political ideas – including socialism and anarchism – were being imported from Europe alongside much-needed labour. Labour unrest, culminating in the first Argentinean general strike of 1902, had brought the fear of violent social revolution to the River Plate, and the question of how to prevent it.

Initially, the preferred strategy of the government was one of concerted oppression, imposing martial law and closing down the opposition press, both socialist and anarchist. In 1902, the Law of Residence allowed the state to deport foreigners it deemed trouble-makers. But strikes and protests continued. In 1907, tenants of 1,000 Buenos Aires *conventillos* refused to pay their rent. May Day demon-strations drew large crowds. In 1909 the chief of police in Buenos Aires, Ramón Falcón, was assassinated. In 1910, the celebrations of the centenary of the Argentinean revolution were disrupted by strikes. Clemenceau was in Buenos Aires when a bomb was thrown into the Teatro Colón. This kind of thing was bad for business, potentially frightening off investors. In an attempt to split off relatively moderate leftist opposition from more intransigent anarchists who opposed voting on the basis that it legitimated the state, President Roque Sáenz Peña proposed and pushed through a new law in 1912 allowing for universal male suffrage, obligatory voting and a secret ballot. It was a historic reform. Now, perhaps, the Argentinean nation could begin to be built not from the top down, but from the bottom up.

There were still deeper questions lurking behind the grand façades of Buenos Aires in 1913: for whom was the country really run? The great mass of Argentineans or foreign investors? 'Is Argentina as bright as it is painted?' asked the *Herald* of its readers in October.[40]

Americans in 1913 worried about the overweening power of a money trust of Wall Street squeezing out Main Street in favour of large companies controlled by the banks. In Argentina, locals complained about a meat trust, driving down the price of meat sold abroad to win market share, and driving up the price of meat sold in Buenos Aires. 'Small wonder that we unfortunates who dwell in this land of plenty have to thank our stars if Bones the Butcher can let us have a bit of scraggy cow beef, miscalled steak, at the paltry price of $1 to $1.50 the kilo', wrote one journalist.[41] What was good for the average consumer in Europe, it turned out, was not necessarily good for the locals in Argentina.

And while the very name 'Argentina' suggested silvery wealth, many who lived in Argentina were struggling, unable to realise their dreams. 'The poor immigrant has an enormous struggle to raise himself above the condition of a serf', wrote John Foster Fraser, having continued his travels from Australia to Argentina.[42] Another writer, an English engineer travelling around Latin America, noted the same phenomenon, blaming 'land monopoly, reckless finance . . . [and] the unscrupulous use of the country's credit for promoting schemes for the benefit of monopolists or private companies, rather than the public'.[43] In the countryside, most of the best land was already taken by large private landowners. Unlike immigrants to Canada, most immigrants to Argentina ended up working the land for others, or trying their luck in Buenos Aires. In the city, working class *Porteños* made a habit of dressing smartly to keep up appearances of affluence, wearing frock coats and ties as they rode the tram to work at five or six in the morning. But such attire, aspiring to middle-class gentility, was quickly abandoned at the docks or the railway yards, where grubby overalls were more suited to the ten hours of underpaid back-breaking labour ahead. May Day demonstrations in Buenos Aires were not simply the creation of foreign agitators, as some conservatives seemed to think; they were also the product of an unequal society, a society which seemed stuck. The national lottery, avidly played by poorer *Porteños*, was perhaps the best substitute for the aspirations of advancement slowly eroded by the reality of Argentinean economic life on the ground.

'Sir –', wrote Harry Jenkings to the *Herald*, 'I have often wondered when I have read in your columns the extravagant encomiums lavished upon this country by exalted personages . . . whether those exalted personages have entirely forgotten the warning . . . "All is not gold that glitters"'.[44] While it was certainly important to keep Argentina shining in the minds of foreign investors so as to keep their money flowing in, the glare of the elite's conspicuous wealth, on display in the grander streets of Buenos Aires, could blind outsiders to a worrying catalogue of unresolved problems:

> To those of us who have lived in Argentina a few years it is irritating to read, for example, that the Lord Knoosoo, after being whirled round the Port of Buenos Aires has expressed unbounded admiration of all that he has seen at a time when the mercantile community have been clamouring at the delays suffered by shipping through local mal-administration and when Insurance Companies have declined to accept responsibility for goods deposited in the Customs Houses owing to a succession of fires attributed to interested incendiaries. It is equally painful to hear Her Grace the Duchess of Timbucto declare after a motor tour extending from the Avenida de Mayo to the Hippodrome at Palermo that there is no crime, no poverty, and in short nothing undesirable in this modern El Dorado.

A closer look at the newspapers revealed a popular obsession with violence and petty crime. For immigrants, life in Argentina was tougher than many anticipated. Disappointment could be in store for investors, too, warned Jenkings: 'I believe that Argentina has reached its climax, that its "phenomenal progress" is a thing of the past . . . and that henceforth its advance will be by arithmetical, not geometrical, progression'.[45] Perhaps Argentina's destiny as a wealthy, powerful nation – like Moretti's monument – was to be delayed after all.

A torrent of letters followed, both to contest and to support Jenkings' broadside. 'Satisfied' responded angrily, suggesting that 'those who are making their living here should be the last to run it down; if they don't like it there are steamers leaving every day for other parts'.[46] This was the argument of the booster, warning that even if things were worse than reported, to make this known was to undercut one's own interests, and those of others. A railway clerk wrote to the *Herald* in disagreement with Jenkings, arguing that his fortunes had certainly improved since leaving Britain and that he was now able to send more money home to his mother in Bristol than both his brothers: 'Doesn't that show which is best for the average man?' More lightly, 'Gourmand' and 'Gourmet' fought it out in the pages of the newspaper over the quality of Argentina's gastronomy, the former criticising it while the latter noted the availability of French, Italian, Spanish and German cuisine, all of which could be washed down in Buenos Aires with Bordeaux or Chianti for less than $5.

More tragic was the letter of a British domestic servant, Anne Robinson, stuck in rural Argentina. 'Although I am no great hand at letter writing', she told the *Herald* nervously, 'I feel impelled to add a few words'.[47] 'I arrived in Argentina just as full of hope and visions of that cottage in the country (which is every domestic servant's ideal) as it was possible for a young woman to be', she wrote. Yet the country had proved a disappointment. In England she had enjoyed a reasonable position in a family with a house by the sea at Brighton, earning £25 a year. There, she chanced upon the brother of a friend, a sailor, who painted Argentina in bright colours and offered to put her in touch with a lady who would pay £60 a year for domestic help. And so, packing her life in a suitcase, she went across the seas. But, once in Argentina, she was quickly disabused of her initial optimism. Her mistress was kind, but she railed against an Irish-*Porteña* fellow servant – 'bad-tempered, dirty, ignorant and lazy'. The work was hard, the mud of the country impossible to wipe clean from the house in winter, and the dust impossible to protect against in the dry summer. 'I have an afternoon off every fortnight from 1 till 7', she wrote, but 'where can I go?' Church offered one possibility, or simply walking around town, but unable to speak Spanish and without the time to learn, she was isolated. She could make her own clothes, but imported materials from Europe were so expensive to almost make it not worthwhile:

> No, sir, when the next six months is up, I'll be glad to hear of a lady who wants a maid or a nursemaid on the voyage home. I'll gladly give my services in exchange for a passage home, but if not, the little I am able to save out of that wonderful £60 a year will have to get me home to England, even if in steerage.

Buenos Aires' southern star did not burn brightly for all.

ALGIERS
The Radiance of the Republic

In 1913, as a Frenchman would remind anyone who cared to listen, the southern extremity of the French Republic – that area legally considered the unitary territory of France, whole and indivisible – did not lie on the shores of the Mediterranean, but in Algeria, at the southern edge of the three French administrative *départements* of Algiers, Oran and Constantine. Formally, these *départements* were as much part of France as Normandy or Provence. It was only beyond them, amongst the undulating dunes of the Sahara, that the French Republic ended and the colonial French Empire began.

Granted, the governance of French Algeria as a whole – comprising both the three northern *départements* of French Algeria, considered an integral part of the French Republic, and a large southern area, treated more as a straightforward colony – differed in several important ways from the system of administration in effect in France north of the Mediterranean. A Governor General wielded substantial administrative powers over all of French Algeria, far beyond those of the French President.[1] There were layers of government unknown in mainland France, including the elected Délégations financières, the decisions of which were subject to approval in Paris. Although all the Algerian and French-born residents of Algeria, both European and non-European, were considered French subjects, most non-Europeans (Arab, Kabyle and Berber) were not considered full citizens, limiting their political rights, subjecting them to a different legal code and to a different (and more onerous) fiscal regime. These were substantial differences from how things were run on the French mainland, rooted in the politics of a white French Algerian population assuming leadership and control over a larger native Algerian population.

Yet, at the same time, parliamentarians representing the European population of the *départements* of Algiers, Oran and Constantine sat alongside those from Lyon, Nantes and Calais in the National Assembly in Paris. '*Liberté, égalité, fraternité*' adorned the doorways of primary schools in Algiers, just as they did those of Dunkerque. Most Frenchmen deemed *l'Algérie française* to be as eternally French as France was herself eternal. The inconsistencies between the principles of the French Republic and its practice in French Algeria were considered either temporary, or inevitable.

The coastline of Algeria had come under French control over eighty years ago, in 1830, when an insult delivered to the French consul by the local representative of the Ottoman Empire – the Frenchman was said to have been struck with a peacock-feathered fly-whisk for his alleged impertinence – had provided a pretext for invasion. Since then, French rule had steadily extended south. In 1848, a year of European revolutions known proverbially as the 'Springtime of the Nations', Algeria was formally annexed to France. By 1913, with France entrenched as the preponderant power in Tunisia and Morocco as well, France was far and away the dominant power in north Africa. Algeria was the centrepiece of France's overseas

Barrels of wine awaiting export from the port of Algiers. In 1913 Algeria was considered administratively part of France, and Algiers was a majority-French city.

expansion, a consolation for the loss of Alsace and Lorraine in the Franco-Prussian War of the 1870s and a frontier for French colonisation to match Britannic frontiers in Canada and Australia.

The proudest advocates of this idea of French Algeria as the radiant extension of France herself were the French Algerian parliamentarians – all of them European, of course – sent to Paris every few years. A tightly knit union of self-interested self-promoters, led by the formidable Eugène Étienne, they spent most of their time lobbying for more investment in Algeria, clamouring for more influence over the central ministries in Paris and rebutting calls for reforms which might undermine the privileged political and economic position of Europeans over Arabs.

Given the sparseness with which parliamentary debates on Algeria were attended by most other members of the French National Assembly, the French Algerian caucus could generally head off any liberal criticism in parliament. But getting the attention, let alone the active sympathy, of government was another matter. When Raymond Poincaré was elected President of the French Republic in January 1913, a telegram was sent by political leaders in Algiers congratulating him as an 'enlightened patriot and proven republican' – and making a request. 'Your Presidency should not pass without a visit to Algeria', the note read, 'to see for yourself its overflowing vitality, to study its legitimate aspirations and to bear witness to the indefatigable devotion of its population to France [and] to its republican institutions'.[2]

If the President himself were to visit French Algeria, the authors of the telegram reasoned, would he not see that here under the warm Algerian sun was a land fit for more widespread colonisation and that the dotted lines of maritime routes from France to Algeria were destined to grow ever more dense? Would he not understand that Algeria was not only France's Canada, or France's Australia, but perhaps even France's India? It was an inalienable aspect of France's greatness. To develop it was imperative, to lose it unthinkable.

Algiers was by some margin the largest city in Algeria, with more than 130,000 inhabitants, most of them European.[3] But it was also the *vitrine* for French Algeria as a whole: the first point of call for most visitors, the chief city of government, and, its denizens would argue, the most beautiful. The gardens of Algiers were filled with purple bougainvillea and white magnolias, its parks with orange and lemon trees, yuccas and palms, the surrounding countryside dotted with blue-green eucalyptus and hardy olive trees. It was precisely this natural beauty, and the proximity to the fresh air of the sea, that had made Algiers a popular city in which to pass a winter away from Europe in the last decades of the nineteenth century, attracting Karl Marx in 1882, amongst others.[4]

And Algiers had other merits, too, as far as many local French Algerians were concerned. The fact that the majority of its European population were of French origin – as opposed to the situation in other Algerian coastal towns, where the European population included large numbers of assimilated French of Italian, Spanish or Maltese descent – gave Algiers additional cachet over Bône (now Annaba), Philippeville (Skikda) and Oran.[5] The city was also the most culturally developed of Algeria's towns, boasting its own university (since 1909), its own municipal museum (since 1910) and its own roster of plays and concerts. In 1913, Beethoven's ninth symphony was performed in Algiers by a French orchestra. 'The ninth in Algiers!' one local was said to have exclaimed, 'it is almost as if the Mediterranean didn't exist anymore'.[6] A visiting Englishwoman, meanwhile, proclaimed the city 'extremely cosmopolitan', its streets 'full of interest'.[7] 'On the electric tramway', wrote Rachel Humphreys, newly arrived on the liner from Southampton, 'you may sit next to French, Germans, Greeks, Turks, Arabs, English, Americans and in the shady squares you may see a smart automobile followed by a curious cart filled with white-draped and veiled women coming in from the countryside'.[8]

In the central raised section of the waterfront – the Boulevard Carnot and the Boulevard de la République – the modern city was at its most splendid, a succession of elegant stone buildings with evenly spaced arcades at ground level, in the style of rue de Rivoli in Paris, and below them ramps leading down to the railway station and port. There, barrels of red wine, Algeria's chief export, awaited shipment to mainland France. In the evening, this would be the place to come to eat fresh crustaceans or *bouillabaisse* fish stew. A short stroll away was the chief square of the city, the Place du Gouvernement. It was here that the city's denizens would arrange to meet – with the equestrian statue of the Duke d'Orléans, the nineteenth-century conqueror of Algiers, acting as an obvious rendezvous – before taking a coffee in the nearby Café Apollon. It was here, on the Place du Gouvernement, that the city's yellow and brown trams converged. On Thursdays and Sundays one could hire a chair for a few centimes and pause to listen to a military band, a reminder of French martial glory and of the force which backed up France's continued presence.[9]

There was something else, too. While three sides of the Place du Gouvernement were shaded arcades – shops, cafés and a hotel – the square was completed on its fourth side by a mosque, the stark white-painted Mosquée de la Pêcherie. This was a reminder of a crucial difference between French Algeria and the French mainland. Outside the cities it was Muslim Algerians – Arabs, Berber and Kabyle – who dominated the country, numbering well over four and a half million compared to 720,000 Europeans (a number which included Jewish Algerians naturalised as French citizens en masse in 1870). The Muslim population of Algeria could not be as readily ignored as the indigenous people of Australia or Canada.

In Algiers itself, Muslim Algerians were more in the background than was the case in the countryside. Here, though never out of view entirely, they were only truly dominant in one part of the city: the Casbah. Once, the Casbah had been all there was of Algiers. Now, it was simply the Arab district of a much larger city, a triangle of white rising high up on the hill behind the modern French town. If the Boulevard de la République was the shopfront of French Algiers, the Casbah was the citadel of its Arab past. The elegant modern city of Algiers turned its back on the crowded Arab Casbah, trying to forget it, facing the sea instead.

'The lanes of old Algiers form the most bizarre muddle imaginable', warned the *Joanne* guide, describing the Casbah for French visitors, 'none is level or straight, they weave and snake, turn back on themselves, get tangled up the one with the other, sometimes climbing up sharp inclines, sometimes precipitously descending almost vertically'.[10] Rachel Humphreys, having struck up conversation (in Esperanto) with two French Algerians, was taken on a quick tour of the Arab town. 'I don't know how I can make you imagine the squalor and the primitive civilisation of the people in this part', she wrote later, 'smell is too mild a word for the appalling odours we encountered'.[11] Humphreys ultimately solved the problem by dousing her handkerchief in perfume and holding it close to her nose while she walked.

She observed the Arab population of the Casbah drinking their coffees in the street, out of the heat of the *'cafés maures'* (Arab cafés), before hurriedly moving on, and back down to the Hôtel Continental – the most highly recommended in the local *Baedeker* – on the Boulevard Bon-Accueil, in the European villa district of Mustapha-Supérieur.[12]

For some, the Casbah did impart a kind of romance. Isabelle Eberhardt – a Russo-German adventurer who fled the boredom of Switzerland to live as a Muslim in Algeria, where she married a French soldier of Algerian origin and became a sometime French spy – cast an indulgent eye over the Casbah of Algiers one summer evening, writing in her diary:

> How can all those fools in social and literary circles say there is nothing Arab about Algiers? There is for instance that lovely moment of the maghreb over the harbour and rooftops of the upper town. The place teems with merry Algerian women all frolicking happily in their pink or grey garb against the bluish-white of the rooftops ... Despite the riff-raff French civilisation has brought over here, whore and whoremaster that it is, Algiers is still a place full of grace and charm.[13]

Indeed, in the first years of the twentieth century, an Arab-inspired architectural style came back into fashion somewhat, the prime example of which was a new *madrasa* religious school built by the state in what was called the *'néo-Mauresque'* style.[14] French Algerian Henri Klein set up a local Comité des amis du vieil Alger (Committee of Friends of old Algiers) dedicated to protecting the city from the architectural encroachments of modernity. Meanwhile, north Africa was becoming fashionable to a new generation of artists looking for inspiration with which to mark their difference from the formal European traditions they sought to challenge. The flat, bleached-white houses of north Africa became the subject of paintings by Matisse (though he found Algiers itself 'vile, ugly' when he visited in 1906).[15] The Hungarian composer Béla Bartók travelled with his wife Marta to Biskra to record Arab music on his phonograph in the summer of 1913, hoping to find new tonalities he could use in his work.[16] Forced by heat to cut short his excursion, Bartók intended to return in 1914 – a plan interrupted by events in Europe.

On the ground in Algiers, however, many Frenchmen felt the Casbah, at least, deserved no such artistic endorsements, or special protection. Some wanted it razed entirely, to clean the slate. When conservationists frustrated his plans to create a new business district where a lower part of the Casbah now stood, Eugène de Redon, a French Algerian involved in the recent development of Algiers, was said to have exclaimed: 'The *historic* houses of the rue du 14 juin?! The *historic* Hamma fountain! It's the shitholes ['chiottes'] of the Casbah which are truly historic'.[17] He had a point. Typhus had overrun the Casbah in 1909. There were occasional bouts of malaria. Death stalked the narrow alleyways of the Casbah far more than in the airy Mustapha-Supérieur.

For many, then, far from being a picturesque corner of the city the Casbah was rather proof of the backwardness of native Algerians or, to a more enlightened few, a squalid reminder of the unkept promises of the French Republic to improve the lot of those same Algerians. To some the Casbah recalled a more uncomfortable truth, that the modern French cities of Algeria remained enclaves in the country as a whole, potentially vulnerable to the anger of the local Algerian Arab, Kabyle and Berber populations.

Bar a small and easily suppressed Algerian rebellion in the north-western village of Margueritte in 1901, it was over forty years since there had been any serious uprisings against the French presence in Algeria, during the Franco-Prussian War. Yet fear of pan-Islamist revolt was easily stoked amongst the French population. In 1913, in the north-eastern city of Constantine, André Servier wrote the popular *Le Péril de l'avenir*, warning that a nationalist current was beginning to take hold of the peoples of north Africa, influenced by events in Tunisia, Egypt and the Ottoman Empire, not to mention across the border in Libya, where Italian troops were in the process of establishing themselves as the new colonial masters against the will of the local Muslim population.[18] A string of similar books made the same argument. In French-language newspapers, standard crimes would be regularly qualified as 'indigenous' or 'Kabyle', as if to suggest a particular propensity for gruesomeness amongst the local Algerian population or an aptitude for crime in general.[19] For the three years leading up to 1913 the French forbade Algerians from undertaking the pilgrimage to Mecca on the basis that the journey risked exposing them to religious and political extremism. In 1913, the Haj was sanctioned once more, though local French officials asked darkly why it was that a German ship turned up to provide transport for the pilgrims.[20]

The same year, in Algiers, a theatre company from Tunis put on a modern Arab play for the first time: *Saladin*, by Najib al-Haddad.[21] The subject was politically piquant. Saladin had been a great Muslim leader, a man who had battled against the crusaders in the Holy Land, conquered Jerusalem, and won honour and respect for his skill, his daring and for his chivalry in victory. He was, in short, a pan-Arab hero. To evoke his life was to remind an audience of a time when Arabs had been the masters, not the subjects. As was painfully obvious, that time was now long gone. Yet educated Algerians were beginning to see themselves in a new light by 1913, as actors in their own history, framed by the French Republic and heavily informed by its values, yet not entirely determined by the dictates of Paris. In 1907, a book published in Algiers provided brief biographies of great figures from the Algerian past, the kind of hagiographical exercise which French republicans, who went in for much the same thing, would understand as being crucial to the formation of a sense of nationhood.

Meanwhile, the eternal French republican values of *liberté, égalité, fraternité* had proved highly malleable when faced with the question of how to organise a small European population amongst a much larger number of Arabs, Berbers and Kabyles. All republicans paid homage to the principle of assimilation, the ideal of turning Algerians into Frenchmen. This, they argued, was France's civilising mission. 'I am of those who have profound confidence in the unity of the human race', said Governor General Lutaud in a speech in May 1913.[22] But, as Lutaud and others saw it, if such unity was to be accomplished at all, it was to be achieved very much on French terms and at French leisure:

> On each occasion that an [indigenous] individual has received the benefits of education and civilisation he comes closer to us. By incre- ments, he can receive the same rights as us. It is the law of evolution, of slow but ineluctable transformation, imperceptible yet sure. The day when the indigenous peoples have the same education as us, the

day they set aside certain prejudices, will be the day that we can accept fully their demands.

From an Algerian perspective the promised transformation was indeed almost imperceptible. As of 1913 tremendous inequality persisted, entrenched in law and in practice. Algerians were French subjects, but not French citizens. It was possible for an Algerian to become one, though doing so would require the renunciation of his or her religion, and acceptance of the consequence that the Islamic clergy (as well as many of one's compatriots) would view this act of naturalisation as an act of apostasy. In the decade before 1909, only 337 Algerians had successfully applied for naturalisation to become French citizens, with a further 214 turned down.[23] Meanwhile, the civil rights accorded to Frenchmen did not apply in full to Algerians. The latter were subject to additional legal constraints, which made it a punishable offence for a Muslim to answer back to a French official or to fire a gun in the air in celebration of a marriage, as was the local tradition. Administrative detention could be used to lock up Algerians for up to three years simply on the say-so of the Governor General.

The same inequality that existed under the law existed under the fiscal arrangements to which Algerians were subject. Algerians paid far higher taxes than Europeans in proportion to their wealth and income, with so-called 'traditional' taxes still being levied, as well as the semi-feudal labour requirements of the *corvée*, abandoned in France at the revolution. No wonder Algerian landowners steadily lost out to French and other European farmers as they were gradually pushed deeper into debt, or into bankruptcy, or off the land and into the towns. While in 1913 half the Algerian population still lived and worked on land they owned, they had become steadily impoverished over time, forced to divide their farms into smaller and smaller parcels. In 1913, thirty years after Karl Marx's visit to Algeria to enjoy its restorative qualities, his acolyte Rosa Luxemburg cited the country as a prime example of the capitalist accumulation of wealth by the colonisers. 'Next to tormented British India', she wrote, 'Algeria under French rule claims pride of place in the annals of capitalist colonisation'.[24]

Despite providing the bulk of Algeria's taxes, Algerians had relatively little say in how that money was then spent, with predictable results in the provision of public services. In rural areas, if there were mayors at all, they were French. In some communes a council might have one-quarter of its seats, but no more, elected by Algerians. In others, what Algerian representatives there were on local commissions were appointed by the French – a lucky few called *Béni Oui-Oui* for their propensity to agree wholeheartedly with whatever the French proposed to them. In Algiers itself, while twenty-one members of the Délégations financières – the body which passed the local budget for the whole of Algeria – were either Arabs or Kabyles, they were outnumbered two to one by Europeans. Moreover, whereas European delegates were elected according to universal male suffrage of French Algerians, Algerian representatives were selected by a small Algerian elite of no more than 5,000, largely consisting of the conservative Algerians who were thought most likely to keep their own people in check.

The gap between the promise of the republic and what it actually provided in Algeria was unmistakeable to anyone who took the time to look more closely at the reality of country. Increasingly, however, an educated and Gallicised Algerian elite was developing, prepared to challenge the gap – in French, and directly to the French government. In 1913, Chérif Benhabylès, holder of a doctorate in French law, put his thoughts down on paper. 'This judgement', wrote Benhabylès, 'is the timid confession of a young native Algerian brought up in a French classroom, who profoundly loves the beautiful name of France, who owes his education to the French administration and who owes it the truth; who wants to be neither the detractor of his sponsors as are some ungrateful souls, nor the obsequious lickspittle of the power of the day'.[25] Benhabylès did not criticise the republic so much as call its bluff.

Algerians should be grateful, Benhabylès argued, for the security provided by France, the establishment of order in what had once been a country of brigands, a base for pirates. And yet, 'consider the monthly pay of a police officer', he continued, 'Mohammed ben Ali, zealous agent, who has earned both the confidence and respect of his superiors, but when it comes to the budget, the scales weigh heavily in favour of François Alberti . . . Why this inequality?' He sharply criticised the traditional Algerian elite, who he viewed as by turns conservative and lazy, content to enjoy the dubious fruits of their position rather than to seek their own improvement – or the improvement of others. In the evening, Benhabylès suggested, the young scions of the old Algerian aristocracy were to be found not learning to be Frenchmen, but at the Dar Zbantout, the house of bachelors, 'where one plucks at guitars, plays cards, binges on soft cakes, smokes *kif,* or even opium while a *houri* [a beautiful girl] her eyes haloed with charcoal, most often a Jewish prostitute, looks after the others'. A few streets away, he continued, 'sobbing mothers and wives wait for our *promeneurs*'. (It was a criticism made not just by liberal, Gallicised Algerians of course, but by their religious counterparts too: the followers of Salafist Islam who sought a purification of religious life, believing it to have been corrupted both by the French and by the traditional Algerian upper crust.)

But Benhabylès argued that the path ahead for a new Algerian elite – the Jeunes Algériens – lay not away from France, but through it, through the same institutions from which he himself had benefited: the school and the university.[26] (The path for Emir Khaled, an Algerian from a prestigious family who rallied to the Jeunes Algériens in 1913, had been through that other great republican institution: the army.[27]) Fundamentally, Benhabylès concluded, French Algerian arguments against the agenda of the Jeunes Algériens were motivated by economic interests; they feared competition from Algerians for jobs and government spending. Their political fears were overwrought. The spectre of pan-Islamism – 'the product of the fertile imagination of a couple of writers' – was simply a smokescreen raised to conceal these rather baser motives.[28] In any case, was not France bound to support reform in Algeria in order to be true to the values of the republic? Indeed, would not reform be 'the most beautiful compensation for a country which has always had trust in her children, whose glorious mission has been to carry through the entire universe and through different epochs of her history, the splendid flag of civilisation'?[29]

As befitted a doctor of law, Benhabylès did not employ the language of revolution. His was the republican language of gradualist assimilation, expressed by an Algerian rather than a Frenchman. After all, the Jeunes Algériens were not seeking full political rights for all Algerians tomorrow, but rather the greater inclusion of a French-educated elite – themselves, in other words – in the management of the country. It was a lessening of the legal and economic burdens that was requested, not a wholesale dismantling of French rule. In many respects, what was surprising about the agenda of the Jeunes Algériens was how moderate it was. In 1908, a delegation of Algerians had travelled to Paris in order to put the case to Prime Minister Georges Clemenceau. In 1912, another group returned with something approaching a manifesto for reform to put to Prime Minister Poincaré. The following year Emir Khaled, a man whose distinguished Algerian lineage, service in the French army and French education meant that he was able to span the worlds of both traditional Algerians and republican Frenchmen, made a series of speeches in France advocating the adoption of the reforms proposed by the Jeunes Algériens. An *Alliance Franco-indigène* was set up, supported by leading French intellectuals (as well as by French socialist leader Jean Jaurès). Momentum for change was building.

There was a powerful new argument to employ in the service of reform in Algeria in 1913, one to which Paris was increasingly sensitive: conscription.

For some years now governments in Paris had considered the option of extending compulsory military service to Muslim Algerians, the vast majority of whom were not French citizens, as a means of boosting the size of the French army. Done right, this would turn Algeria from a drain on the troops of metropolitan France, who were required to garrison the place, into a reservoir of fresh conscripts. French Algerians opposed the idea, on the one hand noting that it would disturb Algerian economic life and, on the other, worried that the army would provide native Algerians with dangerous organisational and military skills. For different reasons, the traditional Algerian elite opposed the extension of military service as well, concerned about what would happen to Muslims in a majority-Christian army, and seeing in it only an additional burden on themselves and their sons.

The Jeunes Algériens took a different line. They were prepared to accept the idea, but they had conditions. If the duties of citizenship were to be extended to Algerians, should not a greater share of the rights of citizenship also be extended? As a matter of justice, but also as a matter of good politics, would it not be wise to placate the Algerians somehow by giving them something they wanted? Theirs was a strategy to use military service as a lever to prise open the structures of *l'Algérie française* and to insist on reform, trusting that Paris was ultimately worried more about troop numbers than about the inevitable howls of protest from a handful of French Algerian parliamentary deputies.

And so it went. Compulsory military service was extended in 1912; promises were made in Paris that reforms would follow. But when? And which reforms? The devil, as always, was in the detail and the timing. In 1913, as Emir Khaled was building support for the agenda of the Jeunes Algériens in Paris, none other than Eugène Etienne – French Algerian member of the French National Assembly, stalwart defender of the political status quo – was made minister of national defence. How, then, would the circle of French national security, Algerian reform, the promises of the republic, and colonisers' self-interest, be squared? Was a new bargain for the French Republic in north Africa waiting to be struck? Or, as so often before, had promises for reform been made which, ultimately, would not be kept? Would the French Republic be truly republican north of the Mediterranean, but only ever superficially republican south of it? As 1913 closed, these questions burned more deeply than ever.

BOMBAY—DURBAN

Tapestry of Empire

On the morning of 23 December 1912 on Chandni Chowk Road, midway between the railway station and the Red Fort, former residence of the Mughal Emperors in Delhi, a bomb was thrown at the *howdah* (elephant carriage) of Charles Hardinge, Viceroy of India, the personal representative of the King-Emperor George V. 'It exploded with terrific force', the official government note recorded afterwards, 'blowing to pieces the attendant who was standing in the *howdah* immediately behind Lord Hardinge and seriously wounding the attendant who was standing behind Lady Hardinge'.[1] 'Her Excellency fortunately escaped', continued the report, 'but parts of the missile struck Lord Hardinge and inflicted the wounds described by the medical report'. A boy standing nearby was killed. Several onlookers were wounded.

An investigation ensued. The Muslim head of the local Criminal Investigation Department, Khan Bahadur Sheikh Abdullah, reported that the bomb used picric acid as its chief explosive and had been thrown on to the *howdah* from the offices of the Punjab National Bank.[2] The perpetrators of the crime, however, could not be identified. In a country of 300 million or more – some parts falling directly under British rule, others coming under the rule of local Indian princes (with British guidance), and the whole presided over by a handful of British civil servants of the Indian Civil Service, with a small number of troops to call on (mostly Indian, with British officers) and limited police resources, even a high-profile political crime such as this could not necessarily be solved without a lucky lead. After all, Hardinge's India – otherwise known as the Raj – stretched from the borders of Afghanistan and Tibet in the north to the waters off Ceylon (Sri Lanka) in the south, taking in everything between Siam (Thailand) in the east and Persia (Iran) in the west. This was a world to itself, and one into which a fugitive could easily melt.

For the time being, therefore, the attempt on the life of the Viceroy simply had to be accepted as part of a broader wave of sporadic anti-British activity over the last few years, particularly in Bengal in eastern India, where anti-British feeling had been aroused by a cack-handed attempt to partition the historic province into two administrative parts – a policy now happily reversed. A boycott – named *swadeshi* in Hindi, meaning self-sufficiency – of non-Indian goods had briefly gained popularity in the wake of the partition proposal, but had never gained nationwide traction, and had now become more of a general slogan for Indian economic development and the protection of Indian craft traditions, something upon which a wide group of Indians and British could agree. Terrorism had been used by some as a political weapon against the British, but it never threatened the hold of the Raj on India as a whole.

That said, the spread of terrorism to Delhi was a cause for particular concern. After all, the city had been proclaimed as the new capital of the Raj only two years previously. In 1911, the King-Emperor George V had visited India and, in a semi-feudal display of allegiance known as the Delhi Durbar, received the magnificent homage of Indian princes. Delhi was thus supposed to be a redoubt and symbol of British strength in India, installing the British in the public mind as legitimate heirs of the Mughal Emperors who had once been based there. The symbolism of the city was reinforced by the choice of architectural style in which it was built, a point made forcefully by Charles Hardinge when he urged a building style 'such as will appeal to Orientals as well as Europeans'.[3] Now, even before that city had been completed, had its purpose as a symbol of British power already been compromised?

It was impossible to know how most Indians saw such things – or even whether they had a view. Besides a tiny minority whose voices were listened to attentively, Indians were unheard at the centre. Most Indians' lives were dictated entirely by local circumstances and concerns.[4] Most British persisted, then, in their belief that their presence in India was broadly welcomed as a benign act of civilisation, bringing railways and enlightenment to the country, spreading the virtues of order and the principles of good government. What they heard from and about India they heard mostly from those close to the Indian government, from retired British members of the Indian Civil Service or superannuated military officers – not quite as self-interested as the French Algerian deputies in the National Assembly in Paris, but nonetheless with a view of themselves as a caste among castes, a select group who better understood the true interests of India than did the Indians themselves.

Meanwhile, the Indian group which did purport to speak for Indians as a whole – the ambitiously named Indian National Congress, in reality an organisation of Indian elites, sometimes chaired by British sympathisers – was split.[5] The moderate wing called only for reform within India, and for the raising of India's status within the British Empire. 'Man for man they are better men than ourselves', said Congress leader Gopal Krishna Gokhale of the British, 'they have a higher standard of duty, higher notions of patriotism, higher notions of loyalty to each other, higher notions of organised work and discipline, and they know how to make a stand for the privileges of which they are in possession'.[6] There was still something to be learned from the British lion; for the moderates, the British Empire continued to be India's natural home.

Others were not so sure. Bal Gangadhar Tilak, a former leading member of the Congress, had suggested enhanced agitation against the British, calling for a quicker path to much fuller *swaraj*, 'self-rule'. Pictures of Tilak were said to be hung on Bombay walls. His conviction in a Bombay courtroom in 1908 on a charge of sedition had led to protests in the streets. But in 1913 Tilak was still in prison – and the pragmatic self-appointed representatives of Indian opinion maintained their calm appeals for reform, reform to which they felt their own moderate demeanour gave them full entitlement. At the Indian National Congress meeting in Karachi at the end of the year, the president of the meeting, the Muslim Nawab Syed Muhammad Bahadur, sensed a reduction in the stresses in British India – and in his own organisation. 'The Indian unrest from which, thanks alike to the good sense of the people and to British statesmanship, we have safely emerged', he told his audience, 'was part of the prodigious waves of awakening and unrest that swept over the whole of Asia during all this period'.[7] From this point forward, he urged, 'let us strive for unity amongst us, for the advancement of the nation, and for bringing the forces of progress and solidarity in line with our achievements in the past and of our expectations for the future'.

The attempt on the life of Viceroy Charles Hardinge in Delhi. India was the lynchpin of the British Empire, a reserve of military manpower and a market for British goods.

Over the course of the first few weeks of 1913, Charles Hardinge was in convalescence. When he was fully recovered, things in India returned to their normal confused state: the jewel of the British Empire, won for Britain as much by chance as by design and as much by commercial interests as by government intention; the greatest asset of empire and its greatest vulnerability; a mystery to many; a multitude of peoples, races and religions which, the British claimed, could be managed only as they did, with skill, disinterest and unflinching composure. Present in India for centuries, the British were now part of the landscape, the story of British India mirroring the growth of British power globally. 'The English connection with India has grown with the growth of England', wrote William Wilson Hunter in his introduction to his history of British India, 'till it now forms flesh of our flesh and bone of our bone'.[8]

A few months after the attempt on Hardinge's life in Delhi, a welcome display of moderate Indian loyalty was put on in downtown Bombay – the gateway to India, the seaside city where King-Emperor George V had landed in 1911 on his way to the Durbar. The occasion now was Empire Day 1913, celebrated in Bombay just as in Winnipeg or Melbourne, albeit with a distinctly Indian touch. 'The premises of Javer Baug were adorned with the Union Flag . . . and the entrance of the Nar-Narayan temple was hung with a placard with the words "Long Live the Emperor and Empress of India"', wrote Purushottam Balkrishna Joshi, a noted historian of Bombay in a pamphlet published to accompany the celebrations, *Empire-Day and Our Duties and Responsibilities*.[9] Portraits of George V and his wife Queen-Empress Mary were decorated with garlands of flowers. 'The Shankaracharya of Karvir who presided was provided with a raised seat covered with the sacred *agin* or black antelope skin', Joshi continued, 'the proceedings commenced with a recitation of a prayer in sanskrit by the Shankaracharya'.

There were advantages to British overlordship, as Joshi saw it. 'English education [particularly the British foundation of five Indian universities] has revolutionized our society, it has dispelled our puerile prejudices and opened to our view a vista of boundless knowledge', at least for the tiny minority able to attend.[10] In this, were not the British following in the best Brahmanic traditions of spreading education and enlightenment to the people, feeling their responsibilities towards Indians just as Hindu aristocrats felt their duties towards others? Were not the British and the Brahmans thus natural partners in this quest? Without improvements in education, he argued, India would have been condemned to backwardness and the British to being unloved:

> India would have remained in the same darkness of ignorance in which Afghanistan and Persia are at present . . . Englishmen would have been shunned and hated as *mlecchas* [barbarians], or if tolerated owing to the might of their bayonets, they would have been considered as the descendants of the monkey heroes of Rama.

Politically, had not the British brought order, after the mutiny of 1857? 'The people of India will never forget the foresight, magnanimity and statesmanship displayed by Queen Victoria [the first Indian Empress] and her able ministers', suggested Joshi, though he added that the British had not yet made good on all of their undertakings to the people of India on matters of government. 'We have not asked for any special rights or privileges', he told his audience at Javer Baug, 'what we pray for and earnestly wish is the fulfilment of the solemn promises given to us by Queen Victoria'. But, like the Indian National Congress, he counselled an approach of patience, loyalty and friendly argument with their British partners, rather than one of terroristic recklessness, which would be bound to antagonise the British and demonstrate the inaptitude for self-rule some ascribed to India and Indians. 'No greater sin do the Indians ever commit than by being ungrateful to the British Raj', Joshi declared, 'which is taking much pains for their sake ever since the British set their foot on these shores'.

According to this view, India was in Britain's eternal debt. The Raj, far from being a device for the British oppression of Indians, was ultimately a tool for India's own self-improvement. In this conception, the relationship of Britain and India was a partnership – unequal at first, perhaps, but tending over time towards a gloriously liberal equality. Did not reforms introduced in recent years – the introduction of sixty elected Indian representatives into the Viceroy's Council, Indian representatives on provincial councils, and the reversal of the partition of Bengal – demonstrate the unalterable path of reform, a step in the right direction, though perhaps a timorous, halting step?

True, India in 1913 was perhaps even less of a democracy than French Algeria. But then Britain had never promised quite as much as the French Republic. For its mandate, it offered law, education and good government, rather than liberty, equality and fraternity. Indeed, might not democracy as understood in the European sense actually run counter to good government in India? For did the British not have a duty to protect minorities – Muslims, for example – from too great an advance of majoritarian principles which would see them swamped by Hindus? Being overcome by force of Hindu numbers was something feared by the newly formed Muslim League, which prefaced petitions for British protection with ample professions of loyalty to the British Crown. Coming from a group of Indians distinctly over-represented in both army and police – precisely because they were considered particularly loyal – this was warmly accepted. Even while British liberals joined some Indian colleagues – including British-Indian MP Dadabhai Naoroji, elected for the London seat of Finsbury Central in 1892 – in criticism of unreformed imperial rule in India, they did not all necessarily believe that unfettered democracy was the answer. The problems of governing India were not to be solved in a single stroke, by the British or by anyone else.

The British might claim a historic mission in India, but no one could doubt that Britain derived clear material and strategic advantages from her presence in India as well. Moral purpose was handily allied with national pride – and self-interest. 'As long as we rule India, we are the greatest power in the world', Lord Curzon, a previous Viceroy, had noted in 1901, 'if we lose it we shall drop straightaway to a third-rate power'.[11] The reason for India's importance was partly economic. In 1913, Britain's single biggest export was still cotton piece goods, for which its biggest market was still India.[12] British money invested in India had developed a giant railway network across the country and Indian purchases of train engines and carriages in turn represented a third of Britain's exports of those goods. But it was also political, and strategic. Control of India brought control of the Indian Ocean, and therefore the maritime routes between Europe and Asia. At the same time, control of India forestalled Russian expansion which would lead to further dominance of the Eurasian landmass. Moreover, troops stationed in India, more numerous than were required for India's own defensive needs yet paid for by taxes raised in India – the so-called 'Home Charges'

– provided a sizeable additional reserve of military manpower should the need arise to bolster other parts of the British Empire. Finally, Indian gold was held in London, adding to Britain's own stocks, and ensuring that, as India's silver-based currency tended to devalue – the subject of a Royal Commission in 1913, ably assisted by John Maynard Keynes – payment of the 'Home Charges' due to Britain would be secured.

In 1913, India was called the jewel of empire, as if it were merely a decorative bauble, an ornamental addition to British possessions, an additional body of British subjects to swell a Londoner's pride at the immensity of the empire of which he was the centre. It might more properly have been referred to as the empire's lynchpin.

For most travellers from Europe, having travelled through the Suez Canal, been funnelled along the Red Sea and then spat out into the Indian Ocean at Aden, their first landfall in India would be Bombay, a former Portuguese colony given to the British crown as part of Catherine of Braganza's dowry when she married King Charles II in 1661.

In the seventeenth century, Bombay had been a city of 10,000 – a fortified island port, one node in a Muslim trading network stretching along the coast of India and across the ocean to Arabia and east Africa. Over time and under British rule the city's physical form had expanded, land had been reclaimed from the sea, and the island of Bombay had been steadily transformed into more of a man-made peninsula, jutting confidently from the mainland into the Indian Ocean. In 1853 a railway line had first connected Bombay to Thana. In later years – up to 1912, when the Mazagon-Sewri reclamation added 583 acres to the land of the city – engineers extended Bombay outwards, connecting the surrounding islands into a single whole.[13] Now, in 1913, Bombay numbered one million residents – a few hundred thousand behind Calcutta. It was an industrial city as well as a commercial one, home to the richest in India as well as some of its poorest, a cosmopolitan, crowded city, where the sounds of Marathi mingled with those of Gujurati and Hindustani, where Muslims of different sects, Hindus, Zoroastrian Parsis, Jews and Christians all found their place.

In 1854, the year after the railway line to Thana was completed, the city's first cotton mill was founded by Parsi businessman Cowasji Dawar, inaugurating an Indian-owned and Indian-run industry which made Bombay the economic and financial capital of India. By 1911, when the Tata Hydroelectric Power Plant opened at Lonavala, Bombay claimed to house half the cotton looms in the whole of the country.[14] 'The year nineteen hundred and eleven will stand out as a red-letter day in the annals of the development of the city of Bombay', gushed one journalist, 'brought to its present stage of development by Indian intelligence and Indian capital'.[15] 'For long India was held an important place in the world because of her vision', the article continued. But now things were changing:

> She [India] has dreamed dreams. She has lived among the stars. When India hitches to the star a waggon of practical life and learning there will undoubtedly be a future for her mightier than even the past has been. India will make, within the next century, mighty advances in science and industry.[16]

Bombay was a city of empire, to be sure, yet not an imperial city in the same way as its peers: Delhi, built for the purpose of impressing upon Indians the claims of the British Raj to be the successors to the Mughal Emperors, or Calcutta, where the traders and industrialists were as much European as Indian.[17] Bombay was not to be a city with its head in the stars, but representative of a practical, commercial, modern, businesslike India: the India of the future, confident and outgoing. Bengal might have produced India's first winner of the Nobel Prize for Literature, Rabindranath Tagore, in 1913, but it was in Bombay that India's first film was premiered in the same year, *Raja Harischandra*. 'SEE – The Royal Tiger Hunt, SEE – The Fire in the Jungle', proclaimed a newspaper advertisement for the movie.[18] Bombay's confidence abounded in its physical environment. In the 1880s the city built the magnificent Victoria Terminus railway station, the largest building in the Raj. All brick archways, crenellations, Gothic spires, and gargoyles, it bore more than a faint resemblance to St Pancras railway station in London, with a few additional concessions to the Saracenic style of north India. At the entrance, visitors were greeted by a British lion and an Indian tiger, and the whole building was topped with a fourteen-foot statue representing Progress. Down by the water, the colossal Taj Mahal Hotel greeted its first guests in 1903, built on the orders of Jamsetji Tata, one of Bombay's leading Parsi businessmen. 'Urbs Prima in Indis' – 'Foremost City in India' – proclaimed the city's crest. It was a boast that the residents of Bombay intended to maintain. 'Of no mean city am I', crowed Bombay-born poet Rudyard Kipling in the dedication to one of his popular collections of poetry, 'For I was born in her [India's] gate/Between the palms and the sea/Where the world's-end steamers wait'.[19]

From the sea, the city could be sensed before it was seen. 'The air is heavy with an indefinable perfume', wrote Serbian Prince Bojidar Karageorgevitch, approaching the city on board ship in the last years of the nineteenth century, 'we are already coasting the Indian shore, but it remains invisible and gives no sign but by these gusts of warmer air laden with that inscrutable aroma of musk and pepper'.[20] Then, the city itself appeared:

Before daybreak, in the doubtful light of waning night, dim masses are visible – grey and purple mountains – mountains shaped liked temples of which two indeed seem to be crowned with low squat towers as if unfinished. The morning mist shrouds everything; the scene inevitably passes through a series of pale tints, to reappear ere long in the clear rosy light which sheds a powdering of glowing gold on the broad roadstead of Bombay . . . As we go nearer, gothic towers are distinguishable among the buildings . . . revived under the burning light of white Asia.

For one German visitor to the city a few years later, Count Hans von Koenigsmarck, it was again the city's smell – 'a blend of musk, of spices, and of the smouldering sandal-wood they burn at prayer and festivals' – which first assaulted his senses.[21] But close behind came its colour: 'the human skin reveals itself here in every shade and tint, and the variety of its garb beggars every colour of the palette'. And it was perhaps the concentrated variety of Bombay which ultimately best characterised the city, in keeping with its traditions as a city of mercantile exchange, a meeting place for those with something to sell and those with money to buy:

The fascination of Bombay lies in its diversity – the diversity of its landscape, of its street scenes, of its population. One would have to have a hundred eyes to be able to take in its exotic, kaleidoscopic *va-et-vient*. Talk of scenes from *The Thousand and One Nights*! The Orient, in its entire fairylike splendour, and alongside it sober businesslike Europe; the drab commonplaceness of the West rubbing shoulders with these teeming crowds drunk with colour and adventure. Bombay is at one and the same time pan-Asiatic and cosmopolitan – a melting pot of races and religions.

In Bombay, on one street, one might see a limp body being taken away to be burned, in the hope that this would help cure the city of its periodic bouts of plague. Elsewhere, perhaps on the Malabar Hill, the grandest residential area of the city, overlooking the Back Bay, one could see the automobile drive past of a Parsi millionaire. 'Who does not recognise the savour, typical here, of blistering human flesh', asked Koenigsmarck, 'mingling with the fragrance of tropical vegetation'?[22]

Stephen Edwardes, an amateur historian of the rise of Bombay and by 1913 the city's police chief, claimed that 'of the human tides which roll through the streets of the cities of the world, none are brighter or more varied than that which fills the streets of Bombay':

Here are Memon and Khoja women in shirt and trousers ('kurta' and 'izzar') of green and gold or pink and yellow, with dark blue sheets used as veils, wandering along with their children dressed in all the hues of the rainbow. Here are sleek Hindus from northern India in soft muslin and neat coloured turbans; Gujurathis in red head-gear and close-fitting white garments; Cutchi sea-farers, descendants of the pirates of dead centuries, with clear-cut bronzed features . . . English soldiers in Khaki; Arabs from Syria and the valley of the Euphrates; half-Arab, half-Persian traders from the Gulf, in Arab or old Persian costumes and black turbans with a red border . . . tall Afghans, their hair well-oiled, in the baggiest of trousers . . . Sindis in many-buttoned waistcoats; Negroes from Africa clad in striped waist cloths, creeping slowly through the streets and pausing in wonder at every new sight; Negroes in Bombay Mahomedan dress and red fez; Chinese with pig-tails; Japanese in the latest European attire; Malays in English jackets and loose turbans; Bukharans in tall sheep skin caps and woollen gabardines, begging their way from Mecca to their Central Asian homes.[23]

This, Edwardes might reflect anxiously, was the city in which he was to keep order. It was quite a task, requiring a permanent balancing act between communities, each with their own interests, festivals, traditions and historic rivalries imported from the wide spaces of the countryside into the close quarters of Bombay. For here in the city, life was uncomfortably compressed. According to the census of 1911, three-quarters of Bombay's population lived in single rooms in four or five-storey *chawls* (tenements). The city government occasionally built new buildings with more light and air, but often they charged too much rent to attract tenants, or else found that these larger, better-ventilated rooms ended up being inhabited by more people than the number for which they were designed.[24] In 1893, eighty people had been killed in intercommunal riots between Muslims and Hindus. Five years later, in 1898, a heavy-handed search party looking for a concealed plague victim was confronted with an angry crowd, upon which they fired, sparking attacks against Europeans in turn. In 1904 traditional Sunni Islamic *tolis* (street bands) celebrating the festival of Muharram were banned from the central Doctor Street at the request of Shi'a Bohras, who subsequently inveighed against Sunnis' irreligious 'rowdy and irregular processions . . . making immense noise both vocally and with tom toms . . . making most indecent gestures and signs and exposing their persons to males and females'.[25] When, in 1911, Edwardes the police chief attempted to prescribe the route which could be taken by the marching *tolis* – the 'roystering and brawling . . . of aboriginal spirit-belief', as he described it elsewhere – twenty people were killed by police gunfire.[26]

The best view of the city, as a whole, was afforded from the ridge of the Malabar Hill at the southern end of one of the promontories of Bombay island. From here, the full range of the town revealed itself, from its spacious new gardens and parks to the crowded old city, the grand administrative edifices of empire and, a little further out, the cotton mills that had made the fortunes of Bombay's Parsi elite. 'Standing by night upon the ridge', described the *Imperial Gazetteer* in 1908, 'one looks down upon the palm groves of Chaupati, and across the sweep of the Back Bay to the Rajabai tower [of the neo-Gothic University of Bombay, designed by Gilbert Scott, the architect of St Pancras station in London], the Secretariat, and the Light-house at Colaba, the whole curve of land being jewelled with an unbroken chain of lights which have earned the appropriate title of "The Queen's Necklace"'.[27] Below, across the bay, lay the old city of Bombay. To the left, was 'the industrial area, with its high chimney stacks and mill roofs', the origin of many fortunes for the owners of the mills, and increasingly hit by strikes of workers protesting against the conditions under which these fortunes were made.[28] In 1913, the chairman of the Bombay Mill Owners' Association, Jehangir Bomanji Petit, foresaw India being affected by the same tendencies as Europe. 'Labour in this city', he noted, 'has now commenced to realise the force of numbers and the power of combination'.[29]

Hans von Koenigsmarck traced Britain's impress in the structures of Bombay. 'You can tell at the outset that this metropolis is the daughter of old England', he wrote with Germanic confidence.[30] The Union Jack flew atop the Governor's residence, certainly. Of the 2,398 cars listed in *Thacker's Bombay Directory* of 1913, the prized registration number 01 fell to British Captain G. H. Hewett, just ahead of the Maharaja of Gwalior, who had to make do with registrations 02, 03 and 04.[31] British architects, meanwhile, were responsible for many of the city's main public buildings. But in most respects the city's British aspect was lightly worn. The city's two leading architects, Scots John Begg and George Wittet, adopted the consciously un-British Indo-Saracenic style for two of the grandest buildings built in Bombay in recent years: the General Post Office building and the Prince of Wales Museum of Western India.[32]

Undoubtedly the most British spot in Bombay was the Royal Bombay Yacht Club, on the Apollo Bunder (a seafront promenade). On a Friday afternoon, the place filled with expatriate Anglo-Indians, awaiting the arrival of the mailboat from Britain while listening to a smartly dressed British military band playing in the club gardens. Indians were excluded. 'One could hardly find a more enjoyable way of passing an hour or two', confided Rachel Humphreys, fresh from her adventures in Algiers, 'than at the Yacht Club, which is essentially English, not a trace of a gentleman of colour allowed'.[33] John Alfred Spender, editor of the *Westminster Gazette*, wrote: 'Tone it all down and in the dim light the view [from the Bombay Yacht Club] might be that from Plymouth Hoe [on the English south coast]'. Spender, visiting India for the Delhi Durbar of 1911, went on, 'the twilight passes quickly, festoons of electric light make a dazzle on a hundred tea-tables, and an excellent military band strikes up a selection from "Samson and Delilah"'.[34] 'While you are here', he continued, 'you forget the great, seething, miasmic city behind you'. Rather, he wrote:

[you] wonder at the cheerfulness, smartness, good looks and good manners of the Bombay English and their womenkind. Civilians or soldiers, they are clearly a strong, self-reliant, well-favoured race, with an indefinable air of being in authority.[35]

The authority, however, was not, at least as Spender saw it, flaunted:

You hear no big talk; it is, indeed, the most difficult thing in the world to induce any of them [the British military and civilian administrators] to talk at all about themselves or their duties. They seem to take for granted that they should be there and doing what they are doing. The first dominant impression you bear away is that they have a great interest in governing and none at all in possessing. Hence, in spite of the alien rule, Bombay strikes you as eminently belonging to itself, as being in fact a real Indian town and as remote as possible from a British colony.[36]

And Bombay was indeed in many respects far more Indian than it was British, the very opposite of Algiers, which was more French than Algerian. If leading Indians were excluded from British clubs, no matter – they had their own. In 1886, the Parsis established their own *gymkhana*, or 'sports club'. A plot of land for a Muslim *gymkhana* was secured in 1892, and a Hindu *gymkhana* two years later. In 1912, for the first time, there was a quadrangular cricket tournament between the four communities: European, Parsi, Muslim and Hindu. Perhaps the leading citizens of Bombay would not meet in each others' homes, or in each others' club-rooms, but they could at least meet on the cricket pitch.

When not competing at cricket, the different communities of Bombay engaged in competitive philanthropy. The winner of this contest was undoubtedly Sir Jamsetjee Jeejeebhoy, a leading Parsi, and the first Indian in Bombay to be granted a baronetcy (a hereditary knighthood). Jeejeebhoy and his successors were well represented in the names of hospitals and fire temples across the city – not to mention Bombay's art school, where Lockwood Kipling, the father of arch-Anglo-Indian Rudyard Kipling, taught architecture. By 1913, seven other Bombay baronetcies had been created in recognition of the local great and good: two more in the Parsi community, three amongst the Sassoon family of Baghdadi Jews, and one each from the Muslim and Hindu communities.[37] It was these leading lights of the Parsi, Muslim, Hindu and Jewish communities who influenced the Bombay City Improvement Trust, the body charged with reshaping the city itself. Occasionally, influential leaders of the Indian community in Bombay would weigh into wider discussions – for example the conditions of Indians in other parts of the British Empire or, for Indian Muslims, the attitude taken by Britain on the wars in the Balkans – convening meetings in the city, or firing off letters to relevant government officials. For these Bombay men and women their city stood not on the fringes of British India, but at the centre of a wider Indian world.

In 1913, the attention of Bombay Indians turned not only to matters in Madras, Mysore or Calcutta. It turned also across the Indian Ocean to the Indian diaspora in Durban, in the province of Natal, in the newly formed Union of South Africa.

The previous year Congress leader Gopal Krishna Gokhale had spent nearly a month in South Africa, following a punishing schedule that took him from Cape Town to the Kimberley diamond mines, and to Johannesburg, Pretoria and Natal, meeting with everyone from the Transvaal Chinese Association to the South African premier, Louis Botha, and his government. Entering Durban, a seaside city like Bombay and home to the majority of South Africa's Indian community, Gokhale was met at the station by the Jewish mayor of the city, F. C. Hollander. The Indian anthem 'Vande Mataram' was sung by local Indian girls as the train pulled in to a platform decorated with British flags. 'Outside', noted an account of the visit, 'a team of four cream horses decorated with pink carnations and rosettes of green, yellow and red ribbon awaited ... Thousands of Indians thronged the streets, and constant cheering was kept up along the route'.[38] Always by Gokhale's side, sometimes

making speeches in reply to his, sometimes welcoming him, sometimes reminding the audience of Gokhale's wider fame – even
suggesting that had he been born British he would be Prime Minister,
and had he been born American he would be President – was
Mohandas Karamchand Gandhi, an English-trained lawyer who
had earned a reputation in South Africa for his integrity, and for
his ability to make himself an unfailingly polite nuisance to the
authorities.

Shuttling between the Tolstoy farm – named after Gandhi's erstwhile correspondent, the Russian author of *War and Peace* – and
Phoenix in Natal, using his knowledge of the law first to defend
Indians in court and then, later, to agitate for their rights, Gandhi
had become a well-known figure locally, more often than not dressed
smartly in the pinstripe suit of an English county solicitor. The visit
of Gokhale was a coup for Gandhi personally, evidence of the
recognition his work was receiving in India, and of the importance
attached to the wider question of the status of Indians in *their*
empire. It was also a moment of revelation for Gandhi himself:
accompanying Gokhale to Dar es Salaam to see him on to his boat
back home at the end of 1912, Gandhi dressed in Indian clothes for
the first time in his adult life.[39]

The Durban in which Gokhale arrived in 1912 was a dusty and
beautiful British outpost, a port competing for South African business with Lourenço Marques in the neighbouring Portuguese colony
of Mozambique, and a coastal resort where people came from inland
areas to warm their feet in the Indian Ocean. 'Best wishes from
Durban' read a postcard of the time, showing white locals playing
in the sea in front of the serried ranks of painted bathing huts.
Surrounding the city to the north and west were the Drakensberg
mountains, rising high above the coastal plain. The climate was
gentle, the sun shone almost every day. To many, South Africa felt
blessed with the certainty of future wealth and power. Already one
of the world's largest producers of gold and with a virtual monopoly
of the production of diamonds, did not the country have the basis
in natural resources for a people as prosperous as the Australians,
destined to be as great as the Canadians? On the beach at Durban,
white South Africans could be permitted to forget, if only for a
moment, the demographic and political realities of their country:
fragile, divided and deeply unequal.

The Union of South Africa dated back only to 1910, forged quite opportunistically out of four British colonies, all with different populations and different political traditions, ranging from the relatively liberal and English-speaking Cape Colony to the Boer supremacist Orange Free State, where Dutch-speaking Afrikaners had the whip hand, and where memories of the Anglo-Boer War were still raw, part of the foundation story of the Afrikaner people. The constitution of the Union of South Africa – agreed upon by the British Parliament in the hope that its racial connotations would, over time, be alleviated – allowed only 'British subject[s] of European descent' to sit in the House of Assembly and the unelected Senate.[40] In the Cape province, the franchise remained theoretically colourblind, though in practice franchise qualifications based on education and wealth excluded the vast majority of non-European residents. The racially exclusive franchise that predominated in most other parts of South Africa was maintained for national elections. This was the price of Afrikaner adhesion to the new national state. In 1910 Prime Minister Louis Botha, a Boer, formed what he hoped would be a truly national government able to bridge the divide between Afrikaners and British. This would not be easy, however. By the beginning of 1913, Barry Hertzog, a Boer nationalist who disliked the ideas of Cape racial liberalism as much as he disliked the subservience of the Union of South Africa to the British Crown, had split from Botha's government, threatening to bring it crashing down. History, race and land provided the combustible ingredients of South African politics. How long the Union would last in its current form was anyone's guess.

Natal, formerly a British colony and now one of the smaller South African provinces, with Durban as its largest city, was something of an outlier. The governing whites here were less numerous than Indian immigrants and in a much smaller minority compared to native Africans than elsewhere in South Africa. In Natal, whites were outnumbered ten to one, compared to two to one in the Free State, and three to one in Transvaal and the Cape.[41] Partly to make up for this weakness in numbers, white Natalians in Durban developed a strongly British identity, clearly marking themselves out from the native Zulu population, the Afrikaners and, increasingly, the Indian population of Durban. A third of the white population of the city had been born in Britain. They had created a city of English gardens and statues of Queen Victoria. In 1899 Lord Milner, the leading British colonial administrator in southern Africa, described Natal as 'a secure outpost of England, loyal in the fashion of Ulster'.[42] In 1910, the sub-tropical African city of Durban repaid the compliment, completing its new town hall as an almost exact replica of that which stood proudly in Belfast, 6,000 miles away under the slate-grey skies of Northern Ireland. In 1913, the city's British pride was redoubled by the visit of battlecruiser HMS *New Zealand*, a reminder that even the smallest of the British dominions could contribute something to the defence and unity of the empire.

Whatever the image of Durban white Natalians wished to present to the world – and to themselves – the economic fortunes of the city and the countryside alike were not simply the product of hardy white settlers battling against the elements. Far from it. From the 1860s up until 1911, when it was stopped, indentured Indian labour – or 'coolie' labour, as whites called it – had flowed into the colony of Natal, to work on coastal sugar plantations, and later on the coalfields of northern Natal and the railways. It was these workers who had provided much of the muscle for development in Natal, as nowhere else in South Africa. The initial period of indenture for such labourers was not more than a few years, but many Indians gave up their free passage back to India once that time was up, and stayed on in South Africa to work as domestic servants, in industry, or growing fruit and vegetables. A few drifted to the mines of the Transvaal. The bulk stayed in Natal. Some, not able to make ends meet on the open market, found themselves back on a new inden-tured contract on the sugar plantations or at the mines, forbidden from travelling more than two miles from their place of work without written permission.[43]

From the 1870s on the population of indentured Indian labour was supplemented by 'free' immigrants from Gujurat, on the west coast of India, who thus extended their trading networks from Mauritius over to southern Africa. Setting up shop in downtown Durban, Gujurati merchants imported rice and ghee for their local Indian clientele as well as engaging in wider trade with India and Britain. In 1908, they had set up an Indian Chamber of Commerce in Durban, viewed by the city's white traders as dangerous compe-tition.[44] What had been an Indian 'solution' to the question of developing the resources of Natal was now viewed, by whites,

as an Indian 'problem', bringing into doubt their economic predominance and perhaps, over time, their cultural and political
predominance too.

Armed with the tools of colonial self-rule since the 1890s – making
it harder for London to dictate policy in local affairs – white Natalians
had set about encouraging non-indentured Indians to re-emigrate.
They made life difficult for Indian traders by allowing local officials
to decide arbitrarily on whether trading licenses should be granted,
eliminated future Natalian Indians from the franchise, and imposed
a £3 annual tax on Indians not returning to India at the end of their
indenture.[45] The British government was petitioned to protect the
rights of Natal Indians compromised by these changes, and to uphold
the principle of basic equality of Crown subjects, irrespective of race
or religion, the principle upon which Indians had come to southern
Africa in the first place and the principle upon which they had been
able to stay. The Indian government, under pressure from outraged
Indian opinion at home, attempted to bring pressure to bear by
threatening to cut off the flow of indentured labour to Natal altogether.
The government of Natal pursued its own policies nonetheless.
Natal's violent suppression of Zulu disturbances in 1906 – 3,000
Zulu deaths, compared to twenty-four white deaths, of which
eighteen were soldiers – had led Winston Churchill to label the
colony the 'hooligan of the British Empire'.[46] Treatment of the
Indian population, though nowhere near as severe, drew similar
brickbats, requiring the government of Natal to trim its policies
towards its Indian population and to alter the wording of its laws
to placate London's sensitivities, though without fundamentally
changing their aims or consequences. Aware of their historic rights
as subjects of the British crown, with a local elite articulate in their
own defence and allies in India to make their case, Natalian Indians
became a cause célèbre of empire – showing up the richness of its
tapestry and, in South Africa, the gap between imperial principle
and local practice.

At the time of Gokhale's visit, the position of Indians in South
Africa appeared under ever-greater assault; they were discriminated
against by carefully crafted provincial and national laws, and by the
established practices of petty officials who felt themselves vested with
the responsibility of protecting 'white' Natal. In Durban, particular
Indian anger was reserved for the immigration officials operating

according to their own interpretation of the rules – 'Little Tin Tsars', as one South African politician put it – with the apparent aim of generalised harassment.[47] Gokhale's visit had raised hopes that the situation would improve. It had not. 'Mr Colborne-Smith's [the Chief Immigration Officer] humour is of a grim and sardonic type', observed *Indian Opinion*, the voice of South Africa's Indian community, 'he appears to imagine that General Botha's promise to the Hon. Mr Gokhale that, in future, the administration of the Immigration Laws of South Africa would be rendered more humane, as an excellent joke, meaning exactly the converse of what it said'.[48]

In February 1913, a letter to the *Natal Mercury* drew readers' attention to the recent case of twelve-year-old Ahmed Kotwal. Ahmed was initially refused permission to land in Durban, despite holding a Natal domicile certificate, on the basis that his father, an Indian merchant at the time touring Europe and the United States, was not in Natal. Dispatched rapidly back to India on the ship on which he had arrived, the *Markgraf*, he did not have time to seek a court injunction. 'Would not the people of Natal rise in revolt', asked Mr Polak, 'were men, women, and children of European origin treated with the same scandalous harshness and inhumanity as are these unrepresented and disenfranchised Indians?'[49] The editors of the newspaper took up the matter on their editorial pages, asking how the matter would be viewed in Delhi or Bombay:

> Had the hardships alleged been inflicted on the subjects of a foreign Power an awkward diplomatic question would have arisen. What are the people of India to think when their loyalty is rewarded with treatment which our officials would not lightly dream of meting out to persons enjoying the protection of an alien flag?[50]

The following month, in March, a court decided that marriages celebrated according to Indian rites should not be recognised in South Africa since Hinduism and Islam allowed for the possibility of polygamy, even if the vast majority of Hindu and Muslim marriages were, in fact, monogamous. 'In effect', complained *Indian Opinion*, 'it [the court judgement] declares that the wife of a Mohammedan, who goes out of the Province, may not return, because her husband is a polygamist, even if he has only one wife'.[51] 'In the latter event', the newspaper noted drily, 'he is termed a monogamous polygamist'. Indian anger was further inflamed when the minister of the interior, Jan Smuts, used disrespectful Boer slang to characterise Islamic divorce, suggesting all that was required was that the man tell his wife to *voetsek* – get lost.

Against this background of legal restrictions and arbitrary administration, a new immigration law made its way through the South African parliament in the middle of 1913. This law gave government officials – and ultimately the minister of the interior – still wider powers, including the power to exclude any group from migrating to South Africa if they were deemed undesirable on economic grounds or, more broadly, 'on account of standard or habits of life' inappropriate to the development of the country. That the intention was to exclude Asian immigration was openly acknowledged. 'We are all agreed that the unrestricted immigration of Asiatics, whether British subjects or not, is a thing which could not be tolerated', editorialised the *Natal Mercury*, explaining that it did not want 'the unlimited addition of an exotic element in the inferior stage of civilization and with the social characteristics distinguishing the mass of Asiatics from the average European'.[52]

Although immigration controls against Indians went against a key principle of the British Empire – the free movement of British subjects – many Indians in South Africa were grudgingly prepared to accept controls, as long as their existing rights were recognised. But the problems with the new law went deeper. Giving so much discretionary power to officials, without a right of appeal, threatened injustice at every turn (the *Natal Mercury* itself complained at this 'reckless arbitrariness').[53] The fact that different provinces of the Union of South Africa restricted Indians' movement and settlement in other ways – it was illegal for Indians to travel from Natal to Transvaal without prior registration, for example – provided further grounds for anger. And behind all this lay the suspicion that the immigration law was only a beginning, that the government would tighten the restrictions until even resident Indians might be deprived of their most basic rights to live in South Africa if they were absent for a short period of time, or else cantoned into new areas of settlement.

Gandhi accused the government of South Africa, in putting forward the immigration law, of a 'breach of trust'.[54] He proposed a campaign of passive resistance to oppose it and, perhaps more powerfully still, to force the abolition of the £3 tax. This grievance was particularly acute now, given that Gokhale, when he visited in 1912, thought he had secured a firm commitment from the government to withdraw the tax. Yet a year later it was still on the statute books. The government had not delivered.

This was not the first time that Gandhi had found the government of South Africa to promise one thing and do another. Nor was it the first time he had tried the strategy of passive resistance, known as *satyagraha*, to force their hand. In Transvaal a few years earlier, protesting against a new requirement for Indians to register themselves – as a prelude to possible further controls – Gandhi had counselled a policy of mass refusal, persuading a meeting of local Indians in Johannesburg's Imperial Theatre to follow his lead. In subsequent negotiations with the government of Transvaal, and with Jan Smuts, then the Colonial Secretary of Transvaal, Gandhi appeared to have secured a compromise – Indians would register

English-trained lawyer Mohandas Karamchand Gandhi, champion of the Indian population of South Africa. He wore traditional Indian clothes for the first time as an adult in 1912.

voluntarily, and the law would be withdrawn. But the law was not withdrawn from the statute books. Registration cards were burned. Gandhi led a march from Natal to Transvaal in violation of the law. He was arrested and thrown in jail for his pains.

This time around, his opponent was again Smuts, now the South African minister of the interior; like Gandhi, he was an English-trained lawyer, albeit a former Boer general as well. In some ways, Gandhi now had a stronger hand, opposing not just a law, a symbol, a nuisance – but the very real financial burden of the £3 tax, which forced a large number of Indians from one period of indentured labour to another. Moreover, he had on his side the righteous anger of Indians in India, furious that Gokhale had been misled. Not all Indians in South Africa were convinced that passive resistance would work, however. 'In the Transvaal many of the leading Indian merchants, who previously provided the sinews of war, have dissoci-ated themselves from the campaign', noted the *Natal Mercury* in early October, 'and in Natal a large section, who on the previous occasion entered into the struggle, are now holding aloof'.[55]

There was one further weapon which could be used: a strike. In October 1913, several thousand Indians working in the coal mines of northern Natal were successfully called out. The critical issue now was time. How long could the strikers be kept out, keeping up the pressure on the mine owners to persuade the government to think again? Gandhi spoke at gatherings of Indian miners, alongside his allies Thambi Naidoo and C. R. Naidoo, urging the miners not to go back to work. But there were limits to this strategy. It was the poorest who were most affected, forgoing their wages and risking their jobs. They could not be expected to stay out forever. Trying to force a confrontation with the authorities before the miners lost their resolve and the strike its strength, Gandhi threatened to take more radical measures: a march from Natal to Transvaal, as before, illegally crossing the border between the two provinces without prior registration. This, it was hoped, would force a response from the government, either bringing them to the negotiating table or forcing them to lock up the marchers, thus further damaging the govern-ment's credibility and inviting still louder criticism from India, from London and from liberal opinion in South Africa. In smaller groups at first, but ultimately building up to several thousand, the marchers began their trek.

But rather than responding by locking up the marchers as they crossed into Transvaal, Smuts decided instead to do nothing. He preferred to play a waiting game, trusting that the strike would ultimately collapse under its own weight. This was astute, for although money was sent from India to support the strikers and now the marchers, the cost of feeding them was still crippling for the meagre resources of the local Indian associations. Gandhi had already come under fire within the Natal Indian Congress for his precipitate action. Now there was a real possibility that the strategy of passive resistance would fail and that Gandhi would be remembered as a failed agitator. Eventually, Gandhi himself was re-arrested and sentenced to another term in jail.

In November 1913, however, the situation began to change again, this time in Gandhi's favour. The Indian agricultural workers of southern Natal also came out on strike. This was in some ways more serious than the coal strike, involving many times more workers. The situation for sugar plantations was particularly serious. A whole year's harvest was at risk, not just a few weeks' lost production, and the employers had no ready replacement labour force they could bring in to do the work. As the economic costs mounted, *Indian Opinion* urged mill owners not to attempt to break the strike, but 'look to the root of the matter' and make a 'strong, united appeal to the Government, not for more police, but for the immediate suspension of the tax'.[56] Consumers began to feel the pinch. Amongst white Natalians, wild rumours spread that black workers, with their own grievances, were waiting for their moment (though Gandhi himself, ever careful to distinguish Indians from Africans, denied that '*kaffirs*' had been asked to strike).[57] Perhaps a generalised revolt was in the offing.

The final blow to the government of South Africa's position of studied inaction, however, came not from within South Africa, but from India. There, fearing that angry home opinion at the situation in Natal would destabilise India, Viceroy Charles Hardinge, now fully recovered from the assassination attempt of the previous year, resolved to act himself. Dragooned into the service of an expatriate Indian community, Hardinge took the remarkable step of openly criticising a fellow member of the British Empire, and calling for an independent Commission of Enquiry to be set up in South Africa to investigate the £3 tax and other Indian grievances in Natal. 'The

Indian community of South Africa cannot be too grateful to Lord Hardinge for the brave stand he has ventured to take', noted *Indian Opinion* approvingly, 'knowing full well that his attitude would be resented and that he would be subjected to adverse criticism [by some in South Africa]'.[58] For Smuts, this was an embarrassment; for some in South Africa it was unwarranted interference in a domestic matter, indeed *The Economist* in London classed Hardinge's intervention a 'constitutional impropriety of the first order'.[59] But it was also an opportunity to compromise. In December 1913, with as much grace as he could muster, Smuts accepted the idea of a commission, with the expectation that it would recommend – as it did the following year – the end of the £3 tax. Mohandas Karamchand Gandhi's passive resistance campaign had proved a success. Even though disagreement remained on the composition of the commission as the year 1913 ended, one thing was clear: *satayagraha* had won.

Durban could now sink back into the background of Indian political consciousness, and South Africa could return to the bickering of British and Boers, and to the still bigger issue of white South African concern: the 'native' problem. Gandhi's reputation, however, was now made. After twenty years amongst a community of Indians counted in the tens of thousands, he could now plan a return to the India of 300 million, with the lessons of South Africa fresh in his memory, his philosophy of political action confirmed, and his sense of mission redoubled.

At the end of 1913, Indians in South Africa had reason to celebrate. However, a much larger group of South Africans, black Africans, looked deeper into a well of despair. Gandhi's success brought no respite for them. Rather, 1913 would be remembered with a dark mark against it, as inequality was more deeply enshrined in law, as opportunities were curtailed, as segregation became a legally enforced reality, and as the world of black South Africans became a little bit smaller. 'Awakening on Friday morning, June 20, 1913, the South African Native found himself, not actually a slave, but a pariah in the land of his birth', wrote Solomon Tshekisho Plaatje a few years later, selecting the date of the passage of the Natives Land Act of that year, a law which heavily restricted the purchase of land by black South Africans.[60]

The black population of South Africa had always been central to the politics of white South Africa, long before the Union of South Africa itself was forged. That black Africans were a numerical majority was obvious, a fact which caused white workers to fear that the price of their labour could be undercut were blacks to enter the skilled workforce, and which caused other whites to fear the possibility of black rule, perhaps brought about by violent rebellion. Unlike in Australia, that blacks had in effect been dispossessed of the lands of their ancestors was broadly admitted by whites in South Africa. But there was disagreement as to the extent of white responsibility for the black population of South Africa, the form this responsibility should take, and the extent to which it might include political rights. In the Cape, if a black farm-owner were wealthy enough and well-educated enough, he might vote in provincial elections. In other parts of South Africa, this was unthinkable. Blacks might be farm-hands, maybe even proprietors, but not voters.

The Anglo-Boer War had been fought, at least as the British presented it, to enforce British interests and British principles in South Africa, including protection of native rights. In making the peace, however, the British accepted that the question of the franchise, and therefore the possibility of a colour bar, would be left to a future South African government, subject only to a special exemption for existing voters in the Cape. When the Union of South Africa was formed in 1910, therefore, London had not insisted upon a colour-blind franchise. 'Union without honour is the greatest danger any nation can incur', thundered William Schreiner, a former Prime Minister of the Cape, urging that non-Europeans should not be denied the vote in national elections, provided they fulfilled the same other criteria as might apply to Europeans.[61] Outvoted at home and outmanoeuvred in London, however, Schreiner failed in his appeals. The Union of South Africa entered the world of states as a constitutionally unequal state, a democracy for some and a tyranny for others.

On the broader question of how to manage the native 'problem', confusion reigned. Complete segregation of black and white was an option in theory – but unworkable in practice. Partial territorial segregation, recommended by the government-appointed Lagden

Commission in 1905, was another option, elevating a piecemeal practice of separation at the provincial level into a potential principle of policy at the national level. The idea of allowing European and non-European communities to evolve along different pathways, on different land, was viewed by some as progressive, avoiding tainting European civilisation with tribal instincts and allowing Africans to develop at their own pace, potentially without competition from European farmers, traders and businessmen.[62] Others viewed segregation as a dereliction of the duty of Europeans to civilise Africans – or simply as a step backwards, away from the unity of the nation and towards ever-greater fragmentation and narrowness of perspective. Everywhere, land was a central issue. In Natal a few years previously a land commission had awarded the land most suitable for farming to whites, leaving Africans with less good land, from which they were expected to pay the heavy burden of the local poll tax. (In 1906, refusal to pay the tax had spiralled into a full-blown Zulu revolt.) In the Transvaal and elsewhere, white farmers worried about an alleged increase in blacks purchasing land – though in fact blacks owned less than five per cent of land in Transvaal, and less than two per cent in the Orange Free State (as against nine per cent in the Cape, and over thirty per cent in Natal).[63] In the Orange Free State, where blacks were now legally disbarred from buying land, Afrikaners feared the steady incursions of black 'squatters', paying white farm-owners rent to work the land, and steadily altering the province's demography. Before he resigned from Botha's government Barry Hertzog, the Boer nationalist from the Free State, was tasked with coming up with a native policy for the Union of South Africa. Unsurprisingly, his approach was one in which assimilation was rejected, and the harshest form of segregation promoted.

The South African Native National Congress had been set up the previous year to provide, at last, a voice for the African majority. It opposed complete segregation not only as unfair, but also as unprofitable to whites – who benefited from black labour – and as preventing the development of blacks themselves. The Reverend John Dube, president of the Congress, and founder of Ohlange Native Industrial School a few miles from Gandhi's Phoenix settlement just north of Durban, argued on the pages of the *Natal Mercury* that 'the system of tribal segregation might have suited very well a period when barbarism and darkness reigned supreme . . . but it had

and has the fatal defect of being essentially opposed to all enlightenment and Christianity'.[64] He continued: 'The times have changed,
and manners must change with them. We natives need the white
man, and cannot any longer live and thrive without his teaching,
his training, his example'.[65]

This was pragmatism of a sort. It implied no shame in being
African. 'Our blackness is our Creator's gift', Dube wrote, 'and we,
for our part, would not have it replaced by any other colour or tint'.
He had no illusions as to what segregation would mean in practice;
not the award of good farmland to the African majority, but rather
the meagre scraps:

> . . . more likely is it you would prefer to drive the native away to
> some barren, inhospitable wilderness, fever-stricken districts
> unwanted by yourselves; make him an outcast in his own fatherland,
> presumably because you find him helpless and powerless to object.
> I have said 'drive' him away, for I think not one of the million natives
> now resident in the Province [of Natal] would, without a murmur
> and without demur, be prepared to sever to your call those sacred
> ties that bind all human beings possessed of a feeling heart to that
> dear spot they call and know to be their birthplace and their home.
> Be assured that no single native would be prepared to move, unless
> compelled by force. But to prostitute your power to so immoral a
> proceeding would indeed be a sad object lesson for us, a shameful
> reflection on a people professing to be guided by the spirit and
> teachings of Christ.[66]

Whatever the morality of the matter, the politics of it were against
the South African Native National Congress. Spurred by the need
to placate Orange Free State politicians who threatened to go their
own way now that Barry Hertzog had left Botha's government, the
government of South Africa introduced a Natives Land Bill in
parliament in April 1913, largely along the lines which Hertzog had
proposed. It would allow blacks to buy land on just seven per cent
of the territory of the Union of South Africa (and prevent whites
from buying land on that same area), and make 'squatting' illegal,
thus forcing blacks to work on white farms as employees rather than
tenants. Shepherded through the House of Assembly by a minister
deemed to be friendly to African interests, the bill was modified

– exempting the Cape almost entirely, and suspending some provisions in the Transvaal and in Natal – and then passed. The process of segregation had been sharply accelerated, an inequality worsened, an injustice made the law of the land. The *Natal Mercury*, noting a gathering of several thousand natives opposed to the law before it was even passed, worried for the security of Durban.[67] Afterwards, as the law was put into effect, it expressed sympathy for Africans being told to 'leave your homes – the homes possibly of your grandfathers, and great-grandfathers – and pay annually for the privilege of your enforced removal'.[68] 'How would this appeal to ourselves were the position reversed?' the newspaper's editor asked.[69]

At the end of June 1913, as existing tenancies came to an end, black farmers attempted to renew their contracts, unaware of the new law. Some white farmers, equally unaware, accepted. 'It was only when they went to register the new tenancies', wrote Plaatje, 'that the law officers of the Crown laid bare the cruel fact that to provide a landless Native with accommodation was forbidden'.[70] 'Then only was the situation realised' by black South Africans, he continued – South Africa had inched further away from being *their* country, perhaps it would never truly be *their* country again. Unlike British-ruled Bombay, where sections of local Indian population had secured themselves a leading position in the life of their city and substantial influence in the future direction of their country, the native population of white-ruled South Africa had been unceremoniously reduced to the status of third-class subjects in a land they had once called their own.

TEHRAN
Under Foreign Eyes

In the distant past, over 2,000 years previously, Persia – as the country we now call Iran was generally known in 1913 – had been a great and feared nation, with an empire which included Turkey, the coastal zone of Egypt, and most of the rest of the Middle East. By 1913, its empire had been pared back. Where once the country's geography – jammed between the Persian Gulf, the valleys of the Tigris and the Euphrates, the Caucasus, Afghanistan, and the Indian Ocean – had provided a springboard for Persia's conquest of its neighbours, the country's geographic position now made it an object of unwelcome interest by newer and more dynamic powers, Britain and Russia in particular, who saw it as a buffer between their respective empires, and as a prospective market for their goods.

Persia's domestic economic development had stalled long ago. Its internal political situation was lamentable. In July 1913, former Viceroy of India Lord Curzon relayed a contemporary description of the country as:

> a country minus a King – true, because he is only a boy; minus a Regent, because the Regent has been travelling about for some time in Europe; minus a Parliament, because the Parliament has been abolished; minus a Government, because no Government can be said to exist; with no army but the robber bands . . . and with no money except that which she can extract from Great Britain and Russia.[1]

In the last few years the country had been convulsed by a constitutional revolution in 1906 as well as by civil war, international intrigue and foreign military intervention. As Curzon described it in 1913, the country was now in an advanced state of dismemberment, the fig leaf of sovereignty barely hiding the role of foreigners in determining its future: a Russian sphere of influence in the north, a British sphere of influence in the south, and a weak government in the middle, with a divided cabinet, a fifteen-year-old boy-Shah and, for much of the year, an absentee Regent. What remained, then, was Persia as an idea – a memory of ancient greatness, catapulted into the twentieth century. But was that enough?

In Tehran, the Persian capital, uncertainty reigned as to the future course of government, with the ship of state leaky and rudderless. Since the Regent's departure for Europe the previous year, noted a British diplomatic dispatch in May 1913, 'His Majesty [the Shah] has done absolutely nothing but waste his time dawdling around eating sweets', contributing to the boy's adolescent chubbiness, and to the sense of the country's political drift.[2] Rather than being encouraged to govern, the Shah's courtiers preferred to 'encourage him in his idleness', the note reported, 'and instil into his mind that women and futile pleasures are much more desirable than intelligence

Ahmad Shah Qajar. Since the departure of the Persian Regent to Europe, wrote a British diplomat in 1913, 'His Majesty [the Shah] has done absolutely nothing but waste his time dawdling around eating sweets'.

and learning'. Two months later, with the Regent still absent, things had not improved. 'There is a lot of "if" and no small share of "but" in the present political situation in Persia', the British minister in Tehran wrote sternly back to London.[3] 'It seems almost inconceivable under the circumstances that the Government coach goes on at all', he continued. And yet it rumbled on, 'for all the world like one of the Noah's Ark vehicles that convey the unfortunate traveller over the stony, bumpy road between Resht and Tehran'.

At the end of that road, in Tehran itself, lay a city of a few hundred thousand, the dilapidated capital of a dilapidated country. 'If you desire comfort, do not travel to Tehran!' advised European resident Dorothy de Warzée.[4] The condition of the city in 1913 compared unfavourably with that of more up-to-date Bombay or Algiers where the crowded compactness of those cities' geography, and the adoption of Western technologies, made even the poorest parts of town appear to be bustling, on-the-make places. Tehran, in contrast, exuded a sense of irretrievably faded magnificence. It straggled haphazardly across miles of open ground. Wide and unpaved roads ran between beautiful and overgrown gardens, hidden from public view by tumbledown walls. The city, to put it mildly, had seen better days.

Around Tehran's old perimeter ran defensive walls, punctured by fourteen colourfully tiled gates, and a moat. But by 1913, the moat had become the city's rubbish dump. 'Into this moat', wrote de Warzée, 'the carcases of all the animals that die are thrown; it is the usual thing to see a gorged circle of pariah dogs sitting in happy repletion after a mid-day meal off these remains.' Although electric lights had been strung up in a few parts of town, Tehran by night was a dark and dangerous city, lit mostly by the 'mitigated darkness of a few petroleum lamps' – and 'woe to the uninitiated who walk or drive unwarily by their faint flicker'.

By day, the city took on a somewhat brighter hue, the streets filling with pedlars and merchants, tea houses opening up, mud bricks being laid out to dry, women washing their linen in the street, men having their hair cut by street barbers and, as was the custom, dyed red, black or brown, to cover up the signs of age. 'There are no old men in Teheran', noted de Warzée, 'for it is not polite to be wiser than the Shah'.[5] Jugglers and masked figures with tame bears and monkeys jostled for attention with beggars – 'worse than those in Italy' – bearing their misshapen limbs, injuries and skin diseases as proof of their poverty, misfortune and worthiness of alms, which it was the responsibility of all Muslims to provide. And at the centre of it all lay the bazaar:

> The Bazaar is a little world; it is roofed in like an immense tunnel, and is always cool, with scarcely any light. It is the centre of all conspiracies and plots, and a sort of gigantic club-house the members of which have different political interests; all the mischief that can be planned comes from the Bazaar, and all the rumours, fantastic and otherwise . . . All criminals, if they can but reach the Bazaar, are safe, because there it is very difficult to discover their whereabouts. It is like a great beehive, with endless cellars and dark little alleys leading by yet darker, cavern-like openings to courtyard or house, with always an outlet hidden somewhere behind, a maze only to be threaded by the native; the foreigner usually finds himself in a cul-de-sac, from which he will have to retrace his steps if he is without a guide.[6]

One might get lost in the bazaar, but for the patient European traveller in 1913 there were bargains to be had. Families were selling off their heirlooms – a piece of intricate jewellery here, a French watch there – to cover the rising price of life in a country where trade was interrupted, and the surrounding countryside beset with difficulties. In the north, where the Russians had imposed themselves, the situation, was, in general, grimly stable. In the south, insecurity reigned. There, brigandage was such, Curzon suggested before the House of Lords, that a case of tea from Bombay bound for the central Persian city of Isfahan would now, rather than being ferried up the Persian Gulf and then overland to Isfahan, more probably be sent around Arabia, through the Suez Canal, through the Dardanelles to the Black Sea, entering Russia at Batumi, and then down to Isfahan via Baku: a detour of several thousand miles. In such ways, by adding time and cost to every exchange with the outside world, rural instability exacted its price in the everyday lives of the peaceful residents of the capital.

Curzon knew well the country whereof he spoke. Having travelled through Persia in his early thirties he had published in 1892 a two-volume book – *Persia and the Persian Question* – which he had intended to be, and no doubt believed still was twenty years later, the definitive account of the country.[7] In it, he described a lonely, dramatic country of extremes. 'It is difficult to bring home to English readers, whose ideas of nature are drawn exclusively from the West, the extremity of the contrast that meets the eye', Curzon had written:

> Mountains in Europe are for the most part blue or purple in colour; in Persia they are flame-red, or umber, or funereal drab. Fields in Europe, when not decked with the green of grass or crops, are crimson with upturned mould. In Persia they are only distinguishable from the brown desert by the dry beds of the irrigation ditches. A typical English village consists of detached and often picturesque cottages, half hidden amid venerable trees. A typical Persian village is a cluster of filthy mud huts, whose outline is a crude combination of the perpendicular and the horizontal, huddled within the protection of a decayed mud wall . . . Rivers do not roll between trim banks, nor do brooks babble over stones. Either you are stopped by a foaming torrent, or you barely moisten your horse's fetlocks in fording a pitiful thread.

Across this vast land – some of it mountainous, some of it virtual desert, some of it fertile, some of it not – there was not a single railway line outside Tehran, even in 1913. There were a few roads deemed suitable for wheeled traffic, mostly in the north of Persia, leading from Tehran up to the province of Azerbaijan in the north, to Mashhad in the east and to Qom and Isfahan in central Persia. 'The remaining roads are either caravan or mule tracks which have existed from time immemorial', concluded a British military intelligence report of the time, 'long stretches of sand, rough mountain tracks covered with boulders and loose jagged stones, slippery rocks, narrow defiles, and steep gradients are the characteristics of most Persian roads'.[8] This was a landscape which reinforced local tribal allegiances, which conspired against strong central government and which provided perfect cover for marauding bands of armed men – troublemakers, brigands or heroes, depending on one's interests; insurgents, outlaws or *mujaheds* depending on one's affiliations. Justice in such parts of the world as these was summary: religious authorities took it upon themselves to mete out punishments for religious offences; civil authorities were responsible for judgement on everything else – drawing their inspiration from past edicts, local custom, Sharia law, or from a simple sense of pragmatism.⁹ More often than not, order was maintained by force – and by force of character. In the distant corners of Persia, the Shah in Tehran might seem as distant as the sun; Europe, as distant as the stars beyond. Epidemics, droughts and famines were common.

Above all, this was a man's world, where women played a traditional family-oriented role, even if some women in Tehran, exposed to the literature and political currents of Europe and America, now chafed more keenly at the injustices of their position. 'Alas!' wrote Taj al-Saltana, a harem-born daughter of a former Shah, 'Persian women have been placed together with cattle and beasts':

> They live their entire lives of desperation in prison, crushed under the weight of bitter ordeals. At the same time, they see and hear from afar and reading the newspapers about the way in which suffragettes in Europe arise with determination to demand their rights: universal franchise, the right to vote in parliament, the right to include the affairs of government. They are winning successes. In America their rights are fully established and they are striving with serious determination. The same is true in London and Paris. My teacher! How I wish I could travel to Europe and meet these freedom-seeking ladies! I would say to them '. . . cast a look at the continent of Asia. Look into the houses, where the walls are three or five metres high and the only entryway is a door guarded by a doorman'.¹⁰

Unable to attend the Budapest meeting of the International Women's Suffrage Alliance in 1913, representatives of the women of Persia sent a telegram instead. They were nonetheless mentioned in the conference proceedings. 'Do not forget', urged Mrs Carrie Chapman Catt, the American woman presiding, 'that this [Persia] is a Mohammedan nation and that a modern liberal element within that religion was slowly but surely lifting people to enlightenment and self-respect'.¹¹ Chapman Catt blamed recent foreign intervention – Russian and British – for undercutting a wider process of national political reform and, therefore, women's hopes of an improvement in their own situation.

Persia's population was divided by more than sex – indeed, as a linguistic and ethnic group, Persians themselves actually only made up half the country's population, out of a total of around twelve million.[12] Another two and half million were Azeri-speaking. Two hundred thousand were Mazanderanis, living on the fertile shores of the Caspian. Additionally, amongst the scattered non-Persian tribes in the country there were Kurds in the west, Arabs in the south at the head of the Persian Gulf, Baluchis in the south-east, Qashqa'is in the south-west and Bakhtiaris, key political players, between the Persian Gulf and Tehran. After these came a dizzying array of smaller groups, including Afghans, Turcomans, Hazaras, Basseris, Tajiks – and the Turkic-speaking Qajars, from which group the Shah himself was drawn. Shi'a Islam predominated throughout the country, providing some of the unifying glue of an otherwise disparate enterprise and making Shi'a religious leaders the custodians of Persian national identity as much as any national political magnate. But there were also 100,000 or more clandestine Baha'is (considered foreign-inspired conspiratorial heretics by Shi'a clergy and dangerous social reformers by the Shah). In Yazd, Shiraz and Tehran and elsewhere there were Jewish communities, and a handful of Zoroastrians, forerunners of the Parsis who dominated the economy and trade of the city of Bombay. There were pockets of Assyrian Christians and Armenian Christians. Franz Joseph, the Austro-Hungarian Emperor in Vienna, would surely have sympathised with the dilemmas facing any ruler of such a country.

In the old despotic Persia, the political regime which survived into the beginning of the twentieth century, the Shah was nominally the central pivot of the country's politics, claiming both the religious sanction of Islam and a link back to more ancient Persian glories symbolised by the lion and the sun on the imperial Qajar crest and on the national Persian flag. As Curzon found in the 1890s, the Shah was praised as high as the snow-capped mountains around – but as a symbol of past greatness more than as a real political leader. Even before the disturbances of the twentieth century, it was an open question how far the Shah's writ ran outside the capital city. Unlimited in theory, in reality his power was circumscribed. Local governors might be linked to him by family ties, by the awards of great titles, and by extravagant and unbreakable oaths of loyalty, but there was no modern bureaucracy to speak of to enforce his will. The foreign ministry, while keeping legations in all the major European capitals, also posted officials in the provincial capitals of

Persia itself – to keep tabs on local governors, it was said. This was hardly a sign of great central authority.

And these were problems of governance which, whether the Shah was bound by a constitution or not, could not be changed overnight, by the stroke of a pen. Dealing with them would require long-term administrative reforms, a change in political culture and a period of security in which reforms could take root. Recent Persian history, however, had provided only spasmodic reform, and precious little security. European countries offered little real help other than lending money to the regime – which left it drowning in debt. On occasion, Russia actively conspired against Persian renewal, preferring a weak neighbour to a strong one. The overall result for Persia was drift, punctured by protest – or, as American William Morgan Shuster preferred to describe it, slow strangulation. Briefly employed as a reforming Treasurer-General of Persia in 1911 – before he was forced out under Russian pressure – Shuster found the odds stacked against him, and against Persia's renaissance. Back in the United States in 1912, he introduced his written account of his time in Persia with a melancholy couplet of his own devising, a prophecy and a lament: 'Time with whose passage certain pains abate, but sharpens those of Persia's unjust fate'.[13]

There had been stirrings of modernisation, or at least the awareness of its necessity, when Curzon was in Persia in the 1890s. Nasser al-Din Shah, who reigned for nearly fifty years up until his assassination in 1896, had travelled to Europe and been fascinated by the march of progress he observed there. But, once back in Tehran, this fascination had not been translated into sustained Persian modernisation, but rather dissipated in the Shah's intense but short-lived passions for the latest novelties. 'He is continually taking up and pushing some new scheme or invention which, when the caprice has been gratified, is neglected or allowed to expire', Curzon had written:

One week it is gas; another it is electric light. Now it is a staff college; anon, a military hospital. To-day it is a Russian uniform; yesterday it was a German man-of-war for the Persian Gulf. A new army warrant is issued this year; a new code of law is promised for the next. Nothing comes of any of these brilliant schemes, and the lumber-rooms of the palace are not more full of broken mechanism and discarded bric-a-brac than are the pigeon holes of government bureaux of abortive reforms and dead fiascos.[14]

But time, like geography, was not on Persia's side.

Irregularly at first, but with accelerating pace, concessions to foreign traders built up. In 1872 the Shah agreed a seventy-year concession for Baron Paul Julius de Reuter, a Jewish German-born British businessman, for just about everything in the country. Local merchants and religious leaders made the Shah relent.[15] Two years later, a German concession to build a railway line from Tabriz to Julfa died a similar death. In 1890 a tobacco concession to the British met with protests in Tabriz and Tehran, and a nationwide tobacco boycott – leading that concession, too, to be withdrawn, at great cost to the state. But the process of chronic indebtedness leading to more loans, and loans leading to more commercial influence and more concessions, was ineluctable. A British bank, the Imperial Bank of Persia, was granted the sole right to issue bank notes. A mirror Russian bank – the Banque des Prêts (later the Banque d'Escompte de Perse) – was set up to act for Russian commercial interests, and to claim interest on Persia's mounting debts. Rights for shipping and fishing excited foreign diplomatic activity. Concessions for oil exploration were granted to British interests in southern Persia and Russia in the north. The best-trained unit of the Persian army consisted of Russian-officered Cossacks. By the time that Curzon was Viceroy of India, at the beginning of the twentieth century, the strategic importance of Persia was axiomatic to British and Russian foreign policy. Britain's telegraph lines to Asia already lay across the country. Russia's southern borders, galloping southward over the Caucasus decade by decade, encompassing an ever-greater share of the Caspian shoreline, and swallowing up and then exploiting the oilfields of Baku, inevitably infringed on areas of ancient Persian influence and interest. The country was trapped in an ever-tightening vice.

In the 1880s and 1890s, steel-tipped arrows rained down on Tehran in the form of essays and pamphlets critical of the Shah and his regime. Sayyid Jamal al-Din 'Afghani' – a Persian-born intellectual who travelled widely in India, Afghanistan and Europe, strongly anti-British, and strongly encouraging of pan-Islamic revival – was forced to leave the country in 1891, ordered out for his overly critical tone.[16] In 1892 he put his revenge on paper, criticising the Shah's regime as tyranny, and blaming it for the economic woes which had come to the country:

> Is it the fault of Persia, land of the sun; land of the date, the pome-granate, the barley, and the wheat; Persia, with her coal-mines, and none to work them; her wealth of iron, and none to smelt it; of copper, of turquoise; her wells of virgin petroleum; her arable land, so fertile that one has but to scratch the soil and harvest after harvest springs as fast as one can reap; and her so-called deserts which need but the restoration of her irrigation works? But all is undone, ruined, blackened, curst.[17]

In 1896, Nasser al-Din Shah was assassinated by a follower of Afghani. But the death of one Shah did not entail a transformation of the country's fortunes. Nasser al-Din's successor, Muzaffar al-Din Shah, was no more able to wake Persia from its torpor, nor escape the pincers of the Anglo-Russian embrace.

In the years immediately before 1913 the pace of events acceler-ated, a bewildering succession of political intrigues, forward marches, retreats and upheavals, with more twists and turns than the passage-ways of the bazaar, more dead ends and more unanticipated open-ings. Suitably enough, it was amongst the *bazaaris* that the trouble began in 1905. Shopkeepers, students and religious leaders combined in Tehran to demand the dismissal of the Belgian head of Persian customs. The demand, ricocheting around the country by telegraph, and adding to other accumulated grievances, set off a cycle of demonstrations, marches and broken promises that continued into the next summer. Faced with possible loss of his control over key army units in Tehran itself, the Shah found himself obliged to accept the formation of an indirectly elected national assembly – the *majlis* – tasked with drawing up a constitution. The old regime had cracked.

The work of drawing up a constitution was quickly done. On the penultimate day of 1906, Muzaffar al-Din Shah accepted the new constitution; in early 1907, on the Shah's death, his successor Muhammad Ali Shah was forced to do the same. It seemed at the time to be a watershed moment. Persia had arrived, wrote an editor of a Persian newspaper, in a 'safe wadi of constitutionalism', having undertaken a journey of 'a thousand years – in the space of eight months'.[18] But the revolution, if that was what had happened, meant different things to different people. A temporary coalition of anger against the old regime was no basis for a stable parliamentary government. The real business of politics – much of which happened outside parliament – remained highly opaque, driven by personal and tribal relationships as much as by parties or principle.

The *majlis* itself was divided between conservatives, who saw the overthrow of the despotic government of the Shah as the beginning of a restoration of a religious authority and the removal of foreign influence, and radicals, who saw it as the starting point for a truly social revolution, and a wider process of Westernisation. Conservatives criticised radicals for going too far, for wanting to undermine Shi'a teaching and the traditional role of religious leaders. External powers, rather than providing a helping hand, preferred to wield the carving knife. In 1907, an Anglo-Russian convention, signed over the heads of the Persians, restricted but did not entirely freeze the competition of Russia and Britain in Persia, agreeing zones of commercial influence for each, in which the other would not interfere. Constitutionalism was immediately discredited.

Sensing his opportunity to re-establish his supremacy, Muhammad Ali Shah attempted a *coup d'état* in 1908, firing on the *majlis*, plunging the country still deeper into the mire, and bringing Russian intervention in the north of the country on his side. The fate of the revolution hung in the balance, the country ablaze. Only in 1909, by dint of good fortune, shifting political alliances and the military organisation of the Bakhtiari tribal military, was the power of the *majlis* re-established. The Shah was forced into exile, with a pension conditional on his future non-interference in Persian affairs. But new battle lines had now hardened in the country's domestic politics, the division between radicals and conservatives overlaying those of different factions, tribes and interest-groups. A new *majlis* was elected, drawn more widely than the last, and more conservative as a result. From his initial exile in Odessa the now ex-Shah was reported to be travelling around Europe, angling for support for a comeback in Persia. His replacement on the throne in Tehran was his twelve-year-old son Ahmad. 'The prospects of Persia being able to evolve from the complicated situation confronting her [to] a reasonably stable and orderly government were far from encouraging', noted Shuster in his memoirs.[19]

It was now that Shuster, the American, had his walk-on role. His plans for reform, involving the rearrangement of government finances and the collection of taxes backed up by a new fiscal gendarmerie – in addition to a Swedish-officered national gendarmerie recently set up as the kernel of a new military force to balance the Cossacks – offered a glimmer of hope. If order could be re-established, the excuse for foreign military presence would evaporate. If the country's finances could be put on a firmer footing, might constitutionalism yet succeed? Such hopes were dashed on the rocks of local intransigence, foreign interests and a worsening political situation. Having travelled across Russia with arms and ammunition disguised in boxes marked 'Mineral Water', Muhammad Ali Shah himself landed in the north of Persia in 1911, in a last attempt to regain his throne.[20] In Tehran, his son Ahmad Shah celebrated his birthday with the gift of a narwhal tusk signed with the name of Captain Peary, newly returned from the conquest of the North Pole, delivered to him by Mr Cairns, Shuster's assistant. 'Sultan Ahmad Shah had never before seen Mr Cairns and through some mistake of the interpreters he for some time labored under the impression that Mr Cairns was the discoverer of the North Pole', reported Shuster, 'who had come to present the tusk in person'.[21] History does not record Ahmad Shah's response in being apprised of the error.

The Russians, meanwhile, objected to aspects of Shuster's plan as interfering with their own interests. Pouring troops into the country to make their point, they issued a series of demands culminating in an ultimatum that Shuster be removed. (The British, following the line of least resistance, eventually came to support the Russian position.) The *majlis* rejected the ultimatum, but with Tehran under direct threat from the Russians the decision was taken out of their hands by another *coup d'état* conducted by the Cabinet, with the *majlis* dismissed and Bakhtiari tribal forces now disbanding the institution which a few years ago they had served to restore. The constitution remained, but the constitutional moment had passed.

By the end of 1913, the situation had recovered a little, but only barely. Corruption had installed itself with a vengeance in the provinces, and in Tehran. The country's finances had settled down under a new Treasurer-General, Mornard – a former thorn in the side of Shuster – but only to the extent of adequately supporting foreign interests. The Regent had returned from his European sojourn, and a new Cabinet was being formed. Elections for a new *majlis* were anticipated for some time over the coming days or weeks, though the British diplomat on the ground observed 'no outward signs' that such an eventuality was being prepared.[22] The propriety of formally crowning the young Ahmad Shah was under discussion, some arguing that he was too young and inexperienced, others that a crowned head instead of the politicking around a Regent was exactly what the country needed.

And yet had not Persia, as a viable independent state, been already hollowed out, as Curzon had remarked earlier in the year? To what? A jumble of ideas, ambitions, slogans, hopes and fears, enemies within and enemies without; a strengthened sense of Persian national identity perhaps, but without the means to give it form; a Russian-dominated north – perhaps permanently so – and a southern portion where robber bands arrived with the spring, and left only with the onset of winter.

All the while, one final aspect of Persia heaved more firmly into view, for the British in particular, worried about the decline of naval pre-eminence, and looking for a solution: oil.

The British commercial quest for oil in Persia had begun ten years before, with the grant of a concession to the Australian-educated William Knox D'Arcy to search for black gold in the southern provinces of the country. Its strategic significance, however, had skyrocketed only much more recently, with the decision by Winston Churchill, British First Lord of the Admiralty, that oil was the fuel of the future for the Royal Navy, allowing for faster ships with greater range than coal, requiring less time and fewer men to refuel, and offering the possibility of all this happening quite easily at sea rather than at Britain's many coaling stations around the world.[23] The only problem with Churchill's strategy, as its critics were keen to point out, was getting hold of the fuel itself at a reasonable price, without being forced to pay ever-higher prices in a crisis, potentially bidding directly against its enemies. For while coal was abundant

First Lord of the Admiralty Winston Churchill. Having pushed for the Royal Navy to be run on fuel oil rather than coal, in 1913 Churchill was instrumental in securing Persian oil supplies for the navy, inaugurating an era of petro-geopolitics.

in the United Kingdom, oil was not. Its price was rising and its relative abundance or scarcity unproven. 'Mr Churchill is of course much too clever to see', noted *The Economist* sourly, 'that in exchanging steam coal, which is almost our [British] monopoly, for oil fuel, in which we are very poor, Great Britain is once more handicapping her fleet and her taxpayers'.[24]

Persia could never be more than one of several prospective sources for British oil. As Churchill told the House of Commons in July 1913, 'on no one quality, on no one process, on no one country, on no one company, on no one route, and on no one oil field must we be dependent. Safety and certainty in oil lie in variety, and in variety alone'.[25] But Persia was a special case. Much of the rest of the world's supply was in Russia, or in the United States, or under the control of consortia in which there was a strong non-British element – a judgement which applied to Royal Dutch Shell, despite the business being based in London, and most of its directors being British. (Mexico was an alternative to Persia, of course; but it was a country on the other side of the Atlantic, with its own political problems attached.)

In south-west Persia, however, following the discovery of oil in 1908 on the concession granted to William Knox D'Arcy, an entirely British operation had sprung up. Known by 1913 as the Anglo-Persian Oil Company – and much later as British Petroleum – British diplomatic assistance, both in Tehran and locally, had been critical to getting the whole thing off the ground. Locally, a secret British guarantee of political support to the local Arab magnate Sheikh Khaz'al of Muhammerah (Khorramshahr, in Persian), allowed British commercial interests to more or less bypass the central Persian authorities entirely, particularly important when it came to shipping in the necessary infrastructure to build a pipeline and a refinery.[26] Britain had already developed a series of strong local relationships at other points along the Persian Gulf, in places where the Admiralty had also considered the possibility of oil, in Kuwait and Bahrain. In 1910, Sheikh Khaz'al was made a Knight Commander of the Most Eminent Order of the Indian Empire for his services.

In 1913, the Anglo-Persian Oil Company raised the possibility – or perhaps the threat – that, were it not to achieve a position of greater financial strength, it might be unable to produce the resources of its concession or else be pushed into a price war with other consortia with more extensive marketing operations, and ultimately be bought out by them. (The Turkish Petroleum Company, a consortium of largely foreign partners set up the previous year, was mooted as a possible buyer.) If, on the other hand, Anglo-Persian was able to strike some kind of financial deal with the Admiralty and the government of India, assuring the firm's long-term future, it would be in a position to offer them a forward contract for oil at a decent price. A key source of British supply would be secured. The strategic risk associated with a shift from coal to oil would be partly mitigated.

That the Admiralty would sign up to such a scheme, essentially turning the British government into the strategic partner of a commercial player, was not a foregone conclusion. The Admiralty had to be won round – by the Anglo-Persian Oil Company, by Churchill himself, and by the weight of positive appraisals Churchill had engineered, including one by Admiral Fisher, the father of the modern Royal Navy. Eventually, however, the job was done. In the autumn of 1913, to settle the matter once and for all on the naval side, a commission under Rear Admiral Sir Edmond Slade, a former Director of Naval Intelligence, was sent through the Strait of Hormuz and up along the Persian Gulf, to Bahrain, Kuwait and, in south-west Persia, up the Karun River to Maidan i-Naphtun and White Oil Springs, inspecting the rock formations, estimating its productive capacity and speaking to the geologists on site. Reaching Muhammerah on 23 October 1913, they celebrated New Year in the region, arriving back in England only at the end of January 1914.

They returned to London full of praise. Persia, it seemed, would fit the bill for British requirements nicely. Thus from a buffer between British India and Russia, a country prized as a market for British and Indian goods, and a route for British telegraph wires, Persia would now, over time, develop into something still more: a vital strategic asset of a foreign nation. From 1913 on, the history of Persia would be intertwined with a new aspect to global power – oil – a fate from which the country could no more escape than from its storied history, or from its awkward present.

JERUSALEM
Zion and its Discontents

As 1913 drew to an end, the Holy Land received two visitors from the sky.

The first was French pilot Jules Védrines, an old-timer in the new world of the aeroplane. Winner of the Paris–Madrid air race of 1911, he was competing in a gruelling air race to Cairo, which had already taken him across Europe, across Turkey, over the Taurus mountain range, and now to the eastern shores of the Mediterranean. In late December 1913, he became the first aviator to land on the bumpy ground of Palestine. Having damaged his landing gear coming down on the coastal plain, Védrines was forced to stay the night. The next day, however, he was off, continuing his journey along the coast to Cairo, after a short demonstration flight over the city of Jaffa.

Behind him came his compatriot Marc Bonnier. Realising that he had no chance of catching the leader in the race, Bonnier decided instead to become the first man to land a plane at Jerusalem itself. In the event, he touched down a mile or so south of the Old City. These landings were double proof of French mastery of the air, evidence that in some fields of endeavour at least, the flair, technology and heroism of the French was still superior to that of other nations. French prestige amongst the local population of the Holy Land was lifted, as the resident German diplomat reported crossly, with cries of '*Vive la France!*' ringing out on the streets. Still, he added, more might have been achieved were it not for the weaknesses of his French counterpart: 'never in his office, sleeps the whole day, conducts no business at all – except with prostitutes'.[1] Bonnier ascended into the air again, leaving the earth behind, the holiest city on earth viewed as no human had ever viewed it before.

Jerusalem in 1913 was not a city on any great trade routes. It was not of any great military significance. Though no one knew the number of its Ottoman and foreign inhabitants with any certainty, it was certainly not a large city by any means, numbering no more than 100,000 at most, of whom perhaps half were Jewish (many of whom were not Ottoman citizens), a little over one-quarter Christian (mostly Arab) and a little less than a quarter Muslim, all living within the broader, overwhelmingly Arab Palestine, itself sparsely populated, punctuated by more recent Jewish colonies.[2] The city's mayors, all Arab, were drawn from the traditional leading families of Palestine – the Husseinis and the Khalidis in particular. Jerusalem's political importance to the Ottoman Empire, of which it was an outlying district or *sancak*, lay above all in its symbolic importance as a holy city for Muslims, for Christians and for Jews. This triple

The first plane to land in Jerusalem, 1913. The local Turkish governor had a hard job managing multiple foreign interests in the Holy Land while keeping a lid on competition between the Jewish majority in the city and the Arab majority in the surrounding countryside.

religious heritage had inspired a complex and sometimes tortured history, and had contemporary consequences for international interest in the city.

This city of three religions could never just be another Ottoman town in 1913, its distant rulers recognised. Its symbolic power was too great, the presence of foreigners too pronounced, and their sense of ownership over the city too well developed. Rights of access to Christian sites had provided the Russian pretext for the Crimean War sixty years before, the French had intervened in Lebanon fifty years ago to protect Maronite Christians, and the defence of Christians still provided an excuse for Russian interests in both eastern Turkey and in the Balkans. Why should Jerusalem be immune to such logic in the future? It was in part for this reason that, for the last forty years, the Ottoman governor or *mutassarif* of the district – uniquely in the Ottoman Empire – did not report to the authorities of the larger province of which the district was a part (traditionally, the *vilayet* of Syria) but rather directly to Constantinople, the capital of the empire as a whole.[3] Jerusalem was a prize – but also a political problem to be managed, delicate and difficult.

From the tower of the Protestant Church of the Redeemer, opened in 1898 by German Emperor Wilhelm II on a grand visit to the city, one could see, virtually at one's feet, the Church of the Holy Sepulchre, built on the site from which Jesus Christ was said to have risen into heaven. Down one hill and up another, on the Temple Mount, stood the golden Dome of the Rock and the Al Aqsa Mosque: the former said to be built directly over the site of the stone where heaven and earth meet, the very spot where Adam was created; the latter the third-holiest site in Islam, after Mecca and Medina, which had for a while been the direction (*qibla*) towards which all Muslims were to pray. Out of view lay the Western Wall, one side of the Temple Mount and all that remained of the ancient Jewish temple, the home of God himself, which had been destroyed by the Romans some eighteen centuries previously.[4] How could such a city, invested with such spiritual power, ever be normal? How could it ever be owned by one people, or by a single religion?

Selma Ekrem, the daughter of the Ottoman *mutassarif*, recalled the string of visitors to visit her father when he first arrived in Jerusalem in 1906, each proclaiming their unswerving loyalty and undying friendship.⁵ First came the French Consul at 9.30 p.m., declaring himself 'the greatest friend of the Governor', the words Holy Sepulchre, Bethlehem, Gethsemane overheard during an hour of conversation. Then came the Russian – 'a new friend of my father, how many proofs of his friendship he brings forth!' After him, the Italian Consul – 'Could the governor find a better and more disinterested friend?' Then, as the hours stretched into the early morning, came a representative of the Armenian Church and then of the Greek Orthodox Church, both declaring their devotion to the Ottoman Empire. But the procession was not finished:

> Twenty minutes to two, arrival of a queer personality, wearing an odd costume with two curls falling on both cheeks. He is cold, restrained but courteous. He is the representative of the foreign Jews, who are not subject to the Turks.
>
> At last the poor governor has found a real friend! The foreign Jews, but they are the most disinterested and the quietest people in Jerusalem.
>
> Three o'clock lets in another Jew. An old man with a long beard, eyes speckled with mischief but amiable and oily mannered. He is the representative of the Turkish Jews.
>
> 'Take care, your Excellency', he begins, 'of that rogue of a Jew who was just leaving and have confidence only in your humble slave'.
>
> Four o'clock: my father runs away at last and goes to bed. But can he sleep? He is up at dawn. He goes before the window. What a splendid city is stretched before him, with its old fortress, its churches and its two big domes of Omar's mosque and the Holy Sepulchre. The houses are all of stones and olive trees cluster round. The sun is reflected on the gilded towers of the great Moscovite church and throws a golden light all over the city.
>
> 'Ah', sighs my father, 'if only I did not have so many friends in Jerusalem.'⁶

On another occasion Selma Ekrem remembered a conversation with her mother, when, as curious and precocious children do, she and her sister had sought to untangle the mysteries of how the three Abrahamic religions of Jerusalem are both related to and divided from each other. Forced to answer the question why Jesus is accepted as a prophet by Muslims but Mohammed is not viewed as a prophet by Christians, Selma's mother replied exasperatedly: 'It shows their [the Christians'] prejudice'.[7] Such things were perhaps too complicated to go into with any longer explanation.

Yet within the Arab population of Jerusalem, Christian and Muslim grew up knowing each other's religion well, understanding which tolling of bells and which procession signified which particular holiday for this or that sect. Such events were the timeless rhythm of Jerusalem, after all. Secular pleasures, such as taking a picnic together in the shade of olive trees on the hills outside the city in the summer, could be shared. Christian and Muslim Arabs alike would go to the Bi'r Ayyub to watch the spring waters in full flow. Wasif Jawhariyyeh, an Arab Christian boy growing up in Jerusalem in these years, went to a school where English, French and Turkish were taught, received lessons on the Qur'an from a local *faqih* (a scholar of Islamic jurisprudence) and ascribed his later career as a singer, sometimes in rather louche circumstances, to the mastery of classical Arabic he had acquired by dint of being taught it through the holy book of Islam.[8] Music was itself a common language of the city. Jawhariyyeh remembered summer evenings spent lolling about amongst the Jerusalemite crowds gathered on the street corners in front of the Austrian Hospice to listen to the singer and *oud*-player Muhammad al-Ashiq, all 'drinking juice and coffee and smoking *argileh*, motionless and mesmerised'.[9]

Jews and Arabs, meanwhile, rubbed shoulders on the streets of Jerusalem in 1913 as they always had. Granted, there was more suspicion now than in the past. After all, the *Yishuv* – the community of Jews in Palestine – had grown considerably over the last decades, not only through the inward migration of religiously motivated Jews but through the migration of those inspired by a new secular philosophy, Zionism, the political ambitions and implications of which were as yet unclear. Palestine had a modern Jewish Zionist city, Tel Aviv. There were scattered settlements of Zionists across the land. Fresh Jewish acquisition of land, controversial for decades, was actively discussed, debated and (mostly) criticised in Arab newspapers – though this did not prevent willing Arab sellers and organised Jewish purchasers from finding ways to circumvent Ottoman regulations, and the steady process of Jewish colonisation continuing as a result.

But what any of this really meant for the future was unknown. Arab voices raised in concern did not yet add up to a certainty of broader conflict. Though much less so in the new suburbs, in the Old City of Jerusalem the traditions of an open city were to the fore. Different quarters seeped into one another rather than being sharply divided by a particular alleyway or street. In the city's cafés, representatives of different communities could wait together for an Ottoman official to answer a petition, sign a document or grant a licence, united in their experience of sullen Ottoman bureaucracy. After 1908 – when censorship was lifted in the Ottoman Empire, more newspapers were published, and the political forms of the empire seemed more up for grabs – the café was where politics was discussed or debated. Some argued that Arabs should have more autonomy in the Ottoman Empire now, and that Jews could be their allies in the process; others argued that the Ottoman identity required all to submit to the central rule of Constantinople, and others that Jewish immigration was undermining the economic and political balance of their part of the world, that the new government in Constantinople was doing too little to prevent it and was perhaps in hock to the Jews. In the Seraii Café in the perfumers' market, such conversations took place under a large mulberry tree.[10] At the Qalonia Café, a nod would guide the visitor to an area for gambling at the back.

All the while, the city was being modernised and expanded. The Arab mayor, Hussein al-Husseini, implemented plans to pave Jerusalem's streets, supported by Muslims, Christians and Ottoman Jews alike. (The re-election of the mayor in 1914 was declared by the Sephardi Jewish newspaper *Ha-Herut* to be the 'only beam of light' in the council elections that year.[11]) A tramway was in the offing. Outside the walls of the Old City, new suburbs were being built and older ones expanded: Mea Shearim and Yemin Moshe as largely Jewish suburbs, and Musrara and Sheikh Jarrah as the preferred new suburbs of well-to-do Palestinian Arabs. For Jawhariyyeh, a young boy from a middle-class Arab family, everyday life was becoming more comfortable, more up-to-date:

During the summer months [of 1904] we would sit around the lowered table for the main meal. Food was served in enameled zinc plates. That year we stopped eating with wooden spoons from Anatolia and

Greece and replaced them with brass ones that were oxidized periodically. We replaced the common drinking *taseh* [bowl] tied to the
pottery jar with individualized crystal glasses. In 1906 my father
acquired single iron beds for each of my siblings, thus ending the
habit of sleeping on the floor. What a delight it was to get rid of
the burden of having to place our mattresses into the wall enclaves
every night.[12]

Jawhariyyeh remembered seeing the one-handed doorman of the
Notre Dame de France church turning on the electric lights of the
building – the first to be electrified in Jerusalem, Jawhariyyeh claimed
– and astonishment that, 'in less than a blink of an eye', the place
went from total darkness to being bathed in white.[13]

Though changing all the time in some ways, Jerusalem was
nonetheless unchanging in others: exalted by three religions, its
particular spirit intact, its texture unique. Over the years, the city
had been conquered by Persians, Romans, Arabs, Christians and
Ottoman Turks, but though their control of Jerusalem had by 1913
lasted nearly 400 years, even the Ottomans were only custodians
of the place. What role could day-to-day vicissitudes of the outside
world play, or petty struggles between families or religious groups,
or even the onset of modernity, when compared to Jerusalem as
an eternal realm of the spirit and the soul, the common heritage
of the whole world?

For Christian Europeans and Americans, Jerusalem was a city of
pilgrimage. A city inaccessible except to the most hardy and the
most motivated a generation or two earlier had now become a
destination for tens of thousands each year. It was overrun with
pilgrims, the paraphernalia of pilgrimage – wooden crosses, tattoos
of the saints, bead-embroidered Madonnas, praying-beads, icons –
and the local hucksters and guides who preyed on pilgrims' religiosity
and credulity to extract a few *piastres* here and there.

The travellers came from all corners. Over the last decades, locals
noted, each Christian group and each European nationality had
established its own particular church or its own hostel or its own
tour groups – a single faith divided by nationality, language and

rites. Different countries even had their own postal services, circumventing the Ottoman telegraph service, which was widely thought to be a nest of spies reporting communications back to Constantinople. On the outskirts of the city the Russians had built a huge compound with its own cathedral, hospital and three hospices, visited in 1911 by Rasputin, Nicholas II's pleasure-seeking *starets*.[14] Near the Damascus Gate, on the Via Dolorosa itself, stood the Austrian Hospice, decorated as if it were on a hillside outside Salzburg, adorned with loving portraits of the moustachioed Austro-Hungarian Emperor Franz Joseph – the first reigning Catholic monarch to visit Jerusalem since the Crusades when he came in 1869 – and his wife. The Protestant Church of the Redeemer laid down a German marker, intended by Wilhelm II to help re-establish Germany as a power in the Holy Land, matched by the German Catholic Dormition Church, dedicated only in 1910. Finally, of course, came the representatives of the confessions which claimed a share in the control of the Church of the Holy Sepulchre – Roman Catholic, Greek Orthodox, Armenian, Coptic, Ethiopian and Syriac – and who squabbled endlessly about their respective rights towards it.

'Whoever has wished to go has already started on the pilgrimage', wrote Stephen Graham, beginning his account of his own travel to the Holy City in 1912, 'and once you have started, every step upon the road is a step toward Jerusalem'.[15] In the event, Graham's journey was undertaken in the company of a group of 500 Russian Orthodox peasants, himself disguised as a peasant. He joined them halfway, on a storm-wracked journey from Constantinople across the Mediterranean on a boat no larger than a Thames steamer and considerably more crowded. Relieved to arrive in one piece two weeks later, the pilgrims rested for a night in Jaffa on the straw-covered floor of a Greek monastery, before the next day travelling to Jerusalem. Those who could afford it took the train; those who could not prepared for a long walk. Eventually they reached the Holy City itself:

> All whispering prayers to ourselves and making religious exclamations, we flocked after one another through the Jerusalem streets; in outward appearance jaded, woe-begone and beaten, following one another's backs like cattle that have been driven from afar; but in reality excited,

feverish, and fluttering like so many children that have been kept up far too late to meet their father come home from long travel.[16]

The very act of pilgrimage, Graham realised, was itself a spiritual, equalising experience, building a communion of the faithful through shared suffering and joy. 'There was no feeling of comparison, of superiority, among any of us', he wrote, 'though some were rich, some poor; some lettered, some illiterate; some with clean bodies, new clothes and naked feet, feeling it was necessary to take off their boots for the ground whereon they trod was holy; others who had not the idea even to wash their faces'. In Jerusalem, gradations of identity so important at home could be forgotten in a single, common faith. Some were overcome with emotion; others with drink. After midnight on Easter Sunday – with only the Jews asleep, remarked a Russian pilgrim – the experience of pilgrimage descended into singing, embracing, 'tangling of beards and whiskers', feasting and the consumption of the alcohol bought from Arab hawkers over the previous few days:

> Every monk or priest I met saluted us with 'Christ is risen!' and we replied 'Yes, He is risen!' and kissed one another. There commenced a day of uproarious festivity. The quantity of wine, of cognac, and arakha consumed at the *Rasgovenie*, the breaking of the fast, would no doubt appal most English. And the drunken dancing and singing would be thought rather foreign to the idea of Jesus. But I don't know. To my eyes it was all an expression of genuine joy . . . At the thought of all their pilgrimage behind them, and of the glorious Easter morning at last achieved, something melted in the heart of every pilgrim. Their faces caught the radiance of a vision, the gleam which shows itself on the countenance of the dying when they catch a glimpse of something of heaven.[17]

Besides the exuberant Russians, and more ascetic pilgrims from other parts of Europe and America, there were the tourists. How different, Graham mused, was his experience as a Russian pilgrim from that of a German with a Kodak camera who took a photograph of him passing by – a photograph which would no doubt be later presented to friends back home as a true likeness of a genuine Russian peasant. How different from the American and English tourists, 'hundreds of them, with their Arab guides and red hand-books', hands clasped tightly over their jackets to protect themselves from pickpockets.[18] Graham recognised a few of the English, though he passed undetected by them. At one point, just past the office of Thomas Cook's the travel agents, he paused with a Russian pilgrim in front of a busty, blonde-haired, blue-eyed English girl, who was having her photo taken in 'local' clothes – 'an ancient embroidered scarlet costume that would serve as a representation of Babylon at a fancy dress ball' – posing sweetly for the camera, a head taller than the surrounding crowd. This was Jerusalem not so much as destination of pilgrimage as an exotic backdrop; Jerusalem as a stage set of half-remembered Bible stories.

By 1913, Christian pilgrims and tourists from Europe and America were perhaps as much the fabric of Jerusalem as the Arab and Jewish residents, some of whom could trace their ancestry back generations into the past. Though transient in one sense, the European and American pilgrims and tourists had become a permanent, indeed a crucial, aspect of the city's economy. Though visitors, their visits expressed deeper and enduring claims to the city and to its meaning. Jerusalem was theirs as well, their presence confirmed.

And of course some pilgrims stayed. Pilgrimage had been the starting point for what became known as the American Colony, begun a few decades previously by the Spafford family and mille-narian Christians from Chicago, and since then added to by converts – Jacob Eliahu, a Sephardic Jew from Ramallah – and, in 1896, by a large number of Swedish Evangelicals.[19] Weaving their own tablecloths, baking their own bread, organising hymn-singing on Sundays, and forming a literary club, choir and band, the American Colony became a prominent part of Jerusalem society, intermixing Jews and Muslims and Christians. Christmas became a festival of gifts from the city's Arabs, Jews and foreigners alike, one of the Spaffords recalled:

Ahmed Effendi sent a sheep; Sheikh Mohammed a basket of rice, the same came from the Mayor of Jerusalem, two turkeys from Hussain, two ducks and two geese and four baskets of oranges from Faidi Effendi al Alami. From others (I can't remember the names) we got four trays of 'buklaway' (Arabic sweetmeat), one tray of geribi (like Scotch shortbread), one tray of 'mamoul' and another of 'Karabidj Halab' (whips of Aleppo – a delicious sweetmeat). Suliman sent a large tray of candy for the tree. A beautiful large tree came from Mr Baldensperger, and many other gifts which I cannot remember.[20]

On 4 July, American Independence Day was commemorated grandly, with the Stars and Stripes raised, despite the protests of the local American Consul, who deemed the colony a fraud and who fought a bitter battle against it.[21] On one occasion Edith Spafford dressed as the Statue of Liberty for a staged photograph to celebrate the occasion. By 1913, what had started as a religious undertaking of a few Evangelical Christians had acquired the characteristics of an extended family business: printing postcards, offering guided tours to tourists, and offering photographic services commissioned, amongst others, by the Zionist Organization and by *National Geographic* magazine.[22] The story of the colony inspired a novel by Selma Lagerlöf, the Swedish laureate of the Nobel Prize for Literature of 1909. In 1913, as the result of a visit to the colony a few years previously, Klas Pontus Arnoldson, winner of the Nobel Peace Prize in 1908, published a book entitled *Jerusalem själ* (*The Soul of Jerusalem*).

What Jewish immigration might ultimately mean for the political destiny of Palestine and for the existing Arab population of the *sancak* of Jerusalem was unclear in 1913.

The Zionist idea of a Jewish homeland was still a dream taking form. Although Jewish immigration to Palestine had begun to increase in the last decades of the nineteenth century, subject to rather half-hearted and ineffective controls by the Ottoman authorities, Zionism as a political movement was essentially a pressure group within the Jewish world rather than the unambiguous representative of all Jews everywhere. If an increasing number of European Jews saw the potential benefits of a homeland where they could develop as a people, safe from the fear of endless persecution and slights experienced by an Alfred Dreyfus or by a Mendel Beilis, there were others who felt that the Zionist project would mean Jews turning their backs on the promise of assimilation into European societies and ghettoising themselves anew – not broadening their horizons, but diminishing them. There were divisions within the Jewish community between educated western European Jews who valued the economic and social status they had achieved in their respective countries, and generally less well-educated eastern European and Russian Jews – let alone north African or Middle Eastern Jews – some of whom seemed to have barely crept out of the Middle Ages. Even amongst convinced Zionists there was disagreement on the means to achieve a Jewish homeland, and on the precise form such a homeland should ultimately take.

It had not been at all obvious, until the very end of the nineteenth century, that the Zionist project necessarily equated to a Jewish homeland in Palestine, as opposed to some other corner of the world. Theodor Herzl's *Der Judenstaat* (*The Jewish State*), published in 1896 in Vienna, did not identify Palestine specifically. But even once that central question had been answered at the first Zionist Congress, held in Basel in 1897, plenty of other questions remained. Did a Jewish homeland entail a majority of Jews within a particular geographical area, or could Jewish security be obtained without Jews being in a demographic majority? Should religion play a strong role in such a homeland, or should it rather be defined by a progressive secular identity, centred more around the university and the opera house than around the synagogue? What should be its language – Hebrew or German, or perhaps both, perhaps many? Should Jews learn Arabic, partly in order to assuage the fears of local Arabs in Palestine that their culture and traditions would be swamped, and partly to more easily negotiate the purchase of land? Should only Jews be employed to work the land of Jewish-owned settlements in Palestine, or should Arabs also be employed, thus allowing for a greater degree of economic interdependence and social assimilation? And, after all this, would Arabs be the contented political equals of Jews in such a homeland, benefiting, as many Zionists saw it, from the economic investment and technical expertise that Jewish migration would bring to Palestine? Or would they be its sullen rivals, either slowly emigrating to other parts of the Ottoman Empire or, more worryingly, remaining entrenched on the land? In the broader political context, what degree of autonomy could or should a Jewish homeland aspire to in the Ottoman Empire; and, as a matter of practical politics, did the route to the establishment of a Jewish homeland lie through Constantinople or rather through Berlin, Paris, Vienna and London?

The role of Jerusalem within a Jewish homeland was itself a question. When Herzl visited in 1898, hoping to persuade the touring German Kaiser to throw his imperial prestige behind the noble idea of a Jewish homeland in Palestine, Herzl found the city cramped, unhealthy, full of dark corners and mysticism – hardly a place to fulfil his vision of a self-confident, liberal, progressive, modern Jewish nation. When, a few years later, he wrote a futuristic novel depicting a Jewish Palestine in 1923 – suitably titled *Altneuland* (*Old-New Land*) – he imagined the northern town of Haifa as its powerhouse, not Jerusalem. Thus while some Zionists saw Jerusalem as the inevitable centre of Eretz Israel – the home of the holiest Jewish site, after all, and a Jewish-majority city – and many more accepted the symbolic power of Jerusalem as a means of raising money for the Zionist project, the city was hardly the sole or even central preoccupation of practical, pragmatic Zionists.[23] Arthur Ruppin, the head of the Zionist Organisation in Palestine, set up his office on Bustrus Street in the city of Jaffa, down on the coast. He corresponded with Zionist headquarters in Berlin in German, not Hebrew.

When the eleventh Zionist Congress met in Vienna in September 1913 then, the task of its delegates from Palestine was essentially to act as promoters: to ensure that European Jewish support for the project was maintained, that positive momentum was given to the push to secure a proper homeland in Palestine and to achieve more than simply a vulnerable set of settlements. In Vienna, they showed maps of Jewish settlements, photographs showing Jews in the fields of their new homeland, even a film. The push was ultimately given new life by the call for a Jewish University – a 'new shrine on Mount Zion', as one delegate called it – to be established in Jerusalem, on land that was bought just outside the city, on Mount Scopus.[24]

Though the Ottoman Empire had, over many years, attempted to forbid land purchases by foreign Jews in Palestine, prevent settlement, control immigration and limit the amount of time Jewish visitors could spend in the region, these policies were not terribly effective in the face of the determination and wiliness which Zionists brought to their cause on the ground. Land could be bought under different names; newly-arrived migrants could disappear into existing populations, or even be declared dead by the consular officials of the country whose nationality they retained, only to reappear a few years later miraculously alive.[25] Given the legal and administrative obstacles presented to migrants, the modus operandi of Zionism was necessarily somewhat underhand on occasion. Messages sent from the Zionist office in Jaffa to headquarters in Berlin were written out in elementary code. In 1913, land already purchased on behalf of Jews would be described as 'Shanghai'.[26] If an offer of sale of land had been made to Jews with ample time to think before a decision had to be made to go ahead or not, this would be conveyed to Berlin with a word describing the tempo of slow-moving music: 'Adagio'. If there was less time, another word would be used: 'Allegro'. The project for a Jewish University was referred to as '*Kunstwerk*', the German word for artwork. Tel Aviv was '*Stadtpass*' (city pass). Opponents of land purchases were '*Stickluft*', implying a stifling atmosphere. Enemies were '*Stickstoff*' (nitrogen), friends were '*Stiefsohn*' (stepson).

Still, noted a letter back to Berlin in November of that year, 'the tempo of colonisation is so slow'.[27] It continued, 'we could say without exaggeration that we could have obtained at least 100,000 more Dunam [an Ottoman unit of land] more than we have'. More money, and more political support was always welcome. In December 1913, Berlin asked Ruppin to take special care of the son of a Christian German industrialist who, having completed his military service in China, now wished to see something of the Middle East. 'We don't know Dr Kruft personally, about as well as we know Christ', the Berlin office wrote, 'but we place importance in German Christians visiting Palestine and offering them the opportunity to construct their own verdict about relationships there'.[28]

Meanwhile, Ottoman authorities in Constantinople, Arabs in Palestine and Arabs across the broader Middle East did not always share the same interests regarding what happened in Palestine. The Ottomans' key objectives were to maintain order, to prevent events in Jerusalem from offering a pretext for further foreign intervention, and to keep Arab nationalism in check. Preventing Jewish immigration was hardly an existential question at this point, as long as immigration did not lead to a movement for Jewish political independence. In any case, any concerns about the demographic balance in Palestine were balanced by wider sets of issues preoccupying the

Ottoman state. In 1913, Constantinople had a much more immediate worry: the very survival of the Ottoman Empire itself. Having lost Libya to the Italians a few years previously, and now on the brink of losing what remained of the empire's historic European possessions to a fractious alliance of Bulgarians, Serbians, Montenegrins and Greeks, the Ottoman Empire needed friends, particularly friends with money. Jewish support could be helpful.

Similarly, for Arabs in Syria or in Egypt, areas far more central to emergent pan-Arab political consciousness in 1913 than Jerusalem, Palestine was a side issue. The causes which motivated Arab elites politically were much broader than the situation in the *sancak* of Jerusalem, however symbolic. They sought either a greater stake in the running of the Ottoman Empire or, if they could not get that, greater autonomy from it. They wanted accelerated economic development. It was not entirely out of the question that Jewish immigration, and Jewish political support, might actually help in achieving these aims. Was there a bargain to be struck between pan-Arabism and Zionism? Victor Jacobson, responsible for the Zionist Organization in Constantinople, suggested in 1913 that 'the first article of our work programme ought to be an entente with the Arabs'.[29] One of the delegates to the very first Arab Congress that year, held in Paris in June, was Sami Hochberg, the Jewish editor of a French-language newspaper in Constantinople called *Le Jeune Turc*.[30]

Some Arabs and some Ottomans were more concerned by Zionism. A number of books and pamphlets were published on the subject. Newspaper articles were written setting out the Zionist challenge in increasingly strident tones, and drawing attention to specific incidents of Jewish land purchases or Arab–Jewish tension. Some articles were themselves countered by Zionists. In 1913, a Moroccan Jew named Shimon Moyal, who had trained in Beirut as a doctor and who previously lived in Cairo, set up an organisation known as HaMagen, which attempted to rebut anti-Zionist articles in the Arabic press and translated such articles from Arabic into Hebrew.[31] But the fact that such an approach was deemed necessary was itself an indication of a worsening atmosphere of mutual suspicion and a rising war of words. Ruppin himself saw the growth of Arab nationalism as something to be worried about. 'If the national consciousness of the Arabs strengthens', he wrote to the central office in Berlin in early 1913, 'then we will face resistance that perhaps we will no longer be able to overcome with money'.[32]

The lifting of censorship in the Ottoman Empire in 1908, and the growth of newspaper print which followed in the Arab world, had allowed grievances to be articulated and spread more readily. In 1911, Najib Nassar published a book in Arabic entitled *Zionism: Its History, Objectives and Importance*. He admired Herzl for what he had done, for the organisation of Zionism and for its political successes, and urged that Arabs in Palestine respond accordingly, through financial and political organisation. 'Why do we, who have spent centuries suffering tragedy and misery, not become men', he asked, 'and go on the way of freedom and live for our patrimony and for ourselves, so that we shall not invoke upon ourselves the curses of our ancestors and our sons by losing the country which our ancestors acquired with their blood?'[33] Ruhi Khalidi, scion of one of Jerusalem's leading families, and now an elected representative to the Ottoman parliament, tried to awaken his fellow deputies to the issue. In 1913, before he passed away, he was preparing a book on the subject, going through the history of Zionism in detail and outlining the challenges it posed for Ottoman sovereignty in Palestine, and for the existing Arab population.

The situation was inflamed that summer, when a squabble on the road between the Jewish settlement of Rehovot and the Arab village of Zarnuqa descended into a shoot-out.[34] Zionists claimed Arabs from the nearby village had been caught stealing grapes from the settlement and that they had attacked a Jewish guard who attempted to interdict them. Arabs claimed the problem stemmed from the militarisation of Jewish settlements, where security had been taken over by an increasingly powerful self-defence organisation, HaShomer. It was claimed that a typically over-zealous Jewish guard had wrongfully accused the Arabs of theft and that he had been disarmed in order to prevent violence. In the confusion immediately following the incident on the road, with Jewish Rehovot settlers and Arab Zarnuqa villagers all thinking they were coming to the rescue of their beleaguered kin, local Jews and Arabs took up arms. A Jewish settler was shot in the ensuing fighting but survived; an Arab villager was fatally wounded. A few days later, a Jewish guard at Rehovot was murdered. Arrests were made. Each side pleaded the justice of their case to the

Ottoman authorities, to their community, and to the wider world. 'No intelligent or impartial person could believe this odious accusation presenting Jewish farmers as provocateurs', wrote Ruppin to the Ottoman Governor of Jerusalem (in French).[35] In the past, he claimed, violence or theft on the part of Arabs had been forgiven: 'thousands of trees harmed, human lives lost in the fullness of youth, hundreds of animals taken, fruit stolen or ripped off'. But there were limits. 'We are ready to reform our security', he wrote, 'but not to suppress it or give in to those who attack and pillage us'.[36]

Would this be yet another incident in the long litany of incidents between Jew and Arab, Christian and Muslim, Christian and Christian – built up over years of close proximity in the Holy Land – to be ultimately overcome by common sense and common interest? Would the case be forgotten, accumulating dust in the files of the Ottoman authorities? Or, as some contended, was a point of no return now being approached? In November of that year a poem was published in *Falastin*, a local Arab newspaper in Palestine, denigrating the Jews and calling upon the Caliph in Constantinople to act:

> Jews, sons of clinking gold, stop your deceit;
> We shall not be cheated into bartering away our country!
> Shall we hand it over, meekly,
> While we still have some spirit left?
> Shall we cripple ourselves?
>
> The Jews, the weakest of all peoples and the least of them,
> Are haggling with us for our land;
> How can we slumber on?
> We know what they want
> And they have the money, all of it.
>
> Master, rulers, what is wrong with you?
> What ails you?
> It is time to awake, to be aware!
> Away with this heedlessness
> There is no more time for patience![37]

In December 1913 ships set sail from Europe bringing new migrants to Canada, Australia and Argentina. The British naval expedition sent to enquire into the petroleum potential of Persia turned back to London. Algerians, both French and Arab, shuttled between Algiers and Paris. Gandhi contemplated a return from South Africa, where he had now made his name, to India. In Kiev, Mendel Beilis, the Jewish clerk who had been locked up, persecuted and demonised for a murder he did not commit, prepared himself, like so many others, to seek a new life in a new land.

> Goodbye, Kiev, farewell my native land, farewell all my friends with whom I have spent my life! I am leaving for the land of our fathers, for the Holy Land, where once flowed milk and honey, and which has always been dear to my heart. I am going to rest body and soul in the Land of Israel.[38]

Next year in Jerusalem: for Beilis at least, the incantation would become reality.

Taking a coach from Kiev in the middle of the night, practically on the eve of the New Year, Beilis met his wife and children in the country town Kozyatyn, from where they caught a train, streaking across the frozen countryside of western Ukraine to the border of the Austro-Hungarian Empire at Podvolochisk. Once across, the way was open to Lemberg (now Lviv), then Vienna, then the Austro-Hungarian port of Trieste on the Adriatic Sea. Though he attempted to conceal his identity, Beilis' secret inevitably came out in the places through which he travelled. Crowds gathered around him, intrigued to see the unassuming spectacled figure whose trial and subsequent acquittal had shamed the mighty Russian Empire.

In the first days of the New Year, 1913 having passed away and 1914 arrived in its stead, Beilis' ship docked first in Alexandria, and then Haifa. 'The Land of Israel had an invigorating effect on me', Beilis wrote warmly afterwards, perhaps in the mode of publicist as much as diarist. Israel, he continued, 'gave me new life and new hope':

> Nature itself, the life of the people, inspired me with vigor and the desire to live. When we had left Kiev, it was cold, and the fields were covered with snow. Here everything was green, and the sun was warm.

It was the most beautiful season of the year in Palestine. Everything was blooming; the hills and the fields were covered with vegetation. I could not get too much of the atmosphere. For quite some time I would wander around, inspecting every corner of the country, breathing the refreshing air, deep-lunged.[39]

Everywhere, he was welcomed with generosity. When he had landed in Haifa, he remembered, a local Arab chief put a coach and horses at his disposal and insisted on riding ahead on the dusty road south, acting as his guard of honour. The welcome from the Jewish community, naturally, was still more enthusiastic. 'The Zionists are in a frenzy of celebration and have dressed Tel Aviv as for the arrival of a prince', wrote the German Consul in Jaffa to the German Chancellor in Berlin in February 1914.[40]

He had reached the Holy Land, but Beilis did not initially go to the Holy City. Despite entreaties that it was at the Western Wall where the most fervent prayers had been said for his release from prison, he delayed. Prayers had been said for his sake at many places other than Jerusalem, he pointed out. In any case, he was quite taken up with engagements in Tel Aviv and Jaffa, dinners and receptions, a visit to the colony at Petah Tikva, and endless requests to shake the hands of tourists, newly arrived migrants and locals – Jews and Arab Palestinians alike.

In April, however, just before Passover, he made the journey inland. Staying in a comfortable hotel by the Jaffa Gate, Beilis did the rounds of the synagogues, hospitals and charitable institutions of Jerusalem, his family and followers in tow. Eventually, he made it to the Western Wall itself. Herzl had found the place a disappointment, finding deep emotion impossible in a place of such 'hideous, miserable, scrambling, beggary'.[41] Beilis' feelings were mixed, those of others in his group were uncontained:

I relived the whole Jewish exile and also re-experienced my own sorrows. As I was standing at the wall, absorbed in thought, I heard a sudden cry. Turning, I saw H. Berlin, one of the members of my party, crying. It was surprising from a man who had no Jewish characteristics whatever; he had been supposed to be far-removed from Judaism altogether. His daughter, a doctor, who could not even speak any Yiddish, was crying hysterically.

There was one final and still more remarkable step to be taken. Ascending to the Temple Mount, Beilis, the Jewish factory super-intendant from Kiev, was granted access to the Al Aqsa mosque itself, the third-holiest site in Islam, guided around by a local Palestinian Arab. Despite all that had happened in Palestine over the previous year, such kindnesses were still possible. The die was not yet cast.

The Galata Bridge, Constantinople. 'We live in a time of surprises', wrote an American observer in 1913, 'Turkey is reforming, China is waking up, the self-satisfied complacency of the white race has received a shock'.

PART IV

TWILIGHT POWERS

Around the world, throughout history, great powers had risen from obscurity to conquer huge tracts of the world or to weld magnificent empires from disparate territories. The Romans, the Persians, the Macedonians of Alexander the Great, the medieval Abbasid Caliphate, the Mongols, the dynasties of ancient China, the Ottoman Turks, the Aztecs and Incas, the seafaring Spaniards and Portuguese, now the British and the French – all had had their day. Some of these imperial creations survived for centuries. Others lasted only a few decades, or even just a few years, only as good as their last military victory, held together by nothing more permanent than fear.

This, to any well-educated citizen of the world in 1913, appeared to be the rhythm of history: empires rose, empires fell, empires were born, and empires died. At any single point in time – sometimes fully conscious of their predicament, sometimes without realising it at all – great and apparently once-invincible empires might be approaching the twilight of their days, after which dusk would surely fall over them, consigning their achievements to history. (It was no surprise that Britons studied the Roman Empire so closely – they wanted to understand how to imitate its success, and how to avoid its end.) Other empires would no doubt rise and take their place, perhaps led by some as-yet obscure people who, through accident of history, good fortune of geography, great leadership or techno-logical innovation, suddenly found itself in a position to extend its dominion over others. For such a people, twilight heralded not dusk but the dawn of their own imperial age.

In 1898, the grand old man of British politics, Lord Salisbury, gave this classic description of the rise and fall of empires a modern, Darwinian twist. He described the world divided into what he termed 'living' and 'dying' powers. On one side of the ledger were those 'growing in power every year, growing in wealth, growing in dominion, growing in the perfection of their organisation'.[1] As such powers appropriated the technologies of the modern world – the railway, advances in armaments, and so on – they became still stronger and more developed, concentrating ever more power in their hands. Their best days lay ahead of them. On the other side lay the 'dying' powers, their best days now in the past:

> Decade after decade they are weaker, poorer and less provided with leading men or institutions in which they can trust, apparently drawing nearer and nearer to their fate and yet clinging with strange tenacity to the life which they have got.[2]

This was a Darwinian world where the 'survival of the fittest' applied to states as well as to the natural world. It offered no room for complacency. And it raised three sets of questions for political leaders looking at their own countries. First, on which side of Salisbury's ledger did their country fall? Second, if their country found itself on the wrong side of the ledger, was decline inevitable or could an active programme of modernisation reverse it? Third, did modernisation imply simply the adoption of the most advanced technologies – or did it also imply deeper cultural, social and political reform? Did becoming modern mean becoming Western?

In 1913, it was fairly obvious that the German Empire and the United States were, by Salisbury's definition, 'living' powers, destined for roles of growing importance in the world. The jury was out on the Russian Empire, although most commentators would put it in the same category of a 'living' power, and some saw Russia as the inevitable Eurasian behemoth of the twentieth century. For other European empires – the Austro-Hungarian or even the French Empire – the outlook was less clear. Beyond these, in the wider world, two old empires – the Ottoman and the Chinese – were in a period of rapid and uncertain transition. To some they appeared to be on their last legs; others saw the stirrings of rebirth. A third non-European empire, the Japanese, was rising rapidly, having made a spectacular entrance into the ranks of great powers by defeating the Russian Empire in the Pacific, an outcome unthinkable to previous generations. Meanwhile, the questions hanging over the future of another empire – the British – grew more insistent with each passing year. This was Britain's moment in the sun – of that there was no doubt. London basked in the glory of the largest empire the world had ever seen. How long this moment would last, however, was unclear. Was Britain heading into the twilight, too?

'We live in a time of surprises', wrote Elizabeth Kendall, an American globetrotter in 1913, 'Turkey is reforming, China is waking up, the self-satisfied complacency of the white race has received a shock'.[3] In Salisbury's day, in 1898, things had been simpler. Then, the Ottoman Empire was the quintessential 'dying power'. Having once extended as far as the gates of Vienna, by the turn of the twentieth century the Ottoman Empire was a mangy beast, thinned out by war, by secession, and by the slow pace of economic development. An independent Greek kingdom had peeled off in the 1820s. Serbia affirmed its independence from Constantinople, the Ottoman capital, in the 1860s. Bulgaria and Bosnia gained autonomy in 1878, and the British became masters of Cyprus. Egypt, the key to the Suez Canal, was firmly in London's orbit by the 1880s. Whereas the populations of all the European Great Powers had increased over the nineteenth century, that of the Ottomans had fallen to barely twenty million, the vast majority of whom were illiterate. Britain produced more coal in a day than the Ottoman Empire did in a year, while the mileage of Ottoman railways was less than that of Brazil or Belgium, and only one-tenth that of India.[4] The Ottoman Empire's financial arrangements had essentially been outsourced to foreign bankers.

China was, if anything, in a worse state in 1898. There, over the previous fifty years, foreigners had turned their economic and military advantages over a technologically backward China into trade concessions along the Chinese coast and along China's inland waterways: Hong Kong, Shanghai, Nanjing and so on. The already-fragile hold of the Qing dynasty in Peking over the country as a whole – beset by a history of regional rebellions, and by regular famines and floods – was further weakened as a result. So-called 'Unequal Treaties' had been signed which resulted in an ever-increasing foreign presence, and made it impossible for China to pursue an economic policy adapted to its needs. Traditional Chinese spheres of influence had been usurped at the fringes of its empire. The Russians took control over a slice of outer Manchuria in the 1860s, beating a pathway to the Pacific and establishing a Russian city at Vladivostok, which subsequently became the terminus of the Trans-Siberian railway. Despite Chinese protests, France occupied the neighbouring Indochinese cities of Hanoi and Haiphong in 1880. (In 1884, a naval battle between China and France destroyed an entire Chinese fleet, within minutes, at the cost of just five French lives.) The British made Burma a protectorate and staked out their position over Tibet. In 1895, a people that most Chinese considered a tributary nation, the Japanese, were victorious against China in war. In consequence, Japan extracted a huge indemnity in the Treaty of Shimonoseki, incorporated Taiwan into its empire, and formally established that it was Japan – and not the Qing dynasty – which had pre-eminence in Korea.

Many inside China and outside the country wondered whether Chinese civilisation was capable of renewal from within, given the country's long history of resisting innovation and the strong interests of the establishment in preventing the kinds of social or political changes that could undermine their position. Many questioned whether China would survive as a political unit at all. (Both Ottoman and Chinese thinkers read Darwin and his acolytes on theories of natural selection – one leading Chinese theorist of reform, Yan Fu, translated the works of Thomas Huxley into Chinese.) A cartoon in a Parisian magazine of 1898 shows a traditionally attired Chinese gentleman, with arched eyebrows, pigtail (also known as the queue), drooping moustache and thin beard, hands raised in an expression of horror as a large cake marked 'C-H-I-N-A' is in the process of being divided up.[5] Kaiser Wilhelm II plants his knife firmly to secure his slice; beside him Queen Victoria's bejewelled fingers stake out the British claim; a wistful-looking Nicholas II of Russia ponders his country's options while Marianne, female personification of the French Republic, looks on. To one side, samurai sword unsheathed, a Japanese figure greedily eyes the scene. This was a picture of a scramble for China along the lines of the scramble for Africa of the 1880s. A more suitable analogy for China's position might have been that of an ancient torture still administered by representatives of the Qing dynasty: death by a thousand cuts.

By 1913, fifteen years later, neither the Ottoman nor the Chinese Empire was out of the woods. Both had experienced further military defeat, loss of territory, and political humiliation at the hands of stronger powers. (In 1913, the Ottoman Empire was battling to retain even a toehold in Europe.) But both had also undergone seismic political shifts at home, destabilising at first, yet fostering expectations of longer term renewal. In Constantinople constitutional government was reintroduced in 1908 as part of the 'Young Turk' revolution, bringing the hope that the Ottoman Empire would now re-establish itself through internal reform, and through the energies of a younger generation of political leaders. In Peking, the child-Emperor of the Qing dynasty had ceased to rule beyond the walls of the imperial palace of the Forbidden City, and the forms of republican government had begun to take shape under a former general, Yuan Shikai. If strong central government could be properly established – a very big 'if' in the context of the anarchy and civil unrest which predominated across the country for much of 1913 – all bets on China's future role in the world were off. Wrote a foreign resident of Peking:

> In the hands of such a [strong] government China will soon become a World-Power, easily able to hold her territory against aggression . . . With her wealth of internal resources and her teeming millions, a Westernised China must sooner or later count as the controlling factor in industrial and military struggles of the world.[6]

'What will happen', he asked, 'when such a China begins to look abroad for markets and colonies?' It was precisely such a fear of a newly-powerful China – a distant but no longer inconceivable prospect – which inspired British writer Sax Rohmer to pen the first of his extraordinarily popular Fu-Manchu novels in 1913. *The Mystery of Dr. Fu-Manchu* described the fantastical dangers of a combination of ancient Oriental wisdom and modern Western technology.

Both China and the Ottoman Empire were still basket cases – but perhaps not forever. In the course of little more than a decade, from 1898 to 1913, both had jolted from a period of slow, steady and apparently ineluctable decline into a new and more uncertain phase, from which they might yet emerge leaner, fitter and better able to survive in the world of the great powers. Meanwhile, both Ottoman and Chinese reformers looked admiringly at a third empire which seemed to have already cracked the secret of surviving and flourishing in a Western-dominated world by beating the West at its own game: Japan.

As late as the mid nineteenth century Japan was an isolated island-nation where the public duty of every Japanese *samurai* was to kill any foreigner who might chance upon Japanese shores, and where an official policy of *sakoku* (closed country) was considered an article of national faith. From the 1850s on, however, Japan began to open up. This was partly the consequence of foreigners' insistence on greater access: in 1854, an American mission led by Commodore Perry barged into the country, overawed the Japanese with its steamships, and demanded trade rights far beyond those traditionally accorded to select foreign traders. But Japan's opening up was increasingly a matter of enlightened policy-making by Japanese leaders themselves, who understood the usefulness of Western military technologies in settling political squabbles at home, and who realised that modernisation was the key to Japan's survival as an independent nation.

Tentative and uncertain at first, the process of opening up to the West accelerated sharply in the 1860s. In 1867, for the first time, the Japanese Empire provided a national pavilion at an international exhibition, the Paris Exposition Universelle, provoking a Western craze for Japanese art and design. Shortly thereafter, in 1868, after seven centuries when Japan had been ruled as a traditional semi-feudal military dictatorship known as the *bakufu* – a hereditary *shogun* calling the shots in Edo (Tokyo) and the Emperor in Kyoto reigning as a purely symbolic figure – the political authority of the Japanese Emperor was restored. The last *shogun* was shunted into an early retirement (though he only died in 1913). The *samurai* class – essentially an aristocratic warrior caste – was pensioned off.

The Meiji Restoration – as Emperor Meiji's assumption of political power in Japan was called – proved a watershed. Although presented initially as a return to more ancient political forms, accompanied by a drive to rediscover native Japanese virtues and religion in place of the Chinese imports of Buddhism and Confucianism, the Meiji Restoration in fact provided the basis for Japan's accelerated Westernisation led by the state. *Sakoku* was out, learning from the West was in. Books such as Fukuzawa Yukichi's 1869 *Introduction to the Countries of the World*, designed to be taught in schools, lauded the civilisational advances of the West.[7] In 1871, fifty high government officials led by Iwakura Tomomi were sent around the world on an intensive study trip to identify the best examples of foreign technology and organisation, spending 205 days in the United States (partly because a few of the group had to travel back to Japan to acquire adequate diplomatic credentials), 122 days in Britain and 23 in Prussia, with side-trips to Paris, Bern, Copenhagen, Stockholm, St Petersburg, Vienna and Rome.

The officials were encouraged. 'The wealth and prosperity that one sees in Europe date to a considerable degree from the period after 1800', noted one of the study trip members in his diary.[8] There was no reason, in other words, why Japan could not catch up. Under the slogan, *Fukoku kyōhei* – rich country, strong army – Japan began to lay the foundations for the country's emergence as the pre-eminent power in East Asia. In 1889 it adopted a constitution, with a parliament known as the Diet. Its aristocracy was reformed to look more and more like that of Britain.

After a quarter-century of political, industrial and economic reform, Japan's easy victory over China in the Sino-Japanese war of 1894–5 demonstrated the extent to which Japan had by then overhauled her Asian neighbour. The financial indemnity won from China allowed for further naval expansion, railway construction and, in 1901, the establishment of Japan's first large-scale steel works. Just as important was the boost to Japanese pride which victory provided – and to the respect which Japan now expected from the rest of the world. From now on, one newspaper claimed hopefully, the West would 'call us as we call ourselves: Nippon, which has a meaning, the rising sun, and there will be no more "Japan" or "Japs" in the foreign press'.[9] In 1902, the greatest empire in the world, the British Empire, consented to make an alliance with Japan. Two years later, in 1904–1905, the Russo-Japanese war resulted in a stunning Japanese victory, the first time an Asian power had so comprehensively humiliated a European one. Although Japan was not able to extract a financial indemnity from Russia as it had from China (indeed the war left Japan close to bankruptcy) and although the territorial gains involved in the American-mediated peace were meagre – regaining Port Arthur, which she had won from China ten years earlier and been forced to give up under Western pressure in peace negotiations – the country's position in the world was transformed. Japan had, through education, frugality, economic transformation, military strength and political determination, elbowed her way to the table of the Great Powers by 1913.

The Meiji era had thus been crowned with success. But with the Emperor's death in 1912 and the accession of his son Emperor Taisho, other, more existential questions about Japan's future came to the fore. Was Japan to be a true popular democracy, or was it to retain the attributes of a traditional oligarchy? Was Japanese society to become a Western consumer society geared towards the satisfaction of individual wants, or was it the role of each individual to serve the collectivity, the nation and the state? Was Japan as respected abroad as much as the Japanese felt it should be, or did Western racism represent a permanent block to Japan's full acceptance into the Western club? In Asia, was Japan to become little more than a European-style colonial power, or was the country destined to wake the countries of Asia and lead a pan-Asian revival? Perhaps both.

And what of Britain? The sun still shone – but were the country's prospects as bright as they had seemed a generation previously? Was the life slowly ebbing from British power? Was the sun beginning to set? Relative decline was hard to square with Britain's unprecedented prosperity in 1913, or with the dominance of the British Empire, or the majestic centrality of London to world affairs, both economic and political. But a quick glance at an almanac, or at a newspaper, was enough to confirm the facts: Britain was no longer in a class of her own; the Americans were richer and the Germans more productive.

As a whole, the British Empire was still remarkably strong. Canada and Australia continued to boom. India flourished. The population of the British Empire far outstripped that of any other empire. But the problems of imperial defence, so crucial in the political debates of Canada and Australia in 1913, loomed larger than ever. The long-term integrity of the empire would not be assured by warm words alone. Britain's own position in the empire had changed. Once, the country had been the engine room of empire, the productive heart of the beast. But was Britain now becoming more like a boardroom, investing money, taking decisions, but essentially living off the labour of others, and off the earnings of the past? At some point in the future, might even this role wither away, and might Britain become little more than a repository of British tradition, a common idealised land into which Britons abroad – in Australia, Canada, New Zealand or South Africa – could retreat, a collective memory of green fields and swooping glens?

In 1897, Queen Victoria's Jubilee year, Rudyard Kipling had shocked British sensibilities with the warning tone of his poem *Recessional*:

> Far-called our navies melt away—
> On dune and headland sinks the fire—
> Lo, all our pomp of yesterday
> Is one with Nineveh and Tyre!
> Judge of the Nations, spare us yet,
> Lest we forget—lest we forget!

A decade and a half later, such dire warnings of the inevitable decline of even the greatest of empires had entered deep into public consciousness. In 1911, *Recessional* was set to music, forming part of the closing ceremony of the Festival of Empire, held in London's Crystal Palace that year.[10] Imperial pomp was now tempered by elegy.

And then there was the worrying situation at home in Britain, which occupied just as many column inches, pub conversations, and university debates as the situation abroad. In 1913, there were suffragettes on the street, challenging the male-dominated political culture of Britain, and claiming the right to vote. At the same time, and quite separately, militant trade unions threatened to shut off the country's food supply. Above all, there was a very real possibility that Home Rule for Ireland, the most divisive issue in British politics for a generation, would finally come about – and be opposed by armed volunteers on the streets of Ulster. Was Britain still a 'living' power – or had it slipped, somewhere along the line from one side of the ledger to the other?

CONSTANTINOPLE
Tides of History

In 1913, the city of Constantinople – known in ancient times as Byzantium, and to modern Turks as Istanbul – was entering the twenty-sixth century of its existence. Founded by the Greeks at a strategic point on the Bosphorus between the Black Sea and the Mediterranean, the city had first flourished as a city of trade. Later, in the year 330, when London was little more than a Roman encampment by the shores of the Thames, Constantinople had become the eastern capital of the Roman Empire. In 1453, fifty years before Columbus arrived in North America, the Christian city of Constantinople had been conquered by the Muslim Turks. Since then, the city had been the capital of the Ottoman Empire, ruled by an Emperor who was at once a mighty temporal potentate – ruling an empire which at its peak covered most of north Africa, all of the Arabian peninsula, and much of south-eastern Europe – and Caliph of the world's Muslims. Much reduced since its medieval hey-day, even now the Ottoman Turks still ruled the heartlands of the Near and Middle East. The holy cities of Jerusalem, Mecca and Medina were all in their hands – and Muslim, Christian and Jewish pilgrims would most likely pass through Constantinople on their way to visit them. In the east, Ottoman territory stretched towards the Russian Caucasus and Persia, in the south it ran along the coast of the Red Sea, in the north it went up to the shores of the Black Sea and, in the west, it retained – just – a small corner of Europe.

The Turkish poet Tevfik Fikret described Constantinople itself as a harlot, yet one which still mesmerised its visitors and its million-odd inhabitants alike:

Oh Decrepit Byzantium, Oh great bewitching dotard
Oh widowed virgin of a thousand men
The fresh enchantment in your beauty is still evident
The eyes that look at you still do so with adoration[1]

It was a fittingly ambivalent description of a city which had experienced massacres in its streets (just five years previously 10,000 Armenians had died in inter-communal violence), which was the regular victim of fires that burned down whole neighbourhoods of wooden houses, which was subject to the periodic shudders of earthquakes, and yet which survived. Even in the decrepitude of old age, Byzantium-Constantinople-Istanbul was still cherished by the different religious and national groups for whom the city played a key part in their communal history. And the city was still coveted by outsiders – particularly the Russians – who saw it as the rightful seat of Christian Orthodoxy and who resented the Ottoman stranglehold on the strategic waterway running through the centre of Constantinople, the gateway from the Black Sea to the Mediterranean.

'Thrice-titled town, jewel of mankind's common heritage', rhapsodised German travel writer Hermann Barth, expostulating on the city which Greeks still called Byzantium, most other Christians (and

Ships at anchor in Constantinople, gateway to the Mediterranean, capital of the multi-ethnic Ottoman Empire, eyed jealously by the empire's neighbours. In 1912–13 Bulgarian troops got to within a few miles of the city limits.

foreign visitors) called Constantinople, and Turks called Istanbul.[2] Like Jerusalem – which the Turks ruled over, but which had resonance for Jews, local Arabs and foreign Christians alike – Constantinople was home to many different populations, all keenly aware of their historical ties to the place, and all sensitive to their relative position within it. To be an Ottoman, in the fullest and most political sense of the word, was to understand and celebrate these different religions and cultures as part of a larger whole, whatever one's own background. But to be a true Ottoman in 1913, whether Turkish, Arab or Greek, was increasingly difficult. To many, the empire seemed to be pulling in different directions, its territory was under siege, and the central government in Constantinople, led by the 'Young Turks', seemed ambivalent towards the traditional heritage of Ottomanism. Was Constantinople, therefore, a multi-ethnic and multi-religious anachronism in an age of nations and nationalism, or was it, like the Austro-Hungarian Empire, a symbol of the possibilities of inter-communal harmony and cooperation?

At different times of the year, the different communities which had been washed up on the shores of the Bosphorus – Greeks, Arabs, Shi'a Muslims, Sunni Muslims, Turks, Kurds, Persians, Armenians, Bulgarians, Jews – would take over parts of the city for their particular religious or national celebrations. The greatest of these was undoubtedly the end of the fasting month of Ramadan, when the city's Muslims – mostly Turks, but also Kurds and Arabs – would pour on to the streets in three days of celebration, paying visits to friends and family, and exchanging gifts of sweets and tobacco, porcelain from the imperial works and perfume. A religious celebration rapidly became an excuse for the secular pastimes of *bayram*, a festival, not unlike those of a country fair in the Australian outback or a village fête in France: 'merry-go-rounds propelled by hand, swings in the form of boats, milder swings for girls . . . so many arguments against Mr Kipling and the East-is-East theory'.[3] More particular to Turkey were the *Karagöz* shadow plays in the city's coffee houses, as bawdy as the audience they entertained. Later in the year came the second great Muslim festival, commemorating Abraham's near sacrifice of his son Ishmael (not Isaac, as in the Christian and Jewish faiths), celebrated by the ritual slaughter of rams shipped in to Constantinople in great number over the weeks before the day itself, the noise of bleating animals encroaching upon the usual bustle of the city, the bark of its many dogs, and the call to prayer of the *muezzin*.

But it was not just the Sunni Muslim Turks, Kurds and Arabs who took to the city's streets. For the city's Shi'a, mostly Turkish-speaking Persians from Tabriz, the key day was Ashura, a commemoration of the death of the Prophet's grandson Hussein, the moment of bifurcation between Sunni and Shi'a Islam. An American observer remembered seeing 'a gruesome company of men in white, who chanted hoarsely and slashed their shaven heads with bloody swords', winter snows swirling around their half-naked bodies.[4] The climax of the Christian calendar was Easter, celebrated by Greeks, who represented nearly a quarter of Constantinople's inhabitants in 1913, and Armenians, who numbered one in every ten. (The Armenian share had been much reduced by communal troubles in the 1890s – since when the city's Armenian street porters had been replaced by Kurds – but still contained many of the city's prominent citizens: shopkeepers, architects, government officials, even the holders of the Ottoman gunpowder monopoly.[5])

These celebrations could be boisterous affairs. In 1909, British resident Mary Poynter noted in her diary that the Greek Orthodox celebration of Easter included 'firing guns and revolvers in the air, and at figures of Judas . . . a few people being killed and several wounded'.[6] Other Christian feast days offered quieter festivities: on a January morning by the shores of the Bosphorus one might see a Greek Orthodox blessing of its waters, accompanied by 'shivering mortals in bathing trunks' who were waiting for the opportunity to rescue a gilt wooden cross tossed into the Bosphorus by the local bishop.[7] In late 1912 the Greek population drew to a silent halt to bury Patriarch Joachim, seventy-eight years old, the streets lined with 'black masts . . . from which hung black gonfalons with white crosses in the centre, while black and white wreaths or garlands decorated all the houses'.[8]

The New Year – ignored by most Muslims, feted by a few thousand Persians as *Nowruz*, and celebrated by different Christian sects on different dates in January – provided a further opportunity for revelry. On the first day of 1913 the Austro-Hungarian Ambassador Marquis Pallavicini held a reception in his embassy, after Mass at the nearby Sainte Marie Draperis church; in the embassy of the French Republic respects were paid to Ambassador Bompard and to his wife, a picture of the 'virtues of French womanhood' according to a local paper.[9]

Besides Ottoman Muslims and Ottoman Christians – and the city's many foreigners – local officials estimated the Jewish population of the city at around 52,000.[10] Amongst these numbered two ambitious young law students, David Ben-Gurion and Yitzhak Ben-Zvi – who were to become the first Prime Minister and second President of Israel – melting into the background of the city in their dark European suits, crisp white shirts and Turkish fezzes.

The bustling midpoint of the city of Constantinople was not a square, or a palace, but an inlet of the Bosphorus known as the Golden Horn – and the Galata Bridge which crossed it from one half of the city to the other.

On the south side of the Golden Horn lay the older part of the city, Stamboul, in which were situated the majority of the city's local population, the bazaar, the old (and by this time abandoned) palace of Topkapi, and the city's main mosques (including the Ayasofya mosque, which for eleven centuries had been a church). On the north side lay Galata, and, above it, Pera (now Beyoğlu). Founded six or seven centuries ago by Genoese and Venetian traders, Galata and Pera were the areas favoured by Constantinople's foreign population – so much so that Turks and Arabs from Stamboul referred to Pera as '*Frengistan*', foreigner-land. A little further along the waterfront, this was also where the imperial court had built several new palaces in the nineteenth century: first the Europeanised Dolmabahçe, then the Çirağan and finally the Yildiz palace complex, a little inland behind high walls, with its own water and electricity supply, and its own harem – everything necessary for the paranoid Sultan who built it, Abdül Hamid II.

It was from the old Galata Bridge that, in the 1870s, the Italian writer Edmondo De Amicis had recommended that visitors could find the best vantage point of Constantinople, able to take in its full scale, and the variety of its peoples and their activities:

The Albanian in his long white garment with pistols thrust in his belt, brushes against the Tartar clad in sheepskin; the Turk guides his richly-caparisoned ass between two files of camels; close behind the aide-de-camp of one of the imperial princes, mounted on an Arabian charger, a cart rumbles along piled up with the odd-looking effects of some Turkish household. A Mussulman woman on foot, a veiled female slave, a Greek with her long flowing hair surmounted by a little red cap, a Maltese hidden in her black faldetta, a Jewess in the ancient costume of her nation, a negress wrapped in a many-tinted Cairo shawl, an Armenian from Trebizond all veiled in black . . . It is an ever-changing mosaic, a kaleidoscopic view of race, costume and religion . . . It is one continuous tramp and roar, a murmur of hoarse gutturals and incomprehensible interjections, among which the occasional French or Italian words which reach the ear seem like rays of light seen through a thick darkness.[11]

At the beginning of the twentieth century a proposal for the rickety old bridge to be upgraded was initially rejected by Sultan Abdül Hamid on the basis that a gallery of shops at water level might provide a strategic location for rebellion against his unloved regime. Eventually, however, a new, wider, iron bridge was built across the Golden Horn by a German company. It was completed in 1912.[12]

Over the years since De Amicis had penned his colourful description of the scene on the Galata Bridge, the Ottoman Empire had continued its steady drift from the status of a Great Power – in the same class as Britain, France and Russia – to a second-rank power, still nominally independent, but clearly on the 'dying' side of the ledger. The sovereignty of the Ottoman state over its own territory was compromised by a special legal regime – the aptly-named Capitulations – which placed foreigners in the empire under the protection of their various embassies. The share of the Ottoman Empire's population protected in this way grew over the course of the nineteenth century, giving external powers a permanent interest in the internal arrangements of the Ottoman state. A free-trade agreement signed with the British in 1838 deprived the Ottoman Empire of a trade policy. Having defaulted on its foreign debts in 1875, the empire was forced to cede domestic financial management to the essentially-foreign Caisse de la Dette Publique Ottomane, which, by 1911, had more employees than the Ottoman Empire's own finance ministry.[13] British advisers were brought in to support the modernisation of the Ottoman fleet; German soldiers advised the Ottoman army. But more thorough reform was avoided. The reason that the Ottoman Empire had survived as a state at all, rather than being carved up, was that too many of the Great Powers had conflicting interests over the potential spoils. This was an empire living on borrowed money but, above all, borrowed time.

Sultan Abdül Hamid, who ruled the Ottoman Empire from 1876 to 1909, was seen by many Ottoman modernisers as part of the problem. On his accession, in a concession to a reform-minded group of officials known as the Young Ottomans, the Sultan had granted constitutional government, overturning centuries of Ottoman administrative autocracy. But the experiment did not last long. In 1878 Abdül Hamid suspended the constitution and returned to the old traditions of Ottoman governance, enforced by the feared agents of the Sultan's secret police, with political prisoners regularly locked up and the key thrown away. For the following thirty years Abdül Hamid presided over a regime which, though it made sporadic efforts to modernise and reform itself, remained essentially conservative and thuggishly authoritarian.

Many Ottomans chafed under the restrictions of the regime, and worried that the Ottoman Empire was being steadily weakened – both from outside and from within. In 1889, the centenary of the French revolution, a group of young reform-minded government officials, soldiers and doctors – Turks, but also Albanians, Circassians and Kurds, well-educated but mostly middle ranking – set up what amounted, at first, to little more than a secret discussion group for Ottoman modernisers.[14] Swearing allegiance to the cause of Ottoman renewal on the Koran and a revolver, and calling themselves the Committee of Union and Progress – but known to others as the 'Young Turks', successors to the Young Ottomans – the group's early leaders were men such as Mehmed Talat, a postal worker in Salonica, and Ismail Enver, a junior military officer posted in the same city. That they were young was seen as a badge of honour, evidence that the future was with them, standing on its head an earlier Ottoman worldview that wisdom goes hand in hand with age. By the early twentieth century, having won strong support in sections of the army, particularly in Macedonia, the discussion group had developed into one of the key political forces of the Ottoman Empire.

The central objectives of the Young Turks were, first, the restoration of the constitution and, second, the renewal of the Ottoman Empire. Prescriptions for how this renewal was to be achieved differed. A few Young Turks saw decentralisation of political authority as the key – later, a couple even wondered about a confederal Turco-Arabian Empire along Austro-Hungarian lines. But the vast majority saw the path to modernisation lying through the power of a revamped central state. Most Young Turks were not ethnic Turkish nationalists at this stage so much as frustrated Ottoman patriots.

The Western world, as they saw it, was something to be admired, and to be learned from – though with the ultimate aim of protecting the Ottoman Empire from foreign powers. For a few years at the beginning of the twentieth century the intellectual headquarters of the Young Turk movement had been Paris, with Cairo and Geneva playing a secondary role, though Salonica – a mixed Jewish, Turkish and Greek city in Ottoman Macedonia – became its forward operating base. (It was also the city of birth of Mustafa Kemal, later Atatürk.) Others saw an alliance with the German Empire as a strategic necessity for Ottoman survival, at least in the short run. In terms of a model, perhaps Japan was the most appropriate: a country which had managed to modernise itself using Western techniques while retaining the essentials of its distinctive culture (and striking an alliance with the British Empire into the bargain). Young Turks spoke of the Ottoman Empire becoming the 'Japan of the Near East'.[15] Could they pull off the same trick?

In 1908, the Young Turks achieved their first objective, the restoration of the constitution, with barely a shot being fired. Army units loyal to the Young Turk leadership began to march towards Constantinople from Macedonia in mid June, threatening to take the city by force. In early July, the military commander sent out to oppose them, Şemsi Pasha, was assassinated in broad daylight by a member of the Committee of Union and Progress. Uncertain of the loyalties of his army, Abdül Hamid decided to cut his losses and reinstate the constitution. Thirty years of tyranny were, in theory, over.

In Constantinople, the news was greeted joyfully. 'Indoors or out one can hear the cheers of the people', Mary Poynter wrote in her diary:

Abdul Hamid's spies have disappeared as if by magic, newspapers [previously heavily censored, and forbidden from writing about the true state of political affairs] cannot be published fast enough to meet the demand for them and have doubled in price. The towns up and down the Bosporus are lined with people who cheer the steamers as they pass.[16]

The restoration of the constitution, coming hand in hand with the release of political prisoners, was widely welcomed. Armenians, for whom Abdül Hamid was a butcher, saw a restored constitution as a guarantee of their rights. Ottoman Greeks saw an opportunity to convert their economic power in the empire into a political role in the Ottoman parliament. (And, asked the nationalists amongst them, might not this provide the first step towards the realisation of the Great Idea: the reunification of all Greek-speakers in a single Greek state?) Turkish women appeared in the street to celebrate, in anticipation of the relaxation of the male chauvinist codes which had received imperial sanction under Abdül Hamid (that Muslim women should not leave the home without male relatives, for example). Across the empire an election was called for a new parliament, providing an excuse for yet more processions in Constantinople. Mary Poynter described a march from the polling stations to the counting houses bearing ballot boxes as if they were holy objects:

> . . . always headed by a band, mounted troops, and carriages filled with brightly-dressed little Turkish girls, followed by the populace on foot, waving the star and crescent and holy green flags, and all singing (when the band is not playing) the new patriotic song called 'Vatan' . . . Turkish women accompany the procession, often in numbers. The ballot box, completely covered in flowers, is carried high in the midst of this enthusiastic multitude.[17]

Out of 288 deputies elected, there were 147 Turks, 60 Arabs, 27 Albanians, 26 Greeks, 14 Armenians, 10 Slavs and 4 Jews.[18]

Not everything was so positive, however. Abdül Hamid had been forced to replace his Grand Vizier and allow elections, but he was still Sultan. The political uncertainty generated by events in Constantinople was exploited by others: Bulgaria declared its formal independence with Ferdinand as Tsar (later downgraded to King), the Austro-Hungarian Empire annexed Bosnia, Crete united with

Greece. Conservatives opposed the social reforms which accompanied the re-establishment of the constitution. In April 1909, a counter-coup led by those who had lost position in the change of regime and carried out by disgruntled Turkish troops in the name of Islam and the restoration of Shari'a law, forced many Young Turks to flee Constantinople.

The counter-coup did not last. A so-called Army of Deliverance, loyal to the Young Turks, marched back to the capital to take it by force. 'The quick tramp of infantry, the rush of the cavalry, and the roar of artillery-wagons over the pavements' left an impression on locals and foreigners alike, reminding them that the Young Turks' power base, ultimately, was the army.[19] Fighting in Constantinople temporarily closed down communications with the outside world. The shutters of the city were pulled down, the steamers normally plying their trade along the Bosphorus motionless but for the swell of the sea. Buildings caught in the crossfire were scarred by bullets, including the residence of the Persian Ambassador – 'he must have thought himself in Persia when the bullets and shells were whizzing past his door', one local commented.[20] But more important than the physical damage to the city was the political fallout. Turks and Muslims had now fought and killed each other. The Young Turks had learned that Islam could be turned against them by religious and political conservatives.

At least Abdül Hamid was gone. At 2.45 a.m. on 29 April 1909, the Sultan boarded the imperial train for the first time – and headed into internal exile in Salonica, the headquarters of his enemies. A few months previously 'the interior of Tibet was easy to reach in comparison' to the Yildiz palace, wrote Mary Poynter in her diary.[21] Now the palace was a sort of tourist attraction for those picking over the remnants of a discredited regime, with a motor car at its gate offering to drive visitors around for a small sum. The gardens, once tended by 400, rapidly fell into a state of neglect. Large safes lay in the courtyard, their doors wide open and contents long gone (some embezzled by the army, it was alleged, other pieces of jewellery sold by the Ottoman government in Paris in 1911).[22] One account, published in English with the support of Mahmud Shevket Pasha – the general who had led the Army of Deliverance into Constantinople and who had been made war minister as a result – described the Sultan's bedroom in the Yildiz palace, left exactly as it had been on the morning of his departure:

Tossed and tumbled about on the couch were a soft Turkish quilt . . . and some half-dozen soft silk cushions. Over a long chair nearby hung a white night-dress and a cincture bearing the letter 'A' both belonging probably to Abdurrahman Effendi, the Sultan's favourite son, who was continually with his father during their last few days in Yildiz. Near the Sultan's bed was a little rest for a coffee-cup or, more probably, for a revolver. In a recess cut into the wall in a corner of a room was a wash-stand and basin hidden by a lacquer screen. On the wall above the couch hung a large Japanese *kakemono* [scroll painting] bearing the figure of a bird, I think an eagle.[23]

Mahomet, the new Sultan, lived quietly in the Dolmabahçe palace, attending prayers at Ayasofya mosque and, for the time being, scrupulously avoiding any political entanglements.

Over the next year or so, with the Young Turks back in the saddle, parliament passed dozens of bills, some liberal, many attempting to put the genie of counter-coup firmly back in the bottle: the slave trade was abolished, the constitution reformed (so as to cement parliamentary rule), laws were passed to provide for new censorship of the press, to restrict public meetings, to allow for the conscription of non-Muslims (for the first time) and to prevent strikes.[24] G. F. Abbott described how the topics of conversation in Constantinople's cafés, 'once temples of thoughtless meditation', were now filled with a single word: change, not of the weather, but of ministers.[25] A reliable budget was drawn up for perhaps the first time, showing Ottoman expenditure to be just one-quarter of that of the Austro-Hungarian Empire and one-sixth of that of the Russian Empire.[26] The tax system was reformed, a process which by 1910 was beginning to bear fruit in the form of increased revenues, albeit below the level of government spending. The fire service was revamped; so was the police. Was the Ottoman Empire finally receiving the shock therapy of reform which it required?

All the while, Constantinople itself was changing. 'Electric lights and telephones are springing up, the streets are being paved', wrote Poynter in the years after the Young Turk revolution, 'and the dogs seem to be disappearing' (in fact they were removed to an island

and collectively dispatched).[27] The city welcomed a renewed flood of foreign visitors coming to see what the Young Turk fuss was all about: Le Corbusier, André Gide, and Leon Trotsky amongst them.[28] 'Constantinople', wrote Abbott, 'outwardly the same great city of magnificent mosques, amorphous palaces, and dirty streets, is essentially a city transformed'.[29]

That was to say too much. The Ottoman Empire could not be reformed overnight; the city of Constantinople would not become London, or Berlin, or Vienna just by cleaning it up a bit at the edges, installing a new mayor, or killing the dogs. Such things would take time. Constantinople had been changing slowly for some time before the Young Turks got hold of it. It would continue to change long after they had gone. But change in Constantinople would never be at a pace which was anything other than stately, befitting a city whose lineage was far more ancient than that of even the Ottomans, let alone their new upstart political leaders.

In 1913, Stamboul in particular – the old city on the southern side of the Golden Horn – was still a rather ramshackle place. English writer Robert Hichens described it as 'a city of wood and of marble, of dusty, frail houses that look as if they had been run up in a night and might tumble to pieces at any moment' and, alongside these, 'magnificent mosques, centuries old, huge, superb, great monuments of the sultans'.[30] To Stamboul's inhabitants, their lives and deaths not much different to those of their grandfathers or their grandfathers' grandfathers, each uneven paving stone was well known, the sound of each creaking gate familiar, their local mosque, or church, or *hamam* all within easy reach. To most Europeans Stamboul was a mystery, the beginning of the East. Wandering its crowded streets, and getting lost in them, they were intoxicated by it – or repelled by it.

The old city of Stamboul was largely unplanned and, despite attempts at civic reform in the nineteenth century, had largely been unmanaged. Garbage piled up in the streets, fresh water was provided from occasional pumps and fountains, the smell of rotting fish lingered by the quayside, pigeons flapped around the yards of mosques. Dogs, fed by local Turks with scraps from their table, fiercely guarded their patches of territory, symbols of Eastern filth or good-luck charms depending on one's perspective. For some visitors, clutching a copy of Pierre Loti's latest book to their breast, the very name Stamboul evoked grand ideas of beauty and tragedy, of exquisite poetry and music, stimulating images of twisting dervishes, or of harems of Turkish beauties and Circassian women from the Caucasus. For others the narrow and crooked streets of Stamboul suggested closed medieval minds, more informed by Eastern mysticism than by modern science, and of a people but a short step away from unfathomable barbarity. It would take more than the ambitions of a Young Turk official or two to replace the practices of centuries.

Walking through Stamboul, Robert Hichens found himself transported by a sense of the city's history: 'What it has seen, Stamboul! What it has known'.[31] Others were carried away more by its degeneration. Ellis Ashmead-Bartlett, a British journalist for the *Daily Telegraph* come to cover the Balkan wars in 1912, described a 'city which nature designed to be a paradise on earth and which man has transformed into a cesspool of vice, decay and blood':

> . . . a city which from the Bosporus looks like a dream of marble hanging on the slopes of purple hills, and which on closer inspection turns out to be a hopeless jumble of tumble-down houses with gangrened and mouldering walls, built along the sides of badly-paved precipitous streets, down which tired horses glide and stumble, with here and there some beautiful mosque rising above the gaudy rubbish-heap of an out-worn faith. The Turks have done nothing constructive to beautify the city since their irruption in 1453. They have merely added minarets to the old Byzantine churches, or erected mosques in garish imitations of the Greek buildings. For the rest, they have allowed the city to fall into hopeless decay.[32]

In late November 1913 the new American Ambassador Henry Morgenthau arrived in Constantinople. Two days later he went to visit the Grand Bazaar, recording his telegraphic judgement in his diary on returning home to the ambassador's residence: 'very odd'.[33]

Things in Pera were rather more modern and, to the American or European eye, more familiar. The foreign embassies were here, the British occupying a large classical block on the crest of the hill above the water. So too the foreign-owned banks. (One of which, the Ottoman Bank, had famously been occupied by the Dashnak Armenian nationalist group in 1896, threatening to blow it and its foreign employees up if demands for greater freedom were not met.)

It was in Pera that technological innovations from the West had always been first introduced: the city's first gas lamps in 1856, the city's first film in 1895 and, in 1875, the city's first underground line, the suitably named Tünel, burrowing from the Galata quayside to the top of Pera Hill.

On either side of the Grande Rue de Pera, and down adjoining streets and alleys, lay Constantinople's European bars, dance halls, and shops – an Italian circus, a French theatre, the Pazar Alman (German Market) department store and the Bon Marché, where shopfloor assistants would call out the prices in French. Here, at one of its 349 outlets across the Ottoman Empire, one could buy a Singer sewing machine and obtain lessons in how to use it to follow the latest Parisian fashions.[34] Mothers could buy tinned Nestlé condensed milk, advertised in the English and French-language papers, for the protection it offered against both cholera and adulterated local milk. On display behind plate-glass windows, or stacked high on shop shelves, one might find Russian Treugolnik galoshes, by appointment to the Romanov court, or 'Parisian' scarves made in Manchester, or bright red Ottoman fezzes with long black tassels (though, in a sign of the times, these were as likely to have been made in an Austro-Hungarian factory as anywhere within a hundred miles of the Ottoman capital).

In Pera one might meet the city's French, German or Russian governesses, a trend which conservative Muslims criticised, worrying that Christian women were being hired by Muslim households.[35] It was inevitably the part of the city where Ottomans would go to drink, or to buy a foreign newspaper or a foreign book. This was where the Young Turk military officer Mustafa Kamal – posted in late 1913 as the Ottoman military attaché in Sofia – would choose to come on leave, to practise his French and demonstrate his flair for dancing.[36] Expatriates and Western-minded locals could send their children to the French Lycée, which had occupied a large area of the district since the 1860s, providing education to Muslims, Christians and Jews alike. A more recent addition to the area, finished only in 1912 and set back a little from the main street, was the Roman Catholic church of St Anthony of Padua, run by Italian monks. The city's leading hotels were all in Pera – the Pera Palace first amongst them – and then those of the second rank, such as the Khedival Palace or the Hotel de Saint Pétersbourg or the

Armenian-owned Hotel Tokatliyan. 'Foreigners may only live in Pera', warned *Baedeker* sternly.[37]

Some found the ostentatious Western modernity of Pera unattractive. Robert Hichens railed against its 'cafés glittering with plate-glass through which crafty, impudent eyes are forever staring out upon passers-by' and its 'pretentious, painted women from second-rate European music-halls', ghostly pale under electric lights.[38] American Harry Griswold Dwight feared the 'deadly levelling of Western civilisation', making the city over to 'German *Liebespaar*, the British old maid, the American mother and daughter who insist on making one place exactly like another'.[39] G. F. Abbott laughed at the 'ostentatious banality of a pseudo-European civilisation . . . all those exotic abominations which, here as elsewhere, are fast turning the East into a colossal, comico-tragic caricature of the West'.[40]

Indeed, it was not just cultured Westerners who found Pera rather fake. The Turkish historian Ahmed Cevdet Paşa warned a foreign acquaintance that Pera gave an entirely inaccurate image of the Ottoman Empire as a whole. 'From here', he said, 'you see Istanbul through a telescope, but the telescopes which you used were always warped'.[41] Turks sniggered at their compatriots who pretended to be more European than the Europeans. The writer Ahmed Rasim lampooned the affectations of a Turk who:

> . . . jumping in his mind from Paris, passing mentally through Vienna, casting a glance at Berlin, having seen a map of the Italian cities of Milan, Rome and Naples, having sent a regretful sigh in the direction of London, having read about the American provinces such as New York, Washington and Philadelphia during the time of the exhibitions from guidebooks, had actually only been as far as Izmir [in western Turkey] and promenaded up and down the corniche.[42]

But was this really just a laughing matter? Was not there something pernicious, dangerous even, in the way in which Western mores were invading Pera, and thereby infecting the city as a whole? 'Do not underestimate the bicycle', wrote Rasim, 'for it has many vices'.[43] It could be used, for example, in the theft of goods and in the seduction of women and young girls. Other Turks commented on the racy European habit of swimming openly in the Bosphorus in skimpy swimsuits, whereas Turks would rather take to the waters, if at all, behind the discreet protection of bamboo shields, in separate men's and women's sea-*hamams*. Some noted the change in Ottoman women's dress over the last few years, and even the change in their walk, from a slow gait to a brisk, assertive, European pace – something which they ascribed to Western influence. This struck at the very heart of Muslim society, for it suggested a dangerous liberation of women from their male masters. Where would it end?

In 1906, the dream of greater Western freedom had led a young Turkish woman, Zeyneb Hanoum, to flee the restrictions of her life in Constantinople, where she was 'kept in glass cages and wrapt in cotton wool'.[44] She travelled widely, spending six years in between Paris, London, Brussels and Italy. Ultimately, however, Hanoum returned to the Ottoman Empire. The West, she had found, was not necessarily any better than the East, it simply had different vices: crassness, greed, violence and selfishness. 'How dangerous it is to urge those Orientals forward', she concluded, 'only to reduce them in a few years to the same state of stupidity as the poor degenerate peoples of the West, fed on unhealthy literature and poisoned with alcohol'.[45] Hanoum had experienced the West and found it artificial; Pera was the symbol of Western artificiality in the heart of Constantinople.

Over several decades' residence in the city, Byzantine scholar Alexander van Millingen had noted much that had changed in Constantinople, not all of it for the better.[46] The city, he wrote at the beginning of the twentieth century, had become perhaps a little less distinctive over the years. Its Eastern mystery had been tarnished by the march of Western technology. The varied clothes described by De Amicis in the 1870s, by which every passer-by's nationality and religion could be discerned by the expert Ottoman eye, were increasingly being swapped for standard European garb: 'now, the order of the day is "à la Franca"'.[47] Latticed screens, which had imparted mystery to the traditional Turkish home and hid its women from an intruder's gaze, were being replaced by Venetian shutters. 'The groups of horses standing at convenient points in the great thoroughfares to carry you up a street of steps or to a distant quarter', noted van Millingen melancholically, 'have given way to cabstands, and to a tunnel which pierces the hill of Galata'.[48] Older people, who had been children in the 1840s, might remember the first steamer on the Bosphorus; now, the water heaved with such vessels, crowding out the fragile but elegant *caïques* of before. Whereas the postal service from Europe had once been a week by boat from Trieste, and three times a month from Marseilles, it now arrived daily by train, at a fraction of the price:

> Little, perhaps, did the crowds that gathered at the Stamboul railway station [Sirkeci – the Asian line terminated across the water at Haydarpaşa] on the 14th of August that year [1888] to witness the arrival of the first train from the Austrian capital, appreciate the significance of that event. But it was the annexation of Constantinople to the Western world. New ideas, new fashions now rule, for better or for worse. And soon the defects of the old Oriental city will be a dream of the past.[49]

The defects of the old city might be going by 1913 – but, in van Millingen's eyes, perhaps some of its charm too.

There were new processions on the Galata Bridge now: Turkish troops, many from the Anatolian hinterland, heading to fight off the Balkan armies which had made it almost to the gates of Constantinople – and refugees, overwhelmingly Muslim, arriving in a city they had never seen, leaving behind the villages and towns in Europe where their ancestors had lived for centuries.

Violence had always been a part of the borderland experience of the Ottoman Empire. The Ottoman authorities had long battled localised revolts in the mixed Muslim and Christian province of Albania, mostly related to the eternal bugbears of tax and conscription and, after the Young Turk revolution, a dispute over which script should be used in Albanian schools.[50] A wider pattern of low-level brigandage and military reprisal had become the stuff of Balkan lore. English traveller Edith Durham quoted a characteristically gung-ho Balkan song in her book *High Albania* in 1909:

> Oh we're back in the Balkans again,
> Back to the joy and the pain –
> What if it burns or it blows or it snows?

We're back to the Balkans again.
Back, where tomorrow the quick may be dead,
With a hole in his heart or a ball in his head –
Back, where the passions are rapid and red –
Oh, we're back to the Balkans again![51]

But the latest round of international wars threatening the
Ottoman Empire – and the domestic political ascendancy of the
Young Turks – had started not in the perennially difficult Balkans
but in sparsely populated north Africa. In 1911, the Italians invaded
the then Ottoman province of Libya, hoping for a quick victory to
erase the memory of the Battle of Adowa (when an Italian force
had been defeated by the Ethiopians in 1896) and confirm Italy's
status as a great power. Tripoli and Benghazi were, as expected,
rapidly occupied. The Ottomans, unable to reinforce Libya by land
– because the British refused them transit across Egypt – and
incapable of reinforcing it by sea, were reduced to subterfuge. Young

The proud pose of Young Turk leader Enver Pasha, hero of Edirne. The Young
Turks sought to modernise the Ottoman Empire in order to better defend it.

Turk military officers, Mustafa Kemal amongst them, travelled to Libya in civilian disguise to organise guerrilla resistance. Such resistance would never dislodge the Italian army from the coast, but it prevented them from securing inland areas. In response, in order to try and force the Ottoman government to make peace, Italian forces occupied the Dodecanese islands in the Aegean in the summer of 1912, just off the coast of Turkey. This provoked a political crisis in Constantinople. The Ottoman Parliament – in which the Young Turks had recently, by means fair and foul, won a renewed majority – was suspended. Young Turk leaders were sidelined from the Ottoman government. A new Grand Vizier was installed who was known for his anti-Young Turk views.

In October 1912 the Ottoman Empire finally agreed to cede Libya in return for an Italian promise to evacuate the Dodecanese. By then, however, the empire was under attack on another front, in the Balkans this time, from the combined armies of Greece, Bulgaria, Serbia and Montenegro loosely allied in the Balkan League.[52] This was an entirely different kind of war to the conflict in Libya – it was a war for survival. In Libya, Ottomans had fought for pride. In the Balkans, they were fighting for the homes of their compatriots and sometimes for their own. In Constantinople, the departure of the Turkish troops for the front was met with raucous cheers and waving handkerchiefs. One Turkish soldier showed an American journalist his shepherd's pipe tucked into his cartridge belt: 'that was the way to go to war, he said – as to a wedding'.[53]

What Ottoman troops found in the Balkans, however, was a bloodbath. The advances of the Balkan League were swift. Salonica fell to the Greeks in November 1912 (a poisoned chalice: King George of Greece was assassinated there, by a Greek, the following year). Edirne (Adrianople), a city which had once been the Ottoman capital, was surrounded. Over the winter of 1912 and the spring of 1913 Turkish wounded returned to Constantinople in ever-greater numbers. The city swelled with new inhabitants; offices and embassies became makeshift hospitals, British doctors and French nurses tended to Turkish wounded. (Mary Poynter's diary, and the foreign-language newspapers, were full of Lady Lowther's war relief committee.) Cholera broke out.

At one point towards the end of the year Bulgarian troops were within a few miles of Constantinople, their planes scouting ahead to catch a glimpse of the city's minarets and to assess the Ottomans' last line of defence around Çatalca. Naval vessels of the European powers stood ready to disgorge soldiers into the city should protection of their citizens be necessary. Bags were packed in preparation for a hasty departure. The cemeteries on the outskirts of the city became encampments. 'There the living had taken refuge with the dead', wrote Poynter, 'upon the very ground where camped the Crusaders, who came to take a Christian city in 1203, and where camped the Turks who took Byzantium on that sunny May morning in 1453':

> Will the [Bulgarian] army from the north, now so near us, if victorious, come into the city through our European quarter or will they go through the cypress cemetery, where so many refugees are camping . . .? And will they hold mass in Sancta Sophia . . .? We shall know in a few days. What moments of waiting these are! One forgets to be afraid, though they tell us we are in danger.[54]

At the beginning of 1913, the Young Turks, sidelined domestically, decided to take matters into their own hands, ostensibly to prevent the government in Constantinople from giving up Edirne in a peace deal backed by the great European powers. Forcing their way into a Cabinet meeting on 23 January 1913 a group of Young Turk officers shot the war minister and forced the Grand Vizier to resign. A new Cabinet was formed. Hostilities against the Balkan League recommenced almost immediately.

Foreign opinion on the rights and wrongs of the Balkan War was divided. Some were sympathetic to the Turks. Pierre Loti saw them as brave defenders of their homeland, and asked what would happen when Edirne was overrun by the Christian armies of the Balkan states. 'When the boots of the bearded hirsute victors have soiled the exquisite mosque of Selim II and its funerary kiosks', he warned, 'then pillage, rape and murder will begin'.[55] (In Constantinople it was suggested that a road should be named after the French writer, as indeed one subsequently was.) Many more Europeans were unmoved by the Ottoman Empire's plight. Harry Johnston, a British colonial administrator, saw the Balkan War as opening the way to what he called 'the final solution of the Eastern Question'.[56] The expulsion of the Ottoman Empire from Europe would be an advance for civilisation. 'The Turk, pur sang, is stupid', he wrote, claiming that their architects, doctors, surgeons, financiers and admirals were all drawn from the peoples who they subjected, not from their own ranks.

But most Westerners looked at events in the Balkans, and the question of the survival of the Ottoman Empire, through the prism of their own national interests. The Russians had no love of the Ottoman Empire, but they did not want the Bulgarians to conquer Constantinople – if any European power was to control the city it should be them, they reasoned. The Austro-Hungarians, again, no particular friends to the Ottoman Empire, worried that the war would strengthen Serbia and Montenegro as a Slav bulwark against their own presence in the Balkans, and wanted to ensure that the Adriatic port of Scutari fell to the Albanians instead (preparing to intervene militarily if necessary). The Germans, who had long had a political alliance with the Ottoman Empire, wanted to ensure that their position was not compromised. The British, who in the past had worried about German influence in Constantinople, expressed concern now that should the Islamic Caliph be forced to leave Istanbul as the result of a Christian invasion this would cause problems in India. (As it was, Indian Muslims were already active in donating money for relief efforts in the Ottoman Empire, and even issued a *fatwa* calling for a boycott of European goods.[57])

On the ground in the Balkans, the situation deteriorated for the Ottomans with the fall of Edirne to the Bulgarians in March 1913. The Great Powers urgently pushed for some kind of peace settlement, ultimately imposing the Treaty of London upon the warring parties in May, by which time the Ottoman Empire had lost nearly all of its territory in Europe. But this was not an end to the affair. Before the ink was dry on the Treaty of London, plans for a new war were afoot. The Balkan League, always a marriage of geopolitical convenience, rather than one of love, was falling apart at the seams. Though Greece, Bulgaria, Serbia and Montenegro had all made startling territorial gains as the result of their war against the Ottoman Empire, they all felt they deserved a little more of the pie. By June, the Bulgarians were fighting the Greeks and the Serbians. The Ottomans saw their chance. Albania and Macedonia were lost forever, but Edirne at least could be reclaimed. In July the Bulgarians, having overplayed their hand, were forced out of the city, and the Young

Turk military leader Ismail Enver (now known as Enver Pasha) was able to claim, at last, an Ottoman victory. The Treaty of London was hastily revised to reflect the changed facts on the ground – it now became the Treaty of Bucharest, confirming Ottoman possession of Edirne.

It had been a bloody and vicious set of wars, behind the lines as well as along them. It was a conflict which would leave deep scars across the Balkans. In areas occupied by Bulgarian troops Muslims were subject to forced conversions, completed by the sprinkling of holy water and the symbolic eating of sausage.[58] When Edirne fell, Ottoman troops were confined to an island where they died by the hundred each day, the bark torn off the trees up to the height of an outstretched hand. A Jew in Salonica, Leon Sciaky, later pinpointed 1913 as the beginning of mass Jewish emigration from the city, many heading to that other corner of the Ottoman Empire: Palestine.[59] Visiting the outlying countryside that year he recalled that 'not even the barking of dogs greeted our coming . . . where the laughter and songs of children had resounded yesterday, an oppressive silence now hung'.

An international investigating committee sponsored by the Carnegie Endowment for International Peace noted that 'the burning of villages and the exodus of the defeated population is a normal and traditional incident of all Balkan wars and insurrections'.[60] Depressingly, there was a circularity to such conflicts: 'what they have suffered themselves they inflict in turn upon others'. Although the Ottoman Turks had been ejected too quickly to be the perpetrators of many atrocities during the first phase of the Balkan wars there was room for revenge in its closing stages. In the village of Kirka, in eastern Thrace, the Greek population which had massacred local Muslims was in turn slain.[61]

In retaking Edirne, a degree of honour had been restored to the Ottoman Empire. The return of the Young Turks to political power in Constantinople had been cemented. If the peace were to hold, the Young Turks could now turn to the pressing challenge of modernising a much-reduced, but perhaps more easily-managed, Ottoman Empire. In September 1913 the congress of the Committee of Union and

Progress proposed a series of administrative and economic reforms for the empire, and proposed that the committee itself become a fully fledged political party, a step towards Western political normalisation.

There was much to be done to secure the future of the smaller Ottoman Empire. It was inevitable, after such a loss of territory and population, that the political arrangements between different groups would now have to be recalibrated. The empire's Arabs, in particular, would have to be placated, so as to be relieved of any temptation to split off. In April 1913, for the first time, the government allowed the use of Arabic in law courts in Arab-majority provinces and provided for Arabic to be used as the main language in schools.[62] The following month, a German military adviser to the Ottoman army suggested that perhaps the capital of the empire be moved to Aleppo – a move which, he argued, would make both military and political sense. That was too much for Young Turks to stomach. But the appointment of an Arab Grand Vizier certainly showed the empire's direction of travel in 1913.

Meanwhile, opined *The Economist*, 'Constantinople is taking things philosophically, and is little concerned by national triumphs and defeats'.[63] A bumper harvest was being collected and trade was returning. (*The Economist* suggested the city be boosted by being made a free port.) Constantinople's first power station was under construction in Silahtarağa. Tram services had begun to be electrified, starting with a few lines on the Galata side of the city. Work was underway to roll out a telephone service with no fewer than twelve telephone exchanges by the following year.[64] In December, much to the Russians' anger, German General Liman von Sanders arrived in Constantinople at the head of a delegation of forty officers – a far larger group than in the past – invited by the government to assist in the continuing modernisation of the army. (Russian protests meant he was subsequently over-promoted and so could not formally serve as Constantinople's garrison commander – as originally intended – though he stayed on to play a major role in the Ottoman army during the Great War.) Between international crises, in other words, the process of modernisation resumed. Might 1913 ultimately be remembered as the beginning of a new chapter in the long history of the Ottoman realms, down, but not out; a moment when the tides of history which had for so long run against the empire, began finally to run in its favour?

PEKING—SHANGHAI
Waking Slumber

'A plate of spinach with some egg yolks', was some foreign wit's description of the view of Peking from the city walls, reported by Alphonse Favier, the city's French Catholic Bishop.[1] 'Nothing but trees, trees, and more trees', Favier explained, 'the yellow-tiled roofs of a few palaces and pagodas peeking through the green'. It was only in 1860 that foreigners had been granted the right to walk along the city's walls – a right denied to most Chinese and a concession which the Chinese imperial court hoped would soften foreign demands on other matters in the wake of the Second Opium War. By the beginning of the twentieth century the view from the city's walls was considered amongst the best for visiting tourists or for new arrivals, a way of grasping the city's dimensions and some elements of its layout, a layout laden with the symbolism of power and with the Confucian ideal of the Chinese Empire and its Manchu Qing dynasty. (Even today, the vastly-extended layout of modern Beijing essentially follows the square layout of the imperial city.)

The view from the city walls was not the very best to be had in Peking, however. That honour was traditionally reserved for one man, the Emperor. Only through the Emperor's eyes could the city be seen in its proper majesty, from a pavilion on the Scenery Hill, at one end of the aptly named Forbidden City.[2] This point in Peking was protected from the outside world by a moat and three sets of walls. Each wall represented – in principle and in reality – a boundary between the Emperor and his people. Cities within cities, walls behind walls, worlds within worlds: such was the ordering of imperial Peking.

The Forbidden City, reserved to the court and to the eunuchs who staffed it, was contained within the larger Imperial City, where aristocrats and high officials could reside, and behind the walls of the

Inner City, where the city's bannermen (soldiers) were based. 'From this "Inside"', wrote Katharine Carl, an American visitor in 1903, 'customs and habits flow and pulse over the rest of China, as the blood flows from the heart, by a thousand arteries reaching to the very confines of the Empire'.[3] Since the end of the Second Opium War, when foreign states had at last been granted the right to have permanent embassies in Peking, the city's small foreign community resided in the Foreign Legation quarter. Complete with its own churches and schools, this area broke up the architectural harmony of imperial Peking with spires and Western architecture. Beyond this lay the Outer City, where commerce was accepted and where the physical ordering of Peking finally began to break down into a mess of low-rise *hutongs*, beautiful courtyard houses hidden behind thick wooden doors, muddy lanes overflowing with garbage, and unpaved streets crowded with rickshaws and pigs, Mongolian camels from the Gobi desert and the stunted horses of northern China.

Katharine Carl's visit to Peking in 1903 was for business as much as for pleasure. She had been hired to paint a portrait of the Dowager Empress Cixi, to be displayed at the world fair the following year in St Louis, Missouri. Carl's first taste of the life of the Chinese imperial court came not in the Forbidden City, but in the Summer Palace, a few miles to the west:

> After readjusting ourselves in the waiting-room, we were met, when we came out, by the Chief Eunuch of the palace, who conducted us to the red-covered Palace chairs, each carried by six men. They bore us past the Imperial Gateway (used only for their Majesties), through a door of entrance at the left, when we were within one of the sacred precincts of one of the residences of the Son of Heaven and within the walls of the favorite palace of the Empress Dowager! Before we could take in our surroundings, we had been rapidly carried through various courts and gardens, and had come at last to a larger quadrangular court, filled with pots of rare blooming plants and many beautiful growing shrubs. Here the bearers put down our chairs; we descended and walked through the court, preceded and followed by a number of eunuchs. The great plate-glass doors of the Palace in front of us, blazing with the huge red character 'Sho' (longevity) were swung noiselessly back, and we were at last within the Throne-room of Her Imperial Majesty the Empress Dowager of China![4]

After an initial interview, during which the Empress dictated the terms on which her portrait was to be painted, Cixi retired to change, returning 'in a gown of Imperial yellow, brocaded in the wistaria vine in realistic colors and richly embroidered with pearls'. Her nails were worn long, as was the fashion, with a nail protector made of jade on one hand and one of gold, set with rubies and pearls, on the other. 'My heart trembled!' confided Carl, 'the inscrutable eyes of the wonderful woman I was about to paint, fixed piercingly upon me, were also disconcerting'. Just then, the clocks in the throne-room, all eighty-five of them, began to strike eleven: 'the auspicious moment had come! I raised my charcoal and put the first stroke upon the canvas of the first portrait that had ever been painted of the Empress Dowager of Great China'.[5]

Carl had good reason to tremble. The Dowager Empress Cixi was a formidable force. She had ruled China, in effect, for forty years. In the 1860s and 1870s she ruled as regent for her son Emperor Tongzhi. When he died, Cixi broke with Manchu tradition and engineered the appointment of her three-year-old nephew Guangxu as Emperor, allowing her to keep the reins of power firmly in her own hands until he reached his majority. When he did, and attempted to break from Cixi through a slew of Western reforms introduced in 1898, the wily Dowager Empress simply had him sidelined, reasserting her power from behind the throne once again.

But it was not just that Cixi had a reputation as a ruthless Machiavellian operator. She also had a reputation for hating foreigners, the result of the so-called Boxer Rebellion of 1900. When Katharine Carl began her portrait in 1903, the massacres of foreigners which the Boxer Rebellion had brought about – and the disastrous consequences for China – were fresh in Western and Chinese memories. Even ten years later, in 1913, the events of that rebellion and its aftermath would be no more distant than the events of 9/11 are today, a vivid and inescapable backdrop to mutual perceptions and misperceptions.

The origins of the Boxer Rebellion of 1900 were hazy, starting with peasant desperation at a succession of floods and droughts in Shandong province, but steadily growing into a wider rebellion against all things foreign. The rebellion was led loosely by the Society of Righteous Harmony, a cultish, rag-tag bunch of desperadoes who promoted a belief in their own invincibility and who provided an anti-foreign focus for all sorts of unconnected grievances. In the West this group came to be known as the Boxers, in reference to their fondness for martial arts. In the first months of 1900 word trickled in to Peking from missionaries in rural China, reporting ugly attacks against all manifestations of the West, particularly Chinese converts to Christianity, who the Boxers viewed as having disturbed the natural order of the Chinese countryside by adopting Western religious practices. Bishop Favier, the man whose book on Peking included delicate renditions of the finer things in Chinese civilisation – exquisite porcelain, musical instruments, fine lanterns, elaborate silks – was under no illusions as to the cruelty and crudeness of Chinese mob violence, or the possible consequences should the Boxers reach Peking.[6] Most foreigners were more sanguine – surely Cixi would quell the violence if it were ever to approach the capital?

In the event, the Dowager Empress did exactly the opposite. She was relieved that the Boxers had focused their anger on foreigners rather than on the Qing dynasty and she was angered that Western forces had seen fit to capture a major Qing fortress at Dagu in order, they claimed, to be better able to protect foreign interests in uncertain times. When the Boxers arrived in Peking in June 1900, rather than attempting to disarm them or dissuade them from attacking Western interests, Cixi issued an ultimatum to the foreign legations to leave by 4 p.m. the next day – or face the consequences. A peasant revolt had become an imperially sanctioned national uprising. The telegraph lines with the outside world cut, foreign legations now faced a dreadful choice: either to take their chances in the open countryside, attempting to reach the coast by God only knows what means, and quite possibly against a swarm of Boxer rebels, or to try their luck in defending the legation quarter itself, with limited weapons – pistols, a few machine guns, a single artillery piece – against the Boxers, and perhaps against the army of the Dowager Empress herself.

After the whole thing was over, it was easy to dismiss the first course of action, and to present the second choice above all in moral terms. 'Picture to yourself what this convoy would be crawling out of giant Peking [had they chosen the first option]', wrote Bertram Lenox Simpson, a Briton working for the Customs Office in China:

... we would be a thousand white people with a vast trail of native Christians following us and calling on us not to abandon them and their children. Do you think we could run ahead, while a cowardly massacre by Boxers and savage soldiery was hourly thinning out the stragglers and defenceless people in the rear? Never![7]

In reality, the calculation was as much one of self-preservation as any desire to protect Chinese Christians. Inside the legation, the foreigners at least had the hope that relief troops – called for before the telegraph wires were cut – would shortly arrive. Outside the legation, who knew what awaited them?

And so, against the initial advice of the diplomatic heads of the foreign legations themselves, the die was cast. As in any conflict, the months that followed saw both heroics – those of Japanese Colonel Shiba were particularly remarked upon – and abject fear in the face of the ever-present threat that the foreign quarter would be overrun, with torture and slow death the likely result.[8] In London the newspapers prepared, and prematurely published, the obituaries of the leading figures of the foreign quarter. As it was, the siege saw the eleven nationalities of the quarter pull together remarkably well, demonstrating ingenuity and resilience. Anything suitable was melted down to make bullets, an ancient cannon found in an antique shop was dusted off and made serviceable, the foreign quarter's mules and horses were swiftly sacrificed for human consumption – a bounty in which the Chinese Christians in the foreign quarter did not share – and the latest fashions were torn apart to make sandbags, or dressings for wounds.

At one point in mid July an informal ceasefire seemed to be taking hold, largely because different factions around the Dowager Empress were beginning to question the wisdom of taking on, in effect, the whole world in microcosm. By the end of July, however, any semblance of a ceasefire had broken down. Fighting resumed, with potshots taken on both sides; no one in the foreign quarter knew when or where there might be another assault, perhaps one which they would be unable to repel.

However, the lull in fighting in the middle of the month had allowed a few messages to reach the besieged Westerners: they now knew that a relief force was being organised. By early August that force, 20,000 strong, was on its way to Peking. Under the ultimate command of a Prussian Field-Marshal, in honour of the fact that the first European killed in Peking during the rebellion had been the German legate Baron von Ketteler, the international force was made up of Japanese, German, American, Italian, French, Russian and British contingents. Much to the annoyance of the other nationalities it was the British-officered troops from the Indian Raj who made it first into Peking, turbaned Sikhs greeted wildly by the remaining foreign population. Simpson recalled the moment he realised what was happening, clambering over a wall and being met with 'the smell of another world . . . the smell of India!'[9] Victory had been snatched from the jaws of defeat, Western fortitude had triumphed in the face of adversity; no wonder the Boxer Rebellion made for such good headlines in European and American newspapers, encouraging books, memoirs and even the odd film.

The siege was broken, and the carnage around it revealed. Walking through Peking a few days later, British writer Henry Savage Landor came across a sobbing mother caressing the face of her son, most likely killed by a Western artillery shell, imploring him to answer her. Landor saw a naked eunuch hanging from a beam, the body covered with the marks of torture. In a courtyard he came across a collection of severed heads. Further on, in an alleyway, he found three adults and three children strung up against a wall, strangled. 'The light was not propitious for a snapshot, as the bodies were in shadow', he wrote coldly.[10] But he took a picture all the same. 'Owing to the state of decomposition of the corpses', he continued, 'I did not give it a very long exposure'.

The situation was similar in other parts of China, where Boxers had killed Chinese Christians, and where columns of foreign troops had inflicted their own reprisals – the Russians around Manchuria, the British and Germans around Tianjin. 'Wield your weapons so that for a thousand years hereafter no Chinese will dare look askance at a German', Kaiser Wilhelm had exhorted German soldiers as they embarked for China earlier that year.[11] They took him at his word. The recently signed Hague Convention, which established the laws of war, was not considered applicable. As far as most Westerners were concerned, it was a case of putting down a semi-colonial revolt, rather than a war between civilised nations.

Taking on the persona of 'John Chinaman', the British pacifist philosopher Goldsworthy Lowes Dickinson put the Chinese case in the pages of the *Saturday Review*. The Boxers might be 'barbarous and cruel', he wrote, but what of the troops of the West, the troops of Christendom?

> Ask the once fertile land from Peking to the coast; ask the corpses of murdered men and outraged women and children; ask the innocent mingled indiscriminately with the guilty; ask the Christ the lover of men, whom you profess to serve, to judge between us who rose in mad despair to save our country and you who, avenging crime with crime, did not pause to reflect that the crime you avenged was the fruit of your own inequity.[12]

It was an appeal unlikely to touch many hearts in London, or San Francisco, or Berlin. There, tales of Boxer barbarity reached Western audiences who were already accustomed to the notion of race war – a book on the subject was written in 1887 by the founder of the Australian Labour Federation – and who associated their own Chinatowns with disease, drugs and crime, dominated by opium dens, triads and fallen white women.[13] (As early as the 1880s the alleged threat to the United States posed by the mores and habits

US Marines in Peking after the international intervention against the Boxer Rebellion, 1901.

of the domestic Chinese population led to the exclusion of Chinese from US citizenship.) As always, it was easier to have one's prejudices confirmed than to have them challenged.

After the violence in Peking, humiliation followed. The Dowager Empress Cixi had fled to Xian. Foreign troops set themselves up in the Chinese capital. The Forbidden City – which foreign troops had left alone in 1860 at the end of the Second Opium War – became a tourist attraction. As with the bedroom of the Sultan at Yildiz palace in Constantinople a few years later, the bedchambers of the Emperor were of particular interest. The ubiquitous Pierre Loti, who swept into Peking with the French marines, noted a piano which the Emperor was said to be learning to play, a music box playing Chinese tunes, and a silk mattress of imperial yellow, still impressed with the shape of the imperial body. 'What disarray there must have been in his unfathomable little mind', Loti pondered:

> . . . the triple-walled palace violated even unto its innermost secrets; himself, the son of Heaven, torn from the home where twenty gener-ations of his ancestors lived inaccessible; him, forced to flee and, in flight, to allow himself to be seen [by commoners] . . . even to implore, and to have to wait! . . .[14]

As Loti left, he heard a cheerful French voice behind him in the thick accent of rural Gascony: 'Well, I'm telling you mate, now we can say we've had a roll in the bed of the Emperor of China!' Looting was common, with treasures stuffed into the greatcoats and knapsacks of individual soldiers – or carted off as the spoils of war to museums in Paris and Berlin.

Despite an injunction against the presence of journalists, Henry Savage Landor managed to talk his way into attending the allied victory parade in the Forbidden City itself, in the company of the Russian General Linievitch. (As it turned out, he discovered that he was not the only journalist to have slipped through: the long-time Australian correspondent for *The Times* of London, George Ernest Morrison, was already there.) The British artillery fired a twenty-one gun salute and, in Landor Savage's words: 'the spell was broken. The deed was done. What Celestials had kept sacred for 500 years, foreign devils desecrated in two seconds'. As he left he noted the demeanour of the Chinese: 'although apparently submissive, even servile, any observant person could note on their stolid faces an expression of hatred and contempt'. This was not a slight which would easily be forgotten. A year or so later, when the Forbidden City was turned over to the Dowager Empress again, the final terms of China's humiliation were set out in the Boxer Convention: a punishing indemnity which was expected to be paid off in 1940, the erection of monuments to the Western dead, permission for the foreign quarter in Peking to have a permanent international force of soldiers guarding it, and a ban on the import of arms to China. In 1903, a memorial arch to Baron von Ketteler was inaugurated in Peking with a march-past by German soldiers.

No wonder, Katharine Carl reflected, that the Empress Dowager had put off coming back to the Forbidden Palace in Peking until the last possible moment, waiting until even the permanently stoked furnaces under the Summer Palace could no longer keep it warm enough to live in: if the Forbidden City was the most hallowed ground in China, and the formal seat of the Manchus, it was now also a tarnished symbol of a tarnished dynasty.

How to overcome China's weakness, so painfully revealed in decades of foreign depredations and now with foreign soldiers having breached the Forbidden City itself?

In the same year that Carl was in Peking, Liang Qichao, who had been an adviser to Emperor Guangxu during his ill-fated reform drive of 1898, was in North America. Like an increasing number of reform-minded Chinese, Qichao travelled abroad – and drew inspiration from what he saw and read there. Yan Fu, the man who translated the works of Thomas Huxley into Chinese – and who had also translated Adam Smith's *Wealth of Nations* and works by John Stuart Mill – had spent time in England as a young man at the Greenwich naval college in London. Sun Yat-Sen, who was one of the leading figures in the opposition to the Qing dynasty and was the Provisional President of the Chinese Republic in 1912, had grown up in Hawaii, was trained as a doctor in Hong Kong and travelled frequently to Japan, the United States and Canada as well as Europe (where he liked to spend time in the British Library, much as Karl Marx had done a few decades previously).

Like Yan Fu and Sun Yat-Sen, Liang Qichao believed that in order to understand China's weaknesses and to prepare the ground for Chinese renovation it was imperative to look beyond the borders of China itself. In New York he wangled a brief appointment with John Pierpont Morgan, who offered him the following piece of sterling advice: 'the outcome of any venture depends on preparations made ahead of time'. At the University of Chicago, he marvelled at the effectiveness of the honour system in operation at the university's library.

Even relatively minor comparisons between China and the West might carry wider meanings. Qichao noted that though Chinese shops were open almost constantly and American shops were closed on a Sunday, American shop-owners were richer.[15] He concluded the importance of resting every seventh day. Whereas any gathering of more than a hundred Chinese was accompanied by noise – 'the most frequent is coughing, next comes yawning, sneezing, and blowing the nose' – American theatre or concert audiences were silent. Whereas Chinese spoke loudly, and interrupted each other constantly, Americans adjusted their speech to their surroundings and interrupted rarely. Qichao's observations even went as far as to note the differences between Western and Chinese ways of walking:

When Westerners walk, their bodies are erect and their heads up. We Chinese bow at one command, stoop at a second, and prostrate ourselves at a third. The comparison should make us ashamed. When Westerns walk their steps are always hurried, one look and you know that the city is full of people with business to do, as though they cannot get everything done. The Chinese on the other hand walk leisurely and elegantly, full of pomp and ritual – they are truly ridiculous . . . Westerns walk together like a formation of geese; Chinese are like scattered ducks.[16]

Taken together, these observations constituted an indictment of China's political development. Qichao argued that China's history had made the Chinese into 'clansmen, rather than citizens', with the mentality of the village rather than that of a nation – indeed the very word 'nation' was an innovation, first appearing in Chinese in 1899 – able to accept despotism but not to enjoy freedom, lacking the ability to set their own national objectives. These fundamental differences – entrenched by millennia of imperial history – inhibited China's political development, and her ability to defend herself. In order to become a respected member of the family of nation-states, China would first have to herself become a nation: a group of individuals linked, as French political theorist Ernest Renan had put it in the 1880s, by 'a common will in the present, to have done great things in the past and to wish to do more'.[17] Qichao was well placed to help the process along, writing as a journalist at a time, at the turn of the twentieth century, when newspapers were multiplying across China and communications improving between the country's far-flung provinces.

But it would take what would amount to a cultural revolution before China could truly be democratic, argued Qichao. (Amongst his admirers was Mao Zedong, then a child in southern China, later the country's first Communist leader – he claimed to have learnt the master's essays off by heart.) As Qichao put it:

If we were to adopt a democratic system of government now, it would be nothing less than committing national suicide. Freedom, constitutionalism, and republicanism would be like hempen clothes in winter or furs in summer; it is not that they are not beautiful, they are just not suitable for us. We should not be bedazzled by empty glitter now; we should not yearn for beautiful dreams. To put it in a word, the Chinese people of today can only be governed autocratically; they cannot enjoy freedom. I pray and yearn, I pray only that our country can have a Guanzi [medieval autocratic reformer], a Shang Yang, a Lycurgus, a Cromwell alive today to carry out harsh rule, and with iron and fire to forge and temper our countrymen for twenty, thirty, even fifty years. After that we can give them the books of Rousseau, and tell them about the deeds of Washington.[18]

Not all took quite such a dark view of the need for autocratic rule to be the handmaiden of the introduction of Western political forms into China. But many concluded, after the defeat of China in the war against Japan, the failure of the government to deal with regular natural disasters and now with the Forbidden City occupied in 1900, that the Qing dynasty – in its present form, at least – was a busted flush. The motto of the Boxer Rebellion had been 'revive the Qing, exterminate the foreign' – but was it not now too late for that?[19] (And weren't the Manchus, from whom the Qing dynasty was drawn, foreign anyway?) What China now needed, it was argued, was wholesale renovation, perhaps even a constitution. Some, including Sun Yat-Sen, went further: China should dispense with the forms of empire altogether and become a republic. In 1905, Sun Yat-Sen brought all the anti-Qing movements into a single umbrella organisation, the Revolutionary Alliance. Between 1906 and 1908 the Revolutionary Alliance launched a number of uprisings against the Qing dynasty in the south of China.

Under pressure abroad and at home the Qing regime undertook a series of dramatic reforms – many of which had been proposed in 1898, but shelved after the Dowager Empress reasserted her authority over Emperor Guangxu. In line with demands made as part of the Boxer Convention, a formal Qing Foreign Ministry was established in 1901. (As a result Chinese diplomats – a class which had previously been publicly scorned, engaged in an occupation traditionally viewed as shameful – were more present internationally. This implied acceptance of China's place in a foreign-run world order, but also an understanding of the need for China to actively defend her interests in that order.) The old *jinshi* system, a gruelling and classically focused set of exams which had formed the basis of entry into imperial state service since time immemorial, was abolished in 1905 – in principle to allow for a wider intake into state service. A Qing ministry for commerce was founded, and another for post and communications. The army underwent a slow process of reform, incorporating Western uniforms and salutes. Some traditional punishments were done away with, at least in principle. A Supreme Court was established in 1906, in the hope that reform of the system of law in China would undercut the foreign powers' traditional argument that the inadequacies of the Chinese system made it imperative for their citizens to be subject only to their own foreign systems of justice.

These administrative reforms were radical enough in themselves, establishing the basis of China as a modern state. But they were accompanied by political reforms which were potentially more far-reaching. Partly to deflect demands for a republic, and partly to reassert central control over processes of political reform already underway in the provinces, the Qing dynasty assembled a high-ranking study group to investigate options for constitutional reform.

In January 1906 – after having escaped an attempt to assassinate them at Peking railway station a few months earlier – the study group travelled to the United States. They returned with suggestions for constitutional government which were subsequently accepted by the Dowager Empress and the court. In 1908 it was announced that full constitutional government would be in place by 1917. When the Dowager Empress Cixi finally died later that year – one day after the long-suffering Emperor Guangxu, still under effective house arrest – power passed to the Manchu regents surrounding the new child Emperor Puyi, ensuring an extended period of jockeying for position at court. In October 1909 provincial assemblies, elected according to a franchise that ensured elite dominance, assembled across the country. In 1910 they forced the Qing court to bring forward the timetable for constitutional government: a provisional national assembly was to gather in Peking before the end of the year.

At the same time, the Chinese government began to grapple seriously with one of the issues which had dogged China for years: opium. It was, in effect, in order to defend the 'rights' of British traders of Indian opium that Britain had first gone to war against the Qing dynasty in 1839. At the beginning of the twentieth century, local anti-opium campaigns – not unlike prohibition campaigns in the United States – spread across China, shaming addicts, closing down opium dens and leading to bonfires of the paraphernalia of drug use.[20] Now Peking decided to get in on the act, proposing to suppress domestic demand entirely, threatening addicts with execution, calling upon the British to help in a moral crusade against the drug, and vastly increasing the customs' duty on opium. In 1907, Britain agreed to a system whereby it would curtail exports from India, reducing them by a tenth every year over a period of ten years. British policy stipulated one condition: it would have to be shown that local eradication and suppression was working, on the basis that if it were not, there would simply be a substitution between Indian supply and local Chinese supply. In 1909, the International Opium Commission held an American-convened conference in Shanghai, with delegates from all the European powers, plus representatives from Japan, Persia, Portugal (which had a colony at Macau), Burma, and the Netherlands (which controlled the Dutch East Indies – Indonesia). The Chinese produced numbers to show the economic burden of opium on the people of the country and, in a move calculated to sway the commercial instincts of foreigners, argued that the impoverishment of China from opium addiction undercut foreign business prospects far more than the value of the trade itself.[21] How much greater would the market for *other* Western goods be if opium were eliminated?

This was a powerful argument at a time when China's economic development – particularly in the coastal areas – was already accelerating. After the Boxer Rebellion, railway construction, which foreign powers hoped would accelerate penetration of Chinese markets (and potentially improve troop movements), took on a new lease of life, financed by Western interests. (Ten times as much track was laid between 1900 and 1905 as between 1896 and 1899.[22]) As early as 1903, Shanghai was connected to the Trans-Siberian Railway, which ran all the way to Europe via Mukden and Harbin. In 1905 a line was completed linking Peking to Wuhan in central China. Foreign investment in China doubled between 1902 and 1914: Britain was far in the lead, and behind her, in order, were Russia, Germany, France, Japan and the United States.[23] (The change in Japanese investment was particularly striking, rising from just $1 million in 1902 to well over $200 million a little over a decade later.) *The China Year Book 1913* noted a steady increase in shipping in Chinese waters – two-fifths of it under the flag of the United Kingdom, nearly a quarter under the flag of Japan, and one-fifth under the Chinese flag.[24] Factories sprang up, particularly in the treaty ports. An oil drum factory was operated by the Asiatic Petroleum Company in Shanghai. The British-American Tobacco Company had factories in Hankow, Shanghai, and Newchwang (Yingkou) in Manchuria. Electric light was said to be available in thirty-one Chinese cities.

In 1907, after having been initially opposed by the Qing authorities, a motor race from Peking to Paris was allowed to start from the city. The following year, less than a decade after foreign troops had had to fight their way from Tianjin to Peking to liberate the foreign quarter, Dutchman Henri Borel covered the same ground by train, in three hours. 'I had certainly heard of reforms in China', he wrote, 'but I had not expected an up-to-date train-de-luxe to take me on modern springs to the Imperial City . . . it was in this way that I had travelled to Nice and Vienna'.[25] Arriving in Peking, Borel found the Grand Hôtel des Wagons Lits staffed by a manager who would not have been out of place in Monte Carlo or Ostend and a bedroom appointed with every modern convenience: 'Did I come to Peking for this? I could not help smiling somewhat bitterly. Have things already gone so far with Peking? I expected to reach to China's mysterious capital, and I find myself landed in a Parisian hotel'.[26]

Whatever Borel's experience, for many the true coming metropolis of China in these years was not Peking, it was Shanghai. Barely touched by the Boxer Rebellion, growing yearly more prosperous, already the undisputed commercial capital of China and untarnished by association with the Qing dynasty, it was Shanghai which came to symbolise the possibilities of Chinese modernity – with foreigners still very much part of the picture. Where Shanghai led, it was felt, the rest of China would surely follow.

Unlike Peking, where ancient tradition and the spirit of Confucian order was supposed to be imprinted on every brick of the city's walls, Shanghai was popularly conceived of as a city of change, ever-ready to adopt a new technological innovation or import a new style of dance. Shanghai's first telephone company was established in 1881, its main streets were lit with electric light from 1883, it showed its first movie in 1896, and saw its first car in 1902 (around the same time as Tokyo, capital of much more advanced Japan).[27] Its printing presses produced more books, newspapers and political pamphlets than any other Chinese city – there were seventy-three Chinese and twenty-five foreign-language newspapers in 1913, as opposed to a total of fifty-two in Peking.[28] For its literary and artistic prowess – or perhaps for its nightlife – Shanghai was dubbed the Paris of the East. While the rest of China was having its opium dens shut down, those in the international settlement of Shanghai, beyond the reach of the Qing authorities, remained open until 1910 (opium shops remained open in the city for another seven years after that).

Whereas Peking had been around for centuries, Shanghai was a relative upstart, the child – indeed the poster-child – of the treaty port system. Unlike many of the other treaty ports, which remained economic backwaters where consular representatives of the foreign powers were sometimes the only foreigners in town, Shanghai's

growth as a Chinese city trading with the rest of the world had
been explosive. Forty-four foreign ships had entered the port in 1844,
shortly after the signature of the treaty ending the First Opium
War. Ten times that number docked in 1855.[29] In 1908, the lavishly
illustrated *Twentieth Century Impressions of Hongkong, Shanghai, and
Other Treaty Ports of China* noted the ceaseless activity of the city's
port:

> From Woosung to Shanghai, a distance of some thirteen miles, the
> river is alive with shipping . . . A constant succession of tenders,
> lighters, junks, and sampans is met at all states of the tide, and it is
> interesting to watch the skill with which the Chinese navigate their
> clumsy-looking and heavily-laden craft . . . Long before the landing-
> stage at Shanghai is reached, the river banks begin to wear a busy
> aspect, cotton mills, silk filatures, docks, wharves and godowns [ware-
> houses] appearing in almost unbroken succession.[30]

By 1913 Shanghai took in nearly one-third of all the customs'
revenue raised in China's treaty ports.[31] While new factories were
built all across China, they were mostly financed by banks in
Shanghai, and their securities traded in the city's stock market. A
Chinese critic of the city noted that, in Shanghai, 'people only care
about the value of gold and silver and do not know the origin of
elegance and vulgarity'.[32] A similar barb could be made by Peking's
foreign residents, looking down on 'Shanghailanders' as a rather
uncultured breed of foreigner, getting their hands dirty in business
while they, in Peking, steeped themselves in the timelessness of
Chinese civilisation.[33]

Whereas the centre of Peking was the Forbidden City, behind
walls and moats, the most prestigious address in Shanghai was
somewhere on the Bund, on one side of the broad Huangpu river,
facing the world. The Bund – its name derived from the Hindi word
'*band*', meaning embankment – was home to the city's leading hotels,
its banks and the social clubs of Shanghai's Western gentlemen.[34]
This was where the Customs House stood, the nationality of the
long-serving head of China's Imperial Customs, Sir Robert Hart,
reflected in its curious design: a Tudor-style building topped with
a four-faced clock tower ringing out Westminster chimes. (Hart
himself died in 1911; a statue was erected to him on the Bund a few

years later.) Many of the Bund's buildings had gone up within the past couple of decades. The Imperial Bank of China building was finished in 1897. The predominantly British Shanghai Club – 'the centre of the business and social life of the settlement' – had just moved into expanded premises.[35] While its new building was being built, the German Concordia Club, the foundation stone of which had been laid by the young Prince Adalbert of Prussia in 1904, had been so good as to provide a temporary home.

In Shanghai, cosmopolitanism was the rule. A missionary report of the time described the Nanjing road as a display of international variety far greater even than the streets of London:

> There walks a tall bearded Russian, a fat German, jostling perhaps a tiny Japanese officer, whose whole air shows that he regards himself as a member of the conquering race . . . there are sleek Chinese in Western carriages, and there are thin Americans in Eastern rickshaws . . . a splendid Indian in a yellow silk coat is struck in the face by the hat of a Frenchman, who finds the pavements of Shanghai too narrow for his sweeping salute; one hears guttural German alternating with cockney slang . . .[36]

During 1913, Shanghai celebrated Kaiser Wilhelm's twenty-fifth anniversary as German Emperor, as well as American Independence Day and French Bastille Day.[37] Advertisements in *The China Yearbook 1913* appealed to an international, well-travelled clientele. One, for the Palace Hotel, noted that 'all principal languages' were spoken by the establishment's staff.[38] Another, for the Hong Kong and Shanghai Banking Corporation, listed its branches around the world, and promised a global banking service to facilitate the lives of its globe-trotting customers. *Plus ça change.*

And whereas in Peking the foreign quarter was a small part of the city, defended as if it were a fortress, machine guns at the ready, in Shanghai the international population felt that this was fundamentally *their* city. This was not obvious from the numbers alone. Among a Chinese population of perhaps one million in the city as a whole, the *Yearbook 1913* listed a foreign population of just 13,346 in the International Settlement – including 4,465 British, 3,361 Japanese, 1,495 Portuguese, 940 Americans, 317 Russians, 113 Danes, 83 Turks, 49 Persians, 11 Egyptians, and 7 Brazilians.[39] But within the International Settlement (and the separate French-managed French Concession) it was these foreigners who ruled the roost. The Chinese residents, who paid most of the taxes, did not get a look in when it came to politics. It was the foreigners who voted for the municipal council and who sat on it, including a Shanghai-born, British-national, Sephardic Baghdadi Jew. It was they who administered justice, a point which had flared into riots in 1905 when Western judges took a different line to their Chinese counterparts. It was they who commanded the local police, including a large Indian contingent – particularly resented by the Chinese – backed up if needed by foreign volunteers, who occasionally marched through the streets in uniform to make the point.

Moreover, foreign Shanghai was expanding. In 1898 the International Settlement, itself the result of a merger between the British and American Concessions, doubled in size. Further expansion was not ruled out. Indeed it was anticipated: roads were built north into the Zhabei district and maps drawn up showing it coloured red.[40] In 1913 Zhabei's future became the subject of a local spat between foreign and Chinese authorities, which, as the local British consul put it in his dispatch to the British Ambassador in Peking, 'does not augur well for the proposed negotiations'.[41] The French Concession, where in the 1890s American visitor Eliza Ruhamah Scidmore had for a moment felt herself on a street corner in Paris, was nonetheless able to push through an expansion the following year, in 1914.[42] Shanghai had long had mission schools, many of them of American foundation, where Chinese children could be provided with a Christian and Westernised education: Mary Farnham Girl's School (American Presbyterian) founded in 1861, St Francis Xavier's College (Roman Catholic) in 1864, St Mary's Hall (American Episcopal) in 1881, Eliza Yates Memorial School (Southern Baptist) in 1897, to name a few.[43] Now, as Shanghai's foreign population came to include families – rather than just men – schools for foreign children were established.

The International Settlement's social life was, as Scidmore put it at the turn of the century, 'formal, exacting, elaborate and extravagant'. As well as the Club on the Bund, there was a Country Club on Bubbling Wells Road 'to which ladies belong as well as men, where everyone who is anyone meets for summer tennis, the afternoon dances, theatricals and balls of the winter season'.[44] Upstream

ON THE BUND. SHANGHAI

A British police officer patrolling the International Settlement in Shanghai.

from Shanghai, 'the finest pheasant shooting in the world' was promised – exactly what a Scottish colonial officer trying his luck with the Shanghai police might want. The Lyceum Theatre, the Yacht Club, the Rowing Club, the Cricket Club, the Baseball Club, the Flower Show and the Shanghai Swimming Bath Club were all plausible occupations for the weekend. The English were no doubt delighted that hunting with hounds was possible in the miles of flat ground around the city. In late 1913 the city's American community waited expectantly for the arrival of the New York Giants and Chicago White Sox baseball teams, on a world tour.[45]

For a Chinese man or woman to live in this city – and particularly in the International Settlement – was to choose to live in a city more modern than any other in China, saturated with radical foreign influences, in the vanguard of the future. It was in Shanghai that the traditional binding of women's feet fell fastest out of fashion. It was in Shanghai that Chinese pigtails, symbols of subordination to the Qing dynasty, were most defiantly cut off. But Shanghai was hardly a nirvana of political or economic equality. Extreme poverty existed alongside great top-hatted Western wealth. The city's Chinese inhabitants were considered distinctly second class by its rulers.

Two articles from the *North China Daily News* in January 1913 starkly made the point. One dismissed the argument that because most taxes in Shanghai were paid by Chinese they should have representation on the council of the International Settlement by noting that 'they knew what to expect when they came to live in the Settlement, and the number of them does not suggest that they are dissatisfied with what they find'.[46] Another, the following day, dealt with the problem of rickshaw drivers earning as little as thirty cents a day, offering to undercut the cost of a tram ride in order to be employed. 'While it is a matter of common knowledge that some coolies reap an occasional harvest from tourists and sailors', a journalist for the newspaper wrote, 'it is equally well established that cases of death from starvation occur':

> No lover of horses fails to visit his stable after a hard ride in order to satisfy himself that the animal is properly tended and fed . . . But the ricsha coolie who runs a mile or so in the blazing summer sun or in winter ploughs his way through mud and cold rain such as Shanghai has experienced this week is paid off, and forgotten. If ever a thought is given to him the little consolation necessary is found in the fact that he belongs to an order of which the average European comprehends little, and that, as a human being, he should be able to take care of himself. But the facts are that gradually his health breaks down, and sooner or later he dies the death of a neglected dog.[47]

In 1913 a Methodist guidebook published in Chinese with the subtitle *What the Chinese in Shanghai Ought to Know* described the city as a 'foreign country', setting out the rules and regulations for using the tram, or eating in a restaurant, or even visiting a public park, accordingly:

> Shanghai has four public gardens altogether. Amongst them, three are for Westerners and one is for Chinese. One of the gardens for Westerners is located by the Huangpu river, and during the week black musicians will be performing. Unless accompanied by a Westerner, Chinese are not allowed to enter. Dogs and bicycles are definitely forbidden to enter.[48]

But if Shanghai was not quite China in terms of its internal functioning, it could not be isolated from the unruly politics of the country which surrounded it. Shanghai did not exist in a vacuum, subject only to the laws of supply and demand, of trade and finance, of dollars and taels. The very fact that the International Settlement was beyond the reach of the Qing authorities ensured that it was a natural bolthole for runaways and political radicals. The commercial importance of the port of Shanghai made the control of it essential to any Chinese government. The dynamism of Shanghai as a city, open to outside influences, churning with new visitors and new ideas, made it suspect to traditionalists, and attractive to reformers and revolutionaries of all stripes. News of the revolution in St Petersburg in 1905, or of the Young Turk coup of 1908, had reached Shanghai before anywhere else in China, and was discussed more fervently there, with obvious relevance for the country's own political trajectory. If ever full-blown political revolution were to come to China, the inhabitants of Shanghai – foreign or Chinese – were guaranteed, whether they wanted it or not, a ringside seat.

When 2,000 years of Chinese empire ended it was with a bang – and with a whimper. The bang took place in October 1911 in the Russian quarter of Hankou, where the casual disposal of a cigarette in a Chinese revolutionary bomb factory caused an accidental explosion, bringing the Qing authorities running, and forcing local army units – who had been heavily infiltrated by revolutionaries – to accelerate a planned rebellion. In Peking, the whimper came in February 1912, when the formal abdication of six-year-old Emperor Puyi was announced, in return for a promise of continued ownership of the treasures of the Manchu court, continued residence in the Forbidden City and an annual subsidy of $4 million to keep the court in the style to which it had, through centuries, become accustomed.

News of the explosion in Wuhan and the uprising which followed reached Sun Yat-Sen via an American newspaper, over breakfast, in Denver, Colorado. Rather than hurrying back, he went first to Europe to persuade Britain and France not to intervene militarily or to continue financial support for the Qing regime should there be any clash. He made it back to Shanghai, which in November had declared its secession from the Qing dynasty, on Christmas Day 1911. The revolutionary flag flew from the rooftops of the city. Pigtails were ceremonially cut. Foreign warships lay at anchor. A week later Sun Yat-Sen travelled by train to Nanjing, the old capital of China and a city which for over a decade in the middle of the last century had been the headquarters of the anti-Qing Taiping rebellion. There, on 1 January 1912, he was proclaimed Provisional President of the Chinese Republic by a meeting of delegates from sixteen provincial assemblies.

For several weeks China had both an Emperor and a President. In the end, the dynasty's fate was sealed by a note from leading commanders of the most effective military unit of the Chinese forces, the Beiyang army, in which the newly appointed Qing premier Yuan Shikai was highly influential. The commanders recommended a republican course for the future government of China. By prior arrangement, Sun Yat-Sen himself now abdicated the presidency in favour of Yuan Shikai, advising the Nanjing assembly of his 'personal opinion' that Yuan Shikai would prove himself a 'loyal servant of the state' and urging them that 'the happiness of our country depends on your choice'. An American observer remarked: 'It sounds like Washington'.[49]

Sun Yat-Sen's decision to pass the presidency to Yuan Shikai, considered to have the confidence of the army, was in some ways noble: a means of potentially avoiding China's disintegration and the foreign depredations which might follow from it. It turned out to be a miscalculation. Yuan Shikai was indeed a masterful political operator with strong support in the most capable units of the army and a quick recognition of the importance of securing foreign support. To that end, he cannily appointed George Morrison, the Australian *Times* correspondent in Peking as one of his political advisers – despite the fact that Morrison did not speak Chinese – and accepted the advice of Charles Eliot, the former president of Harvard University and representative of the Carnegie Endowment for International Peace, that the Provisional President should really have an American law professor by his side in drafting the country's new constitution. Frank Goodnow arrived in Peking in May 1913.

But Yuan Shikai's modus operandi was that of a strongman not a democrat, a fact which became clearer as China prepared itself for the 1912 parliamentary elections. American Ambassador Paul Reinsch later recalled having been told by Wu Tingfang, a former Chinese Ambassador in Washington, that Yuan Shikai 'has no conception of free government [and] is entirely a man of personal authority'.[50] 'Beware, when you get behind those high walls of Peking', Wu Tingfang warned Reinsch: 'The atmosphere is stagnant. It seems to overcome men and make them reactionary. Nobody seems to resist that power!' His judgement proved accurate. In 1912 the new Provisional President successfully resisted a pre-agreed move of the capital from Peking to Nanjing – away from his own stronghold – on the basis that the north of the country was not yet sufficiently pacified. Traditionalist that he was at heart, Yuan Shikai felt that Peking was a city he could trust – unlike Nanjing, where Sun Yat-Sen had been elected China's first Provisional President, and still less Shanghai, that capital of sedition, metropolis of modernity.

To fight the parliamentary elections at the end of 1912, Sun Yat-Sen formed a new political party, the Kuomintang (commonly referred to as the KMT) under the leadership of the thirty-year-old Song Jiaoren. (Liang Qichao, former adviser to Emperor Guangxu and publicist for the idea of Chinese nationhood, led another grouping: the Progressive party.) When the results began to be announced in January 1913, it was clear that the Kuomintang had won the bulk of support of China's forty million electors. In the end, the party took 269 out of 596 seats in the new National Assembly. China had, it appeared, taken a giant step towards popular democracy. The average age of the nation's new representatives was young, under the age of forty. About one in five had been educated in Japan, the United Kingdom or the United States.[51]

Not untypical of the euphoria in some quarters was Ching Chun Wang's article at the beginning of 1913 on the pages of *The Atlantic*, which attempted to convince an American audience that now was the time to diplomatically recognise the new China, something all of the Western powers had so far singularly failed to do:

The Chinese millions have given the world the greatest revolution of modern times in the most civilized manner known to history. We have emancipated ourselves from the imperial yoke, not by brute force but by sheer reasoning and unparalleled toleration. Within the amazingly short period of four months, and without shedding over one hundredth part of the blood that has been shed in other similar revolutions, we have transformed our immense country from an empire of four thousand years' standing into a modern democracy

... Now we come forward with hands and hearts open to join the sisterhood of nations, and all we ask is that the world will permit us to join its company. We ask for recognition of our Republic because it is an accomplished fact.[52]

Others were distinctly more sceptical. One of them was Edmund Backhouse, probably the most famous British expert on China and a resident in Peking. Backhouse, who had made a name for himself as the publisher of the intimate diaries of a high official at the court of the Empress Dowager – in the 1970s these were shown to be highly-capable fakes – was scathing about Westerners' naive views about what had really happened in China. Old wine in new bottles, he argued in a book written in 1913 with former *Times* journalist and Shanghai man-about-town John Otway Bland. The republic would not last:

Those who have followed the course of events in the Far East during the past two years, that is to say, since the ignominious collapse of the Manchu power and Young China's little hour of brief authority, must have been struck by the general, almost unanimous concurrence of opinion, expressed in Europe and America alike, that, with the establishment of a Republican form of government, China has undergone sudden and radical transformation; that the essential qualities of the people had been completely changed . . .[53]

Students of history, he wrote, were familiar with 'the imperishable vitality of this Utopian fallacy'. The truth, he suggested, was somewhat different:

It is true of China, as of India, Persia and Turkey (and, for that matter, of Japan) that, on the surface of the deep sea of national life, rapid phenomena of disintegration are perceptible, and new structures are forming; but the social conditions of the masses and their incapacity for self-government remain at a stage generally similar to that which existed in Southern Europe before the Christian era.

His prognosis was that tradition and authority – 'throne and court' – would reassert themselves in some shape or form, and indeed that this would be best for China's future development.

The events of the year seemed to support the case. On 20 March 1913 Song Jiaoren, leader of the Kuomintang party and premier-elect, was shot twice in Shanghai railway station as he boarded a train bound for Peking, where he was to attend the opening of the new National Assembly. Though taken to hospital, he died from his wounds two days later. Song Jiaoren's murderer was swiftly arrested. But most suspected that the order for the assassination came from much higher up: perhaps even from President Yuan Shikai himself. 'It is not impossible that some over-zealous follower of Yuan may have thought he was aiding the President's cause by planning such a crime', an American diplomat in Shanghai noted, hedging his bets.[54] For KMT supporters the crime confirmed their suspicions – frequently voiced by Song Jiaoren during and since the 1912 campaign – that what the President really wanted was to dispense with parliament altogether and rule as Emperor in all but name. A little over a year after Sun Yat-Sen had stood aside for Yuan Shikai in the national interest – and in recognition of his own military weakness – the two were at each other's throats. In Shanghai, republicans threatened that Song Jiaoren's death would be 'avenged by a reign of terror more frightful than that of the French revolution'.[55] The city became a 'storm centre' of 'secret plottings'.[56]

No wonder that the opening of the National Assembly in Peking in early April 1913, was a dull affair. 'The sun shone, bands played, complimentary addresses were delivered', the *North China Daily News* reported. But, on the whole, it was an 'anti-climax'.[57] Yuan Shikai was not there, pleading his own assassination fears. A large number of elected representatives failed to appear, too. And amongst those who did, instead of the 'mass of brilliant colors which always characterized a Chinese crowd in the old days', the choice of clothing was sober, formal and Western: black frock coats and silk hats.[58] As the event got under way, a circular was handed round to members of the new National Assembly advising them that, with several hundred foreigners anticipated to be coming along to watch, it was imperative to 'maintain a dignified and graceful demeanour . . . so that we may command the respect and win the friendship of foreigners'.[59] The whole thing seemed more about saving face than about saving China.

The foreign powers still resisted pressure to formally recognise the Chinese Republic. After all, some argued, they were not sure which way the chips would fall. Earlier in the year, an American diplomat reported the bleak view of one of his French colleagues: 'his government had no confidence in the stability of the present government in China . . . things were going from bad to worse'.[60] In any case, foreign powers had not yet received what they wanted from Peking – to give recognition too early would be to give up an aspect of their diplomatic leverage. Quite apart from confirmation of the status of their trade concessions in China, the Russians insisted that China fully respect Mongolia's 1911 declaration of independence (under Russian tutelage). The British wanted guarantees of Tibetan autonomy. The Japanese wanted their economic preponderance in Manchuria confirmed. All the while the foreign powers were embroiled in negotiations – with China and with each other – over the terms of a large 'Reorganisation' loan to be extended to Yuan Shikai. Better to withhold recognition at least until these negotiations were completed. Such was the logic of foreign diplomacy.

Reports back to Washington revealed the full pettiness of the discussions amongst the powers. All sought to place their men in positions of influence. At one point, the American delegate presented a compromise proposal to accept a German, a French and a British appointment to the office responsible for the management of the salt *gabelle* – the tax on salt, one of the most reliable sources of income for the Chinese state. The Russian representative 'promptly and vigorously objected' however:

> He said his government had the largest interest of all the powers in the Salt Administration because it had the largest percentage of the Boxer Indemnity [from 1901] . . . He said the British already had the Maritime Customs; the French the Post office and military adviser to the War Department; the Japanese and Germans also had appoint-ments . . . but the Russians had nothing.[61]

The Japanese agreed to support the American proposal, but only as long as others would offer 'moral support' for Japan getting some other undefined appointment further down the line. Now the Germans objected. Since the German in question was already in place at the salt *gabelle*, he should not be considered part of the German quota: Germany would require an additional position, too. And so on it went until May, when a deal was finally struck with

Yuan Shikai, despite the opposition of Sun Yat-Sen and the Kuomintang who, correctly, feared that the Provisional President was settling in to rule China very much as he wished to.

American banks did not participate in the loan. The newly elected President Wilson went on the record to state the end of so-called 'dollar diplomacy' and the beginnings of a new foreign policy based on principle. (At the time of America's withdrawal from negotiations the *North China Daily News* accused Wilson of abandoning China to her fate, to be carved up all the better because there was no American around the negotiating table of the great powers to stand up for her.[62])

It was not that the United States was uninterested in what happened in China. Far from it. American missionaries had long been present in the country. The prospect of China becoming a Christian country, however far-fetched, had always resonated widely in the United States. Before the opening of China's new National Assembly in April, public appeals had been made to American Christians to pray for the new Republic. More to the point, there was money to be made in China, and American businesses, having conquered Europe, might now conquer Asia, with its almost unimaginable potential for the consumption of beer, cars, sewing machines or whatever else American factories might churn out in the future. As American businessman B. Atwood Robinson described the situation as he saw it in 1913:

> Among the articles which are enjoying an increased demand, with every promise of a rapid and continued increase for many years, may be mentioned the following: clothing, boots and shoes, cotton and woolen goods, bicycles, clocks and watches, hats, caps, gloves, hosiery, haberdashery and underwear, phonographs, photographic and optical supplies, lamps, machinery, railway and electrical appliances, automobiles, hardware and building material . . . Now, therefore, is the time to secure a firm foothold and establish commercial relations that will gain for us the confidence and respect of the Chinese against the time of their great commercial activity.[63]

Whether driven by the desire to demonstrate principle, or to provide support to a fellow republic against the empires of the West, or to establish a friendly basis for a future commercial relationship

– or all three – in May the United States became the first of the major powers to formally recognise the Republic of China, though it was a few weeks behind Brazil, whose flags fluttered briefly and bizarrely in the streets of Peking that spring. Britain, Japan, Russia and France did not recognise the Chinese Republic until October.

By then, however, the dream of a Chinese parliamentary democracy had been conclusively smashed by the reality of Yuan Shikai's rule. Over the summer, a number of provinces declared their autonomy from Peking, and skirmishes broke out around the country's arsenals. In Shanghai, one of the cities thought to be most sympathetic to the Kuomintang cause, sporadic fighting developed between government troops associated with Yuan Shikai and Kuomintang forces associated with Sun Yat-Sen. Foreign soldiers prepared to defend the city. Foreign journalists wrote breathless accounts of their exploits running between the lines, referring to the events grandly as the 'second revolution'.[64] But the second revolution never really got off the ground in many places; everywhere, it was crushed. In Shanghai, it barely dampened the city's social life. Nor, looking back at the end of the year, did it greatly affect its trade. Cigarette imports were up despite an anti-smoking campaign, the British Foreign Office report on Shanghai's trade noted, adding sagely that 'the merchant, even in Shanghai, cannot expect as his birthright the safety of life and limb afforded by London, Paris or Berlin but that periodic danger is an incidence of life in China'.[65]

In September, forces loyal to Yuan Shikai entered Nanjing and, despite undertakings ahead of time, followed their conquest with 'wanton murder, looting, rape . . . the unchecked amusements of the victorious soldiery'.[66] The death of a small number of Japanese civilians and the destruction of Japanese property in the so-called 'Nanking incident' – to be repeated a hundred-thousandfold by Japanese forces in 1937 – led to demands for reprisals in Tokyo, and a flurry of concern in other capitals that Japan would intervene more directly in favour of the Kuomintang, some of whose leaders had been educated in Japan. But the Japanese government was restrained, even if the crowds in Tokyo were not.

The Kuomintang routed, in October Yuan Shikai forced the National Assembly, after several rounds of voting, to elect him to a five-year term as President, running until 1918. The Kuomintang party was banned the following month, and the National Assembly effectively shut down. Sun Yat-Sen fled to Japan. The message was clear: authority was to replace experimentation, order was to replace revolution.

The British Ambassador did not mince his words in his end of year report to London. 'Sun and his fellow champions of the Southern cause are completely discredited', he wrote, 'there appear at the present moment to be no individuals of sufficiently striking personality to challenge seriously the position of the President'.[67] Frank Goodnow, the American lawyer sent out to China with President Wilson's blessing to help write a new republican constitution, wrote home in early 1914, frustrated: 'Young China has lost control, the old ideas of Chinese absolutism are now in the ascendancy, the prospect of adopting a constitution on western lines has been set back for perhaps 25 years; indeed such a constitution may never be adopted'.[68]

But then, as the old China hands had always insisted, and as many businessmen in Shanghai agreed, what China needed was strong, not popular, government, and that was what it was getting. The *North China Daily News* declared the outlook to be brightening for China: 'a movement has been made in the direction of centralising and consolidating authority, and that public opinion grows calmer and more reassured'.[69] China has 'immense recuperative power', readers of the paper were promised. It would recover from political disturbance more rapidly than most.

And in Peking, at the heart of the ancient empire? An Australian, writing in the *Sydney Morning Herald* earlier in 1913, described his impressions of the city at the end of a day spent at the funeral of China's Dowager Empress Longyu, the woman who had signed the abdication of the Qing dynasty two years earlier:

An impressive pathos steals into one's consciousness as the hues of sunset soften into the twilight that quickly passes over this great old city in shadows of night that obscure palace and temple and pagoda and shrine. The memory of all that is passing gives a touch of melancholy to the deepening purple haze that lies above the horizon; and in some pessimistic moment one wonders whether China, with her great ancient past, now in her poverty and in her difficulties, and her struggles, will ever merge her early Eastern glory into both the splendours and the shadows of Western civilisation, and even Western Empires; but the melancholy passes with the night, and soon one feels the thrill of a new spring day; and the tinge of green is deeper upon the trees, the beauty of the early blossoms suffuses the grey old background with a delicate beauty, and one realises that this is the spring-time of the national life of this great old race. There are new buds that China's destiny, which is mightier than wealth or armaments, may one day develop into gorgeous blooms that shall make her the best civilised splendour of the Orient.[70]

The former Emperor Puyi, now seven years old, still lived in the Forbidden City, perhaps unaware of all that had happened over the course of his short life. But now, the Qing mantle of power had passed. Yuan Shikai, its inheritor, was driven around the city in an automobile. China, a once and future great power, had begun to wake from her centuries-long slumber.

TOKYO
Rising Sun

In the late morning of 10 November 1913, the Imperial Japanese Navy put on the most impressive display of naval power the Far East had seen since the return of the Japanese fleet from the Battle of Tsushima in 1905. On that occasion, the display had been a celebration of Japan's comprehensive defeat of the Russian Baltic fleet, an event which echoed around the world, upending the prevailing view that Europeans (and Americans) won wars – and everyone else lost them. On this occasion, eight years later, the display of Japanese naval might was intended to placate a nation burdened by high taxes for naval expenditure, to convince them of the case for further expansion planned in the years ahead – under Premier Yamamoto, himself a retired Admiral – and to showcase the super-dreadnought *Kongo*, one of the most powerful warships anywhere in the world, newly arrived from the shipyards of Vickers Ltd, Barrow-in-Furness, England.[1]

Having departed Tokyo's Shimbashi railway station on a special train at seven that morning, Emperor Taisho – accompanied by the premier, foreign minister and other ministers – arrived on the coast at Yokosuka to be greeted by a hundred officers of the navy, all the primary schoolchildren of the town, and bunting, brass bands and waving flags.[2] Later, from the deck of the battleship *Katori* the Emperor and his entourage watched the manoeuvres of twenty-eight large warships and twenty-seven destroyers. From various other points around Tokyo Bay, binoculars were trained on the sight of ships sailing abreast of each other at one point, then turning abruptly into a new formation, and finally sailing in a line past the *Katori*. No wonder some called Japan the England of the Far East, an island power which placed its navy at the heart of its national defence.

Premier-Admiral Yamamoto had reason to be proud of his

stewardship of the Japanese navy. Only the German fleet – and the much smaller Austro-Hungarian navy – had grown faster than that of the Japanese over the last decade or so, from 187,000 tonnes in 1900 – just over half that of the United States and under a fifth that of Britain – to 700,000 tonnes now – two-thirds that of the US Navy and more than a quarter of the Royal Navy (still the benchmark of global maritime power).[3] Indeed, it was the strength of the Japanese navy that made Japan an attractive ally for the British Empire, able to reassign Royal Navy vessels to competitive European waters as a consequence of the alliance in the Far East.

The weaponry of the *Kongo* – eight fourteen-inch guns, sixteen six-inch guns and eight twenty-one inch torpedo tubes – was well advertised in the local papers.[4] So was the fact that, although this first ship in its class had been built in England, a sister ship, the *Kirishima*, would be launched at the Mitsubishi dockyard in Nagasaki in December and a third ship, the *Haruna*, at the Kawasaki yard in Kobe shortly thereafter. New ships meant new jobs, not just new taxes – an important political consideration these days. The *Kongo* notwithstanding, nine out of every ten new ships in the Japanese navy were built at home – an extraordinary feat and a reminder that, while Japan was still essentially an agricultural country, the country was adopting the industrial technologies of the West in record time.[5] Japan's first major steel works had only opened in 1901.

The only disappointment of the morning was that an American-built Curtiss hydroplane flown by Sub-Lieutenant Fujise got lost in fog, passing once over the *Katori* at a height of a hundred metres, but not taking its full part in the day's events. The requisite impression of Japan's power and modernity was made nonetheless. 'Majestic and inspiring', wrote a reporter for the *Japan Times* sent to cover the event.[6] 'The grandeur of the spectacle', he continued, 'was even increased in brilliancy in the evening as the warships were placed under the glamor of powerful electric illumination', glinting off the dark waters of the bay of Tokyo. A country which had been all but sealed off from the rest of the world fifty years previously was now the Far East's leading naval power, and an empire in her own right. 'From Karafuto and the Kuriles in the north to Taiwan and Pescadores in the south, Korea and all Japan', ran a school song of the time, 'the nation our *taikun* [commander] rules, and the fifty million countrymen over whom waves the flag of the rising sun'.[7]

Japan was now a force to be reckoned with – a country that could not be ignored, whose interests were to be made to count in the world.

The best time to visit Tokyo, noted Chamberlain and Mason in the 1913 edition of their *Handbook for Travellers in Japan*, was in April. For a few weeks the most populous city in east Asia would be transformed into a 'garden of blossom', an explosion of cherry petals signalling the arrival of spring and covering the city's public parks – the Ueno park most famously – in a dream-like canopy of pink.[8] 'Not the Bois [de Boulogne, in Paris], Cascine [in Florence], or the Tiergarten [in Berlin] can vie with Uyéno on this blossom Sunday', American visitor Eliza Ruhamah Scidmore had written in the 1890s:

> Czars and Kaisers may well envy this Oriental ruler, whose subjects gather by the thousands, not to throw bombs and riot for bread or the division of property, but to fall in love with cherry-trees, and write poems in their praise . . . Tattered beggars gaze entranced at the fairy trees, and princes and ministers of state go to visit the famous groves.[9]

So much that was picturesque about Tokyo had faded over the last fifty years, as old Edo, the pleasure capital of the feudal *daimyo* lords and the *samurai* warrior class, became modern Tokyo, the political centre of a centralised, bureaucratic state. But cherry trees planted along the city's new avenues and its parks brought a flush of beauty to the city nonetheless. When Tokyo's mayor, Ozaki Yukio, visited the United States in 1912, his gift to the capital of the American Republic from the capital of the Japanese Empire was, naturally enough, several thousand cherry trees, following through on a suggestion Scidmore made some years earlier that Washington DC be beautified in the same way as Tokyo. Perhaps Americans would thereby come to see Japan not only as powerful, but as elegantly civilised and aesthetically refined. Perhaps as the cherry trees blossomed, so too would the relationship between the two rising powers of the Pacific.

Tokyo's recent history had been a roller coaster. Just before the

Meiji restoration in 1868 the population of Edo – its name under the shogunate – had stood at over one million, making it the largest city in the world, larger even than London, the great metropolis of the West. The Emperor lived at Kyoto, and the life of Edo revolved around *shogun* and *samurai*, *bakufu* and *daimyo*, tea house and temple, market and geisha parlour. For some time after the *shogun* had abdicated, the population of Edo had fallen. The *daimyo* lords and their retainers left the city, gutting its economic life. Edo became a shadow of its former self, buildings left abandoned. Even though it was renamed Tokyo ('capital of the East') in 1868, and even though the city was chosen to host the new national Yasakuni shrine – celebrating those fallen both fighting for the Meiji Restoration and against it – it was not clear what exact role Edo would play in the country's political life for several years after the restoration. The Emperor himself preferred to process around Japan rather than live permanently in Tokyo, where a new palace built in the grounds of the old *shogun*'s castle was only finally opened in the late 1880s. In 1872, 1876, 1878, 1880, 1881 and 1885 the Emperor Meiji was away on one of his so-called 'Great Circuits', showing himself to his people, and forging Japan into a nation united in worship of the office of the Emperor, rather than divided between the local loyalties of individual clans or regions. Tokyo wondered whether the Emperor's eye might not fall on some other city on one of these long trips. It took until 1890 for Tokyo's population to surpass that of Edo before the Meiji Restoration. In the 1860s it had been possible to buy land cheaply in downtown Tokyo at less than thirty yen an acre at one point – thirty years later such purchasers were rich men.[10]

By 1913 the city had far outstripped the *shogun*'s capital, reaching two million, and then hurtling past it. The population of Tokyo was now clearly ahead of Osaka and Kyoto – its traditional rivals within Japan – and was indeed larger than any other city in Asia, equivalent to St Petersburg, capital of the Russian Empire. 'Now is the age of cities', said Japanese intellectual Yokoi Tokiyoshi in 1907, 'for those who have learning and seek honor to those who want to make money or to sell their labor – everyone and his brother is setting out for the cities, as if gripped by a kind of fever'.[11] The proportion of the Japanese population living in cities doubled between 1888 and 1913 – though it still remained far below the level in England, Germany or the United States.[12] And as elsewhere in the world, the city in Japan became associated with modernity, a meeting place for disruptive influences, a symbol of commercialisation, a place where money was worshipped before beauty, and success was prized over honour. The village remained the mythological locus of the Japanese people, but it was in the city that the modern nation was being built. Tens of thousands of new immigrants to Tokyo every year, fresh from the Japanese countryside, found themselves thrust into another world – into the centre of the dynamic, modern country which Japan was becoming, faster than anyone had expected, least of all the Japanese themselves.

The changes in the city were remarkable. 'The *yashiki*, or Daimyo's mansions, have been pulled down to make room for public buildings, better adapted to modern needs', wrote Chamberlain and Mason, 'everywhere overhead is a network of telegraph, telephone and electric light wires'. The palanquin sedan chairs of old had disappeared, replaced by rickshaws and, increasingly, electric trams and petrol-driven automobiles. Where once there had been 'drunken samurai returning from orgies in brothels or taverns ready to use their terrible swords', noted the diplomat Joseph Henry Longford, the streets of nocturnal Tokyo were now as 'populous, noisy and safe as Piccadilly'.[13] Where once the city had been dark at night, it was now lit up. Where once there had only been narrow lanes of wooden single-storey houses, there were now, in some parts of the city at least, wide avenues of brick buildings which would not look out of place in the suburbs of Stockholm or Melbourne. (In Marunouchi, the redevelopment of an old parade ground by the Mitsubishi company was popularly known as *Iccho Rondon*, 'One Block London'.[14])

As recently as the 1880s there had been no foreign hotels in Tokyo, and most foreigners lodged in Yokohama. Visitors to the capital city would be entertained in the specially built Rokumeikan (literally, 'Deer Cry Pavilion') in a style that the Japanese considered the height of Western sophistication, but which foreigners found a gaudy, second-rate imitation of the West. (Pierre Loti, dancing to Johann Strauss's waltz *The Blue Danube* with the fifteen-year-old daughter of an army officer, described the place as rather like a 'casino in some seaside resort'.[15]) By 1913 the Rokumeikan was no longer needed as an official house of entertainment, and had instead been converted into a private club for the Japanese aristocracy. Some foreigners lived permanently in Tokyo. Visitors would be put up at the Imperial Hotel, a grand hotel much like any other in a major world metropolis. A new railway station was under construction in Marunouchi, modelled on Amsterdam Centraal station in the Netherlands.[16] Tokyo even had its own twelve-storey skyscraper, the Ryounkaku – or 'Cloud Surpassing Pavilion' – in the Asakusa district of the city, the whole thing lit up at night like a Christmas tree, with Japan's first elevator taking visitors as far as the eighth floor. 'To compare Tokio of the present day with Yedo as it was', Longford concluded, 'would be like comparing London of the days of Charles II with London as we now daily see it'.[17] It was to compare two different eras, two different worlds, he wrote.

Central Tokyo's Westernising facelift, impressive though it was, was less than what some reformers had initially wanted. Should not the European or American visitor be as impressed by Tokyo as the men on Iwakura Tomomi's tour of the world had been by what they saw in Paris, London or Berlin in the 1870s? Grand plans were drawn up to reshape the city as a whole into a Western metropolis, inspired above all by the transformation of Paris under Baron Haussmann. In the 1880s Foreign Minister Inoue Kaoru pushed a plan by German architects Wilhelm Böckman and Hermann Ende to turn Tokyo into a grand city of ceremonial avenues.[18] Tokyo was an imperial city – run essentially as an adjunct of the central state – should it not now be rebuilt to reflect the growing power and glory of the empire?

But however splendid such plans looked on the drawing board, they faced formidable obstacles on the ground. Unlike some other growing cities of the late nineteenth century, Tokyo already covered a large area. Edo had, after all, been the biggest city in the world. As a consequence, any new development required pulling down existing buildings – perhaps in the face of the opposition of owners and residents. And then there was the small issue of finance. Already weighed down by the costs of railway construction and military development, the government could not afford to redevelop the city at its own expense, in one dramatic all-encompassing move. In the event, therefore, changes to the fabric of the city occurred more opportunistically, district by district. Fire, flood and earthquake (as in 1894) were often the handmaidens of redevelopment, but these could only be relied upon to destroy parts of the city at irregular

Tokyo, a hybrid Asian and Western metropolis, 1913.

intervals. When they did, the government would have to move fast, decisively, either ignoring or co-opting local interests.

Such was the history of the Ginza district. In February 1872 a fire destroyed 3,000 buildings in the area. Within six days of the fire being put out, senior officials had presented their plans for the area's reconstruction, with wider roads, pavements and brick buildings.[19] But it was not until 1888 that an ordinance covering the whole city was enacted – providing for the widening of 315 streets, new bridges, public parks, and new crematoria and cemeteries for the city's dead – and this was itself eventually scaled back due to financial constraints at the beginning of the twentieth century.[20] Priorities shifted over time. In the 1890s, attention was focused on getting clean water into the city, identified as the best means of reducing outbreaks of cholera. After 1900, emphasis shifted to building tram lines, a sore point with Tokyo's 46,000 rickshaw drivers, who saw the new vehicles undercutting their livelihood.[21] The following decade, a hundred miles of electric trams having now established the sprawling modern geography of the city, the time had finally come to address sewerage of the city's residential areas, some of which still got by with bucket, horse and cart.

As a consequence of uneven developments, driven as much by opportunity and expediency as any grand plan, by 1913 the so-called High City, the *Yamanote*, which occupied the area north and west of the imperial palace, came to look more and more like a hybrid Japanese-American-European city. It was here that the ministries were located in the new government quarter near Hibiya Park. It was here that the richer citizens of the city now lived, in grand houses with gates and porches in the Japanese style. It was here that most of the amenities for foreign visitors were concentrated. From Shimbashi station, the *Handbook for Travellers in Japan* noted, one could reach the Imperial Hotel in five minutes by rickshaw, the Tokyo Club and American Embassy in ten minutes, and the British Embassy in eighteen. The Mitsukoshi department store provided a Japanese variation on a European and American theme. The Home Ministry building looked every bit as imposing, and as forbidding, as the justice ministry in any European capital – designed to impress citizens and foreigners alike with the weighty power of the state.

But not all of Tokyo had been transformed in quite this way. And even in areas which had an outward European or American appearance, the interior reality could be different. The home was relatively untouched, wrote Jukichi Inouye in his account of *Home Life in Tokyo* in 1910. 'Globe-trotters who advise their friends to visit this country with as little delay as possible for fear that in a few years Old Japan would cease to be, do not reckon with our domestic life', he wrote, explaining that 'woman is in Japan as elsewhere the greatest conservative element of national life and within her sphere of influence tradition reigns as supreme as ever'.[22] These would be places the casual European or American visitor would be unlikely to see, allowed to imagine that the inner and outer life of the city were the same. And while the newer parts of Tokyo were indeed radically different from what had gone before, the old low-rise Edo – and its inhabitants, the *Edokko* – was still embedded within the new Tokyo, a little off the beaten track perhaps, but never far.

South and east of the imperial palace lay Shitamachi, the Low City, historically the poorer part of the city, a large, mixed and ill-defined area. Although regularly ravaged by floods and by fires, most recently by the great flood of 1910 and a fire in 1911, large parts of the area had nevertheless miraculously survived. In the inner quarters of the Low City the memory of old Edo lived on in a maze of lanes and streets dotted with shrines and temples where *Edokkos* had worshipped since the foundation of the city 300 years previously. It was in the Low City that *kabuki* theatre was born. This was where the art of wood-block printing had been refined. This was where the traditional festivals of Edo would still be celebrated, and where women would still wear Japanese-style clothing rather than the modern European equivalent. Here, shops were open to the street and there were no pavements. However grand the central business and government districts of the city many felt that the soul of Tokyo was still here, amongst these wooden houses, less sturdily built than the brick buildings of Ginza perhaps but more traditional, more Japanese.

The artisans and merchants of Tokyo still lived in the inner parts of the Low City, alongside the odd sentimental aristocrat who had not bothered to move. A newer class, born from Japan's economic transformation, lived in the outlying parts, particularly to the east: Tokyo's 80,000 factory workers.[23] Although Yokohama was far more industrialised, with its easy access to the sea and open flat land available for building factories, Tokyo had not been immune to the rise of industry over the last few decades. In Honjo, on the far side of the Sumida river, lay the Sapporo brewery and a string of much smaller factories involved in everything from electroplating to the manufacture of rubber tyres. Conditions here were poor, wages low and job tenure was brief. It was not until 1911 that Japan had passed its first law properly regulating such places of work. In 1913, a hundred girls who lived and worked at the Fuji Gas Spinning Company came down with what looked like typhus.[24] In the same year, the novelist Shusei Tokuda had a novel published, set in Honjo, describing the life of a former prostitute and bearing the inimitable title *Festering*. The everyday realities of life in the more industrial areas of the Low City of Tokyo worried the government. Concerned at the political potential of urban discontent, they occasionally sought to mobilise nationalism as a handy means of turning the populace away from outright criticism of the state. But these were areas that foreigners would be unlikely to see, well off their itineraries of temples, shrines and tea houses.

More familiar, at least by reputation, would be Yoshiwara, the old courtesan district of the Low City, where prostitution had tradition-ally been licensed, shocking and fascinating Western sensibilities,

particularly those of American Christian missionaries. Though Edo
had passed into history, Yoshiwara, perhaps the area of Tokyo most
closely associated with the drama and licence of the old Edo, had
survived. It had lost some of its poetry over the years, some said.
'The courtesan has degenerated into a tasteless chalk drawing',
Japanese writer Osanai Kaoru complained, 'the stylish clientele has
given way to workmen's jackets and flat-top haircuts and rubber
boots, and mendicant musicians'.[25] The brothels were now subject
to medical inspections and to government regulation, taking away
something of Yoshiwara's old style, and some of its panache. More
to the point, complained Osanai, it had also lost its attraction as a
place in which to set plays:

> One had no trouble seeing why playwrights of Edo so often set their
> plays in Yoshiwara . . . The daimyo with his millions, the braves of
> whom everyone was talking, robbers in the grand style who aimed
> at aristocratic houses, all of them gathered in Yoshiwara. When an
> accidental meeting was required, therefore, the Yoshiwara was the
> obvious place to have it occur. No playwright would be silly enough
> to put the Yoshiwara of our day to such use. A chance encounter
> under the lights of the beer hall at the main gate would most likely
> involve a person with a north-country accent and a home-made cap,
> and his uncle, in the city with a petition to the Ministry of Commerce
> and Agriculture.

But then perhaps that was a kind of modernisation too, and a
suggestion of the future: a Tokyo less enchanted than in the days
of Edo, but a city more in keeping with its times, a city not of bards
and poets but of salarymen and newspapers, a city not of whispered
sweet nothings but of slogans and headlines, stock reports and naval
displays.

'Be a success!', ran a Meiji-era slogan – and Japan surely was, by
any modern measure, a success as a nation-state, demonstrated by
the naval display at Yokosuka, confirmed by the bustling port of
Yokohama and by the goods available in shop windows of the Ginza.
Still, the mood of the country in 1913 was not one of easy pride and

Crown Prince Taisho. In 1912, he succeeded his father as Emperor of Japan.
Over the previous half-century Japan had emerged onto the world stage,
adopted Western technologies, and become a Great Power.

self-satisfaction, able to sit back and enjoy the fruits of its labour.
Japan had become modern, it had become powerful, it had even
become rich – but this did not always seem to translate into respect
abroad, nor stability at home, nor even into comfortable material
prosperity. The Japanese mood in 1913 was strident: proud of the
nation's achievements, but sensitive as to its proper placement
amongst the nations of the world, alive to any suggestions of inad-
equacy, its old political hierarchies questioned more vigorously than
before.

Some might have put it down to the passing of an emperor.
Emperor Meiji, guardian of Japan for the dramatic four decades of
Japan's rise, had died only the previous year, in July 1912, plunging
the country into mourning. The immediate impacts of his death in
Tokyo were substantial enough, but temporary: shops closed their
shutters, theatres cancelled productions, economic activity drew to
a respectful halt. More significant was the psychological shock. In

an era of dramatic change since 1868, Emperor Meiji had been a constant focus for national adulation, and a constant and reassuring presence in his country's life. The emperor had not only given his name to an era – Meiji meaning 'enlightened rule' – he had embodied it. Now he was gone. His successor Emperor Taisho inspired little of the blind faith that his father had. At a time when the country needed reassurance about Japan's direction, a symbol around which the nation could unite, the young Taisho was better known for drinking and womanising than for governing. He might be surrounded with familiar faces and names – Prince Katsura, the premier at the beginning of 1913, amongst them – but this seemed to confirm the weakness of the Emperor himself and the reassertion of oligarchical power, rather than instilling confidence in the dynamism and intentions of the regime. The year 1913 was the first of the new Taisho era. But what would the era bring?

The Meiji narrative – of Westernisation and modernisation driven forward by an enlightened government – had run its course. The slogans of the past could not be endlessly recycled. The old loyalties could not be relied on forever. Having built a modern nation, Japan would now need to live with its creation. At the beginning of 1913 the country found itself in a deep crisis revolving around the key question of the country's political development: should Japan continue to be governed by a political oligarchy cloaked in the constitutionalism of 1889 – with premiers such as Katsura effectively chosen by the *genro*, Japan's unelected elder statesmen – or should Japan's government be a true popular democracy, however fractious that might be, with members of the Diet calling the shots?

For most of the Meiji period premiers, nominally appointed by the Emperor, had emerged from the deliberations of the *genro* oligarchs, often alternating with one another when things got difficult. Political courtesy dictated that a premier should never be embarrassed by abject failure but rather given a face-saving means of withdrawing from office – most probably to return a few years later. Such premiers did not bother with political parties, even after the establishment of the Diet under the constitution of 1889, indeed political parties were looked down upon by the *genro* oligarchs. They emerged nonetheless. Indeed, because the Diet held the nation's purse strings, party support had increasingly become a political requirement for any effective ministry, whatever the *genro* might have wanted. With the accession of the Emperor Taisho in 1912 the old structures of politics, as much defined by cultural practice as by constitutional niceties, were up for grabs. In early 1913 a simmering conflict between the new party politics and the old oligarchy came to a head.

The proximate cause of the crisis was the resignation of the army minister over the government's refusal to push for two new divisions for the army. Under Japanese law, both army and navy ministers were required to be serving officers, giving both forces key influence at the centre of government. Now, with no officer willing to become army minister, the cabinet as a whole was forced to resign. Long-time oligarch Prince Katsura – a military commander in the Sino-Japanese war and premier during the Russo-Japanese war, now serving at court – returned a third time as premier, persuading the Emperor to issue the necessary order for his transfer from court, and to prorogue parliament while he built a support base. This, his detractors claimed, was to bring the Emperor more directly into politics and to treat parliament with high-handed disrespect. 'They pay lip service to loyalty and patriotism as if it were their monopoly', former Tokyo mayor Yukio Ozaki told the Diet, criticising Katsura and his allies, 'but just look at how they behave':

> They hide behind the throne, lying in wait to ambush their political foes. They have made the throne their breastplate, and the rescript [imperial orders] their bullets to destroy their enemy![26]

Crowds gathered to protest Katsura's political manoeuvrings, and against what they saw as the oligarchs' arrogant manipulation of Japanese politics. Eventually, the crowd's anger spilled over into violence. On a single day in February 1913, in a string of events across the city, the offices of the government-supporting *Miyako Shimbun* newspaper were attacked and burned, two men were crushed underfoot by mounted police protecting the offices of *Japan Times*, a transportation worker was shot dead from an office of the besieged *Kokubim Shimbun* and another wounded in the shoulder. The drawn swords of the police 'glittered terribly in the dark'.[27] Police stations were attacked, fire trucks pelted with stones and trams were stopped in their tracks. Troops were put on alert. Katsura was forced to resign. Admiral Yamamoto, a key player in Katsura's downfall, replaced him – not a full step towards a premier chosen by parliament perhaps, but a powerful demonstration that the age of the oligarchs was drawing to a close. Was this, then, to be the new pattern of Taisho politics – a politics of crisis and protest?

In some respects, life in Japan seemed not to be getting easier, but more difficult. 'One frequently hears it said that business in Japan is played out', wrote a British diplomat in the annual report back to London, 'that the "good old days" when it was possible in a few years to make enough money on which to retire, have gone, never to return'.[28] As a result of the glorious but expensive Russo-Japanese War – from which Japan won no indemnity under the terms of the controversial American-backed peace – Japan had run up substantial debts, a large part of which were owed to foreigners. Besides increasing military expenditures, which allowed for a massive expansion of the Imperial Japanese Navy in particular, financial retrenchment was the order of the day. Emperor Meiji had spent his last ten years urging frugality upon his people. Taxes had risen three-fold since 1897.[29]

Worse, while Japan had spent decades scrimping and saving and struggling her way towards joining the elite circle of Western nations, it increasingly seemed that that club was closing ranks against her. Many Japanese reasonably felt that they deserved the world's respect for what they had achieved as a nation. Yet abroad too often they found that they were belittled, as in the light comic operettas of Gilbert and Sullivan, or else presented as a mortal threat to the very ideals of Western civilisation from which Japan had sought to learn. Apparently a weak Japan was laughable; but a strong Japan was immediately transformed into the prime exhibit for the existence of a 'Yellow Peril'. Might Japan be forever stuck in a kind of no man's land between East and West, not allowed to assimilate into the international order of the Western nations as an equal, forever grouped with the countries of the East amongst which she felt herself superior, and respected fully by neither group?

In the 1880s the question of whether Japan should be a Western or Eastern nation had only one answer. The path of Japanese independence was clearly marked. It led west. 'Our basic assumptions', Fukuzawa Yukichi wrote in the 1880s, 'could be summarized in two words: "Good-bye Asia"':

It is better for us to leave the ranks of Asian nations and cast our lot with civilized nations of the West. As for the way of dealing with China and Korea, no special treatment is necessary just because they happen to be our neighbors. We simply follow the manner of Westerners in knowing how to treat them. Any person who cherishes a bad friend cannot escape his bad notoriety. We simply erase from our minds our bad friends in Asia.[30]

By the turn of the twentieth century doubts had crept in to this view of the world. 'Asia is one', argued prominent Japanese intellectual Okakura Kakuzo dramatically in *The Ideals of the East*.[31] In regular correspondence with the circle of Bengali intellectuals around Rabindranath Tagore – the two had met in Calcutta in 1902 – Okakura became a practitioner of intra-Asian cultural exchange as well as its advocate.[32] He argued for Asia's cultural distinctness from the West, and the necessity for political unity. 'The Himalayas divide', he wrote grandly, 'but not even the snowy barriers can interrupt for one moment that broad expanse of love for the Ultimate and the Universal, which is the thought-inheritance of every Asiatic race'. It was this sense of the universal which distinguished Asians from 'those maritime peoples of the Mediterranean and the Baltic, who love to dwell on the particular, and to search out the means, not the end, of life' – peoples whom Okakura Tenshin was able to observe at close quarters in his day job as curator of the Asian collection at the Boston Museum of Fine Art. Asian traditions and ideals were integral to Japan's own identity, Okakura suggested, and were something to celebrate, not denigrate – or replace.

After the Russo-Japanese conflict in particular, Tokyo became a metropolis for political pan-Asianism: Vietnamese nationalists and Chinese republicans rubbed shoulders with Japanese students, reminding each other that the West had no monopoly on civilisation, nor on modernity, nor on rights of political control. But how did Japan fit in? After all, on the one hand Japan was now a colonial power in east Asia, just like the Western powers, enjoying concessions in China just like they did and defending her acquired rights every bit as vigorously as the German or the Russian Empires, perhaps more so. On the other, Japan occasionally chose to dress up colonisation in the language of Asian emancipation, or the language of pan-Asian development. 'It is to be regretted that some see in our progressive rule in Formosa a revelation of inherent racial power that gives rise to the cry of "Yellow Peril"', Goto Shinpei, the Japanese governor of Taiwan, wrote in an article in the otherwise anti-colonial *Africa Times and Orient Review*, 'that we have any reason to cry "White Peril" never, of course, occurs to them'.[33] Meanwhile, British diplomats in Japan accepted that Koreans were 'better governed, materially better off in almost every way' under Japanese rule, than they had been under the Korean Empire – still, 'one can discern at times a tendency to exploit rather than to control'. A case of the pot calling the kettle black, certainly – but one which showed the inherent ambivalences of Japanese colonisation in Asia.[34]

In 1913, two events in particular brought home Japan's delicate place in the ordering of the world. The first came in April, when the Californian legislature introduced a law restricting Japanese immigrants from owning land in the state. For many Japanese this was a slap in the face. The numbers of Japanese in the United States likely to be affected by the law were themselves relatively few. As it was, a quiet 'gentlemen's agreement' had been made a few years back to limit Japanese immigration into the United States; Japanese already living there had long been excluded from holding American citizenship. But, as President Wilson himself noted, the issue now was not so much the details of the California legislation itself – which he insisted that as President of a federal state he had no power to change – as what the Japanese thought it said about wider American attitudes, confirming a 'feeling on our part that they [Japanese] are not on the same plane with us [Americans]'.[35] The California land law was, in Japanese eyes, a public rebuke – and a racist one, at that. 'It touches a man's pride', Wilson noted – offering an explanation for Japanese anger, but not a solution to it.

Japan's government and society swept into action to oppose the proposed Californian legislation. A formal diplomatic protest was lodged by the Japanese Ambassador in Washington. Japanese emissaries were sent to California to plead Tokyo's case directly. The Tokyo, Kobe, Osaka, Yokohama and Kyoto chambers of commerce sent stiffly worded telegrams to their American counterparts urging them to lobby the California legislature on their behalf, so as to prevent negative consequences for trade. Others appealed to international law or to American traditions of justice and equality – to no avail. Some, including former Mayor of Tokyo Yukio Ozaki, threatened direct retaliation – refusing to take part in the planned Panama–Pacific exhibition of 1915, for example, or boycotting Californian ports in favour of Seattle.[36] In Washington, the Department of the Navy reported to the President on the likelihood of war.

But the matter was not easily settled. Indeed, its ramifications spread. Within a matter of months, the Californian land law dispute rapidly had become the subject of international attention and comment. Andrew Fisher, a former Labor Prime Minister of Australia, voiced his support for California on a visit to New York: Australia no more wanted to be overrun by Asians than did the Pacific coast of the United States, he noted.[37] Japan's proper place in the world was debated on the pages of the London *Times* and other foreign newspapers, vividly exposing the feelings of many Westerners that the Japanese were not now and perhaps never would be their true equals, and subjecting the Japanese to arrogant judgements about their aptitude for assimilation into 'civilised' society. In turn, leading Japanese journalist Tokutomi Soho launched a campaign against *Hoku Batsu*, or white snobbery, in the pages of his newspaper.[38] In a much-reported speech in Kyoto Dr Sanjiro Ichimura of the Imperial University in Tokyo listed the following characteristics of whites:

> 1. White men consider that they alone are human beings, and that all coloured people are on a lower scale of creation. 2. The whites are extremely selfish. They insist on their own interests to the utmost, but persist in unreasonable treatment of those whom they regard as their inferiors. 3. White men are full of racial pride and conceit. When they gain an inch they grasp a mile. To make a concession to them is to lay up a store of humiliation. 4. White men run to extremes. They excel the Japanese both in greatness and in vileness. 5. White men worship money as omnipotent, and believe that it is the key to all things.[39]

Elder statesman Count Okuma warned that the racial prejudice behind the Californian legislation meant that 'even if the present agitation is successfully suppressed troubles of a similar nature will continue to crop up'.[40] But was Japan therefore compelled to indefinitely accept the prejudices of the West, bearing them as best she could? Was Japan forever to be slighted?

Nor was this the end of it. For in some ways the worst thing about the California land law was not that it was discriminatory against Japanese, but that it *failed* to discriminate between Japanese and other Asians. 'Classifying the Japanese with the Mongolians [the Chinese] . . . when the former are attempting to become a great nation, naturally hurts their feelings', Professor Yokoyama of Johns Hopkins University explained to the *Los Angeles Times*.[41] William Elliot Griffis, an American academic who taught at the Imperial University and who had written a number of noted books on modern Japan, declared it 'absurd' for Californian law to place the Japanese alongside the 'Mongolians', a group for which there was a quite proper 'instinctive cuticular repulsion'.[42] The Japanese were racially distinct from the Chinese, he noted: how else could one explain Japan's conspicuous success?

Japan's fragile sense of her place in the ordering of the world was revealed in a different way in China later in the year when, in the midst of that country's brief so-called Second Revolution, Japanese interests were looted in Nanjing, and several Japanese subjects killed. Though the number of Japanese deaths was relatively small – just three died in the first instance – the Japanese flag had been burned, the empire insulted and the Japanese community put into a state of panic. Back home, public opinion was reported to be 'sizzling with indignation'.[43] Angry demonstrations followed. The Chinese are worse than the 'unspeakable Turk', it was said in the *Japan Times*, helpfully adopting a long-standing European prejudice and applying it to the East Asian context. Chinese government troops were presented as 'bandits'. 'A pack of wolves would not work so much havoc', wrote one journalist, 'a band of tigers would have caused less panic'.[44] This time, Count Okuma appeared to be in a less conciliatory mood. 'All this outrage is the outcome of the contempt in which the Chinese government holds the diplomacy of Japan', he told a reporter, 'we should first occupy strategic points in China, and then carry on negotiations with the Chinese government'. The Japanese army was said to be supportive, seeing an opportunity to prove the worth of its men and kit, and to reassert its position as the more important of Japan's armed services.

As the situation got worse in Nanking – the behaviour of Chinese soldiers now qualified as an 'inexcusable crime in this enlightened age', proof of Chinese barbarity – the anger of some Japanese turned them against their own government.[45] Dr Moritaro Abe, director of political affairs at the foreign office, who had been reported as having urged that 'we must not return violence for violence' in the Nanjing case, was ambushed outside his home at 31 Reinanzaka-cho.[46] According to the official statement from the foreign office, 'two men appeared . . . one man held him from the back, while the other stabbed him with a dagger in the abdomen and thigh, and ran away'.

The following Sunday a meeting of 20,000 took place in Hibiya Park, a former parade ground which in recent years had become a popular site for pro and anti-government demonstrations. It was here that crowds had met in 1905 to protest what nationalists saw as the unacceptable peace terms of the Russo-Japanese War, a protest which had become a riot, injuring hundreds and killing several. Now, in 1913, speeches denouncing the foreign office were made again and 50,000 copies of a resolution distributed demanding immediate Japanese military intervention in China. 'Among the more attractive figures on the rostrum was a young woman dressed like a student', the *Japan Times* reported. 'Her appearance was hailed with such encouraging remarks as "Brave girl!" "Give us stuff and fire!" and "A New Woman!"', the *Times* continued:

> Raising her voice above the hum of the multitude she concluded her speech with the following patriotic fulmination: 'The rescue and redress of our fellow-countrymen in China is the duty that we women of the age of Taisho owe to the nation'[47]

The foreign office was then besieged by a crowd seeking to 'interview' the foreign minister. Only a heavy police presence and the iron gates of the ministry prevented it from being stormed. A gathering a few days later at the Meiji Theatre threatened to keep on holding popular meetings until government policy was changed – or the government itself overthrown.[48]

In Autumn 1913, the trees in Ueno Park now bare, Prince Katsura, master of the old order, died. 'Ozaki killed me' were said to have been Katsura's last words, in reference to the denunciation he had received in the Diet earlier that year.[49] 'Prince Katsura was one of the most brilliant and successful soldier statesmen the country has ever produced', the *Japan Times* opined.[50] A symbol of the heroic era of Japanese nation-building was gone. In Britain, Katsura's death was met politely, though there could be little hiding that the man had long been thought to be pro-German. In America, country of science, there featured a letter to the *New York Times* by American neurologist and anatomist Edward Charles Spitzka discussing the reported weight of Prince Katsura's brain and what this said about Japanese race. At 1,600 grams, Sptizka noted, Katsura's brain weight placed him sixteenth in a list of 108 eminent men whose brains had been measured at their death.[51] This augured well for Japan's future, Spitzka wrote:

> . . . the brain weight of the Japanese compares favorably with that of Europeans of similar stature, and it may be shown to be superior in this respect to other races of the same general stature. These facts are not of a little significance in relation to the learning, industry and aptitudes of this progressive rae.

Katsura's death represented the passing of a generation, and the passing of certainties associated with it. Within the span of his life, from 1848 to 1913, Japan had become a country on the threshold of modernity, with all the ambivalences that that entailed. Born into a semi-feudal regime, Katsura died in a nation-state. When he was born, Japan feared for its very existence as an independent political entity in an age of empires. By the time he died the sun had risen on a new era in Japan's history, as an imperial great power itself – albeit one which looked around itself warily, and was looked at suspiciously by others. To what ends would Japanese power be directed? Would Japan prove a factor of stability and Western order – or would it be an expansionist force? Was Japan's rise merely the presage of a still grander awakening – of Asia itself?

LONDON
Beyond the Horizon

'What will be the standing of the British Empire in AD 2013?', asked the *Evening Standard* of its London readers in 1913.[1] Certainly, it answered, it would not be an empire held together by force; rather it would be most probably a collection of 'allied autonomous states under a common head'. The *Standard* speculated that Canada would have a population of 100,000,000 and the federal capital of the Anglo-Saxon Federation would be along the Canadian border with the United States. India might be a self-governing entity by 2013 – but probably not. Britain itself might have become an agricultural country again, its home population having peaked in 1950:

> Of one thing we may be certain. Even if the centre of the Empire shifts across the Atlantic, the love and veneration of the entire race for its original home must preserve it inviolate from alien hands, and its monuments and antiquities will form the objective of thousands of overseas pilgrims, who will look with pride upon the handiwork of their forefathers, to whom they owe their lands their liberties, and their proud position among the peoples of the earth!

It was an intriguing image of a future Britain – a kind of Britannic theme park, or imperial shrine – and a strange vision of a twenty-first century British Empire: still the dominant force in global politics, but its structures transformed, even its capital city moved.

London in 1913 was still in its midday pomp. But the setting of the sun was not as inconceivable as it once had been. Empire could no longer be taken as a given, a God-given right extended to the British, the natural inheritors of the earth. For a hundred years the empire had expanded, almost without forethought, and with remark-ably little effort. Now, it was widely recognised that the empire was entering a new and potentially much more difficult phase.[2] Although it seemed fantastical to imagine a world without the British Empire, it was not impossible. 'Will the Empire which is celebrating one centenary of Trafalgar survive for the next?' wrote James Louis Garvin, editor of the pro-empire *Outlook* magazine, in 1905. 'It is a searching question', he continued, 'and, despite the narcotic optimism which is the fashion of the hour, national instinct recognises that the answer is no foregone affirmative'.[3]

For many, the alarm bells had begun to ring during the Boer War, more than a decade previously. The war was, in plain military terms, an embarrassment. For years, a relatively small population of Boer settlers had pinned down the might of the British Army in a distant, drawn-out conflict leading to tens of thousands of casualties and costing a small fortune to win. And if dealing with a bunch of Dutch farmers in the open *veldt* of South Africa proved a strain on the empire militarily, how on earth would Britain cope with the defence of its other scattered realms, should the time come? While international mobility enhanced links between different parts of the empire, it also made the British Empire, spread out over so much of the world, uniquely vulnerable: could Britain truly be expected to fight and win a war in Asia, the Middle East and Europe at the same time? It was for this reason that in 1902 Britain entered an alliance with Japan – unthinkable a decade previously – allowing Britain to focus its naval forces in Europe and perhaps start a long roll-back of its global position. It was in the same year, at the Colonial Conference held on the occasion of the coronation of King Edward VII, that Colonial Secretary Joseph Chamberlain uttered words forever associated with the challenges of Britain's comparative decline, and the risks of her imperial overstretch: 'The Weary Titan staggers under the too vast orb of its fate'.[4] A titan still, but one worn down by the consequences of success.

But it was not just the cost of the Boer War in blood and treasure which shocked public opinion back home in Britain, convincing some that Britain's efforts at imperial reform needed to be redoubled, and convincing others that the old imperial game was on its way to being up. There was also the question of the *way* in which the war was fought. The policy of internment of Boer families, for example, was seen as unequal to the prize of placing all South Africa under British rule, and unworthy of Britain's world-historical mission to bring peace, civilisation and British institutions alongside British control. Still more fundamentally, there was the question of *why* the war was fought. In 1902, the economist John A. Hobson argued in his study of empire that it was finance which was the motive force behind imperialism these days, not a quest to spread civilisation, nor a moral crusade: 'Finance is . . . the governor of the imperial engine, directing the energy and determining the work'.[5] Imperialism was not a process of equal benefit to colonised and coloniser, it was not a noble undertaking, but rather a 'depraved choice of national life, imposed by self-seeking interests which appeal to the lusts of quantitative acquisitiveness and of forceful domination surviving in a nation from early centuries of animal struggle for existence'. Most Britons in 1913 saw the empire as a moral creation – or else as a self-justifying proof of British superiority – rather than analysing it in the same terms as Hobson. Still, if the Boer War was what imperialism had come to in the modern age, there were many in Britain who wanted none of it.

To those who saw the empire as essential to British greatness, some kind of imperial renovation was now urgently required. But they disagreed on how this was to be brought about. For some of them – including members of the so-called 'Round Table', a self-appointed elite of colonial administrators which started life as the 'Kindergarten' of imperial civil servant Lord Milner – formal and wide-ranging reform of the empire's internal structures was key. This might entail the creation of some kind of imperial federation, perhaps even an imperial parliament where strategic imperial issues would be discussed at length by imperial representatives, rather than in the Westminster Parliament where domestic British issues inevitably dominated debate, attention and time.[6]

Other imperialists were sceptical of the idea. As Briton Richard Jebb discovered on a tour of empire at the turn of the century:

The assumption which underlines such phrases as the 'Expansion of England' or 'Greater Britain' and suggests the familiar principle of federation as the logical form of closer union is not justified by the tendency either of instinctive sentiment or of actual developments in Canada and Australia. So far as generalization is possible, it may be said that there is not, in fact, any growing consciousness of a

common nationality, but exactly the reverse. In other words, the basis
of imperial federation, instead of expanding and solidifying, is melting
away.[7]

Manifestations of Britannic identity aside, the political economy of
any potential imperial federation was perhaps being eroded by the
internationalism of trade and finance, substituting traditional
economic ties to the mother country with a much wider set of
commercial relationships. Some British politicians, foremost amongst
them Joseph Chamberlain, sought to answer this by proposing tariff
reform, backtracking on Britain's traditional support for free trade
and instead envisaging an imperial trading block.[8]

As it was, the greatest imperial innovations up to 1913 had been
the creation of the self-governing Dominions – Canada, the
Commonwealth of Australia, New Zealand and, from 1910, the
Union of South Africa. The Dominions looked to London for
guidance on some policy issues, but were not controlled by it.
Besides the occasional get-togethers of the colonial premiers –
most recently in London, in 1907 and again in 1911 – imperial
government with regard to the Dominions boiled down to a
constant negotiation between the empire's unequal parts, with
London sometimes cajoling, sometimes playing the role of arbi-
trator, and only very rarely actually dictating outcomes, something
she was in most cases constitutionally unable to do. The debate
over imperial defence in Canada in 1913 or the public criticism
of South Africa's Indian policy by the British Viceroy in India
the same year were examples of the way in which the empire
often functioned – as a loose network of political entities with
different interests and aspirations, rather than as a vertically
managed hierarchy. In a 1913 book entitled *The Britannic Question*,
Richard Jebb provided four diagrams of possible structures for
the British Empire, ranging from 'Colonial Dependence' (which
was now of the past), to 'Britannic Alliance' (Jebb's preferred
option, essentially a free alliance of self-governing 'Britannic'
states), and two versions of 'Imperial Federation' (one without
racial equality, and one with racial equality – the latter implying
Indian equality with Australia, Canada and the others).[9] It was
not clear which path would ultimately be chosen – perhaps a
combination, perhaps none.

Some outsiders anticipated that Britain would remain a great imperial power for the foreseeable future. 'It is possible that the day will come when the costs of empire will surpass the resources of the nation', wrote the French historian Elie Halévy.[10] But in Halévy's mind, these were problems shared by other empires. Reform could put off Britain's day of reckoning for a long while yet:

> Why should imperialism present more difficulties or dangers [for the British] than it does for the North Americans, or for the Russians, or for the Japanese, if the Japanese indeed succeed in establishing an Empire of their own? The same causes, scientific and technical, which have driven industrial and commercial concentration encourage military and political concentration: the twentieth century will be the century of empires.

Others presented more dire, but not entirely unreasonable, scenarios. In 1905 a pamphlet entitled the *Decline and the Fall of the British Empire*, purporting to be published in Tokyo a hundred years in the future, in 2005, imagined a world where India was now ruled by Russia, South Africa by Germany, where Egypt had gained her independence, where Canada had joined the United States and Australia was now a Japanese protectorate. In this pamphlet, supposedly published for the edification of Japanese imperial strategists, the Britain of the future provided a case study of an empire in decline, and perhaps finally extinguished:

> As Babylon and Assyria have left us their monuments, Egypt her pyramids, Carthage her Queen, and Rome her laws, so too England has bequeathed to posterity Shakespeare and her world-wide language. And, while these endure, so long will her history be the schoolroom of mankind, and the story of her fall a reminder to living Empires of those subtle influences which are ever present, to quicken the germs of national decay, and transfer the sovereignty of the earth.[11]

The key 'subtle influences' were enumerated as: the rise of the city over the countryside, the loss of Britons' maritime skills, the growth of refinement and luxury, the absence of literary taste, the decline of the physical form of Britons, the decay of the country's religious life, excessive taxation, false systems of education and, finally, the inability of the British to defend their empire. All of these problems were there in 1905. It only took a small effort of imagination, extrapolating these forward a century, to come to the conclusion that Britain's empire was not indeed guaranteed to last forever. The seeds of its fall were already there. Perhaps the rot was already beginning to set in.

For many Londoners in 1913, the rot seemed to start rather closer to home, in labour unrest, in a radical campaign to secure votes for women, and in the oldest and most politically difficult imperial problem of them all: Ireland. Grand theorising about the possible future structure of the British Empire was an enjoyable parlour game for imperialists with time on their hands, but the situation in Ireland was a more immediate threat to the integrity of the British Empire. In London itself, the rise of militancy – both within the labour force and amongst the suffragettes – was represented by others as a direct challenge to the stability and even the security of the United Kingdom. The Roman Empire had degenerated from within, from Rome itself – would the same be true of the British Empire? Affairs in Australia, New Zealand and Canada could hardly compete with protest marches in Dublin, or broken windows in Westminster, or the threat of strikes in London's docks.

London was rich, and it was powerful. It was the conductor of a worldwide empire, and its black-suited clerks held the reins of global finance in their hands. It was the biggest city on the face of the earth. But London's greatness could not by itself deflect demands for reform of the British polity of which it was the head. One crucial political reform had already been passed – the Parliament Act of 1911, whereby the ancient and unelected House of Lords lost its indefinite veto over legislation supported by the House of Commons. This was a seismic shift in a country which had had an aristocratic Prime Minister as recently as ten years previously, and it was a sign that, for better or worse, democracy was overhauling privilege. But demands for political reform in Ireland, for social change, for greater equality between the sexes did not stop there. Britons were no longer content to simply accept what they were given; they wanted more.

The existence of a great empire overseas did not solve Britain's domestic problems. In some cases, empire now magnified and relayed them. Britain exported the divisions of Ireland in the form of Protestant–Catholic tensions in Australia, Indian nationalists drew inspiration from the Irish example, and British suffragettes could point at Australia and New Zealand as examples of British imperial societies where women had already won the right to vote. Why could women vote on the periphery of empire, but not at its heart, suffragettes could reasonably ask? Why was it that political freedoms granted in one part of the empire were not available in another? The inconsistencies of the British Empire, in many ways the secret to its rise, were now turned against it.

The question of Irish Home Rule – the formation of a Dublin parliament and the granting of powers to manage Ireland's domestic arrangements – had been trawled over by British Parliaments for years. Up until 1801 there had been an Irish parliament under the British monarchy; in that year Ireland was made an integral part of the United Kingdom. In the second half of the nineteenth century Irish nationalists had become increasingly vocal about their desire for powers to be repatriated. The subject was politically toxic to many Irish Protestants and to many in Britain, bound up as it was with the historical narrative of the birth of the British state as a Protestant entity facing off against Catholic Europe in the sixteenth and seventeenth centuries. It was an issue charged with emotion, full of claims of Papist disloyalty and counter-claims of treachery, double-dealing and broken promises. It was clear that the last century had hardly been a bright one in Ireland's long history. Its population had steadily declined throughout. The Great Famine of the 1840s had accelerated the trend. Many Irish had emigrated, setting up new homes on the east coast of the United States but never forgetting the troubled lives of their compatriots on the other side of the Atlantic.

More recently some things had got better in Ireland. Educational opportunity for Irish Catholics had widened in recent years. Tenant farmers had become wealthier (though at the expense of agricultural labourers). The census of 1911 showed the slowest decrease in Ireland's population yet recorded.[12] But the nationalist genie was out of the bottle. In the meantime, Home Rule for Ireland remained stuck. Too much had passed between Ireland and Britain for them to live comfortably together in the same house now – each knew the other's faults too well, and had their prejudices and assumptions – and yet an amicable divorce, or even a trial separation, was opposed by those in Britain who saw it as the first step to imperial disintegration, as giving in to Catholic pressure and selling Ireland's Protestants down the river. Two bills for Irish Home Rule had reached the floor of the Westminster Parliament in the last quarter of the nineteenth century. One failed to pass the House of Commons in 1886, voted down by Conservative MPs; the other failed in the House of Lords in 1893, voted down by Conservative peers.

By 1913, it was twenty years since that last defeat. But the Irish Parliamentary Party, led by John Redmond, still sent over seventy Irish MPs to Westminster. Alongside them sat the eight members of the anti-sectarian All-for-Ireland party, which supported Irish Home Rule yet was wary of replacing a Protestant ascendancy with a native Catholic one. Irish MPs held the balance of power between Conservatives and Liberals in Parliament, a disruptive single-issue force in British politics, albeit one with justified complaints about the past and reasonable aspirations for the future.

The British Liberal government of Herbert Asquith was committed to trying for Home Rule once again. Though many Conservatives were certain to oppose this, it was considered not impossible that the Conservatives would propose a constructive alternative, perhaps invoking the kind of federalism which some sought as the future structure for the empire as a whole.[13] Irish nationalists were in many respects natural partners for British Conservatives on social and even some wider issues. They tended to support protectionism; Redmond himself spoke out against female suffrage. Might the Conservatives stomach some degree of greater Irish autonomy in return for political support? In the end however, the Conservatives reverted to the blustering positions of the past, opting for all-out opposition, seeking to force an election in the process.

The crux of the problem for the government in London – the Conservatives' point of leverage, and the Home Rulers' nightmare – was Ulster. Here, in the north, rule from Dublin was strongly opposed. Protestants, who were the majority in most of Ulster, feared the prospect of being ruled by the Catholic majority in the south who, as they saw it, was more loyal to Rome than to London.

Historic sectarian antagonisms, an accepted reality of everyday life in northern Ireland, could easily flare up when appropriately fired by the rhetoric and conviction of religious and political leaders. As the Liberal government in London proposed to try again for Irish Home Rule, Sir Edward Carson, member of Parliament for Dublin's Protestant Trinity College and leader of the Unionist party, became the master and mouthpiece for Ulster's fury.

Over the course of 1912, a new Home Rule Bill made its stormy way through Parliament, being voted down in the House of Lords but reintroduced in the House of Commons. The Conservative leader Andrew Bonar Law, struck by Protestant Ulster's apparent unity at an Easter church service outside Belfast, went further and further in his denunciations of Home Rule. In July, calling the Liberal government a 'revolutionary committee', he proclaimed that 'I can imagine no length of resistance to which Ulster can go in which I should not be prepared to support them', including force, adding that he felt this view would be supported 'by the overwhelming majority of the British people'.[14] This was strong stuff. The leader of His Majesty's Loyal Opposition had virtually endorsed a challenge to the decisions of the legally constituted authorities of the United Kingdom. In September, Carson organised the signing of Ulster's Solemn League and Covenant, describing plans to set up a Dublin parliament as a conspiracy and pledging the signatories to refuse to recognise such a parliament should one be formed. Rudyard Kipling penned an incendiary pro-Ulster poem, a warning of dark forces being unleashed, and of bloodshed foretold:

> The dark eleventh hour
> Draws on and sees us sold
> To every evil power
> We fought against of old.
> Rebellion, rapine, hate,
> Oppression, wrong and greed
> Are loosed to rule our fate
> By England's act and deed
>
> . . .
>
> The blood our fathers spilt,
> Our love, our toils, our pains,
> Are counted us for guilt

And only bind our chains.
Before an Empire's eyes,
The traitor claims his price.
What need of further lies?
We are the sacrifice.

We know the war prepared
On every peaceful home,
We know the hells declared
For such as serve not Rome –
The terror, threats, and dread
In market, hearth and field –
We know, when all is said,
We perish if we yield.[15]

But the Home Rule Bill inched forward into 1913, nonetheless. 'The world moves slowly, and yet it moves', editorialised the sympathetic *Daily Chronicle* in January that year, after the bill had passed the House of Commons a second time.[16] 'No doubt we will be told in a day or two by speakers in the House of Lords that an irreparable injury has been done to Empire', it continued, anticipating the House of Lords' ongoing opposition. But, under the stipulations of the Parliament Act passed in 1911, the opposition of the Lords could not prevent Home Rule from eventually coming into effect: 'We can assume that the Home Rule Bill will suffer the full delay permissible under the Parliament Act and in 1914 will become law'.

The situation in 1913, therefore, became a three-sided deadlock. A Unionist movement prepared to use force to defend themselves against what they viewed as the depredations of a Dublin parliament. A beleaguered British government, without a majority in the House of Commons, committed to delivering a Dublin parliament. And a nationalist movement unable and unwilling to countenance Ulster's exclusion from the workings of Home Rule. All sides recognised the causes of the deadlock; but no side had the means, or perhaps the will, to break it. And so the bloody union of Britain and Ireland began to slide towards bloody disunion. Civil war could not be excluded. Some counted it likely.

*

Londoners could at least console themselves that if arguments over Home Rule spilled over into violence this would most likely be played out on the streets of Dublin, Belfast and Londonderry, rather than in the City or in the East End or around Leicester Square. London would be affected, if at all, indirectly.

The same was not true of labour militancy. In the years to 1913 a rising tide of labour unrest had hit the country's mines, railways and docks. While the Labour Party represented the interests of the workers in Westminster – alongside the Liberal and Conservative MPs still elected in working-class districts – on the streets of working-class towns and in the factories it was often the more militant trade unions who wielded power and influence. London, particularly the docks, would inevitably be a major part of any national labour unrest – with the potential for wider civil conflict. And London, dependent on the rest of the country for fuel, and on the nation's transport networks for food supplies, could not expect to be immune from the material consequences of a prolonged strike in any one of the main strategic sectors of the economy.

The language of union militancy gave succour to this fear. In 1911, during a transport strike involving the port of London, a manifesto had been sent to government departments which read:

> You know the Transport workers have the Key to the Nation's indus-trial position, also we hold the power over the food supply, and if the Shipowners and Dock Companies still persist in their War against the Port Workers of the Country, then we shall bring about a state of war . . . Hunger and poverty has driven the Dock and Ship workers to this present resort, and neither your police, your soldiers, your murder and Cossack policy will avert the disaster coming to this Country . . .[17]

That summer, the then Home Secretary Winston Churchill had called the troops on to the streets of east London and other cities throughout the country. Though previously sympathetic to the trade unions, Churchill now pivoted to 'order' as the maxim of the day. After the event, he justified his actions to Parliament contending that:

> I am sure the House will see that no blockade by a foreign enemy could have been anything like so effective in producing terrible

pressures on these vast populations as the effective closing of those great ports coupled with the paralysis of the railway service.[18]

In 1912 Tom Mann, a British trade unionist instrumental in the London dockworkers' strike of 1889 and who had subsequently spent time as a union agitator in Australia, was jailed for writing an article which urged soldiers not to shoot at strikers, the argument being made that this constituted an incitement to mutiny. The same year his firebrand colleague Ben Tillett led dockworkers in a violent chant directed at the chairman of the London Port Authority: 'He shall die, he shall die'.[19] Tillett called the House of Commons 'the rich man's Duma', a reference to the post-revolutionary Russian parliament, which appeared to confirm a willingness to pursue extra-parliamentary means to achieve his political ends. Though a founder member of the Independent Labour Party, he now became involved with the British Socialist Party, further to the left. In 1913 Parliament passed the Trade Union Act allowing unions to donate money to political parties – something which a court judgement had previously banned them from doing – in the hope that labour militancy would now be subsumed into the more pragmatic aims of the parliamentary Labour party. But Londoners lived on tenterhooks – uncertain of when the next strike would come, the next industrial stoppage, and what its consequences might be.

Meanwhile, of still greater concern even than labour unrest to some Londoners – and certainly more visible, most of the time – was the sharpening militancy of the movement for women's suffrage. By 1913 Britain had, in effect, been engaged in civil conflict over votes for women for a decade or more. Families and political parties had been divided. Common civility had been tested. The conflict had claimed victims and created martyrs. The suffragettes' struggle was endlessly in evidence on London's streets – in a scuffle with police on a street-corner, in an unfurled banner, in a voice raised to claim women's right to vote, or one condemning it as unwelcome agitation, as likely to harm women as to advance them. Nearly a thousand suffragettes had gone to prison; a handful had died.[20] Thus far, they had little to show for their sacrifice.

The normal political process seemed stuck. At Westminster many MPs supported women's suffrage of one sort or another – in principle, in broad terms, as an idea whose time was coming. Women's suffrage bills were regularly introduced by individual members of Parliament, and received support in the House of Commons. But it would take government intervention to provide the parliamentary time to allow private suffrage bills to have a chance of becoming law. This, governments had been generally unwilling to do. Even if a bill was actually debated in Parliament there were other obstacles to its passage. Every permutation of women's suffrage had its drawbacks – Irish MPs might argue that it was taking time away from discussing Home Rule and vote against it, Liberals might oppose it on the basis that if only wealthy women were granted the vote then this would be a boon to the Conservatives, Conservatives might oppose votes for women for the damage that this would supposedly do to home life. Unlike Irish Home Rule, for which there was a substantial and permanent caucus of Irish MPs in Westminster willing to vote and lobby for their own particular cause, women's suffrage was a political orphan, with many supporters, but few willing to make it the objective of their career.

In debate, questions of expedience masqueraded as questions of principle and vice versa. Should the vote be extended to women on the same basis as it was extended to men (in which case women voters would outnumber men)? Should some more limited franchise be adopted? In May 1913 a private member's bill opted again for the limited option, with far greater qualifications on which women could vote than applied to men. The bill, its sponsor claimed, charted a course 'as Ulysses steered between Scylla and Charybdis'.[21] Had it become law no more than one in every ten British women above a certain age would have won the vote. But even this was too much for some. Speaking in the debate, the Prime Minister himself, a Liberal, launched into the nonsensicality of a partial franchise – only to then oppose votes for women on any basis. 'Democracy', he informed its sacred (male) guardians, 'aims at the obliteration of arbitrary and artificial distinctions'. But not in this case:

> Democracy has no quarrel whatever with distinctions which nature has created and which experience has sanctioned. If I may put in one sentence which seems to me to be the gist and core of the real question the House has to answer tonight, it is this: Would our political fabric be strengthened, would our legislation be more respected, would

our social and domestic life be enriched, would our standard of manners
– and in manners I include the old-fashioned virtues of chivalry, courtesy, and all the reciprocal dependence and reliance of the two sexes
– would that standard be raised and refined if women were politically
enfranchised?[22]

Having placed an impossible burden of proof on the advocates
of women's suffrage, Asquith answered his own question in the
negative.

Asquith's Foreign Secretary, Sir Edward Grey, took the opposing
view. Why should five million working women not be able to influence the conditions under which they worked? Was it not wrong
to argue that women could not be granted the vote because it was
only men who served in the country's army, and therefore only men
who bore the ultimate burden for the nation's security? Grey could
not see 'on what grounds of justice, logic, reason, or even expediency'
women's suffrage could be opposed.[23] But his fine words did not
carry the votes of his colleagues. On 6 May 1913 most Liberal and
Labour MPs, and some Conservatives, voted in favour of a modest
number of women being granted the right to vote. Most Conservatives
voted against it. So too did Irish parliamentarians, desirous of greater
freedom for their nation but not for their wives, and thinking the
suffragette cause distracted from their own, more noble, endeavours.
Tramping into the lobby beside them was not only the Prime
Minister, but one of his most controversial ministers: Winston
Churchill.

Faced with repeated parliamentary standoffs of this nature, militant suffragettes began to adopt a different strategy, a long way from
the genteel garden parties that were the polite form of female
engagement with national politics. On the night of 6 May, a bomb
in a mustard tin was placed under the Bishop of London's chair in
St Paul's Cathedral, at the very heart of London, primed to go off
at midnight. 'Only the fact that an electric switch was turned in the
wrong direction had prevented the infernal machine exploding',
reported the *Daily Chronicle* the next day.[24] 'Those who set themselves
to do the Devil's work often cannot even do that right', remarked
the bishop smartly in the following evening's sermon, after thanking
God for delivering the cathedral from the bombers.

This attack had failed, but it was not an isolated event. As the

Bishop of London was delivering his riposte in St Paul's, a suffragette was preparing herself to burn down a bowling pavilion in Fulham and seed the grass with acid. A postcard claiming responsibility read: 'When men play the game and give votes to women they will be allowed to play their own games in peace'. In the first two weeks of May alone, a suffragette plot to blow up London's dockyards was reported in the press, an MP's mansion in Lancashire was destroyed by fire, postboxes were attacked, a brown-paper packet marked 'Nitroglycerine, Dangerous' was found in Piccadilly Circus tube station, and a bomb containing fifty bullets was found in the Empire Theatre in Dublin.[25] A visitor to London would find the Tower of London, the National Gallery, the Tate Gallery and Hampton Court Palace partially or entirely closed, with the shutters of Kensington Palace fastened against the possibility of attack. While the British Museum remained open, its security was upgraded. A letter writer to the *Daily Graphic* – signing himself 'Centurion' – recommended local vigilante groups be formed as the last line of defence. 'Let the vigilantes find them [the suffragettes] out, and mark them down', he suggested.[26]

Born of understandable desperation, did militant action risk alienating supporters and further distancing adversaries who saw it as blackmail, if not terrorism? The suffragettes had succeeded in generating fear and loathing; but could they direct this towards their stated goals? They could not, responded *The Economist*. The consequences of militancy, it contended, were that 'enthusiasts become apathetic [and] apathetic people become strong opponents'. The cause was thus set back. Those already predisposed against women's suffrage would argue that militancy proved their case, that 'frenzy and lawlessness' were women's politics, as against the steady and sensible deliberation of men.[27] The one should not be allowed to infect the other. Had the Suffrage Bill passed in this atmosphere of violence, the editors suggested, would not other varied discontents have felt direct action was the way to achieve their aim? While the suffragettes had stopped at arson, might others – 'in Ulster, perhaps' – go as far as murder?[28]

A few weeks later the *Daily Express* concluded that even that threshold had now been passed. Editorialising on the actions of Emily Davison, the suffragette who ran in front of the King's horse at the Epsom Derby, its editors condemned Davison's intentions as 'murderous', likely to result in the loss of two if not three human lives. (In the end it was only Davison herself who was killed.[29]) The suffragettes had gone too far, it warned: 'perhaps the Derby tragedy of 1913 is the real deathblow of feminist hopes for many years to come'. More eloquent than the *Daily Express* was ever likely to be was *The Suffragette*, the magazine of the Women's Social and Political Union, in whose militant cause Davison had died. On its cover, Davison was portrayed as an angel. 'Greater love hath no man than this', it read underneath, 'that he lay down his life for his friends'.[30] It was a noble thought, in a noble cause, the ideal of sacrifice for an idea of equality, for one's mates, for one's freedom: it was an ideal which reverberated through the age. Yet by the end of 1913 women were no closer to winning the vote than they had been at the beginning of the year. Parliamentary action had come to a dead end. Had extra-parliamentary action reached the same?

Or was it just a matter of time? 'That women's suffrage will pass over the body of Mr Asquith', wrote the British-Jewish playwright Israel Zangwill in November 1913, 'is one of the few certainties of the near future'.[31] Though not in agreement with the militant strategy as a whole, he could not help but admire the fortitude of its foot-soldiers. 'They have been stoned and beaten, ducked in horseponds, obscenely maltreated, imprisoned in third class with drunkards and pickpockets, sentenced to penal servitude, loathsomely fed by tubes and pumps', he wrote. They had compelled the state to resort to violence in force-feeding hunger striking suffragettes. They had then made the state appear both devious and weak by adopting a policy of 'cat and mouse' whereby hunger-striking suffragettes would be released as soon as they fell ill, and reimprisoned when they had recovered. 'Captain Scott, perishing in Antarctic snows for lack of food was less essentially heroic', he contended, 'than Miss Wallace-Dunlop, the fragile inventress of the hunger-strike, starving with luxuries heaped beseechingly around her'.

Surely the suffragettes' sacrifice would ultimately be repaid in justice for their cause. If not this year, then perhaps next year, or the year after. Progress could be slowed, after all – but not stopped.

'The turn of the year', wrote Clarence Rook in the *Daily Chronicle* on 31 December 1913, 'is the point at which the world seems to turn over a new leaf':

> It is the moment when your calendars and almanacs and time-tables and books of reference suddenly become obsolete and even the date you put at the top of your note-paper must undergo a change. It gives a man a jerk to change the superscription from 1913 to 1914 and realise that he is a year's march nearer his long home.[32]

As 1913 ended, the newspapers of London looked back on the year and, as the city's pubs, bars and hotels filled with revellers for the Christmas season, they looked ahead.

The Lord Mayor of London told readers in the *Evening Standard* that his greatest wish was for the 'uninterrupted prosperity of London, the commercial centre of the world', predicated on international peace.[33] Sir Arthur Conan Doyle, author of the Sherlock Holmes mysteries, wrote of his ambitions for the commencement of a Channel Tunnel to connect Britain to Europe by train. British comic writer Sir Francis Burnand wrote of his hope that 'John Bull may see clearly and have no trouble with his "I's" – i.e. Ireland and India'. Lord Desborough, a sportsman and politician, wished above all for 'discipline'; Israel Zangwill for the granting of the vote to women. Mr H. Gordon Selfridge, owner of the London department store, replied to the *Standard* that 'if one could have his wish mine would be for 1914 a year which will develop in every nook and corner of the world of commerce ever broader ideas, a wider horizon and bigger ideals'.

'Although there are some awkward problems ahead', editorialised *The Economist*, 'there is no reason why the inhabitants of this prosperous little kingdom should not enjoy a merry Christmas'.[34] Financial conditions had been tight over 1913. Stock prices had not been as stellar as in previous years, indeed they had been subject to the 'relentless, unvarying monotony of falling prices'. War in the Balkans had dampened economic optimism, as had the rising toll of military expenditures on the European continent. The European situation remained a worry, but apparent outbursts of Anglo-German friendship were greeted warmly. Public opinion was viewed as peaceful the world over. 'The Reichstag and the French Chamber, the American Congress and innumerable resolutions passed by political and commercial associations in this country, all point in the same direction', *The Economist* reported: in favour of peace. Economic conditions in Mexico were tough as the result of civil war, and the new government in China, it was noted, was 'up to its neck in difficulties'. Yet the reduction in American tariffs was sure to accelerate the pace of the global economy. Overall, it was concluded, 'with an improvement in political conditions abroad, we should look for some amelioration of the financial stringency before the next summer'.

There were sourer notes. The *Daily Graphic*, while welcoming the fact that European peace had weathered the storms of wars in the Balkans, saw problems in Mexico and in the Middle East as particularly worrying. 'With every opportunity of doing otherwise', the newspaper noted, 1913 'has spared us Armageddon'.[35] But for 1914: 'wherever we look we see the grim apparatus of war, ever growing, ever more and more viciously on the alert, clogging the wheels of industry and squandering the fruits of peace. Well may we pray for a Happy New Year!'

'Where will it all end?' asked the editor of another London paper, launching himself into criticism of increases in military expenditure over the course of the year.[36] 'It requires no gift of prophecy', he noted, 'to foretell that this mad competition in military expenditure will end in disaster'. The check on such madness could only come from the people themselves: 'Where aristocracies and plutocracies have signally failed, democracy may yet succeed. May its reign soon dawn!'

At the printing presses of the *Daily Chronicle*, rushing to complete their work before the end of the day, the newspaper's typesetters put into order the letters of the year's final poem before going out into the cold London night, the air rich with the smell of roasting chestnuts. Tonight they would celebrate, consigning 1913 to history and beginning a fresh year – for them, for their families and friends, at the heart of their city, their country, their empire, the greatest on earth, the centre of the universe:

> I do not mourn your passing, shed no tear,
> As you are whelmed in shadows of the past:
> I only sigh and say – Please God next year
> Will be more fruitful, fuller, than the last

I mourn not your dead roses, nor the day
When life stood tiptoe for a little space;
Roses will bloom again, and I can pray
For such another crowning hour of grace.

Pass, then, to those grey shades where memory dwells
Inviolate, but mourns not. You shall bear
From me no heavy burden of farewells;
I turn to watch the year dawn that shall be.

At the stroke of midnight 1913 died. The year was 1914.

EPILOGUE
The Afterlife of 1913

The world went to war in 1914. For four years – in the mud of Flanders, in the Alps, along the Eastern Front, in the Dardanelles, and elsewhere across the globe – men attempted to kill other men, sometimes as a matter of national survival, sometimes in the service of some higher ideal, sometimes because they were told to and sometimes because death and killing had become a way of life for them. Millions fell; others, not necessarily more fortunate, were wounded. The hopes and dreams of a generation were ground into dust by the pounding of artillery shells. Families were ripped apart. Humanity looked into the abyss and, peering into the depths, found its own dark, disfigured reflection staring back.

Though the ferocity of the military conflict was concentrated in Europe, and although most combatants were European, this was a global war. Naval battles were fought in the South Atlantic and in the North Sea. The shipping of initially neutral countries such as the United States and Brazil came under German U-boat attack. In the mountains of East Africa and on the high Persian plateau skirmishes of the Great War were fought between the great powers. Indians, Canadians, Australians, New Zealanders, South Africans and Irishmen fought alongside the British all over the world. Algerians and Senegalese fought alongside the French. In an effort to win favour with the British and the French, the young Chinese Republic sent tens of thousands of Chinese labourers to dig trenches in Europe. Americans, who had stayed aloof from war in 1914 and who elected Woodrow Wilson president for a second term in 1916 on a platform promising peace, entered the war nonetheless the following year, pouring troops and resources into the Western Front at a rate that only American scale and organisation could achieve. On the Eastern Front, soldiers from every corner of the Russian Empire – Latvians, Estonians, Lithuanians, Finns, Armenians, Kyrgyz, and Kazakhs – had been sent to die for Tsar and Motherland. German colonies in the Pacific were occupied by troops from Australia and New Zealand. The German concession of Qingdao in China was overrun by the Japanese. At the outset of war German spies had hoped that the banner of Islamic *Jihad* (holy war) raised by their allies the Ottomans would bring about a Muslim rising against British interests in the Middle East and India.[1] In the end, it was British spies who were more successful: turning Arab nationalism into a weapon against Constantinople's hold on its southern flank. Ottoman Armenians, long seen by Turkish nationalists as being the enemy in their midst, suffered gruesome retribution as the Ottoman Empire, beset on all sides, began to fall apart. Everywhere, disease followed where war had led.

In 1918, the guns fell silent. Harry Kessler, the Anglo-German intellectual, archetype of the pan-European aristocracy of 1913, returned from his duties at the front to his home in Weimar in western Germany:

> The old coachman was waiting at the station. My dog greeted me with effusive and moving joy. My house seemed, after years of such violent events, to be almost miraculously unchanged: new and bright in the dying hours of the day, as if a Sleeping Beauty, brilliant lights turned to illuminate her; the Impressionist and Neo-Impressionist paintings, the shelves of French, English, Italian, Greek and German books, the statues and statuettes of Maillol [a French sculptor], his buxom, lusty women, his beautiful, naked youths . . . all as if it were still 1913, and as if the many people who had been here and who are now dead, missing, scattered or who have become enemies, could just come back and European life would begin again where it had left off. It was like a temple to the Thousand and One Nights, full of all sorts of priceless baubles and half-faded tokens and memories . . . I found an inscription by d'Annunzio [the Italian poet and nationalist], Persian cigarettes brought from Isfahan by Claude Anet [the French writer], gifts from the baptism of the youngest child of Maurice Denis [the French painter], a programme of the Ballets Russes from 1911 with pictures of Nijinsky . . .[2]

On the surface, little had changed. And yet, as Kessler knew too well, the ballroom switch could not be flicked back on, the chandeliers dusted off and the conversations of 1913 magically resume. The physical and psychological scars of war were too deep. The clock could not be turned back.

Europe, in particular, was changed by the war, and by the peace which followed. Everywhere, even amongst the victorious nations of the Great War, the political cultures of the past were challenged. For the defeated states, the end of the war signalled the beginning of fresh political and social convulsions. Kaiser Wilhelm II, who had celebrated his twenty-fifth year on the throne with such pomp and ceremony in 1913, was forced to flee into exile in the Netherlands. The German Empire became the German Republic. In the immediate aftermath of war Communist revolutions were put down in Berlin and Bavaria by returning battalions of far-right troops, dragooned into the service of the incoming Social Democratic government. The German capital was moved from Berlin to Kessler's quiet hometown of Weimar. Within a few years of the end of the war the German middle classes suffered a second trauma, almost as bad as the war itself, the destruction of their savings by runaway inflation. Many Germans came to feel that their country had not really lost the war – after all, German troops were still on French soil when the armistice came into effect in 1918 – but that German politicians had lost the peace. At the Versailles peace conference Germany's new masters accepted responsibility for the war, took on a substantial burden of reparations, and agreed to a number of measures designed to reduce the largest continental European power besides Russia to the status of a geopolitical minnow.

The fate of the Austro-Hungarian Empire was equally disastrous. After holding up better than many expected in the first few years of the war, the empire imploded at its close. Out of the patchwork domains of the Habsburgs, built up over centuries, the peacemakers of Versailles carved out the new states of Czechoslovakia (with a substantial German-speaking minority), Hungary (much more homogeneous than before, but correspondingly reduced in territory) and Austria (almost completely German-speaking, but forbidden from uniting with its German cousins to the north). The grand imperial capital of Vienna began a new life as the over-sized capital of a small central European country, its horizons reduced to a tiny portion of the lands that the Viennese had become accustomed to think of as their inalienable heritage as Habsburg subjects. In eastern Europe, the map was redrawn to allow the re-emergence of Poland as an independent political entity after more than a century carved up by her neighbours. The state of Yugoslavia was conjured out of the morass of the Balkans, fulfilling the old Habsburg nightmare of a single south Slav kingdom.

To the east, meanwhile, the Russian and Ottoman empires spiralled into the abyss. Russia, forced by domestic upheaval to exit the Great War before it had finished in the west, lurched from the one revolution to another in 1917 and then to a drawn-out civil war. The Tsar and his family were shot. The capital was moved from Petrograd (the post-1914 name for St Petersburg) to Moscow. Foreign forces intervened in an attempt to keep the Bolsheviks at bay. When the victors of the Great War met at Versailles to establish the terms of the peace in 1919, Russia, one of the undisputed powers of 1913, was not even formally represented (although plenty of anti-Bolshevik Russians milled around seeking Western support for their side in the civil war).[3] Japan, on the other hand, was.

Within a few years, Russia would return to greatness, not as the old Tsarist empire, but as the Soviet Union. The exit of the Ottoman Empire from the stage of history, however, was final. At the end of the Great War, the Arab territories of the empire fell under the political influence or direct control of Britain and France, with London replacing Constantinople as the ultimate master of Jerusalem. In the heartlands of Turkey a new war of survival was fought against the invading armies of Greece – a war which finally ended in 1923 with mass exchanges of Turkish and Greek population, the burning of the Greek city of Smyrna and resentments to last each country for lifetimes to come.

These changes in the constellation of European power were a serious enough break from how the world had looked in 1913. But, as many saw it, they were merely symptoms of an even greater world historical process: the beginning of the end for Europe's predominance in the affairs of the world, and for its claim to civilisational superiority. For if the Great War had shown one thing, was it not that European civilisation, once hailed as the most progressive and most advanced in the world, was really nothing more than a thin veneer for barbarism? Chinese intellectual Yan Fu noted that 'the European race's last three hundred years of evolutionary progress have all come down to nothing but four words: selfishness, slaughter, shamelessness and corruption'.[4] The French writer Paul Valéry wondered aloud whether Europe, which once had been the magnetic centre of the world and the chief source of foreign capital invested abroad, would ultimately become little more than a geographic expression, 'a little promontory on the continent of Asia'.[5] The German writer Oswald Spengler wrote a surprisingly popular pseudo-historical tract on the subject, published in two volumes in 1918 and 1922, entitled simply *Der Untergang des Abendlandes* (*The Decline of the West*).

To be sure, London and Paris remained the capital cities of the world's largest empires after the Great War – indeed the territory under their control was somewhat expanded by the award of quasi-colonial mandates by the newly founded League of Nations. But this was not quite a return to the situation in 1913. The war had eroded Europe's civilisational credibility. The dependence of Britain and France on the armed forces of their empires in order to defend their home territory had been exposed. And though it was not immediately applied beyond Europe, the principle of national self-determination enshrined in the Versailles Treaty signalled that henceforth nations, not empires, would be considered the essential units of world order. Over the course of the 1920s, bushfires of colonial unrest flared in Egypt, Iraq, Indonesia and India. Ireland became an independent Dominion under the British monarchy in 1922. The model of a world ruled – and thereby civilised – by European empires had begun to fray.

The only countries to emerge from the Great War stronger, richer and more influential than they had been in 1913 were Japan and the United States. The presence of Japan at the Versailles peace conference confirmed its great power status, as a global rule-maker rather than a global rule-taker. But it was the delegation of the United States, led by President Wilson, which arrived at the Versailles peace conference with the greatest international credit. Unlike Britain, which had spent money hand over fist during the war, and which had run down its foreign investments and gold reserves substantially in the process, the United States' economic and financial position in the world had been boosted by war. Having played a crucial role in settling the outcome of the war militarily,

President Wilson intended the United States to play a key role in the peace. In the following decade, however, rather than leading the world, America retreated from it. The US Senate voted to keep the United States out of the League of Nations which its President had done so much to establish, ensuring that the new organisation, rather than breaking the European balance of power, would enshrine its importance to international relations. American trade tariffs increased. New restrictions on immigration came into force, with the aim of protecting the wages of American workers and maintaining the ethnic and national composition of the American population. Domestic policy trumped foreign policy.

With Europe weakened as the core of the global system and the United States unable and unwilling to take the reins of leadership, many of the certainties of 1913 – amongst them an expectation of ever-increasing global economic integration – turned into question marks. Internationalism had been a fact of life before the Great War. Now it became a cause in itself.[6] The Gold Standard, lynchpin of the pre-war financial order, was re-established in the 1920s, with London attempting to recreate itself as the hub of global finance that it had been in 1913. But with so much gold now drained across the Atlantic, London's monetary hegemony, and therefore its credibility as the conductor of the world's financial affairs, was eroded. Worse, as countries re-entered the Gold Standard at pre-war rates of exchange which no longer reflected their true economic and financial position – forcing themselves into a financial straitjacket which no longer fitted – the Gold Standard came to be seen as a mechanism for generating economic insecurity rather than one for achieving financial stability. In 1931, in the face of the Great Depression, Britain left. The principles of liberal free trade – and of the economic interdependence which this implied – were replaced with aspirations to economic self-sufficiency, with the result that global trade did not reach its 1913 share of global output again until 1970. The flows of global migration which had bound the world together in a web of human relationships in 1913 were interrupted by the Great War. After the war, they atrophied.

Somehow, somewhere, the world of 1913 had gone.

*

'All the bridges between our today and our yesterday and our yester-years have been burnt', wrote Stefan Zweig in the early 1940s, in his memoirs of the Vienna before the war, a time he termed the 'golden age of security'.[7]

To those who had not known it – and even to some of those who had – the world of 1913 eventually became a kind of dream world, a metaphor for a time before disenchantment, an Eden to which one could not return. In Europe, the Great War was memorialised both in the monuments to the dead raised in towns and villages across the continent, and also in published war diaries, memoirs written long after the event and fictional accounts of the war, sometimes written by authors not even born when the events they described had taken place.[8] Individual memories of war were now elided into the collective tragedy of a generation, the collective catastrophe of a world now out of reach. For Lara in Boris Pasternak's 1950s novel *Dr. Zhivago*, the war lay at the origin of Russia's slide into contemporary darkness: 'I believe now that the war is to blame for everything, for all the misfortunes that followed and that dog our generation to this day'.[9]

Viewed in the light of the disasters Russia had experienced since, the world before the war appeared a more straightforward, more moral time:

> I remember quite well how it was in my childhood. I can still remember a time when we all accepted the peaceful outlook of the last century. It was taken for granted that you listened to reason, that it was right and natural to do what your conscience told you. For a man to die by the hand of another was a rare, an exceptional event. Something quite out of the ordinary run. Murders happened in plays, newspapers and detective stories, not in everyday life.
>
> And then there was a jump from this calm, innocent, measured way of living to blood and tears, to mass insanity and to the savagery of daily, hourly, legalised, rewarded slaughter.

Rightly or wrongly, this is the culturally-received image we now have, a century on, of the world of 1913 – a world bathed in the last rays of the dying sun, a world of order and security, a world unknowingly on the brink of the seminal catastrophe of the twentieth century. It is an image full of pathos and poetry, of figures moving silently towards their destiny, flickering shadows on the surface of time. It provides 1913 with an afterlife which speaks to us today – a parable of lost times. But it also provides us with an opportunity to consider our own times in fresh perspective, to take stock of our past and consider our future, not as a foregone conclusion, not as a pre-determined course of events, but as a future we have yet to build.

Notes

1   F. W. Hirst, *The Six Panics, and Other Essays*, 1913
2   Hamburg-American Line, *Girdling the Globe: Around the World on the Palatial Steamship 'Cleveland'*, 1911
3   To take just a few of the more well-known and the most recent: Fritz Fischer, *Griff nach der Weltmacht: Die Kriegszielpolitik des kaiserlichen Deutschland*, 1962; Eckart Kehr, *Primat der Innenpolitik*, Hans-Ulrich Wehler, ed., 1965; A. J. P. Taylor, *War by Timetable*, 1969; James Joll, *The Origins of the First World War*, 1984; Niall Ferguson, *The Pity of War*, 1998; Sean McMeekin, *The Russian Origins of the First World War*, 2011; Christopher Clark, *The Sleepwalkers: How Europe Went to War in 1914*, 2012
4   Jack Beatty, *The Lost History of 1914: How the Great War was not Inevitable*, 2011
5   Op. cit. (1998), Ferguson
6   For accounts of the war itself, or aspects of it, see Hew Strachan, *The First World War*, 2001; David Stevenson, *1914–1918: The History of the First World War*, 2005; Norman Stone, *The Eastern Front, 1914–1917*, 1998
7   Niall Ferguson, ed., *Virtual History: Alternatives and Counterfactuals*, 1997
8   Op. cit., Clark
9   Barbara W. Tuchman, *The Proud Tower: A Portrait of the World before the War, 1890–1914*, 1966
10 Michael S. Neiberg, *Dance of the Furies: Europe and the Outbreak of World War I*, 2011
11 Norman Angell, *The Great Illusion: A Study of the Relation of Military Power to National Advantage*, 1913 edition (originally published 1910)
12 Leopold von Ranke, *Geschichte der romanischen und germanischen Völker von 1495 bis 1514*, 1824
13 E. J. Hobsbawm, *The Age of Empire*, 1987
14 There are a number of leading historians who have explored the

themes of globalisation, and the idea of 'global history', in the late nineteenth and early twentieth century. For example: C. A. Bayly, *The Birth of the Modern World: Global Connections and Comparisons*, 2004; John Darwin, *The Empire Project: The Rise and Fall of the British World System, 1830–1970*, 2009; Niall Ferguson, *Empire: How Britain made the Modern World*, 2003; Gary S. Magee and Andrew S. Thompson, eds, *Empire and Globalisation: Networks of People, Goods and Capital in the British World*, c. *1850–1914*, 2010; Sebastian Conrad, *Globalisation and the Nation in Imperial Germany*, trans. Sorcha O'Hagan, 2010 (original German edition 2006); Duncan Bell, *The Idea of Greater Britain: Empire and the Future of World Order, 1860–1900*, 2011

15 G. P. Gooch, *History of Our Time, 1885–1911*, 1912

I Centre of the Universe

1 Commandant Renier, *L'Oeuvre civilisatrice au Congo. Héroisme et patriotisme des Belges*, 1913
2 Adam Hochschild, *King Leopold's Ghost: A Story of Greed, Terror and Heroism in Colonial Africa*, 1998
3 Quoted in M. Puel de Lobel, *Exposition Universelle et Internationale de Gand, 1913*, 1914
4 *The New York Times*, 28 August 1913; 7 September 1913
5 Laird McLeod Easton, *The Red Count: The Life and Times of Harry Kessler*, 2002
6 Robert Skidelsky, *John Maynard Keynes: Hopes Betrayed*, 1983
7 Ronald Storrs, *The Memoirs of Sir Ronald Storrs*, 1972
8 Thomas Mann, *Tod in Venedig*, 1912
9 Michael S. Neiberg, *Dance of the Furies: Europe and the Outbreak of World War I*, 2011
10 Stefan Zweig, *The World of Yesterday*, English edition, 1943
11 Barbara W. Tuchman, *The Proud Tower: A Portrait of the World Before the War, 1890–1914*, 1966
12 Op. cit., McLeod Easton
13 *Futurist Manifesto*, 1909
14 Friedrich Nietzsche, *Beyond Good and Evil*, 1886, quoted in Stefan Elbe, '"Labyrinths of the future": Nietzsche's genealogy of European nationalism', *Journal of Political Ideologies*, vol. 7, no. 1, 2002
15 Liliane Brion-Guerry, ed., *L'année 1913: Les formes esthétiques de l'œuvre d'art à la veille de la première guerre mondiale*, vols 1 and 2, 1971; vol. 3, 1973
16 Quoted in David Blackbourn, '"As dependent on each other as man

and wife": Cultural Contacts and Transfers', in Dominik Geppert and Robert Gerwarth, eds, *Wilhelmine Germany and Edwardian Britain: Essays on Cultural Affinity*, 2008

17   Romain Rolland, *Jean Christophe*, ten volumes, 1904–1912

18   Quoted in E. Malcolm Carroll, *French Public Opinion and Foreign Affairs, 1870–1914*, 1931

19   *The Daily Graphic*, 22 May 1913

20   Ibid.

21   *The Daily Graphic*, 23 May 1913

22   *The Daily Graphic*, 22 May 1913

23   *The Daily Chronicle*, 24 May 1913

24   The Duke of Windsor, *A King's Story*, 1951 (reprinted 1998)

25   Friedrich von Bernhardi, *Germany and the Next War*, trans. Allen Powles, 1912 (original in German)

26   Quoted in Charles F. Horne, *Source Records of the Great War*, 1923

27   *The Daily Graphic*, 24 May 1913

28   *The Daily Chronicle*, 25 May 1913

London

1   Ford Maddox Hueffer, *The Soul of London: A Survey of a Modern City*, 1905

2   *The Nineteenth Century and After*, February 1913

3   F. O. Mathiessen and K. B. Murdock, eds, *The Notebooks of Henry James*, 1947 (entry from 1881)

4   Karl Baedeker, *London und Umgebung: Handbuch für Reisende*, 1912

5   *The Economist*, 24 May 1913

6   Joseph Conrad, *Heart of Darkness*, 1902

7   Humayun Ansari, *The Infidel Within: The History of Muslims in Britain, 1800 to the Present*, 2004

8   Felix Driver and David Gilbert, 'Imperial Cities: overlapping territories, intertwined histories', in Felix Driver and David Gilbert, eds, *Imperial Cities: Landscape, Display and Identity*, 1999

9   *The Evening Standard*, 1 January 1913

10   *The Fortnightly Review*, August 1913

11   *Daily Express*, 25 July 1913

12   Op. cit., Baedeker (1912)

13   Jan Rüger, 'Revisiting the Anglo-German Antagonism', *The Journal of Modern History*, vol. 83, 2011

14   *The Daily Chronicle*, 13 May 1913

15   Dominik Geppert, '"The foul-visaged anti-Christ of journalism"?: The Popular Press between Warmongering and International Cooperation',

in Dominik Geppert and Robert Gerwarth, eds, *Wilhelmine Germany and Edwardian Britain: Essays on Cultural Affinity*, 2008

16 *Daily Mail*, 17 June 1913, quoted in Virginia Cowles, *1913: An End and a Beginning*, 1967

17 Antony Phillips, ed., *Sergey Prokofiev Diaries: Prodigous Youth, 1907–1914*, 2006

18 N. Ramunajaswami, *My Trip to England*, 1912

19 Theodore Dreiser, *Traveller at Forty*, 1913

20 John Robert Seeley, *The Expansion of England*, 1883

21 *The Nineteenth Century and After*, February 1913

22 Dennis Hardy, 'From Garden Cities to New Towns: Campaigning for Town and Country Planning', in Stephen V. Ward, ed., *Garden City: Past, Present and Future*, 1992

23 Ellis T. Powell, *The Mechanism of the City: An Analytical Survey of the Business Activities of the City of London*, 1910

24 *The Economist*, 12 April 1913

25 Op. cit., Powell

26 E. M. Forster, *Howard's End*, 1910

27 *The Economist*, 4 January 1913

28 David Kynaston, *City of London: The History, 1815–2000*, 2011

29 *The Economist*, 4 January 1913

30 Quoted in op. cit., Kynaston

31 *The Economist*, 1 February 1913

32 League of Nations statistics quoted in Aaron Friedberg, *The Weary Titan: Britain and the Experience of Relative Decline 1895–1905*, 1988

33 *The Economist*, 4 January 1913

34 John Dunning and Sarianna Lundan, *Multinational Enterprises and the Global Economy*, 2nd edition, 2008

35 Charles Feinstein, 'Britain's Overseas Investments in 1913', *The Economic History Review*, vol. 43, no. 2, 1990

36 Gary B. Magee and Andrew S. Thompson, *Empire and Globalisation: Networks of People, Goods and Capital in the British World, c. 1850–1914*, 2010

37 Quoted in op. cit., Kynaston

38 Ibid.

39 Quoted in Jean-Louis Robert, 'Paris, London and Berlin on the Eve of War', in Jay Winter and Jean-Louis Robert, eds, *Capital Cities at War: Paris, London, Berlin, 1914–1919*, 1997

40 M. Pember Reeves, *Round About a Pound a Week*, 2nd edition, 1914

41 Quoted in ibid.

42 Thomas Holmes, *London's Underworld*, 2nd edition, 1913

43 Jérôme de Wiel, 'Austria-Hungary, France, Germany and the Irish Crisis from 1899 to the Outbreak of the First World War', *Intelligence*

and National Security, vol. 21, no. 2, 2006, quoted in Jack Beatty, *The Lost History of 1914: How the First World War was not Inevitable*, 2012

44   *The Daily Graphic*, 25 June 1913
45   Ibid.
46   Laird McLeod Easton, *The Red Count: The Life and Times of Harry Kessler*, 2002
47   *The Economist*, 28 June 1913

Paris

1   Dreiser, *Traveller at Forty*
2   J. F. V. Keiger, *Raymond Poincaré*, 1997
3   Michael E. Nolan, *The Inverted Mirror: Mythologizing the Enemy in France and Germany, 1898–1914*, 2006
4   David Clay Large, *Berlin*, 2000
5   Neiberg, *Dance of the Furies*
6   Quoted in Malcolm Carroll, *French Public Opinion and Foreign Affairs*
7   David Schoenbaum, *Zabern 1913: Consensus Politics in Imperial Germany*, 1982
8   Maurice Barrès, *La terre et les morts: Sur quelles réalités fonder la conscience française*, 1899
9   Owen Chadwick, *A History of the Popes, 1830–1914*, 1998
10   Quoted in Robert Gildea, *Children of the Revolution: The French, 1799–1914*, 2008
11   Eric Deroo, 'Mourir: L'appel à l'Empire', in Pascal Blanchard and Sandrine Lemaire, *Culture Coloniale: La France conquise par son empire, 1871–1931*, 2003
12   Ramunajaswami, *My Trip to England*
13   Karl Baedeker, *Paris and its Environs: Handbook for Travellers*, 1910
14   L. Houllevigue, 'Le problème de l'heure', *La Revue de Paris*, August 1913
15   Ibid.
16   Stephen Kern, *The Culture of Time and Space, 1880–1918*, 1983
17   Patrice Higonnet, *Paris: Capital of the World*, trans. Arthur Goldhammer, 2002
18   Henri Murger, *Scènes de la vie Bohème*, 1851
19   Claire Hancock, 'Capitale du Plaisir: The Remaking of Imperial Paris', in Felix Driver and David Gilbert, eds, *Imperial Cities: Landscape, Display and Identity*, 1999
20   Otto Friedrich, *Olympia: Paris in the Age of Manet*, 1992
21   Op. cit., Gildea
22   Detlef Briesen, 'Weltmetropole Berlin?', in Gerhard Brunn and Jürgen

Reulecke, eds, *Metropolis Berlin: Berlin as deutsche Hauptstadt im Vergleich europäischer Hauptstädte 1871–1939*, 1992

23 Op. cit., Clay Large

24 David McCullough, *The Greater Journey: Americans in Paris*, 2011

25 Henry James, *The Ambassadors*, 1903

26 Adelaide Mack, *Magnetic Paris*, 1913

27 Phillips, *Sergey Prokofiev Diaries*

28 Ibid.

29 Op. cit., Dreiser

30 Op. cit., Baedeker (1910)

31 Op. cit., Phillips

32 Guerry, *L'année 1913*

33 *The Daily Graphic*, 26 June 1913

34 Jacques-Emile Blanche in *La Revue de Paris*, December 1913

35 *Le Figaro*, 20 February 1909

36 Modris Eksteins, *Rites of Spring: The Great War and the Birth of the Modern Age*, 1989

37 Liliane Brion-Guerry, 'L'évolution des formes structurales dans l'architecture des années 1910–1914', in op. cit., Guerry

38 Op. cit., Blanche

39 Jacques Bertillon, *La dépopulation de la France: Ses conséquences – Ses causes – Mesures à prendre pour la combattre*, 1911

40 Beatty, *The Lost History of 1914*

41 'Agathon' (Henri Massis and Alfred de Tarde), *Les jeunes gens d'aujourd'hui: Le goût de l'action, la foi patriotique, une renaissance Catholique, le réalisme politique*, 1919 edition (first edition 1913)

Berlin

1 Dreiser, *Traveller at Forty*

2 Clay Large, *Berlin*

3 Baron Beyens, *Deux Années à Berlin, 1912–1914*, 1931

4 Charles Huard, *Berlin Comme je l'ai Vu*, 1907

5 Phillips, *Sergey Prokofiev Diaries*

6 *Berlin für Kenner*, 1912, quoted in Jürgen Schutte and Peter Sprengel, *Die Berliner Moderne, 1885–1914*, 1987

7 Warren G. Breckman, 'Disciplining Consumption: The Debate about Luxury in Wilhelmine Germany, 1890–1914', *Journal of Social History*, vol. 24, no. 3, 1991

8 Quoted in Charles W. Huxthausen, '"A New Beauty": Ernst Ludwig Kirchner's Images of Berlin', in Charles W. Huxthausen and Heidrun Suhr, eds, *Berlin: Culture and Metropolis*, 1990

9   *Weltwirtschaftliches Archiv*, 1913
10   Peter Hall, 'The Pioneer Technopolis: Berlin 1840–1930', in Peter Hall, *Cities in Civilization*, 1998
11   Archives of American Art at the Smithsonian Institution (AAASI), Walter Kuhn and Kuhn family papers, letters from Walter Kuhn, Series 1/Box 1, Berlin, October 1912
12   Op. cit., Beyens
13   Op. cit., Dreiser
14   Edith Siepen, *Peeps at Great Cities: Berlin*, 1911
15   William Durick, 'Berlin 1916', in John E. Findling and Kimberly D. Pelle, *Encyclopedia of the Modern Olympic Movement*, 2004
16   Op. cit., Siepen
17   Richard Evans, *Death in Hamburg: Society and Politics in the Cholera Years*, 1987
18   Gottfried Korff and Reinhard Rürup, *Berlin, Berlin : die Ausstellung zur Geschichte der Stadt*, 1987
19   Quoted in op. cit., Schutte and Sprengel
20   Op. cit., Dreiser
21   Op. cit., Clay Large
22   Robert, 'Paris, London and Berlin on the Eve of War'
23   Werner Sombart, *Das Proletariat: Bilder und Studien, 1906*, quoted in Joachim Schlör, *Nights in the Big City: Paris, Berlin, London, 1840–1930*, 1998
24   Op. cit., Korff and Rürup
25   Rosa Luxemburg, *Im Asyl*, 1912, quoted in op. cit., Schutte and Sprengel
26   Madame de Staël, *De l'Allemagne*, 1810
27   Paul Kennedy, *The Rise and Fall of the Great Powers: Economic Change and Military Conflict from 1500 to 2000*, 1988
28   Op. cit., Dreiser
29   Op. cit., Clay Large
30   Karl Scheffler, *Berlin: Ein Stadtschicksal*, 1910
31   Walter Rathenau, 'Die Schönste Stadt der Welt', *Die Zukunft* 26, 1899, quoted in op. cit., Schutte and Sprengel
32   Op. cit., Robert
33   *Chicago Daily Tribune*, 3 April 1892
34   Karl Scheffler, *Berlin: Ein Stadtschicksal*, 1910
35   Karl Scheffler, *Die Architektur der Großstadt*, 1913
36   Anne Topham, *Memories of the Kaiser's Court*, 1913
37   Op. cit., Clay Large
38   Bernd Sösemann, 'Hollow-sounding Jubilees: Forms and Effects of Public Self-display in Wilhelmine Germany', in Annika Mombauer and Wilhelm Deist, eds, *The Kaiser: New Research on Wilhelm II's Role in Imperial Germany*, 2003

39 Ibid.
40 Quoted in Jeffrey R. Smith, 'The Monarchy versus the Nation: The "Festive Year" 1913 in Wilhelmine Germany', *German Studies Review*, vol. 23, no. 2, 2000
41 Ibid.
42 Op. cit., Beyens
43 Duke of Windsor, *A King's Story*
44 *The New York Times*, 8 June 1913

Rome

1 E. M. Forster, *Where Angels Fear to Tread*, 1905
2 *Futurist Manifesto*, 1909
3 Quoted in Christopher Duggan, *The Force of Destiny: A History of Italy since 1796*, 2008
4 Op. cit., Forster (1905)
5 Richard Bagot, *My Italian Year*, 1911
6 Ibid.
7 Michael Paris, 'The First Air Wars: North Africa and the Balkans, 1911–1913', *The Journal of Contemporary History*, vol. 26, no. 1, 1991
8 Filippo Marinetti, *Le Bataille de Tripoli*, 1911
9 Quoted in op. cit., Duggan
10 Filippo Marinetti, *Le Monoplan du Pape*, 1912
11 David Atkinson, Denis Cosgrove and Anna Notaro, 'Empire in modern Rome: shaping and remembering an imperial city, 1870–1911', in Felix Driver and David Gilbert, eds, *Imperial Cities: Landscape, Display and Identity*, 1999
12 David Atkinson and Denis Cosgrove, 'Urban Rhetoric and Embodied Identities: City, Nation, and Empire at the Vittorio Emanuele II Monument in Rome, 1870–1945', *Annals of the Association of American Geographers*, vol. 88, no. 1, 1998
13 Op. cit., Duggan
14 Dreiser, *Traveller at Forty*
15 Op. cit., Bagot
16 Quoted in op. cit., Duggan
17 Op. cit., Marinetti

Vienna

1 Karl Baedeker, *Austria-Hungary, with excursions to Cetinje, Belgrade, and Bucharest*, 1911

2   Alison Fleig Frank, *Oil Empire: Visions of Prosperity in Austrian Galicia*, 2005

3   Ibid.

4   Archibald R. Colquhon and Ethel Colquhon, *The Whirlpool of Europe: Austria-Hungary and the Habsburgs*, 1907

5   Deborah R. Coen, 'Climate and Circulation in Imperial Austria', *Journal of Modern History*, vol. 82, December 2010

6   Henry Schnitzler, '"Gay Vienna": Myth and Reality', *Journal of the History of Ideas*, vol. 15, no. 1, 1954

7   Gordon Brook-Shepherd, *The Austrians: A Thousand-Year Odyssey*, 1996

8   Robert Musil, *The Man Without Qualities*, trans. Sophie Wilkins and Burton Pike, 1995 (originally published in German between 1930 and 1942)

9   Op. cit., Brook-Shepherd

10   John W. Mason, *The Dissolution of the Austro-Hungarian Empire, 1867–1918*, 1985

11   Brigitte Hamann, *Hitler's Vienna: A Portrait of the Tyrant as a Young Man*, 2010 (first published 1999)

12   Ibid.

13   Robert Service, *Lenin: A Biography*, 2000

14   Frederic Morton, *Thunder at Twilight: Vienna 1913/1914*, 1989

15   Op. cit., Mason

16   Kennedy, *The Rise and Fall of the Great Powers*

17   Op. cit., Brook-Shepherd

18   Zweig, *The World of Yesterday*

19   Op. cit., Mason

20   David F. Good, 'Stagnation and "Take-Off" in Austria, 1873–1913', *The Economic History Review*, vol. 27, no. 1, 1974

21   H. Gordon Skilling, *Masaryk: Against the Current, 1882–1914*, 1994

22   Op. cit., Musil

23   Henry Wickham Steed, *The Hapsburg Monarchy*, 1913

24   Jill Steward, 'The Potemkin City: Tourist Images of Late Imperial Vienna', in Driver and Gilbert, *Imperial Cities*

25   Op. cit., Schnitzler

26   Op. cit., Morton; Leon Trotsky, *My Life: An Attempt at an Autobiography*, English translation, 1960

27   Juliane Mikoletzky, 'Die Wiener Sicht auf Berlin, 1870–1934', in Gerhard Brunn and Jürgen Reulecke, eds, *Metropolis Berlin: Berlin as deutsche Hauptstadt im Vergleich europäischer Hauptstädte 1871–1939*, 1992

28   Op. cit., Schnitzler

29   Op. cit., Zweig

30   Maria Hornor Lansdale, *Vienna and the Viennese*, 1902

31 Dominique Jameux, 'Le goût musical dans un centre de haute tradition: Vienne en 1913', in Lilliane Brion-Guerry, ed., *L'année 1913: Les formes esthétiques de l'œuvre d'art à la veille de la première guerre mondiale*, vol. 1, 1971

32 Op. cit., Hamann

33 *The Economist*, 11 January 1913

34 Op. cit., Brook-Shepherd

35 Virginio Gayda, *Modern Austria: Her Racial and Social Problems*, 1915, quoted in op. cit., Cowles

36 Allan Janik and Stephen Toulmin, *Wittgenstein's Vienna*, 1973

37 Op. cit., Zweig

38 Op. cit., Hamann

39 Op. cit., Jameux

40 Op. cit., Zweig

41 Op. cit., Jameux

42 Op. cit., Mason; op. cit., Hamann

43 Op. cit., Jameux

44 Op. cit., Janik and Toulmin

45 Ibid.

46 Op. cit., Zweig

47 Carl E. Schorske, 'Politics and Patricide in Freud's Interpretation of Dreams', *The American Historical Review*, vol. 78, no. 2, 1973

48 Hermann Bahr, *Wien*, 1906

49 Op. cit., Schnitzler

50 Op. cit., Hamann

51 Ibid.

52 Op. cit., Zweig

53 *British Medical Journal*, vol. 2, no. 2753, October 1913

54 London *Standard*, 1 January 1913

55 Op. cit., Zweig

56 Georg Markus, *Der Fall Redl: mit unveröffentlichten Geheimdokumenten zur folgenschwersten Spionage-Affaire des Jahrhunderts*, 1985

St Petersburg

1 Richard Wortman, *Scenarios of Power: Myth and Ceremony in Russian Monarchy from Peter the Great to the Abdication of Nicholas II*, 2006

2 Harold H. Fisher and Laura Matveev, *Out of My Past: Memoirs of Count Kokovtsov*, 1935

3 Quoted in Robert K. Massie, *Nicholas and Alexandra*, 1967

4 Robert D. Crews, *For Prophet and Tsar: Islam and Empire in Russia and Central Asia*, 2006

5   *Petersburgskaia gazeta*, 23 February 1913

6   Dmitri Smirnov, 'Moia poezdka na Romanovskie prazdnestva v S Petersburg', *Tobol'skie eparkhial'nye vedemosti*, no. 11, 1913

7   Orlando Figes, *A People's Tragedy: The Russian Revolution, 1891–1924*, 1997

8   *Petersburgskaia gazeta*, 22 February 1913

9   Op. cit., Smirnov

10   Quoted in op. cit., Wortman

11   Op. cit., Smirnov

12   Op. cit., Figes

13   Phillips, *Sergey Prokofiev Diaries*

14   Op. cit., Figes

15   Ibid.

16   Wayne Dowler, *Russia in 1913*, 2010

17   Ibid.

18   Op. cit., Figes

19   Andrei Bely, *Petersburg*, trans. David McDuff, 1995 (first published in Russian in serial form in 1913–1914; and in book form in 1916)

20   Louis Réau, *Saint-Pétersbourg*, 1913

21   Op. cit., Figes

22   Katerina Clark, *Petersburg, Crucible of Cultural Revolution*, 1995

23   Op. cit., Smirnov

24   Op. cit., Dowler

25   Ibid.

26   Halford J. Mackinder, 'The Geographical Pivot of History', *The Geographical Journal*, vol. 23, no. 4, 1904

27   *Petersburgskaia gazeta*, 17 and 19 March 1913

28   Op. cit., Dowler

29   *The Economist*, 16 August 1913

30   William C. Wohlforth, 'The Perception of Power: Russia in the pre-1914 Balance', *World Politics*, vol. 39, no. 3, 1987

31   Ibid.

32   Op. cit., Dowler

33   Bernard Pares, *Russia and Reform*, 1907

34   Quoted in op. cit., Figes

35   *Darkest Russia*, 26 March 1913

36   Mark D. Steinberg, *Petersburg: Fin de Siècle*, 2011

37   Quoted in Nina Gurianova, *The Aesthetics of Anarchy: Art and Ideology in the Early Russian Avant-Garde*, 2012

38   *Petersburgskaia gazeta*, 3 December 1913

39   Luigi Villari, *Russia under a Great Shadow*, 1905

40   Ibid.

41   Sergey Witte, *The Memoirs of Count Witte*, trans. Abraham Yarmolinsky, 1921 (Russian text completed 1912)

42 Mikhail Loukianov, 'Conservatives and "Renewed Russia" 1907–1914', *Slavic Review*, vol. 61, no. 4, 2002

43 Ibid.

44 Op. cit., Witte

45 *Vestnik Evropy*, December 1913

46 Zoza Szajkowski, 'The Impact of the Beilis Case on Central and Western Europe', *Proceedings of the American Academy for Jewish Research*, vol. 31, 1963; Hans Rogger, 'The Beilis Case: Anti-Semitism and Politics in the Reign of Nicholas II', *Slavic Review*, vol. 25, no. 4, 1966

47 Anders Henriksson, 'Nationalism, Assimilation and Identity in Late Imperial Russia: The St. Petersburg Germans', *Russian Review*, vol. 52, no. 3, 1993

48 *Journal de Saint Pétersbourg*, 14 July 1913

49 Sally West, 'The Material Promised Land: Advertising's Modern Agenda in Late Imperial Russia', *Russian Review*, vol. 57, no. 3, 1998

50 Vladimir Nabokov, *Speak, Memory: An Autobiography Revisited*, 1966 (2000 edition consulted)

51 Solomon Volkov, *Saint Petersburg: A Cultural History*, 1996

52 Op. cit., Phillips

53 George Dobson, *St Petersburg*, 1910

54 Op. cit., Dowler

55 *Birzheye vedomosti*, no. 174, July 1913

56 *Petrogradskaie gazeta*, January 1913

57 Op. cit., Figes

58 John Maynard Keynes, *The Economic Consequences of the Peace*, London, 1919

II *The Old New World*

1 William Thomas Stead, *The Americanization of the World*, 1901; Guglielmo Ferrero, 'The Riddle of America', *The Atlantic*, November 1913

2 Edward Mandell House, *Philip Dru, Administrator: A Story of Tomorrow, 1920–1935*, 1912

3 Jackson Lears, *Rebirth of a Nation: The Making of Modern America, 1877–1920*, 2009; Alan Valentine, *1913: America Between Two Worlds*, 1962

4 For example, *Scientific American*, 20 September 1913

5 *The New York Times*, 26 January 1915

6 Burton J. Hendrick, *The Life and Letters of Walter H. Page*, 1924

7   Woodrow Wilson, 'Democracy and Efficiency', *The Atlantic*, March
     1901
8   John Milton Cooper, Jr, *Woodrow Wilson: A Biography*, 2009
9   'Red hot imperialist' from the *New York Herald*, October 15, 1900; the
     suggestion for the Stars and Stripes from the *North American Review*,
     February 1901
10   Woodrow Wilson, *The New Freedom*, Arthur S. Link, ed., 1956 (orig-
     inally published 1913, based on campaign speeches throughout 1912)
11   Ibid.
12   Ibid.

Washington, DC

1   *The New York Times*, 2 March 1913
2   *Harper's Weekly*, 11 January 1913
3   *National Geographic*, June 1913
4   *Harper's Weekly*, 8 March 1913
5   Both German and Russian comment from *The American Review of
     Reviews*, January 1913
6   Cooper, *Woodrow Wilson*
7   *The Economist*, 8 March 1913
8   *Harper's Weekly*, 8 March 1913
9   Woodrow Wilson, *The Papers of Woodrow Wilson*, 7 March 1913
10   Henry James, *The American Scene*, 1907
11   Op. cit., Wilson papers, 22 March 1913
12   Op. cit., Wilson papers, 26 May 1913
13   *Harper's Weekly*, 22 February 1913
14   Ibid.
15   Ibid.
16   Paul-Henri d'Estournelles de Constant, *Les États-Unis D'Amérique*,
     1913
17   Ibid.
18   Op. cit., Wilson papers, 1 October 1913
19   Charles Frederick Weller and Eugenia Winston Weller, *Neglected
     Neighbors: Stories of Life in the Alleys, Tenements and Shanties of the
     National Capital*, 1909
20   Ibid.
21   Ibid.
22   Ibid.
23   Cited in Arthur S. Link, 'Woodrow Wilson: The American as
     Southerner', *The Journal of Southern History*, vol. 36, no. 1, 1970
24   Ibid.

25 Ibid.
26 *The American Review of Reviews*, August 1913
27 Ibid.
28 Op. cit., Wilson papers, 28 June 1913
29 Op. cit., Wilson papers, 4 July 1913
30 Gary Gerstle, 'Race and Nation in the Thought and Politics of Woodrow Wilson', in John Milton Cooper Jr, ed., *Reconsidering Woodrow Wilson: Progressivism, Internationalism, War and Peace*, 2008
31 Op. cit., Cooper
32 Henry Blumenthal, 'Woodrow Wilson and the Race Question', *The Journal of Negro History*, vol. 48, no. 1, January 1963
33 Nancy J. Weiss, 'The Negro and the New Freedom: Fighting Wilsonian Segregation', *Political Science Quarterly*, vol. 84, no. 1, March 1969
34 Op. cit., Wilson papers, 5 August 1913
35 Ibid.
36 Op. cit., Wilson papers, 15 August 1913
37 Op. cit., Wilson papers, 14 October 1913 (although the report was undertaken in September, it apparently reached the White House the following month)
38 Ibid.

New York

1   W. T. Stead, *Satan's Invisible World Displayed or, Despairing Democracy: A Study of Greater New York*, 1898
2   Henry Bruère, *The American Review of Reviews*, October 1913
3   Op. cit., Stead (1898)
4   *Harper's Weekly*, 27 December 1913
5   Lyman Beecher Stowe, 'Vice, Crime and the New York Police', *The American Review of Reviews*, July 1913
6   John H. Girdner, *Newyorkitis*, 1901
7   *The New York Times*, 14 March 1908
8   Mark Girouard, *Cities & People: A Social and Architectural History*, 1985
9   *Harper's Weekly*, September 6 1913
10 *L'Illustration*, 31 May 1913 (author's translation from the French. An English version of this article – slightly different from the French – had been published in *The Century Magazine* in February and March 1913)
11 Ibid.
12 Ibid.
13 As reported in *The New York Times*, 23 February 1913 (the diary entry referred to was for 30 September the previous year)

14   *The New York Times*, 25 April 1913
15   Sarah Bradford Landau and Carl W. Condit, *Rise of the New York Skyscraper, 1865–1913*, 1996 and following
16   'Mr FW Woolworth's Story', *World's Work*, 25 April 1913
17   Op. cit., Girouard
18   Keith D. Revell, 'Regulating the Landscape: Real Estate Values, City Planning, and the 1916 Zoning Ordinance', in David Ward and Oliver Zunz, eds, *The Landscape of Modernity: New York City, 1900–1940*, 1992
19   Across the country a Campanile tower was under construction in 1913 at the University of California at Berkeley
20   Archives of American Art at the Smithsonian Institution (AAASI), Walter Kuhn and Kuhn family papers, letters from Walter Kuhn, series 1/box 1, Berlin, October 1912
21   Laurette E. McCarthy, 'The "Truths" about the Armory Show: Walter Pach's Side of the Story', *Archives of American Art Journal*, vol. 44, nos 3–4, 2004; Milton W. Brown, *The Story of the Armory Show*, 1963
22   *The Outlook*, 29 March 1913
23   *Harper's Weekly*, 15 March 1913
24   Op. cit., Walter Kuhn archives, series 1/box 2
25   *Evening Mail*, 15 March 1913
26   Moses Rischin, *The Promised City: New York's Jews, 1870–1914*, 1962
27   Israel Zangwill, *The Melting Pot*, 1909
28   Ibid.
29   Meri-Jane Rochelson, *A Jew in the Public Arena: The Career of Israel Zangwill*, 2008
30   Op. cit., Zangwill
31   Henry Smith Williams, *Harper's Weekly*, 26 July 1913
32   Ibid.
33   Most of the sources for this section are from the J. P. Morgan archives, held in the J. P. Morgan library in New York City, particularly series 1, subseries A.
34   *The North American Indian*, J. P. Morgan archives
35   *The Independent*, 3 April 1913
36   J. P. Morgan archives, series 1, subseries B
37   J. P Morgan archives, series 1, subseries A
38   *J. P. Morgan's Testimony: The Justification of Wall Street*, 1912/1913
39   J. P. Morgan archives, series 1, subseries B
40   *The New York Evening Journal*, April 1 1913
41   Quoted in *The Philadelphia Record*, April 1 1913
42   Ibid.
43   J. P. Morgan archive, series 1, subseries A
44   *Le Figaro*, 1 April 1913

45 J. Lawrence Broz, 'Origins of the Federal Reserve System: International Incentives and the Domestic Free-Rider Problem', *International Organization*, vol. 53, no. 1, 1999

Detroit

1 *Guide to Detroit*, 1916, Henry Ford Archives
2 *Detroit Free Press*, 7 September 1913
3 Op. cit., *Guide to Detroit*, 1916
4 Ibid.
5 Henry Ford Archives, photographic print P.P. 7227, 4 July 1917
6 Quoted in Jean-Louis Cohen, *Scenes of the World to Come: European Architecture and the American Challenge, 1893–1960*, 1995
7 Clarence Hooker, *Life in the Shadows of the Crystal Palace, 1910–1927: Ford Workers in the Model T Era*, 1997
8 *Detroit Free Press*, 13 August 1913
9 *Detroit Free Press*, 30 December 1913
10 *Ford Times*, August 1913
11 *Detroit Free Press*, 8 September 1913
12 *Harper's Weekly*, 22 February 1913
13 Quoted in Valentine, *1913*
14 *Ford Times*, May and August 1913
15 *Ford Times*, October 1913
16 *Ford Times*, February 1913
17 *Ford Times*, October 1913
18 *Ford Times*, June 1913
19 *Ford Times*, March 1913
20 Steven Watts, *The People's Tycoon: Henry Ford and the American Century*, 2005
21 Robert Casey, *The Model T: A Centennial History*, 2008; *Ford Times*, January 1913
22 *Ford Times*, September 1913
23 Charles R. Morris, *The Tycoons: How Andrew Carnegie, John D. Rockefeller, Jay Gould, and J. P. Morgan Invented the American Supereconomy*, 2005
24 *Los Angeles Times*, 1 January 1913
25 *Ford Times*, September 1913
26 Quoted in op. cit., Watts
27 Simon Nelson Patten, *A New Basis for Civilization*, 1907
28 Ferrero, 'The Riddle of America'
29 Stead, *The Americanization of the World*
30 *The New York Times*, 11 July 1916

Los Angeles

1   *The Economist*, 4 January 1913
2   Quoted in *The American Review of Reviews*, October 1913
3   Margaret Leslie Davis, *Dark Side of Fortune: Triumph and Scandal in the Life of Oil Tycoon Edward L. Doheny*, 1998
4   Lionel V. Redpath, *Petroleum in California: A Concise and Reliable History of the Oil Industry of the State*, 1900
5   John Steven McGroarty, quoted in William Deverell, *Whitewashed Adobe: The Rise of Los Angeles and the Remaking of its Mexican Past*, 2004
6   D'Estournelles de Constant, *Les États-Unis D'Amérique*
7   *Harper's Weekly*, 7 June 1913
8   *Los Angeles Times*, 20 April 1913
9   Wilson, *The Papers of Woodrow Wilson*, 13 May 1913
10   Quoted in Robert M. Fogelson, *The Fragmented Metropolis: Los Angeles, 1850–1930*, 1967 (reprinted 1993)
11   *Los Angeles Times*, 1 January 1913
12   Ibid.
13   Ibid.
14   *Los Angeles Times*, 5 November 1913
15   Catherine Mulholland, *William Mulholland and the Rise of Los Angeles*, 2000
16   *Los Angeles Times*, 11 May 1913
17   *Los Angeles Record*, 20 October 1913
18   Kim Hernandez, 'The "Bungalow Boom": The Working-Class Housing Industry and the Development and Promotion of Early Twentieth-Century Los Angeles', *Southern California Quarterly*, no. 92, Winter 2010/2011
19   Peter Hall, 'The Dream Factory: Los Angeles, 1910–1945', in Peter Hall, *Cities in Civilization*, 1998
20   *Harper's Weekly*, 18 January 1913
21   *Los Angeles Record*, 22 October 1913
22   Helen Hunt Jackson, *Ramona: A Story*, 1911 edition (originally published 1884)
23   Phoebe S. Kropp, *California Vieja: Culture and Memory in a Modern American Place*, 2006
24   George Wharton James, *Through Ramona's Country*, 1909

Mexico City

1   Report from John Lind to William Jennings Bryan, in Wilson, *The Papers of Woodrow Wilson*, 19 September 1913
2   Jonathan C. Brown, *Oil and Revolution in Mexico*, 1993
3   Quoted in Frank McLynn, *Villa and Zapata: A Biography of the Mexican Revolution*, 2000
4   Charles Macomb Flandrau, *Viva Mexico!*, 1908
5   Emil Harry Blichfeldt, *A Mexican Journey*, 1912
6   Michael J. Gonzales, 'Imagining Mexico in 1910: Visions of the Patria in the Centennial Celebration in Mexico City', *Journal of Latin American Studies*, no. 39, 2007
7   Quoted in ibid.
8   John Kenneth Turner, *Barbarous Mexico*, 1911
9   John Foran, 'Reinventing the Mexican Revolution: The Competing Paradigms of Alan Knight and John Mason Hart', *Latin American Perspectives*, vol. 23, no. 4, 1996
10 Op. cit., Flandrau, 1908
11 Frederick C. Turner, 'Anti-Americanism in Mexico: 1910–1913', *The Hispanic American Historical Review*, vol. 47, no. 4, 1967
12 Report from William Bayard Hale to Woodrow Wilson, in op. cit., Wilson papers, 18 June 1913
13 Op. cit., McLynn
14 *The Economist*, 15 February 1913
15 Quoted in Jerry W. Knudson, 'The Mexican Herald: Outpost of Empire, 1895–1915', *International Communication Gazette*, 63, 2001
16 Report by William Bayard Hale to Wilson, op. cit., Wilson papers, 18 June 1913
17 Op. cit., Wilson papers, 7 March 1913
18 Note from John Bassett Moore, Assistant Secretary of State, to the President, op. cit., Wilson papers, 14 May 1913
19 Op. cit., Wilson papers, 18 April 1913
20 Holger H. Herwig and Christon I. Archer, 'Global Gambit: A German General Staff Assessment of Mexican Affairs', *Estudios Mexicanos*, vol. 1, no. 2, 1985
21 Op. cit., Wilson papers, 26 May 1913
22 Op. cit., Wilson papers, 8 July 1913
23 Op. cit., Wilson papers, 24 July 1913
24 Note from Federico Gamboa, op. cit., Wilson papers, 16 August 1913
25 Letter from John Lind to William Jennings Bryan, op. cit., Wilson papers, 19 September 1913

26 Beatty, *The Lost History of 1914*
27 Letter from Walter Hines Page to Wilson, op. cit., Wilson papers, 12 September 1913
28 *The Daily Chronicle*, 8 May 1913

III *The World Beyond*

1   Rudyard Kipling, *Rudyard Kipling's Verse, 1885–1932*, 1934 (the poem was first published in 1896)
2   Christopher Bayly, *The Birth of the Modern World, 1780–1914*, 2004
3   V. I. Lenin, *The Three Sources and Three Component Parts of Marxism*, 1913
4   Kwasi Kwarteng, *Ghosts of Empire: Britain's Legacies in the Modern World*, 2011
5   Quoted in Edward Said, *Culture and Imperialism*, 1993

Winnipeg–Melbourne

1   *Manitoba Free Press*, 16 May 1913
2   Ibid.
3   *Manitoba Free Press*, 24 May 1913
4   Ibid.
5   *The Argus*, 14 May 1913
6   *The Argus*, 24 May 1913
7   Quoted in Carl Berger, *Imperialism and Nationalism, 1884–1914: A Conflict in Canadian Thought*, 1969
8   John Foster Fraser, *Australia: The Making of a Nation*, 1911
9   Ibid.
10 *The Argus*, 28 June 1913
11 *The Argus*, 1 July 1913
12 *The Argus*, 11 July 1913
13 *The Argus*, 12 July 1913
14 *Victorian Yearbook 1913–1914*, 1914; *The Argus*, 20 September 1913
15 *Sydney Morning Herald*, October 6 1913
16 Ibid.
17 Quoted in op. cit., Berger
18 Ibid.
19 Ibid.
20 *Manitoba Free Press*, 7 January 1913
21 *Manitoba Free Press*, 19 February 1913

22 *Manitoba Free Press*, 7 May 1913

23 Quoted in D. C. M. Platt, 'Canada and Argentina: The first prefer-
    ence of the British investor, 1904–1914', *The Journal of Imperial and
    Commonwealth History*, vol. 13, no. 3, 1985

24 *The Illustrated Souvenir of Winnipeg, Manitoba*, 1905

25 Ibid.

26 *Canada Newspaper Directory*, 1913

27 Alan F. G. Artibise, 'Boosterism and the Development of Prairie
    Cities, 1871–1913', in Alan Artibise, ed., *Town and City: Aspects of
    Western Canadian Urban Development*, 1981

28 Photograph Archives of Manitoba, Winnipeg

29 Alan F. J. Artibise, ed., *Gateway City: Documents on the City of Winnipeg,
    1873–1913*, 1979

30 Op. cit., Artibise (1981)

31 Quoted in op. cit., Artibise (1979)

32 *Manitoba Free Press*, 20 May 1913

33 Jim Blanchard, *Winnipeg 1912*, 2005

34 Henry J. Boam, *Twentieth Century Impressions of Canada: Its History,
    People, Commerce, Industries and Resources*, 1914

35 *Scanlon's Guide to Winnipeg*, 1913

36 *The Canada Newspaper Directory*, 1913

37 Op. cit., Artibise (1979)

38 *Manitoba Free Press*, 30 May 1913; J. M. Bumsted, *Dictionary of
    Manitoba Biography*, 1999

39 *Manitoba Free Press*, 31 May 1913

40 *Manitoba Free Press*, 3 January 1913

41 Graeme Davison, *The Rise and Fall of Marvellous Melbourne*, 1978

42 *Victorian Year Book 1913–1914*, 1914

43 Alex Hill, *Round the British Empire*, 1913

44 *Victorian Year Book 1913–1914*, 1914

45 Miles Lewis, 'The Dome', *La Trobe Library Journal*, no. 72, 2003

46 The film *Marvellous Melbourne: Queen City of the South* is available at
    www.archive.org

47 Op. cit., Hill

48 *The Argus*, 29 April 1913

49 *Victorian Year Book 1913–1914*, 1914

50 *The Argus*, 13 December 1913; *The Argus*, 23 October 1913

51 *The Argus*, 22 November 1913

52 *The Argus*, 22 August 1913

53 *The Argus*, 31 March 1913

54 *The Argus*, 28 January 1913

55 Geoffrey Blainey, *A History of Victoria*, 2006

56   *The Argus*, 18 November 1913
57   Edwin J. Brady, *Australia Unlimited*, 1910
58   *The Illustrated Souvenir of Winnipeg, Manitoba*, 1905

Buenos Aires

1   Reginald Lloyd, *Twentieth century impressions of Argentina: Its history, people, commerce, industries, and resources*, 1910
2   Platt, 'Canada and Argentina . . .'
3   Carlos F. Díaz Alejandro, *Essays on the Economic History of the Argentine Republic*, 1970
4   Albert B. Martinez, *Baedeker de la République argentine*, 1913
5   Georges Clemenceau, *South America Today: A Study of Conditions, Social, Political and Commercial, in Argentina, Uruguay and Brazil*, 1911
6   C. Knick Harley, 'The World Food Economy and Pre-World War I Argentina', in S. N. Broadberry and N. F. R. Crafts, *Britain in the International Economy*, 1992
7   *Buenos Aires Herald*, 6 February 1913
8   Op. cit., Martinez
9   Quoted in op. cit., Martinez
10   Op. cit., Lloyd
11   *Buenos Aires Herald*, 13 November 1913
12   Ibid.
13   Op. cit., Clemenceau
14   Op. cit., Lloyd
15   *The Standard* (Buenos Aires), 4 December 1913
16   Ibid.
17   *Buenos Aires Herald*, 25 December 1913
18   *Buenos Aires Herald*, 12 September 1913; John Fraser, 'The Diaghilev Ballet in South America: Footnotes to Nijinsky, Part One', *Dance Chronicle*, vol. 5, no. 1, 1982
19   Quoted in op. cit., Fraser
20   *Buenos Aires Herald*, 5 October 1913
21   Op. cit., Díaz Alejandro
22   *The English Address Book of British and North American Residents, Business Houses, Institutions, etc. – Argentine Republic*, 1913
23   *Buenos Aires Herald*, 8 May 1913
24   *Buenos Aires Herald*, 12 February 1913
25   *Buenos Aires Herald*, 24 May 1913
26   Leandro Losada, 'Sociabilidad, distinción y alta sociedad en Buenos Aires: Los clubes sociales de la elite porteña (1880–1930)', *Desarrollo Económico*, vol. 45, no. 180, 2006

27 James R. Scobie, 'Buenos Aires as a Commercial-Bureaucratic City, 1880–1910: Characteristics of a City's Orientation', *The American Historical Review*, vol. 77, no. 4, 1972

28 *Buenos Aires Herald*, 31 January 1913

29 *Standard* (Buenos Aires), 6 February 1913

30 Op. cit., Clemenceau

31 J. P. Daughton, 'When Argentina was "French": Rethinking Cultural Politics and European Imperialism in Belle-Époque Buenos Aires', *The Journal of Modern History*, vol. 80, no. 4, 2008; *Buenos Aires Herald*, 8 February 1913

32 *Buenos Aires Herald*, 28 January 1913

33 Op. cit., Clemenceau

34 Ibid.

35 Op. cit., Daughton

36 Luis Tosoni, 'Gaetano Moretti et su obsesión americana', lecture given to the Instituto de Arte Americano e Investigaciones Estéticas, Buenos Aires, 26 September 2008

37 Op. cit., Clemenceau

38 *Buenos Aires Herald*, 6 March 1913

39 Op. cit., Lloyd

40 *Buenos Aires Herald*, 3 October 1913

41 *Buenos Aires Herald*, 13 April 1913

42 John Foster Fraser, *The Amazing Argentine: A New Land of Enterprise*, 1914

43 C. Reginald Enock, *The Republics of Central and South America: Their Resources, Industries, Sociology and Future*, 1913

44 Ibid.

45 Ibid.

46 *Buenos Aires Herald*, 5 October 1913

47 *Buenos Aires Herald*, 10 October 1913

Algiers

1 John Ruedy, *Modern Algeria: The Origins and Development of a Nation*, 2005

2 *L'Afrique française*, January 1913

3 Jean-Jacques Jordi and Jean-Louis Planche, '1860–1930: une certaine idée de la construction de la France', in Jean-Jacques Jordi and Jean-Louis Planche, *Alger 1860–1939: Le modèle ambigu du triomphe colonial*, 1999

4 Jean-Jacques Jordi and Pierre Enckell, 'Le temps des hiverneurs', in op. cit., Jordi and Planche

5   Gilbert Meynier, *L'Algérie révélée: La guerre du 1914–1918 et le premier quart du XXe siècle*, 1981

6   Quoted in op. cit., Meynier

7   Rachel Humphreys, *Algiers, the Sahara and the Nile*, 1913

8   Ibid.

9   Guides Joanne, *Algérie et Tunisie*, 1905

10   Ibid.

11   Op. cit., Humphreys

12   Karl Baedeker, *The Mediterranean: Seaports and Sea Routes, including Madeira, the Canary Islands, the Coast of Morocco, Algeria and Tunisia*, 1911

13   Quoted in Ursula Kingsmill Hart, *Two Ladies of Colonial Algeria: The Lives and Times of Aurelie Picard and Isabelle Eberhardt*, 1987

14   Xavier Malverti, 'Entre orientalisme et mouvement moderne', in op. cit., Jordi and Planche

15   Op. cit., Meynier

16   Kirsty K. Riggs, 'Bartok in the Desert: Challenges to a European Conducting Research in North Africa in the Early Twentieth Century', *Musical Quarterly*, vol. 90, no. 1, 2007

17   Quoted in op. cit., Meynier

18   André Servier, *Le Nationalisme Musulman en Egypte, en Tunisie, en Algérie: Le Péril de l'avenir*, 1913

19   Op. cit., Meynier

20   Ibid.

21   Ibid.

22   Ibid.

23   Op. cit., Ruedy

24   Rosa Luxemburg, *The Accumulation of Capital*, 2003 (first published as *Die Akkumulation des Kapitals* in 1913)

25   Chérif Benhabylès, *L'Algérie française vue par un indigène*, 1914

26   Belkacem Saadallah, 'The Rise of the Algerian Elite, 1900–1914', *The Journal of Modern African Studies*, vol. 5, no. 1, 1967

27   Ahmed Koulakssis and Gilbert Meynier, *L'Emir Khaled, Premier za'im?: Identité algérienne et colonialisme français*, 1987

28   Op. cit., Benhabylès

29   Ibid.

Bombay–Durban

1   *Attempt upon the Life of His Excellency the Viceroy and Governor General, on the occasion of the State Entry into Delhi, 23rd December 1912*, India Office archives, L/PJ/6/1216, file 183

2   Ibid.
3   Quoted in Thomas R. Metcalf, *An Imperial Vision: Indian Architecture and Britain's Raj*, 1989
4   Lawrence James, *The Making and Unmaking of British India*, 1997
5   Gordon Johnson, *Provincial politics and Indian nationalism: Bombay and the Indian National Congress*, 1973
6   Quoted in op. cit., James
7   Report of the 28th INC, Karachi, December 1913, India Office archives, L/PJ/6/1341, file 5311
8   William Wilson Hunter, *A History of British India*, two volumes, 1899, vol. 1
9   Rao Bahadur P.B. Joshi, *Empire-Day and Our Duties and Responsibilities*, 1913
10   Ibid.
11   Quoted in Dennis Judd, *The Lion and the Tiger: The Rise and Fall of the British Raj, 1600–1947*, 2004
12   D. K. Fieldhouse, 'The Metropolitan Economics of Empire', in Judith M. Brown and William Roger Louis, eds, *The Oxford History of the British Empire: The Twentieth Century*, 1999
13   W. R. S. Sharpe, *Bombay: The Gateway of India*, 1930
14   S. M. Rutnagur, ed., *Electricity in India: Being a History of the Tata Hydro-Electric Project, with notes on the mill industry and the progress of electric drive in Indian factories*, 1912
15   *The Indian Witness* (Calcutta), quoted in ibid.
16   Ibid.
17   Prashant Kidambi, *The Making of an Indian Metropolis: Colonial Governance and Public Culture in Bombay, 1890–1920*, 2007
18   Suresh Chabria, ed., *Light of Asia: Indian Silent Cinema, 1912–1934*, 1994
19   Rudyard Kipling, *The Seven Seas*, 1896
20   Bojidar Karageorgevitch, *Enchanted India*, 1899 (first published in French)
21   Count Hans von Koenigsmarck, *A German Staff Officer in India: Being the Impressions of an Officer of the German General Staff of his Travels through the Peninsula*, trans. P. H. Oakley Williams, 1909
22   Ibid.
23   S. M. Edwardes, *By-Ways of Bombay*, 1912
24   Op. cit., Kidambi
25   Ibid.
26   Ibid.; op. cit., Edwardes
27   Quoted in R. P. Karkaria, ed., *The Charm of Bombay: An Anthology of Writings in Praise of the First City in India*, 1915
28   Ibid.

29   Quoted in S. B. Upadhyay, *Dissension and Unity: The Origins of Workers' Solidarity in the Cotton Mills of Bombay, 1875–1918*, 1990

30   Op. cit., Koenigsmarck

31   *Thacker's Bombay Directory*, 1913

32   Christopher W. London, 'Edwardian Architects of Bombay: George Wittet and John Begg', in C. London, ed., *Architecture in Victorian and Edwardian India*, 1994

33   Rachel Humphreys, *Travels East of Suez*, 1915

34   J. A. Spender, *The Indian Scene*, 1912

35   Ibid.

36   Ibid.

37   Preeti Chopra, *A Joint Enterprise: Indian Elites and the Making of British Bombay*, 2011

38   *Honourable Mr G. K. Gokhale's Visit to South Africa*, special edition of *Indian Opinion*, 1912

39   Quoted in Sugata Bose, *A Hundred Horizons: The Indian Ocean in the age of global empire*, 2006

40   South Africa Act, 1909

41   South African Census, 1911

42   John Lambert, '"The Last Outpost": The Natalians, South Africa, and the British Empire', in Robert Bickers, ed., *Settlers and Expatriates: Britons over the Seas*, 2010

43   Maureen Swan, 'The 1913 Natal Indian Strike', *Journal of Southern African Studies*, vol. 10, no. 2, 1984

44   Goolam Vahed, 'Passengers, Partnerships and Promissory Notes: Gujurati Traders in Colonial Natal, 1870–1920', *The International Journal of African Historical Studies*, vol. 38, no. 3, 2005

45   Robert A. Huttenback, 'Indians in South Africa, 1860–1914: The British Philosophy on Trial', *The English Historical Review*, vol. 81, no. 319, 1966

46   Quoted in Ronald Hyam, 'African Interests and the South Africa Act, 1908–1910', in Peter Henshaw, ed., *The Lion and the Springbok: Britain and South Africa since the Boer War*, 2003

47   Quoted in *Natal Mercury*, 11 April 1913

48   *Indian Opinion*, 8 February 1913

49   *Natal Mercury*, 14 February 1913

50   Ibid.

51   *Indian Opinion*, 8 October 1913

52   *Natal Mercury*, 9 May 1913

53   Ibid.

54   *Natal Mercury*, 20 June 1913

55   *Natal Mercury*, 7 October 1913

56   *Indian Opinion*, 13 November 1913

57 *Natal Mercury*, 28 October 1913
58 *Indian Opinion*, 10 December 1913
59 *The Economist*, 6 December 1913
60 Solomon Tshekisko Plaatje, *Native Life in South Africa before and since the European War and the Boer Rebellion*, 1916
61 Quoted in Martin Meredith, *Diamonds, Gold and War: The Making of South Africa*, 2007
62 Harvey M. Feinberg, 'The 1913 Natives Land Act in South Africa: Politics, Race, and Segregation in the Early 20th Century', *The International Journal of African Historical Studies*, vol. 26, no. 1, 1993
63 Ibid.
64 *A National Symposium: Essays on South African Subjects by South African Writers* (pamphlet of articles originally published in the *Natal Mercury* in November 1912)
65 Ibid.
66 Ibid.
67 *Natal Mercury*, 6 June 1913
68 *Natal Mercury*, 18 July 1913
69 Ibid.
70 Op. cit., Plaatje

Tehran

1   *Hansard*, 28 July 1913
2   R. Jarman, ed., *Iran: Political Diaries, 1881–1965*, vol. 3, 1997, May 12 1913
3   Op. cit., Jarman (1997), July 8 1913
4   Dorothy de Warzée, *Peeps into Persia*, 1913
5   Ibid.
6   Ibid.
7   George Nathaniel Curzon, *Persia and the Persian Question*, 1892
8   *Military Handbooks of Arabia, 1913–1917*, vol. 1: *Strategical Study of Persia and the Persian Gulf, 1913*, 1998
9   Ervand Abrahamian, *A History of Modern Iran*, 2008
10 Taj al-Saltanah, *Crowning Anguish: Memoirs of a Persian Princess from the Harem to Modernity, 1884–1936*, Abbas Amanat, ed., trans. Anna Vanzan and Amin Neshati, 1993
11 *Collier's Weekly*, 2 August 1913
12 Ibid.
13 W. Morgan Shuster, *The Strangling of Persia: Story of the European Diplomacy and Oriental Intrigue That Resulted in the Denationalization of Twelve Million Mohammadans, A Personal Narrative*, 1912

14   Op. cit., Curzon

15   Firoozeh Kashani-Sabet, *Frontier Fictions: Shaping the Iranian Nation, 1804–1946*, 2000

16   Michael Axworthy, *Iran: Empire of the Mind: A History from Zoroaster to the Present Day*, 2008

17   Quoted in op. cit., Kashani-Sabet

18   Ibid.

19   Op. cit., Shuster

20   Percy Sykes, *A History of Persia*, vol. 2, 1930

21   Ibid.

22   Op. cit., Jarman (1997), 23 December 1913

23   Marian Kent, *Moguls and Mandarins: Oil, Imperialism and the Middle East in British Foreign Policy, 1900–1940*, 1993

24   *The Economist*, 26 July 1913

25   *Hansard*, 17 July 1913

26   Denis Wright, *The Persians Amongst the English: Episodes in Anglo-Persian History*, 1985; Ronald W. Ferrier, *The History of the British Petroleum Company*, 1982

Jerusalem

1   Israel State Archives (ISA), German consular note, 443/7, December 1913

2   Roberto Mazza, *Jerusalem: From the Ottomans to the British*, 2009

3   Ibid.

4   Simon Sebag Montefiore, *Jerusalem: The Biography*, 2011

5   Quoted in 'Selma Ekrem – Jerusalem 1908: In the Household of the Ottoman Governor', *Jerusalem Quarterly* 50, 2012 (extracts taken from Selma Ekrem's memoirs printed in Turkey in 1931)

6   Ibid.

7   Ibid.

8   Salim Tamari, 'Jerusalem's Ottoman Modernity: The Times and Lives of Wasif Jawhariyyeh', *Jerusalem Quarterly* 9, 2000

9   Wasif Jawhariyyeh, *Al Quds Al Othaminyah Fi Al Mutbakrat Al Jawhariyyeh*, Issam Nassar and Salim Tamari, eds, 2001

10   Salim Tamari, 'The Vagabond Café and Jerusalem's Prince of Idleness', *Jerusalem Quarterly* 19, 2003

11   Abigail Jacobson, 'Alternative Voices in Late Ottoman Palestine: A Historical Note', *Jerusalem Quarterly* 21, 2004

12   Op. cit., Tamari (2000)

13   Op. cit., Jawhariyyeh

14   Op. cit., Sebag Montefiore

15 Stephen Graham, *With the Russian Pilgrims to Jerusalem*, 1913
16 Ibid.
17 Ibid.
18 Ibid.
19 Helga Dudman and Ruth Kark, *The American Colony: Scenes from a Jerusalem Saga*, 1998
20 Bertha Spafford Vester, *Our Jerusalem: An American Family in the Holy City, 1881–1949*, 1951
21 Op. cit., Dudman and Kark
22 Ibid.
23 Sufian Abu Zaida, '"A Miserable Provincial Town": The Zionist Approach to Jerusalem from 1897–1937', *Jerusalem Quarterly* 32, 2007
24 Amy Dockser Marcus, *Jerusalem 1913: The Origins of the Arab-Israeli Conflict*, 2007
25 Ibid.
26 Central Zionist Archive (CZA), L2/27
27 CZA, L2/26/3
28 Ibid.
29 Quoted in Neville J. Mandel, *The Arabs and Zionism before World War I*, 1976
30 Ibid.
31 Op. cit., Jacobson
32 CZA, L2/26/3, letter dated 26 January 1913
33 Ibid.
34 Op. cit., Dockser Marcus
35 CZA, L2/26/3
36 Ibid.
37 Quoted in op. cit., Mandel
38 Mendel Beilis, *The Story of My Sufferings*, trans. Harrison Goldberg, 1926
39 Ibid.
40 ISA 415/10, German consular note, February 1914
41 Theodor Herzl, *The Diaries of Theodor Herzl*, Martin Lowenthal, ed., 1978

IV Twilight Powers

1 *The New York Times*, 18 May 1898; Kennedy, *The Rise and Fall of the Great Powers*
2 Ibid.
3 Elizabeth Kendall, *A Wayfarer in China*, 1913
4 Erik J. Zürcher, *The Young Turk Legacy and Nation Building*, 2010
5 *Le Petit Journal*, 16 January 1898

6   Anon., *China as it Really Is*, 1912
7   Marius B. Jansen, *The Making of Modern Japan*, 2002
8   Quoted in ibid.
9   Quoted in Carol Gluck, *Japan's Modern Myths: Ideology in the Late Meiji Period*, 1985
10   Peter H. Hoffenberg, *An Empire on Display: English, Indian, and Australian Exhibitions from the Crystal Palace to the Great War*, 2001

Constantinople

1   Quoted in Ebru Boyar and Kate Fleet, *A Social History of Ottoman Istanbul*, 2010
2   Hermann Barth, *Constantinople*, 1906 (French version; original German published in 1901)
3   H. G. Dwight, *Constantinople Old and New*, 1915
4   Ibid.
5   Stanford J. Shaw, 'The Ottoman Census System and Population, 1831–1914', *International Journal of Middle Eastern Studies*, vol. 9, no. 3, 1978; Servet Mutlu, 'Late Ottoman Population and its Ethnic Distribution', *Turkish Journal of Population Studies*, no. 25, 2003; Philip Mansel, *Constantinople: City of the World's Desire, 1453–1923*, 1995
6   Mary Poynter, *When Turkey was Turkey*, 1921
7   Op. cit., Dwight
8   Ibid.
9   *Levant Herald and Eastern Express*, 2 January 1913
10   Op. cit., Shaw
11   Edmondo de Amicis, *Constantinople*, trans. Maria Horner, 1896 (originally published in Italian in 1877)
12   Zeynep Çelik, *The Remaking of Istanbul: Portrait of an Ottoman City in the Nineteenth Century*, 1986
13   Feroz Ahmad, *The Young Turks: The Committee of Union and Progress in Turkish Politics, 1908–1914*, 1969
14   Zürcher, *The Young Turk Legacy and Nation Building*
15   Renée Worringer, '"Sick man of Europe" or "Japan of the Near East?": Constructing Ottoman Modernity in the Hamidian and Young Turk Eras', *International Journal of Middle East Studies*, vol. 36, no. 2, 2004
16   Op. cit., Poynter
17   Ibid.
18   Op. cit., Ahmad
19   Op. cit., Poynter
20   Ibid.
21   Ibid.

22 Op. cit., Mansel

23 Francis McCullagh, *The Fall of Abd-Ul-Hamid*, 1910

24 Op. cit., Ahmad

25 G. F. Abbott, *Turkey in Transition*, 1909

26 Op. cit., Zürcher

27 Op. cit., Poynter

28 Op. cit., Mansel

29 Op. cit., Abbott

30 Robert Hichens, *The Near East*, 1913

31 Ibid.

32 Ellis Ashmead-Bartlett, *With the Turks in Thrace*, 1913

33 Henry Morgenthau, *United States Diplomacy on the Bosphorus: The Diaries of Ambassador Morgenthau 1913–1916*, compiled by Ara Sarafian, 2004

34 This and following from advertisements in the *Levant Herald and Eastern Express*, 6 and 9 January 1913

35 Op. cit., Boyar and Fleet

36 Andrew Mango, *Atatürk*, 1999

37 Karl Baedeker, *Konstantinopel und das Westliche Kleinasien*, 1905

38 Op. cit., Hichens

39 Op. cit., Dwight

40 Op. cit., Abbott

41 Quoted in op. cit., Boyar and Fleet

42 Ibid.

43 Ibid.

44 Zeyneb Hanoum, *A Turkish Woman's European Impressions*, 1913

45 Ibid.

46 Alexander van Millingen, *Constantinople*, 1906

47 Ibid.

48 Ibid.

49 Ibid.

50 Nicola Guy, *The Birth of Albania: Ethnic Nationalism, the Great Powers of World War I and the Emergence of Albanian Independence*, 2012

51 Quoted in Edith Durham, *High Albania*, 1909

52 Richard C. Hall, *The Balkan Wars, 1912–1913: Prelude to the First World War*, 2000

53 Op. cit., Dwight

54 Op. cit., Poynter

55 Pierre Loti, *Turquie Agonisante*, 1913

56 *The Nineteenth Century and After*, March 1913

57 Azmi Özcan, *Pan-Islamism: Indian Muslims, the Ottomans and Britain*, 1997

58 Justin McCarthy, *Death and Exile: The Ethnic Cleansing of Ottoman Muslims, 1821–1922*, 1996

59 Leon Sciaky, *Farewell to Salonica: City at the Crossroads*, 2007
60 Carnegie Endowment for International Peace, *Report of the International Commission to Inquire into the Causes and Conduct of the Balkan Wars*, 1914
61 Op. cit., McCarthy
62 Hasan Kayali, *Arabs and Young Turks: Ottomanism, Arabism, and Islamism in the Ottoman Empire, 1908–1918*, 1997
63 *The Economist*, 5 July 1913
64 Murat Gül, *The Emergence of Modern Istanbul: Transformation and Modernisation of a City*, 2009

Peking–Shanghai

1   Alphonse Favier, *Péking: Histoire et Description*, 1902
2   Madeleine Yue Dong, *Republican Beijing: The City and its Histories*, 2003
3   Katharine Carl, *With The Empress Dowager*, 1905
4   Ibid.
5   Ibid.
6   Julia Boyd, *A Dance with the Dragon: The Vanished World of Peking's Foreign Colony*, 2012
7   B. L. Putnam Weale, *Indiscreet Letter from Peking*, 1907
8   Op. cit., Boyd
9   Op. cit., Putnam Weale
10 A. Henry Savage Landor, *China and the Allies*, two volumes., 1901, vol. 2
11 Bickers, *The Scramble for China*
12 Anon., *Letters from John Chinaman*, 6th impression, 1904
13 Julia Lovell, *The Opium War*, 2011
14 Pierre Loti, *Les Derniers Jours de Pékin*, 1902
15 Quoted in Patricia Buckley Ebrey, ed., *Chinese Civilization: A Sourcebook*, 1993
16 Ibid.
17 Xu Guoqi, *China and the Great War: China's Pursuit of a New National Identity and Internationalization*, 2005
18 Quoted in op. cit., Ebrey
19 Op. cit., Bickers
20 Op. cit., Lovell
21 'Report of the International Opium Commission, Shanghai, China, February 1 to February 26 1909', *North China Daily News & Herald*, 1909
22 Jonathan Spence, *The Search for Modern China*, 2nd edition, 1999
23 Ibid.

24   H. T. Montague Bell and H. G. W. Woodhead, *The China Year Book 1913*, 1913

25   Henri Borel, *The New China: A Traveller's Impressions*, 1912

26   Ibid.

27   F. L. Hawks Pott, *A Short History of Shanghai: Being an Account of the Growth and Development of the International Settlement*, 1928

28   Op. cit., Bell and Woodhead

29   Op. cit., Spence

30   Arnold Wright, ed., *Twentieth Century Impressions of Hongkong, Shanghai, and other Treaty Ports of China: Their History, People, Commerce, Industries, and Resources*, 1908

31   Op. cit., Bell and Woodhead

32   Lu Hanchao, *Beyond the Neon Lights: Everyday Shanghai in the Early Twentieth Century*, 1999

33   Op. cit., Lovell

34   Christian Henriot, 'The Shanghai Bund in myth and history: an essay through textual and visual sources', *Journal of Modern Chinese History*, vol. 4, no. 1, 2010

35   Op. cit., Wright

36   Op. cit., Hanchao

37   Op. cit., Bickers

38   Op. cit., Bell and Woodhead

39   Ibid.

40   Op. cit., Bickers

41   Robert L. Jarman, ed., *Shanghai: Political and Economic Reports 1842–1943: British Governmental Records from the International City*, vol. 11, 2008 (report dated 23 January 1913)

42   Eliza Ruhamah Scidmore, *Westward to the Far East: A Guide to the Principal Cities of China and Japan with a Note on Korea*, 1900

43   Op. cit., Hawks Pott

44   Op. cit., Scidmore

45   James E. Elfers, *The Tour to End All Tours: The Story of Major League Baseball's 1913–1914 World Tour*, 2003

46   *North China Daily News*, 22 January 1913

47   *North China Daily News*, 23 January 1913

48   Quoted in Catherine Yeh, *Shanghai Love: Courtesans, Intellectuals and Entertainment Culture, 1850–1910*, 2006

49   Frederick McCormick, *The Flowery Republic*, 1913

50   Paul S. Reinsch, *An American Diplomat in China*, 1922

51   P'eng-yuan Chang and Andrew J. Nathan, 'Political Participation and Political Elites in early Republican China: The Parliament of 1913–1914', *The Journal of Asian Studies*, vol. 37, no. 2, 1978

52   Ching Chun Wang, *The Atlantic*, January 1913

53 E. Backhouse and J. O. P. Bland, *Annals and Memoirs of the Court of Peking*, 1914

54 US National Archives, RG84/350/2/4 – 175, note, consular archives for Shanghai, 1 April 1913

55 Ibid.

56 Op. cit., US National Archives, 11 April 1913

57 *North China Daily News*, 9 April 1913

58 Note from Chargé d'Affaires Williams, op. cit., US National Archives, 11 April 1913

59 Op. cit., Guoqi

60 Op. cit., US National Archives, 25 February 1913

61 Ibid.

62 *North China Daily News*, 29 March 1913

63 B. Atwood Robinson, 'America's Business Opportunity in China', *The Journal of Race Development*, vol. 3, no. 4, April 1913

64 St. Piero Rudiger, *The Second Revolution in China, 1913: My Adventures of the Fighting around Shanghai, the Arsenal, Woosung Forts*, 1914

65 'Report for the Year 1913 on the Trade of Shanghai', in op. cit., Jarman (2008)

66 Robert L. Jarman, ed., *China: Political Reports, 1911–1960*, vol. 1, 2001, letter to Foreign Secretary, L/PS/11/65 P4217/1913, 12 September 1913

67 Ibid., annual report from Sir John Jordan, FO 495/229, 23 January 1914

68 Jedidiah Kroncke, 'An Early Tragedy of Comparative Constitutionalism: Frank Goodnow and the Chinese Republic', *Pacific Rim Law and Policy Journal*, no. 533, 2012

69 *North China Daily News*, 29 December 1913

70 *Sydney Morning Herald*, 7 June 1913

Tokyo

1 J. Charles Schencking, 'The politics of pragmatism and pageantry: selling a national navy at the elite and local level in Japan, 1890–1913', in Sandra Wilson, ed., *Nation and Nationalism in Japan*, 2002

2 Ibid.; *The Japan Times*, 11 November 1913

3 Kennedy, *The Rise and Fall of the Great Powers*

4 *The Japan Times*, 6 November 1913

5 Jansen, *The Making of Modern Japan*

6 *The Japan Times*, 11 November 1913

7 Gluck, *Japan's Modern Myths*

8 Basil Hall Chamberlain and W. B. Mason, *A Handbook for Travellers in Japan*, 1913

9 Eliza Rumahah Scidmore, *Jinriksha Days in Japan*, 1900 edition

10   Jukichi Inouye, *Home Life in Tokyo*, 1910

11   Quoted in op. cit., Gluck

12   Op. cit., Gluck

13   Joseph Henry Longford, *The Evolution of New Japan*, 1913

14   André Sorensen, *The Making of Urban Japan: Cities and planning from Edo to the twenty-first century*, 2002

15   Pierre Loti, *Japoneries d'Automne*, 1889

16   Stephen Mansfield, *Tokyo: A Cultural History*, 2009

17   Op. cit., Longford

18   Op. cit., Sorensen

19   Ibid.

20   Ibid.

21   Op. cit., Inouye

22   Ibid.

23   Op. cit., Gluck

24   Sally Ann Hastings, *Neighborhood and Nation in Tokyo, 1905–1937*, 1995

25   Quoted in Edward Seidensticker, *Low City, High City, Tokyo from Edo to the Earthquake, 1867–1923*, 1983

26   Ozaki Yukio, *The Autobiography of Ozaki Yukio: The Struggle for Constitutional Government in Japan*, trans. Fujiko Hara, 2001

27   *The Japan Times*, 11 February 1913

28   R. L. Jarman, ed., *Japan: Political & Economic Reports, 1906–1970*, vol. 4: *Economic Reports, 1913–1926*, 2002

29   Op. cit., Gluck

30   Quoted in David John Lu, *Japan: A Documentary History*, two volumes, 1997, vol. 2

31   Okakura Kakuzo, *The Ideals of the East*, 1903

32   Rustom Bharucha, *Another Asia: Rabindranath Tagore and Okakura Tenshin*, 2006

33   *Africa Times and Orient Review*, February 1913

34   Op. cit., Jarman (2002), vol. 1: *Political Reports, 1906–1922*

35   Wilson, *The Papers of Woodrow Wilson*, 19 May 1913

36   *The Japan Times*, 17 April 1913

37   Marilyn Lake and Henry Reynolds, *Drawing the Global Colour Line: White Men's Countries and the International Challenge of Racial Equality*, 2008

38   Ibid.

39   *Japan Weekly Chronicle*, quoted in *Africa Times and Orient Review*, June 1913

40   *The Japan Times*, 13 April 1913

41   *Los Angeles Times*, 21 April 1913

42   William Elliot Griffis, *The Japanese Nation in Evolution: Steps in the*

Progress of a Great People, 1907; William Elliot Griffis, 'Japan and the United States: Are the Japanese Mongolian?', *North American Review*, vol. 197, no. 691, June 1913

43 *The Japan Times*, 5 September 1913
44 Ibid.
45 *The Japan Times*, 6 September 1913
46 *The Japan Times*, 7 September 1913
47 *The Japan Times*, 9 September 1913
48 *The Japan Times*, 11 September 1913
49 Op. cit., Ozaki
50 *The Japan Times*, 12 October 1913
51 *The New York Times*, 20 November 1913

London

1   *The Evening Standard*, 2 January 1913
2   Ronald Hyam, 'The British Empire in the Edwardian Era', in Judith M. Brown and Wm. Roger Louis, eds, in *The Oxford History of the British Empire: The Twentieth Century*, 1999
3   James Louis Garvin, 'The Maintenance of Empire: A Study in the Economics of Power', *The Empire and the Century: A Series of Essays on Imperial Problems and Possibilities by Various Writers*, 1905
4   Aaron L. Friedberg, *The Weary Titan: Britain and the Experience of Relative Decline, 1895–1905*, 1988
5   J. A. Hobson, *Imperialism: A Study*, 1902
6   Simon J. Potter, 'Richard Jebb, John S. Ewart and the Round Table, 1898–1926', *English Historical Review*, vol. CXXII, no. 495, 2007; John E. Kendle, *The Round Table Movement and Imperial Union*, 1975
7   Richard Jebb, *Studies in Colonial Nationalism*, 1905
8   Op. cit., Friedberg
9   Richard Jebb, *The Britannic Question: A Survey of Alternatives*, 1913
10 Elie Halévy, *L'Angleterre et son Empire*, 1905
11 Anon., *The Decline and Fall of the British Empire: A brief account of those causes which resulted in the destruction of our late Ally, together with a comparison between the British and Roman Empires*, 1905
12 Deirdre McMahon, 'Ireland and the Empire-Commonwealth, 1900–1948', in op. cit., Brown and Roger Louis
13 Jeremy Smith, 'Bluff, Bluster and Brinkmanship: Andrew Bonar Law and the Third Home Rule Bill', *The Historical Journal*, vol. 36, no. 1, 1993
14 Quoted in Alan Megaghey, '"God will defend the right": The

Protestant Churches and opposition to home rule', in David George Boyce and Alan O'Day, *Defenders of the Union: A Survey of British and Irish Unionism since 1801*, 2000

15 Rudyard Kipling, *The Years Between*, 1919 (poem from 1912)

16 *The Daily Chronicle*, 17 January 1913

17 Quoted in Jonathan Schneer, *Ben Tillett: Portrait of a Labour Leader*, 1982

18 House of Commons Debates, quoted in Chris Wrigley, 'Churchill and the Trade Unions', *Transactions of the Royal Historical Society*, vol. 11, 2001

19 Op. cit., Schneer

20 Andrew Rosen, *Rise Up Women! The Militant Campaign of the Women's Social and Political Union, 1903-1914*, 1974, quoted in Krista Cowman '"Incipient Toryism"? The Women's Social and Political Union and the Independent Labour Party, 1903–1914', *History Workshop Journal*, issue 53, 2002

21 *Hansard*, 5 May 1913

22 Ibid.

23 Ibid.

24 *The Daily Chronicle*, 8 May 1913

25 *The Daily Chronicle*, 3, 6 and 14 May 1913

26 *The Daily Graphic*, 10 May 1913

27 *The Economist*, 1 February 1913

28 *The Economist*, 10 May 1913

29 *Daily Express*, 5 June 1913

30 *The Suffragette*, 13 June 1913

31 *The English Review*, November 1913

32 *The Daily Chronicle*, 31 December 1913

33 *The Evening Standard*, 29 December 1913

34 *The Economist*, 27 December 1913

35 *The Daily Graphic*, 31 December 1913

36 *The Daily Chronicle*, 26 December 1913

Epilogue

1 Sean McMeekin, *The Berlin-Baghdad Express: The Ottoman Empire and Germany's Bid for World Power*, 2010

2 Harry Kessler, *Das Tagebuch, 1880–1937*, vol. 4, 2004

3 Margaret MacMillan, *Peacemakers: The Paris Conference of 1919 and its Attempt to End War*, 2001

4 James Reeve Pusey, *China and Charles Darwin*, 1983

5 Paul Valéry, *The Crisis of the Mind*, 1919

6   Zara Steiner, *The Lights that Failed: European International History,*
     1919–1933, 2007
7   Stefan Zweig, *The World of Yesterday,* English edition, 1943
8   Paul Fussell, *The Great War and Modern Memory,* 1975
9   Boris Pasternak, *Dr. Zhivago,* trans. Max Hayward and Manya Harari,
     1958

Selected Bibliography

Archives and Libraries

British Library, London
India Office archives at the British Library, London
Central Zionist Archives (CZA), Jerusalem
Israel State Archives, Jerusalem
Center for Jerusalem Studies, Al-Quds University, Jerusalem
Bibliothèque nationale de France (BNF), Paris
Benson Ford Research Center, Dearborn, MI
Archives of American Art at the Smithsonian Institution (AAASI), Walter
    Kuhn and Kuhn family papers, Washington, DC
Library of Congress, Washington, DC
US National Archives, College Park, MD
State Library of Victoria, Melbourne
National Library of Russia, St Petersburg
Morgan Library Archive, New York
New York Public Library, New York
Los Angeles Public Library, Los Angeles
Archives of Manitoba, Winnipeg
www.archive.org

Newspapers and Magazines

The Atlantic (Boston)
North American Review (Boston)
Buenos Aires Herald (Buenos Aires)
The Standard (Buenos Aires)
Levant Herald and Eastern Express (Constantinople)
Detroit Free Press (Detroit)
Ford Times (Detroit)
Indian Opinion (Durban)
Natal Mercury (Durban)

Darkest Russia (London)
Africa Times and Orient Review (London)
The Daily Chronicle (London)
Daily Express (London)
The Daily Graphic (London)
Daily Mail (London)
The Economist (London)
The English Review (London)
The Evening Standard (London)
The Fortnightly Review (London)
The Geographical Journal (London)
The Nineteenth Century and After (London)
The Suffragette (London)
Los Angeles Times (Los Angeles)
Los Angeles Record (Los Angeles)
The Age (Melbourne)
The Argus (Melbourne)
The American Review of Reviews (New York)
The Century Magazine (New York)
Collier's Weekly (New York)
Evening Mail (New York)
Harper's Weekly (New York)
The New York Times (New York)
Scientific American (New York)
World's Work (New York)
L'Afrique française (Paris)
Le Figaro (Paris)
L'Illustration (Paris)
Le Petit Journal (Paris)
La Revue de Paris (Paris)
North China Daily News & Herald (Shanghai)
Birzheye vedomosti (St Petersburg)
Le Journal de Saint-Pétersbourg (St Petersburg)
Novaia zhizn' (St Petersburg)
Novoe vremia (St Petersburg)
Petersburgskaia gazeta (St Petersburg)
Pravda (St Petersburg)
Rech (St Petersburg)
Teatr i zhizn' (St Petersburg)
Vestnik Evropy (St Petersburg)
Sydney Morning Herald (Sydney)
The Japan Times (Tokyo)
Wiener Allgemeine Zeitung (Vienna)

National Geographic (Washington, DC)
Manitoba Free Press (Winnipeg)

Selected Further Reading

The following is intended as a short list of books which may be of interest to the reader, continuing and in many cases enlarging on the themes of *1913: The World before the Great War*.

Politics and Economics
Cemil Aydin, *The Politics of Anti-Westernism in Asia: Visions of World Order in Pan-Islamic and Pan-Asian Thought*, 2007
Christopher Bayly, *The Birth of the Modern World, 1780–1914: Global Connections and Comparisons*, 2004
Duncan Bell, *The Idea of Greater Britain: Empire and the Future of World Order, 1860–1900*, 2011
Robert Bickers, *The Scramble for China: Foreign Devils in the Qing Empire, 1832–1914*, 2012
Sugata Bose, *A Hundred Horizons: The Indian Ocean in the Age of Global Empire*, 2009
Judith M. Brown and William Roger Louis, eds, *The Oxford History of the British Empire: The Twentieth Century*, 1999
Christopher Clark, *The Sleepwalkers: How Europe Went to War in 1914*, 2012
Sebastian Conrad, *Globalisation and the Nation in Imperial Germany*, trans. Sorcha O'Hagan, 2010 (original German edition 2006)
John Darwin, *The Empire Project: The Rise and Fall of the British World-System, 1830–1970*, 2009
Amy Dockser Marcus, *Jerusalem 1913: The Origins of the Arab-Israeli Conflict*, 2008
Wayne Dowler, *Russia in 1913*, 2010
Niall Ferguson, *Empire: How Britain Made the Modern World*, 2003
——, *The Pity of War: 1914–1918*, 1998
Orlando Figes, *A People's Tragedy: The Russian Revolution, 1891–1924*, 1997
Aaron L. Friedberg, *The Weary Titan: Britain and the Experience of Relative Decline, 1895–1905*, 1988
Robert Gildea, *Barricades and Borders: Europe 1800–1914*, 1996
Carol Gluck, *Japan's Modern Myths: Ideology in the Late Meiji Period*, 1985
Xu Guoqi, *China and the Great War: China's Pursuit of a New National Identity and Internationalization*, 2005
E. J. Hobsbawm, *The Age of Empire: 1875–1914*, 1987

Marius B. Jansen, *The Making of Modern Japan*, 2002

Hasan Kayali, *Arabs and Young Turks: Ottomanism, Arabism, and Islamism in the Ottoman Empire, 1908–1918*, 1997

Paul Kennedy, *The Rise and Fall of the Great Powers: Economic Change and Military Conflict from 1500 to 2000*, 1988

Kwasi Kwarteng, *Ghosts of Empire: Britain's Legacies in the Modern World*, 2011

Jackson Lears, *Rebirth of a Nation: The Making of Modern America, 1877–1920*, 2009

Margaret Macmillan, *Peacemakers: The Paris Peace Conference of 1919 and Its Attempt to End War*, 2001

Mark Mazower, *Governing the World: The History of an Idea*, 2012

Justin McCarthy, *Death and Exile: The Ethnic Cleansing of Ottoman Muslims, 1821–1922*, 1996

Sean McMeekin, *The Berlin-Baghdad Express: The Ottoman Empire and Germany's Bid for World Power, 1898–1918*, 2010

Simon Sebag Montefiore, *Jerusalem: The Biography*, 2011

Michael Neiberg, *Dance of the Furies: Europe and the Outbreak of World War I*, 2011

Gary S. Magee and Andrew S. Thompson, eds, *Empire and Globalisation: Networks of People, Goods and Capital in the British World, c.1850–1914*, 2010

Sevket Pamuk, *The Ottoman Empire and European Capitalism, 1820–1913: Trade, Investment and Production*, 1987

John Ruedy, *Modern Algeria: The Origins and Development of a Nation*, 2005

Edward W. Said, *Culture and Imperialism*, 1994 edition

David Schoenbaum, *Zabern 1913: Consensus Politics in Imperial Germany*, 1982

Norman Stone, *Europe Transformed, 1878–1919*, 1983

Jay Winter, ed., *1914–1918: The Great War and the Shaping of the Twentieth Century*, 2001

Richard Wortman, *Scenarios of Power: Myth and Ceremony in Russian Monarchy from Peter the Great to the Abdication of Nicholas II*, 2006

Culture and Society

Philipp Blom, *The Vertigo Years: Change and Culture in the West, 1900–1914*, 2008

Ebru Boyar and Kate Fleet, *A Social History of Ottoman Istanbul*, 2010

Julia Boyd, *A Dance with the Dragon: The Vanished World of Peking's Foreign Colony*, 2012

Liliane Brion-Guerry, ed., *L'année 1913: Les formes esthétiques de l'œuvre d'art à la veille de la première guerre mondiale*, 1971 (volumes 1 and 2), 1973 (volume 3)

Preeti Chopra, *A Joint Enterprise: Indian Elites and the Making of British Bombay*, 2011

Peter Conrad, *Modern Times, Modern Places: Life and Art in the Twentieth Century*, 1999

Vincent Cronin, *Paris on the Eve, 1900–1914*, 1989

Modris Eksteins, *Rites of Spring: The Great War and the Birth of the Modern Age*, 1999

Amos Elon, *The Pity of it All: A Portrait of the Jews in Germany, 1743–1933*, 2002

Felix Driver and David Gilbert, *Imperial Cities: Landscape, Display and Identity*, 1999

Martin Evans and Amanda Sackur, eds, *Empire and Culture: The French Experience, 1830–1940*, 2004

Paul Fussell, *The Great War and Modern Memory*, illustrated edition 2012

Jocelyn Hackforth-Jones and Mary Roberts, *Edges of Empire: Orientalism and Visual Culture*, 2005

Peter Hall, *Cities in Civilization*, 1998

Florian Illies, *1913: Der Sommer des Jahrhunderts*, 2012

Allan Janik and Stephen Toulmin, *Wittgenstein's Vienna*, 1973

Hanchao Lu, *Beyond the Neon Lights: Everyday Shanghai in the Early Twentieth Century*, 1999

Philip Mansel, *Constantinople: City of the World's Desire, 1453–1923*, 1995

Frederic Morton, *Thunder at Twilight: Vienna 1913/1914*, 2001

Jean-Michael Rabaté, *1913: The Cradle of Modernism*, 2007

Alex Ross, *The Rest is Noise: Listening to the Twentieth Century*, 2008

Edward Seidensticker, *Low City, High City, Tokyo from Edo to the Earthquake, 1867–1923*, 1983

Yuri Slezkine, *The Jewish Century*, 2004

Mark D. Steinberg, *Petersburg: Fin de Siècle*, 2011

Solomon Volkov, *St Petersburg: A Cultural History*, 1997

Memoirs, Biographies and Selected Contemporary Writing

G. F. Abbott, *Turkey in Transition*, 1909

Norman Angell, *The Great Illusion: A Study of the Relation of Military Power to National Advantage*, 1913 edition

E. Backhouse and J. O. P. Bland, *Annals & Memoirs of the Court of Peking*, 1914

Mendel Beilis, *The Story of my Sufferings*, trans. Harrison Goldberg, 1926

Henri Borel, *The New China: A Traveller's Impressions*, 1912

Vera Brittain, *Testament of Youth: An Autobiographical Study of the Years 1900–1925*, 2009 edition

Carnegie Endowment for International Peace, *Report of the International Commission to Inquire into the Causes and Conduct of the Balkan Wars*, 1914

Winston Churchill, *The World Crisis, 1911–1918*, 1939 edition

Georges Clemenceau, *South America Today: A Study of the Conditions, Social, Political and Commercial, in Argentina, Uruguay and Brazil*, 1911

Price Collier, *Germany and the Germans from an American point of view*, 1913

Theodore Dreiser, *Traveller at Forty*, 1913

H. G. Dwight, *Constantinople: Old and New*, 1915

George Dobson, *St Petersburg*, 1910

S. M. Edwardes, *Byways of Bombay*, 1912

William Elliot Griffis, *The Japanese Nation in Evolution: Steps in the Progress of a Great People*, 1907

Paul-Henri d'Estournelles de Constant, *Les États-Unis d'Amérique*, 1913

Guglielmo Ferrero, 'The Riddle of America', *The Atlantic*, November 1913

M. K. Gandhi, *Hind Swaraj, or, Indian Home Rule*, 1921 edition

Harold H. Fisher and Laura Mateev, *Out of My Past: Memoirs of Count Kokovtsov*, 1935

John Foster Fraser, *Australia: The Making of a Nation*, 1911

——, *The Amazing Argentine: A New Land of Enterprise*, 1914

Zeyneb Hanoum, *A Turkish Woman's European Impressions*, 1913

Burton J. Hendrick, *The Life and Letters of Water H. Page*, 1924

Alex Hill, *Round the British Empire*, 1913

Rachel Humphreys, *Algiers, the Sahara and the Nile*, 1913

Jukichi Inouye, *Home Life in Tokyo*, 1910

Wasif Jawhariyyeh, *Al Quds Al Othamaniyah Fi Al Mutakrat Al Jawhariyyeh*, eds Issam Nassar and Salim Tamari, 2001

Richard Jebb, *Studies in Colonial Nationalism*, 1905

——, *The Britannic Question: A Survey of Alternatives*, 1913

R. P. Karkaria, ed., *The Charm of Bombay: An Anthology of Writings in Praise of the First City in India*, 1915

Harry Kessler, *Das Tagebuch, 1880–1837*, vol. 4, 2004

Laird McLeod Easton, *The Red Count: The Life and Times of Harry Kessler*, 2002

W. Morgan Shuster, *The Strangling of Persia: Story of the European Diplomacy and Oriental Intrigue That Resulted in the Denationalization of Twelve Million Mohammadans, A Personal Narrative*, 1912

Joseph Henry Longford, *The Evolution of New Japan*, 1913

Pierre Loti, *Les derniers jours de Pékin*, 1902

——, *Turquie agonisante*, 1913

Vladimir Nabokov, *Speak, Memory: An Autobiography Revisited*, 1966

Bernard Pares, *Russia and Reform*, 1907

Simon Nelson Patten, *A New Basis for Civilization*, 1907

Antony Phillips, ed., *Sergey Prokofiev Diaries, 1907–1914: Prodigious Youth*, 2006

Mary Poynter, *When Turkey was Turkey: In and Around Constantinople*, 1921

Paul S. Reinsch, *An American Diplomat in China*, 1922

D. Sarason, ed., *Das Jahr 1913: Ein Gesamtbild der Kulturentwicklung*, 1913

Karl Scheffler, *Berlin: Ein Stadtschicksal*, 1910

J. A. Spender, *The Indian Scene*, 1912

Leon Trotsky, *My Life: An Attempt at an Autobiography*, 2007 edition

Solomon Tshekisko Plaatje, *Native Life in South Africa before and since the European War and the Boer Rebellion*, 1916

John Kenneth Turner, *Barbarous Mexico*, 1911

Fredrick McCormick, *The Flowery Republic*, 1913

Bertha Spafford Vester, *Our Jerusalem: An American Family in the Holy City, 1881–1949*, 1951

Luigi Villari, *Russia under the Great Shadow*, 1905

Dorothy de Warzée, *Peeps into Persia*, 1913

Steven Watts, *The People's Tycoon: Henry Ford and the American Century*, 2005

Henry Wickham Steed, *The Hapsburg Monarchy*, 1913

Woodrow Wilson, *The New Freedom*, ed. Arthur S. Link, 1956 (originally published 1913)

Sergey Witte, *The Memoirs of Count Witte*, trans. Abraham Yarmolinsky, 1921

Stefan Zweig, *The World of Yesterday*, trans. Anthea Bell, 2011 edition

Picture Credits

Acknowledgements

1913: The World before the Great War has been a labour of love, a book idea rattling around my head for years but which took a lot of other people's guidance, patience, wisdom and research to make into what you are holding in your hands today.

After a couple of false starts, Jennifer Joel at ICM and Melissa Pimentel at Curtis Brown helped me get the ideas from my head on to paper. Will Sulkin and subsequently Stuart Williams bought the book at Bodley Head, Lisa Kaufman for PublicAffairs. It has been excellent to return to two wonderful publishing operations that still believe in good, serious, non-fiction books. Kay Peddle was at Bodley Head at the outset. Since then, Gemma Wain has been with me in the trenches throughout the writing and production – hopefully without any resulting shell shock. Her expert guidance, occasional cajoling, preternatural calmness and forbearance is tremendously appreciated. This book would not exist without her work. The wonderful cover to the book was designed by Kris Potter. Bernice Davison copy-edited the text to perfection (with the sorry consequence that any remaining errors are entirely my own). Anna Cowling has been in charge of production. Emma Young and Sophie Mitchell at Bodley Head and Jaime Leifer at PublicAffairs have been responsible for getting the book out there to the public and to our friends in the media. I was fortunate enough to undertake most of the writing of this book while on (an almost complete) sabbatical from the Royal Institute of International Affairs (Chatham House), with particular thanks due to Robin Niblett, Bernice Lee and my colleagues there, who universally flourished in my absence.

I owe an extraordinary number of historical debts, too many to list here, more amply accounted for in the bibliography and footnotes. But there are a few which might slip through the cracks if I do not give them particular mention here. The historical profession has produced great researchers, great polemicists, and great writers. I am a great believer in the value of history as an aid to contemporary reflection, and in the necessity for history to have eloquent exponents. I have always been deeply inspired by the awesome narrative skill of the late Eric Hobsbawm, the humanity of the late Tony Judt, the endlessly engrossing writing of Simon Schama, the historical exposition of Norman Stone, the sheer verve of Niall Ferguson.

I remember reading Paul Kennedy's *The Rise and Fall of the Great Powers* one summer holiday when I was really far too young to be interested in such things, and beginning to dimly perceive the vistas that a great history book can open on to our own times, and the really big questions of power and politics. Timothy Garton Ash's ability to bring historical perspective on the present, and contemporary perspective on the past – and all this with wit – is a model for how a historical frame of mind can inform our understanding of contemporary politics, interests and ethics. If Britain does such things as 'public intellectuals' he must surely be one of the most eloquent and elegant of the breed. At Oxford University, I was lucky enough to be taught by Martin Conway – with a black-and-white photograph of Atatürk brooding permanently on one wall – Robert Gildea, Katya Andreyev, Ruth Harris, Jan Palmowski, Christopher Haigh, Patrick Wormald and W. E. S. Thomas. Studying history at Oxford is probably the single most intellectually exciting thing I have ever done.

Occasionally one reads a history book so sparkling with insight and intelligence, so definitive, or so massive – Margaret Macmillan's *Peacemakers*, Christopher Clark's *The Sleepwalkers*, John Darwin's *The Empire Project*, Chris Bayly's *The Birth of the Modern World* – that one is left rather terrified at the prospect of attempting anything oneself. *1913* is necessarily a more impressionistic endeavour than these works. I hope, nonetheless, that it is able to throw a sidelight on the works of other historians, provide their ideas with a different frame, and hopefully lead the reader gently down the garden path into deeper thickets of historical scholarship.

I am indebted further to a number of people who have helped me more directly with the research for this book, either by spending time poring over the newspapers for a particular city in the year 1913 in the British Library Newspaper Reading Room in Colindale, or through looking at diplomatic and other documents, or in other ways. The extraordinarily capable Angus McLaren helped me conduct research on Buenos Aires and Durban (and with the infinitely tricky business of pictures), Rhiannon Evans-Young looked through pages and pages of newspapers for Melbourne and Winnipeg, George Moore attacked Constantinople and helped me get to grips with Japanese politics, while the ever-thoughtful Tom Smith took on Shanghai, Peking and Tokyo. Many thanks to Hugo Service and Martin Conway for sending a number of these historians my way. In between learning Turkic languages, Thomas Welsford guided me to *Crowning Anguish* by Taj al-Saltanah. In Los Angeles, Walter Dominguez pointed me towards *Whitewashed Adobe* by William Deverell and the fascinating *California Vieja* by Phoebe Kropp. Dr Thalia Kennedy helped look through documents on Tehran and Bombay, bringing her eye for the Indo-Saracenic and uncovering hidden gems from the India Office archives in the British Library. (My favourite single line in the book, from a British diplomatic dispatch about Ahmad Shah Qajar, was found by her.) On the recommendation of Tommy Wide, Scott Liddle in Algiers helped translate extracts from Wasif Jawhariyyeh's diaries from Arabic. Dr Maria Mileeva helped me to fill out and stamp the necessary forms in order to gain access to the wonderfully antique National Library of Russia in St Petersburg, and then talked me through the Russian newspapers for 1913, the originals of which one can still look at. The memoirs of Dmitri Smirnov, the priest from Tobolsk, were found, lost and re-found by her. The first person I outlined the whole book to, in a London pub, was Masha. I am yet to discover where she gets her energy from to be so actively involved in working on European and Soviet art history at the Courtauld Institute of Art and still to have some enthusiasm left to impart to me for my own projects. Masha has been my comrade-in-arms on *1913*. Her love has sustained me throughout.

Though the last words of this book were sent back to Bodley Head from a motel in Wickenburg, Arizona, most of *1913* was written at my sister's house in Lyme Regis, in Melbourne and the British Library – a great institution and a fabulous working environment. Having spent so much time there I now rather consider it (worryingly) as a home from home. But I have also benefitted from access to a number of other libraries and archives, and to the helpful staff who make them work so effectively: the Central Zionist Archives, Israel State Archives and Center for Jerusalem Studies in Jerusalem, the US National Archives at College Park, Maryland, the Morgan Library Archive and New York Public Library in New York City, the Archives of American Art at the Smithsonian Institution and the Library of Congress in Washington, DC, the State Library of Victoria in Melbourne, the Bibliothèque nationale de France in Paris, the Benson Ford Research Center in Dearborn, Michigan, the Los Angeles Public Library, the India Office records at the British Library, the Archives of Manitoba in Winnipeg, the National Library of Russia and the extraordinary resource that is www.archive.org – where you can watch *Raja Harishchandra* (India's first feature film, from 1913) and read digitised versions of an extraordinary number of travel books of the era – hugely helpful in working on this book. The organisation and dissemination of knowledge and memory which these institutions represent is of huge value.

In addition, I am lucky enough to have a wonderful group of friends, who inspire me by all the interesting things they are doing and who are very good to talk to about the book – some are BL regulars and have an assiduous record of attendance at The Last Word – but also about pretty much anything else. In one way or another, a huge number have helped me to write this book. They know who they are, and I cannot list all of them, but let me list a few, or even a few more than a few: Alex Burghart and Hermione Eyre, Teresa Drace-Francis and Ronald Grover, Ed Sebline and

Cicely Fell, Jacky Klein, Alex von Tunzelmann, Leo Tomlin and Sarah Bryce, Anna Morgan, Judy Fladmark, Zoe Flood, Michael Shaw, Andrew Harrop, Matthew Morrison, Naureen Khan, Nick and Bel Davis, Henry Hitchings, Tannaz Banisadre, Maya Mailer and Dan Vexler, Jasper Goldman, Alison and Jamie Carpenter, Alissa de Carbonnel, Dario Thuburn, Maria Sanchez, Séverine Hubert, Reg Otten, Aurélie Vandeputte and Richard Osman, Keith Campbell, Nina Hobson, Victoria de Menil, Michael Byers, Joanna and Rob Gray, James and Camilla Smith, Phoebe and Ric Clay, Caroline Boon, MK and Hamish Gilder, James Skidmore, Rob Lilwall, Joey Bryniarska, Daphna Jowell, Hugo Service and Anita Hurrell, Alex Hurrell and Clemmie Franks, Victoria Mackay, James Fox, Victoria Elles, Sophie and Ian Irvine, Anna and Mike Palmer, Emma Castagno, Alex Nash, Alix Duff, Toby Stone, Esra Bulut, Pelin and Tom Luff, Galia Rybitskaya, Natasha White, Nick de Mestre, Jesse and Lisa Fahnestock, Alena Mileeva, Nina Butslova, Hema Kotecha, Will MacNamara and Naomi Wood.

Finally, my family. I discussed this book extensively with my mother Alexandra before she died in 2010. She was very enthusiastic about the idea – as she was about most things which were fun, and interesting, and different. I hope she would approve of the final product. I think she would. My dearest sister Chloe and brother-in-law JB – and the best niece and nephew in the world, Genevieve and Theo – have been wonderful throughout. So, too, in a rather different way, my uncle John Emmerson, and Robert and Pirjo Gardiner, whose flat is ever a haven of calm, good taste and civilisation. But my greatest thanks are reserved for my father. I think he knows the book now better than I do, having read it at all different stages. He never seems to tire of the job of looking at one more version of another chapter – or at least does an excellent job of pretending not to be tired of it. He has my love, and my respect, and my heartfelt gratitude.

Index

Charles Emmerson was born in Australia and grew up in London. After graduating top of his class in modern history for Oxford University, he took up an Entente Cordiale scholarship to study international relations and international public law in Paris. The author of *The Future History of the Arctic* (2010), he writes and speaks widely on international affairs. He is a senior research fellow at Chatham House (the Royal Institute for International Affairs).

PublicAffairs is a publishing house founded in 1997. It is a tribute to the standards, values, and flair of three persons who have served as mentors to countless reporters, writers, editors, and book people of all kinds, including me.

I. F. STONE, proprietor of *I. F. Stone's Weekly*, combined a commitment to the First Amendment with entrepreneurial zeal and reporting skill and became one of the great independent journalists in American history. At the age of eighty, Izzy published *The Trial of Socrates*, which was a national bestseller. He wrote the book after he taught himself ancient Greek.

BENJAMIN C. BRADLEE was for nearly thirty years the charismatic editorial leader of *The Washington Post*. It was Ben who gave the *Post* the range and courage to pursue such historic issues as Watergate. He supported his reporters with a tenacity that made them fearless and it is no accident that so many became authors of influential, best-selling books.

ROBERT L. BERNSTEIN, the chief executive of Random House for more than a quarter century, guided one of the nation's premier publishing houses. Bob was personally responsible for many books of political dissent and argument that challenged tyranny around the globe. He is also the founder and longtime chair of Human Rights Watch, one of the most respected human rights organizations in the world.

.　　.　　.

For fifty years, the banner of Public Affairs Press was carried by its owner Morris B. Schnapper, who published Gandhi, Nasser, Toynbee, Truman, and about 1,500 other authors. In 1983, Schnapper was described by *The Washington Post* as "a redoubtable gadfly." His legacy will endure in the books to come.

Peter Osnos, *Founder and Editor-at-Large*